AFRICAN HISTORICAL DICTIONARIES
Edited by Jon Woronoff

1. *Cameroon*, by Victor T. LeVine and Roger P. Nye. 1974. *Out of print. See No. 48.*
2. *The Congo*, 2nd ed., by Virginia Thompson and Richard Adloff. 1984. *Out of print. See No. 69.*
3. *Swaziland*, by John J. Grotpeter. 1975.
4. *The Gambia*, 2nd ed., by Harry A. Gailey. 1987.
5. *Botswana*, by Richard P. Stevens. 1975. *Out of print. See No. 70.*
6. *Somalia*, by Margaret F. Castagno. 1975.
7. *Benin (Dahomey)*, 2nd ed., by Samuel Decalo. 1987. *Out of print. See No. 61.*
8. *Burundi*, by Warren Weinstein. 1976. *Out of print. See No. 73.*
9. *Togo*, 3rd ed., by Samuel Decalo. 1996.
10. *Lesotho*, by Gordon Haliburton. 1977.
11. *Mali*, 3rd ed., by Pascal James Imperato. 1996.
12. *Sierra Leone*, by Cyril Patrick Foray. 1977.
13. *Chad*, 3rd ed., by Samuel Decalo. 1997.
14. *Upper Volta*, by Daniel Miles McFarland. 1978.
15. *Tanzania*, by Laura S. Kurtz. 1978.
16. *Guinea*, 3rd ed., by Thomas O'Toole with Ibrahima Bah-Lalya. 1995.
17. *Sudan*, by John Voll. 1978. *Out of print. See No. 53.*
18. *Rhodesia/Zimbabwe*, by R. Kent Rasmussen. 1979. *Out of print. See No. 46.*
19. *Zambia*, 2nd ed., by John J. Grotpeter, Brian V. Siegel, and James R. Pletcher. 1998.
20. *Niger*, 3rd ed., by Samuel Decalo. 1996.
21. *Equatorial Guinea*, 2nd ed., by Max Liniger-Goumaz. 1988.
22. *Guinea-Bissau*, 3rd ed., by Richard Lobban and Peter Mendy. 1996.
23. *Senegal*, by Lucie G. Colvin. 1981. *Out of print. See No. 65.*
24. *Morocco*, by William Spencer. 1980. *Out of print. See No. 71.*
25. *Malawi*, by Cynthia A. Crosby. 1980. *Out of print. See No. 54.*

Historical Dictionary
of
Zambia

Second Edition

John J. Grotpeter
Brian V. Siegel
James R. Pletcher

African Historical Dictionaries, No. 19

The Scarecrow Press, Inc.
Lanham, Md., & London
1998

SCARECROW PRESS, INC.

Published in the United States of America
by Scarecrow Press, Inc.
4720 Boston Way
Lanham, Maryland 20706

4 Pleydell Gardens
Kent CT20 2DN, England

British Library Cataloguing in Publication Information Available

Library of Congress Cataloging-in-Publication Data

Grotpeter, John J.
    Historical dictionary of Zambia / John J. Grotpeter, Brian V. Siegel,
James R. Pletcher — 2nd ed.
        p.   cm. — (African historical dictionaries ; no. 19)
    Includes bibliographical references (p.).
    ISBN 0-8108-3345-X (cloth: alk. paper)
    I. Siegel, Brian V., 1950–NN.   II. Pletcher, Jim.   III. Title.   IV. Series.
    DT3037.G76   1998   97-18917
    968.94—dc21   CIP

ISBN 0-8108-3345-X

⊗ ™ The paper used in this publication meets the minimum
requirements of American National Standard for Information
Sciences—Permanence of Paper for Printed Library Materials. ANSI
Z39.48–1984. Manufactured in the United States of America.

To the people of Zambia

To Dick Hobson, John Storm Roberts, and the late William Watson, all of whom contributed in one form or another to this project; and to Kathryn, Jacob, and Elsa Siegel, who patiently attended its plodding progress

To Emily Gilde, Mary Rose, and Joseph, who gave so much to its completion

Contents

Editor's Foreword

When Zambia became independent in 1964, it had a head start on many other African countries of the region, enabling it to create new state institutions and to revamp its economy earlier than these others. One false move, however, was the emergence of a single-party state (although this was admittedly gentler, under Kenneth Kaunda, than in other African states). Other problems were related to a declining economy; although its economy was not rooted in African socialism, it was still far from liberal. Now Zambia is ahead again, among the first African nations to permit multiparty democracy and to experience a transfer of power. It is also among the first to liberalize its economy.

Further, Zambia's location, on the borders of other independent states that could regroup around a democratic and economically dynamic South Africa, could make it a major player in any revitalization of the region. These changes make the appearance of a revised *Historical Dictionary of Zambia* particularly welcome. Like its predecessor, this edition is extraordinarily comprehensive, covering a broad range of topics and fields: politics, economics, sociology, anthropology, and others. It follows Zambian history from Kabwe (Broken Hill) Man to today's leaders, and, in many ways, serves as a who's who of major and minor figures. It also defines ethnic and linguistic groups, political parties, trade unions, religious bodies, state and private corporations, and significant places and events. The bibliography is more extensive than before and structured in a manner that facilitates research.

The first edition of the Zambia volume was written by John J. Grotpeter, who sadly passed away recently. His work was taken up by Brian V. Siegel and James R. Pletcher, who revised, updated, and expanded that volume. They have provided, here, an excellent guide to Zambia.

Jon Woronoff
Series Editor

Preface to the Second Edition

This dictionary is a collaborative effort between the living and the dead. When Jon Woronoff, the series editor, invited Brian Siegel to bring out an updated version of John Grotpeter's *Historical Dictionary of Zambia*, Brian asked Jim Pletcher to help document and describe the many (and sometimes sordid) political changes in Zambia since the mid-1970s. We worked out a convenient, if often untidy, division of labor, one in which Jim, the political scientist, would concentrate upon political and economic affairs, while Brian, the anthropologist, would focus upon historic and cultural affairs. Ours has been a genial and productive partnership.

Jim returned to Zambia, where he collected recent census and political data. Brian proofread the computerized text, rewrote or revised many of John Grotpeter's entries, researched and wrote additional ones, and began an updated bibliography. By August 1995 we began exchanging draft entries. Dick Hobson's *News from Zambia*, a newsletter drawn from the Zambian newspapers, and the Economist Intelligence Unit's quarterly country reports for Zambia provided material for further revisions and additional entries. Jim then sent off a form soliciting biographical data from leading Zambian political figures, while a six-month sabbatical provided Brian the opportunity to complete the dictionary text.

With such a laborious enterprise as this, nothing is ever completely finished. We apologize in advance to readers who may find fault with our efforts and invite them to make our errors or omissions known to us.

We would like to thank Sandra Mead, Craig Saunders, Holly Dumm, and Christy Trager for their patient assistance through what was sometimes a tedious process.

Brian Siegel
Jim Pletcher

Acronyms

AIDS	acquired immune deficiency syndrome
ALC	African Lakes Company
AME	African Methodist Episcopal Church
AMU	African Mineworkers Union
ANC	African National Congress
ARC	African Representative Council
BBC	British Broadcasting Company
BCC	Bank of Commerce and Credit
BIAO	Banque Internationale pour l'Afrique Occidental
BSAC	British South Africa Company
CAA	Central African Airways Corporation
CABS	Central African Broadcasting Service
CAP	Central Africa Party
CAPU	Central African People's Union
CNU	Caucus for National Unity
FDP	Federal Dominion Party
FEMAC	Foreign Exchange Management Committee
FFF	Federal Fighting Fund
FINDECO	Financial Development Corporation
FNDP	First National Development Plan
GDP	gross domestic product
IBM	International Business Machines
IMF	International Monetary Fund
INDECO	Industrial Development Corporation of Zambia, Ltd.
IRLCO-CSA	International Red Locust Control Organization for Central and Southern Africa
K	kwacha
LMS	London Missionary Society
MASA	Mines African Staff Association
MEMACO	Metal Marketing Company of Zambia
MINDECO	Mining Development Corporation
MLSA	Mines Local Staff Association
MMD	Movement for Multiparty Democracy
MUZ	Mineworkers Union of Zambia

NAMBOARD	National Agricultural Marketing Board
NCCM	Nchanga Consolidated Copper Mines, Ltd.
NCEC	North Charterland Exploration Company
NDP	National Development Plan
NECZAM	National Educational Company of Zambia
NP	National Party
NPP	National Progress Party
NRAC	Northern Rhodesia African Congress
NWLG	National Women's Lobby Group
OAU	Organization of African Unity
PAFMECA	Pan-African Freedom Movement for East and Central Africa
PAFMECSA	Pan-African Freedom Movement for East, Central, and Southern Africa
PDC	People's Democratic Congress
PFP	policy framework paper
PMS	Paris Missionary Society
PTA	Preferential Trade Area
RCM	Roan Consolidated Mines
RST	Roan Selection Trust, Ltd.
RTUC	Reformed Trade Union Congress
SDR	special drawing right
SNA	Secretary of Native Affairs
SRAS	Southern Rhodesian Air Services
STD	sexually transmitted disease
TANKS	Tanganyika Concessions, Ltd.
TAZAMA	Tanzania-Zambia Oil Pipeline
TAZARA	Tanzania-Zambia Railway Authority
TUC	Trade Union Congress
UAC	United African Congress
UCCB	Union Church of the Copperbelt
UDP	United Democratic Party
UFP	United Federal Party
UMCA	Universities' Mission to Central Africa
UMCB	United Missions in the Copperbelt
UMHK	Union Minière du Haut-Katanga
UMU	United Mineworkers Union
UN	United Nations
UNICEF	United Nations Children's Fund
UNIP	United National Independence Party
UNITA	União Nacional para a Independência Total de Angola (National Union for Total Independence of Angola)
UNZA	University of Zambia

UP	United Party
UPP	United Progressive Party
URP	United Rhodesia Party
WENELA	Witwatersrand Native Labour Association
WHO	World Health Organization
WTBTS	Watch Tower Bible and Tract Society
ZACCI	Zambia Confederation of Industries and Chambers of Commerce
ZAMANGLO	Anglo-American Corporation of Zambia, Ltd.
ZANC	Zambia African National Congress
ZANU	Zimbabwe African National Union
ZAPU	Zimbabwe African People's Union
ZARD	Zambia Association for Research and Development
ZAUW	Zambia Association of University Women
ZCCM	Zambia Consolidated Copper Mines
ZCF	Zambia Cooperative Federation
ZCEA	Zambia Civic Education Association
ZCSD	Zambia Council for Social Development
ZCTU	Zambia Congress of Trade Unions
ZEMA	Zambia Expatriate Miners Association
ZEMCC	Zambia Elections Monitoring Coordination Committee
ZIMCO	Zambia Industrial and Mining Corporation
ZIMT	Zambia Independent Monitoring Team
ZIPRA	Zimbabwe People's Army
ZIS	Zambia Information Services
ZMU	Zambia Mineworkers Union
ZNFU	Zambia National Farmers Union
ZNPF	Zambia National Provident Fund
ZNBS	Zambia National Broadcasting Services
ZPA	Zambia Privatisation Agency
ZPF	Zambia Police Force
ZR	Zambia Railways
ZRA	Zambia Revenue Authority
Z-VOTE	Zambian Voters Observation Team
ZYS	Zambia Youth Service

Chronology

123,000–107,000 B.C.	Kabwe (formerly Broken Hill) Man lives in area (possibly as early as 248,000 B.C.).
A.D. 50	Iron Age begins in Zambia.
A.D. ca. 1200	Tonga settle at Sebanzi Hill in Zambia.
1350–1450	Southern Zambian trading community, Ingombe Ilede, is in its prime period.
1500–1800	Major migrations enter Zambia, primarily from the Congo.
1514	Portuguese first enter Zambia.
1798	Dr. Lacerda, Portuguese governor of Sena, travels in Northern Rhodesia; he dies near Kazembe's capital, close to Lake Mweru.
1802	Traders Pedro Baptista and Amaro José leave Angola and visit Kazembe during a journey across Africa to Mozambique.
1832	Major Monteiro and Captain Gamitto visit Kazembe.
1835	Ngoni, under Zwangendaba, cross the Zambezi and move north.
1851	David Livingstone meets Sebituane, chief of the Kololo, on the Chobe River near the Zambezi.
1853	Livingstone revisits Barotseland at the outset of his great trans-African expedition.
1855	Livingstone "discovers" Victoria Falls (November 16) during his crossing of Africa from Luanda on the west coast to Quelimane on the east.
1872	First English traders arrive at the court of Sipopa of Barotseland.
1873	Livingstone dies at Chitambo's village (May 1).
1877	London Missionary Society begins work in Central Africa.
1878	Lewanika becomes king of the Lozi.
1886	François Coillard of the Paris Evangelical Mission Society is received in Barotseland by King Lewanika and sets up permanent mission station.

1887	Coillard sets up mission school in Barotseland.
1889	Lewanika makes first request for British protection over Barotseland (January).
	Lewanika signs Ware Concession (June). Cecil Rhodes buys concession.
	Royal charter is granted to Cecil Rhodes' British South Africa Company (BSAC).
1890	Lochner-Lewanika treaty is signed in Barotseland (June 27).
	Alfred Sharpe and Joseph Thomson conclude various treaties in the Luapula, Luangwa, and Copperbelt areas.
1891	Anglo-Portuguese treaty is signed (June 11), under which Portugal abandons claim to belt of land across Africa.
1895	Mwenzo Mission is opened by Free Church of Scotland.
	BSAC territories formally named Rhodesia by proclamation (May 3).
1896	Forbes is appointed first deputy administrator of North-Eastern Rhodesia (July).
1897	Coryndon arrives in Barotseland in office of British Resident (October).
1898	Lawley and Lewanika meet at Victoria Falls and sign a treaty giving BSAC exclusive mineral rights (June 25).
	British force defeats Mpezeni's Ngoni in North-Eastern Rhodesia.
	Last slave cargo is stopped at Chipata.
1899	North-Western Rhodesia order in council is signed (November 20).
	BSAC deputy administrator moves from Blantyre to Fort Jameson (Chipata).
1900	Lewanika treaty is renegotiated.
	North-Eastern Rhodesia order in council is signed (January 29).
1902	Cecil Rhodes dies (March 26).
	Mining starts at Broken Hill, Northern Rhodesia.
	William Collier "discovers" Bwana Mkubwa and Roan Antelope Mines.
1904	Railway reaches Victoria Falls (April 25) and opens (June 19); bridge opens (September 12).
1905	King Victor Emmanuel of Italy sets frontier between BSAC territory and Portuguese Angola.
1906	Railway from the south reaches Broken Hill (Kabwe). Broken Hill mine is discovered at Kabwe.

1907	Seat of administration of North-Western Rhodesia is moved from Kalomo to Livingstone.
	Robert Codrington is appointed administrator of North-Western Rhodesia, Lawrence Wallace of North-Eastern Rhodesia.
1909	Wallace becomes administrator of North-Western Rhodesia.
	Railway reaches Congo border (November).
1910	Moffat Thompson discovers Nkana copper source.
1911	Northern Rhodesia order in council unites North-Western and North-Eastern Rhodesia as Northern Rhodesia (May 4). Wallace becomes administrator of the whole territory.
1912	First copper concentrator is erected in Northern Rhodesia at Bwana Mkubwa.
	Mwenzo Welfare Association is founded by Donald Siwale, David Kaunda, and others.
1917	Advisory Council of five elected members is set up in Northern Rhodesia.
1921	Fossil of Kabwe Man is discovered at Broken Hill (Kabwe).
	Sir Drummond Chaplin is named administrator of Northern Rhodesia.
1922	Major development of Northern Rhodesian Copperbelt begins.
1923	BSAC and British government agree on future administration of Northern Rhodesia (September 29).
	Large oxide ore body is discovered at Nchanga.
1924	BSAC rule ends and Northern Rhodesia Protectorate under British colonial rule is established. Sir Herbert Stanley becomes first governor (April 1).
	Kenneth Kaunda born (April 28).
1926	Anglo-American Corporation of South Africa is established in Broken Hill (Kabwe).
1927	Roan Antelope Mining Company is formed.
	Sir John Maxwell becomes governor of Northern Rhodesia.
1929	Hilton Young Report on closer association of East African territories is published (January 24).
1930	Copperbelt construction work booms. It is terminated at end of year by limitation of output due to fall in world prices.

	Colonial officials suggest that Northern and Southern Rhodesia unite in federation.
1931	Price of copper drops rapidly due to world depression.
1932	Sir Ronald Storrs is named governor of Northern Rhodesia.
1933	Copper slump is ending.
	Work at Mufulira copper mine begins.
1934	Sir Hubert Young becomes governor of Northern Rhodesia.
1935	African workers call first strike on the Copperbelt.
	Capital of Northern Rhodesia is transferred from Livingstone to Lusaka.
1936	Southern Rhodesia Parliament resolves in favor of amalgamation with Northern Rhodesia; conferees at Victoria Falls conference demand amalgamation.
1938	Sir John Maybin becomes governor of Northern Rhodesia.
1939	Munali Secondary School for Africans is established in Lusaka.
	Bledisloe Report on closer association between the Rhodesias and Nyasaland is published (March 21).
1939–1945	World War II causes boom in copper prices.
1940	Second Copperbelt African strike is called.
1941	Sir John Waddington is named governor of Northern Rhodesia.
1944	Central African Council is set up (October 18).
1946	Federation of African Welfare Societies is established.
	Colonial government forms African Representative Council.
1947	Sir Gilbert Rennie becomes governor of Northern Rhodesia.
1948	Dalgleish Report, "The Place of Africans in Industry," is published.
	Northern Rhodesia African Congress formed from Federation of Welfare Societies.
	First African mineworkers union is organized.
	Northern Rhodesia Legislative Council is changed to include two African members elected by African Representative Council and two European members for African interests nominated by government.
1949	Victoria Falls Conference on federation (Southern Rhodesia and unofficial representatives of Northern Rhodesia) is held (February).

1950	Northern Rhodesia government and BSAC agree to transfer of BSAC mineral rights to government in 1986 and to payment of 20 percent of company's revenue from mineral rights in the intervening period. Compulsory education for Africans begins.
1951	Harry Nkumbula elected president of Northern Rhodesia African Congress, which is renamed African National Congress. Kenneth Kaunda is appointed northern provincial organizing secretary of Congress. Official conference on federation is held in London; report is published (June 14). Victoria Falls Conference on federation is held; representatives of United Kingdom, Southern Rhodesia, Northern Rhodesia, and Nyasaland attend (September).
1952	Further conferences are held in London on federation; draft scheme is published.
1953	Queen Elizabeth II signs order in council establishing federation (August). Federation is endorsed by legislatures of all three territories and by United Kingdom Parliament; federation begins operation (October 23); Lord Llewellyn becomes first governor-general. First federal general election is held (December). Sir Godfrey Huggins becomes prime minister.
1954	African National Congress (ANC) boycotts butcheries in Lusaka and other towns (January). Sir Arthur Benson is named governor of Northern Rhodesia. Sir Gilbert Rennie is appointed federal high commissioner in London.
1955	Kaunda and Nkumbula are sentenced to three months' imprisonment (January).
1956	Northern Rhodesia government declares state of emergency on Copperbelt (September). Welensky succeeds Huggins (Lord Malvern) as federal prime minister (October). Kariba hydroelectric project begins.
1957	Congress boycotts beer halls (July). Disturbances begin in northern provinces (August). Earl of Dalhousie is sworn in as second governor-general of the federation (October 8).

1958   Benson Constitution is published (March).

      Copperbelt mines struck (September).

      ANC holds emergency conference; Kaunda and others "split" from Nkumbula; Zambia African National Congress (ZANC) is formed (October).

      Second general election in federation is held (November 12).

      United Church of Central Africa in Rhodesia is organized.

1959   ZANC is banned in Northern Rhodesia (March 12).

      First multiracial elections are held in Northern Rhodesia (March).

      First session of Second Federal Parliament is opened (April 7).

      Sir Evelyn Hone is appointed governor of Northern Rhodesia (April).

      Kariba dam wall is completed (June 22).

      Kaunda is sentenced to nine months' imprisonment (June).

      Mainza Chona leads United National Independence Party (UNIP) (September).

1960   Kaunda is elected president of UNIP (January).

      Monckton Commission is created by British government to study federation problems (April).

      UNIP is declared an "unlawful" society (May).

      Federal Review Conference is held in London (December).

1961   London Constitutional Conference on constitution of Northern Rhodesia is held (January).

      Macleod constitution proposed, allowing some prospect of African representation in future government.

      UNIP Conference is held at Mulungushi. Cha-cha-cha movement starts (July).

1962   Maudling announces modified constitutional plan (February).

      General election produces deadlock (October).

      Kaunda's *Zambia Shall Be Free* is published.

      UNIP and ANC form coalition government (December).

1963   Tension rises between members and nonmembers of Lumpa Church in Northern Province (January).

      Victoria Falls Conference to dismantle federation is held (June).

New constitution for Northern Rhodesia is announced (September).

Federation is officially dissolved (December 31).

1964   UNIP wins general election: Kaunda is appointed prime minister (January).

London Conference on Zambian independence is held (May).

Lumpa "war" begins (July).

Kaunda is proclaimed president-elect of Zambia (August).

BSAC royalties end (October).

Republic of Zambia is born (October 24).

1965   Rhodesia unilaterally declares independence from Great Britain (November 11).

1966   First National Development Plan goes into effect.

1967   Lusaka International Airport is completed.

1968   Kenneth Kaunda is reelected as president, announces philosophy of Zambian humanism.

Mulungushi Declaration introduces major economic reforms (April 19).

1969   Kwacha becomes official unit of currency (January).

First class graduates from University of Zambia.

Lusaka Manifesto is accepted.

1970   Lusaka is host of third Nonaligned Nations Summit Conference.

Rhodesia declares itself a republic (March 2).

1971   Kariba North power station construction begins.

1972   Second National Development Plan is put into effect (January).

One-party participatory democracy is officially created (December 13).

First stage of Kafue hydroelectric project and dam is completed.

1973   President Kaunda approves new constitution after passage by Parliament (August).

Kaunda is elected president of Zambia in first elections of Second Zambian Republic (December).

1974   TAZARA railway reaches Zambia's border (April 7).

World copper prices begin a lengthy plummet after reaching a record high.

1975   Zambia arrests fifty Zimbabwe political activists over murder of Herbert Chitepo, one of the Zimbabwe leaders in Zambia (March).

TAZARA railway reaches Kapiri Mposhi (March).

Times of Zambia and privately owned land are nationalized (June).

1976   University of Zambia is closed (February to May) after student disturbances.

President Kaunda allows Zimbabwe nationalists to use Zambia for a base of operations against the Smith government of Rhodesia (May).

1977   Kaunda places army on full alert and announces that Zambia is "in state of war" with white-ruled Rhodesia (May).

Rhodesian planes attack across the border in Feira District (September).

Government plans major economic cutbacks and a "back to the land" campaign as copper prices continue at extremely low level (November).

1978   Daniel Lisulo replaces Mainza Chona as prime minister. Chona becomes secretary-general of UNIP (June).

Rhodesian troops invade deeply into Zambia, attacking Zimbabwe guerrilla bases.

Kaunda is reelected president (December).

1979   Rhodesian forces destroy critical rail and road links across Chambeshi River in Northern Province (October 12).

Rhodesia announces cessation of maize shipments to Zambia through Rhodesia (November 6).

Rhodesian forces destroy 11 rail and road bridges (November 20–23).

Christian churches, especially the Roman Catholic Church, publish a pastoral letter criticizing the teaching of Marxism-Leninism at the President's Citizenship College (September 19).

President Kaunda announces Third National Development Plan (October).

1980   Simon Kapwepwe dies of a stroke at age 57 (January 26).

Lancaster House agreement settles war in Zimbabwe. Robert Mugabe elected first president of Zimbabwe in landslide.

President Kaunda verbally attacks dissidents, including Elias Chipimo, chairman of Standard Bank Zambia, accused of seeking to overthrow government.

Zambian troops discover 50 armed guerrillas on farm

once owned by Aaron Milner near Chilanga, south of Lusaka (October 16); eventually charge of treason is leveled against 13 defendants.

ZCTU announces its support of Mineworkers Union of Zambia's suspension of 16 shop stewards for breaking ranks and running for offices in UNIP's ward elections, which the union had boycotted (December).

1981   UNIP suspends 17 union leaders from ZCTU and MUZ (January 9), including ZCTU chairman, Frederick Chiluba. ZCTU reinstates shop stewards following UNIP's suspensions; however, suspensions are not lifted.

Senior politicians are reshuffled (February): Mainza Chona is replaced by Humphrey Mulemba as secretary-general of UNIP; and Prime Minister Nalumino Mundia is replaced by Daniel Lisulo.

Government and IMF agree to three-year program and loan of SDR 800 million, then second-largest loan ever given to an African country (May).

Government announces that two state-controlled mining companies, Nchanga Consolidated Copper Mines and Roan Consolidated Mines, are to be merged into one company, Zambia Consolidated Copper Mines (May). Merger takes effect March 25, 1982.

New round of labor unrest hits copper mines, as workers strike over pay grievances (July).

President Kaunda orders the detention of senior trade union leaders, including ZCTU chairman, Frederick Chiluba, ZCTU general secretary, Newstead Zimba, ZCTU assistant general secretary, Chitalu Sampa, and MUZ deputy chairman, Timothy Walamba, blaming them for causing the country 205,681 man-days of lost work because of wildcat strikes aimed at overthrowing the government (July 27). The constitution is amended to abolish primary elections; candidates for National Assembly elections must be approved by Central Committee of UNIP (November).

Zambia hosts an international conference; nine nations sign a preferential trade treaty and found the Preferential Trade Area (PTA) (December 21).

1982   President Kaunda meets with South African Prime Minister Botha to discuss improved relations between South Africa and majority-ruled countries to its north (April 30).

PTA headquarters opens in Lusaka (March).

Archbishop Mutale replaces Archbishop of Lusaka,

Emmanuel Milingo, who had been forbidden to practice faith healing and was associated with widespread criticism of the government.

University of Zambia is closed for three months over a dispute about the establishment of a school of human relations.

First phase of treason trial for those arrested in October 1980 ends; charges of treason are lodged against eight, including Valentine Musakanya and Edward Shamwana (August).

Zambia National Holdings, a subsidiary of UNIP, announces takeover of the *Times of Zambia* and the *Sunday Times of Zambia* from Lonhro, bringing all Zambia's daily papers under the control of the government (October 1).

Adamson Mushala, leader of the Mushala Gang, is killed by government troops (November).

1983   In treason trial of those arrested in October 1980, seven of eight defendants are found guilty of treason and sentenced to hang; the eighth is found guilty of misprision of treason (knowledge of the plot) (January).

Government completes a new round of negotiations with IMF and receives a standby credit of SDR 211.5 million. IMF conditions, however, require austerity (April).

General elections give President Kaunda strong victory, a significant improvement over 1978 returns. Yes votes for Kaunda come to 93.06 percent of total votes cast (October).

1984   Riots break out at Ndola and Lusaka campuses of University of Zambia over student allowances and meals (February).

President Kaunda and President Mobutu of Zaire meet over smuggling between their Copperbelt and Shaba provinces (June). Two armed clashes between Zambian and Zairean forces occur in June.

President Kaunda convenes Zambia's Third National Convention, with representatives of all parts of the population and economy (July 23).

President Kaunda authorizes large increases in the price of maize meal in an attempt to reduce subsidies (July).

IMF approves new standby loan of SDR 225 million, to supplement SDR 664.5 million loan already in force, to run through April 1986 (July).

1985   IMF suspends SDR 225 million standby due to arrears on repayments to the fund (February).

President Kaunda bans strikes in all "essential" sectors, including communications, transport, food, fuel, mining, health, sanitation, water distribution, teaching, and banking (March).

Representatives from Zambia and Zaire sign draft treaty in Lubumbashi in response to continuing border disputes (March).

Mineworkers strike to protest Mukuba pension scheme, introduced in 1982, which requires additional pay deductions (June).

Zambia's consultative group pledges aid monies to address Zambia's international payments situation (June 25–26).

President Kaunda is elected chairman of Front Line States at their summit in Maputo, Mozambique (16 September).

Joint permanent commission with Zaire meets for first time and agrees to exchange detained nationals (September).

President Kaunda announces that the kwacha's exchange value is no longer pegged to a trade-weighted basket of currencies but that a foreign exchange auction for the import of most goods will be held each week (October 4). The first auction is held on October 11, effectively devaluing the kwacha by about 57 percent.

UNIP's 20th National Congress focuses on the deterioration of the economy (October).

Taxi and minibus drivers protest increasing fuel prices and become involved in stone-throwing scuffle (October 18).

1986   President Kaunda announces the abolition of NAMBOARD's monopoly on maize and fertilizer marketing, allowing private traders and cooperatives to operate in the market on their own (January).

IMF agrees to provide credits worth SDR 298.6 million (February), but the accumulation of arrears leads to its suspension in July.

President dismisses Luke Mwananshiku, minister of finance, David Phiri, governor of Bank of Zambia, and Dominic Mulaisho, presidential economic advisor (April 4).

South Africa stages raid against ANC facilities in Makeni, west of Lusaka, the first overt case of South African aggression inside Zambia (May 19).

Maize meal subsidy on breakfast meal is removed,

doubling prices (December 3). Riots break out in Ndola and Kitwe (December 9) and spread to Lusaka and rest of Copperbelt; 15 people die and hundreds are injured. Maize meal subsidies are reinstituted and grain mills nationalized (December 11).

1987   President Kaunda suspends auction system for allocating foreign exchange (January 28).

Bank of Zambia governor Leonard Chivuno announces (March 17) that foreign exchange auction will resume March 28.

President Kaunda announces that Zambia is ending four-year IMF plan for economic restructuring and will instead achieve "growth from our own resources" (May 1).

Government publishes its "New Economic Recovery Programme—Interim National Development Plan," which lays out strategy and targets for economic policy in lieu of IMF program (August 15).

IMF declares Zambia ineligible for further borrowing until it clears its arrears, which amount to about US$370 million (October 2).

1988   UNIP General Conference is held at Mulungushi Rock near Kabwe. UNIP constitution is changed: Central Committee grows to 68 members and 23-member Committee of Chairmen is created (August 18–23).

Official announcement is made that Christon Tembo and eight others have been arrested, reportedly for being involved in a coup plot (October 7).

President Kaunda receives 95.5 percent yes votes in election (October 26), but voter turnout is down from 1983.

1989   A coupon system is introduced to ration maize, in order to cut food subsidies (January).

University students block streets and stone vehicles in Lusaka and Kitwe, protesting lodging and tuition fees (April).

About 200 people are arrested in clampdown on illegal marketing activities (May 24).

Wide-ranging talks with IMF are held to negotiate new agreement (May).

Minister of agriculture and cooperatives, Justin Mukando, announces that government will liberalize pricing of all crops except maize (May).

Kaunda announces a 37.5 percent devaluation of the kwacha, to K16 = US$1, the abolition of all remaining price controls except on maize meal, and a 30–50 percent increase in public sector wages (June 30).

NAMBOARD is dissolved and its functions and staff are taken over by Nitrogen Chemicals of Zambia (for fertilizer) and Zambia Cooperative Federation (July 5).

The government announces a series of economic reforms, including interest rate increases and maize price increases (July).

President Kaunda orders closing of University of Zambia and University of the Copperbelt following campus disturbances over meal allowances (November 23, 26).

1990   President Kaunda announces that a Canadian, Jaques Bussieres, will become governor of Bank of Zambia (January 7).

Treason trial of four army officers, including Lieutenant General Christon Tembo, opens in Lusaka (January 16).

Bank of Zambia announces dual exchange rate system, in which official exchange rate window will exchange currencies at a higher rate than will the market exchange rate window (February 13).

UNIP holds its fifth National Convention (March 14–17); main issue is whether Zambia should consider multiparty democratic system. President Kaunda favors a referendum on the issue.

Extraordinary session of UNIP National Council endorses referendum on multiparty politics (May 28–29).

Government announces that maize meal prices will be doubled (June 19).

Protest march (June 25) by students in Lusaka erupts into rioting (lasting until June 28).

At least 23 people are killed, 100 to 200 are treated for wounds, and 1,000 or so are arrested.

Security forces close University of Zambia (June 29).

President Kaunda announces that referendum on multiparty politics will be held October 17, 1990 (June 29).

Lieutenant Mwamba Luchembe seizes radio broadcast studios of Zambia Broadcasting and announces that the president has been overthrown (June 30). Though incorrect, the announcement sparked dancing in the streets. Luchembe and a few accomplices are soon arrested.

Zambia's High Court rejects Christon Tembo's confession to treason as inadmissible, saying it was extracted under duress (July 4).

Paris Club of official creditors of Zambia agrees to reschedule Zambia's US$2.4 billion official foreign debt (July 11–13).

Seventeen-year ban on politically organized groups is lifted (July 17).

Movement for Multiparty Democracy (MMD) is founded at meeting in Lusaka's Garden House Motel (July 20). Arthur Wina is chosen chairman of its National Interim Committee for Multi-Party Democracy, and Vernon Mwaanga and Frederick Chiluba are chosen as vice chairmen.

Zambia's foreign donors meet in Paris and confirm their intention to provide US$500 million in concessionary finance in 1990 (July 20).

President Kaunda announces that referendum on multiparty democracy will be delayed 10 months, to August 13, 1991 (July 25).

President Kaunda announces amnesty for all political prisoners (July 25), including Christon Tembo, Edward Shamwana, and Mwamba Luchembe.

Parliament unanimously adopts report of the special select committee convened to consider ways to democratize UNIP (August 9).

MMD holds its first three rallies in Kabwe, Lusaka, and Kitwe, which attract large crowds (August 18, September 8, September 15).

Minister of finance, Gibson Chigaga, announces that maize marketing will be liberalized (September 13).

UNIP National Council endorses President Kaunda's suggestion to skip referendum on multiparty democracy and hold elections (September 27).

Twenty-two-member constitutional review commission, under chairmanship of Patrick Mvunga, is sworn in (October 9) and begins to implement the return to multiparty democracy (October 18).

Frederick Chiluba and eight other MMD members are arrested and charged with unlawful assembly (October). Rioting breaks out at opening of their trial (November 13).

Minister of finance announces that Foreign Exchange Management Committee is to be abolished (November 16).

Parliament unanimously approves an amendment to constitution repealing provisions for a one-party state (December 4).

Editor in chief of *Times of Zambia*, Komani Kachinga, is replaced after he says that demand for a free press is "an avalanche that cannot be stopped" (December).

Government introduces new industrial relations bill in Parliament designed to weaken union power in national partisan politics (December). ZCTU responds by leaving UNIP.

MMD is launched as a political party, the first opposition party in 17 years (December 20).

1991   President Kaunda announces that he will allow other UNIP members to run against him for party's presidential nomination (February 18).

High Court rules that President Kaunda acted unconstitutionally on November 1 when he ordered *Times of Zambia* and *Zambia Daily Mail* not to cover MMD activities (February).

MMD holds its first national convention as political party and elects Frederick Chiluba as its president (February).

World Bank approves second policy framework paper for Zambia (March 5). This PFP is a revision of the PFP approved by IMF in July 1990.

Frederick Chiluba and eight other MMD members are acquitted in a Choma court on charges of unlawful assembly and belonging to an unlawful society (March 20).

President Kaunda closes University of Zambia, claiming that students are planning a demonstration in support of an interim government (April 18). In fact, the grievances are among lecturers, who are angry that a promised pay increase has not been implemented.

MMD unveils its economic platform, called Programme of National Reconstruction and Development through Democracy (April).

Bank of Zambia announces that the two foreign exchange windows are being unified (May 1).

Industrial Relations Act, 1990, comes into effect (June).

Mvunga Commission, which has proposed constitutional amendments to make Zambia a multiparty democracy, publishes its report amid controversy about the powers of the president under its proposals (June).

Weekly Post, an independent newspaper owned by some 20 businesspeople, is launched (July 26).

At UNIP Congress, President Kaunda is chosen (unopposed) as UNIP's candidate for president in

October 1991 multiparty elections; Central Committee is reduced from 68 to 34 members (August 6).

President Kaunda signs Constitution of Zambia (Amendment) Bill, which allows for multiparty democracy (August 24).

President Kaunda announces that parliamentary and presidential elections will be held on October 31 and November 1 (September 4).

World Bank announces that it is suspending aid to Zambia because of Zambia's failure to meet deadlines for clearing arrears (September 13).

Frederick Chiluba and MMD sweep multiparty elections (first since early 1970s) (October 31). MMD takes 126 of 150 parliamentary seats, and Chiluba wins with over 80 percent of the vote, on a turnout of only 45.4 percent.

Frederick Chiluba is sworn in as country's second president (November 2).

Finance minister Emmanuel Kasonde announces that the maize meal subsidy is being removed, effectively increasing high-grade meal from K215 to K750 and lower-grade meal from K158 to K320 per 25-kilogram bag (December 13).

1992   Two-tier exchange rate system is put into effect again (June).

Caucus for National Unity withdraws from MMD and splits into two factions, one registering as Caucus for National Unity, the other as Congress for National Unity (July).

Paris Club meeting of donors agrees to reschedule US$650 million of debt repayments, reducing Zambia's annual debt service from about US$500 million per year to US$220 million (July).

Kebby Musokotwane is elected president of UNIP, replacing Kenneth Kaunda, at the party's National Congress held outside Lusaka (September).

Bank of Zambia merges its dual exchange rates for foreign currency (a system reintroduced in June 1992) into one rate and removes the controls on Zambian residents purchasing up to US$3,000 worth of hard currency at *bureaux de change* (December 1).

1993   President Chiluba declares state of emergency, following discovery of a UNIP plot, called Zero Option, to destabilize the country and drive MMD government from power (March 4).

Parliament debates extension of state of emergency for 10 hours and, eventually, passes it. Only three MMD members of Parliament vote against the extension, though several others do not attend the debate (March 9, 10).

Fifteen UNIP members are detained in connection with Zero Option plot; over the next 10 days an additional seven are arrested, including three sons of former President Kaunda: Wezi, Panji, and Tilenjyi (March 11).

Rioting by soldiers in North Western Province follows discovery of a murdered comrade.

Rioting in downtown Lusaka erupts after officials try to remove street vendors (March).

Donors pledge assistance, which falls US$115 million short of Zambian requests (April).

President Chiluba announces sacking of four cabinet ministers, including minister of agriculture, Guy Scott, finance minister, Emmanuel Kasonde, minister of mines, Humphrey Mulemba, and education minister, Arthur Wina (April 15).

State of emergency declared on March 4 is lifted (May 25).

About 5,000 Lozi assemble at royal court in Western Province and call for secession of Western Province from Zambia, claiming that Kaunda's government seized some K78.5 million from the royal Barotse treasury at independence (July).

Nine MMD members of Parliament announce their resignation from MMD and their intention to form political party, eventually to be known as National Party (NP) (August 12).

NP is formally registered as political party (September 10).

By-elections are held in six constituencies from which former MMD members of Parliament resigned to form NP. NP wins four seats in by-elections and becomes, along with UNIP, an opposition party in the National Assembly (November).

1994   President Chiluba's cabinet is reshuffled, with the resignations and dismissal of several ministers, including Vernon Mwaanga, minister of foreign affairs, Sikota Wina, deputy speaker of the National Assembly, and Nakatindi Wina, minister of community development and social welfare (January).

Supreme Court rules that all members of Parliament who resign from the party on whose ticket they were elected must stand for reelection (January).

Lusaka Stock Exchange begins operation (February 21).

Constitution Review Commission, under chair John Mwanakatwe, begins hearing evidence in Lusaka (March).

Congress for National Unity, formed in 1992, is dissolved; members join MMD (March).

Zambia Revenue Authority is launched (March).

MMD defeats NP in six by-elections; voter turnout is low (April 7).

NP holds its national convention; Baldwin Nkumbula is elected party president (May 7–10).

Vice President Levy Mwanawasa announces his resignation from the government but not from Parliament or MMD (July 3).

National food disaster is officially declared, following drought and turmoil in agricultural marketing arrangements (July).

Kenneth Kaunda announces he is reentering politics and begins tour of country (July).

Kenneth Kaunda's son, Wezi Kaunda, is sentenced to three months at hard labor for possession of "Zero Option" plan; the sentence is suspended (September 30).

Police, with support of paramilitary units, raid offices of *Times of Zambia* and the *Post*, looking for seditious material, after the papers published a series of articles alledging that President Chiluba has had an extramarital affair (December 7).

Consultative Group of multilateral and bilateral donors pledge record US$2.1 billion in aid to Zambia for 1995 (December 9).

1995   Angolan President Eduardo Dos Santos and UNITA leader Jonas Savimbi meet in Lusaka to attempt to end civil war in Angola. The meeting, which follows by six months the signing of the Lusaka Accord, is heralded as a breakthrough in negotiations (May 6).

Constitutional Review Commission, established in 1993 to review the 1991 constitution, makes its report amid allegations that two of its clauses referring to qualifications for the presidency were inserted to prevent former President Kaunda from taking office again (June).

Special UNIP congress reelects Kenneth Kaunda as leader of the party, with 83 percent of the votes cast, replacing Kebby Musokotwane (June 25–30).

Government rejects the Constitutional Review

Commission's proposal for a constituent assembly to adopt new constitution and recommendations for further political liberalization (September 26).

1996   New constitution adopted by Parliament (May).

Chiluba reelected to second term, and MMD sweeps 131 of 150 parliamentary seats in national elections, which UNIP boycotts (November 18).

Introduction

The Republic of Zambia was officially born on October 24, 1964, when the British flag was lowered and the multicolored (green, red, black, and orange) flag of Zambia was raised. The people of Zambia, however, have roots in the territory that are traceable in some cases to ancestors who were there 13 centuries before. Others are more recent immigrants, but even they have traceable roots that go back about three centuries.

Bordering a huge neighbor such as the Democratic Republic of Congo (Zaire) makes Zambia appear smaller than it actually is. Its area of 752,618 square kilometers (290,586 square miles) compares, for example, to a combined total of about 795,130 square kilometers (307,000 square miles) for the United Kingdom and France. It is about 1,300 square kilometers (500 square miles) short of the combined areas of the American states of Indiana, Illinois, Michigan, Wisconsin and Minnesota, but its population of about four million in 1969 was roughly equal to that of the state of Maryland that year, which gave Zambia a population density of only 5.3 people per square kilometer (14 people per square mile). The 1990 census records a population of 7,818,447, which gives an overall population density of 10.4 people per square kilometer (26.9 people per square mile).

The peculiar shape of Zambia is owed, of course, to the colonial process which carved Africa into many pieces. One of these became known as Northern Rhodesia. The British South Africa Company acquired rights throughout the territory, starting in late 1889. One of its agents was unsuccessful in securing the signature of the Yeke emperor, Msiri; otherwise, the copper-rich area of Katanga (now Shaba) would be part of Zambia today. Instead, it became King Leopold's territory as part of the Congo (today Democratic Republic of Congo, formerly Zaire) and now cuts deeply into Zambia, creating a distinctive "waist. " Zambia's shape has been aptly compared to that of a butterfly heading north. At its widest point Zambia is about 1,167 kilometers (725 miles) east to west: a north to south trip (crossing the Katanga Pedicle) would cover about 1,046 kilometers (650 miles).

The climate of Zambia could be compared to that of southern California but with more rainfall. In the coolest season the night-time temperature rarely dips below 4 degrees Celcius (40 degrees Fahrenheit), while the hottest season will not normally have day-time temperatures above 35 degrees Celcius (95 degrees Fahrenheit). The annual median rainfall ranges from 114 to 127 centimeters (45 to 50 inches). All of these figures are subject to variation, of course, as certain parts of the country are somewhat colder than others, and rainfall likewise decreases from the northeast to the southwest.

The topography of Zambia is gently undulating, with plateaus (elevation about 1,067–1,372 meters, or 3,500–4,500 feet) broken by occasional hills. In eastern Zambia, however, the Muchinga Mountains rise to 1,830 meters (6,000 feet) in some places; a huge escarpment is created as the eastern side of the mountains plunge to the Luangwa River valley, about 915 meters (3,000 feet) below. Several important lakes are found either along or within the borders of Zambia. Lake Mweru and Lake Tanganyika, both along its northern border, are part of the East Africa Rift, and their waters are shared with the Democratic Republic of Congo (Zaire) and Tanzania. Lake Bangweulu and its adjacent swamps are a little farther south but still in northeastern Zambia. Along Zambia's southern border is the manmade Lake Kariba, part of a hydroelectric system on the Zambezi River that is shared with Zimbabwe.

There are four major rivers in Zambia. The largest, from which the country derives its name, is the Zambezi. It starts in the northwestern part of the country on a southern route, picking up tributaries along the way, then turns east and serves as the southern border of the country en route to the Indian Ocean. Its major tributary is the Kafue, which begins in north-central Zambia and heads generally southwest before hooking back to the east and eventually joining the Zambezi in south-central Zambia. The Luangwa River begins in northeastern Zambia and flows southwesterly before merging with the Zambezi River in southeastern Zambia. The Luapula River is not a part of the Zambezi system, developing just east of the Katanga Pedicle, near Lake Bangweulu. It ultimately forms the Zambia-Democratic Republic of Congo (Zaire) border as it flows north into Lake Mweru.

The people of Zambia are almost all within the Bantu language family. Most of them claim either Luba or Lunda origins, but some have East African roots, and one group, the Ngoni, migrated from South Africa in the 19th century. There is archaeological evidence at Ingombe Ilede dating to an amazingly early time, between ca. A.D. 1350 and ca. 1450. Ingombe Ilede may have been a backwater beneficiary of the coastal interest in the Zambezi River—Great Zimbabwe gold trade. The ancestors of most of today's Zambians arrived in the country by 1800.

Figures about the number of "tribes" and "languages" found in a country are almost meaningless unless definitional ground rules are first explained. It is generally agreed, however, that there are more than 70 African peoples in Zambia, and one source calculates 30 different languages. Only the Tonga and the Bemba peoples constitute close to 10 percent of the population each, while there are about nine groups in the 2.5–6 percent range. Ci-Bemba speakers account for about a third of the population. Ci-Tonga and ciNyanja speakers combine to account for another third. English is the language that links people from distant parts of the country. Zambia also has fairly small populations of Asians, Eurafricans, and Europeans, some of whom are now Zambian citizens.

Zambia's political history must be separated into regions, as sections of the country have their own individual histories, only occasionally linked with other sections. The history of the western part of the country revolves around that of the Luyana or Lozi nation, which eventually came to dominate much of that area. Southern Zambian history has been influenced heavily by the Tonga, although its lack of a centralized kingdom reduced its power considerably. Southeastern Zambia was first controlled by the Chewa people, who entered from the east (Malawi today), but the Ngoni became 19th-century conquerors in that area. Many groups were important in the history of northeastern Zambia, which was dominated by the Bemba and, along the Luapula, by the Lunda of Kazembe.

Europeans first touched parts of Zambia in the early 16th century, but few non-Africans spent much time within the present borders until the early 19th century, when the Portuguese entered from the southeast, and a little later, Arab traders entered from the northeast. The object at this point was purely trade, primarily for slaves and ivory. Some of the stronger African chiefdoms, especially among the Bisa, Bemba, and Lunda, became major partners in this trade, often prospering at the expense of their neighbors. The Swahili (Arabs) set up some villages for trading purposes, but only in a few instances did they establish permanent settlements. The Portuguese, coming up the Zambezi River from Mozambique, were interested in little more than trade.

Missionaries did not arrive until the middle of the 19th century, with Dr. David Livingstone being the first of this new breed of

Europeans. His activities and writings encouraged others to follow his path. Thus Frederick Arnot and François Coillard entered southern and western Zambia, while the Livingstonia Mission of the Free Church of Scotland and the White Fathers (Catholic) entered northern and eastern Zambia. They met with varying degrees of success; ultimately, mission posts and schools were established at opposite ends of the country.

The coming of colonial rule to Zambia was the result of the efforts of Cecil Rhodes, the South African mining magnate. He persuaded the British government to grant a charter to his British South Africa Company (BSAC) in October 1889. The BSAC immediately sought to acquire signatures from African leaders throughout the country. With the slave trade creating a great deal of insecurity among some northeastern peoples, the BSAC was successful in winning concessions from several of the more insecure chiefs. Company posts in this area led to a decline in both the slave trade and the inter-African fighting associated with it. In southwestern Zambia there was a similar insecurity, as the king of the Lozi, Lewanika, sought British protection against the Ndebele. Thus, he signed documents in which he unwittingly opened the door to extravagant BSAC claims to the western half of Zambia. The inaccuracy of the claims was not of concern to unscrupulous seekers of fortune. When the railroad from South Africa crossed the Zambezi in 1905, the interior of Zambia became fair game for any Europeans seeking land for farming or, preferably, the mining of precious minerals. While initial discoveries hinting at the country's copper resources were made about this time, development of the Copperbelt was still about two decades away.

The BSAC controlled Zambia administratively until 1924, when the British Colonial Office officially took over. With the opening of several major copper mines during the 1920s, European interest in Northern Rhodesia began to grow. Increasing numbers of Europeans entered the territory to gain their fortune. The interests of the Africans were secondary. For two decades the Europeans had taxed the Africans in order to force them to work at European enterprises in order to pay the tax. Now a new effort to promote European interests began. Southern Rhodesia had attained self-rule in 1923. It was now proposed that the two Rhodesias be amalgamated under one rule. Africans north of the Zambezi opposed this from the beginning, recognizing the oppressed state of their fellow Africans to the south. The British government was also reluctant to move in this direction, proclaiming that its duty was to promote African interests in Northern Rhodesia. The all-European Legislative Council of Northern Rhodesia supported amalgamation and its subsequent variations—incorporation and federation.

Finally in 1953 the Central African Federation of the Rhodesias and Nyasaland was born. Its leading forces would be Godfrey Huggins and Roy Welensky. The federation would last just months past its 10th birthday, for African nationalists had decided that they could tolerate European rule no longer. Harry Nkumbula and Kenneth Kaunda had begun their political efforts prior to the coming of the federation but failed to prevent its birth. They now set about to ensure its quick demise. The African National Congress (ANC) was the first major nationalist organization to have a nationwide effect, but Nkumbula's leadership did not please many of the younger activists. Thus, men like Kaunda, Simon Kapwepwe, and Reuben Kamanga broke away and formed a new group in 1958. It was soon banned by the government, however, and the United National Independence Party (UNIP) arose with the same leadership. UNIP soon demonstrated national strength, and by March 1961 it was obvious that it would be only a matter of time before the federation would break up and Zambia would be free.

Independence for Zambia came on October 24, 1964. Kenneth Kaunda became its president and UNIP its ruling party. The years since then have not been easy for the country. When white-ruled Southern Rhodesia unilaterally declared its independence from Great Britain in 1965, Zambia found it necessary to cut off all links with the territory that had been its most important trading partner and the principal outlet for Zambia's copper exports. The TAZARA railway neared completion in 1974 and promised a safe outlet for the copper, but that same year world copper prices reached a peak and then began to plummet to new lows. The Zambian economy was hard hit. It was not until Zimbabwe was liberated in 1980 that pressures on Zambia from the south began to recede—and then not completely, due to the continuing struggles in Mozambique, Angola, and South Africa.

UNIP dominance was overwhelming in the early years of the republic, with only rump ANC opposition in the National Assembly. Nonetheless, UNIP itself faced serious factional divisions along ethnic and regional lines. At the 1967 UNIP General Conference, Bemba politicians, led by Simon Kapwepwe, mounted a challenge for the leadership positions of the party. Their success provoked an anti-Bemba backlash among UNIP members, which led to moves to unseat Kapwepwe as vice president of the republic at the 1969 UNIP conference. That challenge was temporarily sidelined, however, by President Kaunda's announcement of sweeping economic reforms, which included a 51 percent nationalization of the copper mines. Still, the Bemba faction within UNIP became more isolated, and in August 1971 Kapwepwe led his faction out of UNIP and formed the United Progressive Party (UPP). Tensions between the UPP and UNIP were soon evident. UPP leaders were arrested in September and accused of threatening the security of the country. Campaigning for the December 1971 by-elections was a bitter and violent affair. In the end, the UPP and the ANC did poorly. Nonetheless, by the end of 1971, President Kaunda was exploring a move to a one-party state, a step that was completed in December 1972 when Kaunda signed into law a constitutional amendment outlawing all political parties but UNIP. Zambia's Second Republic was thus launched.

Over the years of the Second Republic (1972–91) political competition was restricted, and President Kaunda's control was firmly maintained through a variety of means. Under the new constitutional arrangements, only one candidate for the presidency was put before the public at election time, and voters were only given the choice of voting yes or no: for or against the candidate. The candidate was nominated by UNIP, a process locked up by President Kaunda, whose stature and whose power of appointment over party positions virtually assured him of the nomination. When President Kaunda's nomination bid was challenged by Simon Kapwepwe and Harry Nkumbula in 1978, UNIP swiftly changed its qualifications for candidature to eliminate both challengers from the race. It was clear that serious challenges to Kaunda would not be tolerated. During the Second Republic, national elections were held in 1973, 1978, 1983, and 1988. President Kaunda won each of these with upwards of 80 percent of the vote—that is, with 80 percent or more of the ballots marked yes. Turnouts, however, declined precipitously after the introduction of the one-party state, a sign that has been interpreted variously as apathy or tacit disapproval of the elimination of meaningful competition.

In addition to maintaining control over the selection of the president, UNIP's Central Committee vetted candidates for National Assembly seats, and vetted party membership applications from former members of the UPP and the ANC. Campaigns for National Assembly seats were managed by the party, and candidates were required to adopt a common party platform. State and party control over the media and coercive powers at the president's disposal under the state of emergency which prevailed throughout the Second Republic were also used to quash opposition. A state of emergency had been declared in 1964 to cope with the disruptions caused by the Lumpa Church, but it was regularly renewed until President Chiluba revoked it on November 8, 1991. Thus, throughout the Second Republic, effective means of challenging the rule of President Kaunda or UNIP elite were curtailed.

Though UNIP maintained its grip on the government throughout the Second Republic, the deterioration of the economy that began in the mid-1970s undermined the legitimacy of the regime. Over the first five years or so after independence, Zambia had established government control over a large part of the economy. Major industries, such as the mines, banks, industrial and commercial enterprises, and agricultural marketing and pricing were all controlled by government parastatals. From 1965 through 1976, Zambia enjoyed fairly steady growth as real gross domestic product (GDP) increased at an average of 4.3 percent per year. However, the price of copper collapsed in the mid-1970s, and this, coupled with economic mismanagement, ushered in a long period of economic decline, which ultimately undermined the government. Real GDP growth rates for the 1976–86 period averaged only 0.07 percent per year, and GDP per capita in this period declined at a rate of -3.5 percent per year. The sharp decline in GDP per capita is explained in part by a population growth rate of 3.9 percent per year in the 1980s.

The decline in the standard of living beginning in the latter 1970s changed the nature of opposition to the government. Whereas ethnic tensions had been paramount in the late 1960s, by the late 1970s the debate had come to focus squarely on the need for economic liberalization to correct the faults of statism and socialism. Criticism of the economic performance of Zambia under UNIP leadership was, for example, a theme of Kapwepwe's challenge to Kaunda in 1978. In addition, opponents increasingly criticized President Kaunda for the sacrifices borne by the country due to its stand against the minority regimes in Rhodesia and South Africa. Economic pressures and guerrilla raids took an increasing toll on Zambia's already shaken economy in the late 1970s. These themes, too, found expression in Kapwepwe's short-lived campaign. Though the Lancaster House agreement ended the war of liberation for Zimbabwe, and pressures on Zambia from this front eased, Zambia's economy was not to recover from the errors of past policies, or from the hostility of the international market conditions, any time soon. And, as the economy continued its downward slide, popular opposition to the regime grew.

The signs of growing opposition appeared on many fronts. Churches in Zambia became vocal opponents of the regime, criticizing especially the teachings of Marxism in public colleges. The *National Mirror*, a publication of the Christian Council of Zambia, became widely read for its interviews highly critical of the government. Relations between the press and the government eroded over the early 1980s, as the *Times of Zambia* reported declining public confidence in the government and covered stories of corruption. In retaliation, the government denounced and harassed reporters and in 1983 dismissed, without explanation, the editor in chief of the *Times*.

The early 1980s were also marked by many labor disputes, often over wage issues, as economic deterioration eroded workers' standard of living. In 1981 trade union leaders, including Frederick Chiluba, were detained in connection with a number of wildcat strikes, and in 1985 strikes in essential industries were banned by President Kaunda. The opposition of organized labor was the logical consequence of the deterioration of the copper industry. The world recession of the early 1980s forced copper prices steeply downward, and subsequent efforts at exchange rate liberalization forced import-sensitive production costs steeply upward. Meanwhile, the shortage of foreign exchange with which to purchase spare parts and other inputs, the declining grade of ore available in Zambia, the bottlenecks in transport along the TAZARA railway, and declining output of copper prevented Zambia from taking full advantage of rising copper prices in the late 1980s. Trade union disputes would continue throughout the 1980s, and though the union leadership was careful to avoid displaying overtly political motives, labor union activity came to represent a significant challenge to UNIP. Frederick Chiluba, president of the Zambia Congress of Trade Unions, gained a national reputation as an opponent of the regime.

The government made efforts during the 1980s to address the economic problems the country faced, though these efforts were characterized by an on-again, off-again rhythm. In 1983 the government negotiated an agreement with the International Monetary Fund (IMF), their fourth since 1976, and began a process of economic liberalization. The kwacha was devalued, price controls on items other than maize products and fertilizer were removed, and interest rates were moderately increased. These reforms were extended in 1985 with the introduction of a foreign exchange auction and further financial liberalization. However, the UNIP elite was not uniformly behind these efforts. The devaluation of the kwacha and import liberalization had fueled inflation and put pressure on import-sensitive industries. In April 1986, President Kaunda replaced his top proreform economic lieutenants with appointees known to oppose liberalization. Public confidence in the auction began to fail. Then, in December 1986, the government announced the removal of subsidies on some types of maize meal, with the consequence that maize meal prices increased. Riots broke out on the Copperbelt, killing 15 people. The subsidy was quickly restored, and private grain milling firms were nationalized.

The December riots clearly shook the government's resolve to carry through with economic liberalization and strengthened the hand of those within UNIP who opposed such measures. From January through March 1987 the foreign exchange auction was suspended, and foreign exchange was once again allocated administratively. Then, on May 1, 1987, Zambia repudiated the IMF reform program altogether and struck out on its own to grow from its own resources. Signs of serious strain, especially in the country's payments position, were not long in coming, and by midyear the "go it alone" approach was showing signs of failure. Though the IMF program had been repudiated, relations with the IMF and the World Bank were not immediately severed. Both organizations sent missions to Zambia in October 1987 to discuss ways to revise Zambia's Interim National Development Plan. These were unsuccessful, however, and in early 1988 talks with the IMF and the World Bank collapsed. The return to efforts at economic reform would have to wait until after the 1988 elections.

After the October elections President Kaunda moved to reinstitute economic reform: the kwacha was devalued, interest rates were increased, and a plan was announced to ration maize meal in urban areas as part of an effort to reduce maize subsidies without provoking riots like those that had followed their temporary removal in December 1986. Over the first nine months of 1989 a series of economic reforms were put in place, and Zambia conducted talks with the IMF and the World Bank. In September 1989 an agreement was reached in a policy framework paper establishing a program to help Zambia clear its arrears to the IMF and the World Bank and qualify once again for balance of payments assistance.

Economic pressures and repeated corruption scandals helped discredit UNIP leadership over the middle years of the 1980s. By early 1988 it was clear that UNIP was feeling embattled. Students and labor unions had long been disaffected, but the riots of 1986 had clearly demonstrated the depth of public frustration, especially since rioters had appeared to specifically target UNIP offices for destruction. The National Assembly, too, was becoming increasingly critical of the government, so beginning in April 1988, the president led an effort to reestablish party control over this body. President Kaunda proposed constitutional amendments that would make National Assembly membership only part-time, would eliminate their salaries, and would add business and farming representatives, chosen by a UNIP electoral college. The National Assembly balked at these efforts to circumscribe its independence and passed only a much-diluted version of the proposal.

Efforts were made to tighten control over the party, too. At its August 1988 General Conference, UNIP's central leadership structures were enlarged and altered, and President Kaunda sought to co-opt opposition elements by inviting Enock Kavindele, a wealthy businessman who had been a strong critic of the government's economic policies, and two top leaders from the Mineworkers Union of Zambia (MUZ), to sit on the Central Committee. (Frederick Chiluba, leader of the Zambia Congress of Trade Unions, had turned down a similar invitation in 1984.) Efforts to place even more power in the hands of the president were made again in 1990, but the National Assembly refused to approve the necessary constitutional amendments.

Deteriorating economic conditions, frequent corruption scandals, obvious mismanagement, and widespread illegal marketing activities, which the government appeared incapable of stopping, combined to add force to the demands for political liberalization. UNIP responded to these pressures by taking up the debate over a return to multiparty democracy at its March 1990 National Convention. President Kaunda stated his opposition to multiparty politics at the outset of the convention, but the extent of the sentiment for a return to multiparty competition even within UNIP surprised him. He soon agreed to hold a national referendum on the issue. Again, however, political calculations were swept along by economic discontent. In June maize meal price increases were announced, and as in 1986, rioting erupted. This time, however, the riots occurred in Lusaka, not on the Copperbelt, and they had distinctly political—and anti-Kaunda—overtones. Peace was restored, and the price increases were not rescinded. The referendum was set for October 1990.

Then a small group of soldiers seized the radio station in Lusaka and broadcast a message that the government had been overthrown. Though untrue, the announcement initiated widespread celebrating in the streets. The jubilation with which the announcement was greeted was not lost on the government.

Shortly thereafter, the ban on political organizations was lifted so that campaigning for the upcoming referendum could begin, and a number of political prisoners, some of whom had become popular heroes, were freed. The referendum, however, was postponed until August 1991, probably in a ploy to buy time for UNIP to organize the no vote. The unbanning of political organizations allowed the birth of the Movement for Multiparty Democracy (MMD), an organization formed to promote the yes vote for a return to multiparty democracy. The movement's first rallies, held in August and September 1990, attracted huge crowds. The momentum had clearly shifted away from UNIP. In an attempt to rob the MMD of its central cause, and to force upon it the task of organizing itself as a party, Kaunda scrapped the referendum proposal and agreed to allow multiparty competition in the next election.

Over the last quarter of 1990 the government hindered and harrassed MMD's efforts to organize the opposition to UNIP. In December the Parliament passed the necessary constitutional amendment allowing multiparty competition again, and the MMD registered as a political party. Over the course of the campaigning for the October 1991 elections, the government continued to use the advantages of incumbency to thwart the efforts of the MMD, but to no avail. Though several parties contested the 1991 elections, only the MMD and UNIP won seats, and the overwhelming majority went to the MMD. Frederick Chiluba won the presidency with over 80 percent of the popular vote, and the MMD claimed 126 of the 150 seats in the assembly. UNIP did well only in Eastern Province, where it claimed all 19 parliamentary seats.

Throughout Chiluba's first term, Zambia's economy struggled under difficult and austere economic reforms. Efforts to return to the path of economic reform and liberalization following the 1988 elections were derailed in the run-up to the 1991 elections. Though Zambia had reached a new agreement with the IMF in April 1991, it proved unwilling to implement the austerity measures required before the elections, and the program was suspended by the donors in September for noncompliance. Once President Chiluba assumed office, however, efforts to reestablish compliance with reform programs were taken up again. The MMD's discipline in implementing reform greatly pleased donors, who made funds, which had been frozen in September 1991, available as early as January 1992. Over the succeeding four years Zambia would remain roughly on its reform course and in the good graces of the donor community, though living conditions for most Zambians, including nationwide epidemics of cholera and AIDS, became difficult indeed. A wide range of consumer goods became available but at prices well beyond the reach of all but a few. The poverty rate soared, and prices rose with the removal of subsidies. Sharp devaluations of the kwacha raised import prices, and in 1993 interest rates rose dramatically. Still, the liberalization of the foreign exchange and other markets proceeded. The privatization of state-owned firms moved forward as well, though at a snail's pace.

The copper mining industry continued its downward slide. Though efforts were made at rehabilitation and reinvestment beginning in the mid-1980s (efforts that bore fruit in the late 1980s), such improvements were short-lived. Continuing problems with the falling copper content of the ore, shortages of spare parts, and the need for massive capital investments resulted in declining output. The MMD government considered privatization of the Zambia Consolidated Copper Mines (ZCCM) the only feasible solution, but progress here was slower than in other industries, for political reasons. Efforts to reorient and restart the economy were made more difficult by several years of poor rains, particularly in 1992, and by the mismanagement of maize market liberalization, which was completed only in 1995. Some backsliding on fiscal discipline in early 1995 kept the donors on edge as well, though overall Zambia has been recognized for making extraordinary efforts to comply with donor strictures under very difficult circumstances.

On the political front, MMD's overwhelming victory at the polls was hardly a harbinger of harmony and stability. First, the voter turnout in 1991 was only 44.8 percent, and voter turnouts averaging only 18 percent in subsequent by-elections would continue to raise questions about MMD's popularity. Moreover, bickering and factionalism within the cabinet broke out from the start, and the Chiluba administration has witnessed the resignation or sacking of many of its original leaders. Virtually all of the MMD officials who left alleged that remaining members of the cabinet were corrupt and insensitive to the plight of the common Zambian suffering from the austerity programs instituted at the insistence of the international donor community. Charges of corruption would continue to plague President Chiluba throughout his term. Minor cabinet changes in 1992 did little to quell the criticism. In April 1993 donors pledged fewer funds than requested in part because of suspicions of corruption, and the following December, Germany suspended its aid. In August 1994 Parliament adopted a ministerial code of conduct, but critics claimed that it came too late to prevent the personal enrichment of some top MMD officials and that it had been adopted only after considerable donor pressure.

Infighting within the MMD led to its fragmentation. For example, in June 1992, Enoch Kavindele formed the United Democratic Party (UDP) after splitting from the MMD. In July 1992 the Caucus for National Unity (CNU) broke away and immediately split into two parties. However, the first serious split in the MMD came in August 1993 when nine members of Parliament resigned from the MMD and formed the National Party (NP). The founding members of the NP included well-known leaders such as Emmanuel Kasonde, the former minister of finance, Akashambatwa Mbikusita-Lewanika, a founding member of the MMD and a former minister, and Baldwin Nkumbula, son of Harry Nkumbula and a former minister. In late 1993 the NP won four of eight seats it contested in by-elections and so became the third party to be represented in the National Assembly. However, the NP has not done well in subsequent by-elections, and none of the several other new political parties has managed to win seats in the assembly. Indeed, some, such as the UDP, have dissolved and rejoined the MMD. In some respects, the fragmentation of the MMD reflects a resurgence of the ethnic and regional politics typical of the First Republic. Many resent what is perceived to be the dominance of Bemba (Northern and Copperbelt Provinces) in the MMD. The CNU was initially led by Lozis (Western Province), who forged an alliance with Tonga (Southern Province) dissidents. UNIP remained strong in Eastern Province.

However, not all the opposition President Chiluba's regime faced originated in the MMD. Labor unions and the Zambia Congress of Trade Unions (ZCTU), the federation that Chiluba led for so many years, moved swiftly into the opposition following the 1991 election. A series of wildcat strikes broke out as early as the first half of 1992, as workers protested their declining standard of living under IMF-imposed austerity. By December 1993 Chiluba's successor in the ZCTU was charging that the government had been taken over by "criminals." Church leaders, too, criticized the regime, especially for the harshness of the austerity programs. And, of course, UNIP remained in the opposition, though its affairs were equally rocky. In March 1993 the *Times of Zambia* reported a plot, known as the "Zero Option," in which UNIP was allegedly planning to foment strikes and disorder in an attempt to force an early election. The government declared a state of emergency, an action many considered overwrought, and cracked down on some UNIP leaders. The differential treatment of the UNIP elite, however, produced a split within the party.

Divisions in UNIP were exacerbated by Kaunda's decision to return to politics in July 1994 and his announcement the following October that he would seek the presidency once again. Kebby Musokotwane, president of UNIP at the time, refused to stand down and accused Kaunda of betrayal. At the June 1995 special UNIP Congress, however, Kaunda won the candidacy of the party and purged Musokotwane supporters from UNIP's elite ranks. As Kenneth Kaunda once again campaigned for the presidency, the government found excuses to harass him. He was arrested in August 1995 for allegedly inciting riotous behavior, and in October he was briefly charged for being "stateless" as the result of having failed to properly apply for Zambian citizenship many years earlier. It was, however, new constitutional proposals which became the focus of the 1996 elections.

In 1992 the government launched a constitutional review commission, chaired by John Mwanakatwe, to propose changes to the 1991 constitution. The commission's recommendations, reported in June 1995, contained two controversial clauses affecting the eligibility of presidential candidates. One prohibited candidacies of persons who had already been elected to the presidency twice, and the other required that candidates' parents be Zambian citizens by birth or descent. Both—but particularly the latter—were interpreted as explicit attempts to prevent Kenneth Kaunda from running for the presidency again. Chiluba's government denied accusations that the clauses were directed against Kaunda, arguing that these suggestions had been made by citizens (and not the government) during the testimony taken by the commission while Kaunda was retired from politics. Despite widespread public outcry both at home and abroad, the new constitution, containing both clauses, was adopted by Parliament on May 28, 1996.

In response to this constitutional gambit, UNIP opted to boycott the upcoming elections under the slogan "No KK, no election." In the months prior to the November 18 poll, UNIP collected the voter registration cards of UNIP loyalists to confront the regime with a poll that was so poorly attended that the election would be discredited. Kaunda repeatedly denounced the constitutional ban on his candidacy, promising to make the country ungovernable, by peaceful means, after the election. Foreign governments, too, condemned the heavy-handed tactics which tainted the elections before they were held. In addition to the boycott, there were reports of errors in, and deliberate manipulation of, the new voter roll, which was constructed by Nikuv, an Israeli computer firm.

The election was held in an orderly and peaceful manner on November 18 as planned. And, as expected, Chiluba was re-elected by an overwhelming majority. But voter turnout was poor. While government statistics show that 54.5 percent of those registered voted (compared to only 44.8 percent in 1991), a much smaller proportion of those eligible had actually registered in 1996, so that the turnout in 1996 was only 29 percent of all eligible voters (compared to 39 percent in 1991). Undoubtedly this was due in part to the UNIP boycott. But there was evidence of growing apathy and disillusionment in Zambia by 1996 as well. This, coupled with the difficulties of the registration effort, and the arrival of the first rains of the season on election day, explain the low turnout.

President Chiluba garnered 72.6 percent of the presidential vote. Dean Mung'omba of the Zambia Democratic Congress came in a distant second with only 12.7 percent, followed by Humphrey Mulemba of the NP with 6.6 percent, Akashambatwa Mbikusita-Lewanika of the Agenda for Zambia with 4.7 percent, and Chama Chakomboka of the Movement for Democratic Process with 3.3 percent. In parliamentary races, UNIP put up only two candidates, neither of whom won. Of the 150 seats in Parliament, MMD won 131, independent candidates took 10, the NP five, and the Agenda for Zambia and the Zambia Democratic Congress took two each.

The difficult conditions of Zambia in the 1990s persist. Though President Chiluba and the MMD won overwhelmingly in 1996, the results hardly constitute a mandate given the constitutional controversy, the UNIP boycott, and low voter turnout. The economic reforms show few signs as yet of improving the lives of ordinary men and women. There is as well a lack of public confidence in the regime and suspicions that many in the elite are dishonest and corrupt. There is a widespread sentiment that donors run the economy from afar and that the suffering of the people means little to them. Meanwhile the epidemic of HIV/AIDS continues to take its ghastly toll. It seems that Zambians still have a hard road to travel.

Map of Zambia

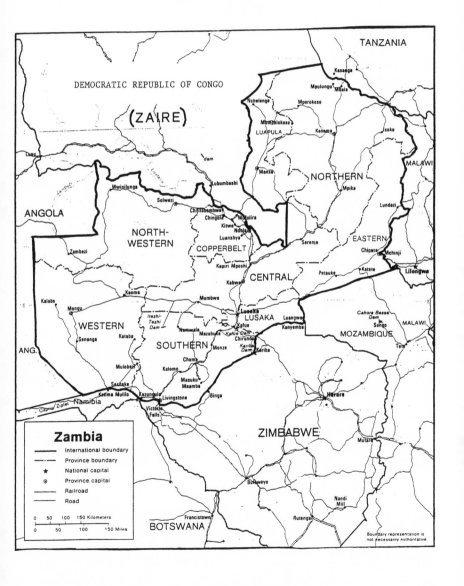

The Dictionary

A

ABERCORN. Renamed Mbala (q.v.) at Zambian independence, the town is about 48 kilometers (30 miles) southeast of the southeastern edge of Lake Tanganyika and 40 kilometers (25 miles) from the Tanzanian border, in the extreme northeastern part of Zambia. It was created as a government post in 1893 and was named for the Duke of Abercorn, then president of the British South Africa Company (q.v.). Hugh Marshall (q.v.) was sent as the magistrate and collector for the Tanganyika District, and Abercorn was to be its administrative center. Marshall had about six Sikhs (q.v.) and a few Nyasaland (q.v.) Tonga to aid him as a police force. The post was near the village of Zombe (q.v.), chief of the Lungu (q.v.). Marshall built an impregnable stockade of 10-foot-high poles. Refugees from the slave raids came there for protection. In September 1914, it was attacked by the Germans but was held when reinforcements came. At the end of World War I, the local German commander, General Paul von Lettow-Vorbeck (q.v.), surrendered to General Edwards at Abercorn on November 18, 1918. Abercorn/Mbala eventually became a major town. In 1969 it had a population of 5,200.

ABERCORN NATIVE WELFARE ASSOCIATION. Founded in 1932 with Franklin Tembo (q.v.) as its first chairman, it was one of only two welfare associations in the Northern Province (q.v.) before World War II. It had some significance as a body in which anticolonial issues could be raised and discussed. It took its complaints to the district commissioner at Abercorn (q.v.). Its jurisdiction was limited to the township of Abercorn itself by the government and never faced problems as serious as those of its sister organizations on the Copperbelt (q.v.).

ABOLITION OF SLAVERY PROCLAMATION, 1906. This rule was imposed upon Barotseland (q.v.) by the British South Africa Company (q.v.) on July 16, 1906, when resident magistrate Frank Worthington (q.v.) of the BSAC forced the Ngambela to read it aloud to a crowd of several thousand gathered in Lealui (qq.v.). As a result, the Lozi (q.v.) ruling class could no longer require workers to assist the *indunas* (q.v.) and headmen to build their homes or cultivate their fields. However, it thereby "freed" Africans to work for Europeans in order to pay the hut tax (q.v.) to the company.

ACTION GROUP. A subgroup of the African National Congress (q.v.), it began organizing and recruiting in October 1953. It was supported by Kenneth Kaunda and Simon Kapwepwe (qq.v.), who saw it as a disciplined and nonviolent way to oppose the colour bar (q.v.), especially in business. Its members were younger and more radical than the ANC leader, Harry Nkumbula (q.v.), who saw in its vigor and enthusiasm a potential threat to his leadership. The ANC national executive council finally tightened its control over it by absorbing the Action Group's funds.

ADMINISTRATION OF NATIVE PROCLAMATION NO. 8, 1916. A rule promulgated by the British South Africa Company (q.v.) administration during World War I, it enabled chiefs and headmen to recruit labor for the war effort. In redefining the powers and duties of the chiefs and the obligations of the commoners to provide "reasonable" requests for free labor, it restored some power to the chiefs that had been diminished for 20 years.

ADVISORY COUNCIL. In response to protests from the new settlers in Northern Rhodesia (q.v.), the British South Africa Company (q.v.) granted the settlers the right to form an elected Advisory Council in 1918. Composed of five settlers, it had no legislative power but merely afforded the settlers a place to have their voices heard. Voting was by white, male, British subjects, at least 21 years old, with £150 in income or property. Four members represented North-Western Rhodesia and one represented North-Eastern Rhodesia (qq.v.). Sir Lawrence Wallace (q.v.), administrator of Northern Rhodesia, had suggested such a council as early as 1914. The council was terminated in 1925, after the British government took over the direct administration of Northern Rhodesia.

AFRICAN AFFAIRS BOARD. A feature of the governing constitution of the Central African Federation (q.v.), the board was a standing committee of the Federal Assembly designed to serve as a safeguard for African interests. It had the power to examine and even veto bills that appeared to discriminate against Africans. The veto, however, could be overridden by the governor-general or, if necessary, by the British Parliament. The board consisted of a nominated chairman, three white members appointed to uphold African interests, and three African members. In the first constitutional discussions, the African Affairs Board was to have been much stronger, to reassure Africans that the federation would protect them. Subsequent constitutional talks reduced its power progressively, however, so that its final form was as outlined above. The demise of the board came in late 1957, when it objected to two constitutional changes passed by the Federal Assembly and the British House of Commons overruled the board. Its chairman, Sir John Moffat (q.v.), resigned, and the board was considered to be dead.

AFRICAN DEMOCRATIC SOCIALISM. The officially stated guiding ideology of the Zambian government at the time of independence, it was heavy on economic goals. It promised to raise the standard of living, to provide a more equitable distribution of wealth, to humanize labor conditions, and to increase social services such as health and educational programs. In 1967 the term was replaced by the new ideology, Zambian humanism (q.v.).

AFRICAN LAKES COMPANY (MANDALA). Originally called the Livingstonia Central Africa Trading Company, this commercial agency was founded in 1878 by James Stevenson and John and Frederick Moir (q.v.), businessmen from Glasgow. Their company intended to supply the Scottish (Livingstonia, q.v.) missions in Nyasaland (q.v.) and offer Africans a commercial alternative to the slave trade. Its initial business was in Nyasaland, but the ivory and rubber trade forced it to build the Stevenson Road (q.v.) through North-Eastern Rhodesia (q.v.). Around the turn of the century the company (reorganized as the African Lakes Corporation in 1893) had trading stations on Lakes Tanganyika and Mweru and along the Luangwa and Kafue Rivers (qq.v.). The company was hindered by many battles with Arab slave traders. Ultimately, Cecil Rhodes (q.v.) acquired a large share in the financially pressed company. His British South Africa Company (q.v.) acquired 11,163 square kilometers (4,310 square miles) of African Lakes Corporation land in the Abercorn area near Lake Tanganyika (qq.v.).

AFRICAN METHODIST EPISCOPAL CHURCH. Founded in America in 1816 by a black preacher, Richard Allen, in reaction to racism in the orthodox American Methodist Church, it became important to Zambia in 1897 when a Sotho (q.v.) evangelist, Willie J. Mokalapa (q.v.), founder of the Ethiopian Church of Barotseland (q.v.), incorporated his church into the AME. Mokalapa eventually became the presiding elder of the African Methodist Episcopal Church in Barotseland. The AME provided an alternative to white missionaries.

AFRICAN MINEWORKERS UNION. Officially the Northern Rhodesia African Mineworkers Trade Union, it was founded in 1947 with the assistance of a representative of the British Labour Party, then in power in England. Lawrence Katilungu (q.v.) became its first chairman. In 1949 he became its president. The union also gained official recognition by the mining companies that year. It gained considerable authority and prestige in the next several years and was recognized as one of the two strongest unions in the country. In 1956 it had a bitter struggle for survival against the Mines African Staff Association (q.v.), a group with strong company backing. This resulted in a series of 15 rolling strikes (q.v.). Though each was brief, copper and lead production was disrupted during a period of peak world demand. Katilungu was replaced as president by John Chisata (q.v.) in December 1960. The AMU was renamed the Zambia Mineworkers Union (q.v.) in January 1965.

AFRICAN NATIONAL CONGRESS (of Zambia). The term African National Congress (ANC) has been used by a number of African political groups, notably in South Africa, but also in Northern and Southern Rhodesia (qq.v.), where it was founded in July 1948 as the Northern Rhodesia African Congress (q.v.) by Godwin M. Lewanika (q.v.). It was previously named the Federation of African Societies (q.v.). Membership surged during the controversy over federation with Southern Rhodesia. Harry Nkumbula (q.v.) became its president in August 1951 and immediately renamed it the African National Congress. This group, led by Nkumbula and Kenneth Kaunda (q.v.), was to be the leading force for Northern Rhodesian nationalism for many years. Kaunda's election as secretary-general resulted in an organizational drive that allowed the ANC to function in most of the country. It bitterly opposed federation and it boycotted shops in which Africans were discriminated against (see COLOUR BAR). Both of its main leaders were imprisoned in

1955 for possessing prohibited literature. In 1957 they visited London and began to receive help from the British Labour Party. Both leaders pressed for constitutional reform and independence for Northern Rhodesia, but they split over the issue of supporting the British-imposed constitution in December 1958. Kaunda formed his own party, the Zambia African National Congress (q.v.). Other officers, notably Mainza Chona and Titus Mukupo (qq.v.), also broke with Nkumbula, who ran for and won a seat in the new Legislative Council (q.v.).

ANC's biggest difficulties seemed to be Nkumbula's lack of organizational skills and his willingness, in contrast to Kaunda's more militant stand, to compromise with white settler groups on some issues. In 1959 and 1960 the ANC lost much of its support to Kaunda's United National Independence Party (UNIP) (q.v.), yet it retained a degree of viability throughout the 1960s in Southern, Western, and Central Provinces (qq.v.). Its greatest support was among the *ci*Tonga-speaking (q.v.) people, especially in Southern Province. For a period of nine months in 1961 and 1962, while Nkumbula served a short jail sentence, the party's acting presidents were Lawrence Katilungu (q.v.) and (after Katilungu's accidental death) Edward M. Liso (q.v.).

The 1962 constitution resulted in elections that year, which produced the necessity for an alliance between the ANC and UNIP in order to have a black majority in the Legislative Council. This sharing of power lasted only until the preindependence election of 1964, which UNIP decisively won. In the 1968 general election the ANC won 23 seats (to UNIP's 105), receiving about 25 percent of the total votes cast. The ANC continued (under Nkumbula's leadership) until the one-party state was officially created by President Kaunda on December 13, 1972. ANC members sat in the Legislative Assembly (q.v.) until it was dissolved in October 1973.

AFRICAN NATIONAL FREEDOM MOVEMENT. The movement was a small political organization founded in May 1959 by Harry Banda, Dauti Yamba, and Paskale Sokota (qq.v.), who announced a "nonviolent campaign for self-government." In June it merged with the United African Congress to form the United National Freedom Party (qq.v.).

AFRICAN NATIONAL INDEPENDENCE PARTY. Founded at the end of May 1959 by Paul Kalichini (q.v.), former deputy president of the Zambia African National Congress (ZANC) (q.v.), and Frank Chitambala (q.v.), also a ZANC activist, in August 1959 the party merged with the United National Freedom Party (q.v.) and formed Zambia's former ruling party, the United National Independence Party (UNIP) (q.v.).

AFRICAN REPRESENTATIVE COUNCIL. The ARC was an advisory body of Africans set up by the British in 1946 to allow the Africans a territorywide voice in government. Although most of its proposals were ignored, it was a place where ideas could be formally exchanged, not just with the British but also between the younger intellectuals and the chiefs. It supplemented the Urban Advisory Councils and Provincial Councils (qq.v.). There were 29 members of the ARC, all but four of them chosen by and from the five Provincial Councils. The Western Province (Copperbelt) (qq.v.) was allotted 10 members and the Southern Province (q.v.), three. The others had four each. The remaining four members were chosen by the Barotse king from among his councilors. It was presided over by the secretary for native affairs. In 1948, ARC was authorized to select two of its members to be appointed as "nominated unofficials" on the Legislative Council (q.v.). The ARC lasted until 1960, when the Northern Rhodesia (q.v.) government, under federation, voted to abolish it.

AIDS (ACQUIRED IMMUNE DEFICIENCY SYNDROME). With infection rates nearing those of Uganda, Zambia is taking its place among Africa's first rank of AIDS-infected countries. Statistics and estimates of the problem are inherently partial and unreliable, but they do convey some sense of just how serious it is. In mid-1995, a UNICEF official estimated that 25–30 percent of urban and 10–15 percent of rural adults were HIV positive; that there are about 500 new infections a day; and that average life expectancy will likely drop to 45 years by 2010. At Lusaka's University Teaching Hospital, over 35 percent of the women attending the antenatal clinics are HIV positive. In early 1994, a WHO-sponsored conference told the assembled permanent secretaries that 250,000 Zambians would die of AIDS from 1994 through 1998, and that another 320,000 would be orphaned. Throughout Africa, AIDS is particularly prevalent among poor women and better-off men. Early 1995 statistics from the ministry of health found that women constitute 52 percent of all cases, and that AIDS is most common in the 30–39-year age bracket; some 70 percent of all known AIDS cases are in the productive 20–39-year bracket. Southern Province (q.v.) had the highest AIDS rate (6.43:1,000), which is locally attributed to the dramatic, post-1990 increase in truck traffic from South Africa. In Eastern Province (q.v.), the Malawian truck traffic is blamed. Central Province (q.v.) (at 1.01:1,000) had the lowest rate. AIDS, however, often exploits other sexually transmitted diseases (STDs); Lusaka Province (q.v.) (34.6:1,000) leads the nation in STDs, while Copperbelt Province (q.v.) (18.3) is a distant second. In Zambia, AIDS is also considered a contributing factor to the country's rising infant mortality rate (from 152:1,000 births in 1977 to 191:1,000 in 1992) and to recent increases in meningitis, malnutrition, and tuberculosis.

AKUFUNA (AKAFUNA), TATILA. A son of Imbuka, Akufuna was king of the Lozi (q.v.) from his installation in September 1884 until he fled his land in July 1885. He was selected for this position after rebels successfully forced Lubosi (q.v.) (later called Lewanika, q.v.) to flee the country. The leader of this revolt was Mataa (q.v.), who was to become his Ngambela (q.v.). Akufuna was young, however, and a weak ruler. His relations with his people were poor. Even Mataa came to despise him. Groups loyal to Lubosi plotted to replace Akufuna in March 1885, but by July, Akufuna fled to Sesheke (q.v.), as Mataa and others were bringing Sikufele to replace him. This never occurred, as Lubosi returned to his former position.

AMALGAMATION. The term as used actively in Central Africa (q.v.) for over two decades meant the absorption of Northern Rhodesia (and Nyasaland) into Southern Rhodesia (qq.v.). It preceded the use of such words as *partnership* and *federation*. It was first used in this context around 1920. Both the Ormsby-Gore Commission of 1925 and the Hilton Young Commission of 1928 (qq.v.) looked into its feasibility. In 1933 members of the Legislative Council (q.v.) voted to suggest that amalgamation would have favorable economic results for all. The Bledisloe Commission of 1938 (q.v.) found that the Africans, chiefs and commoners alike, abhorred the possibility of amalgamation, mostly because of Southern Rhodesia's record on race relations.

AMBO. A small ethnic group in southeastern Zambia near Mozambique (q.v.), the Ambo are an offshoot of the Lala (q.v.). Neighbors of the Nsenga, they are sometimes referred to as the Kambonsenga (qq.v.). They represent almost 1 percent of Zambia's population.

AMERY, LEOPOLD S. He was Great Britain's colonial secretary from November 1924 to June 1929 and secretary of state for dominion affairs from July 1925 to June 1929. He favored close union between Britain's East and Central African territories. In 1927 he persuaded the British government to make this official policy, but it took no immediate action and, instead, appointed the Hilton Young Commission (q.v.) to investigate and report.

ANGLO-AMERICAN CORPORATION OF SOUTH AFRICA, LTD. A multipurpose company engaged in commerce, investment, finance, manufacturing, and mining, it was established by Sir Ernest Oppenheimer in 1917. In 1926 Oppenheimer made plans to start a branch in Northern Rhodesia (q.v.) with headquarters at Broken Hill (q.v.); it was incorporated two years later. The corporation quickly became one of the two dominant mining companies in the country, a dominance that was to grow as the country's economy came to depend on the copper (q.v.) industry. After independence, the minister of commerce and industry decided that no companies controlled from South Africa could operate in Zambia. The company quickly reincorporated its Zambian firm as the Anglo-American Corporation of Zambia, Ltd. (ZAMANGLO). It has also made great strides in staffing its company with young Zambians. The establishment of the Metal Marketing Company of Zambia (q.v.) in 1968 gave the government some influence over the pricing and marketing of copper. In 1970, the government acquired a 51 percent interest in the ownership of all the operating mines, including those of Anglo-American, which had been renamed the Nchanga Consolidated Mines, Ltd. (q.v.). Its Zambian subsidiary, usually called ZAMANGLO, moved its operations to Bermuda, where it created a new subsidiary, Zambia Copper Investments Limited, which now holds all of ZAMANGLO's mining assets that have not been nationalized. The individual mining companies that had been controlled by the Anglo-American group, namely those at Chililabombwe (formerly Bancroft), Nchanga, and Rhokana, were first amalgamated into Bancroft Mines, Ltd., which then changed its name to Nchanga Consolidated Copper Mines, Ltd. (qq.v.).

ANGLO-GERMAN CONCORDAT, 1890. This agreement made the Caprivi Strip (q.v.) German territory, allowing the Germans access to navigation on the Zambezi River (q.v.). It also drew the 338-kilometer (210-mile) boundary line between North-Eastern Rhodesia and German East Africa (Tanzania) (qq.v.), which was formally approved by Germany and Great Britain in 1901.

ANGLO-PORTUGUESE AGREEMENTS, 1891, 1893. These agreements between the British and Portuguese governments resulted in a provisional boundary along the Zambezi and Kabompo Rivers (qq.v.), dividing Portuguese West Africa (Angola) from North-Western Rhodesia (q.v.). By these agreements, the Lozi (q.v.) king lost a substantial amount of the territory he claimed. Protests to the British high commissioner by the Barotse Litunga, Lewanika (qq.v.), were to no avail. These agreements were finally altered as a result of a decision in 1905 by a commission led by King Victor Emmanuel of Italy (q.v.).

ANGOLA. Independent since November 1975, this former Portuguese colonial territory is the neighbor immediately west of Zambia. For centuries people have migrated east across the present border, especially those moving east within the great Lunda (q.v.) empire. Within the last several centuries the Lozi (q.v.) established hegemony over a large region of western Zambia, including over the people in the border region. These people included the Luchazi, the Chokwe, and the Mbunda (qq.v.). The establishment of a Northern Rhodesian-Angolan border occurred in stages. The first of these were the Anglo-Portuguese Agreements of 1891 and 1893 (q.v.), which set a provisional boundary along the Zambezi and Kabompo Rivers (qq.v.). Ultimately, the final border was set as a result of an arbitration decision by King Victor Emmanuel of Italy (q.v.) in 1905. This was needed because Lewanika (q.v.), the Lozi (q.v.) king, was greatly disturbed by the construction of Portuguese forts in "his" territory. The final border was moved somewhat west, dividing the disputed area evenly along the 22nd parallel. The Zambia-Angola border did not become a problem again until the advent of the anti-Portuguese warfare in the early 1960s by African nationalists, some of whom used Zambian territory as a staging area for troops. This invited retaliation by the Portuguese rulers of Angola, who controlled the Benguela Railway (q.v.). This railway, then considered a major outlet for Zambian copper (q.v.) exports, runs through the Democratic Republic of Congo (q.v.) (Zaire) and Angola to the coast at Lobito (q.v.). Problems with Angola continued even after its independence in November 1975. Zambia was not quick to support Agostinho Neto, the winner among the warring Angolan nationalists, and guerrilla activity basically shut down the Benguela trade and transport route during a crucial period of Zambian history.

ANGONI. The term is colonial British English for the Ngoni (q.v.) people.

ARABS. These traders have been bringing East African and Indian Ocean trade into Central Africa (q.v.) for many centuries, trading beads, cloth, and shells for gold, copper (q.v.), and ivory (q.v.). Later, guns were brought in and slaves were taken out. A Portuguese explorer described the Arab trade in Zimbabwe in 1514, but other sources indicate the trade was going on among the Nsenga (q.v.) of Zambia even earlier. Arab traders were recorded later in both southern and western Zambia. Often the Arabs were referred to as either Balungwana (q.v.) or Swahili (q.v.). From 1750 to 1820, dissension among the coastal Arab communities slowed the trade considerably. However, Arab trade hit its peak in the final two-thirds of the 19th century. Slaves, ivory, and salt were among the products sought from Zambia. The peoples most influenced by the trade were the Bemba (and their northeastern neighbors) and the Lunda of Kazembe (qq.v.) along the Luapula River (q.v.). Arab settlements dotted the interior countryside, controlling the trade. In 1872 they even helped a refugee Lunda prince overthrow the Kazembe. Among the most significant Arab leaders or traders involved in Zambia were Mlozi, Tippu Tib, Kumba Kumba, and Abdullah ibn Suliman (qq.v.). Many of the Arabs were of African ancestry; few were "pure" Arabs. Only the extension of British control over North-Eastern Rhodesia (q.v.) around the beginning of the 20th century diminished their influence. British intervention was motivated by the reports of Dr. Livingstone (q.v.) and others.

ARNOT, FREDERICK STANLEY. Arnot was a missionary who came to Barotseland (q.v.) representing the Plymouth Brethren (q.v.), a lay body that had seceded from the Anglican Church. He was their first missionary to southern Africa and a friend of David Livingstone's (q.v.) family. He entered Barotseland in 1882 through the intercession of trader George Westbeech (q.v.) and met the Litunga, Lubosi (qq.v.). He was warmly received and stayed at Lealui (q.v.), the Lozi (q.v.) capital, for 18 months. Lubosi permitted Arnot to open a small school for royal and noble children. Arnot's books claim that he was an advisor to Lubosi and persuaded him to make an alliance with Khama of the Ngwato rather than with Lobengula of the Ndebele (qq.v.). Silva-Pôrto (q.v.), a Portuguese trader based in Angola (q.v.), carried the deathly ill Arnot out of Barotseland in 1884, just as a civil war broke out. Arnot then refocused his energies on chief Msiri and the Yeke empire in Katanga (qq.v.), where he and his colleagues, whom Msiri affectionately referred to as his "white slaves," were able to document the climax and collapse of the Yeke empire. He passed through Lealui again in 1910 and visited with Lubosi, who was known as Lewanika (q.v.) by this time.

ASIANS. Almost all of Zambia's Asian residents derive from Gujarat Province (q.v.) in western India. There are over 11,000 of them in Zambia. About three-quarters of them are Hindu. Over 86 percent of the families are in commerce, mostly in large cities, especially in Ndola, Kitwe, and Lusaka (qq.v.). Most of them came in the late 1940s from Southern Rhodesia (q.v.), though the earliest ones came through Nyasaland (Malawi) to settle in Fort Jameson (Chipata) (qq.v.). Throughout East Africa and Southern Africa, Indians were brought in as a middleman minority to engage in direct interpersonal relations with Africans. Their special niche as retail traders was widely resented by their African customers. The Mulungushi Declaration (q.v.) of 1968 had a major impact on the Indians in Zambia, as it took non-Zambian (i.e., Asian) traders out of rural shopkeeping and limited them to the largest towns. The Kaunda (q.v.) regime thus generated a lot of popularity at the expense of the Asian majority, who had held onto their Commonwealth passports instead of taking Zambian citizenship. Few citizenship applications were granted to Asians after the Mulungushi Reforms. Some left the country, even though the government placed a strict limit on the amount of money they could take out of Zambia.

ASKARI. This term was used for an African soldier serving with the North-Eastern or North-Western Rhodesian Native Police. Men enrolled in the armed forces during World War II were also called *askaris*. Some considered this demeaning to the soldiers.

AUSHI (USHI). This people were said to be of Luban origin. They live in the area north and east of the upper Luapula River and west of Lake Bangweulu (qq.v.). They were under the influence of Kazembe's Lunda for much of the 19th century and, later, became independent allies of Msiri's Yeke (qq.v.). There were, in 1969, some 90,000 Aushi speakers in Zambia.

AWEMBA. *See also* WEMBA. These are variant spellings for the Bemba (q.v.); the initial A represents the plural personal prefix found in the Bantu languages (*see* BA-), and the W of Wemba appears without its circumflex. The name carried over to Awemba District, one of the first administrative districts to be delineated by the British South Africa Company (q.v.). It had Lake Bangweulu (q.v.) as its border in the southwest, and the middle section of the Chambezi River (q.v.) almost dissected it diagonally from southwest to northeast.

AWEMBA WAR. The term is used by the British to describe their last battles against Bemba (q.v.) groups. In early 1899 a contingent led by Charles McKinnon and Robert Young (qq.v.) defeated Ponde (q.v.), who was determined to be Mwamba's (q.v.) successor, at his new village. Shortly afterwards, in April 1899, a force led by H. T. Harrington (q.v.) and Andrew Laws fought an entire day before capturing the stockaded town of Mporokoso (q.v.). The town's defenders were led by Arabs under Nasoro bin Suliman (q.v.). This marked the end of Bemba resistance to the establishment of white rule in Northern Province (q.v.).

AYRSHIRE FARM. The site is southwest of Lusaka (q.v.), near the Kafue flats, where a group of rock engravings are found. The metal tools (axes and hoes) depicted are fairly modern, thus the engravings are of comparatively recent origin.

B

BA-. This is the standard personal plural prefix in the Bantu languages of Africa south of the equator. Thus the *-ntu* root of *bantu* denotes a thing, while the *ba-* prefix indicates that they are people; *bantu* itself means "people." Thus the Barotse and Babemba (written as "Awemba" around 1900) are the Lozi and Bemba (qq.v.) peoples. In the Southern Bantu languages, the personal plural prefix is usually *ma-*; thus the Makololo and

Matabele are the Kololo and Ndebele (qq.v.) peoples. For nearly 50 years now, it has been conventional to drop the Bantu personal prefix in published works.

BAKABILO. These hereditary priest-councilors among the Bemba (q.v.) play very important ritual roles. Although they are, as commoners, ineligible for chiefly positions, they are important both in a chief's installation and, for some of them, his burial. They usually trace their family descent to the legendary first arrival of the Bemba to their land. In addition to legitimizing the chief through a series of rituals, each of the approximately 40 *bakabilo* has his own village near the capital. During interregnums, they serve as regents and guide the government. Once the new chief receives his predecessor's personal relics (*babenye*) from the *bakabilo*, they are subordinate to him. But as nonremovable hereditary leaders, they continue to act as constitutional checks on the chief. Their neutrality (as commoners) gives them special respect from contestants for the position of chief. A group of six senior *bakabilo* is the most important in dealing with crucial issues. Group members are referred to as *bashilubemba* (masters of Bembaland).

BAKAFULA. This name, surviving into fairly recent times, was applied to some of the "little people" who once inhabited many parts of Zambia. While it may refer to pygmies, it more likely was applied to the Bushmen (q.v.) (San) hunter-gatherers of Late Stone Age times.

BALDWIN, ARTHUR. Along with the Reverend and Mrs. H. Buckenham, the Reverend Baldwin served among the Ila (q.v.) in the Ila-Tonga Mission of the Primitive Methodist Missionary Society (q.v.). They reached the Zambezi River at Kazungula (qq.v.) in 1889 but were stopped by the Lozi (q.v.) who resented white men aiding their traditional opponents. In 1891, after the intercession of the Reverend François Coillard of the Paris Mission (qq.v.), they were allowed to come to the Lozi capital and spent two years at the Sefula Mission (q.v.). Finally, in June 1893, they were allowed to proceed to Ila country. In December of that year they set up a Primitive Methodist Mission at Nkala in the Kafue Hook (q.v.), where they soon hosted native commissioner Val Gielgud and prospectors from the Northern Copper Company (qq.v.). Baldwin's journal tells much about the dominance of the Lozi over their neighbors in the 1891–93 period.

BALOVALE DISTRICT. *See* ZAMBEZI DISTRICT.

BALUNGWANA (or BANGWANA). The term was often applied to Arab and Swahili (qq.v.) traders.

BANCROFT MINE. *See* CHILILABOMBWE MINE.

BANDA, HARRY. Banda was one of the founders of the African National Freedom Movement (q.v.) in May 1959. He was just a young clerk, but had been active in Nkumbula's African National Congress (qq.v.). In June he merged the group with the United African Congress to form the United National Freedom Party (qq.v.), of which he became secretary-general.

BANDA, HASTINGS KAMUZU. He was the first president of Malawi (q.v.), Zambia's southeastern neighbor. His leadership of the Nyasaland African Congress led Britain to break up the Central African Federation (q.v.) by giving his country independence. This announcement was further stimulus for Zambian nationalists to fight for the same, especially since Banda and Kaunda (qq.v.) had worked together on several antifederation efforts. Dr. Banda was born May 14, 1906, in northern Nyasaland (q.v.) (Malawi). He received higher education in the United States, including a medical degree from Meharry Medical College. He practiced in England for many years and in Ghana for five years. He returned home triumphantly on July 6, 1958, to lead his people to independence and, as one of Africa's first "life presidents," a chillingly repressive state. Dr. Banda, nearly 20 years older than Kenneth Kaunda, was forced to hold elections at the end of 1992 and was emphatically turned out of office.

BANDA, HAYDEN DINGISWAYO. An Ngoni (q.v.) bookkeeper from the Eastern Province (q.v.), this militant United National Independence Party (UNIP) (q.v.) member also worked with the African National Congress, and the Zambia African National Congress (qq.v.) since 1954. He was imprisoned in 1960 and 1961, while serving as UNIP provincial chairman for the Copperbelt (q.v.). From 1961 to 1969 he served as UNIP's director of youth. A close associate of Kenneth Kaunda (q.v.) for many years, he served in a series of cabinet ministries before his brief suspension for misappropriating government funds and his two-year dismissal from the cabinet in 1971. In 1980 he was jailed for using his government driver to poach elephants on his behalf and was dismissed by President Kaunda in August of that year. He remained in UNIP, though, and following the 1991 electoral victories of President Chiluba and the Movement for Multiparty Democracy (qq.v.), he continued to serve UNIP as leader of the parliamentary opposition. He was suspended from Parliament for three months for accusing the speaker, Robinson Nabulyato (q.v.), of being biased towards the MMD. When, however, Kenneth Kaunda regained the informal leadership of UNIP in 1995, Banda, at age 70, was removed as opposition leader, and he joined the MMD.

BANK OF ZAMBIA. The central bank, set up by the government in August 1964 with power to regulate credit in the country, was created to serve as a counterweight to the foreign-owned "giants," Barclays Bank and Standard Bank. In fact, there was a requirement that commercial banks keep fixed percentages of their deposits as balances at the Bank of Zambia. It issues the national currency and controls foreign exchange.

BANTU EDUCATION CINEMA PROJECT. *See* NATIVE FILM CENSORSHIP BOARD.

BANTU BOTATWE GROUP. This linguistic term refers to the closely related languages and customs of the Tonga, Ila, and Lenje (qq.v.) peoples of Southern and Central Provinces (qq.v.). In the late 1960s, the same term was used to refer to one of the sectional subgroups that formed within the United National Independence Party (q.v.) in response to the perceived domination of UNIP by the Bemba (q.v.).

BANTU LANGUAGES. This is one of the major linguistic families in Africa. With the exception of a few Khoisan speakers (or "Bushmen," (q.v.)), all of the African languages indigenous to Zambia (and to the rest of Africa south of the equator) are Bantu languages. *See* BA-.

BANYAMA (sing., *munyama*). These "vampire men" were the focus of a Northern Rhodesian rumor panic between the mid-1920s and the mid-1960s. Though known by different names, the *banyama* myth seems to have begun along the Swahili (q.v.) (east) coast or in the interior of Tanzania (q.v.) and was then spread by labor migrants to modern Democratic Republic of Congo (q.v.) (Zaire), Zambia, and Malawi (q.v.). The *banyama* supposedly used isolated sites or darkness to abduct their African victims, whom they then delivered to evil Europeans. The Europeans then either extracted their blood and brains or transformed their victims into zombielike slave laborers. In short, the *banyama* myth "explained" the evils of colonialism in terms of witchcraft.

In the late 1930s, *Mutende* (q.v.), the government-run newspaper for Africans, tried but failed to discredit these rumor panics, which were only fed by the wartime blood collection drives. Such fears took particularly virulent forms just before and during the federation (q.v.) era, when sugar sold to Africans was said to contain sterility-causing medicines and certain canned meats were said to contain the flesh of Africans. Europeans like Arthur Davison (q.v.), together with certain chiefs and messengers and the African forestry and tsetse control officers, had long been suspected of being *banyama*. But after the war, Africans associated with the Capricorn Africa Society and the Central African Broadcasting Service (qq.v.) also fell under suspicion. Though such rumors declined after independence, African mothers still use the fears of *banyama* to control unruly children. People still disappear from time to time, and such fears appear to underlie the occasional reports of suspected ritual murderers and their supposed international trade in human organs. Some of these organs are supposedly required for royal rainmaking medicines in Southern Africa, but still others are supposedly required for organ transplant operations in Europe and America.

BAPTISTA, PEDRO JOÃO. A Luso-African from Angola (q.v.), he and Amara José (q.v.), were sent by the Portuguese from Luanda, Angola, across the continent to Tete, Mozambique (qq.v.). The trip started in 1802 and took nine years. They returned then through the territory of Kazembe and Mwata Yamvo (qq.v.). They were detained for four years by Kazembe (q.v.) and were released only after negotiations with traders from Mozambique. Baptista's diary mentions a war between the Lunda and the Bisa (qq.v.) over the Katanga (q.v.) trade and also refers to Africans mining copper (q.v.) there.

BARK CLOTH. Pounded bark, especially from the *Brachystegia* genus of tree, was a traditional source of cloth for clothing, especially among the people in the northeastern part of the country.

BAROTSE ANTI-SECESSION SOCIETY (or MOVEMENT). An organization founded in November 1960, by Nalumino Mundia (q.v.) and other reform-minded Lozi living outside Barotseland (qq.v.), its goal was to attract Lozi support against the Litunga's (q.v.) desire to separate Barotseland from the rest of Northern Rhodesia (q.v.). Some of its organizers had been members of the Barotse National Association (q.v.). Mundia was to become a major organizer for the United National Independence Party in Barotseland before forming the United Party (qq.v.) several years later.

BAROTSE NATIONAL ASSOCIATION (or SOCIETY). The group was started by Lozi (q.v.) along the line of rail (q.v.) circa 1954 to advocate reform in the Barotse native government. Among its leaders were Godwin Mbikusita and, later, Sekeli Konoso (qq.v.), a Lusaka (q.v.) businessman.

BAROTSE NATIONAL COUNCIL. Sometimes referred to as the Barotseland Parliament, this council served as the traditional advisory body to the Lozi (Barotse) Litunga (king) (qq.v.). It did not have regular meetings, sometimes gathering only once or twice a year. It usually met to discuss matters such as new treaties or the selection of a new king. Its membership was about 30, half of them councilors living at the capital, Lealui (q.v.), and half representing the five district councils. Often, meetings were held by smaller groups. The leader or prime minister of the National Council was called the Ngambela (q.v.).

In 1963 the British government reformed the National Council by creating 25 elected seats, all of which were won by UNIP (q.v.) candidates. In mid-1965, the Zambian government introduced the Local Government (q.v.) Bill, which abolished the National Council and replaced it with five district councils. None of these new councilors could be appointed by the Litunga. The bill was signed by President Kaunda (q.v.) in October, and the council was abolished in November 1965. *See also* MULONGWANJI.

BAROTSE NATIONAL SCHOOL. Founded in 1906, it was for many years the best school in Northern Rhodesia (q.v.) as well as the only one not run and financed by a mission society. The school was sanctioned by the British South Africa Company (q.v.) and had the strong support of King Lewanika (q.v.). Its initial curriculum included the teaching of English and "useful technical knowledge." It was financed from part of Lewanika's income from the hut tax (q.v.). Its student body included many sons of ranking Lozi (q.v.) leaders. As a result of its success, the missions were forced to improve their schools in Barotseland (q.v.). Decades later, Lozi held most of the jobs open to indigenous Northern Rhodesians. See also MUPATU, YUYI W.

BAROTSE NATIVE AUTHORITY ORDINANCE, 1936. This special ordinance for Barotseland was passed by the government of Northern Rhodesia with the approval of the Barotse Litunga and *kuta* (qq.v.). The Native Authorities Ordinance of 1936 (q.v.) did not apply to Barotseland because of its special status. The main differences were the provisions that recognized the special status of the Litunga as Lozi (q.v.) king and the necessity of the government to consult with him.

BAROTSE NATIVE COURTS ORDINANCE, 1936. This was a special ordinance involving judicial procedure in Barotseland (q.v.) and differed from that authorized elsewhere by the government of the Northern Rhodesian (q.v.) protectorate. One difference was that administrative officers of the government could intervene only in criminal cases. Also, in certain cases, government action was permissible only after recommendation by the Litunga (q.v.).

BAROTSE NATIVE POLICE. This North-Western Rhodesian force was formed in 1898. Its first commander was Colonel Colin Harding (q.v.), formerly a major in the British South African Police. It was formed to establish order and keep the peace, which it did by, for example, sending patrols against the Mambari (q.v.) slave traders, collecting the hut tax (q.v.), and suppressing the occasional hut tax rebellion. The Barotse Native Police, however, were forbidden to apprehend Europeans, no matter what the complaint against them. The police were primarily recruited among the Lozi and Ngoni (qq.v.). After North-Western and North-Eastern Rhodesia (qq.v.) were united in 1911, the Barotse Native Police were merged into the Northern Rhodesian Police (q.v.).

BAROTSE PATRIOTS. This short-lived political group was formed in the early 1960s to urge governmental reform in Barotseland (q.v.). The group wanted also a commission of inquiry, ultimately led by Sir Charles Hartwell, to investigate local unrest and political agitation.

BAROTSE PROVINCE. From independence (October 24, 1964) until October 1969, when the Barotseland Agreement of 1964 (q.v.) was disavowed by the government, the area known historically as Barotseland (q.v.) was called Barotse Province. The name was changed to Western Province in October 1969. (The previous Western Province was renamed Copperbelt Province (qq.v.).) With the name change there was also a loss of special privileges.

BAROTSE TREATY, 1890. *See* LOCHNER CONCESSION.

BAROTSELAND. This area in the southwestern part of the Republic of Zambia is today referred to as Western Province (q.v.). It was formerly (1964–69) Barotse Province (q.v.). It is adjacent to Angola (q.v.), Zambia's western neighbor, the border between them being finalized in 1905. The Lozi (or Barotse) king, or Litunga (qq.v.) maintains his capital at Lealui (q.v.), 644 kilometers (400 miles) west of the line of rail (q.v.) and substantially isolated from the rest of the country. While parts of this Lozi homeland include part of the Kalahari Desert and forestland, much of it is composed of the rich alluvial floodplain (called *ngulu*, or *bulozi*) along the upper Zambezi (q.v.). Other areas, especially to the north and east, were conquered by 18th- and 19th-century Lozi kings. British protection was first brought to the area as a result of the Lochner Concession, a treaty between the Lozi Litunga and the British South Africa Company (qq.v.). As Northern Rhodesia (q.v.) sought independence from England in the late 1950s and early 1960s, the Barotse native government sought independent statehood. A petition to the British government in September 1961 specifically sought this. The British opposed subdividing the future Zambia. Ultimately, the Barotseland Agreement of 1964 (q.v.) between Kenneth Kaunda (q.v.) and the Litunga acknowledged the traditional Barotse rights within an independent Zambia. The agreement was canceled by the Local Government Act (q.v.) of 1965.

BAROTSELAND AGREEMENT, 1964. The agreement was signed in London on May 18, 1964, by Kenneth Kaunda and the Litunga of Barotseland (qq.v.). It was approved for the British Crown by Duncan Sandys (q.v.). The Litunga assumed that this agreement gave Barotseland a permanent part of the new Zambia but with all traditional privileges maintained. Kaunda saw it as a way of getting the Lozi (q.v.) to accept the new constitution through an act that could be changed later. Indeed, the

Local Government Act (q.v.) of 1965 canceled the agreement and made Barotseland just another province.

BAROTSELAND NATIONAL PARTY. *See* SICABA (NATIONAL) PARTY.

BAROTSELAND NORTH-WESTERN RHODESIA ORDER IN COUNCIL, 1899. *See* ORDER IN COUNCIL, 1899.

BASUNGU (BAZUNGU) (sing., *musungu, muzungu*). A common categorical term for whites in Eastern and Central Africa (q.v.), it carries a lot of emotional baggage, most of it negative. *Also see* BANYAMA.

BATOKA GORGE. An area below Victoria Falls (q.v.) near the city of Livingstone (q.v.), it was noted for its exposed walls of basaltic lava.

BATOKA PLATEAU. A highlands area in southern Zambia, east of Livingstone and north of Lake Kariba (qq.v.), it was free of many disease-bearing insects and thus desired by invaders. The local Toka (q.v.) defended it against the Kololo of chief Sebituane (qq.v.) in the 19th century; the Toka lost, and the Kololo dominated the area for some years, raiding among the Toka as far east as the confluence of the Kafue and Zambezi Rivers (qq.v.). The plateau dwellers were isolated from most trade routes that ran up the Zambezi valley.

BAYETE. A royal salute among the Ngoni (q.v.) and other Nguni-speaking peoples (e.g., Swazi, Zulu), it is roughly translated as "hail." Usable in many contexts, the salute is given on festive occasions to a variety of important leaders, including important political figures.

BAZIMBA. This chiefly Leopard Clan of the Lungu and Tabwa (qq.v.) peoples was a matrilineal clan. Its first chiefs came from the western shores of Lake Tanganyika (q.v.) in the late 18th century to settle north and west of the Bemba (q.v.). The main group settled in Itabwa (q.v.) under a chief called Nsama (q.v.). This was the beginning of the Tabwa chiefdom of Nsama (qq.v.). Dr. Livingstone (q.v.) described Nsama III Chipili as "the Napoleon of these countries."

BECHUANALAND EXPLORATION COMPANY. The company was a subsidiary of the British South Africa Company (q.v.), which in 1902 sent William Collier into what is now called the Copperbelt (qq.v.). He discovered ore deposits at places he named Bwana Mkubwa and Roan Antelope as well as at Chambishi (qq.v.). All were to become important sources of Zambia's copper (q.v.).

BEERHALL SYSTEM. First instituted in Durban, South Africa (q.v.) in 1909, then later in Livingstone and Broken Hill (qq.v.), the beerhall system became a central feature of Northern Rhodesian towns after the Native Beer Ordinance of 1930 (q.v.). The beerhall system, first of all, limited the production, sale, and consumption of Africans' "opaque beer" to municipal or mine-owned and operated beerhalls. Second, beerhall revenues became the major funding source for such African welfare services as films, recreation halls, soccer fields, and on the mine compounds, schools, clinics, and reading rooms. Located in each town's African "location" (q.v.), or mineworkers' compound, the fenced-in grounds of a typical beerhall contained a brewing house; a cavernous beerhall, with its service counter, tables, and benches; and scattered trees and kiosks for smaller groups of drinkers. Its cheap prices and limited hours— typically 9 A.M. to noon, and 3 to 6 P.M.—encouraged heavy and boisterous drinking.

While initially disruptive of traditional patterns of social drinking, and always considered an infringement upon the economic opportunities of private, African brewers, the beerhalls soon became popular centers of African working-class culture. They also generated such substantial revenues after World War II that neither the mining companies, the central government, nor their African or European critics could persuade the town councils to consider any alternative to the system of large beerhalls.

In the mid-1940s, some of the mines opened smaller, branch beerhalls and allowed Africans to buy beer for off-premise consumption. By 1948 the beerhalls could also sell wine and bottled beer, and by the time of the 1957 African National Congress (q.v.) national beerhall boycott, Africans on the urban Copperbelt (q.v.) could buy bottled beer at African-run bottle stores (q.v.) and at licensed bars and social clubs. Only the violent Copperbelt beerhall confrontations, in early 1963, between rival factions of the ANC and the United National Independence Party (q.v.), persuaded the town councils of the necessity for smaller drinking establishments. Finally, in April 1964, the government closed the old, large beerhalls, though smaller ones were opened, and Africans were free to buy bottled beer and liquor in all bars but those in private (predominately European) clubs.

BEIRA. An Indian Ocean port city in Mozambique (q.v.) that became an increasingly important trading port for Zambia from 1965 to 1976. Beira is reached via the Great East Road (q.v.) from Lusaka to Salima in Malawi (qq.v.) and from there south by rail.

BELL, JOHN M. An administrator for the British South Africa Company (q.v.), he was the collector for Chambeshi District at Fife (q.v.) near the end of the 19th century. Although involved mostly with the Bemba (q.v.), he is remembered for his attacks on Arab (q.v.) and Bemba slave caravans and for using his police to put down African resistance to forced labor in 1896 by the Inamwanga (q.v.) people of headman Ilendela (q.v.). He burned the village when the Africans resisted, and one African was killed by gunshot.

BEMBA (AWEMBA, WEMBA). The ethnic group is one of Zambia's largest and most influential (the stereotype is "pushy"). Though only about 11 percent (about 741,000) of Zambians are Bemba, over a quarter of the population speaks *ci*Bemba (q.v.) as its native tongue. This is due to the spread of Bemba political control in the last half of the 19th century and to the disproportionately large proportion of Bemba-speaking labor migrants to the Copperbelt (q.v.) mines beginning in the mid-1920s. The United National Independence Party (q.v.) was considered Bemba dominated in the late 1960s, and similar charges were made against the MMD (q.v.) in the mid-1990s. The following superficial outline of Bemba history is based upon the work of Dr. Andrew D. Roberts.

The Bemba seem to have been 18th-century Luba (q.v.) immigrants into modern Northern Province (q.v.). Originating in the legendary land of Kola or Luba (qq.v.), they were led by the sons and daughter of a man named Mukulumpe (q.v.), who were all members of the Crocodile Clan (Bena Ng'andu), the matrilineal clan of the Bemba chiefs. They established a settlement on the Kalungu River (q.v.) and created the senior chiefship, Chitimukulu (q.v.), named after Chiti (q.v.), their first leader. The Bemba have nearly two dozen ranked chiefships, each with his own chiefdom, and a given individual may be promoted to a number of chiefships in the course of his lifetime. Each Bemba chiefdom is autonomous, yet each owes some allegiance to the Chitimukulu.

Early Bemba men saw themselves more as great hunters and warriors than as farmers or herdsmen. They were thus not closely tied to one area of land. They also attacked weaker neighbors, thus absorbing them and their land (causing the creation of new chiefdoms). In the 19th century, Chief Mwamba, Chitimukulu Chileshye, and Chitimukulu Chitapankwa (qq.v.) involved the Bemba in the East African and Indian Ocean trade in African ivory, copper (q.v.), and slaves. Their expansion came at the expense of their southern neighbors, the Bisa (q.v.), who had been major traders, and brought them into conflict with the northerly moving Ngoni (q.v.). One should not assume, however, that the militaristic spread of the Bemba was based on ethnic unity, for, in fact, the Bemba chiefs had different and, in many cases, contradictory interests in the region's trade and no particular love for one another.

The coming of the British to Central Africa (q.v.) had a great impact on the Bemba in that it cut out the slave trade (q.v.), warfare, and raiding. Missionaries, notably the Roman Catholic order called the White Fathers (q.v.), had a settling effect on the Bemba through conversion and education. The Bemba had participated in migrant labor before World War I, most notably to the mines in Katanga (q.v.), but from the mid-1920s on, Bemba speakers formed the lion's share of the underground miners on the Copperbelt (q.v.). Both on the Copperbelt and in their home provinces the Bemba responded readily to the appeal of modern political activity. Bemba like Justin Chimba and Simon Kapwepwe (qq.v.) were very able organizers of the Zambia African National Congress and UNIP (qq.v.), as the Bemba speakers in Northern, Central, Copperbelt, and Luapula Provinces (qq.v.) were the political backbone of the nationalist parties. In fact, this influence has required Zambian leaders to be conscious of ethnic balance in the government, as such jealousies have caused political difficulties.

BENA CHISHINGA. One of Zambia's middle-sized ethnic groups, its territory is sandwiched between that of the Lunda and the Bemba (qq.v.), north of Lake Bangweulu (q.v.). These people appear to have been of Luba (q.v.) origin, seemingly splitting off from those migrants who later founded the Bemba nation. Chishinga chiefs belong to the Bena Ng'oma, or Drum

Clan, and the people follow a matrilineal descent system. In the 19th century they were noted iron producers. At the same time, however, they paid tribute to the Lunda of Kazembe (q.v.). Their territory, a little south and east of Lake Mweru (q.v.), was also subject to raids by Arab (q.v.) ivory traders. The Chishinga chief Mushyota defeated a Lunda, Kumba Kumba (q.v.), in 1873, and in the early 1890s, a Bemba force sent by Mwamba III (q.v.) defeated the Chishinga chief Chama and took most of his territory.

BENA MUKULU. This small ethnic group lives north and west of Lake Bangweulu (q.v.) near the Chimipili Hills. They are members of the Bena Ng'oma, or Drum Clan. Their chiefs hold the title Chungu (q.v.). Their location made them vulnerable to attack from both the Lunda of Kazembe and the Bemba (qq.v.), especially in the 19th century. They periodically came under the control of the latter, and like the Bemba, with whom they often intermarried, they are matrilineal. Cassava (q.v.) became a staple in their diet. Iron working, which they used in trade, was an important industry. The White Fathers (q.v.) spent much time among them, eventually publishing (1949) the history of the Mukulu chieftainship of Chungu.

BENGUELA RAILWAY. One of Zambia's less effective outlets to the coast, this railway was built in 1931 by Robert Williams' Tanganyika Concessions, Ltd. (qq.v), which was also a major shareholder in the Belgian Congo mining company, Union Minière du Haut-Katanga (q.v.). The railway runs from Lubumbashi, in the Democratic Republic of Congo (q.v.) (Zaire), to Luso, Angola, and then to the coast at Lobito (qq.v.). To reach Lubumbashi, Zambia Railways (q.v.) connected with a branch of the Congolese (Zairean) rail system. This route to Lobito is about the same distance from the Copperbelt (q.v.) as the routes that terminate at Beira (q.v.) and Maputo (Lourenço Marques). Nevertheless, an agreement with Rhodesian Railways (q.v.) kept Zambian trade off the Benguela route from 1936 to 1956. While Zambian imports and exports on this route increased considerably after 1956 (especially because of Lobito's location on the Atlantic shipping route), the railway was effectively closed by the fighting in Angola both before and after its independence in 1975, thus fostering Zambia's reliance upon the TAZARA (q.v.) railway route to Dar es Salaam.

BENSON CONSTITUTION. This constitution for Northern Rhodesia (q.v.) was drawn up by Sir Arthur Benson (q.v.) and was presented to the Legislative Council (q.v.) in March 1958. It went into effect the next year and thus is sometimes called the 1959 constitution. Benson prepared it after many consultations with white political groups and African members of the Legislative Council—but few with African nationalists. It was a multiracial constitution based in part on the Moffat Resolutions of 1954 (q.v.). Simply put, a political balance had to be found so no race predominated and all were protected. Despite the complicated set of voter qualifications, which provided for a gradual transition to African majority rule, Kenneth Kaunda's (q.v.) supporters opposed it as providing too little, too slowly. Revisions in the plan in a September 1958 white paper favored European voters over Africans. The constitution provided for 30 members on the Legislative Council (22 elected) and 10 members on the Executive Council (six elected, two of them Africans). Native authorities (q.v.) were also given added powers. The African National Congress (q.v.) finally accepted the Benson Constitution and participated in the 1959 elections. Kaunda's Zambia African National Congress (q.v.) boycotted them. The Benson Constitution was replaced by another constitution in 1962.

BENSON, SIR ARTHUR EDWARD TREVOR. Governor of Northern Rhodesia (q.v.) from 1954 to 1959, Benson was born in England on December 21, 1907. He attended Oxford, where he received a master of arts degree. He joined the Colonial Office in the 1930s, and after service in the War Office he came to Northern Rhodesia as a district commissioner after World War II. He was also secretary of the Central African Council (q.v.) and served in major posts in Uganda and Nigeria before becoming governor in 1954. At that point he was given the task of preparing a constitution that would take the territory into its next stage of political development. His job became very difficult, as both Africans and settlers were becoming more militant. While he sometimes came into conflict with Sir Roy Welensky (q.v.), he was even more determined to oppose more African self-rule and to destroy, if possible, the African nationalist parties, especially Kenneth Kaunda's (q.v.). He arrested many Zambia African National Congress (q.v.) leaders, blaming a Copperbelt (q.v.) state of emergency on them and comparing them to Chicago racketeers. He said that the problems were the result of a few men who threatened others, much like "Murder Incorporated." He banned ZANC in 1959, claiming that most other Africans favored federation (q.v.). He was responsible for drawing up the Benson Constitution (q.v.).

BILONDA. This Lunda (q.v.) leader and warrior led an army of his people in the early 18th century. The army traveled eastward across the Luapula River (q.v.), defeating the Shila (q.v.) people, and then moved northwest across the Tanganyika plateau. Bilonda returned in triumph. By 1740, his successor, Kazembe II (q.v.), had further tightened Lunda control of the Luapula valley.

BISA. The Bisa constitute about 3 percent of Zambia's population. These matrilineal people live mostly in the central part of eastern Zambia and essentially share a common language with the Lala (q.v.), their western neighbors. There were, in 1986, some 354,000 Bisa/Lala speakers in Zambia. The Bisa chiefs are members of the Bena Ng'ona, or Mushroom Clan. The Bemba (q.v.) are now their northern neighbors. The 18th and early 19th centuries saw the peak of Bisa power; their lands stretched to Yombe (q.v.) country, near the present border with Malawi (q.v.). Land to the north, where Bemba now live, was also controlled by the Bisa. The Bisa were heavily involved in trade, dealing in ivory, slaves, and copper (q.v.) as well as cloth they made from their own cotton. The Bisa were so large that one subgroup, the Tambo (q.v.), apparently broke off and moved north to a less crowded area, eventually losing their Bisa identity. Between 1760 and 1860 the Bisa, along with their allies, the Lunda of Kazembe (qq.v.), dominated Zambia's northeastern trade to the coast. Near the end, however the Bisa chiefs found their land being attacked by the Bemba, the Lunda (to whom they paid tribute), and even the Ngoni (q.v.) to the east and south. Part of the problem was that the five principal Bisa chiefs—Matipa (Lubumbu), Kopa (Mwansabamba), Mungulube, Mukungule, and Chibesakunda (qq.v.)—never united. As five separate chiefdoms (and there were other smaller ones) without binding alliances, they were vulnerable to more centralized groups, especially the Bemba.

BLEDISLOE COMMISSION. Led by Lord Bledisloe, a former governor-general of New Zealand, this commission (appointed at the end of 1937) spent three months the next year in the Rhodesias and Nyasaland (qq.v.) interviewing people of all races concerning the future government of these areas and possible amalgamation (q.v.). Reporting in early 1939, it noted that greater cooperation between the territories would inevitably develop but that current differences, in native policies and ratios between the races for example, would not allow amalgamation for some time. It did suggest that Northern Rhodesia and Nyasaland could be combined without delay and that an interterritorial council to advise in coordinating future development for all three could be set up. The war in Europe that same year prevented the implementation of the proposals. The council, called the Central African Council (q.v.), was formed in 1945. Some observers note that the commission was significant because of the attention it paid to African critics of current native policies, the result being a postponement of amalgamation with Southern Rhodesia.

BOMA. This was the common African term during the colonial period for any government headquarters. The early British South Africa Company (q.v.) *bomas* in North-Eastern Rhodesia (q.v.), for example, consisted of a few dwellings surrounded by a protective palisade. Today, the same term denotes district and provincial governmental headquarters.

BOTSWANA. Because of the Caprivi Strip (q.v.), Zambia's only common border with this, its southwestern neighbor, is a small point on the Zambezi River (q.v.) (*see* BOTZAM ROAD). Before Sir Seretse Khama led it to independence from Great Britain on September 30, 1966, it was known as the Bechuanaland Protectorate. ("Chuana" is a variant of "Tswana.") Many peoples traversed this border region, notably the Kololo of Sebituane (qq.v.) in the mid-19th century. They had a great impact on the history of various Zambian peoples, especially the Lozi (q.v.). Many missionaries also entered Zambia by this route, some as friends of Tswana leaders, notably the great Bamangwato leader, Khama the Great (q.v.).

BOTTLE STORE. A bottle store is licensed to sell bottled beer and may also sell wine or liquor. The beverages may be consumed on or off the premises. Such bottled beverages are far more prestigious and expensive than such "opaque" beers as *chibuku*. In the mid-1940s, some of the mine compound beerhalls allowed Africans to buy beer for off-premise consumption. In 1948 the beerhalls (*see* BEERHALL SYSTEM) were allowed to sell cider, wine, and bottled beer, and by the 1950s, the mines allowed Africans to operate bottle stores in the Copperbelt (q.v.) mine compounds.

BOTZAM ROAD. This 365-kilometer road in Botswana (q.v.) from Nata to Kazungula was opened formally on January 20, 1977. It was built largely with American financial aid. At Kazungula (q.v.), the road ends at a ferry, where, since 1994, two 100-tonne-capacity pontoons transport South African trucks to the Zambian side of the Zambezi River (q.v.). This dramatic increase in road traffic from South Africa has substantially reduced traffic on the TAZARA (q.v.) railway. It was significant as a controversial point of contact, as white minority-ruled South Africa used to maintain that Zambia and Botswana had no common border point.

BRELSFORD, WILLIAM VERNON. Author of numerous books on Zambian history and its peoples, he was born in England and educated at Oxford University. He came to Northern Rhodesia (q.v.) with the colonial service in 1930, when he began his studies of the Bemba (q.v.). He established and edited the *Northern Rhodesia Journal*, which focused upon the territory's colonial history, from 1950 until its final numbers in 1965. Made director of the Department of Information (q.v.) in 1951, he moved to Salisbury (q.v.) (Harare) in 1953 to become director of the new Federal Department of Information. There he edited the 800-page *Handbook of Rhodesia and Nyasaland* (1960). Considered too scholarly for the business of "selling" federation (q.v.) at home and abroad, he was retired in 1960, and served as a Southern Rhodesian member of Parliament (q.v.) from 1962 to 1965.

BRITISH CENTRAL AFRICAN PROTECTORATE (BRITISH CENTRAL AFRICA). The term was used from 1893 to 1907 to denote the territory of modern Malawi (q.v.). It was first declared a protectorate in 1891, but the official order in council came in 1893. In 1907 it was renamed the Nyasaland (q.v.) Protectorate. After independence in 1964 it became the Commonwealth of Malawi.

BRITISH COLONIAL OFFICE. On April 1, 1924, administrative control of Northern Rhodesia (q.v.) was passed from the British South Africa Company (q.v.) to the British Colonial Office. The first colonial governor was Sir Herbert Stanley (q.v.), a South African. The change was initiated by settlers, who protested a company-imposed income tax. The coming of formal rule by the Colonial Office (rather than just supervision of company administration) brought also a 14-member legislature composed of five white settlers and nine Colonial Office men.

BRITISH SOUTH AFRICA COMPANY. A company devoted primarily to exploiting the mineral resources of South Africa, Queen Victoria granted it a Royal Charter on October 29, 1889. The petitioners were led by Cecil Rhodes (q.v.) but included the Dukes of Abercorn and Fife (qq.v.), Lord Gifford, and George Grey (q.v.), among others. Action soon followed as explorers and company representatives quickly made contacts with African chiefs in the area, mostly limited to what became the Rhodesias and Nyasaland (q.v.). Harry Johnston and Albert Sharpe (qq.v.) made treaties in 1890 with chiefs in Nyasaland (soon called British Central Africa) and eastern Northern Rhodesia (q.v.). Lozi king Lewanika (q.v.) (*see* MBIKUSITA) signed with Frank Lochner of the company in 1890 to give the BSAC rights in much of the western part of the country (*see* LOCHNER CONCESSION). Agreements with Africans in Southern Rhodesia (q.v.) were signed the same year. In exchange for Rhodes' promise to pay administrative costs and to supervise the territory, Great Britain granted the BSAC all mining rights and the right to allocate lands and settle whites in the area. The company had little real interest in Northern Rhodesia; it was included only because of the suspicion that gold existed there and further north, in Katanga (q.v.). Tanganyika Concessions, Ltd. (q.v.), a BSAC subsidiary, found and began exploiting the Northern Rhodesian and Katangan copper (q.v.) deposits around 1900, and a railway to Katanga was completed in 1910. A hut tax (q.v.) on Africans to help meet administrative costs forced Africans to find work on white farms or mines in Northern or Southern Rhodesia or Katanga. The presence of the administrators also helped end the slave trade (q.v.) and warfare. Finally, resentment of the company by white settlers pushed it to transfer administrative control to the British Colonial Office (q.v.) in 1924.

Although the BSAC's interest was initially in Southern Rhodesia, its most profitable mineral royalties came from Northern Rhodesia. By its charter, these mineral royalty rights would not be terminated until 1986. It also became involved through investment in many of the mining companies. In the year prior to Zambian independence, Kaunda (q.v.) and his government offered to buy out BSAC royalty rights for US$150 million, equal to about six years of normal royalty payments. BSAC negotiators hesitated to accept this, and Kaunda reduced the offer to US$12 million and forced a settlement. Early the next year, in February 1965, the company announced it was terminating its activities in Zambia and selling its real estate to the government.

BROKEN HILL. This was the colonial-era name for Kabwe (q.v.).

BROKEN HILL MAN (RHODESIAN MAN). *See* KABWE MAN.

BROKEN HILL MINE. This was the original, colonial-era name for Kabwe Mine (q.v.).

BROKEN HILL NATIVE WELFARE ASSOCIATION. The association was formed in 1930 by a civil servant, P. J. Silawe, to assist Africans in taking matters of common interest, such as schools, hospitals, and markets, before the government. The Broken Hill Association was similar to other native welfare associations found in other communities in Northern Rhodesia prior to an elected Legislative Council (q.v.).

BRUCE-LYLE, WILLIAM. He was the High Court (q.v.) justice who chaired the commission of enquiry into illegal transactions in emeralds. The commission's report, submitted in August 1979, accused three Central Committee of UNIP (q.v.) members, a cabinet minister, and other prominent citizens. In all, the sales of illegal emeralds amounted to as much as K100 million per year. In 1981, Bruce-Lyle was appointed to head an anticorruption commission created as a result of the Corrupt Practices Bill, which was passed by Parliament (q.v.) in August 1980.

BUILD-A-NATION CAMPAIGN. A special program begun in November 1961, by the United Federal Party (q.v.), it was organized to win African support for the Central African Federation's (q.v.) principle of racial partnership (q.v.). It was a well-financed campaign clothed in the guise of nonpartisan politics, but Africans recognized its origin in Roy Welensky's United Federal Party (qq.v.), and it failed after several months.

BULOZI (NGULU). The floodplain of the Zambezi River (q.v.) running north to south through Western Zambia (q.v.), the Lozi (q.v.) consider it to be the core of their homeland. It is about 161 kilometers (100 miles) long and 16 to 48 kilometers (10 to 30 miles) wide. It is usually flooded for the first several months of the year. It is bordered on east and west by forests and higher ground. Additionally, the term may be used to refer to all of the land belonging to the Lozi, for in the Bantu languages (q.v.), the *bu-* prefix preceding the name of a people denotes the country of that people.

BULUBA. *See* KOLA.

BURTON, LILLIAN. She was a white housewife and the victim of a violent attack that provoked much reaction throughout Northern Rhodesia (q.v.) and elsewhere. While driving through Ndola (q.v.) on May 8, 1960, her car was stopped, purportedly by an angry crowd of United National Independence Party (q.v.) supporters, whose rally (held in defiance of a ban) had been broken up by the police. Gasoline was thrown into the car and ignited. Mrs. Burton saved her two daughters but, after a week, she herself died of burns. Many of all races were horrified and outraged. Hundreds of UNIP members were arrested, and UNIP was banned on the Copperbelt (q.v.). Kaunda (q.v.) apologized to the widower, Robert Burton, saying that he preached only nonviolence but that hooligans often spoil good intentions. Some Africans said that too much fuss was being made over one white death, given the centuries of cruelty to black Africans. In later political campaigns, the "Burton murder" was used by some white politicians to oppose black nationalists.

BUSH, RONALD. He was secretary for native affairs in Northern Rhodesia (q.v.) in the early 1950s, succeeding Rowland Hudson (q.v.) in that position in 1949. Bush was not sympathetic to the founders of the African National Congress (q.v.), and worked toward persuading African masses to favor federation (q.v.), in opposition to the ANC.

BUSHMEN. This is a common—and in its Dutch origins, pejorative—term for the small, copper-colored, Khoisan-speaking peoples who have long been considered the original Stone Age inhabitants of Africa south of the equator. Only a few now remain in Zambia, mostly the Hukwe, called the *Ma*Kwengo by the Lozi (q.v.). These are woodland/forest hunter-gatherers who live in temporary camps of small, beehive huts made of poles and thatch.

BUTLER, ROBERT AUSTEN He was Britain's home secretary in March 1962, when Prime Minister Harold Macmillan (q.v.) appointed him secretary of state for Central African affairs. Roy Welensky (q.v.) favored this; Africans were suspicious. "Rab" Butler visited Northern Rhodesia (q.v.) in May 1962 and pressured federation (q.v.) officials to accelerate voter registration among Africans. Ultimately, in December 1962, it was Butler who agreed in principle that Nyasaland could secede from the Central African Federation (qq.v.), confirming that federation was dead.

BUXTON REPORT, 1921. The product of a commission led by Lord Buxton, it was primarily a report to the British South Africa Company (q.v.) encouraging a referendum in Southern Rhodesia (q.v.). It also recommended establishing a Legislative Council in Northern Rhodesia (qq.v.) and a survey of settler ideas. It also suggested that Northern Rhodesia's Africans could claim that much of the land belonged to them.

BWALWA. This is the common African name for a homemade millet- or sorghum-based beer.

BWANA. This Swahili (q.v.) honorific term of address, roughly meaning "boss," was given by many Zambians to white men during the colonial period. The term is also found in other parts of Central and East Africa. See BWANA MKUBWA MINE.

BWANA MKUBWA MINE. This, one of the oldest copper (q.v.) mines in Zambia, was located on the southern end of modern Ndola (q.v.). Excavation and smelting operations, provisionally linked to the people of the Luangwa ceramics tradition (q.v.), were well under way at Bwana Mkubwa, Kansanshi (q.v.), and Kipushi by the 14th and 15th centuries but were abandoned long before Chiwala's Swahili (qq.v.) settled nearby in 1898. In 1902, prospectors William Collier (q.v.) and Jack O'Donohogue, like George Grey's (q.v.) prospectors at Kansanshi and Kipushi, were shown the old workings—a 750-meter-long cut, some 10 to 12 meters deep and seven meters wide—and claimed the site for the Rhodesia Copper Company (q.v.). Site development languished until the arrival of the railway in 1909, and production was always sporadic. It was abandoned in 1988, and in 1993, with French aid, work began to transform this huge, open-pit mine into a badly needed water reservoir for Ndola.

Bwana is a corruption of the Swahili (q.v.) term for "great boss" or "master." There is no consensus as to who (if anyone)

Collier and O'Donohogue intended to memorialize by the name Bwana Mkubwa. Chirupula Stephenson (q.v.) considered it to be the nickname for Frank Smitheman (q.v.) and a whole series of domineering Europeans.

BWEMBYA. The predecessor of the great Chitimukulu Chitapankwa (qq.v.), he served as principal leader of the Bemba (q.v.) nation for only a brief period around 1860. He succeeded his brother, Chileshye (q.v.), despite speech difficulties and some mental impairment. As it soon became evident that raids by Ngoni (q.v.) warriors would endanger the nation, the *bakabilo* (q.v.) agreed that Bwembya must be replaced. Chitapankwa was given the chiefly personal relics (*babenye*) and installed as Chitimukulu. Bwembya retired to another village, where he died. In the mid-20th century, another Bwembya rose to prominence. This man served as Chikwanda IV from 1935 to 1946, when he became Nkula IV. He relinquished this post in 1970 to become the Chitimukulu.

BWILE. This very small group of Bemba-(q.v.) speaking people lives on the eastern edge of Lake Mweru (q.v.) on the northern border of Zambia. Their economy is based mostly on fishing. In the mid-18th century they were defeated by the Lunda of Kazembe (q.v.), further south, along the Luapula River (q.v.).

C

CABINET. The Zambian cabinet consists of the ministers of a large and variable number of executive departments plus ministerial heads for each of the eight provinces, all of whom serve at the president's pleasure. Historically, these cabinet ministers were rotated among the ministries, or in and out of the cabinet, every 18 to 24 months. Such shifts were presumably designed to prevent any minister from establishing an independent power base, but critics also claim such shifts meant that the ministers had little control or influence over their respective ministries. Under the Second Republic, or one-party state, established in 1973, all cabinet decisions were subordinate to those of the Central Committee of UNIP (q.v.).

CAPRICORN AFRICA SOCIETY. A very controversial organization with branches throughout East and Central Africa (q.v.) (including the area near the Tropic of Capricorn, thus its name). In Zambia it influenced the formation of the Constitution Party and the Central Africa Party (qq.v.). It was founded in 1949 by Colonel David Stirling (q.v), with the idea of supporting an East and Central African federation. Ultimately, Stirling's vision switched to the idea of encouraging a common citizenship or patriotism that would unite people of all races. After a couple of years of preparation it produced the Capricorn contract, which called for rights and freedom for all, the end to all racial discrimination, and the establishment of a qualified right to vote—which would give some better-qualified individuals (usually Europeans) as many as six votes, while most Africans would have only one or two. While some Europeans saw this as a moderate organization with realistic goals based on ideals such as the establishment of racial harmony in a true multiracial society, most considered it far too liberal in its concessions to the Africans. Most Africans, on the other hand, saw it as just another clever scheme to perpetuate white minority rule. Thus throughout the antifederation struggle of the 1950s, the Capricorn Society was considered a front for the *banyama* (q.v.).

CAPRIVI STRIP. A long finger of land stretching between northern Botswana (q.v.) and southern Angola (q.v.) and Zambia, it is now governed by Namibia. This stretch of land was once under the Kololo rule of Sebituane (qq.v.). The Lozi (q.v.) claimed it after the Kololo were defeated, since one of the major Lozi administrative centers was just across the Zambezi at Sesheke (qq.v.). Germany got the Caprivi Strip and access to the Zambezi as part of the Anglo-German Concordat of 1890 (q.v.), despite Lozi protests to the British that it was a legitimate part of Barotseland (q.v.). Following World War I, a League of Nations mandate placed the Caprivi and all of Namibia (then called German South-West Africa) under South African control. The area took on added significance in 1965, when South Africa opened an air base just across from the Zambian border and, again, in the 1970s, when the South West African People's Organization freedom fighters began resisting South African rule and set up offices in Lusaka (q.v.). Refugees from both Angola and Namibia have used the strip as a route to and from Zambia. South Africa bitterly contested Zambia's and Botswana's claim to a common border at the tip of Caprivi. This is the site of the Kazungula (q.v.) ferry, where the old 60-tonne pontoon has since been replaced by two 100-tonne pontoons to accommodate the heavy truck traffic from South Africa to Zambia.

CARLTON HOUSE TERRACE CONFERENCE. Held in January 1953 in London, this was the final intergovernmental conference that decided upon the constitution for the Central African Federation (q.v.). All the delegates were Europeans, as the Africans, who were opposed to the idea of federation (q.v.), boycotted the meeting.

CASSAVA. Called manioc in South America and the main component of tapioca, this starchy root is the staple crop in some of the poorer agricultural regions of Zambia, such as the western third of the country and up along the Luapula River and Lake Bangweulu (qq.v.). Cassava will grow almost anywhere and requires little labor. It is filling and rich in calories. But it provides hardly any of the vitamins and minerals required by growing children and pregnant women. The Portuguese brought cassava from South America to the slave camps in Angola and Mozambique (qq.v.) in the 18th century. Since cassava is impervious to both drought and locusts, the British and Belgians, after 1930, periodically required Africans to grow "famine gardens" of cassava for their own food security; these were not particularly popular. Both the sweet and poisonous varieties of cassava are grown in Zambia. Whereas the sweet varieties can be roasted in the coals and eaten like sweet potatoes, the more common, poisonous varieties must be mashed and steeped in water to remove the prussic acid before being dried into flour. *Nshima* (q.v.) made from cassava flour has a rubbery, elastic texture.

CAUCUS FOR NATIONAL UNITY. Formed in March 1992 as a pressure group within the Movement for Multiparty Democracy (q.v.) after the 1991 elections, the caucus was led by the financially independent MMD members outside of Parliament who called for investigations of the corruption allegations made against MMD cabinet ministers. By mid-1992, CNU leaders had resigned from the MMD and announced their intention of forming another political party. At that time they announced their desire for constitutional revisions to reduce the president's powers, for primary elections in the selection of the MMD's parliamentary candidates, for measures to ensure accountability in the privatization of Zambia's parastatal corporations, and for greater representation of women in government. There was also a regional and ethnic flavor to the CNU's composition, as it was dominated by Lozi from Western Province (qq.v.) who criticized the MMD for being dominated by *ci*Bemba (q.v.) speakers. In July 1992 the CNU split into two factions, one registering as the Caucus for National Unity and the other as the Congress for National Unity. Neither party attracted prominent politicians, nor wielded any obvious political influence.

CENTRAL AFRICA. In the Zambian context, this vague term refers to either Nyasaland (q.v.) (modern Malawi, (q.v.)), which was known as the British Central African Protectorate (q.v.) from 1893 to 1907, or to the territories covered by the Central African Federation (q.v.), which included Northern and Southern Rhodesia (qq.v.) and Nyasaland (modern Zambia, Zimbabwe, and Malawi).

CENTRAL AFRICA PARTY. This party was formed early in 1959 as a liberal (actually moderate), multiracial party to compete in the 1959 territorial elections. Like its predecessor, the Constitution Party (q.v.), it was inspired in part by the principles of the Capricorn Africa Society (q.v.). Its best-known leader was Garfield Todd (q.v.), former prime minister of Southern Rhodesia (q.v.) and past leader of the old United Rhodesia Party. After splitting from the United Federal Party (q.v.), his URP was firmly defeated in the June 1958 elections. The CAP was formed from the liberal wing of the URP, combined with many of the members of the merging Constitution Party, notably John Moffat and Harry Franklin (qq.v.). It was a moderate party of whites and blacks who believed in a multiracial state based on true partnership. They wanted the principles behind the federal constitution fully supported, therefore bringing Africans eventually to full leadership in the federation (q.v.). This approach satisfied neither the African nationalists nor the European supremacists, yet it attracted some support from each race. It also advocated an immediate end to all racial discrimination. In the 1959 elections Todd and his supporters failed to win a single seat in Southern Rhodesia. Moffat and his colleagues were more successful in Northern Rhodesia (q.v.); Moffat and Franklin beat UFP candidates in the two European-reserved constituencies, and A. H. Gondwe (q.v.), an African, won a "special constituency." When Todd resigned from the party in 1960, the Southern Rhodesian section became even weaker and less effective. Meanwhile, in October 1960, Moffat changed the name of the Northern Rhodesia section of the CAP to the Northern Rhodesia Liberal Party (q.v.).

CENTRAL AFRICAN AIRWAYS CORPORATION. The parent company of Central African Airways, the national airline of the Central African Federation (q.v.), the CAA was created on June 1, 1946. Its roots go back to the Rhodesia and Nyasaland Airways, Ltd., that was formed in 1933 but that was absorbed into the war effort in 1939 and became known as the Southern Rhodesian Air Services (SRAS). Despite its name, the SRAS operated essential air services in all three territories. After World War II, the CAA took over the SRAS fleet of planes. Capital for new equipment came from all three territories: 50 percent from Southern Rhodesia (q.v.), 35 percent from Northern Rhodesia (q.v.), and 15 percent from Nyasaland (q.v.). It provided services between the parts of the federation and to and from outside territories. It became an international agency when the federation was dissolved at the end of 1963, but it began to formally break up after Southern Rhodesia's unilateral declaration of independence (q.v.) in November 1965. Its assets were to be divided, with Malawi (q.v.) receiving 10 percent and Zambia and Rhodesia splitting the remaining 90 percent equally. Final dissolution of the CAA occurred at the end of 1967, several months after Zambia Airways began operations.

CENTRAL AFRICAN BROADCASTING SERVICE. This predecessor of the Zambia National Broadcasting Services (q.v.) began in Lusaka (q.v.) in 1941, when the government established a small, shortwave radio station to circulate news of the war. In 1945, Harry Franklin (q.v.), director of the Department of Information, persuaded the British government to fund a Lusaka station for the education and entertainment of Africans throughout modern Zambia, Malawi (q.v.), and Zimbabwe. As few Africans had electricity or could afford the monthly fee for wired (cable) radio service, the station's real popularity began in 1949, after the introduction of the battery-operated "saucepan special" (q.v.). Each day of the week featured programming in a different language—*ci*Bemba, *ci*Nyanja, *ci*Tonga, *si*Lozi (qq.v.), *si*Ndebele, *ci*Shona, and English. In addition to unbiased world and district news reports, its programs included fables, plays, educational talks, personal messages to distant relatives, and the latest records from America and Southern and Central Africa (q.v.).

From 1948 to 1954, the CABS also broadcast its own field

recordings of traditional African music. The field recorders' itineraries were broadcast in advance, and for weeks at a time they would drive their pickup truck (with their Presto tape recorder) to schools and community halls to record the assembled performers. Suitable tapes would then be sent to the Lusaka studio and aired on Saturday mornings. The few recordings that still survive have been transferred to new master tapes on deposit at the National Archives of Zambia. Though the CABS was refreshingly free of the racism common to that era, its African listeners felt betrayed by its factual reports on the events leading toward federation (q.v.), and its African announcers were both shunned and harassed as suspected *banyama* (q.v.). Yet when broadcasting director Michael Kittermaster resigned in 1954, he became the first European official to be paid a spontaneous tribute by the African members of the Legislative Council (q.v.). The CABS was the first African radio station to broadcast to Africans. With its listener surveys and man-in-the-street interviews, it achieved real success in its pioneering endeavor. And by fostering the recording career of broadcaster Alick Nkhata (q.v.), the CABS also gave birth to Zambian popular music.

CENTRAL AFRICAN COUNCIL. A forerunner of the Central African Federation (q.v.), it was originally suggested by the Bledisloe Commission (q.v.). Its formation was announced in 1944, and it held its first meeting in June 1945. It met twice a year, thereafter, until 1953. It consisted of the governors of Northern and Southern Rhodesia and Nyasaland (qq.v.) and three lay members chosen by the government of each territory. In fact, the latter were always leading political figures. The council coordinated communications between the territories, solved some problems concerning migrant labor, and extended some Southern Rhodesian services to other territories. While it was seen by some as a step toward amalgamation (q.v.), it didn't go far enough to satisfy many settler leaders; it was purely an advisory body with no real executive powers. It was, however, concerned with a very broad range of problems, and in this way laid the groundwork for many activities of the later federation.

CENTRAL AFRICAN FEDERATION. Also called the Federation of Rhodesia and Nyasaland, it came into being in October 1953 as the result of many years of urging by Europeans in Northern and Southern Rhodesia and Nyasaland (qq.v.) who saw many possible benefits from increased cooperation. Southern Rhodesian whites were especially attracted by the copper (q.v.) wealth of the north, whereas those in the two northern territories saw greater security coming from associating with the higher percentage of Europeans south of the Zambezi River (q.v.). Godfrey Huggins (q.v.) and Roy Welensky (q.v.) were major figures in the establishment of the federation. The bill passed the British Parliament in May 1953 and was approved by Queen Elizabeth I on August 1, 1953. The federation was ruled by a federal Parliament based in Salisbury (q.v.), Southern Rhodesia, and by a prime minister. Each of the three territories also had its own legislature.

The end of the federation was the result of rising movements of African nationalism led by Hastings Banda, in Nyasaland, and Kenneth Kaunda (qq.v.) in Northern Rhodesia. When they precipitated the failure of the Federal Review Conference (q.v.) of December 1960, and Banda soon got approval to move Nyasaland toward secession, the end of the federation became inevitable. The federation flag was lowered for the last time at the end of December 1963.

CENTRAL AFRICAN FILM UNIT. *See* DEPARTMENT OF INFORMATION; ZAMBIA INFORMATION SERVICES.

CENTRAL AFRICAN MAIL. The newspaper was founded in 1960 with financial aid from the London *Observer* and was first called the *African Mail.* It was at that time the only newspaper in Northern Rhodesia (q.v.) oriented toward Africans supportive of nationalist goals. As such it had a strong impact on African public opinion. The paper changed its name to the *Central African Mail* in 1962. Its editorial policy was strongly antifederation and in favor of "one man, one vote" as well as independence. It was a weekly newspaper in 1965 when the *Observer* withdrew its support and the government bought the paper and called it the *Zambia Mail.* It is now the *Zambia Daily Mail* (q.v.).

CENTRAL AFRICAN PEOPLE'S UNION. A party that existed during 1962, but mostly only in the mind of its president, Dixon Konkola (q.v.), it surfaced early in 1962 when Konkola campaigned for a seat in the federal Parliament (q.v.). The April 27, 1962, election chose two Northern Rhodesia Africans for the Parliament. Konkola and Edward Mukelabai actually campaigned under another party name, the National Republican Party (q.v.). They received only 22 and 25 votes, respectively, but they won, as only 1.37 percent of the eligible electorate voted. The CAPU supported the continued existence of the federation (q.v.). It reportedly received aid from both the United Federal Party and from Moise Tshombe (qq.v.) in Katanga. Late in 1962 the CAPU reportedly "merged" with the African National Congress (q.v.).

CENTRAL COMMITTEE OF UNIP. As in its beginning, the United National Independence Party (q.v.) Central Committee is now the executive committee of the party. In August 1967, elections to the Central Committee caused a major split in the party, only partly smoothed over by President Kaunda (q.v.). It remained disunited. This surfaced again in August 1969, when Simon Kapwepwe (q.v.) resigned from the vice presidency. Several hours later Kaunda dissolved the Central Committee and assumed party power directly, aided by a hand-picked, interim Executive Committee. In March 1970, the Chuula Commission (q.v.) issued a draft for a new UNIP constitution. Its proposals for the Central Committee, however, were rejected. Instead, new provisions in 1971 called for a 25-member Central Committee consisting of 20 members elected by the general party conference every five years, the secretary general, and four nominated members. At the May 1971 conference, a geographically balanced slate was presented and elected. As a result of the 1973 constitution that made Zambia a one-party state, UNIP's Central Committee became superior to even the cabinet. In 1988 the Central Committee was expanded to 68 members, and a Committee of Chairmen was added to UNIP's structure, as part of an effort by Kaunda to exert more control over the party. In 1991, following a 1990 report from Parliament on democratizing UNIP, the Central Committee was reduced to 34 members.

CENTRAL PROVINCE. Central Province lies south of the Katanga (Shaba) Pedicle (q.v.). When Luangwa (formerly Feira) and Lusaka Urban and Rural Districts were split off to become Lusaka Province, Central Province was whittled down to Serenje, Mkushi, Mumbwa, and Kabwe Urban and Rural Districts. The total population of these five districts, some 359,000 in 1969, was 725,600 in 1990. The major ethnic groups in this province are the Ila, Lenje, Swaka, and Lala (qq.v.).

CEWA. This is a variant of Chewa (q.v.).

CHA-CHA-CHA CAMPAIGN. The term reportedly made its first appearance at a speech Kenneth Kaunda (q.v.) gave to the Mulungushi (q.v.) party conference on July 9, 1961. It eventually came to symbolize a campaign of political consciousness and civil disobedience that would compel the British and Northern Rhodesian governments to concede independence to Zambia. The term most likely refers to Le Grande Kalle's hit record, "*La Table Ronde* (Cha Cha)," which celebrated the 1960 talks leading to the Congo-Kinshasa's (q.v.) independence. Kaunda's impassioned speech stressed the need for immediate action, but he insisted that all action must be nonviolent. As he spoke, the audience repeatedly chanted the phrase "cha-cha-cha." Interpretation varied, but to many it meant that it was time to "face the music" and everyone was expected to join in the "dance." Even Sir Roy Welensky (q.v.) and the Queen will have to learn the cha-cha-cha, it was said. Despite Kaunda's plea for nonviolence, United National Independence Party (q.v.) youths in some provinces burned schools and destroyed bridges and roads. But many demonstrations were peaceful, such as making bonfires of identification cards, or passes (q.v.). Perhaps the widespread nature of the campaign convinced the British that this unified nationalist movement could not be ignored.

CHADIZA. A town in the extreme southeast part of Eastern Province (q.v.) it is near the sites of several good examples of rock art (q.v.), notably that at Sejamanja (q.v.) and Mbangombe. The flat plateau country nearby has some kopjes and outcrops of granite and quartzite. Much game formerly roamed the area, and the area was populated by hunter-gatherers.

CHAFISI HILL. At this site between Chipata and Chadiza (qq.v.) in southeastern Zambia, there are some good examples of rock art (q.v.), notably outline drawings of "reptiles."

CHAKULYA, WILSON MOFYA FRANK. A long-time political and labor activist, he began in the African National Congress (q.v.) Youth League in the early 1950s and eventually followed Kaunda (q.v.) into the United National Independence Party (q.v.). Chakulya was active in the Reformed Trade Union Congress and became an officer in the combined United Trade Union Congress (qq.v.). Chakulya became general secretary of the Zambia Congress of Trade Unions (q.v.) in 1967. He persuaded the ZCTU's largely autonomous member unions to accept a new ZCTU constitution, which required each member union to obtain ZCTU approval before going out on strike. The Mineworkers Union of Zambia (q.v.) resented this centralization of power and tried, unsuccessfully, to remove Chakulya from ZCTU leadership.

In 1969, Chakulya became the first trade union officeholder to be elected to Parliament (q.v.) and in April 1971 became cabinet minister for Central Province (q.v.). After becoming managing director of Nchanga Consolidated Copper Mines (q.v.), he entered the diplomatic service as an ambassador in 1976. He served as minister of foreign affairs in 1978 and 1979 and as minister of defense from 1980 to 1983.

CHAMBESHI (CHAMBEZI; CHAMBESI) RIVER. Beginning in the northeastern corner of Zambia, the river flows in a southwesterly direction, passing through the Bangweulu swamps in a large number of channels. Some of them find their way to Lake Bangweulu (q.v.), but most of them empty into the Luapula River en route to Lake Mweru (qq.v.). Among its tributaries are the Luchindashi and Kalungu Rivers (q.v.).

CHAMBEZI (CHAMBESHI) DISTRICT. A district created in the northeastern corner of Zambia by the British South Africa Company (q.v.) in the late 1890s, it became the location of several of the company's early *bomas*. It was later renamed North Luangwa District of Northern Province of Northern Rhodesia. Today the area includes parts of Isoka, Chinsali, and Lundazi (qq.v.) Districts.

CHAMBISHI MINE. Pegged by George Grey's (q.v.) 1899 expedition, it was one of the major Copperbelt (q.v.) mines and is located about halfway between Nchanga and Kitwe (qq.v.). It has been closed since 1987. Zambia Consolidated Copper Mines (q.v.) put all but its operating cobalt and acids plants up for sale in early 1995 but it failed to attract a single bid by the end of six months. The Chambishi exemplifies the shared problem faced by ZCCM and the Zambia Privatisation Agency (q.v.), that of finding buyers for relatively useless and unattractive assets.

CHANGUFU, LEWIS MUTALE. This Zambian businessman was one of the early nationalist activists and remained active in both United National Independence Party (q.v.) and numerous cabinet positions until his defeat in the December 1973 general elections. Born in Kasama, October 5, 1927, he attended school in both Kasama and Ndola (qq.v.) before entering the civil service. He entered politics in 1950, joining the Congress movement. In 1953, as Congress branch chairman for Lusaka (q.v.), he became active in bringing a successful end to discrimination in some of the butcheries that the African National Congress (q.v.) was boycotting. He lost his civil service job in 1954 because of his political activities. He then became manager of a printing company.

In October 1958, Changufu joined with Kenneth Kaunda (q.v.) and others in forming Zambia African National Congress (q.v.) and was appointed to its executive committee. When the government detained many ZANC activists in 1959, Changufu was arrested and sent to Chadiza for seven months. He returned to become UNIP's chief national trustee and transport officer in January 1960. After a brief period of study in America, he returned home in 1963 and was elected to Parliament from Mansa. In the January 1964 government, he was appointed Kaunda's parliamentary secretary. Later that year he helped put an end to the Lumpa uprising of Alice Lenshina (q.v.). At independence he was made minister of state for defense and security, but several months later, in January 1965, he entered the cabinet as minister of information and postal services. He then changed positions almost annually, serving in a variety of successive ministries. He may have lost some of his Bemba political support when he failed to join Simon Kapwepwe's United Progressive Party (q.v.). He failed to win reelection, and returned to private business.

CHAPLIN, SIR FRANCIS DRUMMOND PERCY. He was the administrator of Northern Rhodesia (q.v.) from March 1921 until February 1924. His appointment to this post stirred up major opposition among many Northern Rhodesians because he was then also administering Southern Rhodesia (q.v.). This seemed like a major step toward the amalgamation (q.v.) of the two territories that was opposed by so many in the north (as well as the south) at that time.

CHEWA (CEWA). This is the third-largest ethnic group in Zambia, and the dominant one in Eastern Province (q.v.) and neighboring Malawi (q.v.). The Chewa speak ciNyanja (q.v.) and likely represented at least 40 percent of the 795,600 ciNyanja speakers in Zambia in 1986. While they seem to have originated in the Congo, leaving there in the 14th or 15th century, those living around Chipata (q.v.) derive from the expansion of a Chewa chiefdom called Undi (q.v.) which was in Mozambique (q.v.) around the 17th century. Some of the Chewa chiefs from Undi moved westward into Zambia, although many of them remained subordinate to Undi and sent back tribute. One group of Chewa under the chieftainship called Mwase (q.v.) moved up the Luangwa (q.v.) valley as early as the 18th century. The Chewa chiefdom of Mkanda (q.v.), somewhat north of Chipata, became independent from Undi in the early 19th century. Despite its prosperity and strength, it fell victim to Mpezeni's Ngoni (qq.v.), who by 1880 had joined with the Chikunda (q.v.) to kill Mkanda and take over his lands. Under colonial rule, the Chewa were split from one another by the border with Nyasaland and, in the late 1920s, were forcibly removed onto overcrowded Native Reserves (q.v.).

CHIBALE. He was a Senga (q.v.) chief in the upper Luangwa (q.v.) valley during the 1890s. An Arab (q.v.) named Kapandansalu (q.v.) built a stockaded village nearby that became a major depot buying slaves from the Bemba (q.v.). Thus the Bemba were disturbed when Chibale, who tolerated the Arabs, also allowed the British South Africa Company (q.v.) to build a station nearby, at Mirongo. He hoped that the company could free his people from Arab dominance, as the Senga had to grow grain and hunt elephants for the Arabs. Chibale told Robert Young (q.v.) of the BSAC that Bemba leaders had threatened to cut off his head for allowing the Europeans to settle. On September 15, 1897, the Arabs and some Bemba attacked Chibale's village. Young arrived with 15 policemen and forced out the attackers, who then laid siege. On September 21, reinforcements arrived for the company forces led by Charles McKinnon (q.v.), and the Arab forces received a crushing defeat. Many were taken captive, including Kapandansalu, their leader; hundreds of slaves were released. The Bemba chiefs, especially Mwamba (q.v.), were disturbed at the company's success, as this was one of several battles in which Bemba vulnerability to European forces was demonstrated.

CHIBALO (CHIBARO). This is a common term in Southern and Central Africa (q.v.) for forced labor. Though retrospectively applied to the "tax labor" exacted during the first years of the hut tax (q.v.) collections in North-Eastern Rhodesia (q.v.), the term probably derives from the word "bureau" in the Rhodesia

Native Labour Bureau (q.v.), which formed in 1903 and was infamous for the ruthless, strong-arm methods its agents used in recruiting laborers for the Southern Rhodesian mines. Essentially, similar methods were then also being used to recruit laborers for Kansanshi (q.v.) and the Katangan mines and for porter work throughout the territory. Thus *chibaro* is also used in reference to the work performed by the 200,000 or more conscripted carriers (or *tengatenga*) of the German East African campaign during World War I as well as to that performed by the African Labour Corps, who were labor conscripts on white farms from 1942 to 1952.

CHIBANGWA, HENRY. In the early 1930s, he was the outspoken leader of the Luanshya Native Welfare Association (q.v.). The association was not granted recognition by the government, in part because of his "subversive activities." Even when brought before J. Moffat Thomson (q.v.), the secretary for native affairs, he repeated his demands for equal treatment and justice for Africans. He especially opposed the pass system (q.v.) that was enforced against urban Africans.

CHIBANZA. A major 19th-century chief of the Kaonde (q.v.) in northwestern Zambia, he controlled a copper mine at Kansanshi (q.v.) from which bullets were cast for muzzle-loading guns. Nevertheless, he was forced to send tribute to the Yeke leader, Msiri (q.v.), in Katanga (q.v.).

CHIBARO. *See* CHIBALO.

CHIBEMBA. This is a variant of *ci*Bemba (q.v.).

CHIBESAKUNDA. This is one of the major chiefships among the Bisa (q.v.) peoples of eastern Zambia. These chiefs belonged to the Bena Ng'ona, or Mushroom Clan, as did many other Bisa chiefs, but they were independent of the others and have kept distinct lineages. During the 1870s much of the land of Chibesakunda was attacked by Bemba (q.v.) leaders, and the Bisa were forced to move further east and north. Some lived as far north as the head of the Luangwa (q.v.) valley in the mid-1880s. Many years later, under the protection of British rule, the Bisa of Chibesakunda were allowed to reoccupy their original territory.

CHIBULUMA MINE. One of the smaller mines owned by Roan Consolidated Mines, Ltd. (q.v.), on the Copperbelt (q.v.), it was opened in April 1956. It is located south of Chambishi and west of the major mining center of Kitwe (q.v.).

CHIBWA (CHIBWE) MARSH AND SALT PANS. A major source of salt in the eastern half of Zambia, it is located along the Lui-tikila River near Mpika (q.v.). The production of salt, which became a major item for trade or sale in the area, involved the labor-intensive process of cutting and burning the marsh's saline grasses, then evaporating the water dripped through ash-filled funnels. Though the Bemba and Bisa (qq.v.) both preferred white trade salt, the marsh and its salt pans were their main source of salt in precolonial times.

CHIENGELE (CIENGELE). A chief (Mwene) of the Mbunda (q.v.) people in Angola (q.v.), he led a band of followers into western Zambia in the early 19th century. They settled near Mongu (q.v.), and the Lozi (q.v.) attempted to integrate them into their system. Chiengele was recognized as the senior chief among the Mbunda in Bulozi (q.v.) (several other groups also settled in the area) and was given the status of a Lozi prince. This included a seat in the Lealui *kuta* (qq.v.). All this was under king Mulambwa (q.v.). When Mulambwa died there was a succession dispute between his sons Silumelume and Mubuk-wanu (qq.v.). Chiengele secretly supported the latter, and arranged an Mbunda war dance in Silumelume's honor. Silumelume was killed there by a dancer's arrow.

CHIFUBWA STREAM. A rock shelter along this stream south of Solwezi in north-central Zambia houses the most important collection of rock art (q.v.) found in Zambia. A mass of engravings are located along the back wall of the shelter. There are good indications that they are from the Late Stone Age, possibly earlier than 2,000 years B.C. if neighboring carbon-dated findings are a good guide. The most common motif of the engravings, which may have been painted, is an inverted V with a vertical bar through the center.

CHIGAGA, GIBSON. A lawyer by training, he was appointed minister of finance in May 1987, after the austerity measures of the structural adjustment program (q.v.) led Zambia to break relations with the International Monetary Fund (q.v.). Chigaga managed Zambia's economy during the period in which it was to "grow from its own resources" and helped engineer a return to the IMF's fold following the 1988 elections. He died suddenly in mid-March 1991 after returning from a meeting in Paris with bilateral and multilateral donors.

CHIKANAMULILO. The senior Inamwanga (q.v.) chief, he successfully beat off a Bemba attack by Chitapankwa and Makasa IV (qq.v.) in 1877 but was defeated and put to flight by a subsequent Chitapankwa raid in 1879. In January 1891, the defeated chief ceded his territory and all his peoples' rights to it in a treaty Alfred Sharpe (q.v.) put together for the African Lakes Company (q.v.). The company paid the chief goods valued at £50. It is very possible that the chief did not understand the nature of this agreement, but it hardly mattered either, since the lands he ceded were in Bemba (q.v.) hands and thus equally inaccessible to the Inamwanga and the British.

CHIKUNDA. This name was given by the Africans to a large and diverse group of slave traders who ravaged the peoples of southeastern Zambia and neighboring territories, especially in the last half of the 19th century. The Portuguese government gave them titles to land west of Tete (q.v.) in order to control it indirectly. Some of the traders had escaped from the black slave armies of Portuguese estates further east. Although of diverse origin (many of them were mulattoes), they developed a common cultural identity and a language (Nyungwe) that was a mixture of several African tongues. Two of the most notorious of this generally brutal breed were known as Kanyemba and Matakenya. Their bases were usually just outside Zambia's present borders, but they terrorized much of the southeastern part of the country. Some, however, got as far as the upper Luapula River (q.v.), and some settled among the Lala, Lenje, and Lamba (qq.v.). Some Chikunda, such as Matakenya, were very wealthy and could put as many as 12,000 armed slaves into a battle. One group, armed with muskets, fought alongside a dissident Lozi (q.v.), Sikabenga, as far west as Tonga (q.v.) country in 1885. Some Tonga also joined with the slave-trading Chikunda, to their mutual advantage. One reason Joseph Thomson (q.v.) was successful in getting treaties with various Zambian chiefs and headmen was that they hoped he could help protect them from the Chikunda.

CHIKWANDA. The title of one of the major Bemba (q.v.) chiefships, it was established around 1830 when the Bemba invaded the Chinama area of Bisa (q.v.) territory, southeast of the Bangweulu swamps. The Bisa moved east, and the Bemba took over the Chibwa salt pans (q.v.), the only source of salt on the plateau. The first holder of the title was Nkumbula Chikwanda I, who built his capital immediately south of the salt marsh. He eventually had a conflict over tribute to be paid to Chitimukulu (q.v.), however, and also angered other senior Bemba chiefs. He was killed, perhaps in the late 1840s, by Bisa whom he had tried to placate after his arguments with the other Bemba.

Mutale Lwanga Chikwanda II was not appointed to the post and the Chinama area until about the 1870s, and he too had difficulties with the Bisa. He reigned until 1913 and was quite successful. In 1898 a visitor reported an army of 600 or more men at his court. Late in his reign, however, a high-handed attitude alienated Bisa chiefs in the area, notably Nkuka (q.v.), with whom he had a long dispute. He also expanded his area into that of the Lala (q.v.), whom he frequently raided for cattle. In addition, he developed his own access to the coastal trade. In 1913 he gave up his title and became Chitimukulu (q.v.) until his death in 1916.

Chief Musungu Chikwanda III left the chieftainship in 1935 and became Nkula and later Chitimukulu. Bwembya Chikwanda IV served from 1935 until 1946, when he became Nkula and finally Chitimukulu. Mutale Chikwanda V served until 1970 when he became Nkula. He followed the nationalist leaders who walked out of the Federal Review Conference (q.v.).

CHIKWANDA, ALEXANDER BWALYA. One of the early political leaders of Zambia, he was born in December 1938 at Kasama (q.v.). He attended Lund University in Sweden, then worked as a clerk at the mines and became active in politics on the Copperbelt (q.v.). He joined the United National Independence Party (q.v.) as a constituency secretary in 1959 and served in several other posts. He won the Kitwe seat in Parliament (qq.v.) in 1964. He was given several administrative posts in 1969 and 1970, the latter in the president's office. In 1971 he was appointed minister of national guidance, moving on to minister of health in 1972. In 1973 he was made minister of planning and finance, in 1975 minister of local government and housing, and from 1977 to 1980, minister of agriculture and water development before resigning from government service.

Chikwanda gave no specific reason for his resignation but warned that "ultraextremists, sham radicals, bootlickers and sycophants" would destroy the nation. He then served as chairman of the Zambia industrial and commercial association in the 1980s. At UNIP's Fifth National Convention in March 1990, he and Vernon Mwaanga (q.v.) circulated a document criticizing the one-party system and calling for a new constitutional commission to take testimony on the kinds of reforms that citizens favored. He eventually left UNIP and became an advisor to the Movement for Multiparty Democracy's president, Frederick Chiluba (qq.v.).

CHILANGA. A town just south of Lusaka (q.v.) along the line of rail (q.v.), it is the site of a major cement plant. The first such plant was built there in 1951; it was expanded in 1968.

CHILESHE, SAFELI. One of the moderate African nationalists, his political career ran from the 1940s to the 1960s. He was a government employee in 1948, when he and another African were flown to London to sit in on talks concerning the possibility of federation (q.v.). The talks also included Roy Welensky and the Northern Rhodesian governor, Gilbert Rennie (qq.v.). When he reported to the Federation of Welfare Societies (*see* FEDERATION OF AFRICAN SOCIETIES OF NORTHERN RHODESIA) about the talks, he was denounced for even attending. Nevertheless, he was elected to the African Representative Council (q.v.) in 1953. Earlier that year, he led a peaceful boycott of butcher shops in Lusaka (q.v.). Although he had been a founding member of the African National Congress (q.v.), he became one of the founders of the multiracial Constitution Party (q.v.) in 1957. He was also one of the Africans appointed to the Northern Rhodesian Legislative Council (q.v.). He was denounced by the ANC for selling out the nationalist movement; he responded by accusing it of using intimidation tactics. When the government banned the Zambia African National Congress (q.v.) in 1959, Chileshe sympathized with the desire for greater African political participation but also said that few Africans approved of gangster methods. In 1964, with independence around the corner, Chileshe was appointed the first non-European mayor of Lusaka.

CHILESHYE CHEPELA. An important Bemba Chitimukulu (qq.v.) of the 19th century, he reigned for over three decades, from the mid-1820s to about 1860. The sister's daughter's son of Chitimukulu Chiliamafwa, he was born with a stunted arm and was abandoned by his mother. Raised by others, he became quite close to Chiliamafwa and, according to some, was his choice to succeed him at his death (around 1820). Instead, the *bakabilo* (q.v.) chose Susulu Chinchinta (q.v.). This

turned out to be a poor choice. Susulu was a harsh Chitimukulu, and the *bakabilo* put up little resistance when Chileshye
raided the capital and deposed Susulu about 1826.

Chileshye was responsible for the considerable expansion of
the Bemba sphere of influence, and annexed the Lunda of Kazembe's (qq.v.) major trade route through Bisa country. Chileshye's capital was at Kansansama (q.v.), on the northern bank
of the Kalungu River (q.v.). But the revival of the Bisa in the
1850s and the coming of the Ngoni (q.v.) left the Bemba with
little more territory when he died in 1860 than when he became
Chitimukulu in the 1820s. One important development, however, was that his accession and long reign switched the ruling
line to a new branch of the chiefly clan.

CHILILABOMBWE. This northern Copperbelt (q.v.) town and
district is extremely near the Katanga Pedicle (q.v.) and thus
near the border with the Democratic Republic of Congo (q.v.)
(Zaire). Prior to independence, the town and its mine were
named Bancroft. The population of the district was about
45,000 in 1969, and 86,600 in 1990. A major labor disturbance
occurred there in August 1968, led primarily by Lozi (q.v.) miners active in the United Party (q.v.). The party was banned soon
afterward.

CHILILABOMBWE MINE. Only about 16 kilometers (10 miles)
from the border with the Democratic Republic of Congo (q.v.)
(Zaire) and 16 kilometers (10 miles) north of Nchanga (q.v.),
this important mine, formerly known as Bancroft Mine, is part
of the Anglo-American Corporation (q.v.) group. Construction
began in 1953, but copper (q.v.) production did not begin until
January 1957. The mine temporarily ceased production early in
1958 but reopened in April 1959. It was named after Dr. Joseph
Austen Bancroft, for many years the consulting geologist to
Anglo-American. "Chililabombwe" is *ci*Lamba for "song of the
frogs."

CHILOLO (pl., *bafilolo*). A common Central African term for an
overseer or *kapitao* (a Portugese loan word), it often is used in
reference to an appointed chief's councilor or advisor.

CHILUBA, FREDERICK JACOB TITUS MPUNDU. He was born
in April 1943 in Luapula Province (q.v.), the son of a miner. His
mother died while he was still young. He was expelled from
Kawamabwa Secondary School for organizing a boycott. He

completed his O-level studies by correspondence, and later passed his A-level exams in two subjects. He was elected general secretary of the Zambia Congress of Trade Unions (q.v.) in 1974 and was always popular with rank-and-file union members for his efforts to keep the unions free of United National Independence Party (q.v.) control.

During the 1980s, Chiluba emerged as the country's foremost spokesman for the plight of Zambian workers, particularly after 1983, when the International Monetary Fund's (q.v.) austerity measures (*see* STRUCTURAL ADJUSTMENT PROGRAM) seriously eroded the living standards of most Zambians. His criticism of government policies and involvement in a number of strikes earned him the enmity of the government. His passport was seized in October 1980, following an alleged discovery of a plot to overthrow the government. He was one of 17 union leaders expelled from UNIP in January 1981 for threatening an election boycott by union members, and one of four labor leaders detained from July to November 1981 for inciting workers to unrest and revolution. The High Court, however, declared his detention illegal and ordered his release. In late 1987, in a move allegedly orchestrated by the government, Chiluba was suspended by the union of building workers. The ZCTU responded by suspending the building union's leaders, and in January 1988 they, in turn, expelled Chiluba. Even then, Chiluba was considered a potential presidential rival to Kenneth Kaunda (q.v.).

He was elected one of the two vice chairmen of the National Interim Committee for Multi-Party Democracy (precursor to the Movement for Multiparty Democracy) in July 1990 and helped lead the many rallies to legitimize competing political parties within UNIP's one-party state. The MMD became an official political party that December, and Chiluba, with 63 percent of the vote, replaced Arthur Wina (q.v.) as party president in March 1991. Chiluba won more than 80 percent of the popular vote in the elections of October 31, 1991, and was sworn in as president of the republic on November 2.

Once in power, Chiluba demonstrated his commitment to economic reform by pursuing the structural adjustment program (q.v.) as mandated by the IMF and donors. Though from time to time the implementation of the various efforts at reform deviated from the rigid conditions set by donors, by and large, President Chiluba's administration complied with their strictures. Politically, his administration was wracked with dissent, and many original MMD leaders left the party to form opposition parties. Furthermore, his administration was plagued by persistent rumors and accusations of high-level corruption, a sore point for donors. His attacks on the *Post* (q.v.), an independent newspaper, were also a cause of concern to many both inside and outside of Zambia.

CHIMBA. A half brother of Chiti (q.v.), the legendary founder and leader of the Bemba (q.v.), Chimba accompanied him on the great migration to their new lands. He became keeper of the bows of both Chiti and Nkole (q.v.), eventually passing them on to their nephew Chilufya, who became Chitimukulu (q.v.). Chilufya allowed Chimba to keep Nkole's bow. Chimba founded a village a few miles north of the Kalungu River (q.v.) at Chatindubwi. Among the Bemba, the current bearer of Chimba's title is also one of the six senior *bakabilo* (q.v.), called *bashilubemba*, who resolve such major issues as chiefly successions. In addition, the current Chimba serves as regent during the long burial ceremonies of the Chitimukulu, just as the first Chimba had done.

CHIMBA, JUSTIN MUSONDA. One of the must prominent of the early nationalist leaders, he became a high-ranking official both in the United National Independence Party (q.v.) and in the government. Born a Bemba in Northern Province (q.v.), he was organizing secretary and later president of the Northern Rhodesian general workers trade union. In 1950 he was cofounder of the antifederation action committee. In 1951 this group joined the African National Congress (q.v.), supporting Harry Nkumbula (q.v.) as its leader. Although Chimba became an active ANC member, he continued his union activities serving in the mid-1950s as a member of the executive committee of the African Trade Union Congress. In October 1958, Chimba was a leader of the walkout from the ANC conference, in protest of Nkumbula's leadership. He quickly became an activist and an Eastern Province (q.v.) organizer for the Zambia African National Congress (q.v.). In 1959 he was detained by the government for these activities and was held in Barotseland (q.v.). From 1961 to 1964 he served as UNIP's representative in Cairo and Dar es Salaam.

Upon his return for Zambia's independence in 1964 he was appointed deputy general secretary of UNIP (a post he held until 1969) and minister of labour and mines. In January 1965 he was made minister of justice. From 1965 to 1969 he was rotated through at least four ministries. In January 1971 he was appointed minister of trade and industry, but shortly became embroiled in controversy and was dropped from the government on January 29, 1971. The problem involved charges by Chimba and John Chisata (q.v.) that the government was guilty of both a coverup and tribalism for failing to prosecute certain non-Bemba political figures for their misuse of funds. These accusations were investigated by the Doyle Commission (q.v.), but the lack of firm evidence resulted in Chimba's dismissal. In August 1971, Chimba joined Simon Kapwepwe's new United Progressive Party (qq.v.), and became its director of youth. He was detained by the government in 1972 but filed suit against the government for false imprisonment and his "degrading and humiliating treatment" by the police. A High Court justice awarded him K7,000 (about U.S.$9,800) damages plus costs in December 1972. On September 9, 1977, he announced that he would rejoin UNIP for the sake of national unity.

CHINA, PEOPLE'S REPUBLIC OF. As a result of China's generous support in financing, building, and maintaining the once vital TAZARA (q.v.) railway, relations between the two countries are historically cordial. Relations began at independence, when China established a charge d'affaires in Lusaka (q.v.), and Zambia announced its recognition of China and support for a UN seat. Numerous visits in 1965–66 by Zambian ministers to China culminated in Kenneth Kaunda's (q.v.) June 1967 visit and China's formal offer to build the railway. Like Tanzania (q.v.), Zambia pledged to match the Chinese's local construction costs with the purchase of Chinese consumer goods, including toothpaste, umbrellas, enamelware, children's clothes, and the all-steel Flying Pigeon bicycles. Zambia has made not one of its scheduled payments on the original interest-free loan since the railway opened in 1975. Yet China refurbished the rail line in the early 1980s and, in 1995, again rescheduled Zambia's loan payments and pledged to help TAZARA establish a light tractor assembly plant at its Mpika (q.v.) workshop. Zambia and China clearly have a long-term relationship.

CHINCHINTA, SUSULA. A harsh and unpopular Chitimukulu of the Bemba (qq.v.) about 1820–26, when Chileshye (q.v.) replaced him. Susula fled to the land of the Mambwe (q.v.) chief, Nsokolo (q.v.), where he soon died.

CHINGOLA. A city and district along the northern part of the Copperbelt (q.v.), it is considered a twin city to its northern neighbor, Nchanga (q.v.). They are often referred to as Nchanga-Chingola. Chingola had some 103,000 people in 1969 and nearly 187,000 in 1990. Such a population increase, along with the long-term pollution of the Kafue River (q.v.) by mining wastes, jeopardizes many Copperbelt towns' drinking water supplies. The seriousness of this problem was first realized in 1988, when women's hair turned green after washing.

CHINSALI. This is a town and also a district in Northern Province (q.v.). The district had only 58,000 people in 1969 and nearly 87,000 in 1990. At the beginning of this century it was part of Chambeshi District (q.v.) and, then, North Luangwa District. Two important religious figures made a name in this area: David Kaunda (q.v.), father of Zambia's first president, was a missionary pioneer in the area near the beginning of this century; and in the mid-1950s, Alice Lenshina began her Lumpa Church (qq.v.) near Chinsali in the western side of the district.

CHINSALI AFRICAN WELFARE ASSOCIATION. Among the many welfare associations (q.v.) that played an important role in fostering African nationalism in colonial Zambia, one of its first major leaders was the Reverend Paul Mushindo (q.v.). Two of its most important young members in the early 1950s were Kenneth Kaunda and Simon Kapwepwe (qq.v.). In the 1950s two of its secretaries were Reuben Mulenga and Samson Mukeya Mununga. The Chinsali Association was strongly opposed to federation (q.v.) because it felt that partnership might not turn out well for Africans.

CHINYAMA. He is one of the legendary founders of the Lunda and Luvale (qq.v.) peoples in northwestern Zambia and neighboring parts of Angola and the Democratic Republic of Congo (qq.v.) (Zaire). Some hundreds of years ago, the Luba (q.v.) clan Tubungu divided over the rights to the chieftainship. Chinyama and his two brothers disputed their sister, Lueji's (q.v.), right to the position. Her husband, Ilunga (q.v.), assumed the chiefly symbols and ultimately led a branch of the Lunda. Chinyama went west with his clan and settled on the Luena River near the upper Zambezi River (qq.v.). By the end of the 18th century, Chinyama was a major chieftainship in the area.

CHIPATA. A town and district in Eastern Province (q.v.), it is located in the southeast. The town—called Fort Jameson (q.v.)

prior to independence—had a population of 13,300 in 1969 and is located only eight kilometers (five miles) from the Malawi (q.v.) border. Fort Jameson was planned in 1898 as the capital of what was called North-Eastern Rhodesia. The Great East Road (q.v.) runs through the town, a stopping point for tourists visiting the game reserves in the Luangwa (q.v.) valley. The district had a population of over 148,000 in 1969 and 294,000 in 1990.

CHIPEKENI. The site of an important battle between the Bemba and Ngoni (qq.v.) around 1870, it was an Ngoni camp east of the Kabishya River in northern Zambia. It was important for two reasons. First, the defeat of Mperembe's Ngoni (qq.v.) forced them to drop plans to subdue the Bemba (q.v.). Second, it was an unusually united force of Bemba chiefdoms that beat the Ngoni, with the Chitimukulu (q.v.) joined by Mwamba (q.v.), Nkula, Shimumbi, and several others in putting together the army.

CHIPEKWE. This is a legendary water rhino, called *chisonga* by the Lamba (q.v.), which supposedly gores hippos to death with a long, white horn it sports on the end of its crocodilelike snout. (Frank Melland, however, lists *chipekwe* as the Kaonde (q.v.) term for a one-tusked bull elephant.) Like the Kaonde's *kongamato* (q.v.), such legendary creatures have, from time to time, fed speculation that the remote areas of Zambia were still inhabited by dinosaurlike creatures.

CHIPENGE. An Ndembu (q.v.) commoner who united his people (after their chiefs failed) in the 1880s, he enabled them to defeat the marauding Luvale forces of Kangombe (qq.v.).

CHIPIMO, ELIAS. He was chairman of Standard Bank in Zambia in 1980 when he made a speech claiming that the country might avoid military coups by returning to a multiparty democracy. Kenneth Kaunda (q.v.) reacted strongly to this statement and linked Chipimo to a number of prominent politicians, whom the president denounced as dissidents. Standard Bank disassociated itself from Chipimo's comments, and he resigned from the bank. Chipimo was arrested and held in detention for two weeks. Others, including Valentine Musakanya and Edward Shamwana (qq.v.), were held as well and were treated much more harshly. Chipimo filed and won a lawsuit against the government-owned Zambia Printing Company for libel. The court granted him K919,000 in damages in 1983.

CHIRENJI. This site near the head of the Luangwa (q.v.) valley northeast of Bemba (q.v.) country was among the first mission stations in northern Zambia. The Livingstonia Mission of the Free Church of Scotland (qq.v.) opened a station there in 1882, but it closed it in 1888, moving west to Mwenzo (q.v.) in 1894.

CHISAMBA. One of the larger towns along the rail (q.v.) line, it is north of Lusaka (q.v.), about halfway from there to Kabwe (q.v.).

CHISANKA. This term refers to the compulsory abandonment of scattered family settlements (*mitanda*, q.v.) and the movement back into large villages. This policy was periodically enforced by the North-Eastern and Northern Rhodesian (qq.v.) administrations between 1902 and 1925.

CHISATA, JOHN. The successor to Lawrence Katilungu (q.v.) as president of the powerful African Mineworkers Union (q.v.) in December 1960, he had been chairman of the Mufulira branch of the union and had represented it at the Miners International Federation in Sweden the previous August. Although a supporter of the United National Independence Party (q.v.), he warned the party's leaders in July 1962 that they should stay out of industrial disputes. This occurred when UNIP workers tried to persuade miners to ignore a strike call because it could have negative effects on the coming election. Chisata himself became a UNIP candidate in the 1962 election and won by over 11,000 votes. He was then appointed a parliamentary secretary. He later served as a minister of state but fell from favor in 1971, when, along with Justin Chimba (q.v.), he accused the government of failing to prosecute certain ministers who were under suspicion for misuse of funds. The two charged that people in the government were showing tribal favoritism through this cover-up. But they were discredited when the Doyle Commission (q.v.) failed to substantiate their charges, and they joined Kapwepwe in the United Progressive Party (qq.v.) in August 1971. On September 9, 1977, they announced that they would rejoin UNIP for the sake of national unity.

CHITAMBALA, FRANK. A close associate of Kenneth Kaunda (q.v.) in politics for over two decades, he was a militant member of the African National Congress (q.v.) in the 1950s. He was imprisoned in 1958 for involvement in some disturbances. When released he became the acting provincial secretary of the ANC for Eastern Province (q.v.), working with Reuben Kamanga (q.v.) and later with Kaunda. In August 1958, he was responsible for getting the Eastern Province executive to pass a motion of "no confidence" in Harry Nkumbula (q.v.). When Kaunda split to form Zambia African National Congress (q.v.), Chitambala followed. He was one of the ZANC leaders detained in 1959, and was rusticated (q.v.) in the Balovale District of North-Western Province (qq.v.) when the case against him failed. Released in May 1959, he cofounded the African National Independence Party (q.v.) with Paul Kalichini (q.v.). He attacked Nkumbula for collaborating with the government and selling out the nationalists. A few months later his party merged with another to form United National Independence Party (q.v.), and he worked hard to build its organization. In October 1959, he was elected its secretary-general. He remained active in it and eventually joined that elect group of late 1970s politicians, the Central Committee of UNIP (q.v.).

CHITAMBO'S VILLAGE. This is the site where Dr. David Livingstone (q.v.), on May 1, 1873, died. His African friends who served as guides and aides buried his heart there but returned his body to England. Chitambo was a Lala (q.v.) chief whose village was then located, by Livingstone's map, about 24 kilometers (15 miles) south of Lake Bangweulu, on the Lulimala River (qq.v.). (Given the *chitemene*, q.v., cultivation system, however, this and other villages migrate within a given area from one decade to the next.)

CHITAPANKWA (CHITAPANGWA). One of the most dominant of the Bemba Chitimukulus (qq.v.), he reigned for over 20 years (from the early 1860s to 1883), a period when Bemba territories more than doubled in size. He was the nephew of a previous ruler, Chileshye (q.v.), and the younger brother of Mwamba II (q.v.). When Chileshye died, he was replaced as Chitimukulu by the elderly and ill Bwembya (q.v.). The *bakabilo* (q.v.) soon realized their error and were willing to assist when Chitapankwa produced a plan to replace Bwembya. Mwamba II declined to switch titles and also supported his younger brother's goal. Thus after a ruse, Chitapankwa obtained the chiefly relics of office (*babenye*) and assumed the throne. One of his visitors a few years later, in February 1867, was Dr. David Livingstone (q.v.). Chitapankwa persuaded him to stay for several weeks, hoping to get from him as gifts most of his European-made possessions. The two men developed a good relationship, and Livingstone was very impressed with Chitapankwa, as was the French explorer, Victor Giraud (q.v.) in 1883.

The first major expansion led by Chitapankwa was south across the Chambeshi River (q.v.), in the mid-1860s. There, he occupied land belonging to Bisa chief Mungulube (qq.v.). He also intervened in a succession dispute in the Bemba chiefdom called Ichinga, ultimately sending his daughter, then his brother, Sampa (q.v.), then a sister's son as regents.

While Chitapankwa was solidifying and extending Bemba power to the south and east, his brother, Chileshye Mwamba II (q.v.) was doing the same to the southwest, notably at the expense of the Lungu (q.v.). This led to a conflict with Munshimbwe, a Lungu chief. Chitapankwa became involved when he killed the son of the Lungu chief. Munshimbwe then called on the powerful Ngoni leader Mperembe (qq.v.) to fight the Bemba. Though the Ngoni came, Mperembe either did not fight then or brought only a small force. Munshimbwe was killed in this battle on the Kafubu River, perhaps in 1867.

The major battle against Mperembe's Ngoni came in about 1870 when, after a series of Ngoni raids from territories bordering the Bemba (in one of which a sister of Chitapankwa was killed and a niece captured), Chitapankwa formed an alliance and army of at least eight Bemba chiefs. The result was an attack on the Ngoni village at Chipekeni (q.v.) and a major defeat for the Ngoni and Mperembe, who now gave up their plans to take over Bemba territory.

Next the Bemba turned to the northeast where Chitapankwa raided, and conquered, such peoples as the Mambwe under Mpande and Nsokolo and the Inamwanga under Chikanamulilo (qq.v.). The latter turned back a Bemba attack by Chitapankwa and Makasa IV in 1877, but a couple of years later the Bemba were more successful. Likewise, the Lungu led by Zombe (qq.v.) repelled a Chitapankwa attack in 1872 but were crushingly defeated by him in 1882 or 1883. The Tabwa (q.v.) were also conquered during this period, but by Chitapankwa's brother, Mwamba II. Both of these great Bemba leaders died of the smallpox in 1883, a year when it swept through parts of northeastern Zambia. Chitapankwa was replaced by his brother, Sampa.

CHITEMENE. The *ci*Bemba (q.v.) name for slash-and-burn, or shifting, cultivation, the system has been used for centuries in

Zambia and still is quite common today. During the dry season, essentially June to November, the men prepare an area of woodland for a garden by cutting branches and trees, stacking them to dry, and then, in October and early November (just before the rains), setting these stacks afire. Whereas the Bemba's "large circle" *(chitemene)* system involves the lopping of branches from a great many trees over a large area, the Lala and Lamba's (qq.v.) "small circle" system cuts down entire trees (at waist height) for burning over a smaller area. Once the rains begin, the softened soil is hoed and strewn with grain seeds. Such gardens are often interplanted with beans and cucumbers or pumpkins, which compete with weeds during the early growth period. After one or two rainy season weedings, the grain crops are ready to be harvested in May and June and then, either before or after threshing, for storage in the wattle and daub granaries built on stilts.

Though the British colonial officers repeatedly tried to discourage this seemingly "wasteful" and "disorderly" cultivation system (*see* CHISANKA; MITANDA), there is—short of massive fertilizer imports—no more effective system of tropical agriculture. The burnings kill weeds and insect pests, while the ash beds supplement the thin, rain-leached topsoil's supply of vital nutrients. Over time, however, the yield of any given garden declines; and once no additional garden extensions can be cut, it is time to move the gardens and, if necessary, the entire village to another forested site. On average, it takes just over 20 years for a site of former gardens to turn back into forest suitable for another cycle of gardens. Village relocations, though, became less common in the 1940s and 1950s, when "permanent villages" of rectangular, mud-brick houses were encouraged. To stay in one place, though, villagers must either defend wide belts of gardens and regenerating forestlands against all encroachers, shorten the fallow period on former garden lands, or place a greater reliance upon root crops like sweet potatoes and cassava (q.v.).

CHITENGE (pl., *fitenge*). An essential item of female clothing in contemporary Zambia, it is a two-meter length of cotton print wrapped around the waist and over a dress or skirt. While its primary function is modesty, that of concealing the knees and upper calves, it also lengthens the life of a dress by serving as an easily washable duster or apron. *Fitenge* are additionally used as baby slings or as spur-of-the-moment carryalls for toting beans, grain, or wild fruit.

CHITI. According to the Bemba (q.v.) origin legend, Chiti was the first of their leaders. He came from a place called Luba or Kola (q.v.), somewhere west of the Luapula River (q.v.). His father was Mukulumpe (q.v.), and his mother, said to have been of divine origin, was Mumbi Mukasa. To catch the moon (and depose their father), Chiti and his brothers, Katongo and Nkole (qq.v.), built a great bamboo tower, which killed many people when it collapsed. Their furious father blinded Katongo and banished Chiti and Nkole, who, with their sister Chilufya Mulenga (q.v.), migrated east, beyond the Luapula River and around the northern part of Lake Bangweulu, to the Chambeshi River (qq.v.). In a subsequent adventure, Chiti died from the poisoned arrow he received while romancing the wife of Senga chief Mwase (qq.v.). He was buried by Nkole in a grove of trees called Mwalule (q.v.), north of the Senga country. Nkole also died soon thereafter, and their nephew, Chilufya, became the first of the line of Bemba paramount chiefs to take the title Chitimukulu (q.v.) (literally Chiti the Great). Historians believe this legend might describe events in the late 17th century.

CHITIMUKULU (CITIMUKULU; KITIMUKULU). The title of the senior or paramount chief of the Bemba (q.v.) people, it literally means Chiti the Great. Derived from the Bemba founder, Chiti (q.v.), this title was first assumed by Chiti's legendary nephew, Chilufya, perhaps around the year 1700. The title and position continue down to the present day. All the Chitimukulus, as well as the holders of lesser chiefships among the Bemba, are members of the Bena Ng'andu, the chiefly Crocodile Clan. Though the major chiefs are all members of this clan, their ties are looser and the Chitimukulu did not possess real control over them unless strong enough to establish this control through force or by influencing appointments of close relatives to the other chiefships. The potential successors to the ruling Chitimukulu are in fact these other Bemba chiefs, some of whom hold three or four of the lesser chieftaincies before being selected as Chitimukulu.

Each chief rules his own territory. That of the Chitimukulu is Lubemba (q.v.). Its first capital was established along the Kalungu River, east of the present-day city of Kasama (qq.v.). The Chitimukulu is considered a divine king with supernatural control over his land and people. His powers traditionally were extensive. He was assisted by a group of councilors, the *bakabilo* (q.v.). (To understand better the history of the Chitimukulu, *see* the entries for the following noted holders of the title: MUKU-UKA, CHILESHYKE, CHITAPANKWA, SAMPA, and PONDE.)

CHITUKUTUKU (pl., *fitukutuku*). This onomatopoeic African term means the wood-burning, steam-powered, traction engine (q.v.) used to haul heavy freight in modern Zambia from 1906 until 1916.

CHITUPA (pl., *fitupa*). The pass (q.v.), or African identification certificate, which preindependence governments required Africans to carry with them at all times. In July 1961, there were mass burnings of *fitupa* in several Northern Rhodesian (q.v.) cities as a symbolic rejection of the Central African Federation (q.v.). Some also burned their marriage certificates (*imichato*). This was during the period of nationalism referred to as cha-cha-cha (q.v.).

CHIVUNGA, JONATHAN KALUNGA. This labor leader became a top-ranking ambassador after serving in a variety of ministerial positions. Born in 1924 in Eastern Province (q.v.), he worked for eight years in the civil service and in business before becoming full-time provincial secretary of Western (now Copperbelt) Province (qq.v.) for the African National Congress (q.v.) from 1956 to 1958. He became president of the union of shop assistants in 1959. In 1958 he switched from the ANC to the Zambia African National Congress (q.v.) and then joined its successor, the United National Independence Party (q.v.). In 1960 he protested Lawrence Katilungu's (q.v.) leadership of the Trade Union Congress and formed the Reformed Trade Union Congress (q.v.), of which he became president. He ran for Parliament in 1964 and became member of Parliament for Kitwe (q.v.) South. From 1964 until 1970 he served in the government as minister of state for six different ministries. In November 1970, he was appointed ambassador to the People's Republic of China, and in 1974 he was transferred to France.

CHIWALA. This is the name (it means "locust" in *ci*Nyanja, (q.v.)) of Majariwa, the Yao leader of a well-armed band of Swahili (q.v.) slave and ivory traders from Nyasaland (q.v.) who, within two years after the 1891 collapse of Msiri's Yeke empire (qq.v.), established a palisaded settlement on the Belgian side of the upper Luapula River (q.v.). The Aushi and Lamba of the Katanga Pedicle (qq.v.) complained of their exactions, and in November 1897 a second Belgian-Yeke expedition drove them out and across the pedicle to Frank Smitheman's (q.v.) prospecting camp at Fort Elwes, in the Irumi Hills of the Rhodesian Lala. Assured of British protection, they headed west into Lamba chief Mushili's (q.v.) area and resumed their operations from a new base on the Itawa Stream, near modern Ndola's railway depot. Christian Purefoy Chesnaye, secretary for North-Eastern Rhodesia (q.v.), led a small party from Fort Jameson (q.v.) through the pedicle in 1900 to establish Chiwala's whereabouts and loyalties and to arrest Bolle and Ziehl, two unscrupulous traders wanted by both the Belgian and British authorities. While Chesnaye saw domestic slavery there— or, at least, hostages held for ransom—he was impressed with Chiwala's friendly attitude and by the Swahili's industrious rice cultivation and orderly, rectilinear houses and village. In 1902, a resident of this village showed the ancient Bwana Mkubwa (q.v.) copper (q.v.) workings to William Collier (q.v.) and Jack O'Donohogue. Chiwala, while detained six months at Chirupula Stephenson's (q.v.) new Ndola *boma* (qq.v.) for running a rival *boma*, was ruined by a 1905 inheritance lawsuit and died in 1912. He was briefly succeeded by his son, Ali, and then, in 1914, by an unrelated, elected chief, Kaimina Chiwala III.

Chiwala's Swahili provided most of the locally grown rice and maize sold to Bwana Mkubwa mine and, after 1909, to the village of Ndola (qq.v.). So when the expanding railway yard and Reserves Commission (q.v.) forced the Swahili to vacate Ndola in the late 1920s, they, unlike the local Lamba, were allowed to choose their own, separate reserve area, one with direct marketing access to the rail line, and were promised £910 compensation for their land losses. The Swahili Native Reserve soon attracted Lamba and other African market gardeners who had been driven off the line of rail (q.v.). The local Lamba have long resented the favoritism shown these former slave raiders during the early colonial period, and in the early 1970s, a small but popular Lamba political faction contested the legitimacy of this Swahili chiefdom, arguing that they were either "foreigners" or, if not, were obliged to acknowledge the seniority of Lamba chief Mushili.

CHOBE RIVER. Also known as the Kwando, Mashi, or Linyati River, it flows in a southeastern direction through parts of Angola (q.v.) until it touches Zambia. It then serves as the Zambian-Angolan border for 222 kilometers (138 miles) until it dips into the Caprivi Strip (q.v.), south of Zambia. It then turns east and becomes the southern border of the Caprivi Strip until it joins the Zambezi River just west of Kazungula (qq.v.). The Kololo (q.v.) people, despite David Livingstone's (q.v.) urgings that they move, chose to live in the unhealthy, swampy area north of the Chobe in the mid-19th century because they saw the Chobe River as the best defensive barrier against the Ndebele of chief Mzilikazi (qq.v.).

CHOKWE. One of the smaller ethnic groups in Zambia, the Chokwe are part of the Lunda-Luvale (qq.v.) language group that lives in northwestern Zambia. These matrilineal people were one of many in this part of Zambia to throw off Lozi (q.v.) domination. They came in from Angola (q.v.) to the west, with whose people they continued to trade. Among other things they acquired were guns from Portuguese slave traders (q.v.). They are skilled artisans who are especially admired for their woodcraft and pottery. As of 1986, there were about 44,200 Chokwe speakers in Zambia and another half a million each in Angola and the Democratic Republic of Congo (q.v.) (Zaire).

CHOLERA. Cholera is contracted when people drink water contaminated by human waste. Thus its reappearance in Zambia is an indicator of a widespread and escalating shortage of healthful drinking water (*see* KAFUE RIVER). During the 1992 epidemic, when cholera was reported throughout all of Zambia, there were some 10,000 cases and 800 deaths from cholera. This problem, though, is far more severe in Zambia's towns, where the water supply and sewage disposal systems—often unmaintained and unrepaired—have been outstripped by several decades of population growth and urban migration.

CHOMA. A town along the line of rail (q.v.) in south central Zambia near Lake Kariba (q.v.), it is also one of the districts in Southern Province (q.v.). The district had a population of 98,000 in 1969 and more than 164,000 in 1990. Up along the northern border with the Democratic Republic of Congo (q.v.) (Zaire), Choma was also the name of an 1890s British South Africa Company (q.v.) station about halfway between Lakes Tanganyika and Mweru (qq.v.).

CHONA COMMISSION. This is the popular name for the national commission on the establishment of a one-party participatory democracy in Zambia. It was established by President

Kenneth Kaunda (q.v.) in February 1972, after he had outlawed the upstart United Party and United Progressive Party (qq.v). Vice president Mainza Chona (q.v.) was named chairman. The 21 members represented a wide spectrum of the country's institutional elites (business, army, churches, chiefs, public service, and United National Independence Party, q.v.). The African National Congress (q.v.) leaders, however, declined to participate. Since the decision had been made to establish a one-party system, this commission was established to sound out the country's views on the structure of the new constitution. Open hearings were held throughout the country for over four months, and oral and written testimonies were taken. An impressive report, filled with recommendations, was presented to Kaunda in October 1972. The new constitution was supposedly based on this report but, in fact, omitted some substantial recommendations. The commission's major suggestions, influenced by Tanzania's (q.v.) previous experience, concerned the supremacy (even monopoly of power) to be held by UNIP. While these suggestions were generally accepted, the government did not adopt the commission's proposals to limit the president's veto powers and tenure in office. Still other recommended reforms, including reform of UNIP, the strengthening of the National Assembly (q.v.), and encouraging electoral competition, were conveniently shelved.

CHONA, MARK CHUUNYU. One of former President Kaunda's (q.v.) most influential and trusted advisors, he was born June 6, 1934, at Monze in Southern Province (qq.v.). His father was chief Chona, and his brother, Mainza Chona (q.v.), was secretary general of the United National Independence Party (q.v.). His studies, including a B.A. in history and economics from Salisbury University, took him to England, Canada, and the United States in the early 1960s, between minor government posts. He joined Kaunda's staff in October 1964. On April 1, 1965, he became permanent secretary for foreign affairs, a post he held for three years. In 1968 he returned to work in the president's office, serving principally as an international representative and troubleshooter, but he was also involved with domestic political matters. Citing ill health, Chona announced his retirement from public service in 1980. His departure coincided with a shift in Zambia's international alignments, which was made most apparent by Grey Zulu's (q.v.) appointment as minister of defense. Chona joined the board of the new and locally owned African Commercial Bank in February 1985.

CHONA, MATHIAS MAINZA. The first president of the United National Independence Party (q.v.), Mainza Chona was born January 21, 1930, at Monze (q.v.), the son of a Tonga (q.v.) chief. He completed Munali Secondary School (q.v.) and worked as a clerk-interpreter at the High Court in Livingstone (qq.v.) for four years, until 1955. He then went to England on a scholarship and studied law at Gray's Inn, London, ultimately becoming Zambia's first African barrister in 1958. Prevented by race from opening a practice in his own country, Chona entered politics and joined the African National Congress (q.v.), with the intent of challenging Harry Nkumubula's (q.v.) accommodationist approach. Though the faction led by Titus Mukupo (q.v.) and Chona failed to gain control, Chona's speeches on national issues brought him and his ANC faction into the newly formed UNIP. He was elected UNIP president in October 1959, but he made it clear that he was only holding the post until Kenneth Kaunda (q.v.) was released from detention. By the time Kaunda was released and made president, in January 1960, Chona had left the country to avoid Northern Rhodesia's (q.v.) sedition charge against him. Returning to London, he served as a UNIP delegate to the Federal Review Conference (q.v.) in December 1960.

Once the sedition charge was dropped, he returned home in February 1961 to become editor of the *Voice of UNIP* (q.v.) and served eight years as a highly effective UNIP national secretary. Elected to Parliament in 1964, he became the first Zambian minister of justice. He then served three years in the ministry of home affairs before becoming minister of presidential affairs, then a minister without portfolio in 1967. Made vice president of Zambia on November 1, 1970, he led the 1972 Chona Commission (q.v.), which determined how to transform the country into a one-party state. Under the Second Zambian Republic's (q.v.) new constitution, his post became that of prime minister until May 1975, when he resigned his post to become minister of legal affairs and attorney general. He was reappointed prime minister in July 1977 and UNIP secretary-general in 1978. He was replaced as party secretary-general by Humphrey Mulemba (q.v.) in February 1981.

CHONDWE. This Early Iron Age site is on a citrus estate about 48 kilometers (30 miles) south of Ndola. It refers as well to its coterminous Chondwe group (q.v.) pottery style. Radiocarbon dates from Chondwe and Kangonga, a similar Copperbelt (q.v.) site, range from the 6th to the 11th centuries A.D.

CHONDWE GROUP. This is the name of an Early Iron Age pottery style found in several rock shelters and *dambo*-side sites in the Copperbelt region north of Kapiri Mposhi (qq.v.). Though this style is not found in Solwezi (q.v.) District, it may extend north into the Democratic Republic of Congo (q.v.) (Zaire). Chondwe pottery features necked bowls and vessels with thickened or undifferentiated rims. These vessels are distinctively decorated with false relief chevron stamping and comb-stamped chordate blocks delineated with broad grooves. Although no evidence of food production has been found, it seems likely that the Chondwe people(s) were mixed grain and livestock farmers whose villages were only briefly occupied before being abandoned. Evidence of iron and copper (q.v.) working exists at many sites. And while the local copper deposits undoubtedly fostered wide-ranging trade contacts, it is assumed that copper mining was on a far smaller scale than that attributed to the people of the Luangwa pottery tradition (q.v.).

CHONGO, JULIUS. Chongo's "Poceza Madzulo" (Evening Story Time), broadcast in *ci*Nyanja (q.v.), was one of the Zambia Broadcasting Services' most popular programs from 1966 to 1976. A collection of his radio narratives, *Fumbi Khoboo!* (1972), was published by NECZAM. The imagery of these narratives is the subject of Ernst Wendland's 1979 Ph.D. dissertation.

CHONGWE, ROGER MASAUSO ALIVAS. Born in Chipata in October 1938, he attended school in Chipata, at St. Marks College in Choma (q.v.), and at Munali Secondary School (q.v.) in Lusaka (q.v.), from which he graduated in 1961. From 1963 to 1967 he earned his law degree at the University of Western Australia and was given an honorary doctorate of law degree in 1987. He practiced as a barrister in Australia until 1969, when he returned to take up law in Zambia. From 1970 to 1977 he was a partner in the Mwisiya Chongwe and Company law firm, but he left in 1977 to found his own firm, R. M. A. Chongwe and Company. During the 1970s and 1980s Chongwe practiced law, traveled widely to participate in international conferences, served as a director for TAZAMA (*see* TANZANIA-ZAMBIA OIL PIPELINE) and Standard Chartered Bank, patronized the arts, and participated in international associations of barristers, including the Commonwealth Lawyers' Association, which he served as president from 1990 to 1993. He was appointed minister of legal affairs in 1991 and served two years in the Movement for Multiparty Democracy (q.v.) government. As such, he became embroiled in controversy when he withdrew the government ban on the possession of pornographic materials. President Chiluba (q.v.) criticized Chongwe's position, and Chongwe resigned from the MMD in November 1993 after being demoted to minister of local government and housing in April of that year.

CHRISTIAN COUNCIL. This ecumenical body represents more than 20 churches, missions, and Christian organizations. It was formed in 1944 to replace the General Missionary Conference of Northern Rhodesia (q.v.). In the early 1980s, these groups became increasingly concerned about the teaching of Marxism in public colleges, and the *National Mirror* (q.v.), a Christian council publication, regularly disseminated interviews highly critical of President Kaunda's (q.v.) administration.

CHUNGA, ELIJAH HERBERT. This civil servant, along with Ernest A. Muwamba (q.v.), cofounded the Ndola Native Welfare Association (q.v.) in 1930.

CHUNGU. This minor Lungu (q.v.) chiefdom gained importance because of its proximity to the Bemba (q.v.). In 1889, the reigning Chungu signed a treaty with Harry Johnston (q.v.), who was attempting to secure territory for Cecil Rhodes' British South Africa Company (qq.v.). Chungu's land was on the northeastern border of Mporokoso's (q.v.). Chungu II managed to defeat a Bemba-Swahili army in the 1890s, and Mporokoso made an alliance with him. Chungu is also the name of a Bena Mukulu (q.v.) chieftainship that was active in the early 19th century.

CHURCH OF CENTRAL AFRICA, PRESBYTERIAN. The name was adopted in 1924 by the Central African branch of the Free Church of Scotland (q.v.). In 1958 it joined the United Church of Central Africa in Rhodesia, which, in 1965, became the United Church of Zambia (q.v.).

CHUULA COMMISSION. The commission was appointed in September 1969 to examine the United National Independence Party's (q.v.) constitution with the hope of recommending changes that would remedy the intense sectional competition then in evidence within the party. Fitzpatrick (Frank) Chuula, the attorney general, was appointed its chairman. Its instructions allowed it also to look into the relationship between the party and the government and the question of party discipline. The commission held hearings and, in March 1970, submitted its report to President Kaunda (q.v.). The report, which was not made public until September 1970, included a complete draft for a new UNIP constitution. Contrary to its goal, the report produced an immediate split in the party, as some of its proposals infuriated some Northern Province (q.v.) party activists. Its most important (and controversial) recommendations attempted to limit the intensely sectional (hence, ethnic) competition for Central Committee posts. But its suggestion that each province be accorded two members was another source of discord. Most of its proposals concerning the Central Committee were substantially changed by the party's national council that met in November 1970 (*see* CENTRAL COMMITTEE of UNIP). The report also recommended the abolition of the posts of president and vice president of the party. UNIP's secretary-general would also be the party's nominee for the presidential elections.

CI-. In the Bantu languages, this is the singular noun-class prefix for a miscellaneous category of things, all of which begin with the same /tʃ/ sound, found in the words "chip" and "church." English speakers often represent this sound with a *ch* spelling to help distinguish it from the *k* sound found in *chemistry*. In the Zambian languages, though, written *c*'s are always soft, and linguists prefer to represent the /tʃ/ phoneme as *ci-* or *ce-*. Thus the Bemba (q.v.) or Nyanja languages, *chi*Bemba and *chi*Nyanja, are usually written as "*ci*Bemba" and "*ci*Nyanja" and the Chewa people as Cewa. For convenience and clarity, this dictionary only uses the *ci-* spellings for African languages.

*CI*BEMBA (*CHI*BEMBA). This Bantu language (q.v.) is spoken throughout Northern and Luapula Provinces (qq.v.) and is the basis for town Bemba (q.v.) in the Copperbelt (q.v.). In 1986, at least 1.7 million Zambians—or 25 percent of the population—spoke *ci*Bemba. Its speakers include two of the largest groups, the Bemba and the Lunda of Kazembe (qq.v.), both of whom also use an archaic form of the Luba (q.v.) language in their praises to their chiefs. *Ci*Bemba is one of Zambia's official African languages.

*CI*NYANJA (*CHI*NYANJA). The third most widely spoken of the languages of Zambia, it is the most common African language in Eastern and Lusaka Provinces (qq.v.). It is used primarily by the Chewa (q.v.), and also by the Ngoni, Nsenga, and Kunda (qq.v.). In 1986, at least 800,000 Zambians—or 12 percent of the population—spoke *ci*Nyanja. One of Zambia's official African languages, it is also spoken by some 300,000 people in Zimbabwe, and the same essential language, though called *ci*Cewa, is the dominant language of Malawi (q.v.). Throughout Southern Central Africa, more than four million people speak *ci*Nyanja as a first or second language.

CITEMENE. This is a variant of *chitimene* (q.v.).

CITONGA (*CHITONGA*). One of the official African languages of Zambia, *ci*Tonga is the dominant language throughout Southern Province (q.v.). In 1986, some 800,000 Zambians—or 12 percent of the population—spoke *ci*Tonga. About two-thirds of these are Tonga, the others being Toka, Totela, Leya, and Subiya (qq.v.). Another 60,000 *ci*Tonga-speakers live in neighboring Zimbabwe and several thousand more in Botswana (q.v.).

CLAN. A clan is a large descent group, composed of its constituent lineages, commonly found among Zambia's matrilineal and patrilineal peoples. Each clan bears the name of a wild or domesticated plant or animal or some other feature of the natural or cultural world. Whereas the members of a given lineage can trace their genealogical links, clan members cannot; they only know that they are related and that they should marry outside their clan. Though some of the chiefly clans, like the Bemba's (q.v.) Bena Ng'andu, are ethnically specific, most clans are widely distributed, making it easy to claim clan relatives across ethnic lines. Indeed, most Africans believe that these clans are far older than contemporary ethnic groups.

But if clan membership is useful for finding fictive kin among strangers, this is even more true of joking-clan relationships, in which people publicly abuse one another on the basis of their clan name. Members of the Iron clan, for example, can berate the Grass clan as their "slaves," arguing that iron (knives and hoes) kill grass. The Grass clansfolk, though, will assert their superiority by saying that grass (thatch) saves iron from being "eaten" by the rain (rusting). The vulgar insults that attend joking-clan interactions are a compulsive and privileged violation of the code of good manners. They are not only highly entertaining icebreakers at any social gathering but serve to establish warm, kinlike relations between relative strangers. Before church groups were so common, joking-clan partners used to bury one another's dead, and they still stand in for absent relatives in ritual performances.

CLARK, J. DESMOND. The father of archeological research in Zambia, he became curator of the museum attached to the Rhodes-Livingstone Institute (q.v.) in 1938 and, apart from his war service in the East African Horn, remained there until he retired as director of the Rhodes-Livingstone Museum on May 1, 1961. He was born in 1916 and studied archaeology at Christ College, Cambridge University. Dr. Clark later became professor of anthropology at the University of California at Berkeley. He is the author of numerous books and articles on the early history of Africa, especially the south-central part. See also LIVINGSTONE MUSEUM; KALAMBO FALLS.

CLARK, J. HARRISON (CHANGACHANGA). See HARRISON CLARK, JOHN.

COAL. After copper, coal is one of the most important minerals found in Zambia. Southern Province (q.v.) has very large reserves. Large-scale coal mining became a high priority of the First National Development Plan, with the goal of making Zambia self-sufficient as soon as possible to eliminate dependence on imports from Rhodesia. Large-scale production at the Maamba Mine (q.v.), begun in late 1968, allowed Zambia to cease its imports from Rhodesia in mid-1970.

CODRINGTON, ROBERT EDWARD. One of the earliest of Zambia's European administrators, he was born in England in 1869 and educated at Marlborough College. He came to southern Africa and became a sergeant in the Bechuanaland Border Police. He later saw action in Matabeleland and then joined Harry Johnston's (q.v.) adminstration in Nyasaland (q.v.). He was hired by the British South Africa Company (q.v.) when it took over North-Eastern Rhodesia (q.v.). In July 1898, he became deputy administrator of that territory and served as administrator from August 1900 to April 1907, during which time he introduced the hut tax (q.v.) in 1901. At that point he replaced Robert Coryndon (q.v.) as administrator of North-Western Rhodesia (q.v.) until his death from heart failure in December 1908. As administrator of the eastern half of the country, he laid the foundation for the country's public service. His preference was to hire young, middle-class, university-educated men fresh from England. He set up a regular, graded civil service, dismissing unsuitable men quickly. He was also something of an autocrat as administrator, seldom compromising his beliefs. When white craftsmen protested that Africans were working in the construction of government buildings at Broken Hill (q.v.), Codrington overruled all opponents. In 1907 he had skilled African workers brought to North-Western Rhodesia from Fort Jameson (q.v.), precipitating controversy, but Codrington stood firm.

As administrator in the northeast, Codrington was responsible for completing BSAC control over the area and, at one point, sent an armed force to pressure the Lunda leader Kazembe (qq.v.) into submitting. Also, he proved to be sympathetic to Bishop Dupont and the White Fathers (qq.v.), supporting them in setting up missions among the Bemba (q.v.). While working later among the Lozi (q.v.), he instituted the practice of referring to the Lozi king as only "Paramount Chief." The demotion was symbolic but typical, as Codrington insisted that all Africans should take off their hats to white men, whom they should always treat with respect.

COILLARD, FRANÇOIS. After David Livingstone (q.v.), he was perhaps the most influential European missionary to live within the boundaries of modern Zambia. Coillard was born in France in 1834 and, as a youth, decided to join the Paris Missionary Society (q.v.). He and his wife, the former Christina Mackintosh, arrived at their first assignment, in Basutoland (modern Lesotho), in 1858. In 1877 they led a large party, which included their niece and four Sotho (q.v.) evangelists, to open a new mission station among Lobengula's Ndebele (qq.v.). When they reached this area in Southern Rhodesia they were not allowed to stay, and they moved west to the territory of chief Khama's Ngwato (qq.v.). Since they knew the Sotho language, he encouraged them to travel north to the Lozi (q.v.) who had adopted that language when it was forced on them by the Kololo (q.v.). Khama even interceded with the Lozi king for Coillard and his party. They then reached the Zambezi River (q.v.) in July 1878 and were permitted to cross to Sesheke (q.v.). There they waited while further messages were traded between Sesheke and Lealui, where the subject of the missionaries' presence was debated in the *kuta* (q.v.). Finally, the answer came that they, apparently mistaken for traders, could not come further north then but would be accepted at a later date.

Coillard was encouraged and returned to Europe to raise money to finance a Barotseland (q.v.) mission. He returned to the upper Zambezi in 1884. With the aid of a respected trader, George Westbeech (q.v.), along with the recommendation from chief Khama, Coillard and his party entered Barotseland. Although delayed by a civil war in which Lewanika (q.v.) was temporarily deposed, the party arrived in the capital, Lealui (q.v.), in early 1885. They remained only briefly but returned in April 1886, after Lewanika had been reinstated. The Lozi king welcomed them and provided a mission site 32 kilometers (20 miles) away at Sefula (q.v.), where a school was opened in March 1887. This was the first of many mission locations of the Paris Missionary Society in Barotseland. Though his wife died and was buried at Sefula in 1891, Coillard remained there until 1896, then returned to Paris for two years. There his famous book *Sur le Haut Zambezi* (On the Threshold of Central Africa) was published in 1898. It came from his letters, his journal notes, and articles he had written for missionary publications. He returned to Barotseland in 1898, where he died in 1904.

The historic importance of Coillard does not rest in his religious conversions, as he was only marginally successful. Even his close friend Lewanika (q.v.), who was so cooperative and who encouraged African youths to study at Coillard's schools, refused to abandon polygamy to convert to Christianity. Coillard's importance was based on Lewanika's confidence in him as an advisor in dealings with Europeans and as one who could help the Lozi acquire the protection of the Queen of England. Thus when Harry Ware (q.v.) arrived in June 1889 and proposed a mining concession, Coillard induced Lewanika to sign it, as a first step toward British protection. Coillard later denied that he had proposed the signing, but he also handled the Lochner Concession (q.v.) in an ambiguous fashion the very next year. His pro-British (and thus British South Africa Company, q.v.) stand reflected a desire to more quickly "civilize" the Lozi, while at the same time he feigned neutrality in order to rebut the accusation of some Lozi that he was encouraging Lewanika to give away their country to the Europeans. As a result of his work, Lozi leaders mistakenly thought that the treaty with Lochner was a treaty of protection with Queen Victoria.

COLLECTORS. The term was used by the British South Africa Company (q.v.) in the early days of its rule to designate many of its administrative officers north of the Zambezi River (q.v.). The company later called these administrators native commissioners and then district commissioners (qq.v.). They were called "collectors" because one of their prime duties was to collect revenue, especially in North-Eastern Rhodesia (q.v.), where hut taxes (q.v.) began.

COLLIER, WILLIAM. One of the early mineral prospectors in Zambia, he was sent into Lamba (q.v.) country in 1902 by the Bechuanaland Exploration Company (q.v.). Near Chiwala's (q.v.) village, he and Jack O'Donohogue were shown the ancient copper workings, which they called Bwana Mkubwa (q.v.). With the aid of a local guide, Collier traveled a little northwest and found a rich lode of copper (q.v.) ore and named the area (Roan Antelope mine, q.v.) after an antelope he had just shot in the vicinity. Several days later he also found the Chambeshi (q.v.) deposit. The Bechuanaland Exploration Company was linked to the Rhodesia Copper Company (q.v.), itself a subsidiary of the British South Africa Company (q.v.).

COLONIAL OFFICE. *See* BRITISH COLONIAL OFFICE.

COLOUR BAR. This is the general term for the discriminatory practices—particularly against Africans—linking racial segregation and European privilege throughout Central and Southern Africa. Towns were considered European domains; coloureds ("mixed race" people) and Asians (qq.v.) were granted separate urban neighborhoods, but Africans were long considered temporary town residents, and their housing rights in urban locations (q.v.) were tied to European employment. The commercial needs of African townsfolk were served by itinerant native hawkers, the town's African market, and by Asian-owned shops in the second-class trading district.

The colour bar entailed separate lavatories, railway coaches, and entrances and service windows at banks, post offices, and railway depots. Many jobs were reserved for whites, and Africans were not permitted to own shops in town. Africans were excluded from commercial cinemas (*see* NATIVE FILM CENSORSHIP BOARD), from hotels, restaurants, and cafes, and from pharmacies, butcheries, and the shops in the first-class trading district. Africans patronized these shops but were required to wait outside at a side or rear wall hatch (*see* HATCH SYSTEM) until the non-Africans had been served, and Africans were often subjected to demeaning language.

African welfare associations and the African Representative Council (qq.v.) voiced their complaints about the colour bar throughout the 1930s and 1940s. By the mid-1940s, Copperbelt (q.v.) town councils allowed Africans to rent structures for retail groceries and bottle stores (q.v.) in the African locations. The gradual erosion of the colour bar quickened in the mid-1950s, when the mines persuaded the European Mineworkers Union (q.v.) to accept the reclassification of certain job categories. Thus by 1960, in the wake of the 1956 rolling strikes (q.v.), over 90 new job categories had been opened to Africans, and the mines had adopted a uniform, nonracial pay scale and promotion ladder. Elsewhere, Africans were admitted to industrial apprenticeships in 1958 and, on the railway, to firemen and engine driver positions in 1960.

Social discrimination also came under attack when Kenneth Kaunda (q.v.) and the younger members of Northern Rhodesia's African National Congress Party (q.v.) ended the hatch system in Lusaka (q.v.) with the 1954 butchery boycott. Their 1956 boycott of European- and Asian-owned stores soon spread to towns all along the line of rail (q.v.). Still other African National Congress (q.v.) members attempted to integrate European eating establishments, cinemas, swimming pools, and churches. In 1960, the Legislative Council (q.v.) officially abolished the hatch system and the colour bar in all public places.

COLOURED. The term, referring to people of mixed racial background, usually means that one of a person's direct ancestors was African and one was European. It is a term rarely used in Zambia today. The term "Eurafrican" (q.v.) is generally preferred. Most of these people are to be found in urban areas such as Lusaka, Chipata, and Ndola (qq.v.). They constitute less than 1 percent of Zambia's population.

COMMITTEE OF THIRTY. This group of many of the best "thinkers" among United National Independence Party (q.v.) members was organized in April 1962 by Sikota Wina (q.v.) for the purpose of drawing up a UNIP platform for presentation to the voters. They drew up specific policies on such subjects as economics, health, agriculture, prisons, the judiciary, education, local government, and foreign trade and commerce. This April conference, also called the Easter School of Political Policies, produced a 60-page election brochure called *UNIP Policy*.

CONCESSION OF 1906. This letter, dated January 23, 1906, from Lozi king Lewanika (qq.v.) to the British South Africa Company (q.v.), reiterated the facts of earlier concessions to the BSAC in 1900 and 1904. The letter reasserted that the king had given the company the right "to dispose of land to settlers" (excluding the heartland of the Lozi) as it saw fit and to retain any money received. The Lozi complained in 1911 to BSAC administrator L. A. Wallace (q.v.) that these concessions had been limited to plowing rights and that Lozi tradition did not allow the king to permanently alienate any of the nation's land. By this time, however, the BSAC was not concerned about how the Lozi construed the Ware and the Lochner Concessions (qq.v.).

CONCESSION OF 1909. This concession was agreed upon by Lewanika of the Lozi (qq.v.) and his Ngambela (q.v.) at meetings held at Lealui (q.v.) on August 6 and 9, 1909. L. A. Wallace (q.v.), acting administrator of the area, was also present. Many doubt the contents of this concession, as it suggests that the Lozi gave the British South Africa Company (q.v.) something for nothing: it seemingly granted rights to the BSAC to use or dispose of large areas of land within Barotseland (q.v.) in exchange for returning to Barotseland the territory between Angola (q.v.) and the upper Zambezi, but, in fact, this area had already reverted to Barotseland as a result of the 1905 boundary decision of the king of Italy, so the Lozi had nothing at all to gain. Thus many suspect that it was never a true concession. This was argued by Lewanika and advisors in 1911, when they reminded Wallace that Lozi tradition did not allow the king to perpetually alienate the nation's land, but only temporary use-rights. The Lozi did not win.

CONFEDERATE PARTY. A very conservative, federal-level party that also contested the territorial elections, it appeared in 1953 as a party opposed to federation (q.v.). It campaigned for partitioning Northern Rhodesia (q.v.) into black and white segments, with the white parts (the Copperbelt and the line of rail, qq.v.) being merged with Southern Rhodesia (q.v.). The party was composed of several disparate elements: Afrikaners who had belonged to the Southern Rhodesia Democratic Party; the Rhodesia Party, composed of old (S. R.) Liberal Party (q.v.) members; elements of the S. R. Labour Party (q.v.) who opposed racial partnership; several former Indian army officers; and a small number of dissident S. R. United Party members, notably J. R. Dendy-Young. The Northern Rhodesians who participated actively and ran for election as Confederates included John Gaunt and Guillaume van Eeden (qq.v.). One source calls van Eeden the founder of the Confederate Party. In the January 1954 federal elections, the Federal Party (q.v.) overwhelmed the Confederate Party, which, despite winning one-third of the votes cast in Southern Rhodesia, won only one seat in the Parliament (q.v.). Dendy-Young was the winner and became the acknowledged party leader. The Confederates had campaigned for separate development within the federation, with "special native representation" in the territorial legislatures. None of the 16 Confederate territorial candidates won in Southern Rhodesia, but two Confederates (John Gaunt being one of them) won as independent candidates in Northern Rhodesia. By mid-1954 the party had vanished as an organization. However, a number of Confederates found their way into the Federal Dominion Party (q.v.) that formed in February 1956. This included Gaunt and, in 1958, van Eeden. In 1960 the name Confederate Party was revived by Stanley Gurland for his white supremacist organization in Southern Rhodesia.

CONGO (KINSHASA). *See* DEMOCRATIC REPUBLIC OF CONGO.

CONGO PEDICLE. *See* KATANGA PEDICLE.

CONGRESS CIRCULAR. Successor to the *Congress News* (q.v.), the *Congress Circular* was published by the African National Congress (q.v.) monthly from 1955 until at least 1958. During most of this time Kenneth Kaunda (q.v.) was its editor and responsible for much of its content. It was antifederation and encouraged Africans to political action.

CONGRESS NEWS. A mimeographed monthly publication of the African National Congress (q.v.), the *Congress News* was started in October 1953, by Kenneth Kaunda, Titus Mukopo, and Wittington Sikalumbi (qq.v.). After its first issue, the police arrested (but did not imprison) Kaunda and Harry Nkumbula (q.v.). Kaunda's name began to be widely known as a result. The publication was not resumed until January 1955, under the title *Official Gazette*. Kaunda, its editor, was imprisoned after the first issue, which was not as large as the original issues of the *Congress News*. A second issue of the *Gazette* was produced by Dixon Konkola (q.v.).

CONSTITUTION AMENDMENT BILL, 1957. This law was passed by the Federal Parliament of the Central African Federation (q.v.) on July 31, 1957. Despite objections by the African Affairs Board (q.v.), it was debated and approved by the British House of Commons. Africans opposed it because, while it increased the membership of the Federal Assembly from 35 to 59, it increased the African representation from nine to only 15. Thus there would be a slightly smaller proportion of African representation in the new assembly. In addition, since the six new African members would be chosen by an electorate dominated by Europeans, they would be more likely to be concerned with European than African interests.

CONSTITUTION OF ZAMBIA (AMENDMENT) BILL, 1991. Signed into law by President Kenneth Kaunda (q.v.) on August 24, 1991, it once again allowed for multiparty competition. It also limited a presidentially declared state of emergency to seven days, after which the president would have to seek an extension from Parliament (q.v.). Other constitutional changes included a stipulation that the president must select the cabinet from among members of Parliament and that the latter remain unicameral. This bill followed some, but not all, of the suggestions made by the Mvunga Commission (q.v.), which sat from October 1990 until it published its report in June 1991. The commission and its report were highly controversial, and the Movement for Multiparty Democracy (q.v.) in particular criticized the provisions for creating too strong an executive. A Constitutional Review Commission (q.v.) was established in 1993 to review the 1991 constitution and made its report in June 1995.

CONSTITUTION PARTY. This multiracial party was founded in Lusaka (q.v.) in October 1957 by moderate to liberal Europeans, such as Alexander Scott, David Stirling, Harry Franklin (qq.v.), and several Africans, including Lawrence Katilungu and Safeli Chileshe (qq.v.), in hopes of dealing "a death blow to the doctrine of racial hatred and malice." Its convention unanimously approved a motion by Chileshe calling for legislation to "abolish the monster of social and economic discrimination" (*see* COLOUR BAR). There was also an attempt to find common ground for cooperation with the African National Congress (q.v.). The party did not limit its activities to Northern Rhodesia (q.v.). In the June 1958 general elections in Southern Rhodesia (q.v.), it did not run candidates but suggested that its supporters vote for the most liberal candidates available. By the time the March 1959 elections for Northern Rhodesia's Legislative Council (q.v.) came around, the Constitution Party had given way to the better organized branch of the Central African Party (q.v.) led by John Moffat (q.v.) in Northern Rhodesia. Many of its members found a home there and also, later, in the Northern Rhodesia Liberal Party (q.v.).

CONSTITUTIONAL REVIEW COMMISSION. The commission, chaired by University of Zambia chancellor and former finance minister John Mwanakatwe (q.v.), was established to review and rewrite the constitution of the Second Zambian Republic (q.v.) for Zambia's new multiparty democracy. The commission's first apppointments were made in November 1992. A team of 25 members, representing five political parties (including the Movement for Multiparty Democracy, the United National Independence Party, and the National Party, qq.v.), was formed in November 1993. Its draft constitution was made public in June 1995 and was distributed as a newspaper supplement in early July. Two controversial clauses in the proposed revisions made it impossible for anyone who had already served two or more terms as president, or whose parents were not Zambian citizens, to stand for the presidency. Each condition disqualified former president Kenneth Kaunda (q.v.) from ever running again.

COOPERATIVES. There was a major drive by the government of Zambia from 1965 to 1973 to develop farming cooperatives. In April 1965, President Kaunda (q.v.) issued his Chifuba declaration on cooperatives, and there was a host of government-sponsored cooperatives in 1966, including two impressive Israeli settlement schemes in the rural Copperbelt (q.v.). The purpose of these farming cooperatives was to foster a feeling of mutual self-help (a goal of Zambian humanism, q.v.) as much as it was to boost agricultural production. The government created a system of subsidies for lands cleared for cash crops by a registered cooperative. Groups clearing 50 or more acres would qualify for a government grant to buy a tractor. The response in the country was immediate and actually overwhelmed the marketing and transportation system of the country. Yet it soon became obvious that much of the cleared land was not being worked and the cooperative movement has yet to recover from the 1973 expulsion of the Israelis, done in the name of Afro-Arab solidarity.

COPPER. First a blessing, then a curse on the Zambian economy, copper exports in the 1970s provided 95 percent of Zambia's foreign exchange earnings. Copper production at Kansanshi (q.v.) dates to the Early Iron Age people of the fifth century A.D. Large-scale production, however, began in the 14th century and is attributed to the Late Iron Age people(s) of the Luangwa pottery tradition (q.v.), who dug the large workings at Kansanshi, Kipushi, and Bwana Mkubwa (q.v.) and cast the flanged copper crosses (q.v.) for long-distance trade.

Though most of the major Copperbelt (q.v.) claims were staked by 1910, development only began in the late 1920s after the British South Africa Company (q.v.) opened the territory to multinational mining firms in 1922. Firms such as the Anglo-American Corporation and Rhodesian Selection Trust (qq.v.) brought in the capital needed to exploit the Copperbelt's low-concentration, copper sulfide ores. Copper production and mine employment dropped dramatically during the Great Depression of the early 1930s but rose again by 1935 and throughout World War II and the Korean conflict.

Following the declaration of the Matero economic reforms (q.v.), the Zambian government acquired a 51 percent interest in the mines and an equal share of their profits. These, in 1969, constituted 54 percent of Zambia's gross domestic product and 59 percent of the government's revenues. Times were never so good again. The world market price for copper fell nearly 40 percent between 1973 and 1975, and the 1976 mine profits constituted only 17 percent of Zambia's GDP and 3 percent of government revenues. Though production was increased to meet the shortfall, increasing production and transport (see TAZARA) costs often meant that copper was sold at or below the break-even point. The mines became a serious drain on government revenues. Throughout the 1980s, Zambia encountered terrible social and political difficulties, as foreign exchange earnings and imports sagged and unemployment and foreign debt soared.

Many of Zambia's mineral ore deposits are now worked out. None are expected to last long past 2001. Some mines are closing down, while others are slated to be sold to private investors. Zambia does have appreciable cobalt, coal, emeralds, and amethyst deposits; and there are recurrent rumors of gold, oil, and uranium deposits. But none of these will ever become what copper once was to the Zambian economy, and the country's long-term future seems to lie in far less remunerative agricultural exports like cotton, sugar, tobacco, and coffee.

COPPER CROSSES. A form of currency found in Zambia and in the neighboring Shaba area of the Democratic Republic of Congo (q.v.) (Zaire), these crossed iron bars were cast in ingots and kept to a fairly standard weight. The earliest ones found indicate that they were used in trade by the 14th or 15th century A.D., perhaps even earlier in the Democratic Republic of Congo (q.v.) (Zaire). Those found at Ingombe Ilede (q.v.) weighed between 2.3 and 4.5 kilograms. Those found in the old Katanga (Shaba) area of the Democratic Republic of Congo (Zaire) are sometimes called Katanga Crosses.

COPPERBELT. Historically, the economic heartland of Zambia, the mining area known as the Copperbelt (as distinguished from the larger Copperbelt Province, q.v.) is about 145 kilometers (90 miles) long and 48 kilometers (30 miles) wide. Back when it regularly produced over 700,000 tonnes per year, it made Zambia the world's third-largest producer of copper (q.v.). Seven of Zambia's 10 largest cities (called "towns") are on the Copperbelt: Ndola, Kitwe, Luanshya, Chingola, Mufulira, Kalulushi, and Chililabombwe (qq.v.). These are home to nearly 90 percent of Copperbelt Province's (and 18 percent of Zambia's) people. The Copperbelt is served by major railroads and highways and shares its northeastern border with the Democratic Republic of Congo's (q.v.) (Zaire's) Shaba (formerly Katanga) Province.

COPPERBELT PROVINCE. Called Western Province until 1969, when Barotseland was renamed Western Province (qq.v.), it includes the area tremendously rich in copper (q.v.) plus a large area to its west and south. The province is divided into eight districts, Ndola Rural District and seven urban ones: Chililabombwe, Chingola, Kalulushi, Kitwe, Mufulira, Luanshya, and Ndola (qq.v.) (Urban). The total population of the province in 1969 was 816,300, and in 1990 1,245,000, or 22 percent of the national population.

COPPERBELT SHOP ASSISTANTS UNION. The first African union to form in Zambia, it was founded in 1948, thus predating the African Mineworkers Union (q.v.) by one year. The British Labour Party government had sent labor advisors to Northern Rhodesia (q.v.) to assist the Africans in its organization.

COPPERBELT STRIKE OF 1935. *See* STRIKES OF 1935, 1940.

CORYNDON, SIR ROBERT THORNE. An administrator of Barotseland in the early 20th century, he was born in South Africa in 1870 and educated partly in England. A trooper in the Pioneer Column, which occupied Mashonaland in 1890, he rose to the rank of major in the 1893 Matabele War and the 1896 Rebellion. He also served for a year as Cecil Rhodes' (q.v.) private secretary. In 1897 he was appointed resident (commissioner) of Barotseland, chosen by the British South Africa Company (q.v.) but approved by the British high commissioner to South Africa. When he arrived in the Lozi capital of Lealui (qq.v.) in October 1897, with one assistant and five troopers, he did not impress Lewanika (q.v.) as the kind of British protective force he had expected. Eventually, however, Coryndon's skill as a hunter and his charm and diplomacy won the respect of the Lozi, and with the aid of Arthur Lawley, he negotiated the Lewanika Concession of 1900 (qq.v.) in June 1898, confirming British power in Western Zambia.

In September 1900, he was appointed administrator of North-Western Rhodesia, a post he held until April 1907. During this time, in order to base the BSAC's claims to the Copperbelt's mineral wealth on the Ware and Lochner Concessions (qq.v.), Copperbelt Province and the entire line of rail (qq.v.) was transferred from North-Eastern to North-Western Rhodesia (qq.v.). Much of Coryndon's influence among the Lozi rested on his claim to be the representative of the English Crown. In obtaining concessions, he appeared to imply that the alternative was that the Lozi would be conquered, either by other Africans or, perhaps, by the British. Coryndon then served as resident commissioner of Swaziland from 1907 to 1916 and, later, of Basutoland (Lesotho). He then served as governor of Uganda and, later, of Kenya. He died in 1925.

COTTON CLOTH. It has been known in Zambia for hundreds of years. The late-14th-century graves at Ingombe Ilede (q.v.), for example, include spinning whorls and fragments of cotton cloth. In the 19th century, the demand for calico, wire, guns, and powder helped fuel the long-distance trade in slaves and ivory (q.v.). And in the 20th century, the demand for cotton clothes brought countless labor migrants to the Kabwe and Copperbelt (qq.v.) mines. Marketed cotton production has varied dramatically in recent years, from 15,000 tonnes in 1979–80 to over 31,000 tonnes in 1983–84 fostering the growth of Kafue

Textiles, Ltd. But while Kafue Textiles exports cloth to Europe, its products are currently far too expensive to compete with the subsidized cloth imports from China and Pakistan or with the *salaula* (q.v.), or used clothing, imports from Europe and North America.

COURT OF APPEAL. Also referred to as the Supreme Court, it is the highest court in the land and is the country's final appellate body. It is higher than the High Court (q.v.), although the chief justice presides over both. Below them both are the magistrates' courts and local courts. The chief justice and other judges of both the Court of Appeal and the High Court are appointed by the president.

COUSINS, C. E. (TED). A former civil servant from the Luangwa (q.v.) area, he was a member of the African National Congress (q.v.) and one of its successful candidates in the 1962 election for the Northern Rhodesian Legislature. This became crucial when the United National Independence Party (q.v.) and the ANC decided to create a coalition to rule the Legislative Council (q.v.), as the constitutional rules required two of the cabinet posts to be held by Europeans. Although the ANC had only seven of the 21 seats in the coalition group, it had the only two Europeans, Cousins and Frank Stubbs (q.v.). Thus it demanded and was given half of the six ministerial posts. Cousins was named minister of land and natural resources. After a series of disagreements with Harry Nkumbula (q.v.) of the ANC over party leadership, Cousins resigned or was expelled (or both) from the ANC late in November 1963. He quickly joined UNIP and became its candidate for one of the 10 reserved roll (European) seats in the January 1964 election, but he narrowly lost to a candidate of the National Progress Party (the former United Federal Party) (qq.v.).

CROWN AND NATIVE TRUST LANDS. The term applies to the unoccupied lands that were alienated from Africans during the creation of the Native Reserves (q.v.). Such lands were to be set aside for an anticipated, but never realized, 1930s influx of white settlers. Urged by Governor Hubert Young (q.v.), the government determined in 1942 that all lands not already apportioned to Europeans or as Native Reserves (q.v.) should be divided into two categories: Crown Land, for European settlers and mining development; and Native Trust Land (q.v.), for progressive African farmers on individual tenure, for African townships, or, pending the approval of the local Native Authority (q.v.), non-African leaseholders. These arrangements were formalized in 1947 with the passage of the Native Trust Land Order in Council. This, for the first time ever, placed clearcut limits upon European land acquisitions in Northern Rhodesia (q.v.).

CROWN COLONY. The term applied to Northern Rhodesia (q.v.) when, in 1924, its governance passed from the British South Africa Company to the British Colonial Office (qq.v.).

CUNNINGHAM, COLIN. This European politician and Lusaka (q.v.) lawyer was especially active during the period of the Central African Federation (q.v.). At one point he was very close to Kenneth Kaunda (q.v.), even meeting him when Kaunda was released from jail. Later, however, he formed the Federal Fighting Fund (FFF), sometimes called the Federal Fighting Force, which pledged support for Roy Welensky and the federation (qq.v.). It favored establishing a federal police force to combat "communism" and all those who opposed federation. Later, Cunningham was a leader of the extremist Rhodesian Republican Party (q.v.).

D

DALGLEISH COMMISSION. This government-appointed commission, chaired by Andrew Dalgleish, a prominent member of the British Trade Union Council, met in 1948 to inquire into the advancement of Africans into industrial jobs (primarily on the mines) reserved for Europeans. It concluded that Africans could not be held back indefinitely; and that Africans should be trained and then moved into European jobs as vacancies arose. The commission's recommendations were ignored by both British and Northern Rhodesian governments and were rejected by the European miners' union.

DAMBO. This is a common African term for a treeless marsh near the source of a stream. While seasonal (rainy season) waterlogging precludes any tree cover at such sites, *dambos* provide reliable grazing areas during the dry season, while, elsewhere, their dark humic soils make excellent dry season gardens for the cultivation of "green mealies" (immature maize, which are roasted and eaten like American sweetcorn) or garden vegetables. *Dambos* cover an estimated 5 percent of Zambia's surface area.

DAMBWA. This Early Iron Age site is in the Zambezi (q.v.) valley, near Livingstone (q.v.). The pottery, dating from the seventh and eighth centuries A.D., is generally similar to contemporaneous pottery found in Zimbabwe. Copper wire from the site suggests its people were involved in long-distance trade, for the nearest copper (q.v.) deposits are in the Kafue Hook (q.v.) and the Gwai River valley in Zimbabwe. The skeletal remains of the Dambwa people suggest a mixture of Khoisan and black African traits. This is often taken as evidence of intermarriage between indigenous hunter-gatherers, like the inhabitants of Gwisho Hot Springs (q.v.), and immigrant Iron Age farmers from the north.

DAVEY, THOMAS G. This Australian mining engineer, employed by Edmund Davis (q.v.), identified the deposits that became Broken Hill Mine (q.v.) in 1902. He and a guide, looking for some old workings, became lost and stumbled upon the mine by accident. He named the area Broken Hill after a similar geological configuration he had known in Australia.

DAVIS, SIR EDMUND. Born in Australia in 1862, this noted financier and mining tycoon dominated the Northern Rhodesian mining industry. He made his way to Cape Town at age 17 and, some 18 years later, formed the Bechuanaland Exploration Company and Northern Copper Company (qq.v.), whose prospectors first claimed, in 1899, the Kafue Hook (q.v.) deposits that became known as the Sable Antelope and Silver King Mines, the first, if short-lived, commercial copper holdings in the territory. He also sent out Thomas Davey (q.v.), who discovered ore deposits in 1902 that became Broken Hill Mine (q.v.). Further south, near Bulawayo, Davis developed the Wankie Colliery, which, once the railway was completed in 1909–10, long supplied coal and coke to the Northern Rhodesian and Katangan copper mine refineries. A long-time associate of Cecil Rhodes (q.v.), Davis acquired a seat on the British South Africa Company (q.v.) board in 1925 and, in 1930, lobbied persistently for making Broken Hill (Kabwe) the new capital of Northern Rhodesia. He died in 1939.

DAVISON, ARTHUR (YENGWE). Davison came from England to Africa in 1904 to work on the Victoria Falls Bridge, during the extension of the Bulawayo rail line. His African nickname, derived from the Sotho (q.v.) word for "lions," refers to the time when he, in foolish innocence, drove a pride of dozing lions off the tracks by throwing stones at them. As a labor recruiter from 1907 to 1912, he supplied and directed Africans during the building of the Lobito (Benguela) and Broken Hill-Congo Border Railways in Angola and Northern Rhodesia (qq.v.) and, then, the Union Minière in Katanga (q.v.). He joined the Northern Rhodesia Rifles (q.v.) in 1914 and, in 1916, the traction engine crew that brought two armed motor launches from Kambove to successfully challenge the German's control of Lake Tanganyika (q.v.). In 1935, with support from the white Railway Workers' Union, he stood for the northern district seat on the Legislative Council (q.v.), but lost to Stewart Gore-Brown (q.v.). During World War II, he was a quartermaster sergeant in East Africa and Ethiopia.

A large landowner, Davison had farms at Abercorn (Mbala), Solwezi (qq.v.), and Bwana Mkubwa, as well as his four-story concrete "castle" on Ndola's North Rise. Africans long suspected him of being one of the *banyama* (q.v.) and to have a special license for exporting kidnapped Africans to the Greek fish traders and Belgian planters in the Congo (q.v.). Though famous for his pursuit of African women, Davison never married nor had any children. His property was left to charitable organizations when he died in 1955. Ironically, the very "castle" in which he was supposed to have warehoused his *banyama* victims was demolished and replaced by Ndola's Arthur Davison Memorial Hospital.

DE LACERDA. *See* LACERDA, FRANCISCO JOSÉ MARÍA DE.

DEMOCRATIC PEOPLE'S PARTY. This short-lived party was formed in March 1972 by Foustino Lombe (q.v.) and other former members of the United Progressive Party (q.v.) after its banning the previous month. It was organized as a protest against President Kaunda's (q.v.) announcement that Zambia was going to become a one-party democracy.

DEMOCRATIC REPUBLIC OF CONGO. The Democratic Republic of Congo (Zaire) is Zambia's neighbor on the north. It was known as the Belgian Congo until independence, and as the Congo until its president, Mobutu Sese Seko, changed its name on October 27, 1971. Following Mobutu's 1997 overthrow, it was rechristened the Democratic Republic of Congo. The intrusion of the copper-rich Katanga Pedicle (q.v.) into the heart of Zambia's midsection gives the two countries much in common. The 1977–78 civil war in Shaba (formerly Katanga, q.v.) overlapped into Zambia, causing temporary concern as planes from the Zaire Air Force attacked a village across the border in Zambia.

DEPARTMENT OF INFORMATION (NORTHERN RHODESIAN; FEDERAL). Presumably linked to the 1936 appearance of *Mutende* (q.v.), the government newspaper for Africans, the Northern Rhodesian Department of Information seems to have begun in 1941, when Harry Franklin (q.v.), director of information, opened a small shortwave radio station in Lusaka (q.v.) to transmit news of the war. In 1945, he created the Central African Broadcasting Service (q.v.). On his retirement into politics, William Vernon Brelsford (q.v.), the first and only editor of the history-minded *Northern Rhodesia Journal* (1950–65), became director in 1951. The department's goals were to interpret government policy and actions to the territory's people, to advise the government on public opinion and public relations, to develop and exploit the media in aid of the administration and its technical departments, and to publicize the territory beyond its borders.

Once the Central African Federation (q.v.) was realized in 1953, Brelsford moved to Salisbury (q.v.) (modern Harare) as director of the new Federal Department of Information. By the late 1950s, given Dr. Hastings Kamuzu Banda's (q.v.) triumphant, nationalist return to Nyasaland (q.v.), the department's four divisions—administration, press, publications, and the Central African Film Unit—were all under pressure to "sell" federation (q.v.) at home and abroad. Thus it assisted C. E. Lucas Phillips in preparing his glowing, federally funded review of the federation's future, *The Vision Splendid* (1960), and it began mailing *Fact*, a free, eight-page monthly newsletter, to anyone who requested a subscription. In June 1960, the federal government hired Voice and Vision, Ltd., the public relations subsidiary of a London advertising agency, to direct its propaganda campaign. Brelsford, who edited the 800-page *Handbook of the Federation of Rhodesia and Nyasaland* (1960), was considered too scholarly for the business of selling federation and was replaced in September 1960 by W. H. (Bill) Hammond.

Apart from *Fact* and the Film Unit's informational shorts, the department had no real contact with Africans. So a variety of exhibition centers were opened in vacant town shops, and in

1962 Fact Convoys began touring with mobile displays and open air screenings of the Film Unit's shorts. In view of the Monckton Commission (q.v.) report of October 1960, few foreigners were surprised that the Department of Information had no success in selling federation to its African peoples.

DEPUTY CHIEFS. A native administration ordinance of 1960 provided for the appointment of deputy chiefs to take over the administrative duties of infirm, aged, or otherwise incompetent chiefs. The position was open to members of the chiefly families, who then competed in an election. In many cases, notably among the Yombe (q.v.), this competition opened traditional chiefships to partisan party politics.

DEVONSHIRE AGREEMENT, 1923. This was the actual agreement between the British Colonial Office and the British South Africa Company (qq.v.) that turned over administration and control of the lands of Northern Rhodesia (q.v.) to the Colonial Office. It also allowed the BSAC to retain mineral rights and its freehold estates. It was formally signed on October 1, 1923. It was named after the ninth Duke of Devonshire, colonial secretary from 1922 to 1924.

DIRECT RULE. The form of administration used by the British South Africa Company (q.v.), it used the chiefs merely as instruments of European rulers. The change to British Colonial Office (q.v.) rule in 1924 brought a gradual shift to indirect rule (q.v.).

DISTRICT. Under British South Africa Company (q.v.) administration, each district was an administrative and tax-collecting unit under its own district commissioner (q.v.) and his subordinate native commissioners (q.v.). Following Northern Rhodesia's (q.v.) establishment as a Crown Colony (q.v.) in 1924, the old districts were replaced by seven provinces. Today there are nine provinces, each of which incorporates between three (Lusaka Province, q.v.) and nine (Northern and Southern Provinces, qq.v.) of Zambia's 57 districts.

DISTRICT COMMISSIONER. Under the British South Africa Company (q.v.), administrators of the major subdivisions of the territory were usually called district commissioners. Under them were native commissioners (q.v.). The district commissioner was also usually a magistrate. Early on, he had to travel extensively, learning languages and customs, and keeping tax rolls (the census). Later, under the Colonial Office and until the birth of Zambian government, the district commissioners were the chief administrators in the district, which now were subdivisions of the provinces.

DISTRICT GOVERNOR. In January 1969, President Kaunda (q.v.) added an additional administrative layer by placing politically appointed district governors over the senior civil servants, the district secretaries (q.v.). By this measure, the civil servants and civil government were formally subordinated to appointed politicians and the United National Independence Party (q.v.) structure. But because district governors were rotated so frequently, district secretaries retained effective control.

DISTRICT SECRETARY. Under the Zambian government, district secretaries, who are professional civil servants, took over the duties of the old district commissioners (q.v.) as the districts' senior administrators. District secretaries found their positions undercut in 1967 when the government gave the position of chairman of the local District Development Committee to United National Independence Party (q.v.) politicians, demoting the district secretaries to committee secretaries. Their positions were further lowered when the government decided in 1969 to appoint district governors (q.v.), who were UNIP appointees, to oversee district governance. Though district secretaries and governors often clashed, the former enjoyed more permanent positions, more knowledge of the district, and all the benefits of institutional inertia.

DOKE, CLEMENT MARTIN. Baptist missionary, anthropologist, folklorist, and, later, Bantu linguist at Witwatersrand University, he worked among the Lamba (q.v.) near Kafulafuta Mission (q.v.).

DOMINION PARTY. *See* FEDERAL DOMINION PARTY.

DONGWE RIVER. This river is one of the major tributaries of the Kabompo River (q.v.), which is itself one of the first tributaries of the Zambezi (q.v.). Rising near the city of Kasempa (q.v.), the Dongwe flows from east to west until it joins the Kabompo in the northwestern part of Zambia.

DOYLE, BRIAN ANDRE. Chief justice of Zambia since 1969 and chairman of the 1971 Doyle Commission (q.v.), he was born in

Burma in 1911 and educated in Dublin. He is the holder of B.A. and LL.B. degrees. He served in various legal posts throughout the Commonwealth from 1937 until he became attorney general of Northern Rhodesia (q.v.) in 1956. From 1959 to 1965 he was both attorney general and minister of legal affairs.

DOYLE COMMISSION. Chaired by Chief Justice B. A. Doyle (q.v.), the commission was impaneled to investigate Minister Justin Chimba's (q.v.) allegations of tribal bias in both criminal prosecutions and civil service appointments. The commission held hearings in 1971, and its report criticized several ministers for their financial irregularities. President Kaunda (q.v.) then dismissed both Justin Chimba and the errant ministers.

DRAPER, CHARLES RICHARD EARDLEY. He was a district commissioner (q.v.) in North-Eastern Rhodesia (q.v.) in 1919 when a series of incidents involving the followers of Hanoc Sindano's (q.v.) Watch Tower Movement (q.v.) caught his attention. He ultimately called in a police force against them. In one incident, he arrested 138 Watch Tower followers in the vicinity of Fife (q.v.). Some see the incidents as early examples of anticolonial activity. Others praise Draper for his restraint.

DRUG TRADE. Since 1981, a number of Zambians—diplomats, businessmen, politicians, airline employees, and police officers—have either been accused of—or detained or imprisoned—for involvement in the international and domestic drug trade. South African cocaine is smuggled through Zambia to Europe and America; Indian heroin and Mandrax (i.e., methaqualone, or quaaludes) are smuggled through Zambia to South Africa; and cannabis is grown in Southern Province (q.v.) for export to South Africa. While some of the charges against certain individuals seem to have been politically motivated, there is no doubt that a number of factors—Zambia's economic deterioration, its relaxed foreign controls and open foreign exchange trading, and its token fines and jail sentences—have fostered a dramatic rise in drug trafficking and money laundering. The national Drug Enforcement Commission claimed to have seized over US$36 million in drugs and equipment in 1994 and estimated that laundered drug money, which deflates the value of the Zambian kwacha (q.v.), ran more than $241 million. It is widely assumed that drug traders were behind the attempted assassination of the commission's deputy director in March 1994.

DUPONT, JOSEPH. A Roman Catholic missionary of the order called the White Fathers (q.v.), Father Dupont came south from East Africa in 1890 to begin a settlement along the Stevenson Road at Mambwe (qq.v.). From there he planned to move further south to convert the Bemba (q.v.). He was personally involved in two notable (and successful) attempts to set up missions among the Bemba, both of which laid the groundwork for British rule, as well. The first was the result of the White Fathers' attempts in 1894 and 1895 to set up a mission near Makasa's (q.v.) village at Mipini, despite Chitimukulu Sampa's (qq.v.) edict prohibiting white men from entering Bemba country. Threatened with an attack by Sampa, Makasa first accepted, then refused the offer. Finally, in July 1895, Dupont visited Makasa again and, by refusing his instructions to leave the village, forced Sampa's hand. When Sampa did not attack, Makasa willingly allowed a mission to be started at Kayambi, near Mipini. Later, Dupont twice refused Sampa's invitation to visit him. In 1897 Dupont was named bishop of the Nyassa region.

The other successful mission came as a result of a request by another Bemba chief, Mwamba (q.v.), to visit his village in 1898. Dupont arrived on October 11 to find Mwamba mentally alert but close to death. Mwamba hoped the bishop could heal him or, if not, succeed him so that the other Bemba leaders would not invade his capital and kill his followers. Dupont built a chapel nearby, provided morphine as a painkiller, and helped Mwamba until his death on October 23. From his mission along the Milungu Stream, Dupont then became Mwamba's regent. In his successful effort to maintain order, however, Dupont began acting more as a chief, knowing that eventually the British would intervene and impose their rule. This finally happened when Robert Codrington (q.v.), administrator of North-Eastern Rhodesia (q.v.), came to settle the matter of succession in May 1899. The new Mwamba was installed in September.

DUTCH REFORMED CHURCH. The principal church of the Afrikaners in South Africa, it instituted missionary work in Nyasaland (q.v.) in 1889 and in North-Eastern Rhodesia (the eastern half of Zambia) (q.v.) near the turn of the century. It never gained a large following except among whites from South Africa, although its missionaries worked among the ciNyanja (q.v.)-speaking peoples for many years. Its successor under African control is called the Reformed Church of Zambia.

E

EASTERN PROVINCE. This easternmost of Zambia's nine provinces stretches between the Luangwa River and the Malawi (qq.v.) border, from the northeastern town of Isoka to just north of Feira (qq.v.), in the south. It consists of six districts: Chadiza, Chama, Chipata, Katete, Lundazi, and Petauke (qq.v.). The provincial capital is in Chipata, which in colonial times was the North-Eastern Rhodesian capital of Fort Jameson (q.v.). The province had 510,000 people in 1969 and 974,000 in 1990, almost 13 percent of Zambia's population. Thirty percent of this province's people live in Chipata District. Among the major ethnic groups in the province are the Chewa, Senga, Ngoni, Nsenga, and Kunda (qq.v.).

ECONOMIC ADVISORY COUNCIL. Formally announced by President Chiluba (q.v.) in May 1993, the council was formed to advise the government on Zambia's economic performance and future development strategies. Though chaired by the minister of finance, it was expected to operate as an independent agency, reporting to the president through the National Development and Economic Committee. The council's 24 members were to be drawn from government, the University of Zambia, and various interest and lobbying groups.

ECONOMIC SURVEY MISSION ON THE ECONOMIC DEVELOPMENT OF ZAMBIA. *See* SEERS REPORT.

ECONOMICS ASSOCIATION OF ZAMBIA. Founded in the 1960s as the Lusaka Economics Club, it was originally dominated by economists from the University of Zambia (q.v.). By the mid-1970s, though, most of its Executive Committee members were practicing economists in government and business, and some became vocal critics of Zambia's system of state capitalism. The association was registered as a society in 1985. In 1991 it became a more formal organization, with a Lusaka office and a published newsletter.

ELWELL, ARCHIBALD H. An experienced British civil servant who was sent to Kitwe (q.v.) in 1944 by the Colonial Office to serve as a social welfare officer, his sympathy for African aspirations led to "the Elwell incident." On the request of a leader of the Kitwe African Society (q.v.), he addressed the group in January 1946 and, just two years before formation of the Copperbelt Shop Assistants Union (q.v.), suggested that such self-help groups might form political or trade unions and that a well-disciplined strike might bring the benefits they desired. His brief speech angered mine officials and the local district commissioner (q.v.). Elwell was soon transferred to Livingstone (q.v.) and, a few months later, was sent back to London.

EMRYS-EVANS, PAUL V. President of the British South Africa Company (q.v.) during the period around Zambian independence, he represented the BSAC during the negotiations that resulted in it agreeing to give up all of its mineral royalty rights in exchange for £4 million. The announcement came just hours before the moment of Zambian independence.

ENGLISH COMMON LAW. This is the basis of jurisprudence in Zambia, in contrast to the Roman-Dutch law adopted in Southern Rhodesia (q.v.) after the pattern in the Republic of South Africa.

ETHIOPIAN CHURCH OF BAROTSELAND. This church movement was run by Africans in Barotseland (q.v.) immediately before and after 1900. With ties to both the Ethiopian movement in South Africa (i.e., churches independent of European control) and the African Methodist Episcopal Church (q.v.), it was led by Willie Mokalapa (q.v.), a Sotho (q.v.) evangelist who broke away from François Coillard's Paris Mission Society (qq.v.) in Barotseland. In 1898 he began to express his displeasure with the treatment of African churchmen by the missionaries. Lozi king Lewanika (qq.v.) responded favorably to Mokalapa's proposal to begin schools that would teach English and practical skills to his people. Lewanika (q.v.) did not favor the religious education taught in the Lozi language by the missionaries. Ultimately, the colonial administration and missionaries had to offer what the Lozi wanted. The result was the creation of the Barotse National School (q.v.) in 1907. Meanwhile, Mokalapa's church grew rapidly as he broke from the Mission Society, taking with him large numbers of African followers, including relatives of Lewanika. The church and schools prospered until late 1905, when Mokalapa was swindled of £750 of Lewanika's money in Cape Town, where he was supposed to buy some large equipment such as boats and carriages. Mokalapa was too ashamed to return, and his church did not long survive his absence.

EURAFRICAN (EURO-AFRICAN). The term refers to people of mixed racial ancestry, the so-called Coloureds in South Africa. The nearly 6,000 such people in the 1980 census then constituted 0.1 percent of the Zambian population. Historically, some of their leaders once formed the Northern Rhodesian Eurafrican Association (q.v.).

EUROPEAN MINEWORKERS UNION. Formed in 1936, the union's goals included the maintenance of racially distinct pay scales and the job reservation system, which limited certain skilled and semiskilled jobs to Europeans. Recruitment from Europe was encouraged when needed to meet demand. In 1955, the Anglo-American Corporation (q.v.) accepted the right of the union to veto any changes in the colour bar (q.v.) as it applied to jobs, although some new job categories were opened to Africans that year. In a November 1960 agreement, the union acknowledged the inevitable, and a majority of its 4,700 members voted to open 60 more job categories to Africans and an equal pay and promotion ladder for all.

EUROPEANS. The term applies to all "white" people and African Americans, regardless of their continent of origin. *Basungu* is the African word. In 1963 there were about 67,000 Europeans in Zambia; in 1969 there were 43,490; and in 1980, only 15,580 (0.3 percent of the population). Many left after independence, either because they feared they would lose their privileged lifestyle under African rule, or because their jobs were Zambianized.

EVANS, IFOR. A justice of the Zambian High Court (q.v.) his decision in July 1969 to release two Portuguese soldiers arrested for illegal entry into Zambia set off violent demonstrations against the court. Even President Kaunda (q.v.) condemned Evans for his decision. In June of that year Evans ruled that eight United National Independence Party (q.v.) members of Parliament (q.v.), including three ministers, had been invalidly elected the previous December, and he criticized the commissioner of police for "deliberate misconduct and mismanagement." Kaunda eventually apologized for his attacks, but Evans and the other justices, including Chief Justice James Skinner (q.v.) resigned or retired.

EVELYN HONE COLLEGE OF APPLIED ARTS AND SCIENCES. Located in Lusaka (q.v.), this is the second largest institution of higher education in the country (after the University of Zambia, q.v.). It offers a wide variety of vocational and trade courses. It was named after Sir Evelyn Hone (q.v.), the governor of Northern Rhodesia (q.v.) at the time of independence.

EXECUTIVE COUNCIL. A body created to advise the governor of Northern Rhodesia (q.v.) on executive matters, it was provided for in the Order in Council of 1924 (q.v.), which established British Colonial Office (q.v.) rule. It was composed entirely of colonial officials. While the governor was required to consult with it, he could reject its advice but then had to report his reasons to the secretary of state for the colonies. Seldom did he reject their advice. In 1939 the election of nonofficial members ("unofficials", q.v.) was provided for. Changes in 1945 left the council with five official members to three unofficials. Only officials held ministerial portfolios. In 1948 the council was expanded to 11 members. Four of them were unofficials; one of them was nominated (not elected) and was designated specifically to represent African interests. In 1949, two unofficials were given portfolios. The Order in Council effective on December 31, 1953, reduced the officials to five, but they retained a five-to-four majority. Constitutional change in 1959 gave the unofficials (dominated by the ruling United Federal Party, q.v.) a majority on the Executive Council and five of the portfolios. However, the membership was composed of four officials, four elected unofficials, and two Africans, both with full ministerial status. The 1964 constitution replaced the Executive Council with a cabinet (q.v.).

F

FAMILY HEALTH TRUST. Registered in 1987 as an umbrella organization for nongovernmental organizations working on AIDS (q.v.) and HIV education, the trust serves as the national clearinghouse for all nongovernmental organizations concerned with AIDS in Zambia. It also supports orphans under 20 years of age through its Children in Distress Project, and provides some home care for AIDS-affected families in Lusaka (q.v.).

FEDERAL DOMINION PARTY. The principal opposition party in the Federal House, the FDP was formed in 1958 when Winston Field (q.v.), leader of the Southern Rhodesia Dominion Party, was elected to the Federal Parliament and joined with G. F. van Eeden (q.v.), head of Northern Rhodesia's Commonwealth Party. This right-wing party had support among white farmers in Southern Province, Northern Rhodesia (qq.v.) and among South African miners on the Copperbelt (q.v.). One of its principal proposals was to subdivide the federation into segregated spheres of influence for Europeans and Africans. Voting rights for Africans would be severely restricted by extreme qualifications. Near the end of federation (q.v.), there were proposals to merge the FDP and the Rhodesian Republican Party (q.v.) to force Sir Roy Welensky's (q.v.) resignation. At the time, the FDP had seven seats. In March 1962, the Dominion Party in Southern Rhodesia merged with various dissident conservatives to form the Rhodesian Front (q.v.).

FEDERAL ELECTORAL BILL. Introduced in the Federation Parliament in September 1957, it became law the following January. It was passed despite the objections of the African Affairs Board (q.v.). Its provisions included two voting rolls, with separate qualifications. Most of those on the upper roll (q.v.) were Europeans, while the lower roll was mostly Africans. Africans objected to the fact that the eight seats to be filled by Africans were to be chosen by members of both rolls, whereas only upper-roll voters could fill the remaining 45 seats.

FEDERAL FIGHTING FUND. A drive to collect money in support of Roy Welensky (q.v.) and the federation (q.v.), the FFF was started by Colin Cunningham (q.v.) in 1960. It was announced at a meeting held in Kitwe (q.v.), where about a thousand Europeans contributed to send a delegation to England to make public appearances in support of the federation. They also pledged support of law and order and opposition to communism. While Cunningham called the African politicians "dirty agitators," Kaunda (q.v.) called the FFF, "Fifteen Fighting Fools."

FEDERAL PARTY. Formed in 1953 in order to contest the January 1954 federal elections, it grew out of the United Central Africa Association (q.v.). Its most prominent members were Sir Roy Welensky and Sir Godfrey Huggins (qq.v.). Pledged to the concept of racial "partnership," it won 24 of the 26 contested seats in the Federal Parliament. In February 1954, it won 10 of the 12 elected seats in the Northern Rhodesia Legislative Council.

Huggins became prime minister but retired in 1956, when Welensky succeeded him both as federal prime minister and as leader of the Federal Party. In March 1958, the Federal Party merged with the United Rhodesia Party and the two became the United Federal Party (q.v.).

FEDERAL REVIEW CONFERENCE. Held in London from December 5 to 16, 1960, it was supposed to review and amend the constitution of the Central African Federation (q.v.). The three African nationalists, Kenneth Kaunda, Joshua Nkomo, and H. K. Banda (qq.v.), had planned to boycott it but finally participated when Britain agreed to schedule conferences for Northern Rhodesia and Nyasaland (qq.v.) in mid-December. The three leaders walked out on December 12, along with the attending Northern Rhodesian chiefs, but Kaunda and his delegation returned in time for a final session on December 16. The abortive conference convinced the British of the irreconcilable differences between the nationalists and the federalists.

FEDERATION. Originally a concept suggested by some settlers in the late 1940s who did not like the concept of amalgamation (q.v.) it came to be seen by many, such as Stewart Gore-Browne (q.v.), as a way to bring the benefits of economic interdependence between the two Rhodesias and Nyasaland (q.v.) while preserving African rights. Ultimately, of course, it became the shorthand name of the Central African Federation (q.v.).

FEDERATION OF AFRICAN SOCIETIES OF NORTHERN RHODESIA (FEDERATION OF WELFARE SOCIETIES). An organization formed on May 18, 1946, it changed its name to the Northern Rhodesia African Congress (q.v.) in 1948. In 1933, the African welfare societies of the country met at Kafue to form a union of concerned Africans within the Protectorate. Officials saw the union as subversive and forbade any political activity. Thus, no organization developed until 1946, when Dauti Yamba, Godwin Lewanika (qq.v.), and representatives of 14 African societies created the federation. Yamba became its president. The government reacted by forming the African Representative Council (q.v.), but this act of tokenism did not defuse the feelings of the budding nationalists. The 14 societies included traders' and farmers' organizations in addition to six welfare societies. Under the leadership of Yamba and George Kaluwa (q.v.), this federation opposed both amalgamation (q.v.) and federation with Southern Rhodesia (q.v.), attempted to get seats on the African Representative Council, and sought representation at London constitutional talks. Although they lost, the government was forced to recognize and deal with them. A general conference of the organization in July 1948 passed a number of resolutions but also made its political goals explicit by changing its name to the Northern Rhodesia African Congress. It was soon to be renamed the African National Congress (q.v.).

FEDERATION (CONSTITUTION) ORDER IN COUNCIL. The official act that created the Central African Federation (q.v.), it passed the British Parliament in May 1953 and received the approval of Queen Elizabeth II on August 1, 1953. Two months later, the federation became a reality.

FEIRA. A small town in Zambia's least-populated district, Lusaka Province's Luangwa (qq.v.) (formerly Feira) District, it had only 7,900 people in 1969 and 16,300 in 1990. It is primarily of historic interest, as a market (Portuguese, *feira*) was established there in 1732, on the Zambezi-Luangwa River (qq.v.) confluence, to tap the gold trade from Zimbabwe. It also became a trade and travel link between the upper Zambezi valley and the Indian Ocean coast. Portuguese soldiers considered it a dangerous outpost, for they had recurrent clashes with Nsenga (q.v.) chief Mburuma. The Portuguese fort at Feira, built in 1806, was abandoned in 1836 due to the decline of the gold trade with Great Zimbabwe and the arrival of Ngoni and Ndebele (qq.v.) raiders. Chikunda (q.v.) slave and ivory (qq.v.) traders then dominated the region from 1850 until the mid-1890s, when John Harrison Clark (q.v.) established his private kingdom there.

FIELD, WINSTON. Leader of the Federal Dominion Party (q.v.) in the Federal Parliament and also a leader of the Rhodesian Front (q.v.) in Southern Rhodesia (q.v.), he became prime minister of Southern Rhodesia as a result of the December 1962 elections. He resigned from this position, under cabinet pressure, in April 1964, and was succeeded by Ian Smith (q.v.).

FIFE. An outpost and trading station founded in 1894 by the African Lakes Company (q.v.), it was situated on the Stevenson Road (q.v.) between Lakes Nyasa and Tanganyika (q.v.), about 161 kilometers (100 miles) southeast of Abercorn (q.v.). It was named after the Duke of Fife, son-in-law of the Prince of Wales and a member of the board of directors of the British South Africa Company (q.v.). In 1914, during World War I, a German force moved into Northern Rhodesia (q.v.) and fired on both Abercorn and Fife, with little effect.

FINANCIAL DEVELOPMENT CORPORATION. This parastatal body was set up in 1971 by the Zambian government to oversee financial institutions run by the government, such as the insurance company, the building society, and government shares in the Commercial Bank of Zambia, Ltd., and in the National Commercial Bank, Ltd. It also helped finance some African businessmen and diversify the rural economy.

FINGER MILLET. This dwarf millet, just 15 to 20 centimeters (six to eight inches) high, is one of the staple grains in the *chitemene* (q.v.) cultivation system of northeastern Zambia. The millet seed is planted in a bed of ash left from burned branches. Harvested in April and May, it is stored until used. *Nshima* (q.v.), made from finger millet flour, tastes like a cross between Wheatena and Malt-O-Meal-brand hot cereals, and its distinctive taste presumably explains why finger millet is the preferred grain for making beer.

FIRST ZAMBIAN REPUBLIC. This is the title now given the Zambian government that ruled from independence (October 24, 1964), until December 1972, when the one-party "participatory democracy" of the Second Zambian Republic (q.v.) began.

FLAG OF ZAMBIA. Introduced to Zambians in June 1964 by President Kaunda (q.v.), its base color is green, representing the grassland of the country and its agricultural products. About one-third of it, however, is taken up by an orange eagle flying over a block of three vertical stripes, colored red, black, and orange. The eagle in flight represents Zambian freedom. The orange stripe symbolizes the country's (copper, q.v.) mineral resources, the black represents the color of most of the population, and the red stripe is symbolic of the blood shed for freedom.

FORBES, PATRICK WILLIAM. Deputy administrator from July 1895 to June 1897 of what soon became North-Eastern Rhodesia (q.v.), Major Forbes led the British South Africa Company's (q.v.) forces in battles against the Portuguese and the Ndebele (q.v.), among others, in the early 1890s. In 1895 he was made the principal administrator of BSAC's land north of the Zambezi and west of Nyasaland (q.v.). His headquarters were actually at Zomba, in modern Malawi (q.v.). His major task was to extend BSAC influence deep into the region between Lakes Nyasa (Malawi) and Tanganyika (q.v.) and to have much of it explored and mapped. He also tried to stop the slave trade (q.v.) and thus set up *bomas* (q.v.) in the northeastern part of his territory near Fife (q.v.) and present-day Isoka (q.v.). He also encouraged Father Dupont of the White Fathers (qq.v.) to establish mission stations among the Bemba (q.v.).

FOREIGN EXCHANGE MANAGEMENT COMMITTEE. The interministerial committee created in May 1987 to allocate foreign exchange after Zambia's break with the International Monetary Fund (q.v.), FEMAC was composed of representatives from the Ministry of Commerce and the Bank of Zambia (q.v.). It was required to allocate foreign exchange according to criteria that gave priority to basic consumer industries and the manufacturers of nontraditional exports. It was established in a political climate critical of the rising cost of living and basic commodities shortages that followed from the austerity measures of the IMF's structural adjustment program (q.v.). During the budget speech of November 16, 1990, it was announced that FEMAC was to be abolished. After the introduction of a dual exchange rate system in February 1990, in which foreign exchange was sold through two windows, one at the official rate and one at the market rate, the government moved to unify the two rates and to expand the list of imports qualifying for use of the market rate window. By late 1990 that list included virtually all imports, so FEMAC's role in allocating foreign exchange at the official rate was virtually eliminated.

FORT JAMESON. Renamed Chipata (q.v.) at Zambian independence, Fort Jameson became an important administrative town for the British South Africa Company (q.v.) when Robert Codrington (q.v.), the deputy administrator of North-Eastern Rhodesia (q.v.), transferred his headquarters there from Blantyre in 1899. It was then a new outpost, created near the town of Ngoni chief Mpezeni (qq.v.), who had been subdued by force only the previous year. Within a year, the town had 20 brick houses and sat astride the Karonga-to-Abercorn telegraph line. As Europeans settled nearby, Fort Jameson became a small center for trade and services, kept busy by European planters and officials. Codrington encouraged colonization, and export tobacco became a popular crop just before World War I. In the succeeding 10 years, there was an influx of Indian settlers many of whom took over petty trade. Still, Fort Jameson never became large. The 1960 population estimate was about 400 Europeans, 3,000 employed Africans, and 300 "other races," mostly Indian.

FORT JAMESON NGONI. The term is frequently used to refer to Mpezeni's (q.v.) group of Ngoni (q.v.), who settled around Fort Jameson (now Chipata, q.v.). Other Ngoni chiefs and their peoples live in Malawi (q.v.).

FORT ROSEBERY. Known as Mansa (q.v.) since independence, the town had its beginning as a British South Africa Company (q.v.) outpost in the 1890s. In 1892, Alfred Sharpe (q.v.), a BSAC representative, chose another site for the town, along the Luapula River, naming it for Lord Rosebery, the current British foreign secretary. While it was never built there, maps recorded its existence on the Luapula for many years. When it was finally constructed years later, the new site was about 48 kilometers (30 miles) east of the Luapula River and 80 kilometers (50 miles) west of Lake Bangweulu (q.v.). It became the administrative *boma* (q.v.) for district commissioners (q.v.). As a district center, its population grew to about 5,700 by 1969 and it had acquired a small airfield. Manganese has been mined nearby. During the 1950s and 1960s, it became a center for Zambia African National Congress and United National Independence Party (qq.v.) political activity.

FOUNDATION FOR DEMOCRATIC PROCESS. Zambia's most prominent organization for civic education and the monitoring of elections, the foundation was formed in April 1992 to strengthen democracy and to protect human rights and the electoral process through the careful monitoring of elections. It was the successor to the Zambia Elections Monitoring Coordination Committee and grew out of a series of coalitions formed among church and other nongovernmental groups associated with the November 1991 elections. In July 1991 the government and the Movement for Multiparty Democracy (q.v.) came together under church leadership to discuss multiparty elections and the constitution being proposed by the Mvunga Commission (q.v.). Together they formed the Christian Churches Monitoring Group. In September 1991 the monitoring group joined with the Law Association of Zambia (q.v.), the Press Association of Zambia, the Women's Lobby, the University Student Union, and other nongovernmental groups to form the ZEMCC to oversee the 1991 elections. It was decided at that time to keep the committee chair in the hands of the clergy. In April 1992 the committee became the foundation.

FOX-PITT, THOMAS S. L. This British colonial officer served in a variety of posts, one of which was provincial commissioner of Barotseland (q.v.) in the late 1940s. Although he retired in the early 1950s, he continued to be a significant advisor and confidante to African nationalists. Before he returned to his home in England he joined the African National Congress (q.v.). He continued to meet Kaunda (q.v.) and others in England and to correspond with them at home. The government of the Central African Federation (q.v.) banned his return there, but Kaunda reversed that after independence.

FRANKLIN, HARRY. Born in 1906, Franklin was Northern Rhodesia's (q.v.) chief information officer (*see* DEPARTMENT OF INFORMATION) from 1941 to 1951. During this time, he founded the Central African Broadcasting Service (q.v.) and fathered development of the "saucepan special" (q.v). When he retired in 1951, he founded Lusaka's (q.v.) nonracial Kabulonga Club and became a specially nominated member of the Legislative Council (q.v.) for education and social services. He was a political moderate but alienated many of the more militant Africans by encouraging Harry Nkumbula's (q.v.) accommodationist tendencies and by persuading him to call off the 1956 shop boycotts. In 1957 he helped form the multiracial Constitution Party (q.v.), which merged with the newly created Central Africa Party (q.v.) in 1959 to compete in the federation (q.v.) elections. Franklin and Sir John Moffat (q.v.) became two of the best CAP candidates in Northern Rhodesia (q.v.), winning two of the seats reserved for Europeans, but with overwhelming support from African voters. Franklin and Moffat also led the Northern Rhodesia wing of the CAP to an independent status as the Northern Rhodesia Liberal Party (q.v.) in 1960. When, after the London Constitutional Conference (q.v.) in February 1961, the United Federal Party (q.v.) resigned from the government, Franklin and two other Liberals took ministerial posts on the Executive Council (q.v.). He died in England in 1995.

FREE CHURCH OF SCOTLAND. This was one of the numerous Central African churches inspired by the work of Dr. David

Livingstone (q.v.). Much of its work was centered in the present-day Malawi (q.v.), notably the Livingstonia Mission (q.v.), which set up stations in Northern Zambia. One was opened at Chirenji (q.v.) in 1882–83; although it was closed in 1888, a new station was opened at Mwenzo (q.v.) in 1894–95. Among the Africans influenced by missionaries from the Scottish Church was the father of Zambia's first president, David Kaunda (q.v.), himself a Livingstonia evangelist. In 1924 its Central African program was renamed the Church of Central Africa, Presbyterian (q.v.). It later became part of the United Church of Zambia (q.v.).

FWAMBO. This is the name of both a town in extreme northeastern Zambia and an important Mambwe (q.v.) chief in the same area. As a location, it became the site of an 1887 mission station of the London Missionary Society (q.v.). By the mid-1880s Chief Fwambo was the most powerful of the Mambwe chiefs. His people were part of the Mambwe living near the Tanganyika border, and were famous for mining, smelting, and exporting iron. Fwambo was one of the few chiefs to successfully fight off the Bemba (q.v.) before the arrival of the British, and he defeated Bemba chief Ponde's (q.v.) forces as late as the mid-1890s. He also was reluctant to welcome British administrators, notably Hugh Marshall (q.v.), the first British South African Company collector (qq.v.) in Tanganyika District (q.v.).

G

GAMITTO, ANTÓNIO. An officer in the Portuguese army, he was stationed in Mozambique (q.v.) in 1830 when a caravan of ivory (q.v.) came from the Lunda chief Kazembe (qq.v.) to the post at Tete. Captain Gamitto and Major José Monteiro (q.v.) were appointed leaders of an expedition to Kazembe's capital along the Luapula River (q.v.). The trip began in 1831 and cut in a northwest direction through eastern Zambia, notably through Bisa and Bemba (qq.v.) territory, before reaching Kazembe. Gamitto's journal tells of the growing power of the Bemba throughout the region, especially through military conquest, and also documents the elegance of Kazembe and his capital. The mission was frustrated in its attempt to establish trade with the Lunda (q.v.), however, as the Arabs (q.v.) were firmly in control of it. After threats on their lives, the two leaders returned their expedition in 1832 to Tete, where Gamitto's negative report long discouraged further Portuguese attempts to establish this trade.

GAUNT, JOHN. A prominent political figure in Northern Rhodesia (q.v.), especially during the federation (q.v.) era, he was born in England in 1905 and went to Africa in 1925. He farmed in Northern Rhodesia briefly before entering the colonial service (q.v.). In 1937 he became a district commissioner (q.v.), serving in Mkushi, Lusaka, Mankoya, and Livingstone (qq.v.). From 1950 to 1953 he was director of african affairs in Lusaka. In 1953 he formed the segregationist Confederate Party (q.v.), and eventually merged its remnants into the new Dominion Party in 1956. He united this with groups in Southern Rhodesia and called it the Federal Dominion Party (q.v.). Winston Field (q.v.) was its head and Gaunt was the deputy leader. Gaunt was elected to the Northern Rhodesia Legislative Council in 1954 as an independent. In 1957 he was expelled from the Dominion Party but was elected to a Lusaka seat in the federal legislature in 1958. In 1960 he founded the Rhodesia Reform Party (q.v.). When Winston Field was elected prime minister in 1962 with his Rhodesian Front (q.v.), he chose Gaunt to be his minister of mines. Considered to be an extremist even by some right-wing friends, Gaunt was antagonistic toward African nationalists, comparing people like Julius Nyerere and Dr. H. K. Banda (qq.v.) to Adolf Hitler. He claimed to favor the "best" leadership, regardless of race, but clearly expected little quality to emerge in Africans. At one point, he favored partitioning Northern Rhodesia into African and European sections, with the Copperbelt and the line of rail (qq.v.) becoming European.

GENERAL MISSIONARY CONFERENCE OF NORTHERN RHODESIA. An attempt at some degree of unity and cooperation among the various mission churches in Zambia, it first met in 1914. It continued to meet regularly until it was replaced by the Christian Council (q.v.) in 1944. Though the Roman Catholics (q.v.) long maintained an associate membership, it was basically a Protestant association.

GERMAN EAST AFRICA. The name belonged to Zambia's northeastern neighbor until the end of World War I, when the British renamed it Tanganyika. After union with Zanzibar in 1964, it became Tanzania (q.v.).

GIBBONS, A. ST. HILL. One of the early explorers of the western part of Zambia, he first visited and mapped out part of the Lozi (q.v.) kingdom in 1895–96. He hoped to determine for European prospectors and settlers whether the area could have much value for them. He returned with a British military intelligence expedition in 1898, sponsored by the British South Africa Company (q.v.) and the Royal Geographical Society, among others. Its goals included making an ethnographic survey of all the Lozi territory, judging the area's economic potential, and determining the exact limits of the kingdom of the Lozi.

GIELGUD, VALDIMAR (VAL). A British South Africa Company (q.v.) official in Southern Rhodesia (q.v.), he and A. C. Anderson were sent to Lenje chief Chipepo's territory in the Kafue Hook (q.v.) in 1900 to report upon local conditions and to provide security to the Northern Copper Company's (q.v.) employees in the region. From his station at Muyanga, he used his 20 Ndebele (q.v.) Native Police to harass the Mambari slave traders (qq.v.) and to impress hostile Ila, Lenje, and Soli (qq.v.) villages with European power and prestige. Though callously tolerant of white miners' and traders' abuses against Africans, his and George Grey's (q.v.) complaints about the slave traders brought Colonel Harding (q.v.) and his Barotse Native Police (q.v.) to patrol the western side of the Kafue River (q.v.) in 1900–01. By the time of the first hut tax (q.v.) collections in 1901–02, he had opened a station at Mwomboshi and there urged African men to seek their tax monies in Bulawayo. He soon thereafter became an agent for the Rhodesian Native Labour Bureau (q.v.).

GIRAUD, VICTOR. This French naval lieutenant and explorer, as part of an unsuccessful attempt to find the rumored gold of Katanga (q.v.), took a small expedition through Bemba (q.v.) territory and the area around Lake Bangweulu (q.v.) in 1883–84. He was attacked and, until his escape into modern Tanzania (q.v.), was held for two months by Lunda chief Kazembe q(q.v.). He visited Chitimukulu Chitapankwa (qq.v.), who reportedly gave him a "splendid reception." When the Chitimukulu died shortly after Giraud's departure, Giraud was suspected of causing the death.

GLENNIE, A. F. B. Provincial commissioner and, later, resident commissioner of Barotseland (q.v.) for 11 years, from the mid-1940s to the mid-1950s, this tough and sober-minded administrator oversaw (and demanded) major reforms in the traditional Barotse government. He especially demanded reform of the Barotse National Council (q.v.) and the reinstatement of another council, the Katengo *kuta* (q.v.). His efforts to modernize the councils by adding younger and better educated Lozi (q.v.) only alienated both traditionalists and the modernizing elements.

GONDWE, A. H. A member of the Central Africa Party (q.v.) he was elected to the Legislative Council (q.v.) in the 1959 elections, the only African among the three CAP members elected. In February 1961, he and the other two (Harry Franklin and John Moffat, qq.v.) received ministerial posts on the Executive Council when the United Federal Party (q.v.) withdrew from the government. He ran again in the 1962 elections and, though defeated, he received more votes than any others in his party—which had been renamed the Northern Rhodesia Liberal Party (q.v.) in 1960.

GONDWE, JEREMIAH. The work of this famous prophet (leader) of the Watch Tower Movement (q.v.) was centered in modern Copperbelt Province (q.v.). Born in the 1890s, this Tumbuka from Isoka (qq.v.) District worked as a domestic servant in Salisbury (q.v.) and returned home just as the Watch Tower teachings of Elliot Kamwana (q.v.) were most popular. He was impressed as a porter during World War I and then, as a Robert Williams and Co. (q.v.) recruit, worked in Katanga (q.v.) before moving on to Zambia's mining towns. In 1923 he was baptized by one of Kamwana's disciples in Broken Hill (q.v.) and was jailed three months for preaching without a license. He moved to the rural Copperbelt (q.v.) in 1924 and spent most of the next five years evading arrest, preaching noncooperation with the government and its chiefly "puppets," and offering baptism as a cure for witches and their witchcraft. He and his disciples also preached among the Lamba and Lala (qq.v.) in Katanga, much to the Belgians' alarm (*see* MWANA LESA). Considered a martyr by his followers, Gondwe was arrested and convicted of sedition in 1929. After a year in a Livingstone (q.v.) jail and another two in Isoka, he was allowed back to the Copperbelt and, in 1941, was given rights to his own village near Ibenga (St. Theresa's Mission). His followers, the *bena* Gondwe (Gondwe's people), live off their substantial cassava (q.v.) gardens and by trading grain to townspeople. Hundreds of Luba (q.v.), religious refugees from Mobutu's Zaire, joined Gondwe Village in 1964, and ever since then the neighboring Lamba and Lima (q.v.) villagers have been keen to make the distinction between proper Jehovah's Witnesses (q.v.) (*bamboni*, "witnesses") and *bena* Gondwe, who have long been accused of practicing sexual communism. Gondwe died and was buried in his village in 1974; he is said to have risen from the grave three days later and to be currently driving a cab in New York City, near the Jehovah's Witnesses' Brooklyn headquarters.

GOODE, RICHARD ALLMOND JEFFREY. Acting administrator of Northern Rhodesia (q.v.) for the British South Africa Company (q.v.) from March 1922 until May 1923, he returned as acting administrator from September 1923 until the British Colonial Office (q.v.) took over in February 1924.

GOOLD-ADAMS, H. A British Colonial Office (q.v.) official in Bechuanaland, he was sent to Barotseland (q.v.) in 1896 to clarify the boundaries of the domain of the Lozi king Lewanika (qq.v.). The major arrived at the capital, Lealui (q.v.), in October, but the intervention of missionary Adolphe Jalla (q.v.) was necessary to convince Lewanika that the major was a representative of Queen Victoria. It was the British hope that Goold-Adams could provide facts to allow a settlement with the Portuguese over the Barotseland-Angola border. Since later expeditions contradicted his report, however, it eventually took international arbitration to settle the matter.

GORE-BROWNE, SIR STEWART. Born in Great Britain, he was one of the most important of the settler-politicians and certainly the one closest to the Africans and their nationalist cause. He first came to Northern Rhodesia (q.v.) in 1911 as an officer with a joint Anglo-Belgian commission seeking to set the Congo-Northern Rhodesia border. He returned in 1921 and set up a farming estate in an isolated part of Bemba (q.v.) country (in northern Zambia). There he built his Shiwa Ng'andu, a virtual baronial fortress, for a home. In 1935 he was elected to the Legislative Council (q.v.) and quickly demonstrated an empathy with the rural African. He opposed racial segregation and favored cooperation between the races in running the country. In 1938 he was picked to represent African interests on the council. In this capacity, he played an important role in introducing urban courts and African Advisory Councils (q.v.) on the Copperbelt (q.v.). A speaker of *ci*Bemba (q.v.), he traveled extensively to discuss problems with the Africans.

He especially made the point that Europeans should listen to educated Africans, not just the chiefs. He frequently spoke to African welfare associations (q.v.) and encouraged the growth of nationalist groups. He came into conflict with the nationalists, however, when he proposed in 1948 that Northern Rhodesia could be partitioned into an African-controlled area and a European-controlled area. He consistently favored African self-rule and thus angered many Europeans, who favored amalgamation with Southern Rhodesia (qq.v.); yet he alienated African nationalists when he advocated self-rule for Africans in Northern Rhodesia but within a Central African Federation (q.v.). He fought hard for federation (q.v.), which he saw as a healthy compromise that would help both Africans and Europeans. Early in 1961, Gore-Browne officially joined the United National Independence Party (q.v.). In April 1962 he accompanied Kenneth Kaunda (q.v.) to give testimony in New York before the UN Commission on Colonialism. In the October 1962 elections he ran on the UNIP ticket for a seat in the Legislative Council, but he failed to get elected despite heavy support from Africans. Kaunda ordered a state funeral after Gore-Browne's death on August 4, 1967. His baronial estate, Shiwa Ng'andu, then became the home of Simon Kapwepwe (q.v.).

GOVERNOR OF NORTHERN RHODESIA. This office was created on February 20, 1924, before Northern Rhodesia (q.v.) became a protectorate (on April 1) under the jurisdiction of the British Colonial Office (q.v.). Executive power was vested in the governor, Sir Herbert Stanley (q.v.), who was appointed by the crown on the advice of the British government. He was directly responsible to the government in London for all matters concerning the government of the territory. He was assisted by an Executive Council (q.v.) of five senior civil servants. If he chose to reject their advice, which he seldom did, he was required to explain his reasons to the secretary of state for the colonies. As election to the Legislative Council (q.v.) became the norm and the unofficials came to dominate the Executive Council, the governor was expected to consult the majority party in the Legislative Council before appointing the Executive Council. All subordinate administrators and provincial commissioners were also responsible to the governor. During the period of peak nationalist activity, notably while Sir Arthur Benson (q.v.) was governor, the use of emergency powers and other formidable powers by the governors brought the latter into considerable conflict with emerging African leaders.

GREAT EAST ROAD. One of the two major tarred roads in Zambia, it starts at Lusaka (q.v.) and travels east for 805 kilometers (500 miles) to Chipata (q.v.) and the Malawian town of Salima. The considerable amount of commercial traffic traveling this road proceeds from Salima, a railhead, to the port of Beira, Mozambique (qq.v.), by means of the railway. This route became important for Zambia after the closing of traffic through Rhodesia (Zimbabwe), and Zambia is only now beginning its 24-kilometer rail link from Chipata to the Salima line at Mchinji.

GREAT NORTH ROAD. One of the oldest and most important routes in Central Africa (q.v.), it carries traffic from near Victoria Falls (q.v.) to its northeastern corner. Cecil Rhodes' (q.v.) dream of a Cape-to-Cairo railway would have followed much of this route. This 2,415-kilometer (1,500-mile) tarmac road goes north from Livingstone to Lusaka and on to Kapiri Mposhi (qq.v.), near the southern edge of the Copperbelt (q.v.). From there it angles northeast to the border, crossing near Tunduma, Tanzania (q.v.). It then heads east to the port at Dar es Salaam. It became a crucial commercial link with the world, especially when the Rhodesian border was closed in 1973. The TAZAMA oil pipeline (1968) and TAZARA (qq.v.) railway (1975) routes parallel this road. Since it remained a gravel road until 1971 and was particularly treacherous during the November to April rainy season, truck drivers who drove this road tagged it "Hell Run." This road is again in bad shape, and 1994 reports claimed that youths in Northern Province (q.v.) were enlarging the existing potholes to slow down the trucks and pilfer them.

GREY, GEORGE. The younger brother of Viscount Grey, the secretary of state for foreign affairs, Grey came to Southern Rhodesia (q.v.) in 1891 to take charge of a Northumbrian prospecting and mining concern. He fought in the Ndebele (q.v.) war of 1893, then formed and led Grey's Scouts during the Shona and Ndebele uprising in 1896–97. Employed by Robert Williams' Tanganyika Concessions, Ltd. (qq.v.), he led the 1899 Congo Border prospecting expedition which founded the Copperbelt (q.v.) mining industry by claiming the ancient copper (q.v.) workings at Kansanshi, Chambishi, and Nkana (qq.v.) on the south side of the border, and the Lufira gold pans and Kipushi copper workings near Kambove. Accordingly, the newly chartered Comité Spécial du Katanga granted TANKS five years' exclusive prospecting and mining rights in southern Katanga (q.v.), as well as a share of all future stocks and profits.

Grey's second and far larger 1901–02 expedition, based at Kansanshi (q.v.), located another 40 Katangan copper deposits, established a network of labor recruitment and grain buying camps, and cut a 563-kilometer (350-mile) ox-wagon road from the Kafue Hook (q.v.) to Kansanshi Mine. Grey's men often encountered Mambari (q.v.) slave traders (q.v.) during their operations, and his complaints brought up Colonel Colin Harding's Barotse Native Police (qq.v.) to patrol the region and end the slave caravans to Angola (q.v.). Meanwhile, Grey's successes in Katanga determined the ultimate terminus of the future railway from Bulawayo.

Grey was famous for his epic, solo bicycle rides. Once, to inform TANKS of his 1899 prospecting success, he rode the 1,385 kilometers (860 miles) to the Bulawayo telegraph in under a week, armed with just a jar of beef spread, some chocolate bars, and his razors. He was the sole manager of Katangan mining operations from 1901 to 1906, when the Union Minière du Haut Katanga (q.v.) took over. When Robert T. Coryndon (q.v.) left North-Eastern Rhodesia (q.v.) to become Resident Commissioner of Swaziland, Grey became his Special Commissioner and, from 1907–10, arranged the fairest possible land apportionment for the Swazi. In 1911, this remarkably modest and able man went hunting in Kenya and, at age 41, was fatally mauled by a wounded lion.

GRIFFITHS, JAMES. The British Labour Party minister who headed the British Colonial Office (q.v.) from March 1950 until October 1951, he replaced Arthur Creech Jones as colonial secretary. Griffiths agreed to the convening of a conference in London in March 1951 (*see* LONDON CONFERENCE, 1951) to discuss Central Africa (q.v.). This conference produced a recommendation for a federal constitution. Griffiths then toured Central Africa and continued to encourage unity, despite finding considerable African opposition. It was he who introduced the soon widely used word "partnership" (q.v.), which he also defined. His party lost its majority, and he his post, soon after. As an opposition member of Parliament (q.v.), however, he served as spokesman for the cause of adequate African influence in the federation. He feared they would be at the mercy of the settlers.

GROUNDNUTS. The British English term for peanuts, this American crop is commonly grown in northern and eastern

Zambia. Apparently brought in by the Portuguese, they were being grown by the Bisa (q.v.) before the end of the 18th century and were fairly common among the Bemba (q.v.) by the mid-19th. Groundnuts are eaten as a roasted and salted snack food but, after pounding, also serve as the basis of a creamy sauce for greens or other vegetables.

GUJARAT PROVINCE. This province in western India is the original home of the families of almost all the Indians in Zambia.

GWEMBE TONGA. One of the subdivisions of the broader ethnic group called the Tonga (q.v.), they live in the Gwembe valley (q.v.). Around 1908 they caused considerable difficulty for the British South Africa Company (q.v.) by vigorously protesting and resisting the imposition of taxes. Problems arose again in the late 1950s. The Kariba dam (q.v.) had been built, and the waters of Lake Kariba (q.v.) were rising and flooding their homeland. About 29,000 people were resettled, 6,000 being moved 161 kilometers (100 miles) away to Lusitu. Again, major resistance occurred, especially among those bound for Lusitu, and in a clash with police on September 10, 1958, eight people were killed and 34 were wounded. The government trained many Gwembe Tonga as fishermen to use Lake Kariba as the source of a fishing industry.

GWEMBE VALLEY. Now partly inundated by the vast, man-made Lake Kariba (q.v.), it was the traditional home of the Gwembe Tonga (q.v.). Located about 100 kilometers (60 miles) east of Victoria Falls (q.v.), the Zambezi River (q.v.) flowed peacefully through this hot and inhospitable, flat-bottomed valley. It was the home of enormous herds of elephants, which the Tonga hunted for their tusks. This created a major industry with Asian traders on the east coast of Africa as early as the second century A.D. The tusks were traded for numerous imports, including glass beads, seashells, and porcelain items.

GWISHO HOT SPRINGS. Located on the southern banks of the Kafue River (q.v.) flats in Lochinvar National Park, west of Mazabuka (qq.v.), the low, waterlogged mounds provide a remarkably complete picture of hunter-gatherer life in Late Stone Age southern Zambia. The 2.4 meters (eight feet) of occupational floors in these mounds were periodically inhabited from 3000 to 1500 B.C. The sites include traces of a stick and grass shelter, hearths, and grass bedding, along with microlithic flake and blade stone tools, a wooden digging stick, and grinding stones for processing seeds or nuts. A bowstave fragment and the pods of a poisonous shrub imply the use of poisoned arrows in hunting game. There are 10,000 plant remains, mostly those of edible fruits and nuts, and bones of grassland grazing animals, like antelope species and zebra. There are also hippo, rhino, and elephant bones. Except for the obvious environmental differences, the Gwisho peoples lived much like the Kung San of the Kalahari Desert, and the skeletal remains recovered from Gwisho's 35 shallow graves are of slight, San-like people, some of whom were decorated with shell beads.

H

HAMMERSKJØLD, DAG. He was secretary-general of the United Nations from April 1953 until his death on September 18, 1961. His plane crashed just west of Ndola (q.v.) while he was on a mediation visit to the Congo (q.v.).

HARDING, COLIN. The later author of several memoirs, Harding was a major in the British South Africa Company (q.v.) police when he came to North-Western Rhodesia (q.v.) in 1898 to become acting resident of Barotseland (q.v.) (1898–99), then acting administrator of North-Western Rhodesia (q.v.) (1900–1901), and to command the newly formed Barotse Native Police (q.v.). The police patrols, with George Grey's and Val Gielgud's (qq.v.) support, stanched the flow of slaves to the Angolan coast in 1900–1901. Harding became disenchanted with the BSAC's duplicitous dealings with the Lozi (q.v.) and resigned his positions in 1906, in protest of forced labor recruitment (*see* CHIBALO) and the use of hut burnings during hut tax (q.v.) collections.

HARRINGTON, HUBERT TYLER (CHIANA). A late 19th-century collector (q.v.) for the British South Africa Company (q.v.) in Luapula-Mweru District, Chiana Harrington opened or occupied stations at Abercorn, Mporokoso, Kalungwishi, Fort Rosebery (Mansa), and Feira (qq.v.). In April 1899, he was called upon by Andrew Law, the Abercorn collector, to support his attack on the Arab (q.v.) slave traders (q.v.) operating out of Mporokoso's (q.v.) stockade. Harrington brought nearly 100 armed men, and the Arabs were defeated after a day-long battle. Mporokoso's defeat marked the last attempt by the Bemba (q.v.) to resist the establishment of European rule in Northern Province (q.v.). Many of his people fled into the Belgian Congo in 1901, when Harrington instituted road work during the first hut tax (q.v.) collections in Fort Rosebery District. And in 1906, he recorded the flow of labor migrants from the Luapula region to the mines of Southern Rhodesia (qq.v.).

HARRISON CLARK, JOHN (CHANGA CHANGA). Born in Natal about 1860 and raised at the Cape, Clark is supposed to have fled some difficulty with the police when he crossed the Zambezi near the ruins of Feira (q.v.) in 1887. There, he raised his own private army among the Nsenga (q.v.), married a Chikunda (q.v.) chief's daughter, and became the self-appointed chief over the region between the lower Luangwa valley and the Kafue Hook (qq.v.). His African nickname supposedly refers to his preference for traveling by *machilla*, which is to say, carried by porters in a pole-slung hammock.

Several years before the first British South Africa Company collectors (qq.v.) arrived from Fort Jameson (q.v.), Harrison Clark stanched the flow of slaves to the east coast by collecting his own license fees and export taxes from the Portuguese ivory (q.v.) and cattle traders from modern Mozambique (q.v.). Between 1895 and 1899 he collected scores of concessionary treaties from African chiefs and headmen, which, along with his labor recruiting services, he tried to parlay into an official BSAC appointment. His offers, though, were declined, as the BSAC already claimed this region under the terms of the 1889–90 Ware and Lochner Concessions (qq.v). The BSAC did grant him rights to Fort Algoa, his 1896 headquarters on the Lukusashi-Lunsemfwa River confluence, and to two successive farms in Mkushi District; but it also charged him several times for running an unauthorized African court. At the end of World War I, Harrison Clark moved to Broken Hill (q.v.) (modern Kabwe, q.v.), where he achieved some prosperity by building and managing the town's first African beer hall (*see* BEER HALL SYSTEM). Like Chirupula Stephenson (q.v.), he questioned the legitimacy of the Lochner Concession and the BSAC's claims to the Copperbelt (q.v.). The year before his death, in his testimony to the 1926 Reserves Commission (q.v.), he denied that Lozi king Lewanika (qq.v.) ever had any authority over the central Zambian peoples north of Lusaka (q.v.). After his death, his friends erected a public drinking fountain in his memory.

HATCH SYSTEM. Until the mid-1950s, Africans were not permitted to enter the main doors of first class (i.e., European) trading district shops, but instead were handed their purchases through hatches at the side or back of the buildings. It was an unwritten law but was seldom violated. As African nationalist consciousness rose, the hatch system became the focus of increasing agitation, especially around 1950 when boycotts of businesses engaged in this practice took place in many cities (beginning in Broken Hill, q.v.). In 1954 the Northern Rhodesian Congress picketed stores in Lusaka (q.v.), notably butcheries, which reserved the poorest cuts of meat for Africans. Success in Lusaka resulted in protests in other cities, many of them also successful. Further boycotts in April 1956 in Lusaka (and later elsewhere) seemed to put an end to the hatch system, especially in major cities. The first step in dismantling the colour bar (q.v.) had been taken.

HEMANS, JAMES. A controversial teacher and agricultural missionary with the London Missionary Society (q.v.), he and his wife, Maria, served at Niamkolo Mission near Lake Tanganyika (qq.v.) from 1888 to 1906, when, because of his ostracism by other LMS missionaries, he was retired. This dark-skinned Jamaican was treated shabbily by his color-conscious British colleagues, who were jealous of his friendship with Bemba chief Ponde (qq.v.), and who objected to his tolerance for "immoral" African customs. Hemans felt that his superiors failed to take advantage of his pigmentation, for Ponde had little trust in the lighter-skinned missionaries. Hemans died in Jamaica in 1908.

HIGH COURT. An Order in Council of 1911 (q.v.) replaced both the High Courts (q.v.) of North-Eastern Rhodesia (est. 1900) and North-Western Rhodesia (est. 1906) (qq.v.) with the High Court of Northern Rhodesia (q.v.). English Common Law (q.v.) was enforced except where modified or changed by an order in council. Native laws and custom could be considered when cases involved Africans and when the justices saw fit. Treason and murder cases and the like were reserved for trial by the High Court. Since independence, the High Court has retained most of its authority. It is presided over by the chief justice. Constitutional provisions maintained the independence of the judiciary, despite the controversy in 1969 involving Justice Ifor Evans (q.v.).

HILTON YOUNG COMMISSION. This commission, chaired by Sir Edward Hilton Young, was sent by the British government in 1928 to investigate the possibility of closer association of the

Central African countries with each other, or even with the East African territories. Its members included Sir Reginald Mant, Sir George Schuster, and Dr. Joseph Oldham. The testimony they took in Nyasaland and Northern Rhodesia (qq.v.) was mainly from the settlers, most of whom favored closer ties with Southern Africa, not with East Africa. Few Africans were heard. Yet its wide-ranging report stressed concern that African interests be safeguarded and not subjugated to those of the European settlers and Southern Africa. It was even proposed that some form of union between Nyasaland and Northern Rhodesia might be attempted, possibly even linking the two with East Africa.

HOLLAND, MICHAEL J. A manager with Robert Williams' Tanganyika Concessions, Ltd. (qq.v.), Holland led the 1900 expedition through Nyasaland (q.v.) that transported, reassembled, and launched the steamship *Cecil Rhodes* on Lake Tanganyika (q.v.). In May 1900 he accompanied Christian Purefoy Chesnaye, the British South Africa Company's (q.v.) secretary for North-Eastern Rhodesia (q.v.), from Fort Jameson and across the Katanga Pedicle (qq.v.) to establish contact with Chiwala's Swahili (qq.v.), near modern Ndola (q.v.), and to arrest Adolphe Bolle and William Ziehl, two unscrupulous Luapula (q.v.) traders who had relocated there. Robert Williams anticipated that the ongoing Boer War might delay George Grey's (q.v.) second Congo (q.v.) border prospecting expedition, so he sent J. R. Farrell, an American mining engineer, to Holland, with instructions to mount a supporting prospecting expedition from Abercorn (q.v.) to Kambove. Holland's party located a dozen Katangan copper (q.v.) deposits before finally joining Grey at Kansanshi (q.v.).

HOLUB, EMIL. Born in Bohemia in the Austro-Hungarian empire in 1847, the young surgeon went to the Kimberly mines to practice in 1872. He visited Victoria Falls (q.v.) in 1875, and from 1883 to 1887 he, his wife Rosa, and a small party of Europeans traveled through South Central Africa (recorded in a two-volume book). It is said that they crossed the Zambezi (q.v.) in June 1886 with the goal of reaching Cairo on a Cape-to-Cairo route. They spent a month or so at Sesheke (q.v.) with the Reverend Coillard (q.v.) in Lozi country, where malaria and other problems cost them both human lives and cattle. With the permission of Lozi king Lewanika (qq.v.) and the help of Toka porters (q.v.), they became the first Europeans to reach the land of the Ila (Mashukulumbwe) (q.v.). They were attacked several times while in the Kafue Hook (q.v.): they lost all their valuables, Oswald Sollner was killed, and they had to fight their way south. Three of the Ila also lost their lives in the raid. After crossing the Kafue, they eventually reached comparative safety across the Zambezi on August 22, 1886. The Reverend Coillard sent them some aid. Holub died in 1902.

HOMO RHODESIENSIS. Rhodesian Man was one of the early names for Broken Hill or Kabwe Man (qq.v.).

HONE, SIR EVELYN DENNISON. Born in Salisbury, Southern Rhodesia (qq.v.), December 13, 1911, he became a Rhodes Scholar and received his B.A. degree from Oxford University. He entered the colonial service in 1935 in Tanganyika and also served in the Seychelles, Palestine, British Honduras, and Aden. He was chief secretary to the governor of Northern Rhodesia (q.v.) from 1957 to 1959, a time when the Zambia African National Congress (q.v.) boycott made it difficult to register Africans to vote. He became governor in 1959 and he quickly began talks with African nationalists. He developed an excellent relationship with Kenneth Kaunda (q.v.) and continued as governor until October 1964. He returned to England and served in a variety of advisory posts, including deputy chairman of the Commonwealth Institute in 1971. (*See* EVELYN HONE COLLEGE.)

HOPKINSON, HENRY (LORD COLYTON). He was Conservative Party colonial secretary (minister of state for colonial affairs) in the early 1950s. He toured Central Africa (q.v.) in 1952 to test African reaction to the impending federation (q.v.). His statements infuriated Africans, as he blamed extremists for the negative responses he received. He also said that 90 percent of Africans knew nothing about federation. He addressed 78 formal meetings with Africans, in each of which he encouraged acceptance of federation. His great error was his inability to recognize the legitimacy of the widespread African rejection of the plan. He also told the House of Commons that it could safely entrust the care and political advancement of the Africans to the settlers.

HUDSON, ROWLAND SKEFFINGTON. Secretary for native affairs in Northern Rhodesia (q.v.) from 1945 to 1949, when he was succeeded by Ronald Bush (q.v.), Hudson was somewhat sympathetic to the African founders of the Northern Rhodesia African Congress (q.v.). He even gave the opening speech at the September 1948 meeting of the Federation of Welfare Societies (*see* FEDERATION OF AFRICAN SOCIETIES OF NORTHERN RHODESIA); it was at this conference that the group shortened its name. Eleven years earlier, however, in a lower administrative capacity, Hudson had opposed such an organization because it could interfere with the work of the chiefs. Hudson began his administrative career in Barotseland (q.v.) and later served in the Lusaka (q.v.) secretariat. During the early 1940s he was labor commissioner and endeavored to introduce the concept of collective bargaining for Africans into the mines, at least at the level of "boss boys." He opposed unionization of the mass of African workers, feeling that they were "not ready." As secretary for native affairs, he recognized the potential leadership of the more advanced Africans, but he opposed their formation of political parties which, he said "would be fatal." In a speech before the African Representative Council (q.v.) in 1948, he suggested that Northern Rhodesia should be based on a "partnership" (q.v.) between Africans and Europeans. The word was later used frequently in regard to federation but had really been introduced in 1935 by Sir Stewart Gore-Browne (q.v.).

HUGGINS, GODFREY MARTIN (LORD MALVERN). A Southern Rhodesian politician, Huggins was the principal moving figure behind the creation of the Central African Federation (q.v.) and its first prime minister. Born in England in 1883, he was educated as a doctor, then emigrated to Southern Rhodesia (q.v.) in 1911. After returning from World War I, he entered politics, taking his first seat in the Southern Rhodesian Parliament in 1924. As leader of the Reform Party he became the prime minister in 1933 on a segregationist platform. He rejected apartheid and merger with South Africa, favoring partnership between the settlers and the more "advanced" Africans, both eventually sitting in the same Parliament (q.v.). Firmly convinced that federation (q.v.) would solve Central Africa's (q.v.) race problems, he urged England to accept the plan. When the federation began, he resigned as prime minister of Southern Rhodesia (a post he held for 20 years) and became federal prime minister and minister of defense. In 1955 he was named Lord Malvern, and he resigned as prime minister on October 3, 1956.

HUMANISM. *See* ZAMBIAN HUMANISM.

HUMAN RIGHTS ASSOCIATION OF ZAMBIA. This society was formed in 1991 to prevent the human rights abuses associated with Zambia's former one-party state. The association's purpose is to work in accordance with the United Nations Bill for Human Rights, to cooperate with the international community on issues of personal rights, and to educate the Zambian public about, and foster awareness of, human rights issues.

HUT TAX. First imposed in North-Eastern Rhodesia (q.v.) in 1901, the hut tax required every adult African man to pay three shillings per year for each hut he claimed, up to a maximum of six, thus penalizing polygynists and those supporting elderly relatives. It was payable in cash or, until 1905, in rubber, produce, or (forced) labor services. It was extended to North-Western Rhodesia (q.v.) in 1904 and by 1913 was being collected throughout the territory. Early administrators were known as collectors (q.v.). Since hut tax revenues paid only a fraction of administrative expenses, the real purpose of the tax was to encourage African men to seek work on the mines or white farms. Many administrators used the tax deliberately to provide cheap labor to Southern Rhodesia (q.v.) (*see* CHIBALO; RHODESIAN NATIVE LABOUR BUREAU). Imprisonment was the penalty for nonpayment. Some of the administrators, like Colonel Harding and Chirupula Stephenson (qq.v.), criticized the tax as being unfair and destructive. In the 1930s, the hut tax was supplemented by the poll tax (q.v.), which was levied upon every able-bodied male of 18 years and above. The hut tax was dropped in the late 1940s.

I

IKAWA. The site of one of the first trading posts established by the British South Africa Company (q.v.) in Northern Province (q.v.), it became the location of the *boma* of the collector (q.v.) of Chambeshi District (q.v.). Located in the northeastern corner of the country, near Fife (q.v.), the post was opened by Major Patrick William Forbes (q.v.) in 1895; collector John Bell (q.v.) was its major administrator.

IKELENGE. He was one of the traditional leaders appointed to attend the Federal Review Conference (q.v.) in London in December 1960. When the three nationalist leaders of Central Africa (Kaunda, Nkomo, and Banda, qq.v.) walked out of the meeting, Ikelenge and the other traditional leaders followed.

ILA (MASHUKULUMBWE). One of the better-known peoples of Zambia, the Ila may have come to south central Zambia from east of Lake Tanganyika (q.v.), not unlike their closely related neighbors, the Tonga (q.v.), with whom they share the awkward combination of matrilineal descent and patrilocal residence. There were some 61,200 Ila-speaking Zambians in 1986. Most important, the Ila and Tonga are among the few Zambian peoples with no tradition of formal chiefships. Together with the Lenje (q.v.) and Tonga, the Ila are part of the so-called Bantu Botatwe ("three people") group (q.v.). The Ila homeland (called Bwila) is not large and consists of the Kafue Hook (q.v.). The authoritative anthropological study of the Ila is the two-volume book by Edwin Smith and Andrew Dale, a missionary and a colonial officer. But one of the first Europeans to mention them was Dr. David Livingstone (q.v.), who referred to them as the "Bashukulompo," his transliteration of the Lozi and Kololo's "Mashukulumbwe" (q.v.). This name presumably derives from Lozi words that refer to the *isusu*, the vertical horn of hair once worn by Ila men. Dr. Livingstone and other Europeans seemed to avoid Ila territory, as they had a reputation as fierce warriors. Around 1860, the Kololo (q.v.) conquered much of southern Zambia, until they were beaten back by the Ila. In 1882, however, the Lozi, under their great leader Lewanika (q.v.), staged a very successful raid on the Ila, winning many thousands of cattle. A similar Lozi raid, their last against the Ila, was successful in 1888. At that point, the Ila went to Lewanika to offer tribute. Though the British South African Company (q.v.) later endorsed Lewanika's fanciful claims to the Kafue Hook and the entire Copperbelt (q.v.), these were denounced as fictions by John Harrison Clark and John E. Stephenson (qq.v.).

ILA-TONGA PEOPLES. A general term of more linguistic than ethnic validity, it refers to the large group of people, the Bantu Botatwe (q.v.) of southern central Zambia, who speak similar languages and have some common traditions. The Ila (q.v.) and the Tonga (q.v.) are separate groups; one thing that bound them together was the Lozi (q.v.) invasion in the 19th century, whereby they came under similar influences. Once under European dominance, both groups responded to the introduction of cash-crop farming.

ILENDELA. He was an Inamwanga (q.v.) headman in the 1890s whose village near the northeastern corner of Northern Rhodesia (q.v.) was the site of the first popular display of resentment of forced labor. His village was near Ikawa *boma* (q.v.), where John Bell (q.v.) was administrator. When Bell sent his police to collect laborers to work on the new *boma*, Ilendela refused and his people fired guns and arrows at the police. The police in turn drove off the villagers' goats and sheep to Ikawa (q.v.). Bell went to the stockaded village to investigate the incident, and Ilendela's people again opened fire. In the exchange of shots, a villager was killed. Bell then burnt down the village. A local missionary, the Reverend Alexander Dewar, wrote a critical letter to collector Bell, urging him to pay compensation. Bell was furious at the meddling of the missionary in administrative affairs.

ILUNGA. A personal name among the Lunda (q.v.), the people whose 18th-century trading empire extended across much of Central Africa (q.v.). According to one legend, a Luba (q.v.) hunter named Chibinda Ilunga married a Luba woman, Lueji, who had inherited a chieftainship. He took possession of the royal symbols of office and assumed the powers of chieftainship. Lueji's brothers, who had disputed her office, migrated to other areas. Soon after, the followers of Lueji and Ilunga called themselves Balunda ("Lunda people"). This may have been in the 17th century. In the late 18th century, Lunda chief Kazembe III (q.v.) was also named Ilunga. During his long reign the Lunda expanded their influence into Katanga (q.v.) and as far east as Malawi (q.v.). The Portuguese traveler, Dr. Lacerda (q.v.), tried to visit him in 1798. The elderly Ilunga refused to meet the traveler, seeing the Portuguese as potential competitors in the business of long-distance trade. Eventually, however, he did meet with Father Pinto (q.v.), who took over the expedition after Lacerda died. But Ilunga would not allow the expedition to continue through his territory to Mwata Yamvo (q.v.). Instead, he demanded the presents reserved for that great Lunda leader be given to himself instead.

IMASIKU, AKABESWA. He was the *ngambela* (q.v.) (prime minister) of the Barotse from 1956 to 1962 under the king, Mwanawina III (q.v.). The king had wanted to appoint him to this position in 1948. Imasiku was related to him through marriage, and he was also chief councilor at the Mankoya *kuta*. Commissioner Glennie (q.v.), however, opposed him, and Muheli Walubita (q.v.) was appointed instead. Under pressure from Mwanawina, Walubita resigned in 1956. When Imasiku was again nominated, a conflict occurred among Lozi (q.v.) leaders. Finally, an election was held, and with Mwanawina counting the votes, Imasiku was declared the winner. Although some charged fraud, Imasiku served as *ngambela* for six years.

IMWIKO. A son of Lozi king Lewanika (qq.v.), Imwiko was himself the king (Litunga) from 1945 to 1948. Upon his father's death in 1916, he was favored for the position by a number of *indunas* (q.v.). Imwiko had been educated in England, and many Lozi felt that he would stand up well to the administration. However, his half brother Litia (later King Yeta III, q.v.) was chosen king instead. When the very infirm and aged Yeta abdicated in 1945, he asked that Imwiko succeed him. Imwiko, now 60 years old, had been appointed chief of Sesheke (q.v.) in 1916 by Yeta and served there until 1945, when be became king. As king, however, Imwiko found that the colonial administration, represented by commissioner Glennie (q.v.), pressured him to make a number of changes in the traditional Barotse government. This attempt at modernization involved especially reforms of the *kuta* (q.v.) and a revival of the Katengo *kuta* (q.v.) with new personnel. While collaborating with the British on the establishment of a Development Center, Imwiko stated firmly that Barotseland (q.v.) would secede from Northern Rhodesia (q.v.) if amalgamation (q.v.) with Southern Rhodesia (q.v.) should occur. Imwiko died in June 1948, presumably of a stroke, although many suspected foul play. Many *indunas* were angry at him, and some felt that his brother and successor, Mwanawina III (q.v.), might have had him poisoned. Likewise some suspected Mwanawina in the mysterious 1959 murder of Imwiko's son, Akashambatwa Imwiko. United National Independence Party (q.v.) leaders used this incident to force the government to investigate the matter thoroughly, thus getting political gain out of opposition to Mwanawina.

INAMWANGA. Though one of Zambia's least numerous peoples, the Inamwanga are among a cluster of patrilineal, cattle-keeping peoples in northeastern Zambia, including the Mambwe and Lungu (qq.v.), who came in from East Africa. The Inamwanga are most closely related to the Iwa (q.v.), an

Inamwanga offshoot, to the Nyakyusa and Kinga peoples of southern Tanzania (q.v.), and to the Ngonde of Malawi (qq.v.). Their chiefs, however, appear to be more recent arrivals from the Luba-Lunda of the Democratic Republic of Congo (q.v.) (Zaire). The senior Inamwanga chief is Chikanamulilo (q.v.). At one point in 1877 he repelled a fierce Bemba (q.v.) attack, but he was defeated by a Bemba raid in 1879.

The Inamwanga, though primarily cattle-keeping cultivators, gained fame as iron smelters and smiths. Their location near the Bemba made them vulnerable to some of the more aggressive Bemba leaders, so they welcomed the arrival of the British South Africa Company's (q.v.) treaty-seeking officials: Mukoma signed with Harry Johnston (q.v.) in 1889 and Chikanamulilo with Alfred Sharpe (q.v.) in 1891. It did not take long for them to regret this, however, and in August 1896, at Ilendela village near Ikawa *boma* (qq.v.), the Inamwanga became the first of Northern Province's (q.v.) peoples to demonstrate against forced labor (*see* CHIBALO). The demonstration was put down by a BSAC official, John Bell (q.v.), who brought in police and finally burned down the village. It was no coincidence, then, that the Watch Tower Movement (q.v.) made its first Northern Rhodesian gains among the Inamwanga and the other northeastern peoples.

INDABA. This Southern Bantu word refers to a public assembly of chiefs and commoners, often called for a specific purpose. Colonial officials made it a practice to ask that *indaba*s be called so that they could talk to the Africans.

INDEPENDENCE CONSTITUTION. Written during final negotiations in London in May 1964, the constitution went into effect with independence on October 24, 1964. No elections were held in the interim, and the constitution specifically named Kenneth Kaunda (q.v.) as the first president of Zambia. It provided for a unitary republic with a strong executive president, modified by some elements of a parliamentary system. While the National Assembly was to be a unicameral legislature, a House of Chiefs with consultative influence (abolished around 1980) also was created. The High Court and the Court of Appeal (qq.v.) topped out the judicial structure, and English Common Law (q.v.) became the basis of jurisprudence. Regional provinces and districts were also provided for. A new constitution providing for a one-party democracy replaced the independence constitution on December 13, 1972.

INDIRECT RULE. This pattern of colonial government was instituted by the British and was credited primarily to Lord Lugard, who developed the concept while in India and Northern Nigeria. His book, *The Dual Mandate in British Tropical Africa* (1922), described the system in which traditional leaders (later called native authorities, q.v.) and their councils were retained, subject however to occasional orders from the colonial administrators. The Native Authorities Ordinance of 1929 (q.v.) attempted to initiate this. Native authorities were allowed to make rules and orders to regulate their districts, subject to veto by the district commissioner (q.v.). They were also given limited judicial responsibility. All this was contrary to the direct rule (q.v.) policy of the British South Africa Company (q.v.), which ended in 1924. Even after 1929, however, district commissioners were reluctant to allow their powers to devolve upon Africans. The system did not work well until 1936, when the British added ordinances to set up native treasuries, acknowledged tribal councilors, and replaced the 1929 Native Courts Ordinance with a new one (*see* NATIVE COURTS ORDINANCE, 1936). Nevertheless, the system never lived up to expectations, especially among the Northern Rhodesian peoples without centralized chiefs, like the Ila and the Tonga (qq.v.), where the British had to appoint native authorities. The system was more successful in Barotseland (q.v.).

INDUNA. This Southern Bantu word, used in various parts of central and southern Africa, refers to a chief's councilor. In Zambia the term has been used most among the Lozi and the Kololo (qq.v.) invaders. Among the Lozi, the importance of an *induna* and the degree of his wealth often depended on the king. Yet since a number of *induna* lived at Lealui (q.v.), the capital, and were part of the important traditional council, their influence was substantial at several points in Lozi history.

INDUSTRIAL CONCILIATION ACT. Although there were several such acts passed in Northern Rhodesia (q.v.) during the colonial period, the one passed by the Parliament of the Federation in 1959 and in operation in 1960 had an important result. By including Africans among "employees," it led to the formation of multiracial trade unions, allowed Africans access to conciliation machinery, and opened the way to multiracial apprenticeship arrangements.

INDUSTRIAL DEVELOPMENT CORPORATION OF ZAMBIA, LTD. Founded by the Northern Rhodesian government in 1960, it became one of three major holding companies for the many parastatal corporations that dominated the state capitalist economy of Kenneth Kaunda's (q.v.) regime. In 1971, INDECO itself became an appendage of the omnibus parastatal holding company, the Zambia Industrial and Mining Corporation (q.v.) (ZIMCO), which once controlled 80 percent of Zambia's formal economy. Following Frederick Chiluba's (q.v.) election in 1991 and the creation of the Zambia Privatisation Agency (q.v.), IN-DECO was dissolved in 1993 and its shares transferred to ZIMCO, which itself was supposed to dissolve in 1995.

INDUSTRIAL RELATIONS ACT, 1990. Kenneth Kaunda's (q.v.) government introduced this bill into Parliament (q.v.) in December 1990. The act weakened labor union support for political parties by making union affiliations with the Zambia Congress of Trade Unions (q.v.) optional, and by limiting union support of political parties to their members' voluntary contributions to a special fund. The act went into effect in June 1991 and was opposed by the ZCTU, which claimed that it would result in "anarchy" in the labor movement.

INGOMBE ILEDE. An archaeological site near the Lusitu-Zambezi River confluence in Southern Zambia, 51 kilometers (32 miles) downstream from the Kariba dam (q.v.), this was an important Iron Age trading community. First occupied by Early Iron Age hunters and farmers from about A.D. 750 to 1,000, the trading community dates from the late 14th to the early 15th century, when 11 young males were deposited in unusual, extended burials. Dressed in bark and cotton (possibly Indian) cloth, they were decorated with conus shells (*mpande*), gold, Indian glass beads, and copper bracelets, along with such prestigious grave goods as copper cross ingots, wire bundles, narrow iron hoe blades, flanged iron bells, and the iron hammers, tongs, and draw plates used for making copper wire. While the people here were able to offer local salt and ivory (q.v.), two Muslim-style amulet holders found near these graves support the belief that these people were involved in the Arab or Swahili (qq.v.) trade known to have existed then between the east coast and the southern gold fields of Great Zimbabwe.

INSTANT JUSTICE. Zambian journalists gave this name to that form of lynching typically associated with market crowds and accused thieves or other criminals. Once the supposed malefactor is identified, the crowd encircles, then beats, him or her until the police arrive and save the accused criminal from death. Occasionally, the police arrive too late. Because of this custom, motorists are usually advised not to stop and offer aid if they should strike a pedestrian. *See also* KABWALALA.

INSTITUTE FOR AFRICAN STUDIES. This was the successor to the famous Rhodes-Livingstone Institute (q.v.). In 1996 it was renamed the Institute for Economic and Social Research.

INTERIM NATIONAL DEVELOPMENT PLAN. This development plan, laying out economic policy and development targets, was unveiled on August 15, 1987, after the government had suspended the International Monetary Fund's (q.v.) austerity measures on May 1, 1987. The interim plan emphasized the philosophy of "growth from our own resources." The plan reestablished a fixed exchange rate for the kwacha (q.v.) and the administrative allocation of foreign exchange through the Foreign Exchange Management Committee (q.v.). By contrast, the IMF program had entailed the auctioning of foreign exchange. The plan also limited debt service to 10 percent of export earnings, net of payments for some invisibles and key imports. The plan set economic targets but left many details vague. Though the plan represented a repudiation of the IMF's efforts to reverse Zambia's declining economic fortunes, relations with donor countries and the IMF did not deteriorate immediately. In fact, quiet talks with the IMF continued in the months following the break, and it was not until October 2, 1987, that the IMF declared Zambia ineligible to receive further loans until it had cleared its arrears with the IMF.

INTERNATIONAL MONETARY FUND. One of the Bretton Woods institutions established at the end of World War II to manage international monetary affairs, the IMF provides balance of payments assistance to countries on conditional terms intended to restore the debtor's payments' balance. The loan conditions, called standby agreements, austerity programs, and structural adjustment programs (q.v.), typically involve the components of demand management (deflation), trade and financial liberalization, and privatization.

Zambia negotiated its first standby with the IMF in 1973. By 1982 four such agreements had been concluded, though none succeeded in addressing the root causes of Zambia's problems. In 1983, Zambia embarked on a more serious effort at reform and liberalization, negotiating three more agreements with the

IMF over the following three years. Results, however, were mixed. In October 1985, however, President Kaunda (q.v.) took the bold step of introducing a foreign exchange auction to try to bring the exchange rate of the kwacha (q.v.) in line with its real value. The subsequent rapid devaluation of the kwacha, and the mismanagement of the auction itself, undermined public confidence in liberalization. Following food riots in late 1986 and a spate of labor strikes in early 1987, President Kaunda in May 1987 suspended attempts to comply with IMF strictures. Zambia launched its New Economic Recovery Program in an attempt to grow from its own resources.

Decreasing inflows of foreign exchange and other failures of the program led the government to approach the IMF once again, after the 1988 elections. In September 1989 a policy framework paper (PFP) was negotiated with donors, setting out a three-year adjustment program for Zambia. The program, however, was not completed: labor militancy and the unwillingness of the regime to stick to the removal of maize price controls led to breaches of the terms and the PFP's suspension in September 1991. Immediately following the victory of the Movement for Multiparty Democracy (q.v.) in October 1991, the government demonstrated its willingness to stick to a rigorous program of adjustment as dictated by the IMF and other donors. By January 1992, funds frozen in September became available. Over subsequent years, Zambia remained roughly on course with the programs it negotiated with the IMF and donors, and it remained in the good graces of the IMF. However, the slow pace of privatization, allegations of corruption in the government, and occasional fiscal indiscipline continued to be causes for concern.

INTER-TERRITORIAL CONFERENCE. This refers to a series of meetings held between 1941 and 1944 by the governors of Northern Rhodesia, Southern Rhodesia, and Nyasaland (qq.v.) and their representatives. It was established by the British to further cooperation between the territories on nonpolitical matters. It even had its own secretariat. The conference was used by settlers and some officials, however, to try to develop closer governmental association, with amalgamation (q.v.) as the goal. The British rejected amalgamation. In 1944, it replaced the conference with the Central African Council (q.v.).

IRON AGE ZAMBIA. In Zambia the Iron Age began as recently as about the fourth century A.D. and is considered to have

closed around the beginning of the 20th century. It is characterized by the use of iron implements by farmers living in small
communities. Among the earliest are the Kalambo group (q.v.)
near Lake Tanganyika (q.v.), the Chondwe group (q.v.) along
the Copperbelt (q.v.), and several groups along and near the
southern border of Zambia from the area near Victoria Falls
(q.v.) eastward as far as the environs of Lusaka (q.v.). In addition to agricultural production, some Iron Age sites show signs
of animal domestication and the techniques of metallurgy, pottery, and permanent or semipermanent buildings. Some Iron
Age people also were responsible for the rock art (q.v.) found
in Zambia.

ISAMU PATI. *See* KALOMO.

ISHINDE (SHINDE). This was a Lunda (q.v.) chieftainship in
what is now Balovale District, north of the Lozi, near the north-
western corner of Barotseland (q.v.). Its founder, Ishinde, was
a captain under the (17th century?) Lunda emperor Mwata
Yamvo (q.v.) in the Congo, who was sent out with several other
leaders to expand the empire. He traveled westward. One of
his descendants had the occasion to meet the adventurous Dr.
Livingstone (q.v.) (who spelled the name "Shinte") in 1854;
Livingstone was impressed by the Lunda and their chiefly
court. Ishinde traded slaves to Portuguese traders for cloth,
guns, and gunpowder, a necessity as Ishinde was not on good
terms with the neighboring Luvale (q.v.). His problems with
Luvale aggressors came to a head in 1885, and in 1890 and
again in 1891 Ishinde requested military aid from Lozi king
Lewanika (qq.v.). In 1892 the Lozi responded by attacking the
Luvale, putting Luvale chief Ndungu to flight.

ISOKA. This town and district are near the northeastern corner
of Northern Province (q.v.). According to the 1969 census the
district contained nearly 78,000 people; by 1990 it was nearly
122,000. During the 19th century, this region hosted many visiting traders from East Africa and was also the site of battles
between the Bemba and the Ngoni (qq.v.). Missionaries and
the British South Africa Company collectors (qq.v.) eventually
calmed the area and made Fife (q.v.) the district's administrative center. In the 1950s and early 1960s, many of the district's
people became supporters of Alice Lenshina's controversial
Lumpa Church (qq.v.).

ITABWA. The land of the Tabwa people (q.v.), it is between Lake Mweru (q.v.) and the southwestern end of Lake Tanganyika (q.v.). Its location made it a very important crossroads for trade, especially with the East African coast. The Arab (q.v.) trader Tippu Tib (q.v.) made the first step toward establishing a permanent settlement of coastal traders there in 1870.

IVORY. Long before the 19th-century slave trade (q.v.), the East African and Indian Ocean trade in ivory was a lucrative one for Zambia's peoples. The people of Ingombe Ilede (q.v.) in southern Zambia, for example, traded in local ivory at least 500 years ago. By the mid-19th century, as hunters gradually depleted the East African elephant herds, the Mbunda, Mambari, Yeke, Arab, Swahili, Chikunda, and Lozi (qq.v.) were all involved in the ivory trade, which often required slaves for transport. Between 1870 and 1890, as supplies became scarce and international demand increased, the price of ivory doubled.

IWA. The Iwa people live in the northeastern corner of Zambia. Originally migrants from East Africa, they are part of a broader family of neighboring peoples. They are an offshoot of the Inamwanga (q.v.) and share a common language. As of 1986, there were 136,000 *ci*Namwanga speakers in Zambia and another 87,000 in Tanzania (q.v.). Living along the Chambeshi River (q.v.), just east of the Bemba (q.v.), they were periodically affected by Bemba raids. Iwa chief Kafwimbi (q.v.) was driven off his lands by the earliest Bemba immigrants sometime in the early 18th century. In the 19th century, the Iwa, like the Mambwe (q.v.), were known for smelting and working iron. They also kept large herds of cattle, but like other East Africans they used them for marriage payments rather than commercial trade. Under pressure, though, they supplied the Bemba with both cattle and grain. The Iwa, on the other hand, similarly dominated the Tambo (q.v.). When European rule eventually came, the Iwa did not provide any real resistance. But when Hanoc Sindano started the Watch Tower Movement (qq.v.) in that region in 1917–18, the Iwa were among the first converts.

J

JALLA, ADOLPHE AND LOUIS. Colleagues of François Coillard (q.v.), these Italian members of the Paris Mission Society (q.v.) worked among the peoples of Barotseland (q.v.) from 1887 on.

While both wrote of their experiences, Adolphe Jalla's writings provided Europe with much new information on Barotseland. They were both accompanied by their wives; Adolphe lost a son to fever; Louis lost a son, two daughters, and his wife, Maria. The two Jalla brothers and Coillard each had influence with Lozi king Lewanika (qq.v.), who used them as intermediaries with the British. Likewise, the British South Africa Company (q.v.) used them to win acceptance for its representatives, Frank Lochner and Robert Coryndon (qq.v.). The Jallas also frequently served as interpreters. It is doubtful that the infamous Lochner Concession (q.v.) of 1890 would have been accepted by Lewanika had it not been for the advice of the missionaries, notably Coillard and Adolphe Jalla.

JEHOVAH'S WITNESSES. Since 1930, this was the common name for the Watch Tower Bible and Tract Society and its members. It was founded by American clergyman Charles Taze Russell in 1872 and incorporated in 1884. From its headquarters in Brooklyn, it provides weekly Bible lessons (in translation) to Kingdom Halls (congregations) in over 90 countries. More than half the witnesses in Africa live in Zambia, where they outnumber Roman Catholics (q.v.), the second-largest denomination, by some 40–50 percent. Jehovah's Witnesses are heavily concentrated in Luapula and Copperbelt Provinces (qq.v.). Watch Tower beliefs were introduced into Northern Rhodesia (q.v.) from Cape Town by 1909, when Elliot Kamwana (q.v.) won some 10,000 followers in the border region with northern Nyasaland (q.v.). Yet while Kamwana and the other Chitawala (Watch Tower) prophets in Central Africa (q.v.) had links to the WTBTS, they soon constituted the independent (African) Watch Tower Movement (q.v.). Though the WTBTS provided literature to these prophets and their disciples, it was not knowingly involved in the mine labor unrest during the 1920s and 1930s, in Tomo Nyirenda's (q.v.) 1925–26 murder spree, or in the Copperbelt's strike of 1935 (q.v.). Seeing the need for closer supervision, Northern Rhodesia permitted the Witnesses to host the 1935 general conference of Watch Tower supporters in Lusaka and to open an office there. Thus the Witnesses came to control several formerly separatist Watch Tower communities.

By the 1950s, the Witnesses on the Copperbelt tended to be sober, industrious, apolitical traders and would-be artisans, with little formal schooling. Most, in fact, had come from the same regions (but less prestigious ethnic groups) that had fostered the earlier Watch Tower movement. Then as now, Witnesses focused upon instructional meetings with, and witnessing for, potential recruits. They share a confident self-esteem and an efficient grassroots organization. Like Witnesses throughout the world, those in Zambia look forward to an imminent Second Coming, when sickness, death, and war will disappear. They believe that the temporal world, including its governments, is under Satan's dominion. So while they pay their taxes, they refuse to salute the flag, sing the national anthem, vote in elections, or perform military service. Such practices run counter to the strain of popular patriotism in many countries. So while the Witnesses in Zambia, unlike those in Malawi (q.v.), have never been outlawed, they have suffered occasional discrimination from politicians and party militants.

JOHNSTON, HENRY HAMILTON (SIR HARRY). This British traveler and colonial officer played an important role in the establishment of British colonial rule in modern Malawi (q.v.) and eastern Zambia. Born in London in 1858 and educated at King's College as a botanist, he traveled widely in North, West, and East Africa from 1879 to 1884. He served as a vice-consul in the Niger River area until 1888. Returning to London, he met Cecil Rhodes (q.v.) in 1889 and the two persuaded Lord Salisbury (q.v.) to act firmly in Central Africa (q.v.). In March 1889, Lord Salisbury sent Johnston, as the consul in Mozambique (q.v.), to work out a settlement that would keep Portugal out of Central Africa. He had permission to sign treaties with the African chiefs. Inspired by Rhodes' drive to obtain a royal charter for his British South Africa Company (q.v.), and by Rhodes' imperialist dreams, Johnston took £2,000 from Rhodes and spent the rest of 1889 in parts of present-day Malawi and eastern Zambia securing 24 concessionary treaties from African leaders, including chiefs among the Inamwanga, Mambwe, and Tabwa (qq.v.). In 1890, he sent Alfred Sharpe and Joseph Thomson (qq.v.) on separate ventures to get Katanga (q.v.) for Rhodes. While this ultimately failed, other concessions were signed. All of these treaties helped to define the borders between British and German territory at the 1890 conference between those nations.

In May 1891, the British declared a protectorate over British Central Africa (today's Malawi) and made Johnston the commissioner. He held this position until the BSAC took administrative responsibility for the area north of the Zambezi (q.v.) in June 1895. In the intervening years, Johnston, working out of

Zomba, solidified British authority in both Malawi and eastern Zambia. With £10,000 a year from Rhodes, he brought in Sikh (q.v.) soldiers from India to stem the east coast slave trade (q.v.). He was in the awkward position of serving two masters: Rhodes and the Foreign Office. And following the Lochner Concession of 1890 (q.v.) with Lozi king Lewanika (qq.v.), Johnston was nominally in charge of North-Western Rhodesia (q.v.) as well. After 1895, Johnston spent much of the rest of his life writing and traveling. He wrote at least 11 books on Africa or other parts of the British empire. He died in 1929.

JOSÉ, AMARO. An Angolan mestizo, he and Pedro João Baptista (q.v.), the two pombeiros (q.v.), traversed the continent from Angola to Mozambique (qq.v.) and back at the beginning of the 19th century.

K

K. This is the symbol for Zambia's unit of currency, the kwacha (q.v.).

KABOMPO. Zambia's fourth-least-populous district, it had 33,400 people in 1969 and 37,000 in 1990. It is located in the remote, northwestern corner of North-Western Province (q.v.), along the border with Angola (q.v.). The town of Kabompo, named for the river, is located north of its confluence with the Dengue River. Kenneth Kaunda, Frank Chitambala, and other Zambia African National Congress (qq.v.) activists were all "rusticated" (q.v.) to Kabompo during the 1959 "emergency." The district's major industry is honey, and in years of adequate rains, the Kabompo honey factory produces over 250 tonnes of exceptionally high-quality honey, 80 percent of which is exported to South Africa, Europe, and America. The ingredients for the Honeysticks-brand lip balm come from the Kabompo honey factory.

KABOMPO RIVER. One of the major tributaries of the Zambezi River (q.v.), the Kabompo drains a major part of North-Western Province (q.v.)before joining the upper Zambezi north of Lukulu (q.v.). One of its own major tributaries is the Dengue River. The Kabompo River has traditionally been the northern border of the Lozi (q.v.) floodplain. During the 19th century, when a split occurred among the Lozi, one of the groups fled north of the Kabompo and established themselves at Luk-wakwa (q.v.).

KABWALALA. This is the *ci*Bemba (q.v.) term for "thief" and commonly used throughout most of Zambia. Like *"chinsoka!"*, the shouted sighting of a large snake, that of *"kabwalala!"* will bring an instant response—in this case people come running, surround the offender, and beat the offender within an inch of his or her life, a process known as instant justice (q.v.).

KABWE. The fifth-largest municipality in Zambia, it had a population of 66,000 in 1969 and 166,600 in 1990. Called Broken Hill during the colonial period, it is the site of the now-closed Kabwe (formerly Broken Hill) Mine. Kabwe is located on the line of rail (q.v.), about halfway between Lusaka and Ndola (qq.v.). Its location on the Great North Road (q.v.) and its position as headquarters of Zambia Railways (q.v.) and a major trucking firm have made it one of Zambia's true transportation hubs. It is also serviced by an airport. Kabwe (Broken Hill) was founded as a British military post. Today it is the capital of Central Province (q.v.).

KABWE, BASIL. A former secretary-general of the Zambia Congress of Trade Unions (q.v.), he was made minister of labour and social services in January 1981. He served as minister of finance for less than a year (1986–87), after which he returned to the ministry of education and culture. In July 1989, he became ambassador to Ethiopia.

KABWE MAN. The earliest known human skeletal remains in Southern Central Africa were found in 1921 during mining operations at Broken Hill (Kabwe) Mine. The skull, with its trepanation (drilled) holes and decayed and abscessed teeth, bears the distinctive, double-arched brow ridges, low cranial vault, and occipital "bun" of the Eurasian Neanderthals. So, like them, Kabwe Man is considered a representative of archaic *Homo sapiens*. Its dating is currently pegged between 110,000 and 130,000 years ago. In 1994 the Zambian government announced its intent to recover the Kabwe finds from the British Museum of Natural History.

KABWE MINE. Formerly called Broken Hill Mine, this multiore mining operation began in 1902, when Australian prospector Thomas Davey (q.v.) discovered the site in 1902 and named it after a similar-looking mine site in Australia. The mine was opened in 1906 and finally closed by Zambia Consolidated Copper Mines (q.v.) in June 1994. Its main products were lead and zinc, but it also produced quantities of silver, cadmium, vanadium, and copper (q.v.). Broken Hill's lead and zinc deposits, together with George Grey's (q.v.) copper discoveries in Katanga (q.v.), determined the railway's route from Bulawayo.

KAFFIR. Arabic for "unbeliever," it became a derogatory and belittling Southern African word for Africans, especially during colonial days. A close equivalent in American English would be "nigger." *Also see* MUNTS.

KAFFIR CORN. *See* SORGHUM.

KAFUE HOOK (HOOK OF THE KAFUE). The Kafue River (q.v.) flows in a southwesterly direction from the Copperbelt (q.v.) into west-central Zambia. It then flows due south until it turns and flows east again into the Kafue flats and toward the Zambezi (q.v.), forming a giant hook. This region was the center of ancient copper (q.v.) mining operations. Northern Copper Company (q.v.) prospectors found and mined copper there in the 1890s. Though the Ila (q.v.) there paid occasional tribute to the Lozi (q.v.) king during the last quarter of the 19th century, it was never, as Lewanika (q.v.) later claimed, under his authority.

KAFUE HYDROELECTRIC PROJECT. Originally conceived in the 1950s as the major project for supplying Northern Rhodesia's (q.v.) electricity needs, it was bypassed by the leaders of the Central African Federation (q.v.) in favor of the Kariba dam (q.v.), a cooperative effort by the two Rhodesias on their Zambezi River (q.v.) border. Soon after it opened, however, Rhodesia pronounced its unilateral declaration of independence (q.v.). So Zambia devised the Kafue hydroelectric project, about 43 kilometers (27 miles) southeast of Lusaka (q.v.), to reduce its dependence upon Rhodesia's Wankie colliery and to secure its power against the arbitrary actions of Rhodesia's white minority regime. It not only supplements the energy supplied by the Kariba dam but it also provides some irrigation water. Thus, with considerable assistance from Yugoslavia, major construction was begun in 1969 at the Kafue Gorge, where a dam controls a 10-kilometer-long (six-mile-long) tunneled race to the turbine house. The dam initially produced 600 megawatts of energy. It produced 920 megawatts in 1980, by which time Zambia was exporting most of its 340-megawatt surplus to Rhodesia-Zimbabwe. The same dam, however, has substantially slowed the river's flow, and recurrent drought and the slower and nitrate-polluted Kafue River (q.v.) have now fostered huge, floating beds of "Kafue weed," which threaten to damage the project's hydroelectric turbines.

KAFUE NATIONAL PARK. A huge game reserve with 22,403 square kilometers (8,650 square miles) of territory, it is located in the western half of Zambia, mostly along the west bank of the Kafue River (q.v.). It is an excellent place to see wild game, including rare species like the aardwolf, the pangolin, and the red lechwe antelope. One of the camps is located on an island in the Kafue and is noted for its fine fishing.

KAFUE RIVER. Called the Loengue River by Portuguese traders and the Kafubu ("Hippopotamus") River by the Ila of the Kafue Hook (qq.v.), the Kafue is one of the three major tributaries of the Zambezi River (q.v.). It rises north of the Copperbelt (q.v.) and soon drifts into a southwesterly flow. When it is joined by the Lunga River in the Kafue National Park (qq.v.), it heads in a more southerly direction. It later hooks back and flows due east until it joins the Zambezi River. On that part of its course, it passes through the Kafue flats floodplain and then through the Kafue Gorge—and the Kafue hydroelectric dam (see KAFUE HYDROELECTRIC PROJECT)—before crashing over a series of rapids and waterfalls. The Kafue basin covers almost 155,400 square kilometers (60,000 square miles), second in Zambia only to the Zambezi basin.

Unfortunately, the Kafue is probably Zambia's most polluted river. The problems begin with mine wastes—including sulphuric acid and copper sulfate—which jeopardize much of the Copperbelt's drinking water supply. The full dimensions of this problem were widely recognized in 1988, when women's hair turned green after being washed in the water. Fertilizer runoffs from Nakambala Sugar Estates (q.v.) and industrial effluent from Kafue township then provide a nitrate-rich medium, which when combined with recurrent droughts and the Kafue dam's reduction in the river flow, produces huge, floating beds of "Kafue weed" (mainly water hyacinth). These river weeds, which the army has to clear by hand, hamper fishing, promote mosquito breeding (and malaria), and threaten to damage the hydroelectric turbines.

KAFULAFUTA MISSION. A small but influential mission among the Lamba (q.v.) of rural Copperbelt Province (q.v.), it was founded in 1905, when the Nyasa Industrial (Baptist) Mission relocated from Blantyre. Now about 16 kilometers (10 miles) southwest of Luanshya (q.v.), it was sited near the village of headman Katanga (q.v.), of later *sanguni* (q.v.) fame. Beginning with the preparation of hymns and religious pamphlets, these missionaries opened a two-year boys' boarding school to teach reading and writing (in *ci*Lamba), as well as plank and brick making. The Nyasa Industrial Mission was about to pull out of Northern Rhodesia (q.v.) in 1913, when the Reverend Joseph Doke and his son, Clement, came for the South African Baptist Missionary Society, looking for a mission to adopt. The Reverend Doke died on the return trip home, and Clement M. Doke (q.v.) and the missionary society took over Kafulafuta in 1915 as a memorial to his father.

Clement helped the earlier missionaries complete their *ci*-Lamba New Testament (1921) and later published his locally inspired *Lamba Folk-Lore* (1927), *English-Lamba Vocabulary* (1933), and ethnography, *The Lambas of Northern Rhodesia* (1931) after his 1921 departure. His sister, Olive C. Doke, remained at Kafulafuta, where she ran the printing press from 1916 until her death in 1972. (She is buried there.) The mission opened a girls' boarding schooling in the later 1920s but abandoned this experiment a month or two later, after all 25 students ran off to the nearby mine compounds. The Reverend Arthur J. Cross then extended the mission's work to include the townsfolk of Bwana Mkubwa and Ndola (q.v.) and so provided advice and encouragement to the fully autonomous Union Church of the Copperbelt (q.v.); about 1936 he left Kafulafuta Mission and moved to Mindolo (q.v.) to join the collaborative Protestant mission, the United Missions of the Copperbelt (q.v.).

In 1930, Kafulafuta Mission gave up its southern territory to the Swedish Independent (now Scandinavian) Baptists at Mpongwe. And following the population shift that attended the creation of the Lamba-Lima Native Reserve (q.v.), the South Africans opened an eastern station, Fiwale Hill, near the railway line and modern highway. They cut a connecting, east-west road between the stations to help deliver grain in the wake of the 1940 famine, and then, from 1943 to 1956, used the mission truck and road to operate a vegetable marketing enterprise between the Lamba villagers and urban Copperbelt markets. Market gardening became so central to the curricula of the mission schools and the Fiwale Hill seminary that middle-aged Lamba now complain that theirs was an education for work as domestic servants. The South Africans turned their work over to the Australian Baptists in 1964, when they were forced to leave Zambia. As of 1985, it all reverted to the Lambaland Baptist Church.

KAFWIMBI. He was a major participant in a succession dispute for the Nsama (q.v.) chiefship of the Tabwa (q.v.) people. The dispute ultimately resulted in the Bemba (q.v.) making major inroads into Tabwa territory. The incident began in about 1868, with the death of Chipili Nsama III. He was succeeded by a nephew, Katandula, who became Nsama IV. Kafwimbi was Katandula's parallel cousin (or classificatory brother) and an unsuccessful challenger for the position. When Katandula later tried to expel Kumba Kumba's (q.v.) Arabs (q.v.) from his area, Kafwimbi came to the Arabs' aid by persuading Bemba chief Mwamba II (q.v.) to join their effort to defeat and kill Katandula. Though Kafwimbi became Nsama V, Mwamba's warriors refused to leave until he gave them a place, called Isenga, where they could settle. Some years later he was killed in a battle with East African traders.

KAKENGE. Title of the most senior of the Luvale's (q.v.) independent chiefdoms, the Kakenge dynasty controls an area in northwestern Zambia very close to the Angolan border—and in fact it was once based in Angola (q.v.). Though the title itself dates to the early 18th century, it is claimed that it is of 16th-century Lunda (q.v.) origin. By the late 18th century, the Kakenge was actively trading with the Portuguese in Angola, exchanging slaves for cloth, guns, and gunpowder. By 1830 the Kakenge were also trading with Lunda chief Kazembe (q.v.) on the Luapula River (q.v.). Around that same time, however, Kakenge had begun paying tribute to the Lozi (q.v.) to his south. That connection was to be responsible for problems between the Lozi and the Portuguese in the early 20th century, when Portugal tried to incorporate the Kakenge's land within Angola's borders.

KAKUMBI, MATEYKO. A carpentry instructor at the Chitambo Mission of the Free Church of Scotland (q.v.), he was elected the first treasurer of the Northern Rhodesia African Congress (q.v.) in July 1948.

KALABO. Located on the western end of Western Province (q.v.) (formerly Barotseland, q.v.), Kalabo District shares a long border with Angola (q.v.). The district contained 94,000 people in 1969 and 101,400 in 1990. Its administrative center is the town of Kalabo, located on the southern bank of the Luanginga River, south of the Liuwa Plain. Some authorities feel that the Lozi (q.v.) kingdom first began to solidify in the Kalabo area and it was certainly the center of the region controlled by Yeta I (q.v.).

KALAMBO FALLS. Close to the southeastern shore of Lake Tanganyika (q.v.), near the Tanzanian border, is Kalambo Falls, a spectacular 725-foot, single-drop waterfall. Above it, the Kalambo River (q.v.) cuts a gorge through the ancient lakes' sediments just behind the falls. There, in 1953, J. Desmond Clark (q.v.) excavated a stratified series of levels representing at least 90,000 years of occupation by Stone Age hunter-gatherers and Iron Age farmers.

At the top of the series, dating from the 11th century A.D., is the Luangwa tradition (q.v.) pottery of Late Iron Age peoples. Below this, dating from the 10th to 4th centuries A.D., are three levels of Early Iron Age farmers—including a village site and its graves—with iron slag and artifacts, a grain-grinding stone, a copper bracelet and earring fragment, and an abundance of Kalambo group (q.v.) pottery. Lower still are levels containing a range of microlithic flake tool types from the Late Stone Age (15,000 to 9,500 years ago) and Middle Stone Age points and choppers from the Lupemban (39,000 years ago) and Sangoan (100,000 to 80,000 years ago) traditions.

The lowest and most remarkable levels are the waterlogged but undisturbed living floors of Early Stone Age humans. While the acidic soils eliminated all bone remains, these lowest floors contained an arc of stones (perhaps a windscreen base) and grass-lined (sleeping?) hollows; charred logs, ash, and charcoal; some of the world's oldest wooden artifacts (a club and a pointed knife, or scraper); nuts, seedpods and fruits; stone flake knives and scrapers; and the Acheulian handaxes (cleavers) associated with *Homo erectus* and early *Homo sapiens*. Now dated to 100,000 to 200,000 years ago, the people who occupied these lowest levels could well have been contemporaries of Kabwe (or Broken Hill) Man (q.v.).

KALAMBO GROUP. Named for the ceramics found at Kalambo Falls (q.v.), this name connotes a heterogeneous collection of Early Iron Age pottery forms from northern Zambia. Kalambo Falls is the only large village site with this pottery, but it has also been found at open sites near Lakes Tanganyika, Mweru, and Bangweulu (qq.v.) and at rock shelter sites between Mbala and Serenje (qq.v.). In the latter case, the association of Early Iron Age pots with Late Stone Age microlithic flake tools (arrowheads?) has been viewed as possible evidence for contacts between indigenous hunter-gatherers and immigrant farming peoples. Kalambo group ceramics commonly consist of undecorated open bowls with undifferentiated or thickened rims. The necked vessels, however, often bear comb-stamped rim bands and stamped or incised lines on their beveled lips. The necks of such vessels are often decorated with crosshatching and broad horizontal grooves, sometimes interrupted by dangling loops or chevrons. It is not clear what, if any, connection Kalambo group pottery has to the contemporaneous Chondwe and Nkope group (qq.v.) ceramics elsewhere in Zambia or to the little-known Early Iron Age pottery types in southern Tanzania and the southeastern Democratic Republic of Congo (q.v.) (Zaire).

KALAMBO RIVER. This small stream in northeastern Zambia forms the boundary between Zambia and Tanzania (q.v.) on its way into the southeast corner of Lake Tanganyika (q.v.). En route from a high plateau region to the lake at the bottom of the Rift valley, the river flows over a 725-foot cliff, forming a spectacular waterfall over twice the height of Victoria Falls (q.v.). The Kalambo Falls is the 12th highest in the world.

KALE (KAHADI). A chief of the Mbwela (q.v.) who brought some of his people from the area of the upper Zambezi valley to settle near the upper Kafue River (q.v.) in the early 19th century, he later welcomed to the area a party of Luba (q.v.) and gave his daughter as a wife to a Luba chief. Quarrels eventually occurred between the groups over the right to wear the *mpande* shell (q.v.), the emblem of chiefship. War ensued and lasted for three years. At one point Kapidi (q.v.) was captured and his head shaven; his people ransomed him, and he resumed the war. The Luba killed Kale's younger brother and were chased across the Kafue River into Ila (q.v.) country. Kale was bitten by a rabid dog just before crossing the Kafue in pursuit and died. The Luba chiefs settled there, in Ila country.

KALELA DANCE. A development of the earlier Mbeni dance (q.v.), this popular Copperbelt (q.v.) dance form originated after World War II among the Bisa (q.v.) inhabitants of the

Chishi Islands in Lake Bangweulu, Northern Province (q.v.). It soon spread to the Copperbelt mining towns, where, on Saturday afternoons, Sundays, and holidays, ethnically homogeneous dance teams gathered on the African compound soccer fields dressed in smart European clothes and bearing titles like "king," "compound manager," and "doctor" and performed original song-and-dance social commentaries. While the 1951 performances described in J. Clyde Mitchell's classic sociological monograph mixed interethnic banter with commentaries on bridewealth, adultery, and divorce, other Kalela lyrics from the 1950s involved such explicitly political themes as the feared loss of lands, praise for nationalist leaders, and appeals for African solidarity against white settler rule. Thus, by the early 1960s, the police often dispersed Kalela dance gatherings, and a number of Kalela dancers were arrested, fined, or imprisoned on politically related charges.

KALICHINI, PAUL. One of the earliest leaders of the Zambia African National Congress (q.v.), he was elected its deputy president at its inaugural, Broken Hill meeting of November 1958. Because of these ZANC activities, however, when the government declared the "emergency" in March 1959, he was arrested and subjected to rustication (q.v.) at Chadiza (q.v.) in eastern Zambia, near Petauke (q.v.). He was released from detention in July and immediately announced the formation of the African National Independence Party (q.v.). Frank Chitambala (q.v.) had laid the party's foundations at the end of May, and the two men became its co-leaders. On August 1, 1959, they merged their party with another small splinter group, called the United National Freedom Party (q.v.), creating the United National Independence Party (q.v.). Two things were clear among all the members: they were waiting for Kenneth Kaunda's (q.v.) release so he could assume the presidency, and they did not want to fraternize in any way with the African National Congress (q.v.). In October 1959, however, Mainza Chona (q.v.), a dissident member of the ANC, joined UNIP, along with a large following. A conference was called to elect interim leaders, and Chona defeated Kalichini for the presidency. Angered by his defeat, Kalichini would not run for any other party post and, ultimately, retired from active politics.

KALIMBA. A musical instrument found almost everywhere in Zambia, it is also called the finger, thumb, or Kaffir piano. It has from eight to 13 metal strips of varying lengths attached by one end to a wooden board or box. The "piano" is played by plucking the free end of each strip with downward thumb strokes. Iron *kalimba* keys appear throughout Early Iron Age Zambia from the fifth century A.D. on.

KALIMANSHILA. War leader and chief councilor to Mwamba III (q.v.), a major late-19th-century Bemba (q.v.) chief, Kalimanshila was the principal councilor opposed to accepting the Europeans—either the British South Africa Company (q.v.) or the White Fathers (q.v.). He especially opposed the growing influence of Father Dupont (q.v.), whom he tried to have sent away. After Mwamba died in October 1899, however, most of Kalimanshila's followers at court chose to accept the Reverend Dupont as a stabilizing force. Kalimanshila also switched sides and made a dramatic speech in which he pledged support to the Europeans as protectors against members of the Bemba's chiefly Crocodile Clan (Bena Ng'andu), who threatened to raid the mourning village.

KALIMINWA. A Lungu (q.v.) chiefship to the northwest of Bemba (q.v.) country, it was influenced strongly by the Bemba (q.v.). The chief at the beginning of the 20th century was not actually of the Lungu royal family but owed his position to the fact that Bemba chief Mwamba III (q.v.) had given him his daughter, Kasonde NaKabwe, for a wife. The majority of the people in the area were Lungu, but there were also many Bemba. Many Lungu left the region rather than accept Kaliminwa's rule, but others—mainly members of the chiefly clan led by Tomboshalo (q.v.)—tried to remove him and were encouraged by the missionaries in this effort. The native commissioner (q.v.) supported Kaliminwa, however, and the incident was resolved with Tomboshalo accepting Kaliminwa's rule. A different kind of struggle involved the chieftainship in 1918–20, when the young Kaliminwa (son of the earlier one) refused to recognize the supervisory rights of Bemba chiefs Mwamba or Mporokoso (qq.v.) over him, claiming they were of "junior standing." Mporokoso demanded that the native commissioner and the British South Africa Company (q.v.) force Kaliminwa to pay tribute and respect to the Bemba chiefs. An inquiry was held on July 9, 1920, and after hearing local testimony, the commissioner agreed with Mporokoso that this Kaliminwa should be dismissed. His reasons seemed to rest in large part upon his respect for Mporokoso's opinions.

KALINDULA. This popular music style, first recorded by Spokes Chola and the Mansa Radio Band in 1977, originated in Luapula Province (q.v.) and clearly benefited from Kenneth Kaunda's (q.v.) 1976 decree that the domestic radio service feature Zambian music. Unlike Zamrock (q.v.) musicians, those playing *kalindula* were relatively immune from the scarcity of electric instruments. It began as a neotraditional dance music featuring one or more acoustic guitars and traditional drum and percussion rhythms over a strong rumba bass line, one originally provided by a homemade bass made from a double-headed drum. *Kalindula* is now a generic name for Zambian dance music and is performed in a variety of languages as well as in *ci*Bemba (q.v.). Prominent *kalindula* bands have included Amayenge, Julizya, Shalawambe, Lima Jazz, Serenje Kalindula, Masasu, Mashabe, and Makishi.

KALOMO. One of Southern Province's (q.v.) southern districts, Kalomo District borders Zimbabwe just west of Lake Kariba (q.v.). Its population was almost 77,000 in 1969 but was nearly 155,000 in 1990. The area has been populated for at least 1,500 years. A few kilometers southeast of the town of Kalomo (which is along the line of rail, north of Livingstone, qq.v.) is the fifth-century A.D. Kalundu mound. Excavations at this site have produced much evidence of Early Iron Age communities, including notable examples of their pottery. Another mound, Isamu Pati, exists a few kilometers west of Kalomo. Later pottery dates have been pinpointed in the period from the ninth to the 13th centuries (*see* KALOMO PEOPLE). During the 19th century there was much activity going on near the site of today's town of Kalomo. Tonga (q.v.) chief Siachitema had a village east of the present town. Kololo leader Sebituane (qq.v.) defeated an Ndebele (q.v.) force near there in about 1840. About a half century later a Lozi (q.v.) rebel, Sikabenga, took refuge with the Tonga chief. The British South Africa Company (q.v.) made Kalomo the headquarters for Robert Coryndon's (q.v.) administration of North-Western Rhodesia (q.v.) from 1900 until 1907, when it was moved south to Livingstone. Kalomo then continued as a small settlement serving the nearby farming areas.

KALOMO PEOPLE. The term is loosely applied to the people who inhabited southern Zambia from roughly A.D. 300 to 1200 and whose mounded village sites are of particular archaeological interest. Many of the mounds are located just a few kilometers in one direction or another from the present town of Kalomo (q.v.) on the Batoka Plateau (q.v.). Among the largest mounds are those called Isamu Pati and Kalundu. The settlements cover a wide area, however, from near Barotseland (q.v.) in the west to the middle Zambezi River (q.v.) in the east. The inhabitants of these small villages cultivated some grain and other minor crops and kept domesticated cattle, sheep, goats, chickens, and dogs. Some of the early Kalomo people were also hunter-gatherers, like the Bushmen (q.v.) they evidently forced out of the area. They also used iron hoes, their mud and pole huts and granaries surrounded a central enclosure, presumably some kind of thorn fence protected them from wild animals and raiders, and they were generally isolated from outside trade.

KALUE, EDWARD. He was the purported leader of the abortive May 1938 coup against Lozi king Yeta III (qq.v.) while the king was away in England. Yeta's well-educated and ambitious second son, he had served earlier as his father's private secretary until British officials judged him an "extremist" and had him replaced. It was often claimed, but never demonstrated, that Kalue was behind the attempted coup. The Lozi *kuta* (q.v.), nevertheless, banished him from the province.

KALULU, SOLOMON. Born in Lusaka (q.v.) on June 18, 1924, this former teacher and headmaster left education in 1952 to become secretary, then treasurer-general, of the African National Congress (q.v.). He left the ANC, however, in 1959 after failing to convince the party congress that Harry Nkumbula's (q.v.) Legislative Council (q.v.) duties best suited him for the post of honorary life president. He soon joined the United National Freedom Party (q.v.) and, as vice president general, helped engineer the creation of the United National Independence Party (q.v.). When Kenneth Kaunda (q.v.) was elected as UNIP's president in January 1960, Kalulu became national chairman, a post he held until 1969. Kalulu was rotated through the leadership of three ministries from 1964 until 1973, when he joined the directing cadre of senior politicians known as the Central Committee of UNIP (q.v.), before becoming ambassador to Egypt. He died in a London hospital at age 68 in 1992.

KALULUSHI. Located in Copperbelt Province (q.v.), Kalulushi is Zambia's 10th-largest town. It had a population of about 32,000 in 1969 and nearly 91,000 in 1990. It is located due west of Kitwe (q.v.) and is one of the newer Copperbelt (q.v.) towns, built almost completely by the mining companies.

KALUNDU MOUND. *See* KALOMO; KALOMO PEOPLE.

KALUNGU RIVER. A minor tributary of the Chambeshi River (q.v.), it is nevertheless important to the Bemba (q.v.) people. It flows from west to east in northern Zambia. Its historical importance is tied to the legendary migration of the chiefly Crocodile Clan (Bena Ng'andu), who settled on the Kalungu River and established the Chitimukulu (q.v.) chiefship. The capital, Ngwena (*ci*Bemba, q.v., for "crocodile"), was established there because they found a dead crocodile on the riverbank and took this to be a good sign.

KALUNGWISHI RIVER. A river in the northwestern corner of northeastern Zambia, it flows into Lake Mweru (q.v.). In 1893 the British South Africa Company (q.v.) established a station called Kalungwishi near the point the river entered the lake. The location was in the heart of the area where the Bemba, Lunda, and Arabs (qq.v.) competed for supremacy. There is also a good example of rock art (q.v.) on a large boulder near Kundabwika Falls (q.v.) on the river: a panel of red schematic paintings, over a large, complex grid of horizontal and vertical lines.

KALUWA, GEORGE W. CHARLES. A Mazabuka (q.v.) storekeeper and farmer, he tried to start an African nationalist movement in the late 1930s. He finally succeeded in May 1946, when he, along with men like Dauti Yamba (q.v.), created the Federation of African Societies of Northern Rhodesia (q.v.). It changed its name in 1948 to the Northern Rhodesia African Congress (q.v.) (a name Kaluwa had used for a 1937 group in Mazabuka), and he was appointed assistant treasurer.

KALYATI, ALBERT. A militant, left-wing member of the United National Independence Party (q.v.), he helped form the Reformed Trade Union Congress (q.v.) in 1960 as a breakaway from Lawrence Katilungu's Trade Union Congress (qq.v.). Kalyati had denounced Katilungu for agreeing to become a member of the Monckton Commission (q.v.). When the United Trade Union Congress (q.v.) was formed by merger in 1961, Kalyati remained as one of its top leaders.

KAMANGA, REUBEN CHITANDIKA. Born to a Chewa (q.v.) village headman's family near Chipata (q.v.) in 1929, Kamanga was educated at mission schools before attending the famous Munali Secondary School (q.v.) in Lusaka (q.v.). Before entering the nationalist movement he worked first as a clerk, then in a government office in provincial administration, and then in private business. He also worked as a trade union organizer. In 1950 he worked with Justin Chimba, Simon Zukas, and Mungoni Liso (qq.v.) as editors of the *Freedom Newsletter* and was a co-founder of the Anti-Federation Action Committee. In 1951 the committee joined Nkumbula's African National Congress (qq.v.). In August 1956, after organizing a colour bar (q.v.) boycott in Fort Jameson, he was chosen to the ANC National Executive Committee.

Kamanga was among the founding members of the Zambia African National Congress (q.v.) that broke from the ANC in October 1958. When the Northern Rhodesia (q.v.) government banned ZANC and arrested its leaders the following March, Kamanga was sent to Sesheke (q.v.). Once released, he traveled to Ghana and then Cairo, where he opened a party office for the United National Independence Party (q.v.). Elected UNIP deputy president in July 1961, he won the Petauke South parliamentary seat in 1962. In the coalition cabinet that followed, he was named minister of labor and mines and, in January 1964, minister of transport and communications. At independence he became Zambia's vice president until September 1967, when he served as foreign minister (1967–69) and minister of rural development (1969–73). During this period he was also charged with criminal misconduct. The Doyle Commission (q.v.), however, cleared him in June 1971, and Kamanga was elected to the Central Committee of UNIP (q.v.) in August 1973.

KAMBONSENGA. Another name for the Ambo (q.v.).

KAMBULUMBULU. The site of some interesting rock art (q.v.) from the Late Stone Age, it is located in Eastern Province (q.v.) in the Luangwa (q.v.) escarpment northwest of Lundazi (q.v.). Many schematic art motifs are found there, including ladders, winged objects, circles, and objects looking like long hairpins. They are done in red.

KAMBWILI. This Bisa (q.v.) chiefship was active in 19th-century trade with the Bemba and Arab (qq.v.) traders. It was also active in the coastal trade with the Portuguese, from whom it acquired guns to defeat a Chewa (q.v.) chief in the 1880s.

KAMWANA, ELLIOT. An early leader of the Watch Tower Movement (q.v.) from northern Nyasaland (q.v.), Kamwana was among the Livingstonia (q.v.) mission-educated elite. Yet he broke from the church when it began collecting school fees and was baptized into the Seventh Day Baptist church of Joseph Booth, the versatile British religious visionary. In 1903 he followed Booth to South Africa, where both became witnesses in the Watch Tower Bible and Tract Society (q.v.). Kamwana returned home to the Lakeside Tonga in 1908 and, taking advantage of Livingstonia's revivalist movement, began preaching that the coming millenium (1914) would soon liberate them from hut taxes (q.v.), labor migration, and white colonial rule. By 1909 he had some 10,000 followers among the Tonga (q.v.), Ngoni, Henga, and Tumbuka (q.v.) of northern Nyasaland and North-Eastern Rhodesia (qq.v.)(*see* GONDWE, JEREMIAH), and the migrant laborers from this region soon spread his message to the mining centers of Katanga, Northern Rhodesia, and Southern Rhodesia (qq.v.). Kamwana's success worried the missions and the government, and he was exiled to South Africa in 1909. From 1911 to 1914 he witnessed near Chinde, Mozambique (q.v.), until the Portuguese arrested him and he was removed to southeastern Nyasaland. Then, suspected of fomenting the Tonga's resistance to the war effort and of being involved in the 1915 John Chilembwe uprising, he was exiled to Mauritius and the Seychelles. Kamwana remained popular, and when he was released from exile in 1937, he found himself head of the Watchman's, or Kamwana Society, Church, which was in correspondence with, but decidedly independent of, the Watch Tower Bible and Tract Society.

KANGOMBE. A Luvale (q.v.) chief in the mid-1880s, he expanded into Lunda, Ndembu, and Lozi (qq.v.) areas until Chipenge (q.v.), an Ndembu commoner, defeated him. This encouraged the neighboring peoples to challenge the Luvale.

KANONGESHA. This is an Ndembu (Lunda) (qq.v.) chiefship in northwestern Zambia between the Lungu and upper Zambezi Rivers (qq.v.) whose existence is attributed to the territorial expansion of Mwata Yamvo's (q.v.) aides. One of them, Kanongesha, established himself among some of the Lukolwe (or Mbwela, q.v.) people in that area. The chieftainship he established became involved with the Ovimbundu slave traders from Angola (q.v.). The Lukolwe retained much of their independence from the chief, and the unity that was imposed was primarily of a ritual nature.

KANSANSAMA. This capital of an important Bemba Chitimukulu, Chileshye Chepela (qq.v.) is located on the northern bank of the Kalungu River (q.v.). It was also the site of an attack by the Ngoni (q.v.) against the Bemba (q.v.) around 1850. The Bemba retained their capital, and the Ngoni moved on.

KANSANSHI. This is the site of an old copper mine in northern Zambia near the modern Solwezi (q.v.). Africans mined the copper for their own use long before Kaonde chief Kapijimpanga brought George Grey's (q.v.) prospectors to the ancient copper workings in the late 1890s. Kansanshi Mine closed in the mid-1910s, but was periodically revived: in 1927–32, 1952–58, and, apart from one two-year interval, in 1969 until the present. Though many Copperbelt (q.v.) mines have either shut down or are slated to be closed (*see* COPPER), Kansanshi produced about four tonnes of copper a day in 1994/95.

KANYANTA. One of the more prominent Bemba (q.v.) leaders of the last century, he held the Nkolemfumu (q.v.) title from 1884 until 1899. Mubanga Chipoya, the Mwamba III (q.v.), died in October 1898. After a brief interim during which Father Dupont (q.v.) kept order, Kanyanta succeeded as Mwamba IV in September 1899. Following a meeting with the headmen, British South Africa Company administrator Robert Codrington (qq.v) and Father Dupont agreed to this succession. When Ponde, the Chitimukulu (qq.v.), died in 1923, a dispute arose over succession, and again Kanyanta was involved, this time in conflict with Bwalya Nkula II. The dispute was resolved in Kanyanta's favor after a lengthy inquiry by H. G. Willis, commissioner of Awemba (q.v.) District. Kanyanta then served as Chitimukulu until his death in 1943.

KAOMA. This is the name of a town and district—both formerly called Mankoya—in the northwestern quarter of Western (formerly Barotse) Province (q.v.). The district had almost 51,000 people in 1969 and 113,000 in 1990. The town (the district's administrative center) is located on the southern bank of the Lwena River (q.v.).

KAONDE. One of the seven largest language groups in Zambia, these peoples primarily reside in North-Western Province's Solwezi and Kasempa (qq.v.) Districts. The people are probably of Luba (q.v.) origin but paid allegiance to a Lunda (q.v.) chief, Musokantanda, when they entered their present area around the 16th or 17th century. The Kaonde combine matrilineal descent with patrilocal residence. They have never been a highly centralized people, although their early history revolves around a young man, Jipumpu, who rebelled against a major chief (his cousin) named Kawambala. After a series of battles and at least one retreat into the Congo area, Jipumpu dominated the area and ruled with the title Kasempa (q.v.). Although the Kasempa chieftainship became a major one in the region, a number of other Kaonde chiefships also emerged, for example, Mushima and Katatola. The Lozi dominated many of these people at different times in the 19th century, especially while the Lozi were led by Lewanika (qq.v.). On the other hand, Kasempa once also defeated a force of Lozi sent by Lewanika. The Kaonde also were noted for sending slave-raiding parties south of the Kafue River (qq.v.) against the Ila (qq.v.).

KAPANDANSALU. An Arab (q.v.) slave-trading chief of the late 19th century, he erected a stockaded village in the upper Zambezi valley near the village of a Senga chief Chibale (qq.v.). This village became a major slave market, attracting traders such as the infamous Arab, Mlozi (q.v.). An army of warriors led by Kapandansalu and several other local Arab chiefs attacked Chibale's village. The force included many Bemba (q.v.) as well. A warning by Robert Young of the British South Africa Company (qq.v.) did not prevent the force from renewing the attack a day later. Young's police and Chibale's forces killed 25 of the attackers, and two Arab chiefs (one of them Kapandansalu) were later taken prisoner.

KAPENTA. This small dried fish is a staple of the Zambian diet. On the Copperbelt (q.v.) in the 1950s, it was also slang for the flashy, well-dressed women who frequented the beerhalls.

KAPIDI. This Luba (q.v.) chief was involved in a three-year war with a Mbwela (q.v.) clan led by Kale (q.v.) in the early 19th century. After Kale's death, Kapidi settled south of the Kafue River in Ila (qq.v.) territory.

KAPIRI MPOSHI. A line of rail (q.v.) town north of Kabwe (q.v.) and south of the Copperbelt (q.v.), it is located just a couple of kilometers south of the Great North Road (q.v.) and Copperbelt highway. It is the site of the Kapiri glassworks and the southern terminus of the TAZARA (q.v.) railway.

KAPWEPWE, SIMON MWANZA. Part of the earliest cadre of Zambian nationalist politicians, he served in the nationalist movement, in the United National Independence Party (q.v.), and in the government until 1971, when he bolted the party. He was born of Bemba parents at Chinsali in Northern Province (qq.v.) on April 12, 1922. His father had been a British South Africa Company (q.v.) policeman who worked his way up to being head messenger at Isoka *boma*. At the age of 12 Simon became a very close friend of Kenneth Kaunda (q.v.). The two met again at the Lubwa Mission School (q.v.), where they qualified as teachers (Kapwepwe in 1945). His political consciousness and dissatisfaction with the government were already in evidence at that time. He began teaching elementary school at Kitwe (q.v.) on the Copperbelt (q.v.) and, in 1948, became a founding member of the Northern Rhodesia African Congress (q.v.). He became a member of the executive and was secretary of its Kitwe Branch. In 1949 he and Kaunda returned to Chinsali and started a group farm, while Kapwepwe continued to teach. They stayed active in the Chinsali African Welfare Association (q.v.), which was, in effect, the local branch of the NRAC. In 1950 he resigned from teaching when the NRAC got him a four-year scholarship to India, where he included journalism in his Bombay studies.

Upon his return to Zambia on January 6, 1955, he found the African National Congress (q.v.)(new name of the NRAC) leaderless, with both Harry Nkumbula (q.v.) and Kaunda in jail for possessing "subversive" literature. Kapwepwe assumed the leadership and began improving the ANC's organization as well as its activities. An inspiring orator, he quickly acquired a reputation as a firebrand. When Nkumbula was released, he appointed Kapwepwe provincial president of the Northern Province Branch of the ANC. In 1956, Kapwepwe was elected party treasurer and soon quarreled with Nkumbula over accounting procedures and Nkumbula's use of party funds. When Nkumbula called an "emergency" NRAC meeting in October 1958 to fend off his increasing critics, Kapwepwe and the other young Turks walked out and formed the Zambia African National Congress (q.v.). ZANC's leaders were incarcerated in March 1959, and Kapwepwe spent nearly nine months in Mongu, Barotseland (qq.v.), organizing UNIP branches.

With UNIP now the major nationalist party, Kapwepwe became its treasurer, a post he held until 1967.

In December 1960, he accompanied Kaunda to London, where they laid the foundation for the final drive toward independence by their actions at the Federal Review Conference (q.v.). In the 1962 election for the legislature, Kapwepwe overwhelmingly defeated Dauti Yamba (q.v.) and a United Federal Party (q.v.) opponent. In the subsequent coalition cabinet with the ANC, Kapwepwe was named minister of african agriculture. When UNIP won control of the Parliament (q.v.) in January 1964, he was made minister of home affairs, and then, for three years, minister of foreign affairs. In this capacity, he was a bitterly vocal critic of British policy, or lack thereof, toward Rhodesia and its unilateral declaration of independence (q.v.).

At UNIP's August 1967 general conference Kapwepwe led an ethnic-based alliance in an attempt to garner Central Committee (q.v.) and party offices for the Bemba and their allies. He succeeded, winning the post of deputy party leader from his old colleague Reuben Kamanga (q.v.). He was also shortly thereafter raised to Kamanga's former position of Zambia's vice president. In that capacity, he became active in economic affairs, both in budgeting matters and in those involving unrest on the Copperbelt. Also in 1970 and 1971 he initiated a campaign to preserve traditional Zambian culture, especially by encouraging the use of Zambian languages in schools. Kapwepwe's political victories, however, were at the expense of deep dissension within UNIP, as other ethnic groups resented what they saw as a Bemba power play. Kaunda himself resented this divisiveness caused by an old friend. Knowing that an effort to oust him from office was under way, Kapwepwe resigned as both vice president and deputy party leader in August 1969 but returned to the cabinet from January 1970 until August 1971, when he resigned to protest the dismissal of four other Bemba-speaking ministers.

Kapwepwe and a number of other prominent former UNIP members formed the United Progressive Party (q.v.). Justin Chimba (q.v.) became one of his chief aides. When the government called by-elections in December 1971 to fill the vacated seats, Kapwepwe defied all odds by winning the Mufulira parliamentary seat for his UPP. His was the only success, however, and the party was banned on February 4, 1972. He and 122 followers were arrested. He was released on December 31, 1972, just a day before the new one-party state came into effect. In February 1973 he was charged in court for possession of two guns, receiving a two-year suspended sentence. In January 1973, Kapwepwe brought a libel suit against the *Times of Zambia* (q.v.) and was awarded K20,000 when he won the case. He also won K10,000 from the *Daily Mail* and K30,000 from the state radio and television services. These cases stemmed from their reports that Kapwepwe was sending people for military training outside Zambia. He then returned to Shiwa Ng'andu, Stewart Gore-Browne's (q.v.) former estate in northern Zambia.

In September 1977, Kapwepwe announced that he would rejoin UNIP for the sake of national unity, and in 1978 he and Harry Nkumbula challenged President Kaunda for the presidential nomination in that year's party elections. UNIP promptly changed the length of party membership required for UNIP candidates and declared Kapwepwe and Nkumbula ineligible. The courts upheld this patently partisan manipulation of UNIP's rules. As a result, there was a large no vote against Kaunda in the popular elections in Kapwepwe's home district. In 1979, Kapwepwe was charged with taking financial support from "foreign powers" (i.e., South Africa), of managing a banned political party (the UPP), and of possessing seditious and obscene materials, failure to secure a firearms license, poaching, and receiving stolen goods. He died of a stroke in January 1980 at age 57.

KAPWIRIMBWE. This Early Iron Age settlement, near a rich iron ore deposit about 13 kilometers (eight miles) east of Lusaka (q.v.), was briefly occupied in about the fifth century A.D. Recovered postholes indicate the existence, but unfortunately, not the layout, of semipermanent structures. Massive debris from collapsed mud structures, either within or immediately contiguous to the settlement, is interpreted as the remains of iron-smelting furnaces. This, together with large amounts of iron slag and bloom, suggests large-scale iron production. The iron objects found here include a razor, a spear point, a ring, and what might have been *kalimba* (q.v.), or thumb piano keys. There was no evidence of copper (q.v.). The people at Kapwirimbwe had domesticated cattle, but there is no other evidence of food production.

KAPWIRIMBWE GROUP. Named for the ceramics at the Kapwirimbwe (q.v.) iron-working site, this is a style of Early Iron Age pottery found around the Lusaka (q.v.) Plateau and as far west as Mumbwa (q.v.) in the first millenium A.D. While broadly similar to the Chondwe group (q.v.) ceramics, the Kapwirimbwe bowls and vessels are marked by a greater frequency of thickened rims and by incised band designs and false relief chevron stamping, rather than the former's comb-stamped decorations. Both the Kapwirimbwe and Twickenham Road sites included perforated pottery colanders, which may have been used in salt making. The Kapwirimbwe people seem to have produced great quantities of iron, but copper appears only late in the sequence. There is no evidence of imported coastal goods. And while they kept cattle, there is no other indication of food production. No rock art (q.v.) is associated with this pottery style.

KARIBA DAM AND HYDROELECTRIC PROJECT. The first of the Kariba power stations was planned and built during the period of the Central African Federation (q.v.). It was completed in 1960. Built on the south side of the Zambezi River (q.v.), and thus under the potential control of the Southern Rhodesian government, it was designed to provide power to both Northern and Southern Rhodesia (qq.v.) from the huge Kariba dam built across the Zambezi. It is 128 meters (420 feet) high and 24 meters (80 feet) thick and caused the creation of Lake Kariba (q.v.), which covers an area of about 5,180 square kilometers (2,000 square miles). When the dam was built, there were numerous political problems concerning the moving of about 60,000 Valley Tonga (34,000 in Zambia) from their homelands. Likewise, thousands of animals had to be moved (Operation Noah).

The South Bank power station (Kariba I) was supplying 70 percent of Zambia's power in 1966, but with its control potentially in the hands of Rhodesian leaders (despite 50 percent ownership by Zambia), the building of Kariba II on the north bank was imperative. The need for it was only partly lessened by the completion of the Kafue hydroelectric project (q.v.) in 1972. Work on Kariba II began in mid-1971. Its goal was to provide 600 megawatts, as did Kariba I (which was later upgraded to 705 megawatts). A future third stage could add another 300 megawatts. British contractors working on Kariba II ran into numerous difficulties and ceased work in February 1973. A Yugoslavian contractor took over a month later, but the project's completion date was pushed back to 1976.

KASABA BAY. Located in the Sumbu Game Reserve on the southwestern shore of Lake Tanganyika (q.v.), Kasaba Bay is noted for its outstanding game fishing.

KASAMA. A town of about 9,000 people (in 1969), it is also the administrative center of Kasama District in Northern Province (q.v.). The district had a population of 108,000 in 1969 and 192,000 in 1990. The town itself is on the TAZARA (q.v.) rail line. The town was founded in 1898 as a station set up by the British South Africa Company (q.v.) on the Milima Stream. It was a few kilometers east of Mwamba's (q.v.) village and a few kilometers north of present-day Kasama. In 1901 the station was moved a little south to its present site. Toward the end of World War I, Kasama was left undefended by the Northern Rhodesia Police (q.v.) and was attacked on November 9, 1918, by a German force led by General von Lettow-Vorbeck (q.v.). During the attack, the Germans blew up the government offices. The troops left the town on November 12. (European women and children had been evacuated from Kasama on November 8 in anticipation of the attack.)

KASAMA NATIVE WELFARE ASSOCIATION. Sanctioned by the Northern Rhodesian government near the end of 1932, this association was limited by a government restriction to Africans living in Kasama township itself. No political activity was allowed, and membership was limited to those who had no allegiance to a local native authority (q.v.). Its chairman was Aaron Nkata and its secretary, John Mulenga. Despite the restrictions, the association became involved in issues such as educational facilities and the operation of lorries. While its membership was never large and in fact declined as the 1930s drew to a close, it was nonetheless one of the few such organizations in Northern Rhodesia (q.v.) before World War II.

KASANKA NATIONAL PARK. This small game reserve and national park is just east of the Katanga Pedicle (q.v.) in the eastern half of Zambia.

KASEMPA. This is the name of both an administrative center and a district in North-Western Province (q.v.). The district's population was 22,900 in 1969 and 22,300 in 1990. It is located west of the Lunga River (q.v.), near the source of the Dengue River. The area presumably got its name from the Kaonde (q.v.) chieftainship that ruled under the title Kasempa. Late in the 19th century Kasempa and his Kaonde warriors crossed to the south of the Kafue River (q.v.) on raids, fighting and capturing slaves among the Ila (q.v.). Kasempa had received guns in his trade with Bié. At one point he defeated a large army of Lozi sent by Lewanika (qq.v.).

KASHINDA. The village was established by Mporokoso (q.v.) after he left his original chiefdom, Maseba, probably late in the 1870s. He located it several kilometers north and east of the Luangwa River (q.v.). The first major mission school of the London Missionary Society (q.v.) in Zambia was established nearby and in 1908 became known as Kashinda Mission.

KASOKOLO, HENRY. He was one of the first two African members of the Legislative Council (q.v.) (he and Nelson Nalumango, q.v., were appointed in 1948). A couple of years later the African Representative Council (q.v.) replaced them with Dauti Yamba and Paskale Sokota (qq.v.). He then became an organizer for the African National Congress (q.v.). In the 1962 election he unsuccessfully opposed Kenneth Kaunda (q.v.) for a seat in the legislature, losing by a margin of 20 to 1.

KASONDE, EMMANUEL. A respected economist and businessman from Northern Province (q.v.), he previously served as permanent secretary at the ministry of finance in the early 1970s before being appointed the first finance minister in the new Movement for Multiparty Democracy (q.v.) government after the 1991 elections. He was later sacked by President Chiluba (q.v.) in April 1993. While his dismissal included vague allegations of corruption or irregular procedures, many believed it stemmed from his leadership of the MMD faction that challenged Chiluba's MMD party leadership. He was replaced by Ronald Penza, the former minister of commerce and industry. In August 1993, Kasonde joined other members of Parliament (q.v.) who left the MMD to form the National Party (q.v.).

KATABA. A town in southwestern Zambia west of the Kafue National Park (q.v.), it is located at the northern end of the Sawmill Railway that runs north from Livingstone (q.v.). The Kataba valley was the site of a major 19th-century battle when Sebituane, leader of the Kololo (qq.v.), confronted and defeated a large force of Lozi (q.v.). This site was nearer the Zambezi River (q.v.) than the present town.

KATANGA. Now called Shaba, it is the southeastern province of the Democratic Republic of Congo (q.v.) (Zaire, formerly the Belgian Congo), Zambia's northern neighbor. But the Congo (or Katanga) Pedicle dips down into the heart of Zambia, causing the latter to have a narrow waist. Geologically, Katanga and Zambia have much in common, notably a large store of ore-bearing rocks. Copper (q.v.) is a major export item of both areas. There are also numerous historical and anthropological similarities. Most Africans in Zambia have at least distant ethnic roots in the Congo, usually in Katanga. Most of the groups in northeastern Zambia claim origins among the Luba (q.v.) people, whose later migrations originated in Katanga. Several other Zambian peoples originated among the Lunda of Mwata Yamvo (qq.v.). While they were a little north of Katanga, the migrations of some, notably Kazembe's Lunda (qq.v.), came through Katanga en route to their current lands. Also 19th-century traders usually crossed back and forth from the Congo to Northern Rhodesia (q.v.), as no real physical borders exist.

Had Cecil Rhodes' agents, Alfred Sharpe and Joseph Thomson (qq.v.), been more successful in the early 1890s or had Kazembe been less dominant, Katanga may also have become part of the British South Africa Company's (q.v.) land rather than part of King Leopold's, and Zambia today might include most of Katanga. As it developed, the copper mines of Katanga attracted many Zambians to jobs prior to the full development of Zambia's Copperbelt (q.v.).

Katanga became important to Zambia again in the late years of the Central African Federation (q.v.). Moise Tshombe's (q.v.) regime in Katanga impressed Northern Rhodesian Europeans, who felt that an African like Harry Nkumbula or Lawrence Katilungu (qq.v.) might play a similar role in Northern Rhodesia. Thus Sir Roy Welensky (q.v.) made several attempts to secure an equivalent to Tshombe. Covert European financing of certain African parties or leaders, sometimes with financial aid promised from Katanga itself, marked the early 1960s.

Problems in Katanga (now known as Shaba) affected Zambia again in 1977 when an invasion force of Lunda fighters (based in Angola, q.v., since the unsuccessful Katangese secession attempt of the 1960s) attempted to retake Shaba Province. Zairian forces counterattacked and inadvertently bombed Zambian territory. Finally the invaders were beaten back, but a similar invasion with similar results occurred in 1978.

KATANGA CROSS. *See* COPPER CROSSES.

KATANGA PEDICLE (CONGO PEDICLE; ZAIRE PEDICLE; DEMOCRATIC REPUBLIC OF CONGO PEDICLE). This copper-rich region of southern Democratic Republic of Congo (q.v.) (Zaire) lies adjacent to Zambia's Copperbelt (q.v.) and dips deeply into the heart of central Zambia. One major road cuts across this area (part of the old Katanga—now Shaba Province of the Democratic Republic of Congo [Zaire]) from the Zambian Copperbelt to Zambia's Luapula Province (q.v.). Though Zambia maintains this 69-kilometer (43-mile) road through the Democratic Republic of Congo (Zaire), this short-cut, which always entails the bribing of unpaid Congolese (Zairean) border guards, is often not the quickest surface route between Luapula and Copperbelt Provinces. The area became part of the Belgian Congo as the result of the three expeditions King Leopold sent to Msiri (q.v.) in 1891. Msiri and a Belgian officer were shot dead, and the Belgians took control. An 1894 treaty between King Leopold and the British then confirmed the borders.

KATENGO KUTA. This *kuta*, or council, has had a varied and disputed history. Under Lozi king Lewanika (qq.v.) in the late 19th century, it had been a secret council called to discuss vital matters such as plots, executions, and witchcraft cases. After Lewanika, however, it became a more formal institution, composed of minor *indunas* (q.v.) and even commoners. Some considered it to be the closest thing the Lozi had to a representative body within their government. Its voice was considered to be closer to the masses than was that of the Saa *kuta* or Sikalo *kuta* (qq.v.). It became a council within the larger Mulongwanji (q.v.) and fell into disuse from the mid-1930s to the mid-1940s. It was revived in 1946–47 by the British, when the resident commissioner of Barotseland (q.v.), A. F. B. Glennie (q.v.), insisted that it be restored as a representative body that would make advisory recommendations to be sent to the National Council (Mulongwanji). Its members were elected by secret ballot under a universal male (and in Senanga, q.v., District, also female) suffrage. However, it met only once a year under the chairmanship of the Ngambela (q.v.), who could control matters for the king. The new Katengo was resented by the traditional elite, and its recommendations were generally ignored. Katengo elections in 1963 were won by United National Independence Party (q.v.) candidates.

KATILUNGU, LAWRENCE CHARLES. A pioneer Zambian trade union leader and politician, he was born in January 1914 at Chipalo in Northern Province (q.v.) and was a cousin of the

Bemba chief Chitimukulu (qq.v.). He was mission educated, becoming first a Catholic mission teacher and then a headmaster before higher wages drew him to seek work in the copper (q.v.) mines in 1936. He was one of the leaders of the famous 1940 mine strikes and then left the country to work in the Congo for seven years. He returned to Nkana in 1947 and soon became a senior interpreter. The same year he worked closely with William M. Comrie, who the British Labour Party government sent to promote African trade unions on the Copperbelt (q.v.). The African Mineworkers Union (q.v.) was formed in 1949 with Katilungu as its president.

Meanwhile, he had also entered politics as chairman of the Kitwe Branch of the Northern Rhodesia African Congress (q.v.). His political interests continued for several years, as he was active on the Congress's Supreme Action Council, which opposed the idea of a Central African Federation (q.v.). In 1952 he went to London with an African National Congress (q.v.) delegation to protest the coming federation (q.v.). But he soon devoted his full time to the union movement.

After encouraging other Africans to form unions in their fields of labor, Katilungu formed the Northern Rhodesia Trade Union Congress (q.v.) in 1950 and was elected its president. For the next decade, his leadership of the mineworkers union was virtually unchallenged. He attended meetings in Britain, led an orderly and successful strike in 1952, and was involved in a controversial and bitter strike in 1955. Some union members claimed he called off the latter strike before the objectives were achieved. He made it a point to keep the union under his own personal control. In 1955, however, he was defeated for TUC president. When he accepted appointment to the controversial Monckton Commission (q.v.) in 1959, some unionists rebelled, resigning to form the Reformed Trade Union Congress (q.v.) in 1960. They were also protesting his moderate approach to union activity. In December 1960 he lost his union power when the AMU branches voted to depose him as president.

Meanwhile, Katilungu had not abandoned the political arena. In 1950 he had been chosen to the Urban Advisory Council and as a member of the African Representative Council (qq.v). While he remained interested in the ANC, he did not encourage his union members to join in a two-day "National Prayer" work boycott in 1953. He was also criticized by the ANC in the mid-1950s for drawing people out of the party and into his union activities. His anger with ANC attempts to undermine his union support led him to support the formation of the Constitution Party (q.v.) in 1957. Nevertheless, when Kenneth Kaunda (q.v.) and his supporters broke away from the ANC in 1958 to form the Zambia African National Congress (q.v.), Katilungu stood by Nkumbula (q.v.). In fact, he applauded the government's banning of ZANC in March 1959. In the 1959 election he ran for the Copperbelt (q.v.) seat in the legislature but lost because of heavy European voting for an African candidate of the United Federal Party (q.v.).

By mid-1959, Katilungu returned to close friendship with ANC's Nkumbula and campaigned with him. Sir Roy Welensky (q.v.) and others increasingly saw him as a moderate leader to be courted by Europeans, especially after his acceptance of a position on the Monckton Commission when most Africans were boycotting it. In March 1961 he was elected ANC's deputy national president, and when Nkumbula was jailed for nine months for drunken driving, Katilungu became its acting president. He also filled Nkumbula's seat in the Legislative Council (q.v.). As leader of the ANC he received further attention from Roy Welensky and the UFP. Katilungu was receptive to the attempts by the Europeans to link him with Moise Tshombe in Katanga (qq.v.), who was in a position as a conservative leader to supply the ANC with both counsel and financial support in their forthcoming electoral struggles with UNIP. Katilungu died in an automobile accident in November 1961.

KATONGO. He was the oldest son of Mukulumpe and brother of Chiti and Nkole (qq.v.), the Bemba's (q.v.) legendary founders. One estimate has it that around 1670, Mukulumpe (his father) deliberately blinded Katongo out of anger and that it was this and a similar threat to Chiti that motivated Chiti and Nkole to lead many followers to new territory, away from their despotic father. The Bemba legend says that the father tried to lure Chiti and Nkole back into a trap, but Katongo warned his brothers by sending a message on the talking drum.

Katongo is also the name of one of the titled chiefdoms of the Bemba. It later changed its name to Chewe and now is the chiefdom of Nkula at Ichinga. Some sources say that Katongo ultimately left his father's village, following Chiti and Nkole, but that he settled on the Luvu River and there began this chieftainship. At least one bearer of the Katongo title has served as Chitimukulu (q.v.).

KAUNDA, BETTY. The deceased wife of Zambia's first president, Kenneth Kaunda (q.v.), she was the mother of nine children.

The daughter of John and Milika Banda, she was born on November 17, 1928, and named Mutinkhe, after a grandmother. Her father had worked for the African Lakes Company (q.v.) and was transferred to Chinsali, where he met David and Helen Kaunda. The family moved again, however, and she was 17 years old before she was introduced to the 22-year-old Kenneth Kaunda. The next year, 1946, she attained an Elementary Teacher's Certificate. The wedding took place at Mpika (q.v.) in August 1946. The couple's first home was at Lubwa (q.v.). Over the next 20 years Betty Kaunda displayed tremendous courage and patience as she kept her growing family alive during long periods of low political salaries and high expenses, the imprisonment of her husband, and his long absences both within Zambia and abroad. Her first six children were boys. The seventh was a girl, and twins arrived in 1964. In later years she traveled abroad and was active in the UNIP Women's Organization.

KAUNDA, DAVID JULIZYA. The father of Zambia's first president, Kenneth Kaunda (q.v.), he was a teacher, an ordained minister, and an early advocate of African rights. Born a Lakeside (i.e., Malawian) Tonga (q.v.) at Lisali in Mwambazi District in 1878, he was named Julizya. He took the name David after being received into the Presbyterian Church (q.v.). His father, Mtepa, was killed in battle when Julizya was a small child.

Around 1885, his mother, NyaChirwa, took her four children to live in the large Ngoni (q.v.) village of Elangeni where he was raised. He grew up with a deep love of religion, as some African evangelists, notably William Koyi, were active in the area. He attended Ekwendi Mission School through standard III and then Overtoun Institute, where he went through teacher training. His wife, Helen, also studied at Overtoun. They were married in 1904. About 1905, David Kaunda began traveling as a part of an Overtoun team, working at evangelistic and educational efforts. He is considered the missionary pioneer of Chinsali (q.v.) District. Around this same time he became close to men like Donald Siwale (q.v.), Peter Sinkala, Hezekiya Kawosa, and Hanoc Mukunka. This group of comrades often discussed the attitude of Europeans toward Africans. Their discussions over the next couple of decades led to the formation of the Mwenzo Welfare Association (q.v.) by Siwale, Kawosa, and Kaunda. It was one of Zambia's first African nationalist organizations.

The Kaunda family lived at Chinsali until 1913 and then

moved to Nkula for two years. David continued as a teacher and missionary. He was tremendously effective everywhere at establishing schools. He traveled extensively among the Bemba and Bisa (qq.v.) peoples, as well as others, establishing numerous schools. Kenneth Kaunda was born in 1924, 20 years after his parents' marriage, and was an unexpected addition to the group of Kaunda siblings. Although David had taught since 1904, he returned to Overtoun for theology studies from 1927 to 1929, when he was ordained. He died three years later, at the age of 54. He had been conducting religious services and was returning home to Lubwa (q.v.) when he was struck ill. He died in his home.

KAUNDA, FRANCIS. No relation to Kenneth Kaunda (q.v.), he was appointed chairman of the new Zambia Consolidated Copper Mines (q.v.) in 1981 and became a member of the Central Committee of the United National Independence Party (qq.v.) in August 1988. He was dismissed from his ZCCM post shortly after the Movement for Multiparty Democracy (q.v.) took power after the 1991 elections. In 1992 he was charged with abuse of office, allegedly for transferring ZCCM funds without authority.

KAUNDA, KENNETH DAVID. The attempt here at a biographical sketch of Kenneth Kaunda must be recognized as being only a token effort. Several major biographies exist, notably Richard Hall's *Kaunda—Founder of Zambia* and Fergus Macpherson's *Kenneth Kaunda of Zambia*. In addition, of course, is Kaunda's autobiography, *Zambia Shall Be Free*, and his numerous other writings.

Born in 1924 at Lubwa (q.v.) Mission, near Chinsali, Northern Province (qq.v.), Kaunda was the eighth child of the 20-year marriage between Helen and David Kaunda (q.v.). Both were teachers, and David was also a missionary for the Livingstonia Mission (q.v.). The Kaundas were of Malawi (q.v.) origin, but Kenneth grew up among the Bemba (q.v.) of Zambia. His education began in Lubwa at the Mission School and continued at Munali Secondary School (q.v.). At Lubwa he became friends with Simon Kapwepwe (q.v.). Kaunda returned to Lubwa as a teacher (after a teacher training course at Munali) in 1943. He served as headmaster there from 1944 to 1947 and was a scoutmaster and athletic coach, as well. In 1946 he married Betty Banda; together they would raise nine children. For part of 1947 and 1948, Kaunda taught in Tanganyika, but he returned in 1945 to teach in Mufulira at the United Missions in the Copperbelt (q.v.) School. He also worked as a welfare assistant at the Nchanga Mine (q.v.).

Kaunda returned to Lubwa in 1949 to begin a group farm with two old friends, Simon Kapwepwe (q.v.) and John Sokoni, where they became active in the Chinsali African Welfare Association, the local branch of the Northern Rhodesia African Congress (qq.v). Kaunda was elected its secretary in 1950. The next year he became a district organizer, as it changed its name to the African National Congress (q.v.). The following year he was named organizing secretary in Northern Province (q.v.), and his skills and boundless energy and dedication led to his being selected as ANC secretary-general in August 1953, second in authority to its president, Harry Nkumbula (q.v.). Two months later he began editing the *Congress News* (q.v.). Because of it he was arrested (but not imprisoned) in November 1953. Kaunda's next arrest came on January 6, 1955: he was ultimately sentenced to two months in prison for possessing banned political literature.

At that time he began his austere lifestyle, forgoing tobacco, alcohol, and meat. In May 1957 he visited England as a guest of the Labour Party, staying six months in order to study the British political system. In May 1958, he traveled to Tanganyika and then to India, returning in October. Upon his return, Kaunda and many of his ANC colleagues rejected the accommodationist leadership of Nkumbula and broke away to form the Zambia African National Congress (q.v.) on October 24, 1958, at Broken Hill. Kaunda was made president. In December he attended the first All African People's Conference in Ghana. A nervous Northern Rhodesia (q.v.) government banned the party in March 1959, and on March 12, Kaunda was arrested. He was sentenced to nine months' imprisonment and sent to Kabompo (q.v.) in northwestern Zambia. Kaunda was released on January 9, 1960, and on the last day of January was elected president of the United National Independence Party (q.v.). In April, *Black Government*, a book that he had written with Colin Morris (q.v.), was published.

Kaunda spent 1960 in a vigorous campaign to get Britain to renounce federation (q.v.) and to allow Zambia to become independent. The first sign of hope came in December 1960, when Kaunda and his nationalist colleagues at the Federal Review Conference (q.v.) in London walked out of the meeting. This precipitated further action on the part of British leaders that led to the demise of the Central African Federation (q.v.).

The first break was when Great Britain indicated a willingness to allow Nyasaland (q.v.) to secede. Zambia would eventually follow. Nevertheless, Kaunda and UNIP bitterly opposed the constitutional proposals being put forth by the British. Still, Kaunda decided that UNIP should contest the October 1962 elections. While UNIP would not win a clear parliamentary majority, it did form a coalition cabinet with the ANC. Kaunda became minister of local government and social welfare and was clearly the dominant African in the government. Also in October 1962, his autobiography, *Zambia Shall Be Free*, was published. He then negotiated a new constitution for his country and led UNIP to a sweeping election victory in January 1964, thus becoming prime minister. The rest of 1964 was spent preparing the country for independence. Only the "holy war" of the Lumpa Church (q.v.) back in his home district of Chinsali caused a serious distraction for Kaunda and his cabinet. Finally, on October 24, 1964, Zambia received independence, with Kenneth Kaunda as its first president.

During 1963, Kaunda was also elected president of the Pan-African Freedom Movement (q.v.). His concern for freedom movements in Southern Africa prompted him to tolerate the existence of their offices in Lusaka, but his close involvement with the Lusaka Manifesto (q.v.) reflected a sincere realism and even a modest approach toward revolution and change. As a leader of the Front Line States, he repeatedly sought moderate solutions to the Zimbabwe crisis as long as they seemed feasible. By 1977 he seemed to have despaired of a peaceful solution. Likewise, Kaunda's policies toward South Africa have reflected both a sense of realism and a willingness to compromise—not in ultimate goals, necessarily, but in the process of change.

While concerned about international issues, Kaunda's first goal was the proper development of Zambia. Although stressing the importance of Zambianization (q.v.) he consistently assured the Europeans that he hoped they would remain as part of a multiracial society in which everyone contributes. Kaunda also developed an ideology for his country's development called Zambian humanism (q.v.). Two of his books deal with the subject: *A Humanist in Africa* (1966) and *Humanism in Zambia and Its Implementation* (1967). Government control of the economy and especially of major industries was essential to his program.

UNIP unity began to splinter at the party's general conference in 1967, when Kaunda 's previous efforts to keep an ethnic balance within the party unraveled as the result of an ethnic electoral coalition set up for the party elections. Great political skill was needed, and while Kaunda patched things up for a while, the roots of serious difficulties for UNIP were firmly set. When Simon Kapwepwe created the United Progressive Party (q.v.) in 1971, he took with him many followers from UNIP. Kaunda's banning of the party and arrest of its leadership would not solve the problem. Finally, Kaunda made Zambia a one-party state and placed the country's civil service administrators under the supervision of UNIP appointees.

Internal unrest mounted in the late 1970s, when the copper (q.v.) economy began to go bad and a host of senior ministers abandoned government for private enterprise. While Kaunda cultivated the image of a statesman, easily moved to tears by the evils around him, he was, in fact, a shrewd and jealous wielder of power. In the early 1980s, a host of former UNIP politicians was implicated in an alleged South African conspiracy to kidnap and assassinate him; toward the end of the decade, similar critics or potential rivals were accused of invovement in the drug trade (q.v.). To support Zambia's heavily centralized economy and its subsidies, Kaunda's government dug itself into a pit of debt so deep that the World Bank and the International Monetary Fund (q.v.) compelled it to adopt elements of its structural adjustment program (q.v.). These unpopular austerity measures led to urban food price riots and brought Kaunda and UNIP into conflict with organized labor, especially the Mineworkers Union of Zambia and the Zambia Congress of Trade Unions (qq.v.), whose leaders brought down Kaunda and his one-party state in the October 1991 elections (see MOVEMENT FOR MULTIPARTY DEMOCRACY). The writing was clearly on the wall when, in June 1990, the people of Lusaka danced in the streets to celebrate the announcement of a (fictitious) military coup (see LUCHEMBE, MWANBA). His subsequent attempt to campaign for the presidency in 1996 was bitterly contested by President Chiluba's (q.v.) administration and only further divided UNIP (see MUSOKOTWANE, KEBBY).

KAUNDA, PANJI. A son of Kenneth Kaunda (q.v.), he served in the military at the rank of lieutenant colonel. He was accused of being involved in the drug trade (q.v.) and of smuggling autos at the beginning of the Mandrax scandal trial in 1985. In March 1993, he was arrested in association with the "Zero Option" emergency (q.v.) and the alleged conspiracy to destabilize President Chiluba's Movement for Multiparty Democracy (qq.v.) government.

KAUNDA, WAZA. The second son of Kenneth Kaunda (q.v.), he won the Chinsali (q.v.) parliamentary by-election in November 1989 by a wide margin, though voter turnout was low.

KAUNDA, WEZI. The third son of Kenneth Kaunda (q.v.), he first stood for parliamentary elections in October 1988, fresh from his postgraduate studies in the United Kingdom. Following his election, his father appointed him minister of state for home affairs, a move that fueled speculation that he was being groomed as his father's heir apparent. He was arrested in March 1993, in association with the "Zero Option" emergency (q.v.), and was found guilty of involvement with a coup plot in 1994. He was also embroiled in an incident in which he scuffled with a Movement for Multiparty Democracy (q.v.) official in 1994; the charges of assault and threatening violence were later withdrawn.

KAVINDELE, ENOCK. A wealthy businessman and head of Woodgate Holdings, he was brought onto the Central Committee of the United National Independence Party (qq.v.) in 1988 when, after the 1988 general party conference, President Kaunda (q.v.) sought to gain greater control over the party by dropping Fines Bulawayo. Kavindele had been a strong critic of the government's economic policies, and his invitation to the Central Committee was seen as both an overture to the business community and an attempt to rein him in. In July 1991, Kavindele announced that he would challenge President Kaunda for the presidency of UNIP and would run for the national presidency in the elections that October. However, at the UNIP Congress that began on August 6, it became clear that Kaunda would command the delegates' overwhelming support, and Kavindele withdrew his candidacy the day before the deciding vote. In the end, Kaunda stood unopposed within UNIP, but he lost the election to Frederick Chiluba and the Movement for Multiparty Democracy (qq.v.). In June 1992, after withdrawing from UNIP, Kavindele founded the United Democratic Party (q.v.), reportedly to oppose Kaunda's reemergence on the national scene and any chance of his political comeback. Kavindele dissolved the UDP in November 1993, joined the MMD, and was appointed chairman of the Finance and Economic Committee.

KAWAMBWA. The largest district in Luapula Province (q.v.), as well as the town that serves as its administrative center, the district had 54,700 people in 1969 and 82,800 in 1990. The district starts on Zambia's northern border and extends about halfway down the eastern edge of the Katanga Pedicle (q.v.). The Zambian shoreline of Lake Mweru (q.v.) is totally within the district.

KAWOSA, HEZEKIYA NKONJERA. One of the earliest of Zambian nationalists, in 1905 he met with such colleagues as David Kaunda and Donald Siwale (qq.v.) to discuss their discontent with the Europeans. Almost 20 years later these same men formed the Mwenzo Welfare Association (q.v.), but it failed to survive the transfer of both Kawosa and Siwale to jobs elsewhere.

KAYAMBI MISSION. A mission established by the White Fathers (q.v.) in Bemba (q.v.) territory, it was started on Kayambi Hill near Mipini along the Luchewe River in July 1895. Permission to begin this work was obtained by Father Joseph Dupont (q.v.) from Bemba chief Makasa V (q.v.). The chief was not originally willing, because he feared reprisals from Chitimukulu Sampa (qq.v.), who had ordered that Europeans should be kept out of Bemba territory. When it became clear that Sampa would not act against them, Father Dupont summoned Father Guille from the Mambwe (q.v.) mission with 200 freed slaves, and they built the mission. Sampa and other Bemba leaders sent messengers and presents as a sign of goodwill. A school started at the mission by the priests soon attracted many students.

KAZEMBE (CAZEMBE). The principal chieftainship of the Lunda (q.v.) people in the eastern half of Zambia, its territorial base is on the eastern shore of the Luapula River (q.v.), adjacent to the Democratic Republic of Congo (q.v.) (Zaire). While the Bemba's (q.v.) origin legend depicts Kazembe as a half brother of the Bemba founder Chiti (q.v.), these eastern Lunda trace their own origins back to the Lunda empire of Mwata Yamvo (qq.v.) in the Katanga (Shaba) area of the Democratic Republic of Congo (Zaire).

The origin of the name Kazembe (and the title Mwata that properly precedes it) begins with Mwata Yamvo's transcontinental trade empire and the Lunda's conquest of the Katangan salt pans. Mwata Yamvo sent his two brothers, Mutanda and Chinyata, out in search of a certain man who had fled him.

They failed to find their man, but they did find excellent salt pans. These cost Chinyata his life, for Mutanda had him killed for revealing their secret to Mwata Yamvo. In turn, Mwata Yamvo appointed Ng'anda Bilonda, Chinyata's son, as the Kazembe; and Ng'anda then moved east of the Lualaba River, where he defeated and killed Sanga chief Mufunga. Kazembe I died, Mwata Yamvo appointed his brother to succeed him, and Kazembe II conquered most of the Luapula and the area that is today's Kambembe's kingdom. This was about 1740.

Kazembe III expanded the territory much more and ruled until about the 19th century. Kazembe IV succeeded and ruled for about a half century. Kazembes V through IX all ruled briefly in a hectic period in which they lost much of their territory to the Yeke (q.v.), who had originated in East Africa and who had even been befriended by the Lunda.

Kazembe X took over in 1874, but about all that could still be claimed was the land in the vicinity of the Luapula valley. He accepted "protection" from the British (through Sir Alfred Sharpe, q.v.) in 1890. He opposed and repulsed a British force sent from a distant *boma* (q.v.) in 1897. But a larger force came in 1899, and he fled to the Johnston Falls Mission, where he acknowledged British rule again. He returned to his capital in 1900 and was recognized as chief when he submitted to the British. The chiefship has continued. In 1957, Kazembe XVI rose to the throne.

The Kazembe is the senior chief (or even king) of the Lunda based along the Luapula River. All other peoples whose lands were conquered accepted his overlordship, while often retaining their own leaders. The royal line continued to be recognized, with the Kazembes controlling a centralized and ethnically heterogeneous state. The Kazembe supervised his governors, many of whom were hereditary rulers from the non-Lunda peoples. Their main task was to collect tribute and send it to Kazembe. Basically a conquest state, Kazembe's kingdom retained a great deal of cohesion among its diverse peoples. Many of the Lunda adopted the Bemba language of their conquered subjects, but the Lunda language remained as the language of the royal court at the capital. Each Kazembe built his own capital somewhere near the Mofwe Lagoon (q.v.), until Kazembe X moved it about 32 kilometers (20 miles) south about 1884. It remains there today on a hill overlooking the swamps. During the hundred years from the mid-18th to the mid-19th centuries, the kingdom of Kazembe dominated the trade routes and much of the political life from Katanga to at least Lake Bangweulu (q.v.) and actually much of northeastern Zambia

KAZEMBE, NASHIL PICHEN. Often said to be a Zairean or Kenyan, this veteran pop music star was born in Luapula Province (q.v.) in 1932. After serving in the Northern Rhodesia Police for a year, he went to the South African mines and there formed the first of his many bands. His father's death brought him back to Zaire (now Democratic Republic of Congo, q.v.), and there, in Kolwezi, in 1953, he formed his second band and toured the country. He moved to East Africa in the late 1950s and for much of the next 20 years was a Zairean rumba stylist in Mombasa and Nairobi with such bands as the Equator Sound Boys and the Orchestre Super Mazembe. Returning to Zambia in the late 1970s, his "Vamhala Vinatha" was the best-selling single (51,000 copies) of 1981. In the mid-1980s, he became a recording engineer with Ndola's Teal Records. He recorded his last album in 1988 and died in 1991. This private but professional musician influenced a generation of musicians in East and Central Africa (q.v.).

KAZEMBE II, KANYEMBO MPEMBA. A brother of the first Kazembe, Chinyanta, he was chosen by Mwata Yamvo (q.v.) to succeed his brother. He thus returned to the Lualaba River and accepted tribute from the Sanga, Lamba (q.v.), and Lomotwa peoples to its east. In about 1740 he crossed the Luapula River and began to conquer the peoples there. He first overcame the Aushi (q.v.) and then successfully overtook the Bisa (q.v.) near Lake Bangweulu (q.v.). He defeated two minor Shila (q.v.) chiefs in the Luapula (q.v.) valley. He died about 1760 in the village of one of them, Katele. This was along the Lunda River, about 19 kilometers (12 miles) east of Mofwe Lagoon (q.v.). He was the first Kazembe to be buried there. During his reign he continued to send tribute back to Mwata Yamvo, in the form of copper (q.v.) and salt. Also during his reign he was opposed by a half brother, Nawezi, who wanted to seize power. Nawezi was killed by the Lunda.

KAZEMBE III, LUKWESA ILUNGA. The son of the first Kazembe, Ng'anda Bilonda, he succeeded his uncle as Kazembe in about 1760 (*see* KAZEMBE II). He resumed his uncle's pattern of conquest and subdued chiefdoms among the Bena Chishinga, Tabwa, Lungu, Shila, and Bisa (qq.v.). By the time he died in about 1804 his rule was acknowledged as far east as the

Chambeshi River (q.v.). On one trip he and his forces proceeded as far east as the Ngonde of Lake Malawi (q.v.) before returning to the Luapula River (q.v.). Through Mwata Yamvo (q.v.), he was actively engaged in the west coast trade with the Portuguese, acquiring guns in return, and in the east coast trade through Bisa traders, exchanging copper and ivory (qq.v.) for beads and cloth. Kazembe was not pleased with having to go through Bisa (q.v.) middlemen, thus he attempted to make contact directly with the Portuguese on the lower Zambezi (q.v.), through the intercession of Gonçalo Pereira (q.v.), a Goan miner and trader with whom he made contact in 1793.

This resulted in a visit to Kazembe's capital by Manuel Pereira, Gonçalo's son, in 1796. Upon his return in 1798, Manuel brought with him two ambassadors from Kazembe who announced that Kazembe wished to trade ivory with the Portuguese at Tete (q.v.) and, in turn, invited the Portuguese to set up a trading post on the Luangwa River (q.v.). This led to an expedition under Dr. Francisco de Lacerda (q.v.), who wished to set up trade through Kazembe that would stretch to Africa's west coast. The expedition included both of the Pereiras and Father Francisco Pinto (q.v.), who took over when Lacerda died shortly after reaching Kazembe's capital. The negotiations failed, as Kazembe feared that his trade with Mwata Yamvo would suffer if he allowed the Portuguese to head west. Kazembe III died in 1804, and his son, Kazembe IV (q.v.) succeeded him. Kazembes V and VI were also his sons.

KAZEMBE IV, FELEKA MAYI. The successor to his father, Kazembe III (q.v.) (Lukwesa Ilunga), in 1805, he ruled for almost 45 years, solidifying the territorial gains of Kazembes II and III. For about 10 years he maintained the trade contacts established with the Portuguese by his father, even exchanging embassies with the Portuguese government at Tete in 1810–11 and again in 1814. Soon after, however, the trade stopped, as Portuguese traders became disinterested in Kazembe's ivory (q.v.) because of the financial rewards of the growing slave trade (q.v.). Nevertheless, the Portuguese governor at Tete (q.v.) attempted to reopen trade with Kazembe throughout the 1820s. Kazembe finally responded by sending an ivory caravan in 1830, and the Portuguese sent an expedition led by two soldiers, Captain António Gamitto (q.v.) and Major José Monteiro in 1831–32. The expedition was beset by sickness and death. Further, Kazembe was not interested in increasing trade.

Although trade did not develop, the expedition resulted in

an excellent literary work, Gamitto's journal, which gives an outstanding description of Kazembe's capital and his wealth. Kazembe's power had peaked, however. He was a brutal dictator, feared by his own people. Also, the Bemba, Luba, and Arabs (qq.v.) were all beginning to chip away at Kazembe's trade routes and his subject peoples. The Portuguese feared that further trade with Kazembe might be unduly interrupted by other forces. When Kazembe IV died, around 1850, his two immediate successors, his younger brothers, did not share the power Kazembe IV had inherited. They reigned briefly, as did Kazembe VII. Kazembes VII, IX, and X were sons of Kazembe IV, Feleka Mayi, and Kazembes XIII, XIV, XV, and XVI were all his grandsons.

KAZEMBE X, KANYEMBO NTEMENA. Reigning from 1874 until his death in 1904, he was the Lunda (q.v.) leader who signed the agreement with Sir Alfred Sharpe (q.v.) in 1890 accepting British dominance in the area. He resisted British rule in 1897 and 1899 (*see* KAZEMBE) but finally submitted in 1900 and was recognized by the British as the chief. It was he who established the present Kazembe capital in about 1884, when he returned from seeking Bemba aid against the Yeke (qq.v.). It is on a hill about 32 kilometers (20 miles) south of the Mofwe Lagoon (q.v.). In 1893 he finally managed to subdue a force of Lunda rebels and their Yeke allies with the aid of the Bemba.

KAZUNGULA. The town is on the Zambia-Zimbabwe border at the point of the confluence of the Chobe and Zambezi Rivers (qq.v.). In early 1973, there were a series of land mine explosions near the town in which many people were killed or injured. The Rhodesians were assumed to be responsible. The town is also the only point at which neighboring Botswana (q.v.) touches Zambia, and Botswana has built a major road up to the opposite river bank, allowing products and people to enter Zambia at Kazungula by two relatively new pontoon bridges.

KELA. He was a Mambwe (q.v.) chief of the late 19th century, and an enemy of Nsokolo (q.v.). As the Mambwe paramount chief, he made a treaty with the Bemba (q.v.) leader, Chitimukulu Chitapankwa (qq.v.). After the latter's death, however, Kela had considerable difficulties with the Bemba, who repeatedly attacked his villages. In 1889, Harry Johnston (q.v.), representing the British South Africa Company (q.v.), made a treaty with Kela.

KHAMA III (THE GREAT). Chief of the Ngwato (Bamangwato) in neighboring Botswana (q.v.) from 1875 until his death in 1923, he came to be a respected friend of the Lozi ruler Lewanika (qq.v.). When Khama agreed to the establishment of a British Protectorate in 1885, Lewanika became convinced that this would also be his own best safeguard against the Ndebele led by Lobengula (qq.v.). Thus the Lozi ruler signed an agreement with the British South Africa Company (q.v.) in 1890. Khama also played an important role in encouraging the missionary François Coillard (q.v.) to go to Barotseland (q.v.), where he ultimately became an important advisor to Lewanika.

KILWA. This Indian Ocean city and trading center (in present-day Tanzania, q.v.) is where many of the East African trade caravans into Zambia started or ended. Through much of the 19th century, both Bisa and Senga (qq.v.) traders traveled to Kilwa frequently with their caravans.

KING VICTOR EMMANUEL OF ITALY. A friend of the kings of both Britain and Portugal, he was asked to be the chairman of an arbitration commission that in 1905 settled the question of the precise location of Zambia's western border with Angola (q.v.). Although a treaty of 1891 had presumably set the border, the Lozi king, Lewanika (qq.v.), complained that the river boundaries chosen had arbitrarily split his land in two and that the British South Africa Company (q.v.) should see to it that his territory be restored. The Italian king and his commission found Lewanika's arguments difficult to evaluate (for example, in determining whether the payment of tribute constituted an acknowledgment of sovereignty) and thus resorted to a straight line border, which was accepted by both the British and the Portuguese.

KITAWALA (CHITAWALA). Another name for the Watch Tower Movement (q.v.) in both Northern Rhodesia (q.v.) and the Congo, it is derived from the English word "tower." The name literally means either the "great tower" or "the tower thing." Thus a member of the movement was sometimes called a Kitawalan.

KITCHEN KAFFIR. Known by a host of other names—Fanagalo, *ci*Lapalapa, *iSi*Lololo, Basic Bantu, Mine Kaffir, and *iSi*Kula

(Zulu for "Coolie language")—this was a colonial-era pidgin language (i.e., an artificial lingua franca, one that is no one's mother tongue). Since it was primarily used by Europeans and Asians when speaking to Africans, it is also a language of command and subordination. It consists of just under 2,000 words, about 30 percent of which come from English (24 percent) or Afrikaans (6 percent), and 70 percent from Zulu and Xhosa. It seems to have originated in Natal around 1830 and was brought to Northern Rhodesia (q.v.) with the South African miners and farmers. South African whites believed that Kitchen Kaffir was understood by Africans all over the continent. Yet the mines dropped its use in the 1950s when they found themselves offering Kitchen Kaffir classes to black and white miners who could already communicate in English. Though the use of this language is considered demeaning to Africans, a number of its words—like *nikishi* ("nothing"), *mbitshana* ("slowly," "slightly"), *haikona* ("no way"), *stelek* ("strong," "thoroughly"), and *pikanin* ("little," "young")— have found their way into most of Zambia's African languages.

KITUTA. The site of an African Lakes Company (q.v.) trading station in the late 19th century, it was located on the southeastern shore of Lake Tanganyika (q.v.). It was the beginning point for many trade caravans heading east along the Stevenson Road to Lake Malawi (qq.v.), and of course much trade followed the reverse path as well.

KITWE. Zambia's third-largest city, after Lusaka and Ndola (qq.v.), it had 200,000 people in 1969 and 349,000 in 1990. The Copperbelt's (q.v.) second-largest city, its history is closely tied to the development of the Nkana Mine (q.v.). It was also the regional administrative and technical center for the Nchanga Consolidated Copper Mines, Ltd. (formerly Anglo-American Corporation of South Africa, Ltd.)(qq.v.) and serves as a retail and service center for the surrounding area. Some manufacturing exists, as well. It is a well-planned city with a central business district, movie houses, educational facilities, television and radio stations, and sporting facilities.

KITWE AFRICAN SOCIETY. Founded in the early 1940s by such later political activists as Godwin Mbikusita Lewanika (*see* MBIKUSITA, GODWIN AKABUWA), its president, and Harry Nkumbula (q.v.), its secretary, it was a typical urban voluntary association. As such it attempted to further the interests of

Kitwe's Africans. One of its meetings, in January 1946, was the occasion of the "Elwell Incident," involving Archibald H. Elwell (q.v.).

KNIFE-EDGE BRIDGE. A short footbridge built by the Zambian government in 1969 to provide easier viewing of Victoria Falls (q.v.) from the Zambian side, the bridge leads to a promontory that directly faces the falls.

KOLA. Also called Buluba, it is the legendary western land of origin for many African peoples in central and northeastern Zambia and southeastern Democratic Republic of Congo (q.v.) (Zaire). Zambians typically claim it to have been of Luba (q.v.) origins, while Congolese (Zaireans) typically claim Lunda (q.v.) origins.

KOLOLO (MAKOLOLO). This Sotho (q.v.)-speaking people from the area of the Orange Free State had significant impact upon the peoples of southern and western Zambia between 1830 and 1870. Like the Ndebele (q.v.), these cattle-keeping warriors moved north to avoid the attacks of Shaka's Zulu. They were followers of Sebituane (q.v.), a chief of the Fokeng, a Sotho group who fled north in about 1823 through what is now Botswana (q.v.). Attracted by the cattle of such southern Zambian peoples as the Tonga and Ila (qq.v.), they crossed the Zambezi at Kazungula (qq.v.), upstream of the Victoria Falls (q.v.), in the early 1830s. (Much of the story of the Kololo is told here under the entries of their two major leaders: SEBITUANE, and his son SEKELETU.) Their main role in Zambian history, however, concerns their conquest and the 25-year rule of the Lozi (q.v.). During this time, the Kololo controlled most of western Zambia and south, across the Caprivi Strip (q.v.), into northeastern Botswana. Their language is still the language of the Lozi (q.v.) today, and in fact they applied the word *Lozi* to the people previously called Luyana (q.v.).

The only other people that caused the Kololo concern were the Ndebele, whom they greatly feared but whom they defeated in several battles. The other major problem they faced was the fact that they sited their capital in a malaria-ridden area near the Chobe River (q.v.), and the fever regularly decimated them. Dr. David Livingstone (q.v.) spent some time with them in the early 1850s and noted the declining number of able-bodied men. Malaria and the succession dispute that followed Sekeletu's 1863 death helped the Lozi defeat their conquerors in August 1864, a defeat so total that a missionary who had worked with them a few years earlier wrote in December of that year that "there is not a vestige left of the tribe as such." Thirty years earlier they had numbered more than 30,000.

KONGAMATO. A pterodactyl-like creature of Kaonde (q.v.) legend, it might refer to sightings of either an out-of-range whale-headed or shoe-billed stork. *Also see* CHIPEKWE.

KONKOLA, DIXON. An important trade union leader of the 1950s and 1960s, he probably set a record for the number of political parties he either founded or belonged to. President of the Railway African Workers Trade Union (q.v.) in the early 1950s, he favored a continuing link between the African National Congress (q.v.) and the union movement. This stemmed in part from the fact that he had been an active organizer for the ANC in Broken Hill in 1952 and 1953. His position differed from that of Lawrence Katilungu (q.v.), whom he defeated as president of the Trade Union Congress (q.v.) in 1955. In January of that same year, with Harry Nkumbula and Kenneth Kaunda (qq.v.) both in jail, Konkola was acting secretary-general of ANC. In that position he edited the second issue of the party's paper, then called the *Official Gazette*.

His political activity continued in 1956 when he organized a brief but very effective boycott of the grocery stores, a movie house, and a butchery in Broken Hill. Nevertheless, in August 1956, he was replaced as the ANC deputy secretary-general by Titus Mukupo (q.v.). Early in 1957, Konkola talked about forming a socialist party; he was opposed by the membership of the Trade Union Congress, although his call for one man, one vote was cheered. Nevertheless he resigned from both the Trade Union Congress and the Railway African Workers Union in mid-1957, claiming Nkumbula was working against him.

When the Zambia African National Congress (q.v.) was formed in October 1958, Konkola wanted the presidency. When he was offered the position of Kaunda's deputy president, he declined. About two months after the ZANC was banned in March 1959, Konkola established the United African Congress (q.v.). In June, however, the UAC joined with the African National Freedom Movement to create the United National Freedom Party (q.v.). Konkola, as its president-general, promised a nonviolent campaign for self-government. By April 1961 there were reports that Konkola was trying to form a republican party in northeastern Zambia. While a National Republican

Party (q.v.) briefly made an appearance as a United Federal Party (q.v.) front organization, Konkola showed up in April 1962 as a successful candidate for one of two federal seats as a member of the Central African People's Union (q.v.). Finally, in June 1964, he applied for membership (and was accepted) into the United National Independence Party (q.v.).

KONOSO, KABELEKA BURTON. A Lozi (q.v.) politician, closely related to the traditional leaders of Barotseland (q.v.), he was named minister of justice in January 1966. He had been active in the United National Independence Party (q.v.) and elected to Parliament (q.v.) in January 1964. In January 1967 he was switched to the post of minister of natural resources and tourism. In the December 1968 elections, he was defeated along with Arthur Wina and Munu Sipalo (qq.v.), two other Lozi cabinet ministers, when the African National Congress (q.v.) received considerable support in Barotse constituencies from the banned United Party (q.v.).

KONOSO, SEKELI. This Lusaka (q.v.) businessman was a leading member of the Barotse National Association (q.v.), which started in communities along the line of rail (q.v.) in the mid-1950s, and which was antagonistic to the Lozi (q.v.) king. Konoso himself was furious over the appointment of Akabeswa Imasiku (q.v.) as *ngambela* (q.v.). His attempt to address the *kuta* (q.v.) at Lealui (q.v.) in 1956 was thwarted, so he returned to Lusaka. In October 1956, Mwanawina (q.v.) (the Lozi king) charged Konoso with passing out pamphlets while in Barotseland (q.v.) that defamed and insulted the Lozi king. Konoso appeared before the Lealui *kuta* in January 1957, accompanied by thousands of chanting supporters. The *kuta* found him guilty, and he was sentenced to three years in solitary confinement (which the federal High Court, q.v., reduced to six months at hard labor). This produced further demonstrations by his supporters and more arrests. As a result, the Northern Rhodesian government appointed the Rawlins Commission (q.v.) to recommend changes in the Barotse native government, but its recommendations were superficial and did not satisfy Konoso or his supporters. Ironically, a few years later Konoso reconciled with the Lealui leaders.

KOPA. A Bisa (q.v.) chieftainship formerly called Mwanasabamba, the chiefs are from the Bena Ng'ona (Mushroom Clan), from which the other major Bisa chiefs also derive. Their common ancestor is Mukulumpe (q.v.). In the last half of the 19th century there were occasional conflicts with Bemba (q.v.) who intruded on Kopa's territory. Chikwanda II (q.v.) came into conflict with Kopa I, Mwanasabamba Mwape Yumba, and both Kopa II Londe and Katepela (later Kopa III) had dealings with Mwamba III (q.v.). The British administrators opened up a major controversy around 1930 when they tried to implement the principle of indirect rule (q.v.). They wished to work with one Bisa leader as "superior native authority," whereas in fact the Bisa had retained almost total autonomy, even those belonging to the same clan. Thus there was considerable resentment when they chose Kopa as the supreme native authority. After hearing the complaints of other Bisa chiefs, they reconsidered the situation but decided finally to leave Kopa as their chosen leader.

KULUHELA. The return trip to the Lozi (q.v.) royal capital after the annual Zambezi (q.v.) flood, it occurs in July and is now an important ritual ceremony. *See also* KUOMBOKA.

KUMBA KUMBA. An Arab (q.v.) trader from the East African coast, he was also the half brother of the famed Tippu Tib (q.v.). His real name was Mohammed ibn Masud el-Wardi. Tippu Tib brought Kumba Kumba on a couple of trading ventures among the Bemba and Nsama's Tabwa (qq.v.) in the 1860s and entrusted Kumba Kumba to guard his goods. In 1873, a group of men under Kumba Kumba's leadership was defeated by Bena Chishinga (q.v.) chief Mushyota, which encouraged Nsama to try to expel the Arab traders. The trader then sought the aid of Kafwimbi (q.v.), who was a challenger to the post of Nsama. Kafwimbi went to the Bemba chief Mwamba (q.v.) for additional support. Mwamba sent 70 men, and the combined force beat the Nsama, named Katandula, who died in the fighting. With some military support from Kumba Kumba, Kafwimbi then succeeded to the post of Nsama. The latter left for the East African coast by 1876.

KUNDA. This *ci*Nyanja (q.v.)-speaking people live east of the Luangwa River (q.v.) in southeastern Zambia. Since their founding ancestor, Chawala Makumba, is shared with the Bisa and Aushi (qq.v.), and since their chiefs later took refuge among the Chewa (q.v.) near Nkhota Kota, it seems likely that they originated as participants—then, later, victims—of the late-19th-century East African slave trade (q.v.). Like the Nsenga (q.v.) in this region, the Kunda vehemently deny the Chewa claims that they are a Chewa offshoot.

KUNDABWIKA FALLS. This tourist site is on the Kalungwishi River (q.v.) in the northern part of Luapula Province near Lake Mweru (q.v.). Near the falls is a large boulder incised with a notable piece of rock art (q.v.) from the Late Stone Age. There is a panel of red schematic paintings and a large grid of horizontal and vertical lines, with additional painted "ladders."

KUOMBOKA. An important ceremonial ritual of the Lozi (q.v.), which is still performed today as a kind of ceremonial pageant, it is as important as the first-fruits ceremonies among other southern African peoples. The Kuomboka commemorates the practice of the Lozi who lived in the capital at Mongu (q.v.), which is in the Zambezi (q.v.) floodplain: when the Zambezi had its annual flood in about February, the Lozi traveled to higher land at Limulunga (q.v.), with the king, or Litunga (q.v.), leading the procession in his royal barge. The return trip, also ceremonialized, occurs in July and is called Kuluhela (q.v.).

KUTA. In the broadest sense, the term is the Lozi (q.v.) word for a council that exercises various governmental functions, especially executive and judicial but also sometimes legislative. In this sense there have been *kuta*s throughout Barotseland (q.v.) for centuries, at both national and local levels. *Kuta*s have assisted councilors (*induna*s, q.v.), for example. At the national (Barotse) level, the word refers to different, often interrelated, councils, for example the Saa *kuta*, the Sikalo *kuta*, the Katengo *kuta*, and the *Mulongwanji* (qq.v.). Some authors use *se*Sotho words in place of *kuta*, the most frequent being *lekhotla* and its variants: *kgotla, kotla, khotla*.

KWACHA. A word meaning either "it is dawning" or "the dawn is here," it was used by African nationalists as a rally cry in the period prior to independence (*see* KWACHA NGWEE). In addition, the word was chosen for the name of the standard currency note when Zambia replaced its pound in January 1968. Two kwacha were then worth one of the old (British-pegged) pounds. By mid-August of 1995, a long history of international debt, economic reforms (*see* STRUCTURAL ADJUSTMENT PROGRAM; INTERNATIONAL MONETARY FUND), and devaluation had made the British pound worth about K1,450 when buying pounds, and more than K1,500 when selling them. By June 1995, when a single daily newspaper cost K500, the Bank of Zambia (q.v.) was preparing to introduce the K1,000, K5,000, and K10,000 notes.

KWACHA NGWEE. The two words were used either separately or together as nationalist slogans during the several years before Zambian independence (they were also used in Malawi, q.v.). As a result, it was declared a criminal offense by the government of Northern Rhodesia (q.v.) to shout out the words. "Kwacha" can either mean "it is dawning" or "the dawn has come," depending on inflection. "Ngwee" is an intensifying expletive, the root of which is derived from a word meaning "light" or "bright." The combination of the two, used as a slogan, meant (in effect), "Cheer up and have faith, for a great new day is almost here."

KWANDO (QUANDO) RIVER. This river is also known as the Mashi, Linyanti, or Chobe River (q.v.).

KWANGWA (MAKWANGWA). A small group of about 72,000 people (1969) living in southwestern Zambia, they are Luyana (q.v.) speaking and are related to the Lozi (q.v.), presumably through a man named Mange (q.v.), who is said to have been the founder of the Kwangwa and a brother (some say a nephew) of the Lozi leader, Mboo (qq.v.). The Kwangwa now live east of the Lozi, mainly in the forest area of the Mongu Lealui District, known as Makanda because of all the lakes there. The Kwangwa are noted for excellent wood carving.

KYUNGU (CHUNGU). This Ngonde (q.v.) chief lived near the north end of Lake Malawi (q.v.) in what is today Malawi (q.v.). A number of northeastern Zambian peoples, including the Lambya (q.v.), Fungwe, and Yombe (q.v.), sent him tribute although they retained political independence.

L

LABOUR PARTY. *See* NORTHERN RHODESIA LABOUR PARTY.

LACERDA, FRANCISCO JOSÉ MARÍA DE. Born in São Paulo, Brazil, he left the university at Coimbra, Portugal, as a doctor of mathematics and was appointed a royal astronomer before returning home to do geographical survey work in Brazil in the 1780s. He returned to Lisbon by 1790 and was in Angola (q.v.) in 1797. In 1798 he was appointed governor of Rios de Sena, Mozambique (q.v.), and was instructed to open a transcontinental route to Angola to fend off British claims to the interior of southern Central Africa (q.v.). At the same time, Lunda chief Kazembe (qq.v.) invited the Portuguese in Mozambique to trade for his ivory (q.v.). Lacerda's expedition of almost 460 people, including 400 porters, left Tete (q.v.) in July 1798 and reached Kazembe's (q.v.) capital in October. Lacerda's journal is one of the earliest accounts of northeastern Zambia's lands and peoples. The Bisa (q.v.), to protect their trading monopoly with Kazembe, made the journey exceptionally arduous, and many of the expedition's porters simply fled. Lacerda died of a fever soon after reaching Kazembe. His chaplain, Father Pinto (q.v.), led the return trip to Tete in 1799, during which Lacerda's bones were lost in a battle with the Bisa.

LAKE BANGWEULU. The only one of Zambia's four major lakes that lies solely within Zambia's boundaries, it encompasses about 2,590 square kilometers (1,000 square miles). The Bangweulu swamps to the southeast of the lake are about twice that size. The Chambeshi River (q.v.) contributes some of its flow to the lake by way of the swamps. On the other hand, the Luapula River (q.v.) drains some water from the lake on its path to Lake Mweru (q.v.). The lake is a fairly shallow basin, about 9 meters (30 feet) deep, and is easily traveled by fishing boats. The Bisa, Unga, and even some Twa (qq.v.) people live in the swampy area. The great Bemba (q.v.) migration to the northeast went around the northern edge of the lake. Generally, the area around the lake has seen a great deal of movement of peoples, and it is still heavily populated.

LAKE KARIBA. Situated on the border with Zimbabwe, Lake Kariba is the third-largest manmade lake in the world (about 5,190 square kilometers, or 2,000 square miles). It is 282 kilometers (175 miles) long and 32 kilometers (20 miles) wide at its widest point. It was developed in 1959 when the Zambezi River (q.v.) was dammed in order to supply electrical power for Northern and Southern Rhodesia (qq.v.) (see KARIBA DAM). The creation of the lake necessitated Operation Noah to rescue the thousands of animals trapped on islands by the rising water and relocate and resettle (not without some forcible means) nearly two-thirds of the Gwembe District's 54,000 residents—primarily the Gwembe Tonga (q.v.) of chiefs Mwemba, Sinazongwe, Chipepo, and Simamba. Each family was moved from 16 to 145 kilometers (10 to 90 miles) from its original home and received £3 compensation—one month's salary for a native authority (q.v.) messenger—for its home and gardens. While the lake's purpose was to supply a source of waterpower, it also created a short-lived fishing industry and tourist attraction.

LAKE MALAWI. Formerly known as Lake Nyasa until Nyasaland (q.v.) became independent and changed its name to Malawi (q.v.), it is located on the eastern border of Malawi, in some places as close as 48 kilometers (30 miles) to Zambia's eastern border. In recent centuries, Africans, especially those engaged in trade, would travel freely between Lake Malawi and the various major lakes of Zambia, where trading stations were maintained.

LAKE MWERU. Part of the great East African Rift system, Lake Mweru is located in the northwestern corner of eastern Zambia, forming a natural border with the Democratic Republic of Congo (q.v.) (Zaire). About two-thirds of the lake's approximately 3,900 square kilometers (1,500 square miles) are considered to be within Zambian boundaries. A great deal of fishing, both commercial and subsistence, occurs there. The first British South Africa Company (q.v.) station was set up on the northeastern corner of the lake in 1891, at Chiengi. In 1893 the BSAC added a post at the mouth of the Kalungwishi River (q.v.), one of Zambia's few large rivers that empties into the lake.

LAKE TANGANYIKA. A major East African lake, its southern edge constitutes part of Zambia's border with the Democratic Republic of Congo (q.v.) (Zaire) and Tanzania (q.v.). This area was heavily traveled by traders, especially in the 19th century, when Arabs (q.v.) from East Africa were involved in both ivory and slave trading (qq.v.) with Africans along the lake's southern edge, an area in which the Bemba (q.v.) were trying to spread their influence at the expense of smaller groups like the Tabwa, Mambwe, and Lungu (qq.v.). The area was the site of many of Zambia's earliest mission stations as well as some of the first administrative stations of the British South Africa Company (q.v.). A resurrected German gunboat, sunk during World War I, ferries people and goods between Kigoma, Tanzania, on the lake's northeastern shore, and Mpulungu, Zambia, on its southeastern end.

LALA. The Lala people stretch from the southern half of the Katanga Pedicle (q.v.) through central Zambia west of the Luangwa River. They are one of many contemporary groups that moved south into Zambia about 1,000 years ago with the Luangwa pottery tradition (q.v.); a Portuguese report from about 1650 indicates they were then already in their present area. The traditions of the Lala indicate that small-statured people were there when they arrived. The Lala, like many other Zambians, follow a matrilineal descent system. They are noted for their artistic wall painting on their houses, and, in the past, for their iron products, which they used in trade. They had a very large open mine at Msomani as well as their own smelters. By the late 19th century, the Bena Nyendwa (Vulva Clan) had attained a monopoly of Lala chiefships. It was then that the Ambo and Swaka (q.v.) peoples broke off from the Lala and that the Lima (q.v.) and Swaka chiefs first became members of the Bena Nyendwa. Almost half of Zambia's 353,600 Lala-Bisa speakers in 1986 were Lala.

LAMBA. A people who speak *ci*Lamba (related to *ci*Bemba, q.v., but closer to *ci*Lala), they live on either side of the Katanga Pedicle (q.v.). Apart from the Seba, a Lamba offshoot just to the west, the Zambian Lamba all live in northern Copperbelt Province (q.v.). The Lamba lost about 80 percent of their former lands to the 1926 line of rail Reserves Commission (qq.v.). They were originally matrilineal and matrilocal *chitemene* (q.v.) cultivators, though a continuous influx of emmigrants from the Copperbelt towns has led to more labor-intensive cultivation systems along the Ndola-Kabwe and Luanshya-Mpongwe roads. Chipimpi and his patricidal son, Kabunda, are the first two chiefs in Lamba myth, much of which seems to be an allegory of their late-19th-century encounters with Msiri's Yeke (qq.v.). Lamba chief Mushili I signed a concessionary treaty with Joseph Thomson (q.v.) in 1890. Unfortunately, Thomson's expedition started a regional smallpox epidemic, which, when combined with subsequent plagues of locusts and rinderpest, left the Zambian Lamba unable to contest the arrival and settlement of Chiwala's Swahili (qq.v.) in 1898. Historically, the Lamba in Zambia and the Democratic Republic of Congo (q.v.) (Zaire) have been considered a low-prestige ethnic group; they, in turn, have historically resented their governments and feel they have been cheated of much of their land and its mineral wealth.

LAMBYA. A small tribe living in the northeastern corner of Zambia, its origins seem connected to peoples in East Africa, especially the Ngonde at the north end of Lake Malawi (q.v.), to whom they once paid tribute.

LANCASTER HOUSE CONFERENCE, 1952. *See* LONDON CONFERENCE, 1952.

LAND ACQUISITION ACT. The law, passed in 1970, which allowed the Zambian government to acquire large tracts of land without compensation if abandoned by their foreign owners.

LANGUAGES OF ZAMBIA. There are reputedly hundreds of languages and dialects spoken in Zambia, some of them not yet properly studied and differentiated. However, English is used as the language of convenience in government and business. There are also seven official African languages: Bemba, Kaonde, Tonga, Lozi, Nyanja, Lunda, and Luvale (qq.v.). Nearly half of all Zambians speak *ci*Bemba (25 percent), *ci*Nyanja (12 percent), or *ci*Tonga (12 percent) (qq.v.), Zambia's three largest languages. Bemba predominates in Northern and Luapula Provinces (qq.v.) and in the Copperbelt (q.v.) towns; Nyanja predominates in Eastern and Lusaka Provinces (qq.v.); and Tonga predominates in Livingstone and Southern Province (qq.v.).

LAW ASSOCIATION OF ZAMBIA. Founded as the Law Society of Zambia, it was renamed the Law Association in 1973. Its objectives are to advance the rule of law, to protect individual rights, and to protect the interests of lawyers. The association serves as a watchdog group, monitoring human rights and the law in Zambia.

LAWLEY, ARTHUR. The administrator of Matabeleland for the British South Africa Company (q.v.) near the end of the 19th century, he traveled to Victoria Falls (q.v.) in June 1898 to conclude a treaty with the Lozi king, Lewanika (qq.v.): the Lawley Concession of 1898 (q.v.). To symbolically dramatize his sense of European superiority, Lawley insisted that the Lozi king cross to the south bank of the falls for the ceremony. That same year, he sent a summary of Frank Smitheman's (q.v.) labor recruitment proposal to Cecil Rhodes (q.v.), leading to the creation of the Rhodesian Native Labour Bureau (q.v.).

LAWLEY CONCESSION, 1898. Concluded by Arthur Lawley (q.v.) of the British South Africa Company (q.v.) in June 1898, it was based on the groundwork laid by Robert Coryndon (q.v.). Lozi king Lewanika (qq.v.) agreed to it and signed it on the south bank of the Zambezi River at Victoria Falls (qq.v.). It differed from the earlier Lochner Concession (q.v.) in three major ways. It allowed the BSAC to grant farmland in Toka and Ila (qq.v.) country to approved white men; it allowed the BSAC to handle and judge all cases of disputes between whites or between Africans and whites; and it cut the annual grant to the king from £2,000 to £850. It also contained a clause urged by Lewanika that excluded the basic Lozi homeland area from BSAC prospecting or settlement. The concession was superseded by the Order in Council of 1899 (q.v.) but served as the essence of the Lewanika Concession of 1900 (q.v.), which Coryndon finalized with Lewanika.

LAWS, ROBERT. An ordained medical missionary from Scotland who founded the Livingstonia Mission (q.v.) (or Overtoun Institute) at Kondowe in modern Malawi (q.v.), he first arrived in Malawi in 1875 with a party of the Free Church of Scotland's (q.v.) Presbyterian missionaries. He set up the mission at Kondowe in 1894. Its school had a great influence on many individuals from northeastern Zambia who studied there, as he taught practical European construction skills and elementary Western medicine in addition to standard education and the Bible. Two of its pupils who had a direct effect on contemporary Zambia were David and Helen Kaunda (q.v.), the parents of Zambia's first president, Kenneth Kaunda (q.v.).

LEADERSHIP CODE. Suggested by the Chona Commission (q.v.) in 1972, it was introduced as a regulation in August 1973. Its purpose was to impose strict standards of financial conduct on national leaders to set an example for the nation. It listed all leadership posts, from president to the civil service, including employees of parastatal boards, and what each could earn or own. All assets had to be made public. Rules prohibited receiving gifts or rewards. Only the president could grant exemptions to the code requirements; a panel administered the code, and penalties were provided for breaking it. Some amendments were added to the code in 1974.

LEALUI. The town was built by Lozi leader Lewanika (qq.v.) (then still called Lubosi, q.v.) to be the permanent capital of the Lozi. Construction began in 1878, and some of the work was still being completed in 1884. The town is located in Zambia's Western (formerly Barotse) Province (q.v.), on the east bank of the Zambezi River (q.v.), immediately south of the confluence of the Luanginga and Zambezi Rivers (q.v.), in the heart of the floodplain. As a result, it is abandoned for several months every year as the residents move to higher ground at Limulunga (q.v.). When the British established Mongu (q.v.), a less flood-susceptible site some 32 kilometers (20 miles) east of Lealui, as the administrative center, it soon came to rival Lealui as a center of Lozi royal activity.

LEGISLATIVE ASSEMBLY. The legislature of Northern Rhodesia (q.v.) between self-rule (January 1964) and independence (October 1964), it was formerly called the Legislative Council (q.v.) and, later, the National Assembly, or Parliament (q.v.).

LEGISLATIVE COUNCIL. A standard feature of British colonial rule, the Legislative Council in Northern Rhodesia (q.v.) was instituted by the Northern Rhodesia (Legislative Council) Order in Council of 1924 (q.v.), when the British South Africa Company (q.v.) turned over the territory's administration to the British Colonial Office (q.v.). The first council consisted of nine official members (the five ex officio members of the Executive Council and four nominated members) plus five elected unofficial members. In 1929 two more elected "unofficials" were added. A 1938 Order in Council changed its composition to eight official and unofficial members each by replacing one official with a nominated unofficial charged with representing "native" interests. With that one new member as an exception, the Legislative Council was totally dominated by settler interests. Most of the members pushed for either a self-rule arrangement, such as Southern Rhodesia (q.v.) had, or for amalgamation (q.v.) with Southern Rhodesia.

In 1941, two new seats were added to the council, one new elected seat and the restored official seat. A major change occurred in 1945, however, when four new nominated unofficial seats were added, three of them to represent African interests. While unofficials now outnumbered officials 13 to nine, only eight of the 13 were elected. This meant, however, that the officials' majority was ended and that the governor had to consider the views of the unofficials when presenting legislative proposals.

During most of the 1940s, the leader of the unofficials was Roy Welensky (q.v.), and in 1948 he won further changes from the government. The council's term was extended from three years to five, and an elected speaker replaced the governor as president of the council. Furthermore, there were to be 10 elected unofficials and 10 officials, plus four nominated unofficials—two Africans and two Europeans—representing African interests. In 1948 the council began to push for the creation of a Central African Federation (q.v.).

With the coming of the federation in 1953, the new Legislative Council was to number 26 seats: 12 elected unofficials, eight officials, four Africans selected from the African Representative Council (q.v.), and two Europeans to represent African interests. As in the past, franchise requirements were such that only a dozen or so Africans could qualify to vote for the elected members.

The Benson Constitution (q.v.), which took effect in 1959, provided for an elected multiracial council. There were to be eight official seats out of the 30 provided. Of the 22 unofficials, 14 were elected in such a manner that they would undoubtedly be Africans. Two of each race would fill "reserved" seats, the remainder, "ordinary" seats. The 1962 constitution was much more complex in its attempt to balance racial interests. It provided for 45 elected members, as many as six officials, and an undetermined number of nominated members to be decided upon later by the British government. Fifteen of the elected members would be chosen by an "upper roll" of voters and 15 by a "lower roll." An additional 15 would be selected from national constituencies by both rolls. One of these national seats was to be reserved for Asian and coloured voters, the rest would be paired in seven two-men constituencies, four of which were to be divided between one African and one European seat. A complicated formula required national seat candidates to secure certain percentages of votes from both the upper and the lower rolls. This proved impossible in some instances, and eight national seats went unfilled. Nevertheless, an African majority then controlled the council.

Under the 1964 constitution that led to independence, the Legislative Council was renamed the Legislative Assembly (q.v.). It was expanded to 75 members: 65 elected by Africans on the main roll, and 10 from reserved roll constituencies by European voters.

LENJE. A central Zambian people speaking a Tonga (q.v.)-related language, there were about 136,000 *ci*Lenje-speaking Zambians in 1986. Like the Tonga, their traditional political organization did not include large, centralized chiefships. The Lenje seem to have come from the Democratic Republic of Congo (q.v.) (Zaire) as early as the 16th century and claim to have found and absorbed the Sala and Soli (qq.v.) groups they encountered south of the Lukanga swamp (q.v.). Many Lamba (q.v.) and neighboring Zambian and Katangan Pedicle (q.v.) peoples sought refuge with Lenje chiefs Chipepo and Ngabwe during the late-19th-century period of warfare and slave raiding. Joseph Thomson's (q.v.) treaty-seeking caravan paid a brief visit to Chipepo in 1890.

LENNOX-BOYD, ALAN. This British Conservative Party member of Parliament (q.v.) served as colonial secretary from 1955 until October 1959, when he was made a viscount and resigned his post. When Harry Nkumbula of the African National Congress (qq.v.) attempted to meet him while in London in late 1955, Lennox-Boyd refused to see him. The secretary visited Central Africa (q.v.) in January 1957 and made it clear that he supported the continuation of federation (q.v.) and Roy Welensky's (q.v.) policies, despite the fact that the African Representative Council (q.v.) had rejected federation. He opposed all such suggestions, telling the Africans in Northern Rhodesia (q.v.), "It is good for you, and you must accept it." In 1958 he assured the traditional leaders of Barotseland (q.v.) that he would allow no constitutional changes affecting their area without full consultation with and consent of the Litunga (q.v.), or "paramount chief."

LENSHINA, ALICE MULENGA. She founded the religious sect called the Lumpa Church (q.v.), or the Lenshina Movement, which was especially active in the United National Independence Party (q.v.) stronghold of Chinsali District (q.v.) from its 1953 founding until its bloody confrontation with and banning by the government in 1964. Alice Lenshina (a corruption of the Catholic "Regina") was a married Bemba (q.v.) convert to the Free Church of Scotland's Lubwa (qq.v.) Mission. In 1953, she claimed to receive a calling as a prophetess from Jesus Christ. This occurred, she claimed, after having died four times and, each time, "rising again." During one of her deaths she claims to have had a long conversation in Heaven with God, who told her to return to Earth and help rid the people of magic and witchcraft. God also gave her the "true" Bible from which to preach. Thus, in September 1953, she began the Lumpa (*ci*Bemba, q.v., for "to travel far," or "better than, or exceeding, all the rest") Church at Kasomo, later renamed Sioni (Zion), which is about 11 kilometers (seven miles) from Chinsali. Membership grew quickly; she had an estimated 50,000 to 100,000 followers at the movement's peak.

At first, the church was neither political nor extreme. It preached a strict morality, forbidding drinking, smoking, dancing, and adultery. Total renunciation of magic and sorcery was necessary to be saved and reborn. Baptism by Lenshina provided protection against sorcery and witchcraft. The only threat the movement posed was to some established churches, especially in northeastern Zambia, as it drew away many of their members.

In the early 1960s, however, Lenshina's church and the major nationalist organization, UNIP, came into conflict. Many of its members had left the church movement for politics. Lenshina countered by forbidding her followers to belong to any political movement or even to vote. It was later alleged, but never proven, that Roy Welensky's United Federal Party (qq.v.) gave Lenshina £8,000 to undermine UNIP. Regardless, animosity between the church and UNIP quickly developed. From mid-1962 to mid-1963 numerous Lumpa churches in Northern and Eastern Province (qq.v.) villages were victims of arson. UNIP organizers saw the church as both a political opponent and an enemy of the nation. Lumpa members sometimes countered UNIP with their own form of harassment, including accusations of witchcraft against some individuals.

Bloody battles finally broke out in 1964, just as Kenneth Kaunda's (q.v.) UNIP administration of Zambia began. The Lumpas had acquired guns and erected stockaded villages. A minor incident led to the killing of two policemen by Lumpa members on July 24. Fighting between armed church members and government forces seeking to restore order resulted in at least 500 deaths in a three-week period. Some of the Lumpa were almost suicidal in their fighting tactics, seeing themselves as "saved" martyrs. In some areas Lumpa fighters killed innocent villagers. Kaunda banned the church on August 3, 1964, and on August 12, Alice Lenshina surrendered to authorities and asked her followers to return home peacefully. Some fighting continued until mid-October, however, and one battle resulted in 60 Lumpa deaths. An amnesty was granted for Lumpa members in 1968, but most resettled in Mokambo, the

Democratic Republic of Congo (q.v.) (Zaire) (just across the border from Mufulira, q.v.). Though some began returning in 1971, and 80 returned in 1993, 2,000 stayed in the Democratic Republic of Congo (Zaire). Lenshina was released from detention in December 1975 but was temporarily restricted to the Lusaka (q.v.) area. When she died in December 1978 in Lusaka, leadership of the banned Lumpa Church passed to Obed Muchinga Chileshe, who died in January 1993. He was succeeded by his widow, (Mama) Ntasa Muchinga Chileshe, who reunited the church's three factions under the name of the Jerusalem Church of Christ.

LETTOW-VORBECK, PAUL E. VON. This wily German general led an impressive campaign of evasion throughout southern Tanganyika (q.v.), Portuguese East Africa, and northeastern Northern Rhodesia (q.v.) during the closing years of World War I. His force of 1,500 soldiers (and as many porters) moved deep into Portuguese East Africa (Mozambique, q.v.) and back again, then into northeastern Zambia in October and November 1918. Pursued by the Northern Rhodesia Police (q.v.) and the King's African Rifles, they came through Fife (q.v.) and traveled southwest to Kasama (q.v.). On November 8, the district commissioner (q.v.) at Kasama, Hector Croad, sent all the women and children to Mpika (q.v.) for safety. One of the town's few defenders (the police had been sent to defend Abercorn, q.v.) had been instructed to burn the town's military stores, but mistakenly burned the government offices as well. Thus, Lettow-Vorbeck found Kasama burning when he arrived on November 9. On November 12, he continued to march his men south to the Chambeshi River (q.v.). On November 13 they began an attack on the rubber (q.v.) factory there. By then, the war was already over in Europe, but the news did not reach the Chambeshi until November 13. The general formally surrendered to General Edwards of the King's African Rifles at Abercorn on November 18.

LEWANIKA (LUBOSI). Litunga of Bulozi (qq.v.) (king of Barotseland, q.v.) in 1878–84 and 1885–1916, he was probably the Lozi (q.v.) leader best known to the European world. His major goals throughout his reign were to restore and strengthen the Litunga's power and to help his nation attain physical security and technical progress, mainly through the establishment of good relations with the Europeans and, preferably, a treaty with the British queen, Victoria. The treaties he signed, however, were all with Cecil Rhodes' British South Africa Company (qq.v.).

He was born in 1842 in Bulozi, the son of Litia (q.v.), himself the son of the noted Lozi king, Mulambwa (q.v.). At the time of his birth, the family was fleeing the Kololo (q.v.) invaders who were dominating his homeland. Thus the child (not known as Lewanika until 1885) was named Lubosi, "the escaped one." About 1856, Litia (q.v.) decided to try conciliation with the Kololo and took his family back to their homeland. In 1863, Litia was executed by the Kololo, but Lubosi was spared. Within two years, however, the Lozi regained their territory, and their leadership was taken over by Sipopa (q.v.), who ruled as Litunga until 1876. A young man, Mwanawina (q.v.), ruled for two years until he was forced to abandon the throne and flee the country. The National Council selected Lubosi as Litunga in mid-1878. His strongest backer in the council was Silumbu, who was then appointed *ngambela* (q.v.) (prime minister) by Lubosi.

There had been others in contention with Lubosi, and their backers would have some success six years later, but for now Lubosi had the upper hand. His forces caught up with Sipopa's sons and killed them. When Mwanawina returned with a military force in 1879, Lubosi's forces defeated him also, although Mwanawina himself escaped. On the other hand, one organizer of the opposition, Mataa (q.v.), remained in Lubosi's court.

Meanwhile, Lubosi was making contacts with the outside world. He began to communicate with a southern neighbor, Khama III (q.v.) of the Ngwato in Botswana (q.v.). It was Khama whose treaty with the British encouraged Lubosi to attempt a similar arrangement, which would perhaps gain him some protection from Lobengula's Ndebele (qq.v.). Thus Lubosi became friends with British traders and travelers, like George Westbeech (q.v.), and gave encouragement to missionaries such as Frederick Arnot and the Reverend François Coillard (qq.v.). An important internal reform by Lubosi was the reintroduction of the old *makolo* (q.v.) system, which had been in disuse since the Kololo invasion. He hoped this action would prevent his opponents from mounting a force for a new civil war.

Despite his efforts, an uprising in July 1884 forced Lubosi to flee the capital to Mashi. The rebel leader, Mataa (q.v.), brought a son of Imbua, Tatila Akufuna (q.v.), back from Lukwakwa to become Litunga in September 1884. Mataa became *ngambela*, a post he had long coveted. Akufuna proved to be a very poor choice, however, and opposition to him quickly surfaced, independent of Lubosi. Mataa was able to defeat one group, but Silumbu gathered a large army for Lubosi in July 1885, and Lubosi mobilized a second one. A major battle in November 1885 was won by pro-Lubosi forces, and both Silumbu and Mataa were killed. Akufuna had fled months earlier.

Lubosi then chose the praise name Lewanika for his name. Its literal meaning is "to add together" but loosely translated comes out, more appropriately, "conqueror." In April 1886, Coillard returned to Lealui (q.v.) and was allowed to set up a mission and school. This was the beginning of a long and close relationship between the two, but a relationship that would serve the king poorly. With Lewanika eager to get protection from Queen Victoria and Coillard eager to bring other Europeans into the area, the missionary assisted several Europeans in working out concessions with Lewanika. An 1889 agreement with Harry Ware (q.v.) soon involved the British South Africa Company (q.v.). This was followed, in June 1890, by an agreement with Frank Lochner (q.v.), a representative of Cecil Rhodes (*see* LOCHNER CONCESSION). Subsequently, the Lawley Concession of 1898, and the Concessions of 1906 and 1909 (qq.v.), resulted in the loss of most of Barotseland to European sovereignty, despite protests by the Lozi that they had been continually deceived by the European negotiators. Lewanika also later charged that the BSAC had voided these agreements by not honoring their provisions for schools, internal development, financial payments, and military protection against the Ndebele. Regular appeals by Lewanika to England brought no satisfaction, and in fact, the Order in Council of 1911 (q.v.) provided for the incorporation of Barotseland into the larger entity of Northern Rhodesia.

Lewanika died in February 1916. He was succeeded by his eldest son, Litia (q.v.). Despite the loss of his nation's sovereignty to the British, Lewanika won greater concessions for his people than any other Central African leader would achieve. Barotseland was to retain a degree of autonomy and separate identity even into the 1960s, and the historic memory of this distinction remains a recurrent factor in modern Zambian politics.

LEWANIKA CONCESSION, 1900. The agreement that affirmed British administrative authority in the western half of Zambia, it was agreed to by Robert Coryndon (q.v.) and the Lozi king Lewanika (qq.v.) at Lealui (q.v.), the Lozi capital. Its basis was the Lawley Concession of 1898 (q.v.). The new concession was needed for technical reasons, as the Order in Council of 1899 (q.v.) had superseded the Lawley Concession. Even this new agreement was not official enough, and the Concession of 1906 (q.v.) was needed to finalize the agreement between the Lozi leaders and the British South Africa Company (q.v.).

LEWANIKA, GODWIN MBIKUSITA. *See* MBIKUSITA, GODWIN AKABUKWA.

LEYA (BALEA). This small group of Tonga-speaking people lives in extreme southern Zambia along the Zambezi River, near the town of Livingstone (qq.v.). Several history books record a 19th-century conflict between Sekute, a Leya chief, and Sundamo, a chief of the Subiya (q.v.), in which Sundamo resorted to calling on the powerful Kololo leader Sebituane (qq.v.) for assistance against the Leya.

LEZA. The word, meaning "the supreme being," is found in many of the Bantu (q.v.) languages of Zambia. Missionaries often used it as an equivalent for "God."

LIBERAL PARTY. *See* NORTHERN RHODESIA LIBERAL PARTY.

LIMA. A *ci*Lamba-speaking people who live in southern Copperbelt Province (q.v.), north of the Lukanga Swamp (q.v.), their chiefs are, with one exception, members of the Bena Nyendwa (Vulva Clan), which is also the chiefly clan of the Lala, Swaka, and Ambo (qq.v.). Though Lima chief Lesa successfully defended his people against Yeke (q.v.) tribute collectors in the 1880s, a Yeke captain established the Bena Nsoka (Snake Clan) line of chief Machiya by marrying the former Lima chief's daughter. The Lamba (q.v.) and Lima have a special regard for Lenje (q.v.) chiefs to the south, for many Lima and Lamba (including those from modern Shaba) sought refuge there from the Yeke.

LIMULUNGA (LIMALUNGA). This is the so-called flood capital of the Lozi (q.v.) to which the Lozi king ceremoniously retires during the Kuomboka (q.v.) ceremony. He stays there from about February until July, the period during which the Zambezi (q.v.) overflows and floods the plain on which the usual capital, Lealui (q.v.), is located. Limulunga was built during the 1930s by the Lozi king Yeta III (q.v.).

LINE OF RAIL. The term is used descriptively of the farms, towns, and mines—and the jobs they offer—along the heavily populated, north-south railway corridor between Livingstone and the Copperbelt (qq.v.).

LINYANTI (LINYATI). The mid-19th-century capital or principal village of chief Sebituane's Kololo (qq.v.), the town was located in what is today the Caprivi Strip, just north of the Chobe (or Linyanti) River (qq.v.). Sebituane maintained his influence throughout most of southern and western Zambia from this location. Dr. David Livingstone (q.v.) met Sebituane at Linyanti in 1851, two weeks before the chief died. Livingstone and his party stayed on for another month after Sebituane's death, and Livingstone's wife gave birth there.

LINYANTI RIVER. This river is also known as the Kwando, Mashi, or Chobe (q.v.) River.

LIONDO. The site of a battle between Lozi forces under Mubukwanu and the Sebituane's Kololo (qq.v.) in about 1838, it is somewhat north of the Kataba (q.v.) valley. During this battle, which was lost by the Lozi, two of Mubukwanu's sons, Sibeso and Lutangu (later better known as Sipopa, q.v.), were captured by the Kololo.

LIPALILE, L. MUFANA. Active in politics, his many positions include vice presidency of the Northern Rhodesia African Congress (q.v.), 1948; vice treasurer of the African National Congress (q.v.) of Zambia, 1952; chairman of the Chingola Welfare Society; and headmaster of the Chingola school. He was an outspoken foe of federation (q.v.). In August 1969 he tried, but failed, to persuade the Zambian government to drop its plans to cancel the Barotseland Agreement of 1964 (q.v.).

LISO, EDWARD MUNGONI. An early fighter for African rule in Zambia, he stayed with his cousin, Harry Nkumbula (q.v.), in the African National Congress (q.v.) until 1973 when he joined the United National Independence Party (q.v.). In 1950, Liso was a founder of the Anti-Federation Action Committee along with Reuben Kamanga, Justin Chimba, and Simon Zukas (qq.v.), who were publishing the *Freedom Newsletter* in Ndola (q.v.). Soon they all joined the ANC. Liso quickly rose to the position of ANC president in Western Province (q.v.). In 1958 he was involved in the Mufulira colour bar (qq.v.) boycotts. He and several other officers of Western Province were put on trial for these activities, but the court acquitted them, finding that they had sufficient justification. In August 1956, at the ANC annual conference, Liso was chosen deputy president, replacing Robinson Puta (q.v.). The next month, however, the police detained Liso and 44 other leaders of the African Mineworkers Union (q.v.), one of them for three years. Liso was soon out again, however, and returned to his party activities. In November 1961 he became acting president of the ANC when Lawrence Katilungu (q.v.), serving as president while Nkumbula was in jail, was killed in a road accident. Two months later, Nkumbula was released from jail and replaced him.

Liso ran for the legislature in 1962 in Lusaka Rural District against UNIP's Solomon Kalulu (q.v.). Relying in part on support by farmers away from the line of rail (q.v.), Liso defeated Kalulu by over 500 votes. In the coalition cabinet with UNIP, he was appointed parliamentary secretary to the chief secretary. In November 1965, there was an attempt by some members of the ANC to run Liso, now the party's secretary-general, for party president against Nkumbula, but Liso refused. He did return to the National Assembly in subsequent elections, although it took a court decision at one point to decide that he held the seat for Namwala (q.v.). In October 1970, however, he was expelled from his assembly seat after charging that the government had provided young women to entertain the delegates to the Summit Conference of Non-Aligned Nations in Lusaka. Despite this, when the one-party state was instituted in 1973, he was chosen a member of the 25-member Central Committee of UNIP (q.v.).

LISULO, DANIEL MUCHIWA. Appointed prime minister of Zambia in June 1978, he had a long record of service to the United National Independence Party (q.v.) and the government. Born December 6, 1930, in Mongu (q.v.), he was educated at Loyola College of Madras University and the Law Faculty at Delhi University, attaining an LL.B. Active in the 1953–63 independence struggle, he continued to serve on UNIP committees, and as its legal counsel, and was admitted to the Central Committee of UNIP (q.v.) in 1972. Lisulo's business experience included working for the Anglo-American Corporation (q.v.) in 1963–64 and running his own law firm since

1968. He became a director of the Bank of Zambia (q.v.) in 1964. In July 1977 he was named minister of legal affairs and attorney general. In June 1978 he was promoted to prime minister by President Kaunda (q.v.).

LITIA (LETIA). The name of both the father and the son of the noted Lozi king Lewanika (qq.v.)(also known as Lubosi), the first Litia was the son of King Mulambwa (q.v.). At the time Lewanika was born about 1842, Litia was fleeing the Kololo (q.v.) invaders. Around 1856 Litia decided to collaborate with the invaders, and returned to his homeland to join the Kololo. In 1863, Sekeletu (q.v.), the Kololo leader, had Litia killed by Mpololo (q.v.) when it was reported that Litia and Sibeso, another returned Lozi, were plotting to overthrow Mpololo and put Litia in his place. The orphaned Lubosi (Lewanika) was adopted by Sipopa and survived to become king of the Lozi. He was succeeded in that position by his son, whom he had named Litia but who ruled under the name Yeta III (q.v.).

LITUNGA. The "owner (steward) of the earth," this title designates the king of the Lozi (q.v.) people. The title implies that one of his responsibilities entails the preservation of Lozi land rights and the power to designate its temporary use. The Litunga has an elaborate court and is involved in royal rituals, the most famous of which is the Kuomboka (q.v.), in which the royal capital is moved out of the floodplain for a few months every year during the rainy season. The kingship of the Lozi stays within the royal family, which is of divine ancestry, according to the Lozi, as all its members are the nominal descendants of Mbuyu (q.v.), the daughter of God. Any member of the royal family may be selected Litunga, but support by the principal *indunas* (q.v.) is crucial to his choice, especially when rival candidates compete for the succession.

Once chosen, the Litunga is the subject of numerous ceremonies and rituals and is elevated to a place above all the other royals. He is installed through a series of purification rites and is soon surrounded by mystery. He does not appear in public frequently and speaks to the people only through someone else. Even after death he is considered special, as it is believed that he takes another form and continues to intervene in earthly events, thus becoming even more powerful than during his lifetime. He is buried at a site chosen by him, which is guarded by an official attendant and medium (the *nomboti*, q.v.) and a number of families who set up a village nearby. After his death, his spirit is regularly petitioned for aid. New kings are confirmed only after having been presented to and accepted by their predecessors at the grave sites.

The term "Litunga" was disallowed by a European administrator, Robert Codrington (q.v.), early in the 20th century. He did not want the Lozi leader to have the status of a king, so he used the term "paramount chief." The Lozi themselves never ceased using the term, however, and in 1961 the British colonial secretary, Iain Macleod (q.v.), approved the use of "Litunga."

LIVINGSTONE. This, Zambia's eighth-largest town (45,000 in 1969; 84,000 in 1990), is located in southernmost Southern Province, near Victoria Falls (qq.v.)(or Mosi-oa-Tunya) and the border with Zimbabwe. It began in the 1890s just east of the Old (or Clarke's) Drift as a Zambezi River (q.v.) ferry settlement on the road from Bulawayo. The town, however, grew appreciably after the completion of the railway bridge (1905) and the railway to Ndola (q.v.) (1909) and Katanga (q.v.) (1910) made it the southern gateway to Northern Rhodesia's line of rail (q.v.). When Northern Rhodesia (q.v.) was officially created in 1911, Livingstone became its administrative capital and remained as such until 1935, when the capital was shifted to Lusaka (q.v.). Though the Liberation War in Zimbabwe led to Livingstone's isolation and infrastructural neglect, the town remains a tourist and commercial center. The Livingstone Museum (q.v.) there contains memorabilia of Dr. David Livingstone (q.v.) as well as examples of African art from the earliest times to the present. Some industry is located in the town, producing textiles and clothing, radios, and other items.

LIVINGSTONE, DR. DAVID. He was the pioneer missionary in Zambia as well as other parts of Central and Southern Africa, and an immense amount of literature has been written about him. (See, for example, the bibliography in George Seaver's *David Livingstone: His Life and Letters*.) His own books constitute an important source of information on 19th-century Zambia.

He was born in Scotland in 1813. While pursuing medical studies at Anderson's College in Glasgow, he decided to become a medical missionary to China and joined the London Missionary Society (q.v.). But when the Opium War closed off China, he joined Robert Moffat at his mission station at Kuruman, South Africa, in 1841. Livingstone soon moved farther inland to work in Bechuanaland (Botswana, q.v.). He also married Moffat's daughter, Mary. In 1851 the doctor (he was called *ngaka,* "doctor," by many Africans) crossed the Zambezi (q.v.) with his family and a small expedition. There at Sesheke (q.v.) he met with the great Kololo leader Sebituane (qq.v.). He also began to realize the extent of the slave trade (q.v.), which became a major object of his opposition throughout his next 22 years in Central Africa (q.v.). He believed that the introduction of Christianity and proper commerce would destroy the slave trade. Later, his work would inspire the African Lakes Company (q.v.) and missionaries from various denominations to pursue the same goal in Central Africa.

In 1853, he made an expedition well into Angola (q.v.) and in 1855 retraced his steps, becoming the first European to see Victoria Falls (q.v.) (which he named). He then traveled through southern Zambia into Mozambique (q.v.), reaching Quelimane (q.v.) on the Indian Ocean in May 1856. He then returned to England, where he received awards and wrote a book. He returned to Central Africa in 1858 and spent most of the next five years near Lake Nyasa (Malawi, q.v.), although he made a trip with his brother and a botanist to Victoria Falls in 1860. They went a little farther, to Linyanti (q.v.), where the doctor renewed acquaintances with Sekeletu (q.v.), the son and heir of Sebituane. The party left the Zambezi valley late in 1860 to return to Lake Nyasa (*see* UNIVERSITIES' MISSION TO CENTRAL AFRICA).

Livingstone returned to England in 1864, returning to Zanzibar in 1866 with an even stronger determination to stop the slave trade. In addition, he was seeking geographical information on the sources of the Nile and Congo Rivers. He crossed through Zambia on several occasions, reaching Lake Mweru and Lake Bangweulu (qq.v.) in 1867–68. His famous meeting with Henry Stanley occurred in 1871. Rejecting Stanley's appeal to return to England, he went southwest again into Zambia and the Congo. He died at Chitambo's village (q.v.), southeast of Lake Bangweulu in Zambia, on May 1, 1873. His heart was buried there by his two constant African companions, who took his body back to Tanganyika and, eventually, on to England.

LIVINGSTONE MAIL. Founded in 1906 in the town of Livingstone (q.v.) by pharmacist Leopold Moore (q.v.), it was Northern Rhodesia's only newspaper for many years. It was important in reflecting and shaping white settler opinion for (European) self-government. Moore invariably framed his attacks on British South Africa Company (q.v.) rule in terms of greater loyalty to the British Crown.

LIVINGSTONE MUSEUM. Formerly the David Livingstone Memorial Museum, the Livingstone Museum was established by Governor Hubert Young (q.v.) in 1934—but was effectively founded by J. Desmond Clark (q.v.), its first curator, in 1938, as part of the Rhodes-Livingstone Institute (q.v.). The two units separated in 1946. Originally housed in Livingstone's old United Services Club in 1937, the first museum contained early maps of Africa, David Livingstone's letters and memorabilia, a sparse ethnographic collection, mineral samples from Broken Hill and the Copperbelt mines (qq.v.), and several boxes of unlabeled, Middle Stone Age artifacts from an early excavation of Mumbwa Cave (q.v.). Clark founded archaeology at the museum with his work on Zambezi valley terraces, his reexcavation of Mumbwa Cave, and his later work at Kalambo Falls (q.v.). While Clark focused upon Stone Age Zambia, he recruited archaeologists Ray Inskeep, Brian Fagan, Joseph Vogel, and David Phillipson to focus upon Iron Age prehistory. The museum is a major tourist attraction with five exhibition galleries and its separate departments in history, prehistory, ethnography, and art and natural history.

LIVINGSTONE NATIVE WELFARE ASSOCIATION. Founded in 1930 by the residents of Maramba, the main African township or "location" (q.v.) of Livingstone (q.v.), it quickly became involved in fighting for social justice. Many of its founders were civil servants from Nyasaland (q.v.), men like Isaac R. Nyirenda, Edward Franklin Tembo, Samuel K. K. Mwase (acting chairman), J. E. C. Mattako (vice chairman) (qq.v.), and Gideon M. Mumana (treasurer). The government, when it granted the association permission to organize, envisioned a social club, but the founders were already protesting police injustices at a general meeting on July 15, 1930. They argued that race was the basis for mistreatment of many people and that the courts always favored Europeans over Africans. At a meeting a month earlier, several local chiefs had expressed their bitter resentment of the Europeans who had taken their land. African grievances continued to flow from the meetings as the years went on, but the government made no effort to satisfy the complaints. Africans began forming similar associations in many other towns throughout the territory.

LIVINGSTONIA CENTRAL AFRICA TRADING COMPANY. This was the original name of the African Lakes Company (q.v.).

LIVINGSTONIA MISSION. This was the working name for the chain of mission stations—including Lubwa (q.v.) Mission—along the western shores of Lake Malawi (q.v.) and into north-eastern Zambia established by the Free Church of Scotland (q.v.) to commemorate the work begun by Dr. David Livingstone (q.v.). All are now incorporated into the United Church of Zambia (q.v.).

LLEWELLYN, LORD. The first governor general of the Federation of Rhodesia and Nyasaland (or Central African Federation, q.v.), he served from September 1953 until October 1957.

LOANGWENI. The 19th-century village of the great Ngoni chief, Mpezeni (qq.v.), it was located near the present Zambian border, southeast of Chipata (q.v.). After the British defeated the Ngoni there in 1898, it was renamed Fort Young. There is now a national monument there.

LOBENGULA. The son and successor of the great Ndebele (Matabele, q.v.) leader Mzilikazi (q.v.), he became chief in 1870. Over the next 25 years, Lobengula's military forces continually threatened their neighbors north of the Zambezi River (q.v.), especially the Lozi (q.v.). Although the Lozi homeland was seldom endangered, their influence over the Ila, Tonga, Toka (qq.v.), and other southern peoples was regularly threatened by Ndebele raids. Nevertheless, at one point in the early 1880s, Lobengula contacted Lewanika (q.v.), the Lozi king, to propose that the two peoples work together to resist the invading white men. Lewanika rejected this overture in favor of closer ties with Ngwato chief Khama (q.v.). In 1891–92, Lobengula did send an army (*impi*) north toward the Lozi heartland, but problems with Europeans south of the Zambezi required Lobengula to recall his men before they could attack. Fear of Lobengula played a big part in Lewanika's search for British protection and, thus, his signing of several treaties that ultimately tied him to British South Africa Company (q.v.) rule.

LOBITO. This important port town of Angola (q.v.) is the end point of the Benguela Railway (q.v.), once one of Zambia's important import and export centers.

LOBOLA. This commonly used Southern Bantu term means "bridewealth." *See* MPANGO.

LOCAL GOVERNMENT ACT. A law passed by the Zambian Parliament and signed by President Kenneth Kaunda (q.v.) in October 1965, it was ostensibly designed to create a uniform pattern of democratically controlled local authorities throughout Zambia. Effectively, it terminated the semiautonomous status of the former Barotseland (q.v.) Protectorate. It abolished the Barotse National Council (q.v.) and replaced it with five district councils. It also had the effect of lowering the status of the Lozi (q.v.) king to "just another chief," as he lost his authority to appoint councilors and judges, to veto legislation, and to control the Barotse treasury. Considerable resentment arose among members of the Lozi traditional elite, and many other Lozi likewise resented the imposition of central government controls.

LOCATIONS. A term used throughout most of British colonial Africa, it referred to the segregated, urban residential areas for African servants, employees, and their families, areas owned and operated by the local (then, European) town councils. Location housing was generally Spartan and shabby, with shared water taps and outdoor toilets. Yet apart from the domestic servants, whose employers provided them separate, backyard quarters, such locations were the only legal residential areas for Africans in town, and rights to a location house depended upon being gainfully employed by a European boss. If you lost your job and could not find another, eviction was inevitable.

LOCH, SIR HENRY BROUGHAM. He was governor of the Cape Colony and British high commissioner in South Africa from 1889 to 1895. A series of letters passed between the Lozi king Lewanika (qq.v.) and Loch between 1890 and 1894 in which Lewanika repeatedly requested assurance that his people would be under the protection of the British government. He feared the neighboring Ndebele (q.v.), and he distrusted the British South Africa Company (q.v.), with whose representative, Frank Lochner (q.v.), he had signed a treaty. Loch assured Lewanika that a resident commissioner would soon be appointed (associated with the BSAC, however, as it turned out) and that, eventually, the Ndebele would be conquered.

LOCHINVAR NATIONAL PARK. One of the smaller national parks, consisting of about 388 square kilometers (150 square miles), it is located in south-central Zambia, and has a small northern border with the Kafue River (q.v.). It is the site of the oldest Tonga (q.v.) settlement known in Zambia, at the top of Sebanzi Hill (q.v.) at Lochinvar Ranch (q.v.).

LOCHINVAR RANCH. An important archaeological site in south-central Zambia, it is more commonly referred to by the specific geographic location, Sebanzi Hill (q.v.).

LOCHNER, FRANK ELLIOTT. A former officer of the Bechuanaland Police, he was working for Cecil Rhodes (q.v.) at Kimberley in 1889 when Rhodes sent him as his agent to negotiate a concession from the Lozi king Lewanika (qq.v.) (*see* LOCHNER CONCESSION). He reached Kazungula (q.v.) in December 1889, crossed the Zambezi (q.v.), and met Lewanika at Sesheke (q.v.) in March 1890. Negotiations continued then in other locations in Barotseland (q.v.) until the Lozi leaders signed the document on June 27, 1890. They undoubtedly would not have agreed to it had Lochner not deceived them into thinking that this was a treaty of protection with the British Crown rather than a business transaction with the British South Africa Company (q.v.).

LOCHNER CONCESSION. Also known as Lochner Treaty of 1890 or Barotse Treaty of 1890, it was one of the most significant documents in Zambia's history. It was signed by Lewanika of the Lozi (qq.v.) and 40 of his major advisors along with Frank Lochner of the British South Africa Company (qq.v.) on June 27, 1890, at the Lozi capital of Lealui (q.v.). The BSAC claimed that this treaty granted the British control over the entire western half of today's Zambia, including the Copperbelt (q.v.). The concession granted mineral rights over all the territory of the Barotse nation to the BSAC and included all future Lozi land, including "subject and dependent territory." The BSAC used the agreement to claim lands well beyond the Lozi's true dominion. The Lozi, misled by both Lochner's and the Reverend Coillard's (q.v.) translations, thought they were signing an agreement with England's Queen Victoria for British protection. The location of a resident commissioner in Barotseland (q.v.) would also provide the "Queen's" presence that Lewanika felt would give him some security, especially against Lobengula's ever-threatening Ndebele (qq.v.). Lewanika understood the agreement to only "loan" Lozi land to the Europeans, not to alienate it—a confusion due in part to Coillard's translation of the agreement. The concession did not actually give the BSAC any administrative rights, only mineral rights over an area estimated by Coillard at about 518,000 square kilometers (200,000 square miles). While guaranteeing to protect the Lozi against outside attack, the BSAC pledged not to interfere with the relationship between the king and his subjects. The fact that Lochner agreed to a £2,000 annual subsidy to Lewanika to buy guns was an important part of the agreement. The BSAC also promised to build schools and industries to help in the "education and civilization of the native subjects of the king." The BSAC failed to fulfill any of its promises, at least for a time. In some instances, it totally ignored them. Lewanika's hopes were totally frustrated, while the BSAC ultimately reaped great profits.

LOCUSTS. Wind-borne clouds of red locusts descended upon various regions of modern Zambia in 1827–31, in the 1850s, in 1892–1910, and again in 1933–35. A single, 97-kilometer-wide (60-mile-wide) swarm of 80 billion insects can travel over 966 kilometers (600 miles) a week and can easily consume all of a district's grain crops in short order. Only root crops like cassava (q.v.) or sweet potatoes are safe from locusts. The 1930s plagues caused much hardship as they hit during the massive Depression-era mine layoffs. The 1890s plagues, however, were the worst in memory, for they coincided with widespread raiding and with smallpox and rinderpest epidemics, the last of which depleted all herding animals just when deathly sick and famished people were most desperate for food. The locusts seem to have originated from breeding grounds in Saudi Arabia and the East African Horn, but have now established permanent breeding areas near Mweru Wantipa and the Kafue flats. The International Red Locust Control Organization for Central and Southern Africa (IRLCO-CSA) claims that the locusts (which, after nearly 60 years, reappeared in Southern and Western Provinces, qq.v., in 1993–94) ultimately derive from breeding grounds in Namibia's Caprivi Strip (q.v.). Zambia, with just one plane and one helicopter to devote to spraying operations, is understandably concerned that Namibia is not a member of the IRLCO-CSA, and it is seeking the cooperation of Namibia, Zimbabwe, and Botswana (q.v.) in eliminating this common threat to their peoples' food security.

LOMBE, FOUSTINO. A former member of the United Progressive Party (q.v.) before it was banned, he founded its short-lived successor, the Democratic People's Party (q.v.), in March 1972.

LONDON CONFERENCE, 1951. A conference held in March 1951 between profederationists, led by Godfrey Huggins (q.v.), and the British Colonial Office (q.v.), represented by James Griffiths (q.v.), the conference produced an agreement that Central Africa (q.v.) must be more closely tied together and that a federal constitution would be desirable. Another result of the meeting was the calling of the Victoria Falls Conference in September 1951 (q.v.).

LONDON CONFERENCE, 1952. Held in Lancaster House in London during April and May 1952, it brought together the colonial secretary with representatives from Northern and Southern Rhodesia and Nyasaland (qq.v.). The African delegates from Nyasaland and Northern Rhodesia boycotted the meeting, but Joshua Nkomo (q.v.) and Jasper Savanhu from Southern Rhodesia did take part. Of course, representatives of the settlers eagerly took part: Julian Greenfield from Bulawayo, Edgar Whitehead, Roy Welensky (q.v.), and Godfrey Huggins (q.v.). The conference produced a draft document for a federation, and commissions were appointed to investigate fiscal, judicial, and civil service concerns.

LONDON CONFERENCE, 1953. This meeting finalized the work of the 1952 London Conference, agreeing upon the constitution for a Central African Federation (q.v.). Representatives from all three governments (the Rhodesias and Nyasaland) met with British colonial officials to set in motion the legal machinery that would allow federation (q.v.) to proceed.

LONDON CONSTITUTIONAL CONFERENCE, 1961. Also called the Lancaster House Conference of 1961, this was hardly a conference at all, in that the representatives of the United Federal Party (q.v.) boycotted the talks. The background for the conference must include the Federal Review Conference (q.v.) of December 1960, from which the African delegates walked out. The British government announced that the Review Conference would not be resumed until the conferences for the individual territories occurred. The Northern Rhodesia Conference began on December 19, 1960, but recessed immediately until January 31, 1961. In the interim, Roy Welensky (q.v.) of the United Federal Party (q.v.) (and federal prime minister) tried to persuade the British colonial secretary, Iain Macleod (q.v.), to not agree to majority rule. Macleod would not guarantee this, however, so on January 28, 1961, Welensky and the Dominion Party delegates announced that they would boycott the talks. The hope was to delay the Northern Rhodesia talks until after the Federal Review Conference was held—or at least until the Southern Rhodesian talks were completed. Macleod was thus forced to cancel plenary sessions and begin a series of informal talks with the various groups. The African parties, in a united front, demanded majority rule based on universal adult suffrage. This was in total conflict with Welensky's ideas, who even tried confidential talks with British Prime Minister Harold Macmillan (q.v.). The boycott succeeded in delaying the conference until after agreement was reached with the Africans from Southern Rhodesia. The conference ended in deadlock on February 17. Some of the delegates continued to discuss the situation with Macleod after the conference closed. On February 20, Macleod presented his own plan to Parliament (q.v.) (*see* MACLEOD CONSTITUTION).

LONDON MISSIONARY SOCIETY. One of the earliest missionary groups active in Zambia, its main concern was in the region immediately south of Lake Tanganyika (q.v.). The missionaries reached the lake from Zanzibar in 1878, and while they built a depot there in 1883, it was 1884–85 before they established a mission on the lake's southern shore at Niamkolo (q.v.). In 1887 they opened a station at Fwambo near the Mambwe (qq.v.) chief of that name. The society also played a different part in Zambian history: stations in South Africa at Kuruman and Kolobeng were the starting points for Dr. David Livingstone's (q.v.) first trips into Zambia. Today, the society's work is done within the framework of the United Church of Zambia (q.v.).

LONRHO ZAMBIA, LTD. A jointly owned British and South African firm formerly known as the London and Rhodesian Mining and Land Company, it had numerous investments and subsidiaries in Zambia. Its interests included mining, newspapers, transportation, breweries, and construction.

LOVALE. This is a variant of Luvale (q.v.).

LOWER ROLL. *See* UPPER ROLL.

LOZI (ROTSE; BAROTSE). One of the most historically prominent Zambian peoples, they reside in Western Zambia (q.v.)

along the Upper Zambezi. There were about 381,000 *si*Lozi-speaking Zambians in 1986, making *si*Lozi the fourth-largest Zambian language. The prominence of the Lozi people stems from several factors. First, they maintained a strong centralized kingship under their leader, the Litunga (q.v.), so their traditions, rituals, and national unity have been preserved through the centuries, despite one desperate period in the 19th century when the Kololo (q.v.) conquered them and controlled their land. Second, the Lozi moved in all directions to dominate their neighbors militarily; many of the peoples west of the Kafue River (q.v.), and a few in southern Zambia as well, paid tribute to the Lozi, especially in the 19th century. Third, they were the first to be involved with the Europeans; missionaries like Dr. David Livingstone, Frederick Arnot, François Coillard (qq.v.), and others wrote back to Europe about their contacts with the Lozi, as did other Europeans such as Emil Holub (q.v.). In addition, Cecil Rhodes (q.v.) secured rights within Lozi territory through concessions secured by men like Frank Lochner and Harry Ware (qq.v.). The British South Africa Company thus opened up Barotseland (qq.v.) to European influence.

The name "Lozi" was given by the Kololo to the Luyi or Luyana (q.v.) people they conquered in the 19th century. The Luyana have been in the Bulozi floodplain for about 300 years. They either drove out or absorbed the existing peoples and set up a strong centralized state along the Zambezi (q.v.). Cultivation of the floodplain was essential to their way of life; gardening, fishing, and herding were also part of their economy and thus affected their village settlement patterns and concepts of land tenure. They are unusual among Zambian people in that they practice bilateral descent and place no importance on clans and lineages other than that of the royal family.

During the 20th century, the Lozi were open to European education and thus provided many of the African civil servants working in other parts of the country, notably along the line of rail (q.v.) and on the Copperbelt (q.v.). The Lozi have long struggled to regain the semiautonomous status they enjoyed as the Barotseland Protectorate, prior to the Local Government Act of 1965 (q.v.). This struggle seems to have intensified since President Chiluba's (q.v.) 1991 election. The Lozi royal establishment is still seeking the £78.5 million it claims to have lost as a result of the Barotseland Agreement of 1964 (q.v.), and President Chiluba has warned those advocating the secession of Western Province (q.v.) (the former Barotseland) from Zambia that they are courting the capital offense of treason.

LUANGWA. Formerly Feira (q.v.) District of Central Province (q.v.), it is now one of the three districts in Lusaka Province (q.v.). It is the least populated district in all of Zambia, with just 7,900 people in 1969 and 16,300 in 1990. It is primarily of historic interest, as its location on the confluence of the Luangwa and Zambezi Rivers (qq.v.) led the Portuguese to establish a market (or fair, *feira*) there in 1732.

LUANGWA NATIONAL PARK. *See* LUANGWA VALLEY GAME RESERVE.

LUANGWA RIVER. There are actually two Luangwa Rivers in Zambia. The lesser of the two is a tributary of the Kalungwishi River (q.v.) in northeastern Zambia, southeast of Lake Mweru (q.v.). Dr. David Livingstone (q.v.) traveled this Luangwa River valley in December 1872.

The better known of the two Luangwa Rivers drains a major part of Zambia on the eastern side of the Muchinga Escarpment, traveling over 644 kilometers (400 miles) on a northeast to southwest path until it joins the Zambezi River at Feira (qq.v.) on Zambia's southern border. The major tributary of this Luangwa is the Lunsemfwa River (q.v.), which joins the Luangwa a little north of the Zambezi. The Luangwa valley is hot, humid, and unhealthy. It is not heavily populated by humans, as malaria (q.v.) is a major problem there. Also, the tsetse (q.v.) fly infects and kills domestic animals. Thus a large central part of the Luangwa valley is taken up by the Luangwa Valley Game Reserve (q.v.) and its animals, wildlife scouts, poachers, and teak forests.

In 1968 the vital Luangwa River bridge on the Great East Road (q.v.) into Eastern Province (q.v.) was blown up, presumably by Portuguese infiltrators seeking to avenge Zambia's tolerance of FRELIMO guerrilla bases in Zambia.

LUANGWA TRADITION. This pottery tradition was the most widespread of Zambia's Late Iron Age ceramics styles and is almost certainly associated with the first large-scale copper (q.v.) workings at sites like Kansanshi and Bwana Mkubwa (qq.v.). This pottery is characterized by necked pots and shallow bowls with tapered, everted rims. The decorated vessels often have elaborate horizontal bands of comb-stamped triangular or herringbone chordate blocks. It appears in such 11th-century sites as Chondwe (near Ndola, q.v.) and Twickenham Road (Lusaka, q.v.) and seems to have displaced the more localized Chondwe, Kapwirimbwe, Kalambo, and Nkope (qq.v.) pottery groups of the Early Iron Age.

Luangwa tradition peoples constructed substantial mud and pole structures and had iron tools and ivory (q.v.) bracelets, hollowed grinding stones (presumably for grain), and dogs and domestic cattle. Since such pottery is today commonly made by women among a variety of central and northeastern Zambian peoples (including the Lamba, Soli, Lala, Nsenga, Chewa, Ngoni, Tumbuka, Bisa, Bemba, Mambwe, and Kazembe's Lunda, qq.v.), it is often assumed that its 11th-century appearance was associated with either a gender switch in pottery manufacture, with women taking over from men, or the arrival of these peoples' ancestors as immigrants from southeastern Democratic Republic of Congo (q.v.) (Zaire).

LUANGWA VALLEY GAME RESERVE. One of Zambia's finest attractions and once one of the best game parks in Africa, it covers 15,540 square kilometers (6,000 square miles), mostly on the western side of the Luangwa River and east of the Muchinga Mountains (qq.v.). The park is almost bisected by a narrow waist, dividing it into the Luangwa North National Park and the Luangwa South National Park. It is heavily populated with animals, including some 20,000 to 24,000 elephants. Poaching is a major problem here, as in all of Zambia's national parks, but it is important to distinguish the very different scale of poaching being pursued by neighboring villagers from that by soldiers and politicians using trucks and automatic weapons.

LUANO. One of the smaller ethnic subdivisions of Zambia, the Luano people live in Lusaka Province (q.v.), east of Lusaka (q.v.).

LUANSHYA. Zambia's seventh-largest town, this Copperbelt (q.v.) mining center had a population of 96,000 in 1969 and 148,000 in 1990. The town is located near the southern end of the urban Copperbelt, a little over 16 kilometers (10 miles) southwest of Ndola (q.v.). Luanshya is one of the older mining centers, the town and its economy being based on the Roan Antelope Mine (q.v.), at which production began in 1931. Luanshya also has some manufacturing plants and other minor industry.

LUANSHYA MINE. *See* ROAN ANTELOPE MINE.

LUANSHYA NATIVE WELFARE ASSOCIATION. This is one of the many welfare associations (q.v.) that played an important role in the growth of African nationalism in Zambia. Its leaders in its important years of existence, the early 1930s, were northerners: Henry Chibangwa (q.v.) and John Lombe from Mporokoso (q.v.) and Kenny Rain, a Bemba from Kasama (qq.v.). The government refused to grant recognition to this organization because it considered their major goals—equal rights, better treatment, "justice to the Native people of this colony," and an end to the pass system (q.v.)—inherently subversive.

LUANSHYA SNAKE. *See* SANGUNI.

LUAPULA PROVINCE. Situated in the eastern half of Zambia, along the eastern border of the Katanga Pedicle (q.v.), the province had a population of about 336,000 in 1969, and 527,000 in 1990. The western border of the province is the Luapula River (q.v.), which separates it from the Democratic Republic of Congo's (q.v.) (Zaire's) Shaba Province. The most famous inhabitants of the province are the Lunda of chief Kazembe (qq.v.) and the Aushi, Bwila, Shila, Bena Chishinga (qq.v.), and Bena Kabende.

LUAPULA RIVER. One of Zambia's major rivers, it forms the border between the Democratic Republic of Congo (q.v.) (Zaire) and Zambia south from Lake Mweru (q.v.) along the eastern border of the Democratic Republic of Congo's (q.v.) (Zaire's) Katanga (Shaba) Pedicle (q.v.). It actually begins as an extension of the Chambeshi River (q.v.), draining the swamps and marshes south of Lake Bangweulu (q.v.). It then turns westward before heading north toward Lake Mweru. At one point it travels through large rocks, becoming rapids and cataracts, until it plunges over Johnston Falls. It then becomes a broad, deep, and peaceful river, the last 160 kilometers (100 miles) of its trip to Lake Mweru. The river is a rich source of fish, supplying a livelihood for many Zambians. The river and its vicinity are justly famous as the location of the great Lunda empire of Kazembe (qq.v) that dominated trade in Central Africa (q.v.) from about 1750 to about 1850.

LUBA. The original home of this major family of Central African peoples is in southeastern Democratic Republic of Congo (q.v.)

(Zaire) near Lake Kisale. According to Luba legend, a member of the royal lineage, Chibinda Ilunga, married Lunda princess Lueji (q.v.), and many Zambian chiefships trace their origins to her grandson, Mwata Yamvo (q.v.). The Bemba's Bena Ng'andu (Crocodile Clan) chiefs, however, actually are of Luba origin. The legendary migration of their leaders (*see* CHITI) began in a place sometimes called Kola (q.v.), or Buluba, by the Bemba. The Lenje (q.v.) of south central Zambia also claim to be of Luba origin. Around 1830, the Congo (Democratic Republic of Congo, q.v.) Luba began to expand, and a Luba army attacked the Lunda capital of Kazembe (q.v.) but was driven off.

LUBEMBA. The land (*chialo*) or territory under the direct supervision of the Bemba senior chief, the Chitimukulu (qq.v.), it is distinct from the rest of Bemba territory, which other Bemba chiefs controlled. Lubemba was larger then the other chiefdoms and was considered the Bemba heartland because of Chitimukulu's senior position. On occasions in the 19th century some of the stronger chiefs on the border of Lubemba intruded into the territory when the reigning ruler was weak.

LUBITA, NGOMBALA. This Lozi (q.v.) politician was active in a number of parties, primarily in the 1960s. Born in 1929 at Lealui (q.v.), and a grandson of Lewanika (q.v.), he was active first in the African National Congress (q.v.) in the 1950s and then joined the United National Independence Party (q.v.). His party activities caused him to be arrested and detained in 1959. In 1960, after his release, he became active in the Barotse Anti-Secession Society (q.v.), an organization with UNIP ties. He resigned in 1962, however, when Munu Sipalo (q.v.) was burned by a firebomb that some blamed on Bemba members of UNIP. He then became active in the Sicaba Party (q.v.) and took over as its president when its previous leaders were about to dissolve it after its overwhelming defeat in the 1962 elections. He made an attempt to affiliate Sicaba with the ANC in 1963; this did not work as planned, and the Sicaba Party was dissolved in 1963. During the next year Lubita went on a lengthy trip into Rhodesia and South Africa on behalf of the Lozi king, Mwanawina III (q.v.). The journey was undertaken in part to secure a better financial arrangement for the Lozi from the Witwatersrand Native Labour Association (q.v.). Contact was also made with the South African government about possible ties with

Barotseland (q.v.), but this failed to develop. Ultimately Lubita returned to membership in UNIP.

LUBOSI (LUBOZI; ROBOSI; LOBOSI). A Lozi (q.v.) leader, son of Litia (q.v.), he became the Lozi king in 1878. He was later challenged by the rebels but regained the throne in 1885. At that point he took the praise name Lewanika (q.v.), which means "conqueror," loosely translated, the name under which he would rule until his death in 1916.

LUBUMBU. A Bisa (q.v.) chiefdom located northeast of Lake Bangweulu (q.v.), it was especially strong in the late 18th century. It evidently once had control over as many lesser chiefdoms as did the great Bemba leader Chitimukulu (qq.v.). In the 19th century, however, its leaders were defeated by the Bemba who were pushing south. At one point in the 18th century the chiefs at Lubumbu were under the dominance of another Bisa chiefdom at Chinama, but by the end of that century this had ceased, and the Lubumbu itself dominated many other chiefs. About this time the sixth Lubumbu chief, Kalenga, moved the capital of the chiefdom from an island in Lake Bangweulu to a land-based location called Mwala by the Lukuta River. In 1831 a Portuguese expedition led by António Gamitto (q.v.) traveled through Lubumbu, and he described the political leadership of the area in his published journal. About 1840 a new chief of Lubumbu, Muma, took the title of Matipa (q.v.) when he succeeded Nkalamo as chief. The latter had put his capital back on Lake Bangweulu because of the imminent danger of Bemba attacks. Matipa reoccupied Mwala on the mainland but was attacked by Mwamba I (q.v.) and returned to an island capital. Bemba raiders killed all the children of Matipa. When Mwamba I died late in the 1850s, Matipa again returned to the mainland, driving the Bemba out of Lubumbu. However, in the 1860s Mwamba II defeated the chiefs subordinate to Matipa and, about 1870, drove Matipa himself back onto an island in Lake Bangweulu. Mwamba then installed a Bemba chief over most of Lubumbu.

LUBWA. The name refers to both a town and a Livingstonia Mission (q.v.) school on the western shore of Lake Bangweulu (q.v.). Kenneth Kaunda (q.v.) was born, schooled, and later taught there. He and Simon Kapwepwe (q.v.) returned to Lubwa in 1949, where they began a cooperative farm and transformed the Chinsali African Welfare Association (q.v.) into a local branch of the Northern Rhodesia African Congress (q.v.).

LUCHAZI. One of Zambia's many small ethnic groups, the Luchazi live in the northwestern part of the country, south of the Ndembu (q.v.). They are of the Lunda-Luvale (qq.v.) linguistic subgroup, and are very closely related to other members of that subgroup, such as the Chokwe (q.v.). These ethnic groups are known for their artistry, and the Luchazi demonstrated special originality in the carving and coloring of their masks. There were over 54,000 Luchazi-speaking Zambians in 1986 and half again as many across the border in the Democratic Republic of Congo (q.v.) (Zaire).

LUCHEMBE, MWANBA. He is the signals officer who, on June 30, 1990, single-handedly seized the Zambia National Broadcasting Service's (q.v.) communications complex and broadcast the (false) announcement (from 3:00 A.M. to 7 A.M.) that the military had overthrown President Kenneth Kaunda's (q.v.) government. The spontaneous street celebrations that followed dramatically demonstrated the widespread unpopularity of Kaunda's regime and its economic austerity measures. The announcement came after a long period of tension and food price riots attending the International Monetary Fund's structural adjustment program (qq.v.) for Zambia. Around 7:00 A.M., Grey Zulu (q.v.), Kaunda's deputy, announced that the coup plot had been foiled.

In the following months, both Luchembe and the government maintained that Luchembe bore sole responsibility for the coup attempt. After his release, however, Luchembe's statements claimed that the plot had included several senior military officers but that he had protected their identities in spite of the harsh interrogation and mistreatment he had endured. For Luchembe's own account of the affair, see John M. Mwanakatwe's *End of the Kaunda Era* (1994).

LUEJI (RUEJI). She was a legendary Lunda (some sources say Luba) (qq.v.) princess of the Tubungu Clan who supposedly lived in the Democratic Republic of Congo (q.v.) (Zaire) during the early 17th century. Her story, widely told in Central Africa (q.v.), tells of the beginnings of many of the peoples in the region. Opposed by her brother Chinyama, supposed founder of the Luvale (qq.v.), she succeeded to a chiefship and retained it through the strength of her Luba spouse Kabala Ilunga (q.v.).

Their followers, according to the legend, became the Lunda. Lueji's grandson, Mwata Yamvo (q.v.), later assumed the chiefship and started the large Lunda empire that dominated the east-west trade in the 18th century and influenced the political development of many Zambian peoples.

LUENA (LWENA) FLATS. A very wet area in the western part of Zambia, it is on the east bank of the upper Zambezi River (q.v.) and the south bank of the Luena River (q.v.). This swampy area is more densely populated than most of the rest of the country. The Lozi (q.v.) came to control the region by defeating its previous inhabitants, the Nkoya (q.v.). The Luena flats were probably once lake beds covering several hundred square kilometers.

LUENA (LWENA) RIVER. A tributary of the Zambezi River (q.v.), it rises in west-central Zambia, just west of the Kafue National Park (q.v.), and flows northwesterly past Kaoma (q.v.) (formerly Mankoya) en route to the Zambezi. It enters the Zambezi north of the Lozi capitals of Lealui and Mongu (qq.v.). The northern Luvale (q.v.) people are also called Luena.

LUFUBU RIVER. This major river in the northeastern part of Zambia takes a winding path northward through the Sumbu Game Reserve into the southwestern corner of Lake Tanganyika (q.v.). It was a popular site for villages and was vigorously contested by Arab (q.v.) traders and Africans (especially the Bemba, q.v.) in the 19th century. The London Missionary Society (q.v.) built a depot at its estuary in 1883.

LUKANGA SWAMP. A large basin south and east of the Kafue River (q.v.) in central Zambia, west of the city of Kabwe (q.v.), it is a permanently flooded area dominated by reeds and other aquatic plants.

LUKULU. A town along the upper Zambezi River (q.v.), a little south of its confluence with the Lungwebungu River (q.v.) in northwestern Zambia, it was the 19th-century site of a fortified village built by the Luyi (Lozi, q.v.) after they had been severely beaten by Sebituane's Kololo (qq.v.) forces. Lozi leader Mubukwanu (q.v.) died there and was succeeded by Imasiku (q.v.). The Kololo then isolated the village, forcing the defenders to the brink of starvation. Imasiku managed to escape shortly before Lukulu surrendered to the Kololo, who with this victory in 1838, then controlled Barotseland (q.v.).

LUKUSUZI NATIONAL PARK. A game reserve in Eastern Province about 40 kilometers (25 miles) southwest of Lundazi (q.v.) and 24 kilometers (15 miles) west of the border with Malawi (q.v.), it encompasses about 2,590 square kilometers (1,000 square miles).

LUKWAKWA. An area in northwestern Zambia near Kabompo (q.v.), north of the Kabompo River (q.v.) but east of the Manyinga River. According to Luyana (q.v.)—later called Lozi, q.v.—tradition, one Luyana group settled there while the rest proceeded south into Bulozi (q.v.). During the succession civil war following the death of the Mulambwa (q.v.), the Kololo under Sebituane (qq.v.) invaded Bulozi in 1833. One of the three warring factions, led by Sinyama Sikufele, fled to Lukwakwa. In 1838, Imasiku (q.v.) fled across the Kabompo also. Sipopa (q.v.) took over the Lukwakwa leadership when Imasiku was killed. When Sipopa later moved south to Bulozi, Imbua (q.v.) moved to Lukwakwa and succeeded Sipopa. The Lukwakwa area continued to be a haven for dissatisfied Lozi for many years and thus was a threat to the Bulozi leadership. In late 1889, Lewanika (q.v.) led a very large force, including many top Lozi leaders, into the area, defeating the Lukwakwa, who ultimately accepted his authority.

LUKWESA ILUNGA. See KAZEMBE III.

LULIMALA RIVER. This very small river flows north into the south-central shore of Lake Bangweulu (q.v.). It is on this river that Chitambo's village (q.v.), the death site of Dr. David Livingstone (q.v.), was located.

LUMBE RIVER. This minor tributary of the Zambezi River (q.v.) joins it south of the Zambezi's confluence with the Luyi River (q.v.). It drains part of southwestern Zambia.

LUMBU. See NANZELA.

LUMPA CHURCH. The religious movement with strong political implications founded in 1953 by Alice Lenshina (q.v.). It remained active at least through the 1960s, despite the problems incurred during its "holy war" against the government in 1964.

The word "Lumpa" is a *ci*Bemba (q.v.) word meaning "better than, or exceeding all the rest."

LUNDA. One of the major ethnic and linguistic groups in Central Africa (q.v.), the Lunda inhabit large areas in Angola (q.v.) and the Democratic Republic of Congo (q.v.) (Zaire) as well as Zambia. The Lunda language is one of Zambia's eight official languages, spoken primarily in North-Western Province (q.v.), where there were more than 177,000 *ci*Lunda speakers in 1986. More than twice that many Eastern Lunda (mostly *ci*Bemba, q.v., speakers) live under Kazembe (q.v.) in Luapula Province (q.v.).

Oral traditions in the Democratic Republic of Congo (q.v.) (Zaire) and Angola suggest the growth and expansion of large Lunda polities in or before the 15th century. By the 18th century, the Lunda under Mwata Yamvo (q.v.) had established a transcontinental trading empire across all of southern Central Africa. As they grew, some Lunda moved south into Zambia, primarily in the 17th and 18th centuries. Among the chiefships that supposedly split away from the Lunda empire are those of the Luvale and Ndembu (qq.v.), who have resided in Zambia for several centuries. Lunda involvement in trade with the Portuguese in Angola also brought that influence into the area. As the Lozi (q.v.) began to dominate western Zambia, some of the Lunda were forced to pay them tribute, but their independence from the Lozi was later reestablished.

The major Lunda ruler to affect Zambia was the emperor in southern Democratic Republic of Congo (Zaire), Mwata Yamvo, whose initiative led to the founding of Kazembe's chiefdom along the Luapula River (q.v.). Kazembe's Lunda at one time controlled large areas of the Katanga (Shaba) Pedicle (q.v.) and northeastern Zambia. Many non-Lunda were thus under Kazembe's role, but he made no attempt to assimilate them (although some became "Lunda" through an act of distinction). Patrilineal descent is practiced among Kazembe's Lunda, as it was at Mwata Yamvo's capital. Centralized authority patterns were established by Kazembe, and district governors served Kazembe in their districts, paying tribute to him just as he continued to send tribute to Mwata Yamvo. In the mid-19th century, Msiri's Yeke (qq.v.) empire broke up the Lunda's transcontinental trading empire, and Kazembe's Lunda became increasingly isolated due to the expansions of the Yeke, Luba, Bemba, and Ngoni (qq.v.).

LUNDAZI. The town of Lundazi is only a few kilometers from Zambia's eastern border and is the administrative center of the district of Lundazi. The district had 92,000 people in 1969 and 173,000 in 1990.

LUNGA RIVER. A major tributary of the Kafue River (q.v.), it begins in north-central Zambia near the Democratic Republic of Congo (q.v.) (Zaire) border and the town of Solwezi (q.v.), flowing due south into the Kafue National Park (q.v.), where it merges with the Kafue on a southern path.

LUNGU. Living generally north of the Bemba (q.v.) along the southern part of Lake Tanganyika (q.v.) in northeastern Zambia, the Lungu people speak a common language with their Mambwe relatives as well as with the Inamwanga, Iwa, and Tambo (qq.v.). In 1986 there were about 211,000 Mambwe-Lungu speakers in Zambia and another 97,000 across the border in Tanzania (q.v.). All of these peoples seem to have come into the area from Eastern Africa and are, to various degrees, related to the Lungu, Fipa, and Nyakyusa of southwestern Tanzania and to the Ngonde of Malawi (qq.v.). While Lungu commoners are patrilineal people of East African origin, their Azimba (Leopard Clan) chiefs are of Luba-Lunda (qq.v.) (Congolese or Zairean) origins and follow matrilineal succession. Because Nsama (q.v.), the senior Tabwa (q.v.) chief, was originally from the Lungu's chiefly Azimba Clan, Tafuna (q.v.), the senior Lungu chief, still claims some proprietary influence over them, even though the Tabwa commoners, while of similar East African origin, now share matrilineal descent and the Bemba language with their Bemba neighbors. The lakeshore Lungu fish and grow rice and cassava (q.v.). They trade some of this to the southern Lungu, who grow millet. The Lungu were also noted in the 19th century for wearing cotton clothes, instead of the then more common barkcloth. They also traded cotton cloth.

During the 19th century, traveling African and Arab (q.v.) traders regularly crossed the territory of the lakeshore Lungu. Thus the Lungu were subject to numerous Bemba and Arab invasions. The Arab influence is still there today in their clothing style and even boat design. To escape the slave traders (q.v.), the Lungu lived in stockaded villages but abandoned them once the British South Africa Company (q.v.) ended the late-19th-century pattern of warfare and slave raiding.

While the northern Lungu were besieged by Bemba and

Arab slave traders, the southern Lungu were concerned with the Lunda of Kazembe (q.v.), to whom they paid tribute in the 19th century. They faced the Bemba in battle, also (for example, against the invading Mwamba II Chileshye, q.v., in the 1860s). A junior Lungu chief, Chitoshi, lost his life in this war. Around the same time, the northern Lungu, under Tafuna, were subject to the domination of Mperembe's Ngoni (qq.v.), who settled in their territory and required the Lungu to both work and fight for them. At a battle on the Kafubu River in the mid-1860s, the Bemba fought both the Lungu and the Ngoni, but the battle was indecisive. A major leader of the Lungu named Zombe (q.v.) fought several battles with the Bemba under Chitapankwa (q.v.). Zombe was victorious, but the Bemba defeated him in a major confrontation in the early 1880s.

Throughout the 19th century the Lungu were noted iron producers. Lungu smiths were in great demand, especially among the Bemba. Sometimes, Lungu smiths would even settle with the Bemba by paying tribute with hoes and axes. One even built smelting furnaces in Mpanda. Some Lungu kept herds of cattle and other livestock in tsetse (q.v.)-free zones. Only the Mambwe and Iwa (qq.v.) among the northeastern peoples shared this pattern with the Lungu.

Perhaps because the Lungu were so frequently attacked by their fellow Africans, they were quick to sign up for European "protection." Harry Johnston (q.v.) found several Lungu chiefs, including Tafuna himself, willing to sign his "treaties." (For the conflict between two Lungu leaders, *see* KALIMINWA; TOMBOSHALO.)

LUNGWEBUNGU RIVER. The first major tributary of the Zambezi River (q.v.) from the west, it rises in Angola (q.v.) and flows southeasterly into the Zambezi. This occurs just south of the Kabompo River's (q.v.) confluence with the Zambezi and just north of the town of Lukulu (q.v.). This point of confluence is considered to be the northern edge of the floodplain that the Lozi (q.v.) people call Bulozi (q.v.), their heartland.

LUNSEMFWA RIVER. This major tributary of the Luangwa River (q.v.) joins it about 80 kilometers (50 miles) north of the Luangwa's confluence with the Zambezi River at Feira (qq.v.). One branch of the Lunsemfwa begins in the Muchinga Mountains (q.v.) and flows southerly, while the other branch moves on a due east course from central Zambia. They merge about 40 kilometers (25 miles) before they join the Luangwa. The

Lunsemfwa basin has been estimated to encompass about 43,512 square kilometers (16,800 square miles).

LUSAKA. The capital city of Zambia since 1935 (although chosen as such in 1931) and Zambia's largest city, Lusaka had a population of 262,000 in 1969 and over 982,000 in 1990. It is located along the line of rail (q.v.) and the Great East and Great North Roads (qq.v.). It also has an international airport. With transportation so accessible, it is the leading industrial, commercial, and financial center of the country in addition to its governmental functions.

The city originated as a railroad siding site in 1905, serving the Broken Hill Mine (*see* KABWE MINE), farther north. The siding was named after Lusaakas, the headman of a neighboring village. Many Afrikaner farm families settled there from South Africa in the 1910s and came to specialize in maize and beef production. A village management board was created in 1913. Real growth began only after it became Northern Rhodesia's (q.v.) capital in 1935 and, again, after independence in 1964. A British planner, Stanley Davenport Adshead, was responsible for laying out the basic plan for the capital city. Today it has grown to take in numerous local African townships and has sprawled far beyond the original plan. The University of Zambia (q.v.) is located at Lusaka. Forty-eight kilometers (30 miles) south of Lusaka is the new town of Kafue (q.v.), slated to be Lusaka's heavy industrial area.

Lusaka is also the name of Zambia's newest province, which formed from the southeastern third of the old Central Province (q.v.). It has grown from 354,000 people in 1969 to 1,208,000 in 1990 (*see* LUSAKA PROVINCE).

LUSAKA AFRICAN WELFARE ASSOCIATION. Founded about 1930 under the name Lusaka Native Welfare Asociation by I. Clements Katongo Muwamba (q.v.) and Henry Mashwa Sangandu (its first chairman and secretary, respectively), it protested the unsanitary and degrading manner in which Africans were compelled to buy meat. It also requested the right to develop farming plots outside the boundaries of the urban townships. This was refused by the secretary for native affairs. In 1932 it began a campaign against legislation that discriminated against Africans, especially the "pass" (q.v.) law. In 1933 the members changed the association's name and at the same time actively protested the proposed amalgamation (q.v.) of Northern and Southern Rhodesia (qq.v.). After Muwamba's attempt to organize a national association of welfare associations late in 1933, the government restricted the activities of all welfare associations. In 1943, however, the Lusaka Association again became active, meeting frequently and again taking up causes in which it could fight for African interests.

LUSAKA MANIFESTO. A manifesto on relations with Portugal, Rhodesia, and South Africa, it was signed by 14 states from East and Central Africa (q.v.) in Lusaka (q.v.) on April 16, 1969, at the East and Central Africa Summit Conference. In September 1969 it was adopted by the Organization of African Unity heads of state and subsequently approved by the United Nations General Assembly. The document was moderate in tone, advocating peaceful change to majority rule and explicitly rejecting black as well as white racism. It noted that the states remaining under European rule all differed in their circumstances, and that African responses to each must also differ. But it also warned that African patience would soon be exhausted.

LUSAKA NATIVE WELFARE ASSOCIATION. This was the original name of the Lusaka African Welfare Association (q.v.).

LUSAKA PROVINCE. This newest of Zambia's nine provinces was carved out of a once larger Central Province (q.v.). It includes Luangwa (q.v.) (formerly Feira, q.v.) and Lusaka Urban and Rural Districts. These same three districts, which had a population of 354,000 in 1969, had over 1.2 million in 1990. Lusaka Urban District, with over 982,000 in 1990, counts for over 80 percent of the province's people. The rural districts include the home areas of the Sala, Soli, Luano, and Senga (qq.v.).

LUSAKA RADIO BAND. There were two successive bands with this name. That in the 1950s consisted of Alick Nkhata's (q.v.) vocal quartet, with Dick Sapseid (keyboards), Pepe Zulu (maracas), and other associates of the Central African Broadcasting Service (q.v.). They made a number of popular records, which fed the demand for dance bands throughout the larger towns in Northern Rhodesia (q.v.). The second band, led by Alick Nkhata and drawn from the United National Independence Party (q.v.) Band, provided political songs for Kenneth Kaunda (q.v.) and UNIP in the early 1960s. As such, the second band's songs were never recorded nor aired on the radio, but the musicians later regrouped as the Big Gold Six, which represented Zambia at the second World Black and African Festival of Arts and Culture in Lagos in 1977, and then as the Broadway Quintet, which won Zambia's best band award in 1981.

LUSAKA STOCK EXCHANGE. It began operation on February 21, 1994, with seven registered companies trading shares. Though the exchange was not fully functional at first, the number of companies traded on the exchange was expected to grow.

LUSENGA PLAIN NATIONAL PARK. A game reserve in Luapula Province (q.v.) in northern Zambia, it is about 40 kilometers (25 miles) southeast of the southeastern shore of Lake Mweru (q.v.). The reserve encompasses about 1,165 square kilometers (450 square miles).

LUSITU RIVER. This minor tributary of the Zambezi River flows into it just south of the Kafue-Zambezi River (qq.v.) confluence. The archaeological trading center of Ingombe Ilede (q.v.) was near the confluence of the Lusitu and the Zambezi, perhaps because of the large salt deposit found there. Dr. David Livingstone (q.v.) noticed the importance of salt in 19th-century trade when he passed through. The Lusitu flows from west to east.

LUTANGU. He was later known as Sipopa (q.v.) or as Lutangu Sipopa.

LUVALE (LOVALE; LUBALE; LWENA). This is one of the major ethnic groups in northwestern Zambia. In 1986 there were over 163,000 Zambian Luvale speakers and more than three times that number across the border in Angola (q.v.). Luvale is one of the eight official languages of Zambia. Legend suggests that Chinyama (q.v.), a Lunda (q.v.) prince and Lueji's (q.v.) brother, left his homeland in the Shaba region of the Democratic Republic of Congo (q.v.) (Zaire) in the early 17th century and moved west to the Luena (q.v.) (or Lwena) River near the upper Zambezi. There he subdued the local Luena people and set up a chiefdom. The senior chiefship today among the Luvale is that of Kakenge (q.v.), founded by a man called Chinyama Kakenge.

The Luvale never established a formal state structure, and chiefships were regularly subdivided, as the formal powers of the chiefs are limited. Lineages played important political and ritual roles for the Luvale, and commoner lineages are traced back 17 generations in some instances. The Luchazi and Chokwe (qq.v.) peoples who live near the Luvale appear to have split from Luvale chiefs in the recent past. Clans, lineages, and even the territory of the three groups overlap. All three also are noted for wood carving and pottery. Luvale lineages combine matrilineal descent systems with patrilocal residence.

The Luvale were hunters and fishers, but their true genius was as middleman traders between the Kafue River (q.v.) and the Angola (q.v.) coast, exchanging cassava (q.v.), ivory (q.v.), slaves, beeswax, and rubber for European cloth, beads, guns, and powder from the 18th century on. The Luvale also engaged in armed conflict with their neighbors, and Dr. David Livingstone (q.v.) indicated that the neighboring peoples greatly feared the Luvale.

In the late 19th century, local Luvale chiefs Kangombe (q.v.) and Ndungu threatened the Lunda of Ishinde (q.v.). An Ndembu (Lunda) commoner, Chipenge (q.v.), stopped Kangombe with an armed force, and Lewanika of the Lozi (qq.v.) helped Ishinde defeat Ndungu in 1892. With this victory the Lozi claimed the right to all Luvale land. But the Luvale, claiming that only one local Luvale leader (Ndungu) had been defeated, denied the claim. Nevertheless, the Lozi claim, supported by the British South Africa Company (q.v.), was allowed until the late 1930s, when the British separated Balovale District (q.v.) from Barotseland (q.v.).

The 1890s were not good years for the Luvale in other ways, beginning with a smallpox epidemic and, in 1895, a plague of locusts. The Luvale were among the last of Zambia's peoples to seek work on the Copperbelt (q.v.). Arriving during the Depression of the early 1930s, they carved out a niche as charcoal burners and night soil removers.

LUWINGU. An administrative center and a district in Northern Province (q.v.), it is located about 64 kilometers (40 miles) north of Lake Bangweulu (q.v.). The district had 47,000 people in 1969 and 67,000 in 1990. An administrative center was established there by the British South Africa Company (q.v.) prior to 1903.

LUYANA (ALUYANA; LUYI). A people, probably related to the Lunda (q.v.) in northwestern Zambia, who moved south and conquered the early inhabitants of what is now Bulozi, or Barotseland (qq.v.). The name means "foreigners." This invasion probably occurred prior to the mid-18th century. In the mid-

19th century the Luyana were conquered from the south by the Kololo (q.v.), who renamed them Lozi (q.v.).

A number of neighboring groups speak languages that belong to the Luyana family of languages, the most signficant of which is siLuyana, the language of the royal court in Bulozi (Barotseland). While of scholarly interest, it is an archaic language now spoken only by a small number of people. SiLozi (q.v.) is the common Lozi language.

LUYI. See LUYANA.

LUYI (LUI) RIVER. A river in Barotseland (q.v.) that joins the Zambezi River (q.v.) south of the town of Senanga, its confluence with the Zambezi is considered to be the southern limit of Bulozi (q.v.), the rich floodplain inhabited by the Lozi (q.v.) people.

LWAMBI. The second or southern kingdom of the Lozi (q.v.) was established by Ngombala (q.v.). Its capital is now at Nalolo (q.v.). Its influence was never as substantial as that of Namuso (q.v.), the northern kingdom, but the proper hierarchical and political relationship between the two was not resolved until the 19th century, when Sipopa (q.v.) began the tradition of appointing a female relative as ruler at Nalolo.

LWENA. This is another name for the Luvale (q.v.).

LWIINDI. The name of the biannual (July and October) Monze (q.v.) rain shrine festival, it is held in a grove south of Monze town, Southern Province (q.v.). While organized by the Plateau Tonga (q.v.) to contact the spirit of the early-19th-century rain shrine's founder, Monze Mayaba (or Monze Mukulu), this regional festival also draws devotees from the Ila, Sala, and Valley Tonga (qq.v.).

LYONS, GEORGE. Resident magistrate of Barotseland (q.v.) from 1916 until his death in 1924, he was very unpopular with Lozi king Yeta III (qq.v.), who had a continuing dispute with him from 1919 until Lyons' death. In fact, in December 1923, Yeta wrote to Richard Goode (q.v.), the acting administrator, requesting that Lyons be transferred. The problem began when Lyons advised a group of Africans that the Abolition of Slavery Proclamation of 1906 (q.v.) freed them from certain traditional obligations to the ruling class. Yeta complained that he was undermining royal authority. Two years later Yeta and his young but well-educated and articulate council presented the British high commissioner in South Africa with a demand that all concessions to and agreements with the British South Africa Company (q.v.) be canceled. The Lozi complained that the BSAC had failed to fulfill its pledges and obligations. When they were turned down, Lyons became the focus of Yeta's anger. Lyons represented the degree to which traditional authority and prerogatives had been undermined by the BSAC. When Yeta demanded in 1923 that Lyons be replaced, Lyons was outraged and demanded a personal apology from Yeta. Yeta refused, and Lyons' sudden death in early 1924 mooted the issue.

LYTTELTON, OLIVER (VISCOUNT CHANDOS). This member of the British Conservative Party replaced James Griffiths (q.v.) as colonial secretary in October 1951. The next month he announced that his government agreed fully with the conclusions of the Victoria Falls Conference (q.v.) held in September and that federation (q.v.) was desirable and even urgent. He announced that a meeting would be held the next year to follow up on the idea. This was then done (*see* LONDON CONFERENCE, 1952). When Lyttelton visited the federation in January 1954, he refused to meet with the leading African politicians of either Northern Rhodesia or Nyasaland (qq.v.). Kaunda and Nkumbula (qq.v.) timed the beginning of new commercial boycotts to coincide with his visit to Lusaka (q.v.).

M

MA-. This is the standard plural personal prefix in Southern Bantu languages (q.v.), like *ba-* or *a-* in the Central and Eastern Bantu languages. It typically appears before the name of a people, as in Matabele, Makololo (qq.v.), or Mazungu (i.e., Basungu , q.v., or "Europeans"). It is conventional to drop these prefixes in the scholarly literature.

MAAMBA MINE. Zambia's major supplier of coal, this source was discovered in the Gwembe valley (q.v.) in 1966. The mine began production in 1968, and it and Nbandabwe Mine allowed Zambia to cut its dependence upon the coal and coke from Wankie Mine outside of Bulawayo, Rhodesia. During the economic troubles of the 1990s, a timely South African loan slated the mine for rehabilitation rather than closure.

MACDONALD, MALCOLM. British colonial secretary for much of the last half of the 1930s, he opposed any amalgamation (q.v.) of Nyasaland (q.v.) and the Rhodesias. He felt it would be detrimental to the best interests of the Africans by favoring the interests of the European minority over those of the African majority.

MACDONELL, PHILIP JAMES. The High Court (q.v.) justice who chaired the Reserves Commissions (q.v.) of 1924 and 1926, he favored developing native reserves (q.v.) to allow Africans to produce economic crops. This, he felt, would help to stabilize village life by preventing the exodus of African workers. He was displeased with the ultimate report of the 1924 commission, feeling that too many concessions were made to Europeans and that an inadequate amount of land was allowed to the Africans.

MACHILI FOREST STATION. *See* SITUMPA FOREST STATION.

MACLEOD CONSTITUTION. As a result of the deadlock at the London Constitutional Conference, 1961 (q.v.), British Colonial Secretary Iain Macleod (q.v.) presented his own plan on February 20, 1961. It provided for a 45-member legislature consisting of 15 upper-roll seats, 15 lower-roll, and 15 "national" constituencies. The plan also insisted that at least two Africans and two non-Africans be included among the six "unofficials" on the Executive Council (q.v.). Kenneth Kaunda and the United National Independence Party (qq.v.) protested that Africans would be unable to get upper-roll support for the national seats but reluctantly accepted the plan. Roy Welensky and his United Federal Party (qq.v.) were critical of the plan and immediately sought revisions.

Both sides seemed to accept the 30 single-member constituency seats to be decided by the upper and lower rolls. The problem was the national seats and the complex vote percentage system involved in determining electoral winners. Welensky feared that it would allow an African majority to be elected. After a series of threats and pressures, in part involving what might happen in Southern Rhodesia (q.v.), Welensky got Macleod to modify his plan on June 26, 1961. The changes included requiring four of the seven double-member constituencies to have one African and one non-African representative. The 15th seat would be for an Asian or a Coloured. In addition, the percentages would be weighted a little differently to aid

European candidates. Finally, by-elections would be called to fill any seats unfilled through lack of proper percentages. African leaders predicted a violent reaction in the African communities, and indeed, strife did begin, continuing for several months. In mid-September, Macleod and Kaunda agreed to further changes in the plan if the disturbances stopped immediately, which they did. Macleod was replaced by Reginald Maudling (q.v.) in October 1961, and talks continued. On March 1, 1962, it was announced that a minor change was made in the percentages needed to win the national seats; this change broke the stalemate and also returned hope to the Africans that they could win a majority of these crucial seats in the election planned for October 1962.

The Macleod Constitution was in force only until January 1964, but it allowed Africans to win control of the Northern Rhodesian government, thus also signaling the end of the Central African Federation (q.v.) and the inevitable independent status for Zambia.

MACLEOD, IAIN. British colonial secretary, 1959–61, this liberal and pragmatic member of the Conservative Party was relatively inexperienced in African matters when appointed but soon made his mark on Central Africa (q.v.). His strength was in his ability to find a middle ground between Africans and Europeans. While his constitutional proposal (*see* MACLEOD CONSTITUTION) was one that neither side wanted, at the same time neither side felt it could reject it. He called for a series of independence constitutions throughout the British colonial empire, an approach approved of by Kenneth Kaunda (q.v.). Macleod arrived in Lusaka (q.v.) in March 1960, and made arrangements to meet with all the participants. This ultimately led to both the Federal Review Conference (q.v.) of December 1960 and the London Constitutional Conference of 1961 (q.v.). On the other hand, when the Litunga and Ngambela of Barotseland (qq.v.) flew to London in April 1961, demanding that Macleod acknowledge Barotseland's right to secede from Northern Rhodesia, Macleod refused. He did reassure the Lozi (q.v.) king that his rights and those of his people would continue to be protected, however. And, significantly, he restored the right to use the title of Litunga (q.v.), rather than the old, limited term, "Paramount Chief" (q.v.).

MACMILLAN, HAROLD. It was under this British Conservative Party prime minister (January 1957–October 1963) that most of the events occurred that brought about the demise of the Central African Federation (q.v.) and the birth of modern Zambia. He created the Monckton Commission (q.v.); he personally visited the federation in 1960, during which a huge rally of African nationalists at Ndola (q.v.) denounced the federation; and he eventually appointed home secretary Robert Butler (q.v.) as minister with special responsibility for the federation, in hopes of resolving the crisis.

MAIZE. One of the most important crops of Zambia, it was brought into the area along the trade routes after being brought from America by the Portuguese. It entered Zambia sometime before the end of the 18th century. Though the fertile Tonga (q.v.) Plateau astride the Kafue River (q.v.) has long been known as the country's "maize belt," farmers in Northern Province (q.v.) dramatically increased their production and sale of maize before the withdrawal of agricultural supports in the early 1990s. Since the mid-1970s, fertilizer shortages, localized locust plagues, and recurrent drought have repeatedly forced Zambia to rely upon maize imports—preferably from elsewhere in Southern Africa, as Zambians far prefer the color and taste of white maize to the yellow maize from America.

MAKASA (MUKASA). The title belongs to a Bemba (q.v.) chiefship begun in the early 19th century by Chitimukulu Chiliamfwa (q.v.). Holders of the title are always sons of a Chitimukulu—but not always the current one. The chiefdom governed by the Makasa is called Mpanda and lies north of Lubemba (q.v.). The territory includes villages conquered from both the Inamwanga and Mambwe (qq.v.), whose inhabitants remained under Bemba role.

Several major sources conflict on the early history of the chiefship, but it appears probable that the first bearer of the title was Kalulu, a son of Chiliamfwa. He evidently reigned for several decades before being killed in a battle with Mpezeni's Ngoni (qq.v.) in about 1850 at Chisenga. Kalulu's brother, Chanso, was evidently the next Makasa, but he too died in battle with the Ngoni.

Makasa III was Bwalya, a son of the reigning Chitimukulu, Chileshye (q.v.). Bwalya ruled not only Mpanda but Chilinda (east of Lubemba) as well. His duty was to protect it against the Ngoni. He set up a village at Manga, located between the Kabishya and Mumbo Rivers. The Ngoni attacked it unsuccessfully and were even followed in retreat by Makasa III. Later, they returned with additional forces and successfully captured Manga, driving Makasa III to a village, where he took refuge. In about 1870 he returned with a large force representing many Bemba chiefships and defeated the Ngoni at Chipekeni (q.v.), the former site of Manga. Makasa III later killed Mpande V (q.v.), an Ngoni ally, in 1871 or early 1872, but Makasa III Bwalya died soon after.

MAKASA, ROBERT SPEEDWELL. Veteran Zambian nationalist politician and diplomat, he was born in January 1922, near Chinsali (q.v.). His education began at Lubwa (q.v.) Mission and concluded at Oxford University. A teacher and headmaster at Nkula, Makasa became actively involved in politics in the late 1940s. He became founder and chairman of the African National Congress (q.v.) branch at Chinsali in 1949. Kenneth Kaunda (q.v.) served as secretary. Makasa's tactics regarding chiefs were widely adopted in rural areas by the United National Independence Party (q.v.) in 1960. He tried to create a split between the chiefs and the government, calling the chiefs creatures of the government and sending them circulars urging them to lead their people in rejecting the government, perhaps even by joining the nationalist movement.

In 1956, Makasa quit teaching and became Northern Province (q.v.) president of the ANC; two years later, there were (he claimed) 165 ANC branches in the province. He spent a year and a half in jail for organizing a boycott against a merchant who discriminated against Africans. At the end of 1958 he led the province's executive from the ANC into the Zambia African National Congress (q.v.). During the mass political arrests of March 1959, Makasa was rusticated (q.v.) to Solwezi (q.v.). When he was released he returned to politics, becoming president of UNIP's Luapula Province (q.v.) branch. From 1961 to 1963 he was in Dar es Salaam, Tanzania, as chairman of the Pan-African Freedom Movement's (q.v.) refugee committee. In 1964 he was elected to Parliament (q.v.) from Chinsali. In 1967 he became minister of state for foreign affairs, and the next year was minister for Northern Province. His subsequent service included diplomatic posts in Ethiopia, Tanzania, and Kenya.

MAKASA IV, CHISANGA CHIPEMBA. The son of Chitapankwa, the Chitimukulu (qq.v.), he was appointed Makasa IV by his father in 1872 after the death of Makasa III Bwalya (see MAKASA). Father and son led their combined forces in attacks on

Inamwanga, Lungu (q.v.), and Mambwe (q.v.) country for about the next decade. Bordering the Mambwe, Makasa IV took advantage of their military weakness. He later married the daughter of Mpenza, a Mambwe chief. One of his greatest military successes was in defeating the Lungu leader, Zombe (q.v.). After his father's death in 1883, he looted his father's capital, taking Chitapankwa's cattle. This angered Sampa (q.v.), the new Chitimukulu, who unsuccessfully attacked him at Chiponde. Makasa did return the cattle, however, and Sampa and Makasa IV later fought together in a campaign against the Mambwe. Makasa IV died in 1890 or 1891.

MAKASA V, MUKUUKU MWILWA. A son of Chitimukulu Chileshye (qq.v.), he was passed over for appointment as Makasa IV by Chitapankwa (q.v.), who appointed his own son instead. As solace, Mukuuku Mwilwa was given territory in Chilinda. When Makasa IV died, Chitimukulu Sampa (q.v.) appointed Mukuuku as Makasa V in about 1891. Nevertheless, he feared Sampa and built his village on the Luchewe River in the north of Mpanda. He became active in trade with the Swahili (q.v.), exchanging ivory (q.v.) and slaves for guns and cloth. His warriors were well armed. In part because of his fear of Sampa, and in defiance of him, Makasa V agreed to allow the White Fathers (q.v.) to set up Kayambi Mission (q.v.) on a hill near his village, Mipini. He was first approached in 1894 and, in fact, sent the missionaries four freed slaves in midyear. At the beginning of 1895, Makasa interceded with Sampa for the missionaries. That April he invited the priests to choose a site, and the mission was begun on July 23, 1895, by the Reverend (soon Bishop) Joseph Dupont (q.v.). While Makasa V never converted to Christianity, he had a deep respect for Dupont, with whom he liked to have intellectual discussions. At least one of his sons was a catechumen.

MAKOLO (sing., *likolo*). Important form of social and political organization among the Lozi (q.v.) until their conquest by the Kololo (q.v.) in the 19th century, they have now vanished from the contemporary scene. They seem to have begun under Mboo (q.v.), the first Lozi king, who allowed some of his "brothers" and "sisters" to create groups of men for military and labor purposes. These *makolo* groups had leaders appointed for them by the royals. Thus territory could be distributed by the king to the royals, who had their own *makolo* to aid them. It is possible in the early days that these groups were actually bands of followers, even relatives of the leader. The tradition may have existed before the Lozi arrived. At its peak, the *makolo* system included all Lozi. Everyone became a member of his or her father's or guardian's *likolo* at birth. Unlike other African "regiment" systems that were primarily military and based on age groupings, the *makolo* were kinship and labor units, each with its own distinctive name, *induna (q.v.)* (councilor), and site at the capital.

As leadership among the Lozi became more centralized in the king, only he could create new *makolo* and appoint their leaders. He could also call upon them for public work or for military duty. Some regular duties were assigned to certain *makolo*, such as providing salt to the capital. Sometimes conquered peoples and land were made subsections of existing *makolo*. Thus the whole system was always being adapted to meet the needs of the nation. When the Lozi were overrun by the Kololo (q.v.) people around 1840, the *makolo* system was disrupted and never regained its old importance.

MAKOLOLO. *See* KOLOLO.

MAKUMBA, CHIMFWEMBE MULENGA. Successor of his cousin Sampa as the Chitimukulu of the Bemba (qq.v.), he reigned from 1898 until his death in 1911. There was some dispute over his succession claim, but he received physical support from Chikwanda II and seized Sampa's wives near the beginning of 1897, thus giving him the traditional right to the title. However, his major opponent, Mwamba III (q.v.), immediately attacked them and took Makumba prisoner. After a series of bad omens, Mwamba released Makumba and conceded the title to him, undoubtedly expecting that Makumba's advanced age would result in a short reign. Mwamba also found it easy to encroach into Makumba's territory without opposition. In 1903, Ponde (q.v.) was able to do much the same, as Makumba became increasingly senile. When he died in 1911, Makumba was succeeded by Chikwanda (q.v.).

MAKWANGWA. *See* KWANGWA.

MALARIA. This, Zambia's most common tropical health problem, affects nearly everyone. Malaria parasites are picked up and transmitted by anopheles mosquitoes, which breed in stagnant water. These plasmodia live in and destroy red blood cells, causing flulike chills and high fever as well as lethargy and anemia. Malaria rarely kills, except in cases of cerebral infection, but it recurs at regular intervals and weakens the body's resistance to other diseases. In the 1950s, malaria control measures meant clearing and draining land and liberal spraying with DDT. When these measures were gradually abandoned after independence, chloroquine (quinine) tablets became the preferred means for avoiding or treating malarial infections (though long-term use can lead to hearing loss). Unfortunately, however, these plasmodia have themselves evolved into increasingly drug-resistant strains.

MALAWI. Known as Nyasaland (q.v.) until its independence in July 1964, it is one of Zambia's two eastern neighbors. The histories of modern Malawi and eastern Zambia were closely entangled in the 1890s and 1900s, and from 1953 to 1963, modern Zambia, Zimbabwe, and Malawi were linked as the Central African Federation (q.v.) (of the Rhodesias and Nyasaland). Though both countries have been independent for over 30 years, their relations were often strained by the philosophical differences between Hastings Kamuzu Banda's (q.v.) pursuit of South African capital and tourism and Kenneth Kaunda's (q.v.) support of the Southern African liberation struggle.

MALUMA. A Tonga (q.v.) spiritualist who led his people in defiance of attempts by the native commissioner (q.v.) to collect taxes in 1909 and 1910, he urged that his people overthrow the colonial regime and "drive all white people out of the country." Maluma led the Tonga in an unsuccessful attack, but British troops arrested him and restored order. Taxes were then collected, albeit irregularly.

MALVERN, LORD. *See* HUGGINS, GODFREY MARTIN.

MAMBARI. The term was applied to the Ovimbundu, or Portuguese African traders, who worked in the region between the Angolan coast to the west and the Copperbelt and Barotseland (qq.v.) to the east. Throughout most of the 19th century, they traded cloth and guns for slaves, ivory (q.v.), beeswax, and rubber. Among their major trading partners were the Lunda, Luvale, Kaonde, Lamba, Lenje, Ila, Tonga, Lozi, and Kololo (qq.v.). They occasionally joined in slave raids on Africans, as when the Kololo leader Mpepe (q.v.) raided the Ila and Tonga. Thanks to George Grey, Colonel Colin Harding, and the Barotse Native Police (qq.v.), the last Mambari slavers disappeared from the country about 1912.

MAMBWE. The Mambwe, who straddle the Zambia-Tanzania border, are one of the larger of the patrilineal, cattle-keeping peoples from East Africa—including the Tambo, Iwa, and Inamgwanga (qq.v.)—who live in northeastern Northern Province (q.v.). They are most closely related to, and share a common language with, the Lungu (q.v.). And like the Lungu, senior chief Nsokolo (q.v.) and the Mambwe's other Azimba (Leopard Clan) chiefs seem to have had a separate, Luba-Lunda (qq.v.) origin in the Democratic Republic of Congo (q.v.) (Zaire). There were nearly 211,000 Mambwe-Lungu speakers in Zambia in 1986 and almost half that many—97,000—living on the Tanzanian side of the border.

The Mambwe were best known for their iron working and their productive, grass-composted, garden mounds. Throughout much of the 19th century, their cattle and gardens were frequently targeted by Bemba and, by the 1860s, Ngoni (qq.v.) raiders. They then hosted Harry Johnston (q.v.) and the London Missionary Society (q.v.) in the 1880s and, beginning in 1891, the White Fathers (q.v.). Late in World War I, Hanoc Sindano (q.v.) brought the Watch Tower Movement (q.v.) to the Mambwe. Hemmed in by an inadequate Native Reserve (q.v.) in 1930, they were one of the few northeastern peoples who seemed to have prospered by their participation in the migration of labor migrants to the Copperbelt (q.v.) mines. With this option no longer open, the patrilineal and patrilocal Mambwe are increasingly (and ironically) reliant upon the cross-border trade based upon mother-daughter links and other kinship ties between women.

MAMBWE MWELA (OLD MAMBWE). This, the first White Fathers' (q.v.) mission station, was established in July 1891 by Father Lechaptois near the Stevenson Road (q.v.), in the eastern part of Mambwe country. The White Fathers used this as a stepping-stone into Bemba (q.v.) territory. At times, the mission became a sanctuary for Mambwe people who feared Bemba attacks. In 1893 Sir Harry Johnston (q.v.) gave the missionaries the right to acquire guns and ammunition to help ward off attacks by Arab slave traders (qq.v.) and Bemba raiders. Later that year, the White Fathers considered abandoning the mission, but conditions eased, and Father (later, Bishop) Joseph Dupont (q.v.) took over its leadership in May 1895.

When Dupont founded Kayambi Mission (q.v.) that July, however, Mambwe became unnecessary, and it closed in September. In August 1896 the missionaries formally abandoned it by selling it to the British South Africa Company (q.v.).

MAMOCHISANE. The daughter of the great Kololo chief, Sebituane (qq.v.), her father appointed her to rule Nalolo (q.v.), the conquered Lozi's (q.v.) southern capital. She was also his chosen successor, and when he died in July 1851 she became the Kololo leader. Sebituane's nephew Mpepe (q.v.) was her proxy during certain ceremonies, but he had ambitions of his own. When he tried to control her politically, Mamochisane tired of the stress of politics and returned to the role of a family woman, abdicating in favor of Sekeletu (q.v.), her younger half brother.

MANDUMELETI. These were the Lozi *indunas* (qq.v.) who represented the Litunga (q.v.) among the subject peoples outside Bulozi (q.v.), such as the Subiya and Nkoya (qq.v.). Their duty was to ensure a steady supply of both laborers and tribute to the Lozi homeland.

MANGE. A brother or probably a nephew of Mboo (q.v.), the first Lozi (q.v.) king, he traveled east into the forest area outside the valley and became leader of the Kwangwa (q.v.) people. According to tradition, he broke away because he was not included in the ruling elite. This area was later reconquered by King Ngalama (q.v.) and restored to Lozi control.

MANKOYA. This word designates both a place in the Western Province (q.v.) of Zambia and the Nkoya (q.v.) people. In about 1970 the town and district called Mankoya were renamed Kaoma (q.v.).

MANNING, WILLIAM. Commander of the British Central Africa Rifles, he led a force of about 650 men from Blantyre on January 2, 1898, to rescue Karl Wiese (q.v.) and the North Charterland Exploration Company's (q.v.) prospectors from the "Ngoni rebellion," led by Nsingu, Chief Mpezeni's (q.v.) son. The battle began on January 16 and lasted for several days. The results were defeat for the Ngoni (q.v.), who had very few guns to use against the heavily armed British force, Nsingu's trial and execution, Mpezeni's surrender, and the confiscation of 12,000 cattle.

MANSA. A town and district in Luapula Province (q.v.) of Zambia, they lie north of the Katanga Pedicle (q.v.) and east of the Luapula River (q.v.). Mansa town and district comprise a major center of entrepreneurs—both men and women, and including many Jehovah's Witnesses and Seventh Day Adventists—most of whom are linked to the local fish trading industry. The district had 80,300 people in 1969 and 142,600 in 1990. The town, nearly 48 kilometers (30 miles) east of the Luapula, was formerly known as Fort Rosebery (q.v.).

MARSHALL, HUGH CHARLIE (TAMBALIKA). A long-time administrator for the British South Africa Company (q.v.), he joined the British Central African (Nyasaland, q.v.) administration in 1891 and was sent by Harry Johnston (q.v.) to be the collector (q.v.) at Chiromo in northeastern Zambia. Two years later he was sent to open Abercorn *boma* (qq.v.) among the Mambwe and Lungu (qq.v.) at the African Lakes Company's (q.v.) Zombe station. There, he and his Sikh (q.v.) soldiers erected an impregnable stockade, which soon became a sanctuary for Africans fleeing Bemba (q.v.) raids. This post, he was told, would also allow him to check on the slave caravan routes to the Indian Ocean and to defend white settlements near Lake Tanganyika (q.v.) from Bemba attack. He was also instructed to establish good relations with the Bemba, as circumstances permitted. One important Bemba leader, Ponde (q.v.), spurned his friendly overtures.

In later years, Marshall served as a higher level administrator for brief periods. From May until August 1911, he was acting administrator of North-Eastern Rhodesia (q.v.). In 1915 he was visiting commissioner and advisor to the Northern Rhodesian administration. And in 1920–21, he was acting administrator of Northern Rhodesia (q.v.). He retired in 1921 and died in England. His African nickname, Tambalika, means "to stretch out" and, figuratively, "to soothe or calm." It presumably referred to either his tall, thin body or to his quiet, reserved character.

MASHASHA (BAMESHASHA). One of Zambia's smaller ethnic groups, they center around the Kahare dynasty's polity in Kaoma (q.v.) District. They speak the Nkoya (q.v.) language and are often considered one of the three geographically dispersed branches of the 19th-century elephant hunters now variously known as the Nkoya (q.v.), Mashasha, and Mbwela (qq.v.) people, all of whom claim a common ethnic identity quite apart from that of their former Lozi (q.v.) rulers. They live in southwestern Zambia, east of the Lozi, south of the Kaonde (q.v.), and west of the Ila (q.v.).

MASHI. One of Zambia's smallest ethnic groups, the Mashi live in Kalabo (q.v.) District, in the extreme southwestern corner of the country, and are among Zambia's 74,800 Luyana-speaking (q.v.) people. Lozi (q.v.) traditions claim that Ilishua, a brother of their first king, Mboo (q.v.), settled there, and in the late 19th century Lozi officials living along the middle Kwando River (q.v.) forced the Mashi to pay tribute.

MASHI RIVER. This river is also known as the Kwando, Linyanti, or Chobe (q.v.) River.

MASHUKULUMBWE. This is the Lozi (q.v.) name for the Ila (q.v.), and is derived from the Ila men's horn-shaped coiffure. Dr. Livingstone (q.v.) spelled it "Bashukulompo." Though the Ila never liked the name, it was commonly adopted by the Europeans who reached their land, the Kafue Hook (q.v.), from Barotseland (q.v.). Thus the name also appears in the accounts of the so-called Mashukulumbwe Rebellion, the name given to a widely anticipated Ila revolt against the first (1906 and 1907) tax collections in their region. Though settlers, missionaries, and prospectors retired to their prepared stockades for their own protection, the Ila revolt never materialized.

MASTER PLAN. Related to the so-called cha-cha-cha campaign (q.v.) in 1961, the master plan was the response of the United National Independence Party and Kenneth Kaunda to the unsatisfactory Macleod Constitution (qq.v.). The burning of passes, or *chitupas* (qq.v.) was the first stage. The destruction of roads and bridges was the next stage. Stage three never was needed, as Colonial Secretary Maudling (q.v.) made adjustments in the election formula that satisfied UNIP.

MATAA. At least two individuals with this name have made their mark in Zambian history. The last of these, Mubukwanu Mataa, became secretary and later principal advisor to Lozi king Yeta III (q.v.) in the 1920s. His father had been appointed *ngambela* (q.v.) late in 1919 and used the title Ngambela Mataa. Father and son were both very close to the king, but in December 1928 they were arrested for the ritual murder of two women. They were both acquitted, but Yeta released them from their positions, perhaps because suspicion remained in the minds of many.

The first Mataa had also become *ngambela* and played an important part in Lozi history. He was an ambitions *induna* (q.v.) who was already seeking a higher post in the 1860s as the Lozi were retaking their kingdom from the Kololo (q.v.). He was the son of Mwala, who had earlier betrayed the Lozi by revealing a revolutionary plot to the Kololo.

With the overthrow of the young king Mwanawina (q.v.) in 1878 by several dissident Lozi groups, Mataa intrigued to get Musiwa, Sipopa's (q.v.) son, on the throne. He was unsuccessful, however, and another group raised Lubosi (q.v.) (later called Lewanika, q.v.) to king. Mataa felt insecure, both because of his support of Musiwa and because his father's actions had resulted in the death of Lubosi's father, Litia (q.v.); he tried to win Lubosi's favor through duplicity but was discovered. Nevertheless, for his aid in defeating Mwanawina, Lubosi appointed him to an official post (*namuyamba*). Unsatisfied with this post (he aspired to be *ngambela*), Mataa became the center of opposition to Lubosi. Mataa and Numwa (q.v.), a king's bodyguard, attempted a coup. The actual uprising occurred in July 1884, and Lubosi barely escaped with his life. Mataa became *ngambela*, and his "candidate," Tatila Akufuna (q.v.), became king. Mataa intended to rule, with the king as his puppet. Other appointments went to Mataa's supporters. He offered the Reverend Coillard (q.v.), whom he had opposed in 1878, a mission site, hoping to add European sanction to his authority.

Mataa's downfall had two roots. First, there was a core of loyalists, who tried to restore Lubosi as king. Second, Akufuna proved to be a very unpopular king, and even Mataa decided that he must be replaced. Mataa managed to defeat one loyalist force, but while he and Numwa were at Lukwakwa escorting their new king candidate, Sikufele, back to the valley, two large forces gathered by Lubosi and Silumbu (q.v.) prepared to attack them. Of the five principals just mentioned, only Lubosi survived the battle in early November 1885. Lubosi was thereafter known as Lewanika.

MATABELE (MATEBELE). The Sotho (q.v.) name for the Ndebele (q.v.), it was incorporated into common British colonial English. *See* MA-.

MATAUKA. Born in 1842, the twin sister of Lubosi/Lewanika (qq.v.) (king of the Lozi, q.v.), she was appointed by him to be

Mulena Mukwae (q.v.) at Nalolo (q.v.), the Lozi second (and southern) capital. Fiercely loyal to her brother, she lost her position after the 1884 coup that led to a Lozi civil war. She was also very active in the counterrebellion that restored her brother to the kingship and, thus, regained her title near the end of 1885. She died in 1934.

MATERO ECONOMIC REFORMS. Announced in a speech by President Kenneth Kaunda (q.v.) on August 11, 1969, at Matero, outside Lusaka (q.v.), the reforms instituted new rules for the sharing of Zambia's copper (q.v.) wealth. First, the government would acquire a 51 percent share in the ownership of the mines. Payment, it was later determined, would come out of the mines' dividends during roughly the next decade. Second, taxes in the industry were recalculated in a manner that gave incentive for expansion, while remaining at about the same level (73 percent of profits). Finally, it was declared that all mining rights in Zambia were being appropriated by the government. The greatest practical effect of this was to give the government more power over the siting of new mines (preferably in less developed areas) and the granting of mining licenses (on the basis of production beginning soon).

MATIPA. One of the most important of the Bisa (q.v.) chiefships, its chief is always a member of the Bena Ng'ona (or Mushroom Clan). The chief rules a territory called Lubumbu (q.v.), which is northeast of Lake Bangweulu (q.v.). The first chief to hold the title of Matipa was named Muma, and had succeeded Nkalamo as chief of Lubumbu about 1840. He became known as Matipa I Muma, and ruled there until his death in 1883.

During the reign of Matipa I, Lubumbu was repeatedly attacked or threatened by the Bemba (q.v.), causing them periodically to flee to either Nsumbu or Chilubi Island on Lake Bwangweulu. Dr. David Livingstone (q.v.) visited Matipa on Nsumbu in 1873. Soon after, Matipa took over Chilubi Island from its occupants, where his people still lived when Matipa I died in 1883.

An early-20th-century Matipa angered several other African groups by supplying canoes to British South Africa Company (q.v.) officials, thus allowing them to reach the islands and tax them. The same administrators had assisted him in gaining the contested chiefship in 1902.

MATOKA, PETER WILFRED. Born in North-Western Province (q.v.) in 1930, this experienced civil servant was educated at

Munali Secondary School (q.v.) and at Fort Hare University College in South Africa (Bachelor of Arts, 1954). After some years as a civil servant, he was awarded an international relations diploma from the American University in Washington, D.C., in 1964. Although he was a civil servant without an active record in nationalist politics, he was appointed minister of information and posts at independence and before 1975 headed at least five other ministries, Luapula Province (q.v.), and was the high commissioner to London. He then became minister of development and planning (1975–76) and of economics and technical cooperation.

MATRILINEAL DESCENT. A form of social and political organization, it is commonly found throughout most of Zambia, with a few exceptions in the extreme northeast and the west. (Most Africans practice patrilineal descent.) Zambia is located directly within the so-called matrilineal belt which stretches across Africa from Angola to southern Tanzania and Mozambique (qq.v.). Matrilineal peoples follow the female line for the sake of tracing descent (or sociological ancestry), inheritance, and political succession. Property or titles may pass from brother to brother, and then on to their sisters' sons, rather than to their own sons. Matrilineal societies are usually matrilocal, meaning that a man lives among his wife's people. But some Zambian peoples—like the Ila, Tonga, and Ndembu (Lunda) (qq.v.)—combine matriliny with patrilocality, in which the wife goes to live among her husband's relatives.

MATTAKO, J. ERNEST C. An early political activist, in 1930 he became a founder and vice chairman of the Livingstone Native Welfare Association (q.v.). A court interpreter by profession, Mattako was transferred that same year to Ndola (q.v.), and late in 1930 he joined with a few others in forming a similar association there.

MAUDLING, REGINALD. Successor to Iain Macleod (q.v.) as British colonial secretary in October 1961, it was his decision four months later that broke the constitutional stalemate. He announced to the House of Commons on February 28, 1962, that he would agree to a slight modification in the Macleod Constitution (q.v.). The change would reduce the qualifying percentage of votes in the national constituencies from 12.5 to 10 percent and remove the "or 400 votes" phrase. While this change seemingly made it all but impossible for anyone to win the seats, it was a plan that the United National Independence Party (q.v.) could accept. Thus the 1962 elections took place, and Kenneth Kaunda (q.v.) became prime minister.

MAXWELL, SIR JAMES CRAWFORD. Governor of Northern Rhodesia (q.v.) from 1927 to 1932, he was educated as a medical doctor at the University of Edinburgh. He served as a medical officer in Sierra Leone early in his colonial service but later was colonial secretary in the Gold Coast (Ghana), where he became familiar with the administrative policy called indirect rule (q.v.). He introduced it in 1929 to all of Northern Rhodesia except Barotse Province (q.v.). He developed a generous and respectful approach to the Lozi (q.v.) king that pleased the latter. Maxwell did cautiously recommend to the Lozi that certain changes in both administration and the courts would correct some obvious abuses.

Maxwell was opposed to amalgamation (q.v.) with Southern Rhodesia (q.v.), a point on which he fully agreed with Lord Passfield (q.v.), the British colonial secretary. He did, however, encourage European immigration as long as it was carefully planned and land was alienated in large enough units to be productive. When the worldwide Depression hit Northern Rhodesia in the early 1930s, Maxwell discouraged unemployed whites from staying in the territory. He feared they would drain the treasury of funds that should be used for Africans or that they might take jobs from Africans. He felt that unskilled and semi-skilled whites should be given the same treatment as Africans by the government, otherwise a colour bar (q.v.) would be created. Maxwell is also remembered for the fact that early work on the construction of the territorial capital at Lusaka (q.v.) began during his term as governor.

MAYBIN, SIR JOHN ALEXANDER. Governor of Northern Rhodesia (q.v.) from 1938 to 1941, he was born in Scotland and was a graduate of the University of Edinburgh. He served in Nigeria and other British territories before being assigned to Central Africa (q.v.). He agreed with the Bledisloe Commission (q.v.), whose report declared that amalgamation (q.v.) of the two Rhodesias and Nyasaland (q.v.) was not desirable at the time. He felt that native policies in the three territories would have to be standardized in a way agreeable to Africans before amalgamation could be considered. Southern Rhodesia's (q.v.) policies toward Africans were totally unacceptable, he felt, and job segregation especially must be rejected. Although there were some economic advantages to amalgamation, these should not come at the expense of Africans. He also saw no advantage to amalgamation with Nyasaland, as there were no real economic ties between the two territories.

Maybin also opposed the formation of the Inter-Territorial Council (q.v.), which he saw as yet another body that would continue to push for amalgamation. While he did meet with leaders of the other territories in 1940 to coordinate war efforts, he did not intend these meetings to have further political ramifications. And while he saw some advantages in increased European immigration, Maybin feared it would result in more land being lost to whites and in the social disintegration of African peoples and their traditions. Policy toward the Africans, he felt, should be based on their traditional institutions, albeit adapted to modern life. To aid in administration, he saw to it that African clerks received improved training.

MAZABUKA. The most populous district in Southern Province (q.v.), it had over 160,000 people in 1969 and 258,000 in 1990. The town of Mazabuka lies along the line of rail (q.v.) south of the Kafue River (q.v.) and serves the major European farming areas nearby. The district is one of the northernmost of Southern Province, and part of it is not much more than 40 kilometers (25 miles) south of Lusaka (q.v.).

MBALA (ABERCORN). Mbala District, Northern Province (q.v.), is in Zambia's northeastern corner. It includes most of the southern shore of Lake Tanganyika (q.v.) as well as about 97 kilometers (60 miles) of land bordering Tanzania (q.v.). The district had a population of 96,000 in 1969 and 138,000 in 1990. The town of Mbala (known as Abercorn, q.v., until after Zambian independence), lies on a branch of the Great North Road (q.v.), which continues on to Mpanda in Tanzania. In 1969, Mbala had a population of about 5,200 people. Its early history is tied to that of the African Lakes Company, the Stevenson Road, and later, Robert Williams and Company (qq.v.).

MBENI DANCE. This form of African popular culture began in German East Africa (Tanzania, q.v.) before World War I and spread to Northern Province and Nyasaland (qq.v.). By 1930, it was being publicly performed by Bemba (q.v.)-speaking labor migrants in the Copperbelt (q.v.) towns. A parody of a military band's drill or march past, the Mbeni was a corporate dance performed by touring dance teams, whose members—as in its successor, the Kalela Dance (q.v.)—occupied a hierarchy of ranked, military-style titles. While the Russell Commission (q.v.) report on the Copperbelt strikes of 1935 (q.v.) reflected the mining companies' view that Mbeni dancers did not organize the strikes, the government was probably correct in assigning these touring dance teams primary responsibility for mobilizing popular opinion.

MBIKUSITA, GODWIN AKABUWA (GODWIN MBIKUSITA LEWANIKA). The word ubiquitous best describes this man, whose life and career tied together virtually all of modern Zambian history. Born in 1907 at the court of King Lewanika (q.v.), he had much success at the Barotse National School (q.v.) and went on to both the University of South Africa and the University of Wales (where he studied social welfare). In 1935, working as a government clerk, he was made private secretary to Yeta III (q.v.). He accompanied Yeta to London in 1938 for the British coronation and a visit to Paris. He did not return home, however, as he was suspected of being involved with Edward Kalue (q.v.) in a plot to overthrow Yeta.

He returned to Zambia in 1941 and eventually became a senior African welfare officer for the Rhokana Corporation (q.v.) in Nkana. A few years later he became the president of the Kitwe African Society (q.v.), which led to his involvement in the creation of the Federation of African Societies of Northern Rhodesia (q.v.) in May 1946, and to his election as president when it became the Northern Rhodesia African Congress (q.v.) in 1948. His leadership of the country's first true African nationalist organization did not satisfy some activists, however, and he was replaced in 1951 by Harry Nkumbula (q.v.). Meanwhile, he had become active in labor unions as well. Mbikusita lost to Lawrence Katilungu (q.v.) in a bid to head the African Mineworkers Union (q.v.) in 1947. In 1953 he became a leader of the rival Mines African Staff Association (q.v.), which was composed of salaried staff and supervising workers in the mines.

Mbikusita returned to Barotseland (q.v.) in 1954 and founded the Barotse National Association (q.v.), which was designed to show support for the Barotse national government (another faction later reversed this). He also went to Switzerland, where he took a course on moral rearmament. He returned to Barotseland in 1956 and was nominated for the post of *ngambela* (q.v.) but came out second in the balloting.

Anxious to safeguard Barotseland's special semiautonomous

status, he supported the Central African Federation (q.v.) and became the first African member of Roy Welensky's United Federal Party (qq.v.). In November 1958 he was elected with its support to the Federal Assembly. He continued to support the concept of partnership and even declared that apartheid was an experiment and, as such, he did not oppose it. He eventually was made a junior minister in the assembly. As a Lozi "royal" and a member of the UFP, he became part of a curious proposal whereby Welensky would allow the breakup of the federation if Southern Rhodesia, the Copperbelt, and Barotseland (to supply labor for the Copperbelt) would be united in a new federation.

In 1967 Mbikusita was appointed to the Lozi House of Chiefs, and the king then appointed him to the post of *natamoyo* (q.v.). When the king died the following year, Mbikusita was appointed his successor and was installed on December 15, 1968. He died in early 1977.

MBIKUSITA-LEWANIKA, AKASHAMBATWA. A founding member of the Movement for Multiparty Democracy (q.v.), he became its first national secretary in July 1990. Once the MMD won the 1991 elections and took power, he was appointed minister of science, technology, and vocational training. Though briefly associated with the Caucus for National Unity (q.v.), a Lozi-dominated pressure group in the MMD, he did not join either of the two political parties eventually generated by the caucus's split from the MMD. He did, though, resign from his ministry and the MMD in July 1992, charging that the MMD's vision of democracy was "clouded and deformed," and he joined eight other members of Parliament who resigned from the MMD to form the National Party (q.v.) in August 1993.

MBIKUSITA-LEWANIKA, INONGE. Born in July 1943 in Senanga (q.v.), she was the daughter of Godwin Akabuwa Mbikusita (q.v.), founder of the Federation of African Societies of Northern Rhodesia (q.v.) and first president of the Northern Rhodesia African Congress (q.v.). Inonge Mbikusita-Lewanika earned a B.S. degree in home economics and education in 1964 and an M.A. in education and psychology in 1965, both from California State University—San Luis Obispo; and a Ph.D. in early childhood and primary education at New York University in 1979. She served as lecturer at Evelyn Hone College and at the University of Zambia (qq.v.) throughout the 1970s. In 1980 she became UNICEF's regional advisor on family planning and child hygiene for Central and Southern Africa. From 1985 to 1987 she served as senior program officer for UNICEF in Kenya and, from 1987 to 1990, as UNICEF regional officer for childhood development and women in West and Central Africa (q.v.). She returned to Zambia in 1991 and entered politics, joining the Movement for Multiparty Democracy (q.v.), winning the parliamentary seat for Senanga in the October 1991 elections. In 1993 she joined several other members of Parliament in leaving the MMD to form the National Party (q.v.), which she served as interim leader from 1993 to 1994. She retained her seat in Parliament in the by-elections following her split from the MMD. Dr. Mbikusita-Lewanika has studied, lectured, worked, and traveled widely throughout Africa and the world. She has won many awards and honors and has been actively involved in nongovernmental organizations in Zambia.

MBOO (MWANASILUMDU; MUYUNDA). He was the son of Mbuyu (q.v.) and is recognized as the founder of the present Luyi dynasty (now called the Lozi, q.v.). His mother, a noted figurehead but not an effective central leader, abdicated in favor of Mboo, her eldest son, who introduced such important institutions as *induna*s, the *makolo* system (qq.v.), and the payment of tribute. All of these were in an elementary stage, however, and the kingdom was not centralized. Nor was it extensive, for while Mboo conquered a number of groups within what is now Kalambo District, he was stopped in attempts to expand eastward along the Lwena flats, probably by an Nkoya group. Essentially, his territory was all within Kalabo District. In addition, several of his relatives, notably Mwanambinyi and Mange (qq.v.), broke away from his rule. Yet all claimants to the Lozi throne are required to trace their ancestry to Mboo.

MBOWE. A small ethnic group, it is concentrated on the Zambezi River above Mongu (qq.v.) and is considered to be part of the Luyana (q.v.) division of the Barotse language group.

MBUNDA. A distinct ethnic group, it belongs to the Lunda-Luvale (qq.v.) linguistic subgroup. These people originated in Angola (q.v.) but today live primarily in North-Western Province (q.v.), where along with several other groups they are sometimes collectively referred to as the Luvale (or Balovale); the Lozi (q.v.), however, often lump the Mbunda, Luvale, Luchazi, and Chokwe under the category of Wiko, or "western people." There were about 102,000 kiMbunda speakers in Zambia in 1986.

The first Mbunda probably arrived in Zambia in the late 18th century, led by two chiefs, Mwene Ciengele and, later, Mwene Kandala. They were a highly decentralized people, relying more on local groups controlled by the elders than on complex state systems. But each small group had its *mwene,* or chief. They brought with them crops that had been introduced by the Portuguese, notably cassava, millet (qq.v.), and a small type of yam. They settled near the Lozi, in the vicinity of Mongu (q.v.) and along the eastern forest. They revolutionized military tactics in the area, being expert with bows and arrows, weapons unfamiliar to the Lozi, and a special fighting axe (*bukana*). The Lozi and Mbunda combined to defeat several groups in the area (the Luvale, the Nkoya (q.v.), and others). Mwene Ciengele was given the status of a Lozi prince and given a seat in the *kuta* (q.v.). The Lozi tried to absorb them through the *makolo* (q.v.) system; however, differences in their religious beliefs and political systems made this impossible.

The Mbunda became directly involved in Lozi politics around 1830, when they participated in a succession dispute involving Silumelume (q.v.), who was killed by an Mbunda warrior. Thirty years later, after the Kololo were evicted from Bulozi, Mbunda groups at Lukwakwa helped Sipopa (q.v.) overthrow and kill Imasiku (q.v.). They also sided with Musiwa, a competitor of Lubosi, in 1880. When Lubosi discovered their involvement in a scheme to protect Musiwa (*see* MATAA), Lubosi ordered many Mbunda killed. Some crossed back into Angola to avoid the attack, but those who remained and survived the murders never forgave the king (Lubosi/Lewanika) and remained his opponents.

MBUYU (MBUYWAMWAMBWA). "The daughter of Mwambwa" or "the daughter of God," she is the ancestress of the royal line of the Lozi (q.v.). She was a Luyana (q.v.) princess who led her people before they settled in Bulozi (q.v.). She abdicated in favor of her son, Mboo (q.v.), who became the first king in the new Luyana (later called Lozi) dynasty. Mbuyu's divine origin is insisted upon by the Lozi, who see this as an important reason for retaining the specific ruling family.

MBWELA. The Mbwela peoples, some of the earliest occupants of western Southern Central Africa, are considered part of the

Nkoya (q.v.) people. They seem to have originally occupied the upper Zambezi River valley in Mwinilunga (qq.v.) District but were driven east toward the Kafue Hook (q.v.) and beyond by western (Luena, Luchazi, and Chokwe, qq.v.) and northern (Luvale, Ndembu, and Kaonde, qq.v.) immigrants from modern Angola (q.v.) and the Democratic Republic of Congo (q.v.) (Zaire). Some of their displacement, though, was presumably linked to their 19th-century occupational niche as elephant hunters, supplying the ivory (q.v.) trade.

MCKINNON, CHARLES (also MACKINNON; M'KINNON). One of the first British South Africa Company (q.v.) administrators to get actively involved in conflicts with the Bemba (q.v.), he was appointed collector (q.v.) at Ikawa (q.v.) early in 1897. From the beginning, McKinnon expressed interest in exploiting splits among Bemba (q.v.) leaders, notably those involving the ambitious Bemba chief, Mwamba III (q.v.). He also requested that the BSAC supply better military equipment, including a Maxim gun (which he never received).

McKinnon's opposition to Mwamba was complicated by the fact that the Bemba leader had the support of Arab slave traders (qq.v.). McKinnon sent his assistant, Robert (Bobo) Young (q.v.), to set up Mirongo *boma* (q.v.), near Senga (q.v.) chief Chibale's (q.v.), to protect him from the Bemba. The next month, September 1897, a combined force of Arabs and Bemba attacked Chibale's village. Young went to protect Chibale with a small force but was soon caught in the stockaded village. Five days later, McKinnon arrived with reinforcements to lift the siege. The unit then went on to destroy a number of Arab stockades and villages, release captured slaves, and arrest Kapandansalu (q.v.), a noted Arab slave-trading chief.

McKinnon's opposition to Mwamba was finally mooted when the Bemba leader died in October 1898. He came to Mwamba's, and was disturbed to find Father (soon Bishop) Joseph Dupont (q.v.) in charge. He ordered both Dupont and Ponde (q.v.), a claimant to the Mwamba title, to leave the village. Early in 1899, McKinnon, Young, and several other BSAC administrators met at Kasama (q.v.) with some company police and attacked and burned Ponde's stockaded village. Though Ponde escaped, this put an end to armed encounters with the Bemba. A decade later, McKinnon became the resident magistrate at Lealui, Barotseland (qq.v.), where he facilitated the establishment of the Barotse National School (q.v.), and became a charter member of Leopold F. Moore's (q.v.) Livingstone landowners' and farmers' association.

MEALIEMEAL. This is the English spelling of the Afrikaans word for (white) maize flour, which, when added to boiling water, makes *nshima* (q.v.). This, dipped into a companion vegetable or meat "relish" (sauce), is the staple dish in most Zambian meals.

METAL MARKETING CORPORATION OF ZAMBIA. The company was formed in conjunction with the Mulungushi and Matero Economic Reforms (q.v.) of 1969. The Zambian government established the Metal Marketing Corporation, with a London office, in 1973, in an attempt to coordinate the sale and price of Zambian metals and minerals, especially copper (q.v.). Following a World Bank study, MEMACO was dissolved in 1994 and replaced by the marketing division of Zambia Consolidated Copper Mines (q.v.).

MICHELLO, JOB E. A nationalist politician of the 1950s and 1960s, he was primarily active in the African National Congress (q.v.). At the time of the ANC's internal splits in 1959, Michello was its provincial secretary for Southern Province (q.v.). Harry Nkumbula (q.v.) then selected him to be party general secretary. When Lawrence Katilungu (q.v.) died in 1961, Michello succeeded to his seat in the Legislative Council (q.v.). Elected to the post in 1962, he became part of the UNIP-ANC coalition government, serving as parliamentary secretary for the ministry of land and natural resources. In 1963 he broke with Nkumbula, however (he had opposed the coalition and also disliked Nkumbula's handling of the campaign), and formed his own People's Democratic Congress (q.v.), a conservative faction aided by both Roy Welensky (q.v.) and the Congo's Moise Tshombe (q.v.). Michello and Nkumbula settled their differences in December 1963, but both groups failed in the 1964 elections, and the PDC folded.

MIDDLETON, GEORGE W. An Englishman who became very active in Lozi (q.v.) affairs in the late 19th century, he first visited there when he became a lay member of the Reverend Coillard's (q.v.) missionary group in 1883. He quit the mission in 1887 and went to South Africa. He returned to Sesheke (q.v.) three years later as a representative of a South African trading and transport firm and began a campaign to convince the Lozi to repudiate the Ware Concession (q.v.) and to sow suspicion against the concession being sought by Frank Lochner (q.v.), Cecil Rhodes' (q.v.) agent. Middleton arrived in the capital in September 1890, after the signing of the Lochner Concession (q.v.) and convinced Lewanika (q.v.) that Lochner and Coillard had misrepresented the British South Africa Company's (q.v.) relationship to the British Crown. Middleton even wrote a letter to Lord Salisbury for the king, in which Lewanika "repudiated" the deal with Lochner. This was smoothed over, however, by the British high commissioner in South Africa, who assured Lewanika that he was under British protection. In 1892, Middleton challenged Lewanika to expel Coillard or cause Middleton to leave the country. He still had hopes of gaining advantages in Barotseland (q.v.) for his firm. Instead, Lewanika declined to dismiss the missionaries, and Middleton was forced to return to South Africa in April 1892.

MILINGO, EMMANUEL. Roman Catholic (q.v.) archbishop of the see of Lusaka (q.v.) from 1969 to 1983, Monsignor Milingo was born in 1930 to an Ngoni (q.v.) farming family in Eastern Province (q.v.). At age 12, he left home to attend a local White Fathers' (q.v.) school. Two years later, he entered seminary training for the priesthood. Father Milingo was transferred to Lusaka in December 1965 as secretary and broadcaster with the Zambian Episcopal Conference's Department of Mass Media. He was soon organizing medical facilities in the townships of Lusaka. Zambians heartily endorsed Pope Paul VI's decision to appoint him to the see of Lusaka in 1969.

Following a dramatic healing success in 1973, Milingo told his cathedral congregation in Roma township that the Holy Spirit had invested him with the power to heal those afflicted by evil spirits. His frequent, public healing sessions attracted hundreds, even thousands, of observers. Other supplicants visited his house or deluged him with mail. Milingo was soon famous throughout much of Anglophonic Africa and enjoyed wide support from the Zambian government. By the late 1970s, however, his fellow Zambian bishops had become uneasy with his casting out of spirits and persuaded him to abandon his public healing sessions in early 1979. A papal investigation followed; Milingo was summoned to the Vatican in 1983, and he resigned the Lusaka see in 1983. As special delegate to the Papal Commission for Migration and Tourism, he oversaw the pastoral care of African refugees. In Rome, he continued to attend the sick and to conduct a monthly healing mass.

MILLET. This is the common English name for two distinct and unrelated grain crops: bulrush millet (*Pennisetum typhoideum*), which looks like a tall, seedy bulrush; and finger millet, or eleusine (*Eleusine coracana*), whose many varieties have five, finger-like, seed-bearing racemes at the top of their short stalks. Regrettably, British writers also use the word "millet" when referring to sorghum (*Sorghum vulgare,* or kaffir corn, q.v.). All three of these grains have been dietary staples since early Iron Age times and are associated with *chitemene* (q.v.) cultivation. They are used to prepare both beer and a gritslike porridge. Like sorghum, both of these millets have been supplanted by maize.

MILNER, AARON MICHAEL. A Eurafrican (q.v.) born in Southern Rhodesia (q.v.), he became a high-ranking officer in both the United National Independence Party (q.v.) and the government before his August 1977 dismissal under suspicion of corruption. Born May 31, 1932, in Bulawayo, he was educated in Southern Rhodesia but left school at age 16 to help support his family. He worked as a tailor and later as a bookkeeper. In 1954 he began working in Northern Rhodesia (q.v.) and gradually got involved in politics. He was elected chairman of the Euro-African Association, which he merged into UNIP in July 1960. In 1961 he was elected deputy secretary-general of UNIP, a post he held for 10 years, and also served on the party's Central Committee (q.v.). In 1964 he was elected to Parliament from Muchinga. He was placed in charge of the Civil Service and served from 1964 to 1967 as minister of state for cabinet affairs and the public service. In the next six years he served in at least four cabinet posts, before becoming minister of home affairs (1973–77). In 1980 the government discovered guerrillas and a cache of arms on a farm south of Lusaka (q.v.) owned by Milner. The discovery led to charges of treason against eight defendants. Milner fled Zambia.

MINDOLO ECUMENICAL CENTRE. The center, three kilometers (two miles) northwest of Kitwe (q.v.), began in 1936 as the Reverend Reginald J. B. (Mike) Moore's headquarters for the newly established United Missions in the Copperbelt (q.v.), a collaborative effort between seven Protestant mission groups and the (African) Union Church of the Copperbelt (q.v.) from 1936–45. Moore used the Mindolo site to hold unity conferences for church elders, to teach catechumens, and to encourage compound evangelism. The UMCB never received the funds or personnel needed to open its planned teacher training school at Mindolo, but it did open a primary school there in 1937. In 1939 in Nkana it also began the Mindolo Women's Centre and an African welfare assistants' class. The Women's Centre eventually offered residential courses in Christian homemaking and became the Copperbelt's only (and elite) boarding school for girls.

The Christian Council (q.v.) of Northern Rhodesia, backed by the World Council of Churches, officially established Mindolo Ecumenical Centre in 1958 as an interchurch center for leadership training, hosting conferences, and training welfare officers. The United Church of Zambia (q.v.) was inaugurated there in January 1965, and until it moved to Nairobi in the mid-1970s, Mindolo served as the home of the secretariat for the All-Africa Conference of Churches.

MINE STRIKES, 1935, 1940. *See* STRIKES OF 1935, 1940.

MINES AFRICAN STAFF ASSOCIATION. Created by the copper (q.v.) companies in 1953, this was a union of African clerical workers and foremen. Led by Godwin Mbikusita (q.v.), it was designed to counter the influence of the African Mineworkers Union (q.v.). The companies gave MASA the right to represent Africans whom they had recently promoted to jobs previously held by whites. In 1956 the animosity between the two unions contributed to a series of rolling strikes that hindered production. In September 1956, the government declared a state of emergency on the Copperbelt (q.v.) and made a number of arrests. MASA changed its name to the United Mineworkers Union (q.v.) in 1963. It was reorganized as the Mines Local Staff Association (q.v.) within a year and, in 1967, joined the Mineworkers Union of Zambia (q.v.).

MINES LOCAL STAFF ASSOCIATION. When the United Mineworkers Union (q.v.) dissolved late in 1963, it was changed to the Mines Local Staff Association. It now claimed only to cover staff and supervisory employees in the mines. In effect, it reverted to the form of the Mines African Staff Association (q.v.). When the United National Independence Party (q.v.) and the government tried to take over the leadership of the miners' unions, it participated in the general Copperbelt (q.v.) strikes of September 1966. As a result, some of its officials were arrested. In April 1967 the MLSA merged with the Zambia

Mineworkers Union (q.v.) and the Mines Police Association to form the Mineworkers Union of Zambia (q.v.).

MINEWORKERS UNION OF ZAMBIA. A union of some 44,000 workers, it represents the April 1967 merging of the Zambia Mineworkers Union, the Mines Local Staff Association (qq.v.), and the Mines Police Association. Each branch sends its delegates to its biannual conferences. Long the most influential union in the country, its members resisted the United National Independence Party's (q.v.) attempts to gain control of the union leadership in the early 1970s.

After 1975, declining living standards, together with government-imposed wage ceilings and subsidies cuts, led the MUZ and its umbrella organization, the Zambia Congress of Trade Unions (q.v.), to increasingly criticize the government and its policies. In January 1981, the union's threat of an election boycott led UNIP to expel 17 Executive Committee members of the MUZ and the ZCTU. The MUZ then staged a popular, eight-day strike to assert the independence of union posts from UNIP membership, and the 17 were readmitted to UNIP in April. That July, after the Railway Workers' Union of Zambia struck to protest government-imposed management changes, and MUZ members burned the minister of mines' official car, MUZ vice chairman, Timothy Walamba—together with Frederick Chiluba (q.v.), Newstead Zimba (q.v.), and Chitalu Sampa (q.v.) (then chairman, general secretary, and assistant secretary of the ZCTU, respectively)—were detained for advocating industrial unrest and the overthrow of the government. They were released in November 1981 after the High Court (q.v.) dismissed all charges. By late 1990, President Kaunda (q.v.) accused the Movement for Multiparty Democracy (q.v.) of inciting the army and the MUZ to disrupt the country and weaken UNIP. In the October 1991 elections, MUZ members were among the many Zambians who gave Frederick Chiluba 81 percent of the presidential vote.

Though Frederick Chiluba and ZCTU leaders played prominent roles in the 1990 formation and 1991 electoral victory of the ad hoc Movement for Multiparty Democracy, job retrenchments in the mines and other industries led the MUZ and 11 other unions to break from the ZCTU in 1994, threatening a considerable loss of members and their annual dues contributions. Given Zambia's continuing copper (q.v.) crisis, the MUZ currently supports the Zambia Privatisation Agency's (q.v.) sale of Chambishi (q.v.) and other mines in the hope this will slow down Zambia Consolidated Copper Mines' (q.v.) retrenchment plans and thus preserve members' jobs.

MINING DEVELOPMENT CORPORATION OF ZAMBIA, LTD. In January 1970, the government vested the 51 percent of its shares in Nchanga and Roan Consolidated Mines (qq.v.) in MINDECO, a new parastatal holding company designed to be a watchdog over the mines' expatriate managers. Andrew S. Sardanis (q.v.) was MINDECO's first managing director. In 1971, MINDECO, INDECO, and FINDECO were placed under an umbrella parastatal, the Zambia Industrial and Mining Corporation (q.v.) with the president as its chairman. In 1974, MINDECO's charge was narrowed to cover only Maamba (q.v.) Collieries, small mining developments, and new mining ventures not controlled by either Nchanga or Roan Consolidated Copper Mines.

MIRONGO BOMA. An administrative post formed in August 1897 by Robert (Bobo) Young (q.v.), an assistant collector for the British South Africa Company (qq.v.), near the present site of Isoka, its purpose was to prevent raids by Arabs and Bemba (qq.v.) on nearby villages. As such, it was welcomed by the Senga. On the other hand, the Bemba and the Arabs, each located about 32 kilometers (20 miles) from the *boma* (q.v.), threatened its inhabitants with death if they did not leave. The situation culminated in a battle at the village of Senga (q.v.) chief Chibale (q.v.), to whom Young provided aid. Another official, Charles McKinnon (q.v.) succeeded in routing the Bemba and the Arabs.

MITANDA (sing., *mutanda*). In North-Eastern Rhodesia (q.v.), this is the term for the temporary huts and scattered, seasonal garden settlements inhabited by *chitemene* (q.v.) cultivators to better protect their crops from bird and animal pests. Once the British South Africa Company's (q.v.) administration ended the late-19th-century threats of warfare and slave raiding, people abandoned their large, congested, stockaded, and conflict-ridden villages and returned to the tradition of smaller villages and seasonal *mitanda*. But this customary settlement pattern made hut tax (q.v.) collections and labor recruitment (*see* CHIBALO) more difficult. And, inasmuch as the officially recognized chiefs were supposed to assist in tax collections, it also appeared to weaken chiefly authority. Thus, from 1903 to 1920, the North-Eastern and Northern Rhodesian administrators periodically outlawed and burned these *mitanda* in what was locally known as *chisanka* (q.v.), or "the confiscation and removal of unauthorized villages." This was part of a futile effort to create a more "orderly" political economy by forcing people back into large villages and by discouraging the "wasteful" *chitemene* system. When combined with tax collection and labor recruitment, such measures caused a lot of hardship, resentment, and unrest.

MKANDA. One of the Chewa (q.v.) chiefships, it straddled the modern Zambian-Malawian border near Chipata (q.v.). The location gave its chief special influence, located as it was along the trade route between Tete, Mozambique (qq.v.), and Zambian traders in either the Luangwa valley (q.v.) or in Kazembe's (q.v.) kingdom on the Luapula River (q.v.). A gold mine was opened on his lands in about 1790. Mkanda easily defeated some of the smaller and less centralized peoples in the area, and by the early 19th century, Mkanda was almost independent of Undi (q.v.), the Chewa paramount chief (q.v.). But his prosperous maize (q.v.) fields and cattle herds attracted Ngoni (q.v.) raiders after 1860, and by 1880 the Ngoni leader, Mpezeni (q.v.), had killed Mkanda and taken over his kingdom.

MKETISO. This institution of the Lozi (q.v.) system required subject peoples to send large numbers of young men and women periodically to Bulozi (q.v.) to provide labor. *Indunas* (q.v.) residing among the subject peoples ensured the Lozi a continuing supply.

MLOZI. A notorious Arab-African slave trader (q.v.), he was the main dealer for Bemba (q.v.) slaves from 1883 to 1895. His base was a stockaded village about 80 kilometers (50 miles) east of Zambia's border, near Karonga, on Lake Malawi (q.v.) (formerly Lake Nyasa). By 1887 he was clashing with both the British and the local Africans. He made a truce with the British in 1889, but in December 1895 a British force attacked and destroyed Mlozi's village and he was hanged. Thereafter, several Arab and Swahili (qq.v.) traders, like Chiwala (q.v.), retreated to the upper Luapula River (q.v.) valley.

M'MEMBE, FRED. He is managing editor of the *Post* (q.v.), an independent newspaper founded in July 1991. The *Post* has been critical of the government of President Chiluba (q.v.) and of the president himself. M'membe has been arrested on several occasions and charged with such offenses as defaming the president, contempt of Parliament (q.v.), possessing state secrets, and possessing a banned publication (after the February 5, 1996, edition of the *Post* was banned). The *Post* has also been sued for libel many times, including a suit filed by President Chiluba. The use of criminal charges to silence or intimidate M'membe and other journalists has drawn the criticism of international groups devoted to the protection of press freedoms. In 1995, M'membe was the cowinner of the *World Press Review's* International Editor of the Year Award.

MOFFAT RESOLUTIONS, 1954. The four resolutions, presented by Sir John Moffat (q.v.) in July 1954, were passed by the Northern Rhodesia Legislative Council with only one opposing vote. They suported fair legislative representation of all racial groups; a transitional period in which neither racial group would have an advantage; protection of everyone's rights and interests; and the right for a person to progress according to his own abilities and efforts without regard to race and color. Some saw Moffat's resolutions as a wishful dream; others, especially Africans, saw them as a way of delaying self-rule. The 1959 Benson Constitution (q.v.) was based on these resolutions.

MOFFAT, SIR JOHN SMITH. A government official and political figure in Zambia for over four decades, he was born in Nyasaland (q.v.) in 1905, a great-grandson of the famous missionary, Robert Moffat. Educated in South Africa and at Glasgow University, he joined the colonial service in Northern Rhodesia (q.v.) in 1927. When the Mufulira miners went on strike in 1935, Moffat was the administrative officer in charge for the secretary for native affairs. He attempted a peaceful settlement, but the strike took place anyway, and he arrested eight of its leaders.

Moffat rose to the position of commissioner for native development. However, in February 1951 he was appointed to an "unofficial" (q.v.) seat in the Legislative Council (q.v.) and to the Executive Council (q.v.) as well. In the Legislative Council he cast one of four votes against federation (q.v.); though he actually approved of it, he didn't think it should be forced upon the disapproving Africans. The next year he introduced the Moffat Resolutions (q.v.) in an attempt to eventually make federation work in the interests of the Africans. He resigned his seat in the Legislative Council, and in December 1954 was appointed as European member for African interests in the Federal House of Assembly. He also became chairman of its

African Affairs Board (q.v.), which could delay bills it considered discriminatory against the Africans. He was bitter, however, when the British Parliament approved several important bills over the board's reservations. He was knighted, however, in 1955.

Disturbed with the action of the Federal Assembly on his new version of the Moffat Resolutions, he resigned in 1958 and in February 1959 became a founding member of the Central Africa Party (q.v.), hoping to enter the Northern Rhodesia elections with an organized policy. His party won four seats, he himself being one of those elected. When Garfield Todd (q.v.) of Southern Rhodesia left the CAP, Moffat's Northern Rhodesian branch broke away and became the Northern Rhodesia Liberal Party (q.v.). In December 1960 he attended the Federal Review Conference (q.v.) in London and stayed for the Constitutional Conference in January and February 1961 (*see* LONDON CONSTITUTIONAL CONFERENCE, 1961).

When the United Federal Party (q.v.) quit the government on February 22 as a result of the Macleod Constitution (q.v.), the governor replaced the three UFP ministers with three members of the Liberal Party. Moffat was appointed minister of land and natural resources. The constitution was revised and presented, finally, in 1962. Moffat supported it as the last chance for Europeans to set up a true and effective partnership with the Africans. He saw the plan as transitional, in which the Liberal Party would participate for about five years while Africans were gaining governing experience. While Kenneth Kaunda (q.v.) liked Moffat, he did not trust the other members of the Liberal Party.

The Liberal Party was not successful in the 1962 elections, and in 1964 Moffat became a United National Independence Party (q.v.) candidate for one of the 10 seats reserved for Europeans. He lost to an NPP candidate. In December 1967 he was appointed by President Kaunda to serve on a three-member Electoral Commission.

MOFFAT THOMSON, JAMES. His first job in Central Africa (q.v.) was shop assistant for the African Lakes Company (q.v.) in 1901. He later worked 14 years for the British South Africa Company (q.v.). In 1910 he discovered the Nkana Mine (q.v.). He took over as secretary for native affairs in 1928. A strong backer of indirect rule (q.v.), he supported the Native Authority Ordinance of 1929 (q.v.), which returned much authority to traditional leaders. On the other hand, he opposed certain nationalistic or progressive movements that did not use the traditional system. He opposed the Watch Tower Movement (q.v.), for example, and although he had spoken favorably of the formation of a Mwenzo Welfare Association (q.v.) when he was head administrator of the Tanganyika District (q.v.) in 1923, he opposed the formation of a United African Welfare Association in the early 1930s. In 1927 he also served as chairman for the Reserves Commission (q.v.) of the Tanganyika District, which was to provide more land to European coffee planters by getting the BSAC to relinquish part of its Tanganyika estate and by resettling local Africans in reserves.

MOFWE LAGOON. Located south of Lake Mweru (q.v.), the area near the lagoon was the site of the capitals of each of the Kazembe (q.v.) kings until 1884, when Kazembe X (q.v.) built his capital about 32 kilometers (20 miles) south of the lagoon, where it remained.

MOIR, JOHN WILLIAM, *and* **FREDERICK MAITLAND MOIR.** In 1878, these Glaswegian brothers helped found the African Lakes Company (q.v.), a private trade and transport company designed to support the Livingstonia Mission's (q.v.) efforts in Central Africa (q.v.) by substituting legitimate commerce for the slave trade (q.v.). John wore spectacles (*mandala*), and his personal nickname soon became the generic name for the ALC's Blantyre headquarters and all its posts. John and Frederick Moir entered the future North-Eastern Rhodesia (q.v.) in the early 1880s. They seemingly worked on the Stevenson Road (q.v.), collected a set of treaties envied by the British South Africa Company (q.v.), and were wounded in the 1889–90 confrontations with Mlozi (q.v.) near Chiengi and Karonga. In addition to introducing Jamaican coffee trees into the Shire Highlands, the Moir brothers played a crucial role in establishing British interests in Nyasaland (q.v.) and North-Eastern Rhodesia.

MOKALAPA, WILLIE J. The founder of the Ethiopian Church of Barotseland (q.v.), he was a Sotho (q.v.) evangelist who had worked for many years with the Reverend François Coillard (q.v.) and the Paris Missionary Society (q.v.) in Barotseland before breaking with them. Mokalapa had studied at the Lovedale Institute, South Africa, at which he heard of Ethiopian, or separatist, church movements and became acquainted with the African Methodist Episcopal Church (q.v.). In 1899 he and his colleagues expressed their grievances against the Coillard mission, complaining about low salaries and about their treatment as inferiors by the missionaries. They requested a greater role to the mission's activities. When this was refused, Mokalapa returned briefly to Barotseland and South Africa, where he became involved with Ethiopians and joined the AME Church. He returned to the Lozi (q.v.) to press for "an African church for Africans."

His first attempt to form an Ethiopian Church in Barotseland was aborted when Coillard intervened with Lewanika (q.v.). Later, however, Mokalapa persuaded Lewanika by promising a school that would teach more English and practical subjects. Africans completely controlled the new church, which was given a mission site in the Zambezi (q.v.) valley and free labor. By 1904 the new church was thriving and had a number of schools. Many of its supporters were drawn from the Paris Missionary Society church.

Late in 1905, Mokalapa was sent to South Africa with some £750 of Lewanika's money to buy him wagons, carriages, and boats, but the South African merchants cheated him out of his money, and he was too ashamed to return. The church quickly declined.

MOKAMBA. Believed by many Lozi (q.v.) to be one of their greatest *ngambela*, he was himself the son of a great *ngambela*, Njekwa (qq.v.). As a youth he was a companion of Lewanika's oldest son, Litia (later, king Yeta) (qq.v.). Litia and Mokamba were among Frederick Arnot's (q.v.) first school students. Mokamba fled into exile with Lewanika in 1884 and helped restore Lewanika to his kingship the next year. As a student of the Reverend Coillard (q.v.), he gained a Western education and an introduction to Christianity. He later married a daughter of Lewanika, and became an important *induna* (q.v.). Although only about 35 years old at the time, he was chosen as *ngambela* by Lewanika over several more mature candidates, the king seeing Mokamba as receptive to modern technology and development, and realistic in dealing with Europeans. As Lewanika grew older, Mokamba increasingly ran the affairs of the nation. After Lewanika's death, he served as *ngambela* for his old friend, King Yeta (Litia), for several years. Mokamba died early in 1919, having served for 20 years as *ngambela*.

MONCKTON COMMISSION. Appointed by the British Conservative Party government to make recommendations for the

Federal Review Conference (q.v.) to be held in December 1960, this 25-member commission was chaired by Lord Walter Monckton, chairman of one of Britain's largest banks. It visited the Central African Federation (q.v.) in February and March 1960 and issued its 175-page report in October: "Report of the Advisory Commission on the Review of the Constitution of Rhodesia and Nyasaland." The commission consisted of many Conservative Party politicians (the Labour Party refused to be part of it) and at least three moderate-to-conservative Africans, including Lawrence Katilungu (q.v.) of Northern Rhodesia (q.v.). The commission's hearings were boycotted by African nationalists, in part because Prime Minister Macmillan (q.v.) had indicated that the commission was not to consider the possibility of secession by any of the territories.

Despite its conservative composition and Macmillan's statement, the commission reached conclusions that were totally unacceptable to the federation's European population and its leader, Roy Welensky (q.v.). It concluded that only force could keep the federation together and that the right of secession should be allowed; that the colour bar (q.v.) prevented political development and must be prohibited by legislation; that a bill of rights should be instituted; that each of the territories should be allowed greater responsibilities; that Africans should be given at least parity in the Federal Parliament and that more Africans must be allowed to vote; and that Britain should provide more economic aid to the federation.

MONGU. This is a district in Zambia's Western Province (sometimes called the Mongu-Lealui District), as well as the urban center that is the capital of Barotseland (q.v.). The district is the most populous one in the province, with 85,500 people in 1969 and 142,200 in 1990. The town of Mongu, located about 676 kilometers (420 miles) west of Lusaka (q.v.), had a population of 10,700 in 1969, a figure double that of six years earlier. Mongu became the administrative center of the Lozi (q.v.) after the British sent a resident magistrate there. It was located about 32 kilometers (20 miles) southeast of the old Lozi capital at Lealui (q.v.). As Lozi leaders regularly traveled to Mongu, it became the royal capital. The Lozi royal village is still there, and the annual Kuomboka (q.v.) ceremony still begins there.

MONGU-LEALUI AFRICAN WELFARE ASSOCIATION. Founded in 1939 by a small number of educated Africans working in Mongu (q.v.), it was formed "to promote cooperation and brotherly feeling between Africans in Northern Rhodesia; to encourage the spread of civilization by education, industrial, and agricultural development; to protect and further African interests generally." The administration in Mongu formally recognized it in 1943. One of its early goals was to persuade the Barotse national government to allow the institution of a provincial council like the ones in the other provinces of Northern Rhodesia (q.v.). It did not succeed. As membership grew to the 1940s to about 100, it consisted of many of the most educated Lozi, along with some clerks and teachers from Nyasaland (q.v.). In general, it was the professional, educated, employed, and well-traveled individual who joined. The association did not want to depose Lozi ruling power; it just wanted to share some of it. It joined the royal house in opposing amalgamation (q.v.)with Southern Rhodesia (q.v.) in the late 1940s. In the next decade many senior members of the organization were co-opted into the Barotse national government, at least in clerical and other minor administrative roles.

MONTEIRO, MAJOR JOSÉ. A Portuguese army officer stationed at Tete, Mozambique (qq.v.), he and António Gamitto (q.v.) led the 1831–32 expedition to Lunda chief Kazembe (qq.v.) seeking a commercial treaty. Their expedition was less than a stunning success, and the report they filed discouraged future traders.

MONZE. The name of a Southern Province (q.v.) district and its capital, Monze District had 79,000 people in 1969 and 157,000 in 1990. The town is located east of the line of rail (q.v.) in Southern Province, south of Mazabuka (q.v.). It is named after a noted Tonga (q.v.) leader who was the rainmaker at one of the principal rain shrines to which many Tonga belonged (see LWIINDI). As such, he had ritual and even some political significance, but was not a chief, as he has been called by some. Monze's village was reached by many visitors in the 1850s, including Mambari (q.v.) traders from the west, Nsenga ivory (qq.v.) traders from the east, and Dr. David Livingstone (q.v.). In the 1880s the Lozi (q.v.), led by a rebel named Sikabenga, raided Monze's cattle, but the Tonga called on the Ndebele (q.v.) for assistance; Sikabenga was killed and other Lozi were routed. In 1902, the Tonga allowed Jesuit missionaries led by Father Joseph Moreau to set up a mission in Monze's area.

MOORE, SIR LEOPOLD FRANK. Perhaps the most interesting political figure in Northern Rhodesia (q.v.) in the early 20th century, he was born in London and studied at night school there to be a pharmacist (chemist). He went to work for a Cape Town company in 1892 but opened up a pharmacy in Mafeking the next year. In 1898 he moved to Bulawayo and in 1904 moved to a frontier post called Old Drift near the Victoria Falls (q.v.). When the bridge across the Zambezi River (q.v.) was completed in 1905, the town of Livingstone (q.v.) was established. The next year Moore began his newspaper, the *Livingstone Mail* (q.v.), for a long time the only Northern Rhodesian newspaper, which he subsidized from the profits of his pharmacy. The newspaper became the voice of the settlers, and Moore quickly plunged into most political issues. He was honest but prejudiced and unrealistic in his political and economic expectations.

He was strongly opposed to rule by the British South Africa Company (q.v.), and felt that the few settlers could run all of Northern Rhodesia (q.v.). Thus one of his goals was the formation of a self-government council. At the same time, he was strongly opposed to the suggestions that amalgamation (q.v.) with Southern Rhodesia (q.v.) should occur. When an Advisory Council (q.v.) was formed in 1918, Moore was one of the five members elected. It was through his additional hard work that the British government took over Northern Rhodesia from the BSAC in 1924 and that a Legislative Council (q.v.) was established.

Moore became the leader of the "unofficials" (q.v.) in the Legislative Council and soon began attacks on the British government. He feared that the Colonial Office would make the territory into a native reserve (q.v.). Thus, in the 1930s, he reversed his position on amalgamation, believing that a union between Southern Rhodesia, Northern Rhodesia, and Nyasaland (q.v.) might prove economically beneficial. One of the major factors in changing his mind was the decision to move the capital from Livingstone to a new town called Lusaka (qq.v.), a move he had vigorously fought. Thus from 1933 on, Moore led the unofficials in the fight for amalgamation. For one thing, he felt that settler votes would be more meaningful when united with those in Southern Rhodesia than they would be under continuing rule by the Colonial Office.

During the 1930s, Moore's views moved to the left; he called himself a socialist and began to echo the anti-imperialist arguments of the world's leftists. He also became slightly more enlightened on native policy, even defending African interests on occasion, notably during the Copperbelt (q.v.) strike in 1935.

While he felt whites were the more intelligent administrators and governors, he believed this could change, since Africans were currently prevented from advancing. By 1937, Moore was arguing in London that an Executive Council (q.v.) should be formed, that unofficials should have equal representation with colonial officials, and that Africans should be allowed to build parallel representative institutions and not be put on white councils. When elections were held in 1941, F. J. Sinclair, a member of Roy Welensky's Labour Party (qq.v.), won the Livingstone seat from Moore, who then left politics. He died four years later.

MORRIS, COLIN. Born in England and educated as a minister, he spent the years 1956 to 1969 in Zambia before returning home. He was president of the United Church of Zambia (q.v.) and became politically involved in Zambia on the left side of the European political spectrum and, ultimately, a close advisor to Kenneth Kaunda (q.v.). Morris joined the Constitutional Party (q.v.) in 1957 and in 1960 became vice president of the Central Africa Party (q.v.). When John Moffat created the Northern Rhodesia Liberal Party (qq.v.) out of the CAP in October 1960, Morris continued with Moffat, again serving as his vice president. He also left his pulpit at Chingola (q.v.) to devote his time to political affairs, and in 1960 he and Kenneth Kaunda coauthored the book *Black Government*. He was at the London talks (December 1960 to February 1961) and played an important part in the constitutional negotiations.

Morris was always an advocate of multiracial government. He felt that Moffat was the only European leader who could gain support from both races. At the same time, he tried to persuade Europeans that they must face reality and work with African leaders, like Kaunda. Morris split with Moffat and the Liberals in 1962 over the question of cooperation with the United National Independence Party (q.v.) during the 1962 election campaign. Morris felt that a collaboration would be desirable. Harry Franklin (q.v.), a close friend of the African National Congress's Nkumbula (qq.v.), opposed this and won Moffat to his view. On March 12 the party executive supported Franklin and Moffat. Morris immediately resigned.

MOSI-OA-TUNYA. The Lozi (q.v.) name for Victoria Falls (q.v.), it literally means "the smoke that thunders."

MOVEMENT FOR MULTIPARTY DEMOCRACY. Begun in July 1990 as a social movement to alter the Second Republic's one-party state, it hastily transformed itself into a political party to contest the October 1991 elections, in which it won 75 percent of the presidential and parliamentary votes and the majority in eight of nine provinces. The organizers of the MMP were academics: Akashambatwa Mbikusita-Lewanika (q.v.), the son of one of the African National Congress's (q.v.) founders, and Derrick Chitala. At the first meeting of the MMD in July 1990, a National Interim Committee for a Multi-Party Democracy was elected, with Arthur Wina (q.v.) as chairman and Vernon Mwaanga (q.v.) and Frederick Chiluba (q.v.) as vice chairmen. From mid-August to mid-September, the MMD attracted huge crowds at its first three rallies, which were formally concerned with mobilizing votes for the upcoming referendum on the return to multiparty politics. The Interim Committee, though, maintained that the referendum was a waste of time and that the government should simply abandon one-party rule.

That is just what happened, probably because the MMD rallies associated with the referendum campaign built support for the MMD at the United National Independence Party's (q.v.) expense. The MMD was launched in December 1990, becoming Zambia's first opposition party in 17 years. Its first national convention was held in February and March 1991, and a national executive committee was elected, with Frederick Chiluba (with 63 percent of the vote) replacing Arthur Wina (with 19 percent) as party president. In April, the MMD unveiled its programme of national reconstruction and development through democracy, which called for a far greater economic role for the private sector, a minimal role for the public sector, the privatization of Zambia's parastatal corporations, the breakup of Zambia Consolidated Copper Mines (q.v.), and an end to the country's historic urban bias in its urban–rural terms of trade.

On October 31, 1991, Frederick Chiluba and the MMD swept the first multiparty elections in Zambia since the early 1970s, taking 126 of 150 parliamentary seats and over 80 percent of the presidential vote. On November 2, Chiluba was sworn in as Zambia's second president. Once in power, the MMD implemented an economic reform program committed to free market principles and to repairing Zambia's relations with former donor countries. Though the reforms won accolades in many circles, they imposed harsh living conditions on the vast majority of Zambians. Furthermore, there was a resurgence of regional and ethnic tensions within the government, and the top ranks of the party were alleged to be corrupt.

The MMD began breaking up in July 1992. The Caucus for National Unity (q.v.) withdrew, cabinet ministers Baldwin Nkumbula and Akashambatwa Mbikusita-Lewanika resigned to protest alleged corruption and antidemocratic abuses of office, and former Prime Minister Daniel Lisulo (q.v.) left to form the United Democratic Congress, a short-lived predecessor to the National Party (q.v.). Following the bizarre "Zero Option" emergency (q.v.) of early 1993, a number of ministers either resigned or were sacked, and in August 1993 at least 10 members of Parliament resigned to form the NP.

MOZAMBIQUE. Zambia's neighbor to the southeast, it was once called Portuguese East Africa and was controlled by the Portuguese until it attained independence on June 26, 1975.

MPANDE. A major Mambwe (q.v.) chiefship in southern Mambwe country, just north of the Bemba (q.v.). The Bemba killed Mpande II, who lived in the early 19th century. Mpande V Chitongwa came under Ngoni (q.v.) influence in the 1860s and became their ally. He even used them against Nsokolo (q.v.), the Mambwe paramount chief (q.v.), whom the Ngoni killed. After the Ngoni were defeated at Chipekeni (q.v.) in about 1870, the Bemba expanded northward and killed Mpande V. His successor fled to take refuge among the Inamwanga (q.v.), and the Bemba made Mpande's people pay them tribute. Twenty years later, in 1892, Mpande returned to settle near the White Fathers' (q.v.) mission in Mambwe country. About a decade later he regained much of his territory from the Bemba. *See also* MPANDE SHELL.

MPANDE SHELL. The *mpande* is a conus (sea) shell disc that has been traded from the East African coast, especially Beira (q.v.), since as early as A.D. 650. The shell became a kind of currency in the slave and ivory (qq.v.) trade. Ingombe Ilede (q.v.) in southern Zambia was a center of this trade. In recent centuries European manufacturers began producing the shells in porcelain and even celluloid. Many Zambian peoples, influenced by the Luba and Yeke (qq.v.), saw it as an emblem of chieftainship. Men and women might wear one or two around their necks, but a chief would wear seven or eight. The Ila also believed that *mpande* must be put on the graves of their dignitaries to ensure their acceptance by God.

MPANGO. This is a *ci*Bemba (q.v.) term for bridewealth (brideprice, in older ethnographies; *lobola,* q.v., in Southern Africa).

This widely used practice involves payment in goods and services made by a bridegroom and his kin to the bride's kin. Often cash is substituted for goods. The concept has nothing to do with buying a wife but is a method of making a marriage legal and binding and of uniting the kinship groups. In case of a divorce, part of the *mpango* is sometimes returned.

MPASHI, STEPHEN ANDREA. Born about 1920, Mpashi became the best-known novelist in Northern Rhodesia (q.v.), capturing the realities of federation-era town life in the idioms of traditional Bemba (q.v.) oral literature. Employed by the Northern Rhodesia and Nyasaland Joint Publications Bureau (q.v.) in Lusaka (q.v.), and a frequent contributor—as speaker, writer, and choirmaster—to the Central African Broadcasting Service (q.v.) programs, his first novelette, *Cekesoni Aingila Ubusoja* (Jackson Becomes a Soldier, 1950), was followed by *Uwakwensho Bushiku* (translated as A Friend in Need Is a Friend Indeed, 1951), a Copperbelt (q.v.) detective story, and its sequel, *Pio Akobekela Vera* (Pio Becomes Engaged to Vera, 1957), in which the hero saves his future brother-in-law from a false charge of murder. *Uwauma Nafyala* (One Might as Well Hang for a Sheep as a Lamb, 1955) is set in the time of the urban *banyama* (q.v.) fears; and *Pano Calo* (Right Here on Earth, 1956) is the allegorical story of a chief. Mpashi, along with Joseph Musapu, published *Amalongo* (Many Pots), a collection of Bemba poems, in 1962. *Betty Kaunda*, Mpashi's biography of the former president's late wife, came out in 1969.

MPEPE. A nephew of Kololo chief Sebituane (qq.v.), he became a prominent leader of his people after his uncle's death. Sebituane's initial successor was his daughter, Mamochisane. Mpepe stood in for her in certain ceremonies and acquired a great deal of personal support as well. Mpepe had been a war leader and cattle raider under his uncle and also assisted the Mambari (q.v.) in raids against the Ila and Tonga (qq.v.) peoples. When his cousin, Sekeletu (q.v.), became the Kololo chief, Mpepe took control of the Kololo forces in Bulozi (q.v.) as a semi-independent ruler. He conspired to surpass Sekeletu and become the chief of the entire nation. Instead, Sekeletu had Mpepe killed at the end of June 1853.

MPEREMBE. Son of the great Ngoni (q.v.) leader, Zwangendaba (q.v.), Mperembe and his brother Mpezeni (q.v.) traveled south of Lake Tanganyika (q.v.) into Bemba (q.v.) territory around

1850. After defeating two Bemba leaders in the Chinsali (q.v.) area, Mpezeni took his force south. Mperembe moved his following to Chibungu, in southern Bemba country near the Bisa (q.v.), so that they could raid in all directions. They destroyed the Bisa trade route to the kingdom of Kazembe (q.v.) and laid waste to numerous Bisa and Bemba villages.

Around 1860, Mperembe took his following north to a new settlement among the Lungu (q.v.), forcing the Lungu to work and fight for them. They also raided the Tabwa and Mambwe (qq.v.) peoples. They routed Makasa and set up their own village (called Chipekeni, q.v.) on the site of his village. In about 1870 a large Bemba force consisting of over half a dozen chiefs and their forces stormed Chipekeni, and Mperembe led his remaining followers north to Inamwanga (q.v.) country, where they stopped for about a year before they continued eastward and settled permanently in what is now Malawi (q.v.).

MPEZENI (MPESENI). Son of the great Ngoni (q.v.) leader, Zwangendaba (q.v.), Mpezeni and his brother Mperembe (q.v.) led their people south of Lake Tanganyika (q.v.) into Zambia around 1850. After their forces defeated a couple of Bemba (q.v.) groups, Mpezeni led his forces further south, establishing the main permanent Ngoni settlement in Zambia. En route to the Chipata (q.v.) region, Mpezeni's followers stopped briefly in the Muchinga Mountains (q.v.) before crossing the Luangwa River into Nsenga (qq.v.) country about 1860. There they also encroached upon the northern Chewa chiefdom of Mkanda (qq.v.), which they totally overran by 1880.

Mpezeni settled his people in a malaria (q.v.)-free area where they could raise cattle (some of which they got in raids) and grow maize (q.v.). As Ngoni people, Mpezeni's followers were organized into age-grade regiments that provided them with organized warrior groups for military purposes. In addition, the Ngoni brought the Zulu short-spear attack method from southern Africa in their earlier migration. Thus they were successful militarily and also succeeded in integrating the vanquished into their structure. On the other hand, the Ngoni adopted the language of their Nsenga wives and concubines.

Mpezeni was ultimately faced with the movement of Europeans from the south and east who coveted his land, which they believed contained gold. In 1885, Mpezeni had given a large mining concession to a German hunter, trader, and advisor, Karl Wiese (q.v.). Wiese made a large profit by selling his concession to a London group that became the North Charterland Exploration Company (q.v.), a British South Africa Company (q.v.) subsidiary, which sent prospectors to the area in 1896. Mpezeni tolerated them but had no intention of accepting British rule. His son, Nsingu, was his leading commander and was eager to take on the British in battle. A force led by Colonel William Manning (q.v.) entered Ngoniland from Nyasaland (q.v.) in January 1898 to protect Wiese and the NCEC prospectors. The large Ngoni force fought valiantly for several days, but their spears were no match for British artillery and machine guns. Nsingu was captured and shot, and Mpezeni surrendered. The British took Mpezeni's large herds of cattle.

MPIKA. This is the name of both a district and its administrative center in Northern Province (q.v.). Geographically the largest district in the province, it had about 59,000 people in 1969 and 117,000 in 1990. The town of Mpika, a former British South Africa Company *boma* (qq.v.), is located on the western edge of the Muchinga Mountains (q.v.) and is near the site of the Chibwa Marsh (q.v.) and its salt pans. Mpika is conveniently located on both the Great North Road and the TAZARA (qq.v) railway.

MPOLOLO. A 19th-century Kololo (q.v.) leader, he was the nephew of Sebituane (q.v.) and the man in charge of the northern region of his people's territory. This was in Bulozi (q.v.), which he ruled from Naliele (q.v.). When his cousin, Sekeletu (q.v.), died, Mpololo led the force that overthrew Mamili, who had seized power. Much of Mpololo's support came from followers who hoped he would serve as a regent for Sekeletu's son. Once in power, Mpololo proved to be a cruel leader who killed all his opponents. He also killed Litia (q.v.), father of the future Lozi king Lewanika (qq.v), in 1863, when Mataa (q.v.) revealed a Lozi plot to overthrow Mpololo. Finally, in August 1864, Njekwa (q.v.) led the Lozi uprising that massacred the Kololo. Mpololo was wounded and committed suicide by drowning.

MPOROKOSO (the chiefdom). This is a secondary Bemba (q.v.) chiefdom, whose chiefs are always sons of the royal Bena Ng'andu (Crocodile Clan) chiefs. Mporokoso I, Mulume wa Nshimba, was given the territory called Maseba in about 1870 and expanded it considerably before his death in 1909. In the interim he used quarrels among other Africans (notably the Tabwa, q.v.) and increased trade with East Africa to became one of the most powerful Bemba chiefs at the beginning of the 20th century. During the 1870s he traveled northwest from Maseba to establish a new village at Kashinda in Tabwa (qq.v.) country, a location that placed him in the middle of a number of battles involving Africans and, on occasion, Swahili (q.v.) traders such as Abdullah ibn Suliman (q.v.). His relations with the latter vacillated: sometimes they were opponents and, at other times, allies. Mporokoso was wary when the first British South Africa Company (q.v.) posts were set up in 1891 but was friendly to, for example, Poulett Weatherley (q.v.). In 1899 he refused to negotiate with Andrew Law, the collector at Abercorn (qq.v.), until a British force overwhelmed his stockade. For an incident involving a later chief Mporokoso, see KALIMINWA.

MPOROKOSO (the district and town). This is the name of both a district in Northern Province (q.v.) and the town that is its administrative center. The district stretches from the border with the Democratic Republic of Congo (q.v.) (Zaire) and the southwest corner of Lake Tanganyika (q.v.) southward for about 200 kilometers (125 miles). It has two major parks and game reserves in the north and is not densely populated. Its population was about 39,000 in 1969 and 54,000 in 1990.

MPULUNGU. Located on the extreme southern end of Lake Tanganyika (q.v.), this town is the terminus of the 42-kilometer (26-mile) tarred road from Mbala (q.v.). Barges leave from Mpulungu to connect with the Tanzania railways at Kigoma, which was important before the completion of the TAZARA (q.v.) railway, and a regular ferry service carries people and cargo between Mpulungu and Kigoma, Tanzania (q.v.).

MSIRI. The leader of a group of Sumbwa Nyamwezi traders from Tanzania (q.v.), he and his followers, who became known as the Yeke (q.v.), settled among the small, copper-mining chiefdoms of Katanga (q.v.), west of Lunda chief Kazembe (qq.v.). From this position they became raiders as well as traders and dominated the area for several decades, until Msiri was killed in 1891 by a member of an expedition sent by King Leopold of Belgium. Msiri's capital was a town called Bunkeya; from this location, the Yeke gun men coerced the neighboring peoples to provide them with food, ivory (q.v.), wives, and human pawns. Msiri turned against Kazembe, taking over some of his previous trade and cutting off his western links to Mwata Yamvo (q.v.) and Angola (q.v.). Msiri also sent his men south into Zambia, where they raided such groups as the Aushi, the Unga, the Bisa, the Kaonde, and the Lamba (qq.v).

Alfred Sharpe, an agent for Cecil Rhodes (qq.v.), attempted to get Msiri to sign a treaty with him late in 1890 but failed, thus explaining the geographical oddity of the Katanga (Shaba) Pedicle (q.v.). On the other hand, when King Leopold's second expedition to the Yeke ended in an argument and Msiri's death, the Yeke meekly surrendered their territory to the Belgians.

MU-. One of two singular prefixes in the Bantu languages (q.v.) (spoken in virtually all of Zambia), it commonly denotes either the noun class of plants or trees (e.g., *muti*, meaning either "tree" or "medicine") or that of people (e.g., *muntu* means "person" and *bantu*, "people"; similarly, a *mu*Aushi is an Aushi person, while *ba*Aushi are Aushi people).

MUBANGA CHIPOYA. *See* MWAMBA III.

MUBITANA, KAFUNGULWA. Born in Namwala (q.v.) in 1938 and educated at Munali Secondary School (q.v.), this writer and ethnographer took a Bachelor of Arts in fine arts from Makerere University in Uganda before joining the Livingstone Museum (q.v.). (*See also* RHODES-LIVINGSTONE INSTITUTE.) Rising from deputy director and keeper of art and ethnography, he became the museum's director in 1972. In 1976 he took his Doctor of Philosophy in social science from the University of Edinburgh. His writings focused upon the song, dance, and dramatic performances of western Zambian peoples. He was killed in 1978 in a car crash.

MUBUKWANU. King of the Lozi (q.v.) about 1840, during the time of the Kololo (q.v.) attack, this son of Mulambwa (q.v.) was the ruler of the southern part of the Lozi kingdom during his father's reign. When Mulambwa died there was a succession dispute between Mubukwanu and his brother, Silumelume (q.v.), the candidate preferred by most of the northern *indunas* (q.v.) and by their father's *ngambela* and *natamoyo* (qq.v.). Silumelume was declared king, but Mubukwanu's supporters conspired to kill him; an Mbunda warrior performed the deed. A civil war broke out, as the northern group produced a new candidate. Shortly after Mubukwanu's warriors prevailed in the war, the Kololo invaded Bulozi (q.v.). The two forces met in three battles: at Kataba near Sefula (qq.v.), at Nea near Nundu, and at Liondo (q.v.). The Kololo won each battle. Mubukwanu either died in battle or of poisoning after his escape to Lukwakwa (q.v.). The period from the first invasion by the Kololo to the abandonment of Bulozi after the third battle was about 1840–48.

MUCHAPE (MCHAPE; MUCHAPI; MCHAPI). The name of a 1930s witch-finding medicine, it also denotes the movement of itinerant witch finders (the *bamuchape*), which originated in central Nyasaland (q.v.) in 1930 and spread (1933–35) to northern and northeastern Northern Rhodesia, southwestern Tanganyika, Katanga, Southern Rhodesia, and Mozambique (qq.v.). Invited by a village headman, young men in Western clothes would enter a village to cleanse it of witchcraft. The entire village would be assembled to hear a Christian-style sermon about the washing of sins and would then be exhorted to surrender all their charms and medicines. When the witch finders returned some days later, they would line up the village residents and examine them with a hand mirror, and the witches thus detected were encouraged to publicly confess their sins. The witch finders sold small bottles of *muchape*, a red, soapy liquid that when drunk, was said to protect the innocent from witchcraft and kill any relapsed witches. This was an offer that few refused, even devout Christians. The administration viewed the *bamuchape* as swindlers and quacks but came to tolerate their practice during a time of locust plagues and Depression-era poverty. And since they never accused anyone of being a witch, they did not violate the Witchcraft Ordinance (q.v.). Though Central Africa (q.v.) has a long history of localized and itinerant witch finders, few have styled themselves as *bamuchape*. However, they are documented in southern Tanzania (q.v.) and northern Malawi (q.v.) in the 1940s and 1960s, in Katanga/Shaba in the 1940s and 1970s, and in Zambia's Eastern Province (q.v.) in the 1980s.

MUCHINGA MOUNTAINS. Situated on the northwestern edge of the Luangwa River (q.v.) valley in the eastern half of Zambia, these mountains jut upward to form an impressive escarpment. They are generally between 1,220 to 1,830 meters (4,000 to 6,000 feet) above sea level, not much higher than the land to their west, but in some places almost 915 meters (3,000 feet) higher than the river valley to the east.

MUDENDA, ELIJAH HAATUKALI KAIBA. Zambian prime minister from May 1975 to July 1977, he had been a member of the

Central Committee of UNIP (q.v.) since August 1973. Mudenda was born in 1927, the son of a Tonga (q.v.) chief. Like many United National Independence Party (q.v.) leaders, he was educated at Munali Secondary School (q.v.). He attended Makerere College in Uganda, Fort Hare University in South Africa, and Cambridge University, where he received a B.S. degree in agriculture in 1954. He spent the next eight years in the study and practice of agricultural methods before entering politics in 1962. After winning a Legislative Council (q.v.) seat in the 1962 elections, he was appointed parliamentary secretary for African agriculture. When UNIP won the 1964 elections, Mudenda became minister of agriculture, a post he held from 1964 to 1967. He then served two years as minister of finance and four as minister of foreign affairs. During the latter service, he became a recognized leader on Organization of African Unity conciliation committees and at the United Nations. He was noted as a skilled negotiator. In 1975, he was appointed prime minister, but in July 1977 he was replaced by Mainza Chona (q.v.) and seemingly received the blame for shortages in some important domestic goods such as sugar and cooking oil.

MUFULIRA. A Copperbelt (q.v.) city of over 108,000 people in 1969 and 175,000 in 1990, its boundaries reach virtually to the Democratic Republic of Congo (q.v.) (Zaire) border. It is one of the urban districts of Copperbelt Province (q.v.) and is the site of the important Mufulira Mine (q.v.).

MUFULIRA MINE. The second-largest underground mine in the world, it is one of Zambia's larger copper (q.v.) mines. Copper was discovered at the site in 1922, drilling began in 1928, and production, as part of the huge Rhodesian Selection Trust (q.v.), began in October 1933. The strike of 1935 (q.v.) began at the mine when taxes were raised. In September 1970, a huge cave-in resulted in the death of 89 workers and a drastic curtailment of production. The mine did not return to normal production for four years. A refinery was installed at Mufulira in 1952 to process the ore.

MUKULUMPE. The father of Chiti and Nkole, the legendary founders of the Bemba (q.v.) nation, he was a chief in an area of the Democratic Republic of Congo (q.v.) (Zaire) called Kola, or Luba (qq.v.). According to one interpretation, he lived about 1670 on the Lualaba River; whether he was Luba or Lunda (q.v.) depends on which legend you accept. He was a powerful chief (Mukulumpe means "the great one") and had many wives. One of them, Mumbi Mukasa, bore him three sons, Katongo, Chiti, and Nkole, and a daughter, Chilufya Mulenga (qq.v.). According to legend, Mukulumpe's sons, trying to surpass him, built a tall bamboo tower to catch the moon; termites caused it to collapse, killing many people. The father was furious, blinding Katongo and banishing the other two. He later called them back from exile but only to trap and kill them. They escaped his trap, but he humiliated them by making them clean the royal courtyard. Eventually, all four children escaped and traveled eastward into Zambia.

The Bemba are not the only Zambian peoples to claim descent from Mukulumpe, as several Bisa (q.v.) chiefships also cite a chief by that name as their ancestor. Similarly, the motifs of the bamboo tower and the cruel chief who sets murderous traps for his sons are common to the origin legends of many Central African peoples.

MUKUNGULE. This Bisa (q.v.) chieftainship was at one time quite strong. Its territory, just west of the Muchinga Mountains (q.v.), was called Mukumbi. Around 1800, Mukungule appears to have been the most prominent of the Bisa chiefs, and Lacerda's (q.v.) 1798 journal describes him ("Mucunjule") as a "kinglet" and an independent ally of Kazembe (q.v.). By 1831, however, it is reported that all Bisa chiefs were independent of him. The reason for his loss of power is unclear. The late-19th-century Bemba leader Chikwanda II (q.v.) occupied some of Mukungule's land, but the area had already been depleted by Ngoni (q.v.) raids. Mukumbi became an elephant-hunting area for the Bemba.

MUKUPA KAOMA. A southern Lungu (q.v.) chiefship, it appears to go back to the late 18th century, when it occupied land to the east of its present boundaries. The second chief in the line was Mukupa Kaoma (q.v.), who lived around 1800. He became involved in a conflict between a couple of Bemba (q.v.) leaders. When it was resolved, they all agreed on the Luombe River area as a common border. Kaoma's successor to the title, his brother, Chikoko, later got into a war with the Bemba chief Mwamba I (q.v.). Chikoko was the weaker of the two, but he was drawn into a border conflict with the Bemba and finally attacked across the river. A Bemba force repelled them, and Chikoko was killed when his men recrossed the Luombe. In the 1860s, Mwamba II (q.v.) attacked Lubula, Mukupa Kaoma

III (q.v.), over his wife's flight to Lubula's village. He destroyed the village, but the Lungu leader and his wife escaped. Lubula asked a Bisa leader, Matipa (q.v.), for aid, but the Bemba beat the combined Lungu-Bisa force in a battle on the Lusenga River. Lubula fled to safety. The chieftainship has continued to the current time.

MUKUPO, TITUS. Experienced in journalism and an active nationalist politician throughout the 1950s, primarily in the African National Congress (q.v.), Mukupo aided Kenneth Kaunda (q.v.) and others in the publication of the *Congress News* (q.v.). In August 1956, he joined the ANC's National Executive Committee as deputy secretary, despite the fact that earlier in the year he had briefly resigned from ANC over Harry Nkumbula's (q.v.) "new look" policy (qq.v.).

In 1958, Mukupo was chosen to be the party's general secretary. Always a man in favor of action, he began a serious campaign against the colour bar (q.v.), to force white-owned cafes, hotels, cinemas, restaurants, and similar facilities to "put partnership into practice" by admitting Africans. Nkumbula provided minimal encouragement or support for such activities since he had become a member of the Legislative Council (q.v.). In June 1959, Mukupo and the party's general treasurer urged Nkumbula to resign as ANC president. On July 4 an informal party meeting did likewise. At the same time, Mukupo was talking to Paul Kalichini (q.v.) of the African National Independence Party (q.v.) about a merger of the two parties. On July 11, Nkumbula suspended Mukupo and seven other dissidents for their boycotts of Indian shops without his permission. Nkumbula also seized all of Mukupo's files.

Mukupo then openly proclaimed his opposition to the ANC president, calling him an incompetent leader and proposing to unify several existing political parties and to reunite the nationalist movement. The next two months were filled with political maneuvering. Mukupo announced that the party's National Assembly would meet on August 23; he hoped to install Mainza Chona (q.v.) as president. The assembly met for a week, with Nkumbula participating; when it ended Nkumbula was still in charge. A series of events followed: Mukupo called for the assembly to reconvene the next day; Nkumbula removed Mukupo from office; Mukupo assembled almost half the delegates, who passed a resolution dismissing Nkumbula; Nkumbula called for a general party conference on September 10. Eventually, the Mukupo-Chona group was outmaneuvered by Nkumbula, and the president was easily reelected. The Mukupo-Chona group met as a separate ANC faction and elected Chona as president on September 13, 1959, with Mukupo as national secretary. The following month, the new faction joined with the recently organized United National Independence Party (q.v.), and Chona was elected UNIP's president.

Due to family difficulties, Mukupo did not run for party office. He became editor of the *Central African Mail* (q.v.), secretary of information, and a UNIP member of Parliament (q.v.). He died in 1992 at age 63.

MUKUUKA WA MALEKANO. He is the first of the historically grounded Bemba Chitimukulus (qq.v.); very little is known about his predecessors. His own dates are not certain, either, although it appears that his reign began around 1770. His praise name, Wa Malekano, means "of the separation" and refers to the fact that he divided Lubemba by establishing the western part, Ituna, as a separate chiefship, and appointed his brother, Chitunda, chief of Ituna. This was one of the major developments during his reign, as it was the first known instance of such an act among the Bemba, a precedent that would be followed often in the future. Upon his death, Mukuuka was succeeded by his sister's son, Chiliamafwa. Another bearer of the name was Makasa V, Mukuuka Mwilwa (q.v.).

MULAISHO, DOMINIC. Born in Feira (q.v.) District in 1933, this economist and novelist was educated at Katondwe Mission, Cansius College, and Chalimbana Teachers' College before studying English, history, and economics at the University College of Rhodesias and Nyasaland (q.v.). Appointed permanent secretary to the Office of the President in 1965, he served in the Ministry of Education and as chairman or manager of the Mining Development Corporation of Zambia, the National Agricultural Marketing Board, and Industrial Development Corporation of Zambia (qq.v.). He was economics advisor to President Kaunda's (q.v.) State House. His first novel, *Tongue of the Dumb* (1971), was followed by *The Smoke that Thunders*.

MULAMBWA. Perhaps the longest reigning Litunga of the Luyana (later called Lozi) (qq.v.), the Lozi consider him one of their best rulers. His reign lasted from about 1780 to about 1830. He was the son of Mwanawina, the Luyana (q.v.) king, and succeeded his brother, Mwananyanda (q.v.), a weak ruler, after a successful military challenge. Mulambwa is remembered in part for his military achievements. Cattle raids among the Ila (q.v.) were recounted a century later to missionaries, and raids for slaves or booty are recorded in oral history. But Mulambwa's reputation is based on solidifying the nation and creating laws to ensure justice. His laws included punishment for thieves, compensation and care for relatives of men killed in war, and rules for tax collecting. Mulambwa refused to deal with the Mambari (q.v.) slave traders (q.v.) who entered Zambia from Angola (q.v.).

Mulambwa succeeded in integrating into the state a large number of Mbunda (q.v.) immigrants led by Mwene Ciengele and Mwene Kandala, who had helped him win several wars. On the other hand, they could not stop the invading Kololo (q.v.), who arrived in Bulozi (q.v.) three years after Mulambwa's death. He was infirm and almost blind in his later years; his death resulted in a civil war for succession between two of his sons, Silumelume and Mubukwanu (qq.v.).

MULASA. In *ci*Bemba (q.v.) and related languages, this is the common name for tribute labor, which was owed to traditional leaders as part of the system of mutual obligations between ruler and ruled. In the period just before World War I, it became unpopular and was generally ignored, even though the British South Africa Company (q.v.) promised to arrest anyone refusing a chief's request. In the mid-1920s, the traditional leaders began to demand it again, but by this time the BSAC was increasingly reluctant to enforce it, maintaining that good leaders would have no trouble recruiting volunteers and that bad leaders did not deserve it. Recruiting tribute laborers became increasingly difficult after the late 1920s, when migrant laborers began flowing to the Copperbelt (q.v.) mines.

MULEMBA, HUMPHREY. A member of the Central Committee of UNIP (q.v.) after 1973, he reached political prominence through his trade union work. Born in 1932 at Lusaka (q.v.), he was educated at Cansius College at Chikuni. He was employed as a miner and then in the personnel office at Nchanga (q.v.). Joining the union, he rose to full-time secretary of the General Workers' Union. In 1959 he was one of the Zambia African National Congress's (q.v.) activists arrested during the "state of emergency." On his release, he became active in the United National Independence Party (q.v.). At one point, he was UNIP's divisional secretary for North-Western Province (q.v.). Later, he was UNIP's representative to Accra and London.

Mulemba was elected to Parliament (q.v.) in 1964 and was appointed deputy speaker that same year. From 1967 to 1969 he served in several positions: minister of state for cabinet affairs and the public service, minister of Luapula Province (q.v.), and minister of Barotse Province (q.v.). In 1969, President Kaunda (q.v.) appointed him to UNIP's interim Executive Committee. He also became minister of trade and industry in 1969 but switched to mines and mining development (1970–74). He then served as chairman of UNIP's Economics and Finance Sub-Committee (1973–77). During this time he had Andrew Kashita—the minister of mines and industry and Zambia's representative to the Intergovernmental Council of Copper Exporting Countries—fired for accepting a 15 percent cutback in copper (q.v.) production. After serving as UNIP secretary-general (1980–85), he became ambassador to Canada (1985).

Mulemba resigned from UNIP in December 1990 to join the Movement for Multiparty Democracy (q.v.) and was appointed minister of mines following the MMD's victory in the 1991 elections. He was fired, however, in April 1993 by President Chiluba (q.v.), who made vague references to corruption. Observers, though, interpret his sacking as an indicator of the president's political insecurity, as Mulemba had challenged his party leadership at the MMD's national convention in February 1991. Mulemba was expelled from the MMD in August 1993 and joined the new National Party (q.v.). At the NP convention in April 1995 he was elected party president over Baldwin Nkumbula (q.v.).

MULEMENA, EMMANUEL. Founder of the popular band Mulemena and the Sound Inspectors, whose songs—in ciKaonde, ciLamba, ciBemba (q.v.), and ciNyanja (q.v.)—included a number of hit singles, he is best known for incorporating a traditional Kaonde (q.v.) beat into his guitar-based music. He was one of the first Africans to abandon drums for a drum machine. He died in 1982, supposedly one of the first Zambian victims of AIDS (q.v.). His band, renamed the Mulemena Boys, continued for some years until death claimed several other members. His name is now kept alive by a younger Kalindula (q.v.) band, the Junior Mulemena Boys.

MULENA MUKWAE. An official position among the Lozi (q.v.), it translates roughly as "princess chief." In Lozi custom, female relatives of the king have always held special rank and a voice in the government, but Lewanika (q.v.) institutionalized this (and solved a vexing problem) by appointing his sister ruler of the southern part of Bulozi (q.v.) and giving her the title Mulena Mukwae. Previously, the rulers of the southern kingdom were men, who then became contenders for a vacant northern throne. The result sometimes was a civil war. Since women were not eligible to become the Litunga (q.v.), the Mulena Mukwae could not be a cause of dissension. As the Litunga's sister (or other close relative), she is usually a strong supporter and a major consultant on important questions. She is also expected to be the Litunga's harshest critic when she feels that he is being unjust.

MULENGA, ALICE LENSHINA. *See* LENSHINA, ALICE MULENGA.

MULENGA, CHILUFYA. The legendary daughter of Mukulumpe (q.v.) and his wife, Mumbi Makasa, she was the sister of Katongo, Chiti, and Nkole (qq.v.). The latter two are considered the founders of the Bemba (q.v.) nation. When Chiti and Nkole fled their father for the second time, they sent a half brother, Kapasa, to free their sister and their blind brother, Katongo. Kapasa later made Chilufya Mulenga pregnant, and he was disowned by the family, which was now migrating eastward. When Chiti and Nkole eventually died, a son of Chilufya Mulenga, also named Chilufya, became their successor as leader of the Bemba people.

MULIKITA, FWANYANGA MATALE. Born in Sefula, Mongu District, in Barotseland in 1928, this writer, playwright, teacher, and diplomat attended Munali Secondary School (q.v.) and, in 1949, passed the Cambridge certificate with distinction in English literature and general science. After two years as a High Court (q.v.) clerk-interpreter, he took his Bachelor of Arts at Fort Hare University College in South Africa, where he studied English and psychology. Between his teaching posts at Mongu Secondary School and Kitwe Teacher Training College, he worked as a Kitwe welfare officer while earning a certificate in freelance journalism. A scholarship at Stanford University led to a Master of Arts in psychology in 1960. Back in Zambia, he opened Chalimbana Secondary School, serving as headmaster before returning to America in 1964, where he took a Master of Arts in diplomacy and international relations at Columbia University. After independence, he served as ambassador to the United Nations (1967–68) and in a long succession of leadership positions in at least six ministries and two provinces before joining the Central Committee of UNIP (q.v.) in 1976. His first book, *Batili Ki Mwanaka* (No, This Is My Child, 1958), a collection of stories in *si*Lozi (q.v.), was followed by the poetic drama *Shaka Zulu* (1967) and a collection of short stories, *A Point of No Return* (1968).

Mulikita was among the nearly 200 civil servants who left government in the late 1970s and early 1980s to become independent businessmen and entrepreneurs. President Frederick Chiluba (q.v.) appointed this former United National Independence Party (q.v.) permanent secretary, Zambian ambassador, and speaker of the assembly to be chancellor of Copperbelt University in August 1992. In December 1993, at age 64, Chancellor Mulikita resigned from UNIP for personal reasons.

MULONGWANJI. The National Council (*kuta*, q.v.) of the Lozi (q.v.) people, it has been the most important advisory body to the Lozi king (Litunga, q.v) and has been consulted traditionally on matters of national importance, especially war but also including a wide range of executive, legislative, and judicial decisions. The extent to which the king abided by its advice varied with the individual king. It is reported that Sipopa (q.v.), for example, regularly ignored its advice and guidance. The membership of the Mulongwanji included *indunas* (q.v.) from several categories. At the discretion of the king, other individuals could be invited to attend for specific purposes. The National Council included within its ranks the individuals who made up four other *kutas*: the Saa, the Sikalo, the Katengo, and the Situmbu sa Mulonga (qq.v.). Each had its specific role and represented a different interest. In the mid–20th century, the British insisted that members of the younger and more educated nonroyalists be added to the National Council to make it more representative and modern. This merely resulted in more conflict between the traditionalists and the nontraditionalists. *See also* BAROTSE NATIONAL COUNCIL.

MULUNGUSHI. Mulungushi Rock is a large, bare, black landmark north of the city of Kabwe (q.v.) chosen by Alexander Grey Zulu (q.v.), a Kabwe resident, as the site of the July 1961 and subsequent annual United National Independence Party (q.v.) General Conferences. It became famous as the site of Kenneth Kaunda's (q.v.) 1968 Mulungushi Declaration (q.v.), which instituted major economic reforms, including the nationalization of many large firms.

Mulungushi Hall is a large conference complex built by the Zambian government in 1970 at a cost of $10 million. It was built north of Lusaka (q.v.) for the Third World Summit Conference held that year.

MULUNGUSHI DECLARATION (REFORMS). These substantive economic reforms announced by former President Kenneth Kaunda (q.v.) at Mulungushi in April 1968 and November 1970 signaled the nationalization of the Zambian economy. Their main points were: (1) that rural retail and trading licenses to non-Zambian residents be limited to Zambia's 10 largest towns; (2) that INDECO, the government's Industrial Development Corporation (q.v.), become a 51 percent owner of 26 major foreign-owned businesses (including breweries, road transport, wholesale, and retail trading companies); (3) that new road service and transport licenses be limited to companies at least 75 percent Zambian-owned; (4) that public works contracts of K100,000 or less be eligible only to Zambian citizens; (5) that all foreign, multinational banks be registered by the government and that all government business be conducted through the newly created National Commercial Bank; (6) that all insurance and building societies be nationalized and become parastatal subsidiaries of FINDECO, the government's Financial Development Corporation (q.v.); and (7) that a wide range of manufacturers—including the leading sugar, distillery, milling, drug, oxygen, soap, cooking oil, and cigarette companies—become subsidiary parastatals of the government's Industrial Development Corporation (q.v.).

These reforms did reorder the Zambian economy and placed the state, rather than multinational corporations or foreign nationals, in charge of its destiny. They opened new opportunities to Zambians in the retail trade and construction industries and created a legion of salaried, bureaucratic positions in the new parastatals (q.v.) for Zambia's educated elite. But this new system of state capitalism also effectively ended foreign investment in Zambia and saddled the state with capital-intensive production systems that required imported parts and raw materials. The entire system of state capitalism depended upon Zambia's copper (q.v.) revenues, and once they began to fail in the mid-1970s, Zambia plunged ever deeper into foreign debt. Thus, beginning in the mid-1980s and again in 1991, the World Bank and the International Monetary Fund and its structural adjustment program (qq.v.) assumed control of the Zambian economy.

MUMBUNA, MUFAYA. A former vice president of the African National Congress (q.v.) and a member of the National Assembly, he became a founder of the United Party (q.v.) and its first president in May 1966. The following year he relinquished the leadership to Nalumino Mundia (q.v.). When the party was banned, Mumbuna returned to activity in the ANC and was reelected to the assembly in 1968. He was one of his party's best-educated spokesmen.

MUMBWA. This is the administrative center of Mumbwa District, Central Province's (q.v.) westernmost district, bordering Western (formerly Barotse, q.v.) Province (q.v.). The district had about 60,000 people in 1969 and 128,000 in 1990.

MUMPANSHYA COMMISSION. Appointed in August 1977 to investigate Zambia Railways (q.v.), its 1980 report charged that the company was rife with tribalism, nepotism, and corruption. It also reported a sharp antagonism between its Tonga and Ngoni (qq.v.) personnel. The most notable charge of corruption was laid against a former foreign minister, who had allegedly intercepted a shipment of Botswana (q.v.) cattle and substituted less attractive animals. Former minister Vernon Mwaanga (q.v.) then sued the government over the commission's allegations.

MUNALI SECONDARY SCHOOL. The first, most important, and best-known secondary school in the country, it became the source of the Zambian educated elite and thus also the breeding ground of African politicians. The Federation of African Societies, for example, became the Northern Rhodesian African Congress (qq.v.) at a 1948 Munali meeting. Eleven of the 14 members of the March 1964 cabinet attended the school, many of them at the same time. Thus, it provided a special unity for the early nationalist politicians as well as for the subsequent government.

Munali was founded in 1939 under the sponsorship of Governor Hubert Young (q.v.) as part of a plan for native training. It was developed by the director of native education, Julian Tyndale-Biscoe, despite the opposition of many of the territory's whites, including some on the Legislative Council (q.v.) who felt that book learning would not instill Africans with the desire to work and would only make them dissatisfied with their position in life.

"Munali" is one of the African names for Dr. David Livingstone (q.v.). Its exact meaning is in dispute. Some say it means "the leader," others say "the red one" (referring to his skin color), and others think it is a corruption of the Dutch *mijnheer*. The school was originally situated on high ground southeast of Lusaka (q.v.), near the home of the governor. Its first head was Frederick Hodgson. Planned as a junior secondary school to prepare pupils for the English General Certificate of Education, its first groups of pupils were limited to about 30 in a class. Kenneth Kaunda (q.v.) spent two years there in its early years.

MUNALULA, MBWANGWETA. *Ngambela* (q.v.) of Barotseland (q.v.) under Yeta III (q.v.) from 1929 until his death in 1941, he began as chief councilor (*induna*, q.v.) of the Libonda *kuta* (q.v.) in Kalabo District. Generally he was a passive man, more likely to cooperate with the British than to resist them. Thus when Yeta was struck by paralysis early in 1939, the provincial commissioner, Gordon Read, appointed Munalula as acting paramount chief (q.v.), and the Barotse national government was run, in effect, by the commissioner. Munalula died in January 1941, predeceasing Yeta.

MUNDIA, NALUMINO. A political figure for two decades, his career includes leadership of three political parties and jailings by several governments. Born at Kalabo in Barotseland (q.v.) in 1927, his education included several years at the renowned Munali Secondary School (q.v.). In 1954 he completed a university degree in commerce while on a scholarship in India. He then studied industrial management at Stanford University. Returning to Northern Rhodesia (q.v.) in 1957, he found the colour bar (q.v.) working against him; he finally found work in Southern Rhodesia (q.v.). In October 1959 he returned to Lusaka, where he protested the Monckton Commission (q.v.) with a public fast outside Government House. He was soon chosen the deputy treasurer of the United National Independence Party (q.v.).

Mundia devoted much of 1960 and 1961 to organizing UNIP in the western part of the country. At first he worked in North-Western Province (q.v.) but also spent time in his native Barotseland, where he formed the Barotse Anti-Secession Society (q.v.) in late 1960. In 1961 he was imprisoned for a month in

Mongu (q.v.) for defying a deportation order (UNIP was still illegal in Barotseland). In January 1964, Mundia ran for and won a seat in Parliament (q.v.) and was given the local government portfolio by Prime Minister Kenneth Kaunda (q.v.). In September, preparing for independence, Kaunda made him minister of commerce and industry, a position he had lost by January 1966 because of conflict of interest.

He was dismissed from UNIP and Parliament in March 1967 but found the year-old United Party (q.v.) to his liking and was elected its president. The UP was soon locking horns with UNIP, especially on the Copperbelt (q.v.). A clash between their supporters in August 1968 led to the banning of the UP and Mundia's arrest. UP supporters quickly switched to the African National Congress (q.v.) for the 1968 elections. Mundia (although in jail) became a successful ANC candidate for the National Assembly from Western (Barotse) Province (q.v.) and helped engineer the ANC sweep of Western Province seats. He remained under restriction in Northern Province (q.v.) until November 1969 and thus was prevented from taking his seat in the assembly for nearly a year after the election. Meanwhile, in January 1969, he was appointed deputy leader of the ANC, a position he used to his advantage once he was in the assembly again. In 1971, he was suspended from the assembly for a three-month period; he was allowed to return but remained a thorn in the side of UNIP leaders. In January 1973 he was detained without trial for several months after the government announced the plan for a one-party state. Three years later, however, Mundia had reconciled himself to UNIP and was back in the cabinet as minister for North-Western Province.

In February 1981, he replaced Daniel Lisulo (q.v.) as prime minister and was given, in addition, the ministry of finance portfolio and appointed chairman of the national commission for development planning. He was dropped as prime minister in April 1985 and appointed ambassador to the United States.

MUNGULUBE. One of the major Bisa (q.v.) chiefships, its chiefs belong to the Bena Ng'ona, or Mushroom Clan. Like the Bemba (q.v.), Bisa chiefs claim descent from Mukulumpe (q.v.). The chiefship was located on the upper part of the Luva River, about 40 kilometers (25 miles) south of the Chambeshi River (q.v.). When the Ngoni (q.v.) came through the area in the mid–19th century, Mungulube fled to refuge among the Senga (q.v.) people. Eventually, the chiefdom, also called Isunga, was occupied by the Bemba chief Nkula, who expanded southward into

Isunga. Mungulube was finally allowed to return to his territory in order to satisfy local ancestral spirits.

MUNTS. One of the derogatory terms used by whites in reference to Africans, it is derived from the word *muntu*, which means "person" in the Bantu languages (q.v.). Like "Kaffir" (q.v.), it is used much like the word "nigger" in American English.

MUNUNGA. One of the major Shila (q.v.) chiefs, his people live by Lake Mweru (q.v.). The ancestors of Mununga are said to have migrated from Bemba (q.v.) country shortly before they were subdued by the Lunda of Kazembe (qq.v.) in the mid–18th century.

MUNWA STREAM. This streamside site in the Luapula valley, about 10 kilometers (six miles) south of Johnston Falls, features rock art (q.v.) of elaborate concentric circles and radiating lines pecked into flat rock outcrops that lack any overhanging protection. While considered to be the work of Late Stone Age peoples, tradition claims a link to the historic Butwa society of this region.

MUPATU, YUYI W. This teacher, shopkeeper, and historian, among Zambia's first generation of literate intellects, was born in late-19th-century Barotseland (q.v.). After completing standard V (grade 6) in 1910, he became a translator at the Lozi (q.v.) royal court. He then taught at the Barotse National School (q.v.) from 1915 to 1928, when a new headmaster dismissed him for refusing to adhere to the prescribed (and inferior) government syllabus. Declining more lucrative teaching offers, he went to Kabanga (Church of Christ) Mission School in the Gwembe valley (q.v.), where he wrote his *Sipeleta Sa Silozi* (The Book of Lozi Spellings). He returned to Barotseland in 1933, where, in spite of much criticism from Lozi councilors and aristocrats, he opened a trading store on the Luyi River (q.v.). Though he returned to the Barotse National School in 1942, he was soon dismissed for leading a protest against a Nyasaland (q.v.) teacher's lower educational standards. Mupatu used his shop's profits to open Makapulwa (primary) School in 1945. He was appointed an *induna* (q.v.) in 1950 but resigned to see his school through a difficult period of growing enrollment. And when the *indunas* cut off his government aid in the early sixties, he got funding from the Reverend J. R. Fell, then principal of the Jeanes School, a government teacher training school in Mazabuka (q.v.). The government took over Mupatu's school in 1966 and renamed it in his honor. Mupatu, author of *Mulwambwa Santulu U Amuhela Bo Mweve* (King Mulwambwa Welcomes the Mbundu Chiefs) and *Bulozi Sapili* (Bulozi in the Past), died in 1982.

MUPUMANI CHESO. One in a line of turn-of-the-century prophets who married Christian and African religious ideas, Mupumani Cheso (i.e., "Jesus") was a solitary Ila (q.v.) leper living near Nanzela (Primitive Methodist, q.v.) Mission in Namwala (q.v.) District. He claimed to have received a heavenly revelation from Shakapanga (the creator), and from June 1913 until early 1914 spread the word that people should put an end to witchcraft and mourning, which then involved the slaughter of sacrificial cattle. He soon attracted pilgrims from all over central and western Zambia, ranging from Serenje (q.v.) and Mkushi Districts in the east to Kasempa, Solwezi, and Mwinilunga (qq.v.) Districts in the west. In addition to the crop and hunting medicines they bought from him, his disciples were told to erect tall, bark-stripped poles in their villages to facilitate their prayers reaching to heaven. The rumor soon spread that this (or another) Jesus had come (or would soon descend) to save them from sickness and death and to bring back the dead. Though the Reverend Edwin W. Smith, whose photo of Mupumani appears in his and A. M. Dale's *The Ila-Speaking Peoples of Northern Rhodesia* (1920), considered him a "sincere and innocent" man, his movement seems to have collapsed when the Mumbwa (q.v.) District magistrate jailed him on charges of vagrancy and false pretensions. The case of Mupumani Cheso suggests that Africans had a tradition of millenarian beliefs well before the appearance of the Watch Tower Movement (q.v.) prophets like Tomo Nyirenda (Mwana Lesa) and Jeremiah Gondwe (qq.v.).

MURANTSIANE SIKABENGA. The principal *induna* (q.v.) at Sesheke (q.v.) in the 1880s and a relative of Mataa (q.v.), who had led the rebellion against king Lubosi (Lewanika, q.v.) in 1884, Murantsiane was himself associated with the rebellion at Sesheke. While destroying the rebellion elsewhere, Lewanika tried to temporarily quiet the situation at Sesheke by offering his sister, Matauka (q.v.) as a bride to Murantsiane. Before the marriage took place, however, Lewanika was ready to purge Sesheke of the rebels—and raided it in 1886. Murantsiane escaped eastward to Batoka, where he joined Tatila Akufuna (q.v.) and continued to foment opposition to Lewanika. The dissidents returned to Sesheke early in 1888 while Lewanika was raiding the Ila (q.v.); they planned to invade the Bulozi (q.v.) valley. Lewanika returned and again attacked Sesheke, and Murantsiane again fled to Batoka. He died there in August 1888, during an Ndebele (q.v.) raid.

MUSAKANYA, VALENTINE. Born at Kasama (q.v.) in 1933 and raised at Nkana Mine (q.v.), he was educated at a Marist Brothers school near Salisbury (q.v.). He took an external degree while a *boma* (q.v.) clerk, later becoming the first African district officer in Northern Rhodesia (q.v.). He was appointed cabinet secretary in 1965, and minister of state for technical education in 1969. Dismissed as governor of the Bank of Zambia (q.v.) in 1972, he entered private business and became the local manager of IBM.

Along with Elias Chipimo and Edward Shamwana (qq.v.), Musakanya was one of eight prominent Zambians arrested in October 1980 on the charge of plotting to abduct President Kaunda (q.v.) and stage a coup. He and Shamwana complained of ill treatment while in detention and, though released, were immediately rearrested. Amnesty International adopted him as a prisoner of conscience, and the treason charge against him was dropped before he had a chance to respond to it. First tried in May 1981, he was sentenced to death by hanging in January 1983. His appeal was heard in August 1984. In April 1985 the Supreme Court acquitted him of treason.

While visiting London to attend his son's university graduation, he "took ill" and died in August 1994. One of the reasons given for Emmanuel Kasonde's (q.v.) April 1993 dismissal from President Frederick Chiluba's (q.v.) cabinet was his decision to send Musakanya overseas "for treatment."

MUSENGA. A 20th-century Bemba (q.v.) leader, he was known as Mpepo III from 1925 to 1942, when he became Nkolemfumu VI and, in 1944, Mwamba VI. He held that chiefship until 1966, when he became the Chitimukulu (q.v.). He died in 1969.

MUSHALA GANG. An armed group led by Adamson (or Damson) Mushala that attacked government camps and terrorized citizens in North-Western Province (q.v.) beginning in 1975. The gang was reputed to have been trained and supplied by South Africa as part of a larger scheme to harass the Zambian government and intimidate the region's residents. In April and

May 1981 government forces captured six and killed two of the gang's members. The gang reappeared in June 1982, allegedly killing three villagers who would not assist them. In November 1982, Adamson Mushala was killed by government troops. Two years later, former members of the gang, led by a man named Saimbwende, joined forces with Angola's (q.v.) UNITA rebels to revive the movement in North-Western Province. They abducted people and terrorized villagers. As a result, an Italian firm, prospecting for uranium in the area, withdrew its team of 200 workers in September 1984; it returned the following February after security was tightened. For one view of this gang, see P. M. Wele's *Kaunda and Mushala Rebellion* (1987).

MUSHILI. Hereditary name of the senior cheiftainship among the rural Copperbelt Province's Lamba (qq.v.) people, this variant of Msiri (q.v.) was given to Lamba chief Kabalu (or Mputu) about 1885, when he sumbitted to a Yeke warlord instead of seeking refuge among the Lenje (qq.v.). This was the Chief Mushili who met Joseph Thomson's (q.v.) smallpox-infected expedition in 1890, and signed the treaty on which the British South Africa Company (q.v.) based its initial claims to the Copperbelt's mineral wealth. Mushili soon began trading with Chiwala's Swahili (qq.v.), who moved into his territory in 1898. When Chirpula Stephenson (q.v.) opened the first Ndola *boma* (qq.v.) in 1904 and began building a road, Mushili fled across the border and remained among the Katangan Lamba until 1912. Before his death in 1917, he saw Ndola become the railhead transit center for the German East African campaign, and witnessed the constant stream of carriers bound across the Katanga Pedicle for the Luapula, from which canoes then delivered cargo to the Chambeshi rubber factory (qq.v.).

Mushili I was succeeded by his nephew, Chamunda Mushili II. The 1924 Reserves Commissions (q.v.) took about 80 percent of his former lands even while Jeremiah Gondwe, the Watchtower Movement (qq.v.) prophet, denounced him as a government stooge. Though many Lamba were able to pay the hut tax (q.v.) by growing and selling vegetables, their lives were increasingly dominated by the mining towns, like Roan Antelope (q.v.). The district officers complained of Mushili II's uncooperative attitude and financial irregularities, and he was deposed in 1938 for raiding the war fund and was replaced by his nephew, "Regent" Kabunda Chiwele.

Shortly after Kabunda's appointment, heavy rains and sandy, overcrowded soils brought on the famine of 1940–41.

This did nothing to inspire the Lamba's confidence in the government, and until Kabunda's death in 1947, he and Mushili II ran rival capitals and courts. These underlying tensions explain the failure of the government's Ndola District Resettlement Scheme (1943–52), which was designed to relieve the overcrowding on Mushili's Native Reserve, south of Ndola and Luanshya (q.v.).

Katepuka Mushili III, Kabunda's nephew and Mushili II's great nephew, who schooled at Kafulafuta Mission (q.v.) before working on the mines, was installed about 1948. The Lamba-Lima Native Authority (q.v.) was opened at Masaiti in 1949, and Masaiti *boma*, the first permanent *boma* in the rural Copperbelt, was opened in 1962. Though Mushili III was cool to African nationalists during federation (q.v.), the Lamba's fear of further land losses were heightened when the government settled Shona farmers from Southern Rhodesia (q.v.) on the old Resettlement Scheme in 1952.

John Lumano Mushili IV was installed in 1963, just two months after his maternal uncle's death. Having earned a Standard 6 pass at Ndola Main School, he briefly attended Chalimbana Teacher Training School before entering a 16-year police career. He was a Sub-Inspector in Southern Rhodesia when elected chief. Known for his bans on beer-drinking during the gardening season, Mushili IV is a shrewd and popular advocate for his people, and is a prime example of why many rural Zambians place more trust in traditional chiefs than in elected or appointed politicians.

MUSHINDO, PAUL BWEMBYA. One among Zambia's first generation of literate intellects, this teacher, translator, pastor, and historian was born in the late 19th century. He entered school in 1906 and, after completing a teachers' course in 1910, taught a number of years with the Livingstonia Mission's (q.v.) schools before completing standard VI (grade 7) in 1920. At the missionaries' insistence, he spent 1923–26 at Nyasaland's (q.v.) Livingstonia Mission to repeat standards V and VI and for further teacher training. He returned to Lubwa (q.v.) Mission as teacher and headmaster during David Kaunda's (q.v.) theological studies at Overtoun Institute; he then taught at the Baptist Mission school in Ndola in 1930–31 before returning to Lubwa, where he worked with the Reverend Robert D. MacMinn on their *ci*Bemba (q.v.) translation of the Bible. Mushindo saw no inherent conflict between Christianity and African culture and viewed his translation work as a gift to all Bemba (q.v.)-speaking peoples. Between his *Imilumbe ne Nshimi* (Proverbs and Folktales) and *A Short History of the Bemba*, he published eight books on Bemba culture and history between the 1920s and early 1970s. Mushindo had no stomach for European claims to racial, cultural, or intellectual superiority. And while he served on the provincial and territorial African Representative Council (q.v.) in the late 1940s and early 1950s, he viewed them as important but necessarily temporary steps toward African majority rule. Mushindo was killed by a car in 1972.

MUSOKOTWANE, KEBBY. He served in two ministries in the early 1980s, becoming prime minister (ousting Nalumino Mundia, q.v.) in a cabinet shakeup in April 1985. In January 1987 he replaced Basil Kabwe (q.v.) as finance minister, then became minister of general education, youth and sports. He was succeeded as prime minister by the former home affairs minister, General Malimba Masheke. In July 1989, Musokotwane became ambassador to Canada. After the United National Independence Party's (q.v.) defeat in the October 1991 elections, Musokotwane became UNIP general-secretary and was elected UNIP president at the National Congress in September 1992, replacing Kenneth Kaunda (q.v.). By November 1994, however, it became obvious that Central Committee of UNIP (q.v.) members wanted to return Kaunda to the party presidency. Musokotwane was expelled from the party by the UNIP party council that December, an illicit action, according to an April 1995 High Court (q.v.) decision. In July, he was ousted from the UNIP presidency by a UNIP special congress, which awarded 83 percent of its votes to Kaunda. In stepping down, Musokotwane claimed he would not accept any position in the party while it was headed by Kaunda. That May, Lucy Sichone (q.v.) had become Musokotwane's second (polygynous) wife (his first wife was described as unhappy but resigned). Musokotwane died in February 1996 at the age of 50 and was buried near his farmhouse. Tensions between Musokotwane and Kaunda supporters were evident even at his funeral.

MUSONKO. *See* HUT TAX.

MUSUMBA. This is the common northeastern Zambian term for a chief's village and capital.

MUSUNGU (KAFULA MUSUNGU). An important 20th-century Bemba (q.v.) leader who served as Chitimukulu (q.v.) from

1946 until his death in 1965, he was born into the royal family about 1890, a son of Mandechanda and grandson of Nakasafya. His brother, Bwembya, became Chitimukulu in 1969. Musungu was named Chikwanda III in 1910 and Nkula III in 1934. His succession to Chitimukulu followed a dispute over the rightful heir. As Chitimukulu he was a thorn in the side of Roy Welensky (q.v.), as he fought the federation (*see* CENTRAL AFRICAN FEDERATION), even traveling to England in 1952 in an unsuccessful protest. He refused to ban the nationalist political parties in his areas and in 1958 refused to meet with Welensky when he toured Bemba country. The government then stripped him of some powers and downgraded him (at least officially) to chief. He died in 1965.

MUTENDE. Meaning "peace" (a greeting), this government-printed newspaper for Africans was begun in March 1936, after the Russell Commission (q.v.) concluded that the strike of 1935 (q.v.)—which it attributed to a poorly publicized tax increase and vernacular Watch Tower (q.v.) tracts—might have been avoided if the government had had its own newspaper to explain its policies to urban Africans. It began as a monthly (then biweekly and, eventually, weekly) news magazine with some 20 pages of parallel columns in English, *ci*Nyanja (q.v.), *ci*Bemba (q.v.), *ci*Tonga, and *si*Lozi (q.v.). The 1938 edition, with a circulation of 12,000, sold for two pence per copy and was distributed not only in Northern Rhodesia (q.v.) but also in the Belgian Congo, Southern Rhodesia (q.v.), and South Africa; during World War II it was also circulated in East Africa, Madagascar, and Burma. Edited by Charles Stevens, then by S. R. Denny, the translations were done by two African clerks, one of whom—Edwin Mlongoti—later read popular stories and radio plays for the Central African Broadcasting Service (q.v.). *Mutende's* Letters to the Editor column provided a popular forum for literate Africans to air their grievances. The paper ceased publication in December 1952. It was replaced by the *African Listener* and the 12-page, multilingual weekly, the *African Eagle*.

MUWAMBA, ERNEST ALEXANDER. A founder and chairman of the Ndola Native Welfare Association (q.v.) in 1930, he was a Lakeside (i.e., Nyasaland, q.v.) Tonga (q.v.) who worked his way up to head clerk at the Ndola *boma* (qq.v.). In the 1920s, he and another clerk trained at the Livingstonia Mission (q.v.) and founded the nondenominational Union (Native) Church on the

Copperbelt (q.v.), though Muwamba eventually joined the more nationalist African Methodist Episcopal Church (q.v.).

He was closely related to Clements Kadalie, the founder of the Industrial and Commercial Workers Union of South Africa, and was the brother of I. Clements K. Mwamba (q.v.). In the early 1950s, Muwamba was still politically active as a member of the Nyasaland Legislative Council and its Public Service Commission. He was among the many African delegates who boycotted the London (Lancaster House) Conference of 1952 (q.v.).

MUWAMBA, I. CLEMENTS KATONGO. A Lakeside (i.e., Nyasaland, q.v.) Tonga (q.v.), he was a founder and the chairman of the Lusaka Native Welfare Association (*see* LUSAKA AFRICAN WELFARE ASSOCIATION) in 1930. One of his first campaigns was against the conditions under which Africans were forced to buy meat; the government refused to intercede with the butchers. In 1933, Muwamba tried to organize an association of welfare associations and was chairman of a meeting at Kafue to which several of the associations from other towns sent representatives. Government opposition prevented such an association from developing further until 1946. Like his brother, Ernest A. Muwamba (q.v.), he was among the African delegates who boycotted the London (Lancaster House) Conference of 1952 (q.v.).

MVUNGA COMMISSION. The commission, chaired by Patrick Mvunga (q.v.), was established in October 1990 to propose the constitutional changes required to return Zambia to a multiparty democracy. Its members were sworn in on October 9, and began work on October 18. Its report, published in June 1991, included the following recommendations: (1) a strong executive president, empowered to declare a state of emergency; to veto all matters related to defense, security, and foreign affairs; and to dissolve the National Assembly if it makes the president unable to govern; (2) the abolition of the House of Chiefs and the creation of a Chamber of Representatives, which would include two chiefs and three representatives from each province; and (3) an extension of the Bill of Rights to guarantee freedom of the press, freedom from discrimination on the basis of sex or marital status, freedom of movement, and an end to exploitative child labor practices.

The Movement for Multiparty Democracy (q.v.) criticized the commission from its founding, attacked its recommendations as "a recipe for another dictator," and initially refused to join with the government to discuss the commission's proposals. However, a conference organized by University of Zambia students in July 1991 attracted representatives from eight of Zambia's 13 parties, including the United National Independence Party (q.v.) and the MMD. Discussions between the government, MMD, and UNIP continued in late July under church auspices and resulted in a UNIP-MMD agreement to establish delegations to work out their differences on the proposed constitutional changes. The Constitution of Zambia (Amendment) Bill of 1991 (q.v.), which reestablished multiparty competition, was signed into law by President Kaunda (q.v.) on August 24, 1991.

MVUNGA, PATRICK. He was chair of the Mvunga Commission (q.v.), which was established in October 1990 to propose the constitutional changes necessary for Zambia's return to multiparty politics. Mvunga was sworn in on October 9, and the commission began work on October 18, 1990. The commission traveled to every province and took testimony from a large number of people. Its report was published in June 1991. During the late 1994 contest between Kebby Musokotwane (q.v.) and Kenneth Kaunda (q.v.) for the party presidency, an extraordinary meeting of the United National Independence Party (q.v.) Council appointed Mvunga as UNIP's interim president until an extraordinary Party Congress (of July 1995) could be held. During this time, the Movement for Multiparty Democracy (q.v.) government refused to recognize any other UNIP leaders but those chosen at its 1992 Party Congress (*see* UNITED NATIONAL INDEPENDENCE PARTY).

MWAANGA, VERNON JOHNSON. Zambia's most experienced diplomat, he returned to government (after a decade of working for Lonrho, q.v.) to become the first minister of foreign affairs in President Frederick Chiluba's Movement for Multiparty Democracy (qq.v.) administration. Mwaanga was born in 1939 near Choma, Southern Province (qq.v.). His academic career was concluded in England at the Institute of Commonwealth Studies, Oxford University, where he read political science and international relations. The British began preparing him for a diplomatic career before Zambia's independence, attaching him to their embassy in Rome. In October 1964 he became Zambia's first diplomat, serving as deputy high commissioner in London and in 1965 becomimg ambassador to Moscow. He returned to Zambia as the president's permanent secretary before being assigned to the delicate negotiations with Rhodesia. From 1966 to January 1972, Mwaanga was Zambia's ambassador to the United Nations. For two of these years he was also on the Security Council, and he spent one year as vice president of the General Assembly. Several other assignments at the UN were concurrent with these. In January 1972 he was called back to Zambia, where he spent two years as editor in chief of the *Times of Zambia* (q.v.). From 1973 to 1975, he was minister of foreign affairs; he later joined the Central Committee of UNIP (q.v.).

Mwaanga took a position with Lonrho Zambia, Ltd. (q.v.), in 1976, when many civil servants left government for the private sector. Following the 1980 release of the Mumpanshya Commission (q.v.) Report, he sued the government over the report's allegations of corruption in the running of Zambia Railways (q.v.). In 1980 the Bank of Commerce and Credit appointed Mwaanga chairman of its new Zambian subsidiary. Throughout the 1980s, he was chairman of both the Curray agroindustrial group and the Zambia Industrial and Commerical Association, a consortium of Zambian entrepreneurs; from that position he issued widely publicized assessments of the economy and criticisms of government policy. In October 1980, his passport was seized following the discovery of an alleged plot to overthrow the government, but Mwaanga was not detained with Elias Chipimo, Valentine Musakanya, and Edward Shamwana (qq.v.) as one of the conspirators.

In September 1985, he was among those detained on Mandrax smuggling charges (*see* DRUG TRADE). Though the charges were never proven, he resigned the chairmanship of BCCI-Zambia. He and 23 other defendants were released without trial in April 1986. Though there were no laws then prohibiting Mandrax imports, his release fueled speculation that these detentions were meant to intimidate the United National Independence Party's (q.v.) outspoken critics. Mwaanga's own version of these events appear in his *The Other Society: A Detainee's Diary* (1986).

Mwaanga was a founding member of the Movement for MMD and was selected one of its two vice chairmen in July 1990. At the MMD's first national convention as a political party in 1991, he was chosen as the party's candidate for minister of foreign affairs and assumed that cabinet post after the October elections. However, Mwaanga resigned that position in January 1994 after Western donors demanded a thorough investigation of allegations of drug trading and corruption against President Chiluba's cabinet. These allegations, however, were evidently targeted at others. Mwaanga then became Chiluba's chairman for international relations.

MWALULE. The name of the sacred grove where the Bemba's Chitimukulus (qq.v.) are buried, it is located east of the Chambeshi River (q.v.), near the Katonga Stream. The official guardian of this graveyard and its shrines is the Shimwalule (q.v.). Such burials were formerly marked by grisly mortuary rites. The location was found by Bemba migrants after the death of their legendary leader, Chiti (q.v.): looking for a suitable gravesite, they found the grove of majestic trees. During the burial ceremonies, Chiti's brother, Nkole (q.v.), accidentally choked to death and both leaders were buried there.

MWAMBA. One of the senior chiefships of the Bena Ng'andu, the Bemba's (q.v.) chiefly Crocodile Clan, its leaders rule the chiefdom of Ituna. It is just west of Lubemba (q.v.), the land of the paramount chief, Chitimukulu (qq.v.). Because of the system of promotion from one royal chieftainship to another, two 20th-century Mwambas later became Chitimukulus, the most recent being Musenga (q.v.). During the 19th century, however, it was more usual that the two chiefships were in competition. For example, Mwamba III (q.v.) (Mubanga Chipoya) had more actual power than his contemporary Chitimukulu, Sampa (q.v.). He regularly extended his rule into areas traditionally dominated by the Chitimukulu. This trend began under Mwamba II (q.v.) (Chileshye Kapalaula), whose sons were chiefs at Mporokoso and Munkonge, thus giving him influence there as well. Mwamba's subordinates held lands closer to the heart of the East African trade route and are said to have channeled their ivory (q.v.) through him.

The chiefship at Ituna goes back to about 1800, but the first of its chiefs to take the title Mwamba was Mutale, the brother of Chitimukulu Chileshye. He received the title in an unusual fashion. Another Bemba royal, Mutale Mukulu, killed a Mambwe (q.v.) chief named Mwamba (the title still exists among the Mambwe) and called himself "Mwamba." He then went on a reign of terror and killed many people, including members of his own family. Mutale stopped the terror by killing Mutale Mukulu and was rewarded with the title of Mwamba.

MWAMBA I, MUTALE. The full brother of Chileshye Chepela (q.v.), one of the more notable of the Bemba Chitimukulus (qq.v.), he was awarded the title of Mwamba (q.v.) and the chiefship of Ituna in about 1830. This came about as a result of Mutale killing Mutale Mukulu, a member of the chiefly clan who terrorized the country after killing a Mambwe (q.v.) chief named Mwamba. Chileshye also gave his brother the right to reign over Miti, whose ruler, Nkolemfumu (q.v.) Chisanga had just died. Mutale built his village, named Kabwe (q.v.), in the Miti portion of his lands.

Mutale faced several threats to his land during his reign. One was when the Lungu chief Mukupa Kaoma (qq.v.) attacked Ituna across its western border. Both Mutale Mwamba I and the Chitimukulu sent soldiers, who routed the raiders and killed Mukupa Kaoma's successor, Matipa (q.v.). Mutale also had trouble to the south with Bisa chief Matipa (qq.v.) over control of Lubumbu (q.v.). Mutale was successful against him, however, and Matipa fled to Nsumbu Island. In the late 1850s, Mutale Mwamba I and Chitimukulu Chileshye went after the Iwa (q.v.) of Kafwimbi as punishment for the aid they gave the Ngoni (q.v.). Mwamba died en route, however. He was succeeded by his eldest sister's eldest son, Chileshye Kapalaula Mwamba II (q.v.).

MWAMBA II, CHILESHYE KAPALAULA. Also known as Malama, he succeeded his uncle as Mwamba in the late 1850s and held this important position until his death of smallpox, in early 1883. He was the elder brother of the great Chitimukulu Chitapankwa (qq.v.), whose reign was almost coterminous with his own. The two succeeded in asserting Bemba (q.v.) hegemony throughout large parts of northeastern Zambia, distributing conquered lands to their sons and other close relatives. Before Chitapankwa became Chitimukulu, Mwamba II was offered the post twice. Once he suggested election of his elderly uncle, Bwembya (q.v.), instead; the second time (when it became obvious that Bwembya had to be replaced) he allowed his younger brother, Chitapankwa, to become Chitimukulu. It has been conjectured that the Chitimukulu's territory was too far from the increasingly lucrative East African trade paths and the power and wealth that went with them. His involvement in East African trade was mainly through the Arab trader Tippu Tib and the Swahili (qq.v.) ivory (q.v.) traders. Shortly after becoming Mwamba, Chileshye moved to strengthen his position, sending a force to the southwest, under his son's leadership, where he defeated the Lungu (q.v.). This brought Mwamba into conflict with the Bisa (q.v.), who were allied with the Lungu. Mwamba's men engaged two Bisa chiefs, Matipa and Mukupa Kaoma (qq.v.), both times emerging victorious. Confrontations continued in this area for over a decade.

During the 1870s, Mwamba turned his attention to the north and west of his home area, Ituna, in order to ensure his influence along the East African trade route. After siding with Kafwimbi (q.v.) in a Tabwa (q.v.) succession dispute, he was given the area called Isenga in southern Tabwa (q.v.) country.

MWAMBA III, MUBANGA CHIPOYA (CHIPOYE). During his reign as Mwamba, from 1883 to 1898, Mubanga Chipoya was the dominant leader of the Bemba (q.v.) nation, even surpassing Chitimukulu Sampa (q.v.). Mubanga Chipoya was Mwamba II's sister's son and also his son-in-law. Mwamba II revived the title of Nkolemfumu (q.v.) for him around 1870 and gave him the territory called Miti, and some Bisa (q.v.) territory, including the Bisa chiefdom of Mpuki.

When Mwamba II died in 1883, Mubanga Chipoya (also called Chisala) was a logical successor. Sampa, though, the soon-to-be Chitimukulu, backed a different and ultimately unsuccessful candidate. The relationship between these two most powerful Bemba leaders was further strained by the deathbed instructions of Chitimukulu Chitapankwa (qq.v.), who instructed the major Bemba chiefs to never obey Sampa. Thus throughout his 15-year reign, Mwamba III had a poor relationship with his "superior," who in fact was now his inferior in both land and influence. Mwamba III maintained his influence in Tabwa (q.v.) country to the northwest, despite a military defeat by the Swahili (q.v.) in 1884. He then strengthened his control to the west and south, partly through the appointment of chiefs at Miti and Mpuki. He also established his son in territory to the south. Under the title Luchembe, his son expanded into the territory belonging to Chikwanda. Mwamba's appointees thus controlled large portions of northeastern Zambia west of the Muchinga Mountains and the Luangwa River (qq.v.).

When the British entered Bemba country in the 1890s, Mwamba treated them with a cautious distrust rather than open hostility. In mid-1896 he made friendly overtures to the White Fathers, and Father (soon Bishop) Joseph Dupont (qq.v) eagerly responded. Meanwhile, Mwamba became a candidate to replace the deceased Sampa as Chitimukulu. His principal competitor was Makumba (q.v.). In the face of several bad omens, however, Mwamba conceded to the elderly Makumba.

Both Dupont and Robert Young (q.v.), the new British South Africa Company collector (qq.v.), visited Mwamba in early 1899. Though neither made much progress with him, there were indications that Dupont eventually might. Mwamba's hopes of extending his area eastward at the expense of a weak Chitimukulu were dashed when the BSAC defeated the Arabs (q.v.) at Mirongo *boma* (q.v.). In fact, a minor confrontation between the BSAC and some of Mwamba's men took place late in 1897 at Mwalule (q.v.), with the Bemba retreating. The British continued to assure Chitimukulu Makumba of their support against Mwamba. The dying Mwamba called Father Dupont to his village in October 1898, and Dupont administered morphine to ease his pain. Fearful of Chief Ponde's (q.v) ambitions, he asked Dupont to assume his chiefship until the next Mwamba was elected, thus implying that Dupont should temporarily succeed him. Mwamba III died on October 23, and when Charles McKinnon (q.v.), the BSAC administrator, rushed to the scene, he ordered both Chief Ponde and Father Dupont out of the village.

MWANA LESA. Literally "Child (Son) of God," it was the title or stage name of the 1920s Watch Tower Movement (q.v.) prophet, Tomo Nyirenda. While working at a mine near Mkushi in the mid-1920s, he listened to the Watch Tower followers preach and had himself baptized into their faith. In early 1925 he began preaching among the Lala (q.v.) of Mkushi and, later, Serenje (q.v.) and Sakania (Katanga (q.v.)) Districts. He aroused enough enthusiasm that the local administrator jailed him. After his release, in April 1925, he declared himself to be "Mwana Lesa."

His doctrines were derived from those of the Watch Tower Bible and Tract Society (q.v.), with a strong emphasis on preparing for the millennium. African American soldiers would drive away the colonists, whose property would be divided among his followers, and those who believed and were properly baptized would enjoy great wealth. His true believers would not sicken or die and would witness the return of the dead; they needed, however, to eliminate witches and witchcraft, the source of unnatural sickness and death. Like his contemporary, Jeremiah Gondwe (q.v.), Mwana Lesa used full immersion baptism to identify the witches hidden among the faithful. But unlike Gondwe, Mwana Lesa involved himself in local political rivalries and either drowned or strangled the witches he "found," beginning in the territory of Lala chief Shaiwila (qq.v.), an illegitimate successor to the chiefship, who used Mwana Lesa to eliminate most of his opponents. In May and June of 1925, 16 Lala were killed as witches, along with another six in Ndola (q.v.) District. At least 170 were killed among the Lala and Lamba (q.v.) in Katanga. Belgian colonial authorities were the first to discover these murders and notified their Northern Rhodesian counterparts. Though Mwana Lesa evaded the Belgian manhunt in Sakania District, he was promptly arrested after crossing the Katanga Pedicle (q.v.) border in September 1925, and he was tried and hanged.

MWANAKATWE, JOHN. One of Zambia's most respected government officials and administrators, he was also the first Zambian to obtain a college degree. He was born at Chinsali (q.v.) in November 1926 into a Bemba (q.v.) family. He attended Munali Secondary School (q.v.) before taking a teaching degree from Adam's College in South Africa in 1948, and his B.A. there in 1950. He taught at several schools, including Munali, before serving as the first African education officer in Livingstone (q.v.). He entered government service in June 1961 as the assistant commissioner for Northern Rhodesia (q.v.) in London, an extraordinary appointment at that time. In 1962 he returned home to enter politics and successfully ran as a United National Independence Party (q.v.) candidate for one of the upper-roll Legislative Council (q.v.) seats. In the coalition government of 1962, he became parliamentary secretary for labor and mines. He was unopposed in January 1964 and was appointed minister of education, a post he held until 1967. One month after independence he also passed his bar finals and received a law degree.

Mwanakatwe served as minister of lands and mines from 1967 to 1968, when he was unexpectedly defeated for reelection. He was appointed to a newly created post, secretary-general to the government. He then ran unopposed in a parliamentary by-election held in July 1969, returned to Parliament (q.v.), and became minister of Luapula Province (q.v.) for a year. From 1970 to 1973 he was minister of finance. He also chaired several fact-finding missions, including the Mwanakatwe Salaries Commission of 1975, which documented the 160 percent increase in government bureaucrats since independence (*see* MULUNGUSHI DECLARATION), and their spectacular growth in salaries. He held that post until October 1973.

He retired from public office in 1978 to join a private law firm in Lusaka (q.v.). Though denounced as a revolutionary "dissident" by President Kaunda (q.v.), he continued his moderated criticisms of Kaunda's regime.

After President Chiluba's (q.v.) election in October 1991 and his acceptance of the International Monetary Fund's structural adjustment program (qq.v.), Mwanakatwe returned to public service with his July 1992 appointment to the newly created Zambia Privatisation Agency (q.v.). That August he was appointed chancellor of the beleaguered University of Zambia (q.v.). In early 1994 he became chairman of the recently created Constitutional Review Commission (q.v.), which reviewed the 1991 constitution adopted as the result of the Mvunga Commission's (q.v.) work. The draft of the Constitutional Review Commission's report was released for public debate in July 1995.

MWANAMBINYI. He was the younger brother of Mboo (q.v.), the first king of the Luyana (Lozi) (qq.v.). According to Lozi legend he outwitted Mboo many times through his supernatural powers. To escape Mboo's threats on his life, he went south with his followers to the present Senanga (q.v.) District. There his people (the Akwandi) conquered the Subiya (q.v.) and the Mbukushi, and he set up a village at Imatonga near the current town of Senanga. During the reign of a later king, Ngalama (q.v.), the people of Mwanambinya were defeated and restored to the original kingdom. During the victory, Ngalama captured the Maoma royal and war drums (which Mwanambinyi had taken from the Mbukushi); they have since become an important part of Lozi installation rituals and ceremonies.

MWANANSHIKU, LUKE. After serving as governor of the Bank of Zambia (q.v.) and chairman of Standard Bank-Zambia, he became minister of finance following the October 1983 elections. When David Phiri, the current governor of the Bank of Zambia, was removed from that post in April 1986, Mwananshiku was shifted from finance to become minister of foreign affairs. These were controversial moves and were widely seen as backsliding on President Kaunda's (q.v.) commitment to the economic reforms of the 1983–86 period. Mwanashiku was replaced by Basil Kabwe (q.v.), and Phiri by Leonard Chivuno, both of whom were proteges of Grey Zulu (q.v.), the United National Independence Party's (q.v.) secretary-general. This shift of personnel was seen as a response to the growing complaints about the harsh austerity measures intrinsic to the International Monetary Fund's structural adjustment program (qq.v.), since the new appointees were known to be concerned about the political impact of the austerity measures and to have little affinity for the IMF. Mwananshiku was seconded to the IMF as an alternate director in November 1990, and was replaced at the Foreign Affairs Ministry by Benjamin Mibenge.

MWANANYANDA. An 18th-century Litunga (q.v.) of the Luyana (later called Lozi) (qq.v.), he succeeded his father, Mwanawina (q.v.), the Luyana king. He was not a particularly good leader and is referred to as "the unlamented." When faced with conflicts between the royal family and the *induna*s (q.v.) (as well as challenges to his position as king), he resorted to suppression and even executions. He defeated a major opponent, Mwanamatia, the nation's southern ruler, but he was unsuccessful in meeting the challenge of his brother, Mulambwa (q.v.), who succeeded him and became one of his people's greatest leaders.

MWANAWINA II. A young man who ruled as Litunga (q.v.) (king) of the Lozi (q.v.) from 1876 to 1878 before being deposed, he was the son of Sibeso, a Lozi prince who had been killed by the Kololo (q.v.) while they ruled Bulozi (q.v.). When the Lozi king, Sipopa (q.v.), was overthrown in 1876, the 17-year-old Mwanawina (who had been living in Sipopa's village) was offered the kingship by Mamili, a very ambitious *ngambela* (q.v.). The young man was popular, and his nomination was acceptable to the major councilors. Mamili, however, quickly demonstrated that he would run the country, and he soon alienated everyone. After he and members of his family were executed, Mwanawina was freer to make his own decisions, but they were not always popular ones. The new *ngambela* he chose was unpopular with everyone, and his appointments to other positions were heavily weighted toward his maternal relations from southern Bulozi. When rumors circulated in May 1878 of a plan to replace the old *induna*s with young ones, the *induna*s redirected an army, organized to raid the Ila (q.v.), to depose Mwanawina, who fled to Sesheke (q.v.). He hoped to raise an army among the Subiya (q.v.). Failing this, he went to Batoka, where he gathered a force. He returned to Bulozi in 1879, but an army under the new king, Lubosi (q.v.), was waiting for him. A fierce battle at the Lumbe River (q.v.) in May 1879 resulted in another defeat for Mwanawina, who again fled to Batoka. He died in exile.

MWANAWINA III. The Litunga (q.v.) (king) of the Lozi (q.v.) from 1948 until his death in 1968, he was the fourth son of Lewanika (q.v.) and was born in about 1888 at Lealui (q.v.). He was educated at Paris Missionary Society (q.v.) schools and attended Lovedale College in South Africa, completing his education in 1913. He then worked as secretary and interpreter for Lewanika. In 1916 he supported his father in promoting cooperation with the British war effort, leading Lozi soldiers in their march to the east. He was twice honored by the British for his support during the two World Wars.

Mwanawina was principal advisor to his brother, Yeta III (q.v.), until 1937, when he was named chief of the Mankoya *kuta* (qq.v.). When Imwiko (q.v.) died in 1948, Lozi leaders selected Mwanawina to succeed him. His major concern during his two-decade reign was the continuation of the semiautonomous status of his kingdom; he opposed both federation (q.v.) and any amalgamation (q.v.) between Northern and Southern Rhodesia (qq.v.). With the rise of young nationalists, he suggested separation from Northern Rhodesia and special status for Barotseland (q.v.) within the federation, or perhaps status as a Barotseland Protectorate within Northern Rhodesia. As independence for Zambia approached, he repeatedly sought British assurances that any Zambian constitution would ensure special status for Barotseland (q.v.), although his preference was to secede from Zambia. After independence, he continued his struggle with the United National Independence Party (q.v.) for the continuation of the powers of the Barotse national government, the traditional ruling class. In all of this he was ultimately unsuccessful, though his cause was resurrected in the early 1990s. He died in November 1968.

MWANDIBONENE. Literally, "I saw you," this is one of the few surviving labels for the "little people" who once inhabited many parts of Zambia. While it may refer to pygmies, it more likely was applied to the Bushmen (q.v.), the original hunter-gatherer inhabitants of Zambia. They were notoriously sensitive about their height, and since it could be dangerous to offend people who used poisoned arrows, when an immigrant Iron Age farmer encountered such a person, it was always polite to exclaim, "I saw you from far, far away" (Mwandibonene kutali saana).

MWANSABAMBA. The Bisa (q.v.) chiefship ruling the Chinama area, near the Chibwa (q.v.) salt marshes southeast of the Bangweulu swamps, it is now known as the Kopa (q.v.) chiefship. Its history goes back well into the 18th century. There was a time in that century when Mwansabamba exercised control over other neighboring Bisa chiefs, including those in Lubumbu, northeast of Lake Bangweulu (q.v.). This was no longer the case by the end of the century.

MWASE. Several Chewa (q.v.) chiefs named Mwase existed in the Luangwa valley (q.v.) as early as the 18th century. The name was also that of an early Senga (q.v) chief, and the Bemba migration legend maintains that Chiti (q.v.) was involved in a fatal battle with a chief called Mwase over Mwase's beautiful wife. It might be conjectured that Mwase was not a name at all but a title meaning "chief. "

MWATA YAMVO (MWATA YAMVWA). The western Lunda (q.v.) king or emperor, he was responsible, directly or indirectly, for several of the chiefdoms and peoples currently inhabiting Zambia. The title is said to mean "lord of wealth" and is still used by Lunda leaders in southern Democratic Republic of Congo (q.v.) (Zaire). Mwata Yamvo's kingdom in Katanga (q.v.) began to expand in the 18th century or earlier, setting up new centers in distant areas. These centers continued to pay him tribute, and their trade enriched him. One such new center was that of the eastern Lunda under Kazembe (q.v.) on the Luapula River (q.v.). West coast trade reached Kazembe by way of Mwata Yamvo, and some east coast trade reached the western Lunda through Kazembe. Meanwhile, other traditions link western Zambians such as the Lozi, Nkoya, Luvale, and Ndembu (qq.v.) with men who were sent out by Mwata Yamvo to broaden his sphere of influence. *See also* ISHINDE; KANONGESHA.

MWAULUKA. The *ngambela* (q.v.) (prime minister) of the Lozi (q.v.) from 1885 until his death in September 1898, he supported Lewanika's (q.v.) attempt to regain power after the 1884 coup, even leading one of the regiments in a major battle near Lealui (q.v.) in November 1885. When Ngambela Silumbu (q.v.) died in the war, Lewanika chose Mwauluka, a strong traditionalist, as his successor. In this position he was a major advisor to Lewanika at the time of most of the major agreements signed with such Europeans as Frank Lochner, Harry Ware, and Arthur Lawley (qq.v.) and was a signatory to these concessions. While Mwauluka was generally a supporter of Lewanika, he saw the king's concern with British "protection" as having potentially dangerous consequences for the traditional Lozi governing structure, and the missionaries as an eroding influence on the traditions of his people. He once even threatened to depose Lewanika if he converted to Christianity. With Mwauluka's death in 1898, the traditionalists lost their strongest voice against change.

MWELA ROCKS. An area of rocky outcrops and boulders near Kasama (q.v.), it is the site of Zambia's richest collection of animal rock art (q.v.), probably produced by Late Stone Age people. They include a very realistic warthog and a group of people surrounding a large animal. More recent paintings, both realistic and schematic, can be found also at Mwela.

MWENYI. These are a small group of Luyana (q.v.)-speaking people whose traditional homeland is north of the Lozi (q.v.) nation, along the Luanginga River in Kalabo (q.v.) District.

MWENZO. The site of one of the early missions in Zambia, it was located among the Inamwanga (q.v.) people near the Tanzanian border in northeastern Zambia. The Livingstonia Mission (q.v.) of the Free Church of Scotland (q.v.) opened the mission station there in 1894–95.

MWENZO WELFARE ASSOCIATION. Perhaps the first true modern protest (or political) organization formed in Zambia, it existed as early as 1912 when Donald Siwale, David Kaunda (qq.v.), and a number of other young Africans trained as teachers met frequently to discuss problems arising from colonial rule. The association was formalized with a constitution in 1923, after Siwale contacted a friend, Levi Mumba, who had been active in a similar Nyasaland (q.v.) association. Mumba's constitution guided Siwale and Kaunda. The association invited others to join, including "educated chiefs and Europeans," but its appeal was primarily to the educated African in a professional position. While the organization was looked on suspiciously by the government, the district commissioner, James Moffat Thomson (q.v.), was convinced that it would be constructive rather than destructive. Indeed, the Mwenzo organization was primarily concerned with providing a forum for Africans to voice their views on social and political questions. The high tax burden on Africans was one such issue, along with that of labor migration and its ramifications for family and village life and agricultural productivity. The organization lasted five years, folding in 1928, largely because its principal leaders had been transferred to other areas.

MWERU WANTIPA NATIONAL PARK. Located east of Lake Mweru in Mporokoso District of Northern Province (qq.v.), it is not far from the border with the Democratic Republic of Congo (q.v.) (Zaire). The park is divided into a game reserve and a hunting area. The total area involved is about 2,590 square kilometers (1,000 square miles). It includes the lake and surrounding swamp, called Mweru Wantipa.

MWINILUNGA. One of the larger districts in North-Western Province (q.v.), it had a population of about 52,000 in 1969 and 82,000 in 1990. It is the extreme northwestern district, jutting northward in such a way that its western border is with Angola (q.v.) and its northern border is with the Democratic Republic of Congo (q.v.) (Zaire). The district's administrative center is the town of Mwinilunga, which is located 40 kilometers (25 miles) south of the border with the Democratic Republic of Congo (Zaire), along one of Zambia's better roads. A canning factory was opened there in 1970, with pineapples being the first of several fruits to be grown and processed.

MZILIKAZI (MOSILIKATSE). The founder of the Ndebele (q.v.) nation, he had been a military leader under Shaka, the great Zulu king. Like many of the great Zulu generals, he and his regiments fled Shaka and drifted through southern Africa before settling in the southwestern section of modern Zimbabwe. They were involved in numerous military conflicts with both Africans and Europeans before they settled down and, as a result, were much feared by their neighbors in southern Zambia and in Bechuanaland (now Botswana, q.v.). Many of the actions of the Kololo and Lozi (qq.v.) can be explained by the fear that their leaders, Sebituane and Lewanika (qq.v.), had for Mzilikazi. Sebituane's cordial relations with Dr. Livingstone and George Westbeech (qq.v.) were efforts to provide a link of goodwill with Mzilikazi. The Ndebele also made frequent raids into southern Zambia, where the large cattle herds of the Tonga and the Ila (qq.v.) were the primary temptation. Mzilikazi died in September 1868 and was eventually succeeded by his son, Lobengula (q.v.).

N

NABULYATO, ROBINSON M. Speaker of the Zambian National Assembly, 1968–88, and again after 1991, he was a teacher at the Kafue Training Institute in the 1940s when, in 1948, he was elected the first general-secretary of the Northern Rhodesia African Congress (q.v.). A political moderate, he also served in the federal Parliament (q.v.) as one of the nominated members. In 1959 he ran for the Legislative Council (q.v.) from Southern Province (q.v.) against Harry Nkumbula (q.v.) but was defeated. Fwanyanga Mulikita (q.v.) replaced him as speaker of the assembly in November 1988. His replacement following the 1988 elections occurred at a time when then President Kaunda (q.v.) was trying to reestablish the United National Independence Party's (q.v.) centralized control over an increasingly independent and critical Parliament. In January 1991, Nabulyato quit the UNIP to join the Movement for Multiparty Democracy (q.v.). Shortly after the MMD's victory in the 1991 elections, Nabulyato was recalled to serve again as the speaker of the assembly.

NACHIKUFU CAVE. This is the site of important archaeological findings near Mpika (q.v.). The major work was done by J. Desmond Clark (q.v.) in 1948. Three levels of Late Stone Age remains were found, along with an Early Iron Age layer. The earliest finds document the presence of microlith-using (presumably bow and arrow) hunter-gatherers between 16,000 and 9,000 B.C. Similar Late Stone Age tools (of the Nachikufan industry) are found in cave and rock shelter sites throughout Zambia east of the Kafue River (q.v.). The cave also includes naturalistic rock paintings of animals and men (*see* ROCK ART).

NACHITALO HILL. The hill, in the southwestern part of Mkushi District, is the site of naturalistic rock art (q.v.), paintings discovered in 1912 by J. E. Stephenson (q.v.). They were the first such paintings reported in the country. Most of them are under an overhang in a small cave near the top of the hill; they depict antelopes, somewhat stylized, done in purple pigment. Red schematic designs overlay the antelopes.

NAKAMBALA SUGAR ESTATES. A large, irrigated, sugarcane plantation in central Zambia, it and its on-site refinery produce virtually all of Zambia's sugar and a good deal for export. Fertilizer runoffs from Nakambala, however, are a major source of the Kafue River's (q.v.) pollution and feed the river's floating weeds (especially water hyacinth), which ruin fishing, promote (malarial) mosquito breeding, and threaten the Kafue's hydroelectric turbines.

NAKAPAPULA. This is the site of a small rock shelter in the northern part of Serenje (q.v.) District. There is a wall painting of a single purple antelope very similar to those at Nachitalo Hill (q.v.). Superimposed on it is a large panel of red schematic painting. *See also* ROCK ART.

NALABUTU. This elderly and respected member of the Lozi (q.v.) National Council argued for the choice of Lubosi (Lewanika) (qq.v.) as Lozi king over the other major candidate, Musiwa. As a result of his successful struggle, the young king looked to him for counsel, and Nalabutu had considerable influence on Lubosi's policies. Nalabutu also led a group of traditionalists that firmly opposed all white men, who were suspected of trying to steal their land. They even opposed the missionaries and resisted conversion. Perhaps the Reverend Coillard's (q.v.) activities during the Lochner Concession (q.v.) negotiations only confirmed their suspicion of all Europeans.

NALIELE. This was the site of the northernmost administrative center of the Kololo (q.v.) while they ruled the Lozi (q.v.). Located on the eastern bank of the Zambezi (q.v.), it was about 24 kilometers (15 miles) south of Lealui (q.v.). From that advantageous location, it was better situated than other Kololo centers to engage in trade with Portuguese in Angola (q.v.). Among those who ruled from there were Mpepe and Mpololo (qq.v.).

NALOLO. Located in the southern part of the Bulozi (q.v.) floodplain, it has been a second capital for the Lozi (q.v.) since the days of their Litunga Ngombala (qq.v.). He found it necessary to appoint a royal representative in the south because of the expansion of the Lozi kingdom by his predecessor's, Ngalama's (q.v.), armies. While this southern chieftaincy was clearly secondary to the northern one, the "chief of the south" was the Litunga's equal in terms of ritual honor and prestige and was the second most powerful person in Bulozi. When a Litunga died, the ruler at Nalolo was always a prime candidate to succeed him; when he was not chosen, a civil war could break out. The problem was ultimately resolved by Sipopa (q.v.), who appointed his sister as ruler at Nalolo. The practice of having a princess as chief has continued and has resolved the problem, as a woman cannot become Litunga. Her successor is not one of her children but a relative of the Litunga making the appointment.

NALUMANGO, NELSON. A pioneer in the struggle for African rights in Zambia, he was literally kicked into political consciousness when, in 1930, a Broken Hill (Kabwe, q.v.) constable beat and kicked him for standing on a sidewalk. In the winter of 1933, he and several other early nationalists like Godwin Mbikusita (q.v.) met in Kafue to try to organize an association of African welfare associations (q.v.). He represented the association he had helped found in Livingstone (q.v.). Nothing came of it then, but in May 1946 some of the same men, including Nalumango, met in Broken Hill and created the Federation of African Societies of Northern Rhodesia (q.v.). In 1948 he was appointed one of the first two African members of the Legislative Council (q.v.). He opposed federation (q.v.). In 1951 the African National Congress (q.v.) persuaded the African Representative Council (q.v.) to replace the two Africans on the Legislative Council (q.v.) (one being Nalumango) with two members of the African National Congress (q.v.).

NAMBOARD. See NATIONAL AGRICULTURAL MARKETING BOARD.

NAMUSO. The principal or northern chiefdom of the Lozi (q.v.), located at Lealui (q.v.), it is ruled by the paramount leader of the Lozi, the Litunga (q.v.). Namuso is superior to the southern chiefdom of Lwambi (q.v.), which has its capital at Nalolo (q.v.).

NAMWALA. One of the districts in Zambia's Southern Province (q.v.), the district had a population of 37,000 in 1969 and 83,400 in 1990. The town of Namwala is the district's administrative center and is situated on the south bank of the Kafue River (q.v.), about 200 kilometers (125 miles) west of Lusaka (q.v.).

NAMWANGA. See INAMWANGA.

NANZELA. A very small group of southern Zambian people living in the western part of Ila (q.v.) territory. They are also sometimes called the Lumbu, the Ila term for "foreigners," for they seem to have originated as Luyi (q.v.) who were driven north by the Kololo (q.v.). Sometimes they are included in the designation "Tonga." One of their outstanding 19th-century leaders was Sezongo I (q.v.).

NASORO. *See* SULIMAN, NASORO BIN.

NATAMOYO. One of the senior official titles in the Lozi (q.v.) traditional political system, the bearer of it is the only councilor to the Litunga (q.v.) who must be a member of the royal family. The word means either "master" or "mother of life." The *natamoyo*'s special significance relates to judicial proceedings: both his person and his house constituted a sanctuary for an accused individual. He could also overrule judgments of the *kuta* (q.v.) or the Litunga (q.v.) if he felt the penalties were unjust or too severe. As the Lozi system modernized in the 20th century, the bearer of the *natamoyo* title was considered to be the minister of justice in the Barotse government.

NATIONAL AGRICULTURAL MARKETING BOARD. As Zambia's government-owned and -operated marketing agency from 1969 until 1989, NAMBOARD was the monopolistic purveyor of most agricultural inputs (seeds, fertilizers, and pesticides) and the monopsonistic purchaser of most field crops (including maize, q.v., sunflower, cotton, and groundnuts/peanuts). Formed by the amalgamation (q.v.) of the Grain Marketing Board and the Agricultural Rural Marketing Board (ARMB), NAMBOARD was designed to promote market-oriented farming throughout Zambia by evening out the differential costs of farming between Zambia's line of rail (q.v.) and remoter rural districts. But NAMBOARD also kept producer prices low in order to subsidize mealiemeal (q.v.) prices for Zambian townsfolk and, thus, only encouraged rural-to-urban migration. By the late 1970s, Zambian farmers lost what little patience they had with NAMBOARD when its checks for the previous season's crop purchases were delayed until well into the next year's planting season, stranding farmers without seeds or fertilizers. NAMBOARD's crop transport and storage facilities became an annual scandal, as outdoor maize stockpiles were repeatedly ruined by rain or rats. With time, Zambia became increasingly dependent upon "emergency" grain imports. Privatization seemed to offer a solution to this problem, so NAMBOARD was abolished in 1989, though the practice of designating official marketing agents for maize continued until 1994.

NATIONAL ASSEMBLY. *See* PARLIAMENT.

NATIONAL DEVELOPMENT PLAN. *See* SECOND NATIONAL DEVELOPMENT PLAN.

NATIONAL MIRROR. The newspaper of the Christian Council (q.v.) of Zambia, it was an important vehicle for the expression of dissent during the latter 1980s, when it published interviews critical of government policies. President Kaunda and United National Independence Party (q.v.) Secretary-General Mainza Chona (qq.v.) verbally attacked the paper for its content.

NATIONAL PARTY. This new political party, formed as a splinter group from the Movement for Multiparty Democracy (q.v.), was created in August 1993 when 10 members of the National Assembly resigned from the MMD after the "Zero Option" emergency (q.v.) and a series of cabinet minister resignations and sackings. These deserters from the MMD included, among others, Emmanuel Kasonde, Akashambatwa Mbikusita-Lewanika, Dr. Inonge Mbikusita-Lewanika, Baldwin Nkumbula, Edward Shamwana, and Arthur Wina (qq.v.). Both the creators of the NP and its new recruits seemed to share the sentiment that the MMD was being "hijacked by corrupt opportunists and drug barons" and that the government was too casual about human rights abuses and the plight of the poor. Other prominent politicians recognized as MMD dissidents, including former ministers Guy Scott and Humphrey Mulemba (qq.v.), attended the NP's inaugural press conference but did not immediately declare their support for the party. The NP was formally registered in September 1993 under the interim leadership of Dr. Inonge Mbikusita-Lewanika, making her the first woman to head a Zambian political party. She lost her position to Baldwin Nkumbula at the party's 1994 convention.

The NP contested six seats in the by-elections made necessary after their occupants, elected as MMD candidates, joined the NP. By the time of the by-elections, 11 members of Parliament (q.v.) had resigned from the MMD, but five of these contested the speaker's decision that they needed to run again for the seats they occupied. As a result of these resignations and by-elections, the NP joined the United National Independence Party (q.v.) as the second opposition party in Parliament, and the number of seats the MMD held fell from the 125 won in 1991 to 113. Following party elections in April 1995, the NP's leaders included Humphrey Mulemba (president), Daniel Lisulo (vice president), Arthur Wina (national chairman), Edward Shamwana (vice chairman), and Amupuwela Mulowa (secretary). Baldwin Nkumbula resigned and returned to the MMD, taking the entire Lusaka Provincial Committee with him. He was killed in an automobile accident a few days later. As with the Unity in the East (q.v.) UNIP faction in the late 1960s, the NP's members seem to be largely drawn from Southern and Eastern Provinces (qq.v.).

NATIONAL PROGRESS PARTY. The party was formed in April 1963 by the Northern Rhodesian branch of the United Federal Party (q.v.). John Roberts (q.v.) continued as party leader, but the party policies did change in recognition that the federation would be dissolved; that European settlers would play a minority role in the territory's future; and that the United National Independence Party (q.v.), not the African National Congress (q.v.), would be the next ruling party. Roberts therefore assured Kenneth Kaunda (q.v.) of his future cooperation and assistance, especially after Roberts understood that Kaunda favored an independence constitution that would establish reserved seats in Parliament for Europeans. Representatives of the NPP participated in the London Constitutional Conference, May 1961 (q.v.). The NPP contested each of the 10 seats reserved for Europeans in the 1964 elections, suggesting it could contribute more as an experienced, loyal opposition than as members of the ruling party. Nine of its 10 candidates had served on the Legislative Council (q.v.), and its slogan was "experience counts." All 10 defeated the UNIP candidates, but the victory margin was not large. Whereas UFP candidates in 1962 had captured 95 percent of the white vote, NPP candidates received only 63 percent. This did not prevent them from being very vocal in Parliament (q.v.). Since UNIP had no backbenchers with parliamentary experience, NPP members presented the only true debate in the first Parliament. The NPP was active primarily on economic questions, especially those affecting European farmers. The constitution "reserved" these seats for only five years; anticipating the end of the reserved seat system, John Roberts announced on August 2, 1966, that the party would disband and that each member of Parliament would decide his own future. In the December 1968 elections for a new Parliament, only one former NPP member ran: Hugh Mitchley successfully contested a safe ANC seat in Southern Province (q.v.). He was an independent candidate but had the clear approval of the ANC. One of his former NPP colleagues in Parliament, R. E. Farmer, was elected as the ANC member for Pemba in a by-election in 1971.

NATIONAL PROVIDENT FUND. *See* ZAMBIA NATIONAL PROVIDENT FUND.

NATIONAL REPUBLICAN PARTY. The "party" seemed to arise only for the sake of sponsoring two candidates for the two federal Parliament (q.v.) seats open to Northern Rhodesia's (q.v.) Africans. They won the election of April 27, 1962, with 25 and 22 votes. Called a front organization for the United Federal Party (q.v.), it was combined in this campaign with a similar group, the Central African People's Union (q.v.) of Dixon Konkola (q.v.), who was one of the two candidates.

NATIONAL WOMEN'S LOBBY GROUP. A nonpartisan group formed in 1991 to encourage the election and appointment of women to public office, the NWLG carries out civic education, advocates human rights and the protection of women, and promotes citizens' participation in the democratic process. The NWLG is one of the most visible and influential groups acting on behalf of women in Zambia.

NATIVE AUTHORITIES (AUTHORITY). A term that developed from the British policy of indirect rule (q.v.). Under this policy, adopted in Northern Rhodesia (q.v.) in the late 1920s, chiefs and principal headmen were recognized as "native authorities" and thus became British agents in a specific territorial unit. While permitted to make rules and orders and to operate courts for their districts, they did so only with the consent of a white district commissioner (q.v.), who could impose his own rules and orders at will. In practice, however, the commissioners did not relinquish much authority to chiefs, so indirect rule was of little practical consequence outside of Barosteland (q.v.). The major native authority ordinances were passed in 1929 and 1936, with numerous amendments added in subsequent years. The importance of the system is that it gave the British colonial rulers a basis for controlling African affairs in rural areas. Yet the Native Treasuries Ordinance of 1936 (q.v.), by fostering the growth of a propertied *boma* (q.v.) class of Africans, later transformed the native authorities into engines of rural social change and class differentiation.

NATIVE AUTHORITIES ORDINANCE, 1929. This act of the Northern Rhodesia (q.v.) government instituted the British policy of indirect rule (q.v.) in 1930. In addition to recognizing limited autonomy for each native authority (q.v.), it continued to keep each chief and headman under the supervision of European administrators. As a result of the ordinance, the chiefs developed their own staffs, each consisting of a clerk, court assessors, and messengers. Secretary for Native Affairs J. Moffat Thomson (q.v.) hoped that the ordinance would defuse potential native unrest by returning to the chief some of the management of his peoples' affairs. Under the previous law, the Administration of Natives Proclamation of 1916 (and amended in 1919), the chiefs and headmen had become, said Thomson, "merely mouthpieces of the government."

NATIVE AUTHORITIES ORDINANCE, 1936. A modification of the Native Authorities Ordinance of 1929 (q.v.), it added native councils and councilors to the chiefs and headmen already included as native authorities. It thus allowed councils of Africans to constitute the native authority in areas where traditional chiefs did not exist. It also recognized the position of the "chief in council" in places where this pattern was more acceptable to the Africans than an independent chief. This ordinance was amended nine times in the following 25 years.

NATIVE AUTHORITIES ORDINANCE, 1960. An ordinance that provided for the election of a deputy chief once the district commissioner determined that the existing chief was too aged, infirm, or otherwise not competent to fulfill his administrative duties, it opened the way for Africans to interject party politics (through the electoral process) into the traditional political system. A notable example of this occurred among the Yombe (q.v.) people in 1962.

NATIVE BEER ORDINANCE, 1930. This ordinance, which gave local townships exclusive control over the production and sale of "opaque," African-style beer, attempted to regularize some 15 years of varied and weakly enforced alcohol control measures. The mines and other white employers wanted sober workers, but they also recognized beer's importance in recruiting and maintaining a stable workforce. White townsfolk, on the other hand, wanted to segregate themselves from African drinkers. The Native Beer Ordinance, based upon the beerhall system (q.v.), which Durban established in 1909, answered the concerns of all parties. It restricted the production, sale, and consumption of opaque beer—until 1948, the only alcoholic beverage deemed suitable for Africans—to enclosed and supervised, municipally licensed beerhalls in the mine compounds or urban locations. Except for official business, the beerhalls were off-limits to whites. Beer pails were sold during limited hours, typically from 9 a.m. until noon, and from 3 to 6 p.m. Though the ordinance forbade rural women from selling beer and their urban sisters from either brewing or selling beer, it actually made such illicit beer, the only source of cash for many women, particularly desirable.

NATIVE COMMISSIONER. The term was originally used by the British South Africa Company (q.v.) to designate the head administrators of the administrative districts in North-Eastern Rhodesia around 1905. Initially the term "collector" (q.v.) was used, instead, since the primary function of the commissioners was to collect taxes from the Africans. After a few years, however, the term "district commissioner" (q.v.) replaced the two others. "Native commissioner" referred to assistants to the district commissioner, each of whom was responsible to the district commissioner for a portion of the district.

NATIVE COURTS ORDINANCE, 1936. The act gave to the governor of Northern Rhodesia (q.v.) the power to appoint African courts and also to prescribe their procedures and powers. However, it gave the territory's regular (white) judiciary the power to reverse, vary, quash, or retry judgments from Native Courts. It repealed and replaced the Native Courts Ordinance of 1929, which had proven relatively ineffective in restoring power to the Native Courts because it ignored the existence of native councils and other officials.

NATIVE FILM CENSORSHIP BOARD. The cinema, or "bioscope," was first shown to African workers and families in 1928 at the Roan Antelope Mine (q.v.). Though old American cowboy films were particularly popular, concerned Europeans questioned the suitability of their gambling, kissing, brawling, and shooting scenes for African audiences. The Native Film Censorship Board was created to screen such films in 1937, by which time Rhodesia Film Productions, Ltd., under a 1935 agreement with the International Missionary Council's Bantu Education Cinema Project, was producing a limited series of documentaries approved for African viewers. The African viewers in Kabwe, Lusaka, Livingstone, and the Copperbelt (qq.v.) mining towns were introduced to British Broadcasting Corporation newsreels in 1940 and, in the 1950s, regional news and feature shorts from the Department of Information's (q.v.) Central African Film Unit. Using funds generated by the beer-hall system (q.v.), the welfare departments in these towns obtained their feature film packages from a South African distributor. The weekly cinema format included noncontroversial (and often unpopular) shorts of news and African life, an old western, an animal cartoon, an adventure (Superman) serial, and the occasional slapstick (Charlie Chaplin) comedy. The South African distributor, along with Metro-Goldwyn-Mayer studios, was often at odds with the Censorship Board for rejecting films that had already passed inspection by its South African counterpart and been shown on the Southern Rhodesian mines. The Censorship Board lost much of its control over African viewers in 1960, when commercial cinemas dropped the colour bar (q.v.) to admissions.

NATIVE RESERVES. Convinced that Northern Rhodesia (q.v.) should be developed as "white man's country" and that African villagers should be protectively isolated from the demoralizing influences of European encroachment, Governor Herbert Stanley's (q.v.) 1924, 1926, and 1927 Reserves Commissions (q.v.) surveyed the Fort Jameson, line of rail, and Abercorn areas (qq.v.). Africans were "chased" onto the duly established Native Reserves between 1928 and 1930, leaving the newly vacated land (Crown Lands, q.v.) available for European purchase. The anticipated influx of white settlers never materialized, however, and most of the Crown Lands remained vacant. Meanwhile, Africans were restricted to the relatively isolated and overcrowded Reserves, far from the railway sidings where they might obtain their hut tax (q.v.) monies by selling produce. In short, the Native Reserves were designed to be overcrowded labor reserves that would provide the mines and white farmers with a supply of cheap African workers. Able-bodied men were supposed to become labor migrants, while the women and the elderly stayed at home and grew their food. Accordingly, male labor migrants were not supposed to need much more money than that required for their taxes and for buying a few clothes. The Native Reserves were the central element of the Southern African migrant labor system, which, in most of the territory, generated rural poverty, stagnation, and underdevelopment.

NATIVE TREASURIES ORDINANCE, 1936. This ordinance gave native authorities (q.v.) the power to collect hut and poll taxes (qq.v.), to pay staff salaries, and after World War II, to finance public works projects (primary schools, clinics, dipping tanks, and dams) and to provide capital development loans. Native treasuries were given an allotted percentage of locally collected hut and poll taxes, but they also received funds from court fines, dog and gun licenses, and fees for brewing, fishing, hunting, butchering, marketing, travel, and cattle dipping. Intended to given African leaders a greater stake in local government activities, the ordinance had at least two unintended consequences: (1) it gave native authorities some degree of political influence by allowing them to determine which regulations they would enforce; and (2) since such authorities had regular salaries, preferential access to salary advances and loans, and access to fees and funds they could embezzle, the ordinance also helped create a propertied and increasingly educated *boma* (q.v.) class, one with its own vested interest in private enterprise, individual land tenure, and inheritance rights. Native authorities were envisioned as a system of indirect rule (q.v.) that would preserve the authority of traditional chiefs and customs. But this ordinance allowed them to become engines of rural social change and class differentiation.

NATIVE TRUST LANDS. This official category of unoccupied lands was effectively established in 1942, at the urging of Governor Hubert Young (q.v.), when lands not explicitly reserved for mining development or white settlers became Native Trust Lands. These were reserved for progressive African farmers on individual tenure; for the creation of African townships; or, pending the approval of the local native authority (q.v.), for non-African leaseholders. This arrangement was formalized in 1947 with the passage of the Native Trust Land Order in Council, which established the first clear-cut limits on European land acquisition and a vision of the territory's future as tied to its African residents. *See* CROWN AND NATIVE TRUST LANDS.

NATIVE WELFARE ASSOCIATIONS. *See* WELFARE ASSOCIATIONS.

NATIVES IN TOWNSHIPS REGULATIONS, 1909. First put into effect in Fort Jameson (q.v.), these regulations from North-Eastern Rhodesia (q.v.) came to typify the colour bar (q.v.) which was imposed upon Africans as nominally "temporary" townsfolk. Under these regulations, Africans not permanently employed by Europeans or Asians were prohibited from living in town. From 5 p.m. to 9 a.m., Africans were required to carry a pass, or *chitupa* (qq.v.), whenever they left their urban "location" (q.v.). In 1914, similar regulations were adopted in Livingstone (q.v.), along with a prohibition on urban beer brewing. *See* NATIVE BEER ORDINANCE, 1930.

NCHANGA. The mining town adjacent to Chingola (q.v.), its "twin town," it is situated farther north on the Copperbelt (q.v.) than all cities except Chililabombwe (q.v.). The town developed as a result of the development of the Nchanga Mine (q.v.).

NCHANGA CONSOLIDATED COPPER MINES, LTD. Formed in 1937 with a capital of £5 million at the time of the sinking of new shafts at the Nchanga Mine (q.v.), the company was a subsidiary of the Anglo-American Corporation of South Africa, Ltd. (q.v.). In the early 1970s, however, 51 percent of Anglo-American's stock (held by another subsidiary, ZAMANGLO) was transferred to Zambia Industrial and Mining Corporation (q.v.). Thus the Nchanga company was amalgamated with Bancroft Mines, Ltd., Rhokana Corporation, Ltd. (q.v.), and Rhokana Copper Refineries, Ltd., and became known as Nchanga Consolidated Copper Mines, Ltd., the effective successor to the strong Anglo-American group in Zambia. In a 1980 attempt to stave off the country's mounting copper (q.v.) crisis, President Kaunda (q.v.) ordered the merger of NCCM and Roan Consolidated Mine into Zambia Consolidated Copper Mines (qq.v.); this was effectively accomplished in 1982.

NCHANGA MINE. Located near the twin Copperbelt (q.v.) cities of Chingola-Nchanga (qq.v.), this enormous mine is one of the largest (if not the largest) open-pit copper (q.v.) mine in the world. Its ore was discovered around 1900 by two prospectors (Frank Lewis and Orlando Baragwanath) sent out by Edmund Davis (q.v.). In October 1923, Raymond Brooks, a mining engineer working for Chester Beatty's Copper Ventures, reported that his crews had unearthed a large oxide ore body at Nchanga. Brooks and copper prospector, William Collier (q.v.), continued drilling despite Beatty's financial difficulties and proved that commercial grade ore was available in quantity. Work ceased at Nchanga in 1931, the result of the worldwide Depression, but new incline shafts were sunk in 1937. Nchanga Consolidated Copper Mines, Ltd. (q.v.), was formed, and production began in 1939. In 1955 the mine began using enormous mechanical shovels in its open-pit mining and quickly became one of the world's largest producing copper mines. It is a unique site on the Copperbelt in that secondary minerals, such as azurite and malachite, are found there ("enriched ore"). The mine was long the largest producer on the Copperbelt.

Nchanga's miners have a history of industrial activism. The Nchanga Mine was the prime target of a series of 1966 work stoppages, when wildcat strikes spread from Nchanga to all parts of the Copperbelt. Another series of wildcat strikes began there in January 1981, when the Mineworkers Union of Zambia (q.v.) succeeded in retaining its union leaders after their (temporary) expulsion from the United National Independence Party (q.v.). Nchanga's open-pit ores are now nearly exhausted, and the Zambia Privatisation Agency (q.v.) scheduled it for sale. As of early 1995, the National Assembly challenged the wisdom of the agency's plans to sell the Nchanga Mine to its allegedly incompetent management.

NDEBELE (MATABELE; MATEBELE). One of the two major groups of Africans in Zimbabwe (Southern Rhodesia, q.v.), they originated in Natal Province of modern South Africa as regiments in Shaka's 1820s Zulu empire. Mzilikazi (q.v.), the founder of the Ndebele people, was one of the last of Shaka's generals to flee the empire with his soldiers. From their bases in the Transvaal, they raided in all directions until Zulu and Boer attacks forced their removal to the Bulawayo region of southwestern Zimbabwe. Mzilikazi died in 1868 and was succeeded by his son, Lobengula (q.v.). The two men were responsible for numerous raids into southern Zambia, and both the Sebituane's Kololo (qq.v.) and the Lozi (q.v.) lived in fear of Ndebele raiders. It was king Lewanika's (q.v.) concern about the Ndebele that led him to seek British protection through treaties. Only once, in 1891–92, was an Ndebele army sent toward the Lozi heartland, but it was recalled before conflict began. Lobengula died in 1894, and there was no successor. The British South Africa Company (q.v.) had signed the Rudd Concession in 1888 with Lobengula, which gave his people mineral rights in his territory. With no obvious successor to

Lobengula, the company took control of the area. *See also* NGABE.

NDEMBU. The Ndembu people are concentrated in Mwinilunga District (q.v.), North-Western Province (q.v.), near the related Luvale (q.v.). The Ndembu seem to have originated during the 16th- or 17th-century expansion of Mwata Yamvo's (q.v.) kingdom, when Lunda (q.v.) immigrants and their Mbwela (q.v.) hosts became the Ndembu. The Ndembu still sent tribute to Mwata Yamvo as late as the 19th century. The Ndembu have been a mobile people, always searching for better hunting or farming land. At one point, however, their mobility reflected a desire to avoid Angolan slave traders (q.v.). The Ndembu did not have a centralized chieftainship; the chiefdoms were autonomous. In fact, individual chiefs had little real authority over their people except in matters of ritual, reflecting the failure of the Lunda invaders to integrate the Mbwela into their value system. When the British instituted indirect rule (q.v.) among the Ndembu, they created an administrative structure and a bureaucracy; headmen became subchiefs with capitals, clerks, and messengers under a British-designated senior chief.

NDOLA. Located near the southern end of the Copperbelt (q.v.), Ndola was the first and is the largest urban area on the Copperbelt. After Lusaka (q.v.), it is Zambia's second-largest town. Its population was 150,000 in 1969 and 376,300 in 1990. It is also the capital of Copperbelt Province (q.v.) and is the distribution center for much of Copperbelt and North-Western Provinces (q.v.). Its airport serves the whole region, and the oil pipeline from Dar es Salaam ends at Ndola. Numerous industries are located in Ndola, and both *The Times of Zambia* (q.v.) and the *Zambia Daily News* are printed there.

Ndola began in 1898, when Chiwala's Swahili (qq.v.) resettled there. The ancient Bwana Mkubwa (q.v.) copper workings there were pegged in 1902, and the Swahili soon supplied the miners with most of their locally grown rice and maize (q.v.). J. E. Chirupula Stephenson (q.v.) opened the first Ndola *boma* (q.v.) in 1904, but the village of Ndola grew appreciably only after the Rhodesia-Congo Border Railway arrived in 1909. Roan Consolidated Mines, Ltd. (q.v.), had its regional headquarters there, and both copper and oil refineries are in Ndola. It is also the location of the former Northern Technical College, now Copperbelt University.

NDOLA NATIVE WELFARE ASSOCIATION. One of the earliest welfare associations (q.v.) formed in Zambia, it was organized in 1930 and was patterned after the one in Livingstone (q.v.). An organizer of the Livingstone association, J. Ernest Mattako (q.v.), had been transferred to Ndola (q.v.) as a court interpreter and joined with two other civil servants, Ernest A. Muwamba (q.v.) and Elijah Herbert Chunga, to set up the welfare association. The leaders proposed that reform be approached in a moderate fashion to avoid government restrictions. They complained about health, housing, and food and water supplies. A new hospital for Africans was eventually built by the government at Ndola.

NEW LOOK. The term was used by Harry Nkumbula (q.v.) and others in the African National Congress (q.v.) in 1956, when some of the nationalists adopted a policy of moderation, rejecting boycotts or other actions which might precipitate violence. They held a meeting with the European leaders of the Legislative Council (q.v.), at which they committed the ANC to gradual reform. Nkumbula promised to keep his followers under control and pledged to try to improve race relations. In exchange, the ANC wanted "respect" from Europeans and help and sympathy from liberal-minded Europeans. Kenneth Kaunda (q.v.) and other members of ANC were bitter in their opposition to the "new look," claiming that it would not gain anything. In September 1956, a strike by members of the African Mineworkers Union (q.v.) led to the government declaring a state of emergency on the Copperbelt (q.v.) (*see* ROLLING STRIKES). It detained 45 union leaders. The government's overreaction led Nkumbula to drop his "new look," and to claim that it had rejected his hand of friendship.

NGABE (NXABA). An Ndebele (q.v.) breakaway from Mzilikazi's (q.v.) group, he and his followers invaded western Zambia in the 1840s in search of land and cattle. Thus, they came into conflict with Sebituane's Kololo (qq.v.), who had just taken over Bulozi (q.v.) and were still pacifying the Upper Zambezi valley. Ngabe's followers got as far north as Kakenge's Luvale (qq.v.) and the Mbundu settlement at Nakalomo, where they obtained guides who took them west toward the Kololo. Sebituane fled southward, and when Ngabe's force followed, their guides abandoned them. The Ndebele were lured to a Zambezi River (q.v.) island, where they were ambushed and killed by the Kololo. Ngabe had not gone into battle and, upon hearing the news, surrendered to the Lozi (q.v.) on the island of Naloy-ela. They then drowned Ngabe and the few remaining men, but retained the women and children.

NGALAMA. The fourth Luyana (q.v.) king, he likely ruled some-time in the 17th century. Some consider him, rather than the legendary Mboo (q.v.), to be the true founder of the Lozi (q.v.) state. Ngalama was a warrior and is remembered for expand-ing the kingdom. His warriors conquered the breakaway states led by Mboo's relatives, Mwanambinyi and Mange. These vic-tories gave the Lozi control over the Upper Zambezi floodplain (Bulozi, q.v.) and destroyed any possible rival.

NGAMBELA. This important, traditional, Lozi (q.v.) appointive position is filled by the king Litunga (q.v.) and is roughly equivalent to prime minister. The term means "spokesman" or "intermediary," for the *ngambela* is the intermediary between the Litunga and his people. He is also the principal councilor to the Litunga and the head of the National Council. It is the highest position to which a commoner can aspire and, in fact, can be held only by a commoner because the *ngambela* is ex-pected to represent the commoners' interests against those of the royals. *Ngambela*s have traditionally opposed kings who they felt were ruling unjustly.

NGOMBALA. According to some calculations, the sixth king of the Luyana (later called Lozi) (qq.v.), he lived probably in the late 17th or early 18th century. Like his predecessor, Ngalama (q.v.), Ngombala was a militaristic leader and was responsible for greatly expanding the area dominated by the Luyana kings. His forces conquered the Subiya (q.v.) and the Mbukushu and then moved further south, overrunning most of the southern border region of today's Zambia, including Sesheke (q.v.) and the area near Victoria Falls (q.v.); they even penetrated south of the Zambezi to the land around Wankie. They traveled east-ward along the northern side of the Zambezi through the land of the Toka as far as the confluence of the Zambezi and Kafue Rivers (qq.v.). His forces also traveled the Chobe River valley (q.v.) along Zambia's western border, where they overcame the Mashi (q.v.) and Makoma peoples and some of the Mbunda (q.v.), all of whom were required to pay regular tribute—food, goods, and labor—to Ngombala and his successors. *Induna*s (q.v.) resided among the conquered peoples to ensure pay-ment. These military conquests were part of Ngombala's plan to supply the homeland in the Zambezi floodplain with products from the surrounding forests. Ngombala set up chieftaincy in the southern floodplain, at what is now Nalolo (q.v.). He first appointed his daughter, Notulu, but after problems occurred, he replaced her as chief with his son, Mbanga.

NGONI. One of Zambia's largest ethnic groups, the Ngoni are mostly *ci*Nyanja (q.v.)-speaking people living in southeastern Zambia. There is a much larger group of them residing in neighboring Malawi (q.v.), however. Like the Swazi and Ndebele (q.v.), the original Ngoni and their leaders fled from Shaka's Zulu empire in Natal, South Africa, to seek new lives in the north, beyond Shaka's reach. Their migration, led by their great leader Zwangendaba (q.v.), took them through parts of Mozambique (q.v.) and Swaziland. In each territory they added to their numbers as other Africans joined the migration. They crossed the Zambezi River (q.v.) in 1835 and continued north through Zambia. They settled for six years among the Senga (q.v.) in eastern Zambia before moving north to the southeastern shore of Lake Tanganyika (q.v.).

After Zwangendaba's death in 1845, the Ngoni split into separate groups under leaders such as Mpezeni and Mperembe, (qq.v.). Some of the Ngoni settled in Malawi; others settled at least temporarily near the Bemba and the Bisa (qq.v), becoming their competitors. Raids were common. Conflicts occurred between the Bemba and the Ngoni in the late 1860s. But the Bemba's guns, which they received in trade with the Arabs (q.v.), held the Ngoni warriors to a stalemate. Ultimately, an Ngoni group under Mpezeni moved further south and by 1880 had defeated the Chewa and the Nsenga (qq.v.) and occupied their territory near the present city of Chipata (q.v.), where they were defeated by a British force in 1898 led by William Manning (q.v.). By that time, the British South Africa Company (q.v.), working in part with a German, Karl Wiese (q.v.), already claimed the area. Mpezeni surrendered, and the large herds of Ngoni cattle (acquired mostly through raids) were confiscated by the British.

The Ngoni people were traditionally a patrilineal society with a warrior-state base. They settled down and even adopted the matrilineal practices of the Chewa and the Nsenga, as well as their *ci*Nyanja language. The traditional Ngoni language is now rarely used. They live by cultivation of maize (q.v.) and cattle herding. Ngoni chiefs have always had a degree of independence under a segmentary arrangement. The traditional age-regiment system, common farther to the south, was maintained by the Ngoni as a method of providing links between the segmented chiefdoms. The Ngoni conquerors were a proud people, and assumed that their subjects—through intermarriage and service obligations—would aspire to complete social assimilation. When Mpezeni was defeated in 1898, many subject people, not tightly controlled by the Ngoni, broke away. Under colonial rule, the British appointed a paramount chief (q.v.) for the Ngoni. He was the administrative head of the area and was assisted by minor chiefs.

NGWEE. A word used by African nationalists as all or part of a rallying slogan in the period prior to independence (*see* KWACHA NGWEE), it is the root of a word meaning "brightness" but also can be an intensifying expletive. When the Zambian pound was replaced on January 1, 1968, by a new currency called the kwacha (q.v.), it was decided that each kwacha could be subdivided into one hundred ngwee (rhymes with "way"). Thus it is also a unit of Zambian currency.

NIAMKOLO (NYAMUKOLO). The first actual mission station established by the London Missionary Society (q.v.) in Zambia, it was founded in 1885 in Mambwe (q.v.) country near the southern shore of Lake Tanganyika (q.v.). It was evacuated in 1888 when another station was opened but it was reoccupied in 1889.

NICOLL, JOHN LOWE. A representative of the African Lakes Company (q.v.), he obtained agreements with several Mambwe and Inamwanga (qq.v.) chiefs between 1891 and 1893. These agreements, in exchange for goods, gave the company rights to mining, game, taxes, and other privileges connected with the territory in northeastern Zambia. It is probable that the full legal and political implications of these documents were unknown to the African signatories.

NJEKWA. This Lozi (q.v.) commoner organized and led the military force that overthrew the Kololo (q.v.) in 1864. The conquest won him so much popularity that Njekwa was offered the position of Litunga (king) (q.v.) despite his lack of royal blood. He declined it and requested that Sipopa (q.v.), a member of the royal family in exile, take the post instead. Sipopa rewarded him with the position of *ngambela* (q.v.). By 1871, Njekwa's power and popularity was so strong, however, that Sipopa was compelled to remove him, making him prince consort (Ishee Kwandu) to his daughter, ruler of the southern Lozi chieftaincy at Nalolo (q.v.). Njekwa left his marriage in 1874, returning to the northern capital to beg for Sipopa's mercy. Njekwa died soon thereafter; many suspected that Sipopa was implicated.

NKANA MINE. Probably named for the Lamba (q.v.) chief of the same name, it is located at Kitwe (q.v.) in the middle of the Copperbelt (q.v.). It was run by Rhokana Corporation, Ltd. (q.v.), a part of the Nchanga Consolidated Copper Mines, Ltd. (q.v.). Copper (q.v.) was first produced there in November 1931, and cobalt production began in August 1933. An electrolytic copper refinery began operation in 1935. The strikes of 1935 and 1940 (q.v.) occurred at Nkana, in addition to Mufulira and Nchanga. The mine was incorporated into Zambia Consolidated Copper Mines (q.v.) in the early 1980s. As of late 1996, the Zambia Privatisation Agency (q.v.) had yet to decide on how the ZCCM's assets would be sold.

NKANDABWE. This site in the Gwembe valley by Lake Kariba (qq.v.) produced coal from 1965 until 1969, when the deposit was exhausted and the mine closed. Fifty percent of the venture was government-owned. While the coal was inferior in quality to that imported from Wankie in Rhodesia, it provided an important supplement to Wankie imports, enabling the Zambian government to resist extortion by the Rhodesian government until a Zambian coalfield at Maamba Mine (q.v.) could begin production in 1968.

NKHATA, ALICK. Born in Kasama (q.v.) District in 1922 of a Bemba (q.v.) mother and a Lakeside (Malawian) Tonga (q.v.) father, Alick Nkhata was the pioneering recording artist of Zambian popular music. Trained as a teacher, this guitar-playing singer served in Burma during World War II as a sergeant in the East Africa Division. Using his serviceman's stipend to further his musical interests, he accompanied Hugh Tracey—a South African musicologist, then director of the International Library of African Music—on his recording trips through Eastern, Central, and Southern Africa. As an announcer and translator with the Lusaka (q.v.) (i.e., African) branch of the Central African Broadcasting Service (q.v.), he became the leading recorder and advocate of traditional Zambian music. He is best remembered for his original songs of social commentary—sentimental, allegorical, or satirical and sung in either ciBemba or ciNyanja (qq.v.)—which he, his quartet, and the Lusaka Radio Band (q.v.) recorded in the 1950s. He also wrote and performed several never-recorded campaign songs for Kenneth Kaunda and the United National Independence Party (qq.v.) in the early 1960s and was appointed director of broadcasting and cultural services after independence. Nkhata retired to his Mkushi area farm in 1974 and was tragically killed during a Rhodesian raid on a nearby Zimbabwean African People's Union camp in October 1978. In 1991, RetroAfric, a British firm, reissued a compact disc collection of his hit songs.

NKOLE. The legendary younger brother of Chiti (q.v.), he led the Bemba (q.v.) migration and became the first great Bemba leader. Nkole and his brothers were sons of Mukulumpe (q.v.), but they fled his rule in the Luba (q.v.) homeland (in modern Democratic Republic of Congo, q.v.) (Zaire) and crossed the Luapula River (q.v.) into Zambia. Chiti was killed in a battle; Nkole carried the corpse to a suitable burial place, the beautiful grove of trees called Mwalule (q.v.). Nkole sent a force to avenge Chiti's death, murdering the other chief, Mwase (q.v.). During the burning of the bodies of Mwase and his wife (Chiti had been involved in a love affair with her), the smoke from the fire choked Nkole and he died. He was buried at Mwalule near Chiti.

NKOLEMFUMU. One of the senior chiefships among the Bemba (q.v.), it is held only by members of the Bena Ng'andu, the chiefly Crocodile Clan. Holders of the title have sometimes given it up to succeed to other chiefships, notably those of Mwamba and Chitimukulu (qq.v.). The Nkolemfumu's territory (cialo) is called Miti and is in the central part of Bemba country. Miti's western border is the Lukulu River.

The title of Nkolemfumu was revived around 1870 for Mubanga Chipoya, a son-in-law of Mwamba II (q.v.). A warrior who had successfully fought the Bisa (q.v.), he now was to rule both Miti and some Bisa (q.v.) territory. In 1873 he expanded into the Bisa kingdom of Mpuki as well. In 1884 Mubanga Chipoya was promoted to Mwamba III (q.v.). From 1884 to 1895, Mubanga continued to rule Miti while also serving as Mwamba. In 1895 he was replaced by Kanyanta (q.v.), who also became a prominent Bemba leader, eventually serving as Chitimukulu from 1925 to 1943. The chiefship continues to the present day.

NKOLOMA, MATTHEW DELUXE. An active trade union leader in the 1950s, he served as general-secretary of both the African Mineworkers Union and the Trade Union Congress (qq.v.). A series of work stoppages in August 1956 (*see* ROLLING STRIKES) led the government to declare a state of emergency in Western Province (q.v.). Nkoloma was one of 45 labor leaders detained; he was held in restriction for three years.

NKOMO, JOSHUA. A major African political leader in Southern Rhodesia during the period of federation (q.v.), Nkomo was the principal African nationalist representative for his country during the 1950s and early 1960s, working alongside Dr. H. K. Banda (q.v.) of Nyasaland (q.v.) (Malawi, q.v.) and Kenneth Kaunda (q.v.). Their cooperation was never more evident than when they staged a walkout from the Federal Review Conference (q.v.) of December 1960. Throughout the late 1970s, Nkomo and his Zimbabwean African People's Union guerrillas were based in Zambia. Once the Liberation War finished, however, Robert Mugabe and his Zimbabwean African National Union party soon dominated the government of Zimbabwe.

NKOPE GROUP. This Early Iron Age pottery group is named after Nkope, a site some 40 kilometers north of Mangochi, along the southeastern shore of Lake Malawi (q.v.). Resembling earlier pottery from the eastern border of Kenya and Tanzania (q.v.), Nkope group ceramics are common to southern Malawi from the third to the 10th centuries A.D. as well as to northern Mozambique (q.v.) and eastern Zambia. Eastern Zambia seems to have been sparsely settled by Early Iron Age peoples. The only known village site with Nkope group ceramics is Kamnama, north of Chipata (q.v.) near the Malawi border. This five-hectare, iron-working community was occupied between the third and fifth centuries. In Nkope assemblies, necked vessels are more common than bowls; the former have everted rims with fluted or beveled lips, while the bowls often have inverted rims. Pots and bowls both tend to be decorated along the rim band with incised or comb-stamped diagonal lines. Both Nkope and Kalambo group (q.v.) ceramics have been found with Late Stone Age microlithic tools at rock shelter sites like Nakapapula (q.v.), Thandwe, and Makwe, fueling speculation that the indigenous hunter-gatherer occupants of these rock shelters were in intermittent contact with immigrant, Early Iron Age farming peoples.

NKOYA (MANKOYA). Close relatives of the Mbwela (q.v.), some of the earliest Congolese migrants into west-central Zambia, the Nkoya live east of the Lozi (q.v.) and west of the Ila and the Kaonde (qq.v.). The Nkoya came under the influence of the Lozi and, in fact, speak a language that is a subgroup of the Barotse language group. There were some 60,000 Nkoya speakers in Zambia in 1987.

Some Nkoya traditions indicate that their ruling lineage may have inspired that of the Lozi. In the 19th century the Lozi established their *induna*s (q.v.) among the Nkoya as representatives of the king of Barotseland (q.v.). Related or not, the Nkoya have resented their position as subject peoples to the Lozi and have long struggled for recognition as a far older, independent people.

NKUBA. This is the principal chieftainship of the Shila (q.v.), a people living in northeastern Zambia, south of Lake Mweru (q.v.). Nkuba IV was killed in about 1760 by Kazembe III of the Lunda (qq.v.), and the Shila have continued to pay tribute to the Lunda since then. Nkuba claimed to be of Bemba (q.v.) origin, even to belong to the Crocodile Clan of Chitimukulu (q.v.). Once defeated by the Lunda, however, Nkuba and his people became "honorary Lunda." The relationship between Kazembe and Nkuba bears some similarity to the British system of indirect rule (q.v.).

NKUKA. This Bisa (q.v.) leader was involved in lengthy, early 20th-century litigation over rights to the area near Mpika (q.v.) called Kasenga. Nkuka claimed to bear the title of an old Bisa chiefship that had lost its Kasenga territory to a 19th-century invasion by the Bemba (q.v.) chief Chikwanda (q.v.), when Nkuka and his followers were forced to flee to the Luangwa River (q.v.) valley. Other observers claimed that Nkuka was never a sovereign chief but was always subordinate to Chikwanda. Nkuka took the issue to the British administrators for a decision during World War I, and in June 1918, Hugh Marshall (q.v.) ruled in favor of Chikwanda.

NKULA I, MUTALE SICHANSA. One of the more active Bemba (q.v.) leaders of the 19th century, he was a nephew of Chitimukulu Chitapankwa (qq.v.), and as a young man stole the bundle of chiefly relics (*babenye*) from Bwembya (q.v.) to enable Chitapankwa to become Chitimukulu. Chitapankwa later appointed him to the Mwaba (q.v.) chieftainship and, in about

1870, to the chieftainship of Nkula (q.v.) and marriage to Mande, Chitapankwa's daughter. Chitapankwa hoped that Mutale Sichansa would help fight the Ngoni (q.v.) from this new post. He held this position until his death in September 1896. During those years he was actively engaged in trading ivory (q.v.) to the Arabs (q.v.), including the famous Tippu Tib (q.v.). French explorer Victor Giraud (q.v.) has described Nkula's trade in detail.

Mutale Sichansa was not content with his territory at Ichinga, moving south into Isunga, the former chiefdom of Mungulube (q.v.), and east into the Bisa (q.v.) chiefdom. In 1884 he was at war with Sampa (q.v.), resisting his claims to the position of Chitimukulu after Chitapankwa's death. Nkula I gained influence over the Bisa territory formerly ruled by Chibesakunda (q.v.) and put a son, Ndakala, in charge of it. After Nkula I's death in 1896, there was an attempt by Chikwanda II (q.v.), Mutale Lwanga, to take over his title and territory, but Bwalya, a son of Chileshye (q.v.), was appointed Nkula II (q.v.).

NKULA II, BWALYA CHANGALA (MUKWIKILE). A son of Chitimukulu Chileshye (q.v.), Bwalya (Mukwikile) was appointed by Chitapankwa (q.v.) to succeed Mutale Sichansa (see NKULA I) as ruler of Mwaba's (q.v.) country in the late 1860s. There were complaints about his rule, however, so he was moved to Ichinga temporarily, until he was given rule over Chingoli (q.v.), the land of the Chinkumba. When Nkula I, Mutale Sichansa, died in 1896 there was a question over succession. A year or so previously, Nkula I had given Bwalya (Mukwikile) part of his land. But the British South Africa Company (q.v.) agent, Charles McKinnon (q.v.), supported Chikwanda II (q.v.), Mutale Lwanga, for the post of Nkula. He was never properly installed, however, and Bwalya received the title of Nkula II. He held the post until he died in 1934.

NKUMBULA, BALDWIN. Son of Harry Nkumbula (q.v.), the father of Zambian nationalism, Baldwin Nkumbula became minister of youth and sports in the Movement for Multiparty Democracy (q.v.) government formed after the 1991 elections. He resigned from that post in July 1992 in protest over the government's failure to respond to allegations of corruption and abuse of office. He subsequently sued Michael Sata (q.v.), then minister of local government and housing, whose ministry, though it was responsible for the purchase of chlorine to treat municipal drinking water supplies, had failed to buy any chemicals for Kitwe's (q.v.) water, which came from the Kafue River (q.v.). Nkumbula maintained that this "recklessness" had contributed to a cholera (q.v.) outbreak. He and eight other MMD members of Parliament (q.v.) resigned from the MMD in August 1993 to form the National Party (q.v.), but he returned to the MMD in August 1995 after losing the party presidency to Humphrey Mulemba (q.v.) the previous April. Nkumbula had always refused to work with Mulemba and other NP members who had once served under the United National Independence Party governments of President Kaunda (qq.v.). He died a few days later, at age 37, when his speeding car overturned on the Kitwe-Ndola road. As one of the two passengers in his car at the time was Castro Chiluba, the son of President Frederick Chiluba (q.v.), a Commission of Inquiry was formed; in its November 1995 report, it ruled out any possibility of foul play.

NKUMBULA, HARRY MWAANGA. The father of Zambian nationalism, Harry Nkumbula was born in January 1916, the son of an Ila (q.v.) subchief, at Maala in Namwala (q.v.) District. During his education at Methodist mission schools he was inspired to stand against white supremacy by George Padmore's *How Britain Rules Africa*. He qualified as a teacher in 1934 at Kafue Training College and taught at Namwala schools for several years. He joined the United Missions in the Copperbelt (q.v.) teaching staff in 1942. He was assigned to Mufulira (q.v.), where he became secretary of the Mufulira Welfare Association (q.v.). His vigorous political activity against the proposed amalgamation (q.v.) with Southern Rhodesia (q.v.) led to his transfer to Kitwe (q.v.). Here he became a cofounder of the Kitwe African Society (q.v.) and, together with Godwin Mbikusita and Dauti Yamba (qq.v), remained actively involved in political affairs. The scholarship he received to Makerere College in Uganda was perhaps intended to divert his political enthusiasm.

In 1946 he received a government scholarship to England, where he earned a diploma in education and studied further at the London School of Economics. While in England he met George Padmore and became active in the Africa Committee with future African leaders such as Kwame Nkrumah, Jomo Kenyatta, and H. K. Banda (q.v.). He left London in 1959 and worked briefly as a salesman in East Africa before returning to Northern Rhodesia (q.v.) in July 1951 to address the Northern Rhodesia African Congress (q.v.). His strong opposition to federation (*see* CENTRAL AFRICAN FEDERATION) led the membership to elect him president of what he immediately renamed the African National Congress (q.v.).

Nkumbula began a vigorous campaign to oppose federation (he and Dr. Banda wrote a notable pamphlet against it in London in May 1949), with primary emphasis on developing new ANC branches, some as far away as South Africa. Provincial officers were established, and a national headquarters was set up at Chilenje, near Lusaka (q.v.), with one full-time employee. The ANC grew quickly in all but Eastern Province (q.v.) and the two westernmost provinces. Nkumbula's militant campaign against the proposed federation included a public burning of a government white paper in March 1953. He also called a boycott campaign, which failed. When federation began, Nkumbula's energy flagged and his leadership seemed to drift just as younger party members, such as Kenneth Kaunda (q.v.), became increasingly active. In January 1955, Kaunda and Nkumbula were jailed for two months "at hard labor" for distributing prohibited literature (the ANC newspaper). In 1958 he burned another white paper, this containing new constitutional proposals. In February 1958, Nkumbula and Kaunda proposed their own constitution to the governor, one calling for universal adult suffrage.

A break in the ANC came at the October 1958 national executive meeting. Nkumbula submitted his resignation to the 300 delegates, but he was reelected president, and the Kaunda-led opposition resigned to form Zambia African National Congress (q.v.). The opposition felt that Nkumbula was not an effective head, had mishandled party funds, and was not enough of a self-sacrificing and committed leader. In addition, his ultimate willingness to try the new constitutional provisions had lost him the support of his more radical followers. Still, he had considerable mass support throughout the country.

Nkumbula and the ANC participated in the March 1959 elections, and he won a seat in the Legislative Council (q.v). But other members were deserting the ANC, and Kaunda's United National Independence Party (q.v.) seemed to feed off Nkumbula's and the ANC's misfortunes. In September 1960, Nkumbula was sentenced to a year in jail for dangerous driving, an incident that had resulted in one death. Out on appeal, he attended the Federal Review Conference (q.v.) in London and the subsequent 1961 London Constitutional Conference (q.v.), during both of which Kaunda was obviously leading the nationalist side. In April 1961 his appeals were denied, and

Nkumbula was jailed until January 1962; meanwhile his seat in the Legislative Council was declared vacant.

The year 1962 was devoted to preparing the ANC for the December elections. The ANC was not nearly as well organized as the rival UNIP, and despite encouragement from Roy Welensky's United Federal Party (qq.v.), the ANC only won seven seats. This was enough, however, to make Nkumbula the power broker. He could join either the UFP or UNIP in a coalition and put that group in power. Although he had an unofficial alliance with the UFP, Nkumbula chose to join Kaunda in an African coalition. He was named minister of African education in the coalition cabinet. With a new constitution, however, the ANC was not as successful in the 1964 elections and at independence Nkumbula was leader of the opposition party in Parliament (q.v.). His party had only 10 seats to UNIP's 55.

The ANC had a resurgence in 1968. Combining Nkumbula's traditional strength in southern Zambia with support from members of the banned United Party (q.v.), the ANC won 23 seats to UNIP's 81. In 1972, Nkumbula fought to prevent the establishment of a one-party state in Zambia, but when it occurred Nkumbula gave in. On June 27, 1973, he announced that he was joining UNIP, saying, "I cannot sit idle or bury my head in the sand." In 1978, both he and Simon Kapwepwe (q.v.) challenged Kaunda for the leadership of UNIP (and the sole candidacy for national president). But UNIP's governing board announced it had rewritten the nomination requirements to exclude them, and the Supreme Court (q.v.) eventually upheld UNIP's freedom, as a "private club," to alter its rules as it saw fit. Harry Nkumbula died in 1983.

NOMBOTI (pl., *linomboti*). A special Lozi (q.v.) official who lives in a village near the grave of a dead king, it is his task to care for the grave, to care for the needs of the deceased leader, and to serve as the intermediary between the departed king and the people. He is believed to have the power to communicate with the king, passing requests and special pleas to him when requested.

NON-GOVERNMENTAL ORGANISATIONS COORDINATING COMMITTEE. It was established in 1985, prior to the UN Decade for Women meeting, to coordinate nongovernmental organizations' activities, to disseminate information, and to establish training services for affiliated organizations. In 1993 it had 29 affiliated member organizations.

NORTH BANK POWER STATION. *See* KARIBA DAM AND HYDROELECTRIC PROJECT.

NORTH CHARTERLAND EXPLORATION COMPANY. The company was organized in May 1895 to exploit the gold that—according to Karl Wiese (q.v.), Ngoni chief Mpezeni's (qq.v.) German trader—existed in Mpezeni's area. Wiese, claiming to own an 1891 concession there, sold it to North Charterland, 30 percent of whose shares were owned by the British South Africa Company (q.v.). The new company immediately sent out a prospecting expedition in Wiese's company. Ngoni warriors resented these intruders and their ownership claims. Several prospectors were killed, and Wiese sent out a call for help in December 1897. Colonel William Manning's (q.v.) British Central African Rifles and its Maxim guns left Blantyre and, in January 1898, rescued Wiese's party and put down the "Ngoni rebellion." Their leader, Mpezeni's son, was tried and executed, and Mpezeni, his village, and the Ngoni cattle were captured.

The North Charterland Company then distributed the heavily populated Ngoni lands to European cattle owners, a move that caused increased friction with the Africans. The problem of relocating Africans continued for four decades. At the end of World War I, anticipating the arrival of new settlers, the company again requested that about 150,000 Africans be moved from their lands in Fort Jameson (q.v.) District so that Europeans could purchase the lands. Despite African and missionary protests, the Africans were removed from the best lands. Though the company owned 25,900 square kilometers (10,000 square miles) in the area, it vigorously opposed a move in the 1920s and 1930s to create several thousand square kilometers of Native Reserves (q.v.) in its territory. It lobbied hard against the British Colonial Office's (q.v.) plan but depleted its own resources in the process. In 1938 it was reorganized with South African money. The new board of directors continued to quarrel over lands for settlement, this time with the Northern Rhodesian government. This was resolved in 1941 after arbitration was instituted, and the company received about £154,000 for 3.8 million acres. This land was opened to both African and European settlers.

NORTH-EASTERN RHODESIA. The term was used from 1895 until 1911 to denote modern Zambia east of the Kafue River (q.v.). It was distinct from North-Western Rhodesia (q.v.), which was merely an inflated Barotseland (q.v.). Given their very real differences of geographical access to travel, transport, and communications—Nyasaland (q.v.) versus Rhodesia—the British South Africa Company (q.v.) considered the two parts different administrative entities. The two were not formally divided until 1899, when the line was drawn at the Kafue River. In 1905, the dividing line was moved father east, so that the BSAC's claims to the Copperbelt's (q.v.) mineral wealth could be based upon the terms of the Lochner Concession (q.v.), rather than on Joseph Thomson's (q.v.) vaguely worded treaties. In August 1911, the two areas were merged into the single administrative unit called Northern Rhodesia (q.v.).

NORTH-EASTERN RHODESIA ORDER IN COUNCIL, 1900. *See* ORDER IN COUNCIL, 1900.

NORTHERN COPPER COMPANY. One of the first European-owned copper (q.v.) companies in Zambia, it operated mines along the Kafue River (q.v.) called the Sable Antelope and Silver King Mines. It was owned by Edmund Davis (q.v.).

NORTHERN NEWS. Since July 1, 1965, known as *The Times of Zambia* (q.v.), this paper was started in 1944 by Roy Welensky (q.v.) as a twice-weekly newspaper. It had a circulation of 2,000 in 1951 when the *Argus* news syndicate of South Africa bought it. It was made a daily in 1953. Five years later, its circulation had reached 18,000 copies. Throughout the 1950s and early 1960s it supported federation (*see* CENTRAL AFRICAN FEDERATION) and, when necessary, argued the cause of the settlers against the British Colonial Office (q.v.). It also supported Welensky's (q.v.) United Federal Party (q.v.) and all of its projects. When the UFP saw the need to cooperate with African politicians, the paper supported the African National Congress (q.v.) along with the UFP. It promoted the continuation of white rule in Southern Africa but also supported Tshombe's (q.v.) secession of Katanga (q.v.) from the Congo. In 1962 it began to treat African nationalists, especially Kenneth Kaunda (q.v.), in a more balanced fashion, recognizing the inevitability of Zambian independence. In December 1964, its ownership was purchased by Lonrho Zambia, Ltd. (q.v.). On May 18, 1965, Richard Hall, a British newspaperman who was a strong supporter of the Africans, was appointed editor.

NORTHERN PROVINCE. Physically dominating the eastern half of Zambia, Northern Province covers an area of 160,269 square kilometers (61,880 square miles). It stretches from Lake Mweru (q.v.) in the west to the upper stretches of the Luangwa River (q.v.) in the east, and from the southern part of Lake Tanganyika (q.v.) to a point just 121 kilometers (75 miles) from Zambia's southern border. It has nine districts: Mporokoso, Kasama, Chinsali, Isoka, Luwingu, Mbala, Mpika (qq.v.), Chilubi, and Kaputa. Their population totaled 545,000 in 1969, and 868,000 in 1990. Kasama, with 20 percent of the provincial population, is the most populous of the nine districts.

Though Northern Province became Zambia's new maize (q.v.)-farming heartland in the 1980s, tsetse (q.v.) fly, infertile soils, and the *chitemene* (q.v.) cultivation system contributed to historically low population densities. Yet Northern Province has long been a transcontinental crossroads. Arab slave traders (qq.v.) from the northeast both fought and traded with its African peoples, and Portuguese traders came through from the southeast. In the late 19th century, European missionaries followed the British South Africa Company's (q.v.) territorial inroads. While most of the African peoples here are linguistically and culturally similar to those in the Democratic Republic of Congo's (q.v.) (Zaire's) Shaba Province, from which they claim to have come, others along the Tanzanian border clearly derive from the patrilineal, cattle-keeping peoples of Eastern Africa. The Bemba (q.v.) and their language dominate the province, but other well-represented groups include the Bisa, the Tabwa, the Lungu, and the Mambwe (qq.v.). A substantial portion of the Copperbelt's (q.v.)population can be traced to Northern Province labor migrants, who began leaving in the late 1920s.

NORTHERN RHODESIA. Though the British Foreign Office gave the British South Africa Company (q.v.) permission in 1897 to use this name for its trans-Zambezi territories, a consolidated Northern Rhodesia first arose in 1911, after the BSAC merged its administratively distinct territories of North-Eastern and North-Western Rhodesia (qq.v.). It became the Republic of Zambia (q.v.) on October 24, 1964.

NORTHERN RHODESIA AFRICAN CONGRESS. The first in a line of African nationalist organizations that culminated in the former ruling party, the United National Independence Party (q.v.), the NRAC was founded in July 1948 at a general conference of the Federation of African Societies of Northern Rhodesia (q.v.) when the conference unanimously voted to change its name. It elected Godwin Mbikusita as president, Robinson

Nabulyato as secretary, and Mateyko Kakumbi (qq.v.) as treasurer. The stated goals of the new organization included promoting the educational, political, economic, and social advancement of Africans. The conference restated African opposition to rule by Europeans and to either amalgamation or federation (qq.v.). It opposed having a European represent the Africans in the Legislative Council (q.v.). It also demanded to be represented at the forthcoming London Constitutional Conference (q.v.). Though the NRAC was generally a very moderate body, it received only negative responses from the Northern Rhodesian government. In August 1951, its leadership was assumed by Harry Nkumbula (q.v.), who immediately changed its name to the African National Congress (q.v.).

In 1937, another organization named the Northern Rhodesia African Congress included a number of successful Plateau Tonga (q.v.)farmers, teachers, and chiefs who lived near Mazabuka (q.v.). It was basically a local group and its interests were mostly in agriculture and land tenure. It was short-lived due to government disapproval. One of its leaders was George W. Kaluwa (q.v.).

NORTHERN RHODESIA AND NYASALAND JOINT PUBLICATIONS BUREAU. To counter Watch Tower (q.v.) tracts in the field of "vernacular" literature, the government began publishing *Mutende* (q.v.) newsmagazine in 1936 and created the African Literature Committee in 1937. The Joint Publications Bureau, successor to the African Literature Committee and the Northern Rhodesia Publications Bureau (1947), was established in 1948. In cooperation with the territorial education departments and some mission societies, it published and distributed books by African authors for African readers. Its subsidized publications were sold through Christian bookshops and, by the late 1950s, were available at schools and missions through the bureau's postbox library service. Most publications were under 100 pages and fell into three general categories: family, manners, and housekeeping guides; African language grammars, dictionaries, and school texts; and African histories, folklore, and fiction. Nearly 40 short novels, including those of Stephen Mpashi (q.v.), were published by or in association with the bureau. Its best-sellers in the early 1950s offered either practical advice for modern living or traditional customs and stories. The bureau's staff then included three Europeans and—as readers, translators, and writers—eight Africans.

NORTHERN RHODESIA COMMONWEALTH PARTY. This minor party was practically the private coterie of the active, conservative politician Guillaume van Eeden (q.v.). He formed it after he had been expelled from the Federal Party (q.v.) in 1955, joining with some individuals who had been active in the Confederate Party (q.v.). The party campaigned on a segregationist platform for partition. In 1958, van Eeden, who held the Kafue seat from Northern Rhodesia (q.v.) in the Federal Parliament, joined forces with the Federal Dominion Party (q.v.).

NORTHERN RHODESIA LABOUR PARTY. The party was formed in 1941 by Roy Welensky (q.v.) and six other members of the Legislative Council (q.v.). Welensky, a strong proponent of amalgamation (q.v.) with Southern Rhodesia (q.v.) and, later, of federation (*see* CENTRAL AFRICAN FEDERATION), became its president and moving force. As a labor-oriented party, it was also against African competition for jobs, especially in the mines and along the line of rail (q.v.) where its European supporters were employed. It also worked for increased power for the "unofficials" (q.v.) in the Legislative Council. Welensky, a railway worker himself, also worked hard for closed-shop agreements with employers. A 1948 visit to England disillusioned him with the British Labour Party, and he disbanded his party to devote himself to the goal of federation.

NORTHERN RHODESIA LIBERAL PARTY. It was formed in October 1960, when Sir John Moffat (q.v.) took his successful Northern Rhodesian segment out of the otherwise floundering Central Africa Party (q.v.) and renamed it. Moffat, Harry Franklin, and A. H. Gondwe (qq.v.) had all won seats in the Northern Rhodesia Legislative Council as CAP candidates in 1959. In February 1961, they received ministerial posts on the Executive Council after the United Federal Party (q.v.) withdrew from the government in protest over a new constitution for Northern Rhodesia (q.v.). The Liberal Party position—in essence, the position of Moffat, its dominant figure—was that the federation should be disbanded and a High Commission should be set up for the three territories. Moffat felt that the constitution should be considered by Europeans as transitional, designed to allow Africans experience in leadership en route to total self-government. During this period of just five years or so, Moffat felt, Europeans would have one last chance to prove to Africans that true partnership was possible. Then a new constitution, presumably to allow for multiracial participation (a key to all Liberal Party thinking), could be established to settle Northern Rhodesia's future. The party opposed the one man, one vote concept but did seek a wider franchise for Africans

The Liberal Party suffered from lack of membership and insufficient funds. In March 1962 it had only 15 registered branches and fewer than 100 truly active members. Its policies were too liberal for most Europeans and too conservative for most Africans. Despite an electoral situation that seemed to aid any party that could get both European and African votes, the Liberal Party was trounced in the 1962 elections. In the upper-roll (European) part of the election, its 12 candidates averaged about 125 votes each, 5 percent of the total cast; its lower-roll total was much worse: 28 of its 30 candidates lost their deposits. Only Gondwe made even a fair showing, but that wasn't good enough to win. The UFP won 90 percent of the European vote. After the election Moffat disbanded the party.

NORTHERN RHODESIA POLICE. Formed in 1912 by a merger of the North-Eastern Rhodesia Constabulary and the Barotse Native Police (q.v.), its membership at that point consisted of 27 British officers and 750 Africans. It was armed with rifles and a few machine guns but no artillery and only minimal motor transport. When World War I broke out, a detachment of Northern and Southern Rhodesia Police left the Victoria Falls (q.v.) bridge and occupied the German post of Schuckmannsburg in the Caprivi Strip (qq.v.). A mobile column of the police rushed north to the Tanganyika border, which was threatened by the German post at Bismarckburg, less than 64 kilometers (40 miles) north of Abercorn (q.v.). The mobile column was in time to assist in the defense of Abercorn and Fife (q.v.) late in 1914. In early 1915, a mobile column of the Northern Rhodesia Rifles (q.v.) provided needed reinforcement, notably at the battles around Saisi in mid-1915. In May 1916, two columns of soldiers, including some forces of the police, moved north into Tanganyika, occupying parts of German East Africa. The German leader there was General Paul E. von Lettow-Vorbeck (q.v.). He evaded a direct confrontation and ultimately moved his troops into Northern Rhodesia, capturing several northeastern towns before the police and other military units could engage him in a battle late in 1918, just as the war was ending in Europe. In 1932 the government of Northern Rhodesia separated the civil and military units of the police, so that in 1933 the military unit became known as the Northern Rhodesia Regiment.

NORTHERN RHODESIA REFORMED TRADE UNION CONGRESS. *See* REFORMED TRADE UNION CONGRESS.

NORTHERN RHODESIA RIFLES. Growing out of a private rifle association, it was a totally European, volunteer military unit in World War I. Its organizer was Major Boyd Alexander Cuninghame, a Scotsman who raised cattle for the market west of Lusaka (q.v.). His force numbered about 300 officers and men, about 135 of whom constituted a mobile column in March 1915. This column marched over 885 kilometers (550 miles) to reach the northern border with German Tanganyika, where most of their clashes occurred. Eventually, however, they were limited to border patrol and garrison duties along the Stevenson Road (q.v.). In 1916 the disgruntled mobile column disbanded, and most of its members joined other military groups, some in Southern Rhodesia (q.v.), which were more actively engaged in battles. Cuninghame died of typhoid fever in 1917, and no strong leader emerged. By 1918 its membership was too low to have it considered a dependable fighting unit.

NORTHERN RHODESIAN EURAFRICAN ASSOCIATION. An organization based in Ndola (q.v.) in the late 1950s, it was composed of politically conscious members of the fairly small "coloured," or mixed race, community of Zambia. In July 1960, its chairman, Aaron Milner (q.v.), led its members into a merger with the United National Independence Party (q.v.), although he had resisted earlier attempts because he feared that its positions were too extreme.

NORTH-WESTERN PROVINCE. Bordering both the Democratic Republic of Congo (q.v.) (Zaire) and Angola (q.v.) in the northwestern corner of the country, this lightly settled province had a population of only 232,000 in 1969 and 383,000 in 1990. Its six districts, Chizera, Kabompo (q.v.), Mwinilunga (q.v.), Solwezi (q.v.), Zambezi, and Kasempa (q.v.), had an average density of about two people per square kilometer (five people per square mile) in 1969. Kasempa had less than one person per square kilometer (two people per square mile). The province is primarily settled by the Lunda, Kaonde, Luvale, Luchazi, Mbunda, and Ndembu (qq.v.) peoples. Historically, the people of the province have had more in common ethnically and commercially with the people of Angola than with people of all other provinces but Western Province (q.v.). The province has some added significance in that a number of important rivers begin in its higher elevations (in some cases as much as 1,525 meters [5,000 feet] above sea level). These feed into the Zambezi and the Kafue Rivers (qq.v.).

NORTH-WESTERN RHODESIA. The term was used until 1911 to denote modern Zambia west of the Kafue River (q.v.). As such, it was distinct from North-Eastern Rhodesia (q.v.). In 1899 its eastern boundary "was placed along the Kafue River, as it was meant to be essentially the territory under Lozi (q.v.) domination or influence which had been acquired from the Lozi by concessions." In fact, it went much further than Lozi influence. In 1905 the eastern boundary was moved to a north-south line at the territory's narrow "waist," so that the British South Africa Company (q.v.) could base its claims to the Copperbelt's (q.v.) mineral wealth on the terms of the Lochner Concession (q.v.) rather than on Joseph Thomson's (q.v.) useless treaties. The move effectively put the richest mining areas under one jurisdiction. In August 1911, however, the two halves were administratively united as Northern Rhodesia (q.v.).

NORTH-WESTERN RHODESIA FARMERS' ASSOCIATION. One of the first politically active settlers' groups in Northern Rhodesia (q.v.), it began early in the 20th century in the newly established farming areas near the line of rail (q.v.). By 1913 it was urging the administrator of Northern Rhodesia, L. A. Wallace (q.v.), to establish a Legislative Council (q.v.), with membership open to the settlers.

NORTH-WESTERN RHODESIA ORDER IN COUNCIL, 1899. *See* ORDER IN COUNCIL, 1899.

NORTH-WESTERN RHODESIA POLITICAL ASSOCIATION. Perhaps the first significant formal political organization in Northern Rhodesia (q.v.), it grew out of the North-Western Rhodesia Farmers' Association (q.v.) around 1920. It had fewer than 100 active members, mostly European farmers living in the western half of the territory. It was led by Leopold Frank Moore (q.v.), a Livingstone (q.v.) pharmacist and newspaper editor. He fought first for an Advisory Council (q.v.) and later for greater self-government. The farmers, notably those near the Kafue River (q.v.), were also eager for amalgamation (qq.v.) with Southern Rhodesia (qq.v.).

NOTULU. The daughter of Ngombala (q.v.) and, according to Lozi (q.v.) tradition, the first ruler of a second chieftaincy located in the southern part of Bulozi (q.v.), accounts say that she requested to go south and her father agreed, giving her royal drums and *induna*s (q.v.) and making her the ruler there. She had a dispute with her brother, Mbanga, who then killed her son. Later, Notulu abdicated, and Mbanga succeeded her as ruler of the southern plain, the center of which is at Nalolo (q.v.) today.

NOYOO, HASTINGS NDANGWA. A Lozi (q.v.) political leader in the 1960s, he was born in Mongu (q.v.) District in 1928. Noyoo was a commoner but ancestors on both sides of his family had served as *ngambela* (q.v.). His schooling led to a medical certificate, and he worked in the Ministry of Health in Mongu. He was a supporter of the African National Congress (q.v.) in the 1950s, even resigning from government service to show his opposition to federation (*see* CENTRAL AFRICAN FEDERATION). He later became active in the United National Independence Party (q.v.). He was elected in 1963 to the Katengo *kuta* (q.v.) as a member of UNIP and was a leader of the elected members. At one point he led a walkout in protest against the traditionalists who were trying to retain their power in the *kuta* (q.v.). Noyoo and his supporters took a middle ground on the issue of Barotseland (q.v.) independence or inclusion in Zambia. They wanted inclusion in Zambia but with special status for Barotseland. This position conflicted with UNIP's. In mid-1964 he was suspended for six months from UNIP for this stand. Meanwhile, he was appointed assistant *ngambela* in March 1964 and *ngambela* in December 1964 by the council. After independence, Noyoo again expressed the will of the council to be associated with, yet independent of, Zambia. The Zambian government did not accept this and passed the Local Government Act (q.v.) to reduce the power of the Lozi leaders. Noyoo again turned to electoral politics, and became active in the United Party (q.v.). When it was banned he joined the ANC and ran for Parliament (q.v.) in 1968. He was one of eight successful Lozi ANC candidates.

NSAMA. The dominant chieftainship among the Tabwa (q.v.), it was founded by members of the Bazimba (Leopard) Clan who settled in Itabwa southwest of Lake Tanganyika (q.v.) late in the 18th century (*see* TABWA). A major controversy over succession to the chieftainship involved a man named Kafwimbi (q.v.), who ultimately became Nsama V.

NSENGA. One of Zambia's largest ethnic groups, the *ci*Nyanja (q.v.)-speaking Nsenga live in southeastern Zambia and are especially strong in Petauke (q.v.) District. Though the Chewa (q.v.) often claim the Nsenga as a Chewa offshoot, their linguistic and cultural patterns suggest a closer connection to the Bisa and the Lala (qq.v.) to the west. In the 18th and 19th centuries the Nsenga traded ivory (q.v.) to the Europeans. They also grew cotton and wove it into cloth. In the 1860s and 1870s, the Ngoni of Mpezeni (qq.v.) invaded and dominated Nsenga territory, both by raiding and by requiring the payment of tribute. Ngoni warriors intermarried with the Nsenga and also adopted their language. Portuguese influence was also strong in the area, but in the three years after 1887 an Nsenga chief, Mburuma, mounted a guerrilla war against the Portuguese, gathering a force of 2,000 warriors to lay siege to Zumbo (q.v.) in 1888. Nsenga chiefs traditionally had firm political and judicial authority based on their rights in their lineage. Each chiefdom was based on a single clan, and all Nsenga chiefs were considered about equal. British colonial officials, however, appointed a senior chief.

NSHIMA. The commonest name for the dietary staple of most Zambians, it is a dish made of boiled mealiemeal (cornmeal) and tastes like stiff grits. It is served with a "relish," the English name for the vegetable—or more rarely, meat and vegetable—stew in which diners dip their lumps of *nshima* before consuming them.

NSOKOLO. The paramount chief of the Mambwe (qq.v.), whose territory is in northeastern Zambia, north of the Bemba (q.v.), this chieftainship suffered in the mid–19th century by being in the path of both the Ngoni (q.v.) and the Bemba. In fact, two holders of the title were killed by the Ngoni in the 1860s. Chitapankwa, a Bemba Chitimukulu (qq.v.), defeated Nsokolo, taking both slaves and cattle from the Mambwe leader. Bemba raids continued, so the Mambwe eagerly accepted the protection promised by British South Africa Company (q.v.) agents. In the early 1920s, however, the reigning Nsokolo vigorously protested the tax increases and other penalties to the secretary for native affairs; the tax was reduced in 1925.

NUMWA. This Lozi (q.v.) warrior and a senior *induna* (q.v.) eventually became a leader of the rebellion against Lubosi (q.v.), the Lozi king. Actually, Numwa is a military praise name; his given name was Muyunda. A son of Muwela, his home area was in Nanga. When Lubosi was one of two candidates for king, Numwa supported him. In fact, a force led by Numwa later found the hideout of Musiwa, Lubosi's opponent, and delivered him to Lubosi to be killed. In 1884, however, Numwa supported Mataa (q.v.), who led a successful rebellion that deposed Lubosi. Numwa had been one of Lubosi's bodyguards but turned against him after Lubosi had one of his close relatives murdered. In addition, he opposed the royal decree compelling the *induna*s to cultivate their own lands. Thus Numwa joined forces with Mataa and ultimately helped to install Tatila Akafuna (q.v.) as king. Lubosi and his followers fought back, and in 1885 a major battle between the opposing forces was won by Lubosi. Both Mataa and Numwa were killed in the battle.

NYAMBE. This is the Lozi (q.v.) name for the God who, they claim, begat the first Lozi king with his wife-daughter, Mbuyu. Misfortunes and disasters that beset the Lozi have been attributed to the anger of Nyambe. The reigning monarch, as Nyambe's direct descendant, is believed to be the only one capable of interceding with Nyambe on behalf of the whole nation.

NYAMUKOLO. This is a variant of Niamkolo (q.v.).

NYAMUNYIRENDA, HELEN, The mother of Zambia's first president, Kenneth Kaunda (q.v.), and wife of David Kaunda (q.v.), she was born around 1885 at Chisanya village near Ekwendeni in Ngoni (q.v.) territory (now part of Malawi (q.v.)). Her father, Mugagana Nyirenda, was a Phoka. In 1893 her parents left the Ngoni and moved to Karonga. In 1900 she went to the Livingstonia Mission's (q.v.) Overtoun Institute, for teacher training. David Kaunda, also an Overtoun graduate, married Helen in 1904. Their first two children were born in Chinsali (q.v.); Katie in 1907 and Robert in 1912. The family lived in Nkula from 1913 to 1915. Kenneth was the eighth child and was born at Lubwa (q.v.), near Chinsali, in 1924. Helen was widowed in 1932. Her oldest was 25.

NYAMWEZI. *See* YEKE.

NYANJA. *See* CINYANJA.

NYASALAND. Known as Malawi (q.v.) since independence on July 6, 1964, the country is immediately east of Zambia. It was called the Nyasaland Protectorate by the British from 1891 to 1893 and again from 1907 until independence. From 1893 until 1907 it was called the British Central Africa Protectorate. Between 1953 and 1963 it was a partner with Northern and Southern Rhodesia (qq.v.)in the Central African Federation (q.v.).

NYENGO. The site, in the northwestern part of Bulozi (q.v.), is where many Luyana (Lozi) (qq.v.) refugees (and most of the royal family) fled after being defeated by the Kololo (q.v.). The group chose Imbua, a younger brother of Mubukwanu (q.v.), as their king (Nyengo). Some of the refugees returned to the valley, where the Kololo eventually executed them. Others moved on to Lukwakwa (q.v.), including Imbua, who was attracted by its iron ore deposits. By the time the Kololo were overthrown, Nyengo had ceased to exist as a separate chieftaincy.

NYERERE, JULIUS. The first president of Tanganyika (later, Tanzania, q.v.), he was a close personal friend and constant inspiration to Kenneth Kaunda (q.v.). When Zambia became independent in October 1964, Nyerere was the only foreign head of state present. In 1963, consultations between Kaunda and Nyerere led to what has become a symbol of their cooperation, the TAZARA (q.v.) railway. Kaunda's organization of the United National Independence Party (q.v.) and his Zambian humanism were both influenced by similar patterns in Tanzania. In the late 1970s the two men worked closely in an attempt to bring about African majority rule in Zimbabwe (Rhodesia).

NYIRENDA, ISAAC RANKIN. A civil servant front Nyasaland (q.v.) working in Livingstone (q.v.) in the 1920s, he and Franklin Tembo (q.v.) founded the Livingstone Native Welfare Association (q.v.) in 1930. Nyirenda presided at its inaugural meeting. Nyirenda and Tembo first suggested the formation of a Northern Rhodesia Native Welfare Association to the government in 1929. Early in 1930 the secretary for native affairs, James Moffat Thomson (q.v.), encouraged them (although requiring that it be limited to Livingstone), even helping the two prepare a constitution for what the government thought would only be a harmless social club. Instead, it soon became a pattern for territorywide political organizations.

NYIRENDA, TOMO. This messianic Watch Tower Movement (q.v.) prophet of the mid-1920s called himself Mwana Lesa (q.v.).

NYIRENDA, WESLEY PILLSBURY. One of Zambia's more prominent politicians in the 1960s and 1970s, Nyirenda was made chairman of the United National Independence Party's (q.v.) subcommittee on appointments and discipline in 1973. Born near Lundazi, Eastern Province (qq.v.), in 1924, he was educated at the Lubwa Mission School and in South Africa. In 1948 he won a medical school scholarship for Witwatersrand University, but family obligations in Zambia forced him to decline it. As a teacher (and later headmaster) he supported his brothers while studying part-time for a B.A. He then studied at the University of London, receiving a B.S. (economics) in 1955. After returning home, he became a principal at Ndola (q.v.) but also became active in the African National Congress (q.v.), where he joined the young Turks who were dissatisfied with Harry Nkumbula's (q.v.) leadership. He accepted an appointment as the ANC's Western Province (q.v.) president in 1958 but resigned after only a few days. He eventually joined UNIP and, in 1962, successfully ran for Parliament (q.v.). In January 1964 he was appointed its deputy speaker, becoming speaker at independence. He continued as the National Assembly's speaker until 1968. In December 1968 he was named minister of education, a title he held until December 1973, when he joined Kenneth Kaunda's (q.v.) elect circle of trusted politicians, the Central Committee of UNIP (q.v.).

He was chairman of the Zambia Olympic Committee for more than 20 years. He also survived President Kaunda's and UNIP's fall from power in the 1991 elections. He was made ambassador to Belgium and died in Brussels, at 69 years of age, in 1993.

O

OLD MAMBWE (MAMBWE MWELA). One of the earliest mission stations in Northern Rhodesia (q.v.), it belonged first to the White Fathers' (q.v.). It opened in July 1891 and was located southeast of Lake Tanganyika (q.v.), not far from what is today the Tanzanian border, near the Stevenson Road (q.v.). At one time the British South Africa Company (q.v.) also had a trading post there. Father Van Oost (q.v.) was its first superior; upon his death he was succeeded by the Reverend (later Bishop) Joseph Dupont (q.v.). In October 1893, the White Fathers decided to abandon the site because the slave caravans through the area hindered their mission work. Subsequent successes, especially Dupont's, with the Bemba (q.v.) kept the White Fathers at Old Mambwe for two more years, when they opened a new mission at Kayambi.

ONE MAN, ONE VOTE. This popular phrase was used by many African nationalists demanding universal adult suffrage and African majority rule. They rejected proposals for weighted votes or separate voting rolls. In the late 1950s, the Capricorn Africa Society and the Northern Rhodesia Liberal Party (qq.v.) espoused a limited, "qualified" franchise for Africans. Harry Nkumbula (q.v.) accepted such a constitutional arrangement for the 1959 Legislative Council (q.v.) elections, thus prompting the more militant African National Congress (q.v.) members to break off and form the Zambia African National Congress (q.v.), which soon became the United National Independence Party (q.v.).

OPERATION FOOD PROGRAMME. This ambitious agricultural program, launched by the government in 1980, envisaged that capital-intensive, high-technology, state-owned farms would produce great quantities of staple food crops. The original plans were to create 18 state farms, two in each province, of 20,000 hectares each. However, few foreign investors came forward to participate. By 1983, a total of only 800 hectares on three farms were under production, and these were part of a pilot scheme.

ORDER IN COUNCIL, 1899. Promulgated by the British Crown in November 1899, this decree provided that administration and justice in the areas known as Barotseland and North-Western Rhodesia (qq.v.) should be carried on by the British South Africa Company (q.v.) under the control of the British high commissioner for South Africa. The eastern border of this territory was to be the Kafue River (q.v.). The BSAC had not told Lozi King Lewanika (qq.v.) that this would remove his sovereign rights over his land. Insofar as administration was concerned, it also superseded the Lawley Concession of 1898 (q.v.), which Lewanika had signed with the BSAC. In 1905, as a result of pressure from the BSAC, the eastern boundary was pushed eastward to the narrow waist of Zambia. This placed all of the line of rail (q.v.) and the Copperbelt (q.v.) under the rules of the 1900 Order in Council (q.v.) even though these territories had never been formally under the jurisdiction of Lozi kings.

ORDER IN COUNCIL, 1900. This British administrative order formally placed the area known as North-Eastern Rhodesia (q.v.) under the administrative jurisdiction of the British South Africa Company (q.v.). It required the appointment of an administrator, whose duties included controlling the development of communications, exercising authority over any Europeans in the area and maintaining law and order through a police force and native commissioners (q.v.). It also created a High Court (q.v.) to dispense justice under English law (except in civil cases between Africans).

ORDER IN COUNCIL, 1911. This order by the British Crown amalgamated North-Eastern and North-Western Rhodesia (qq.v.) into Northern Rhodesia (q.v.), something that the British South Africa Company (q.v.) had been encouraging for a long time. No approval by Africans was needed for it to take effect. Certain provisions were included to safeguard some previously attained rights of the Lozi (q.v.) people. The Lozi, however, did object to the clause that the BSAC could sell land outside the reserve areas to Europeans. Otherwise, it bore great resemblance to the Order in Council of 1900 (q.v.). It provided for an administrator for the whole territory to be appointed by the BSAC with the approval of the British secretary. A High Court (q.v.) was also set up, but no council.

ORDER IN COUNCIL, 1924. There were actually two separate orders in council promulgated at this time. The Northern Rhodesia Order in Council of 1924 provided that the territory would be removed from the jurisdiction of the British South Africa Company (q.v.) and placed under the direct administration of the British government. There would be a governor and an Executive Council nominated by the crown. Article 41 recognized Barotseland's (q.v.) special status. The Northern Rhodesia (Legislative Council, q.v.) Order in Council of 1924 also provided for the territory's first legislature, consisting of nine officials and five unofficial elected members. Ordinances were to respect native laws and customs where they did not conflict with the crown's prerogatives, and no laws were allowed that would discriminate on racial bases, except those concerning arms, ammunition, and alcoholic beverages.

ORDER IN COUNCIL, 1953. *See* FEDERATION (CONSTITUTION) ORDER IN COUNCIL.

ORDER IN COUNCIL, 1953 (BAROTSELAND). At the time of the creation of the Central African Federation (q.v.), the British government promulgated a separate Order in Council. The Lozi Litunga (king) and *kuta* (council) (qq.v.) had made this a prerequisite for their acceptance of the federation. It merely stated that Barotseland (q.v.) was a protectorate within Northern Rhodesia (q.v.) and restated the rights guaranteed to Lozi (q.v.) traditional authorities by the 1924 Order in Council (q.v.).

ORDER IN COUNCIL, JANUARY 3, 1964. This British administrative order formally conferred self-rule upon Northern Rhodesia (q.v.). Only defense, public order, the police, and foreign affairs remained in the governor's control until the date of final independence.

ORMSBY-GORE COMMISSION. This British Parliament commission headed by William Ormsby-Gore (Lord Harlech) was sent to Africa in 1925 to investigate the desirability of establishing a closer association among the British East and Central African territories. It limited its hearings in Northern Rhodesia (q.v.) to the southernmost city, Livingstone (q.v.), however, and did not seem to have consulted Africans. It learned that the governments of Northern Rhodesia and Nyasaland (q.v.) preferred a southern economic association to a northeastern one. The Ormsby-Gore Commission thus recommended improving the infrastructure between East and Central Africa (q.v.) before considering a broad federation. Ormsby-Gore served as undersecretary of state for the colonies from 1922 to 1929. As colonial secretary from 1936 to 1938, he refused to encourage those who wished to amalgamate Northern Rhodesia and Southern Rhodesia (q.v.). He specifically expressed concern that no concessions be granted to the settlers that would endanger the interests or security of native Africans. From May 1941 to May 1944, he served as British high commissioner for South Africa.

P

PAN-AFRICAN FREEDOM MOVEMENT FOR EAST, CENTRAL, AND SOUTHERN AFRICA. The movement for East and Central Africa was formed at Mwanza, Tanganyika, in 1958. It was a loose, regional grouping of political parties designed to encourage the success of the independence movements. Julius Nyerere (q.v.) and Tom Mboya were its prominent leaders. Kenneth Kaunda (q.v.) was active from the beginning. At Addis Ababa in February 1962, Kaunda was elected president of PAFMECA, and the group decided to concentrate political and financial aid on Zambia. That same year, when both South Africa's African National Congress (q.v.) and Pan-Africanist Congress joined, it added "Southern" to its title. When the Organization of African Unity was formed in May 1963, PAFMECSA became redundant and ceased operation.

PAPER ZAMBIANS. This derisive term was often used by black Zambians to refer to Asians and Europeans during the early years of independence. They felt that many of these minority peoples took advantage of the economy without becoming citizens or investing in long-term projects.

PARAMOUNT CHIEFS. The term was used in areas under British colonial rule to designate the supposed single, overall leader of a people, one superior to all other chiefs or headmen. It also served the purpose of denying the use of such royal titles as "king," which would have implied a prestigious sovereign ruler. When Robert Codrington (q.v.) became administrator of North-Western Rhodesia (q.v.)in 1907, he specifically ordered that "paramount chief" be used to describe the Lozi (q.v.) leader, Lewanika (q.v.), and that terms such as "king" and "prince" should be discontinued.

PARAMOUNTCY, DOCTRINE OF. This British colonial policy, enunciated originally by the Duke of Devonshire in 1923 regarding East Africa and extended to Northern Rhodesia (q.v.) and Nyasaland (q.v.) by Lord Passfield (q.v.) in 1930, stated that African interests would be paramount when they came into conflict with the interests of immigrant peoples. Whereas Devonshire had only meant Asians when he said "immigrant peoples," Passfield also applied it to Europeans, thus stirring up a hornet's nest in Central Africa (q.v.). As a result of settler protests, a Joint Select Committee of Parliament issued a report in late 1931 slightly modifying the doctrine. Three years later the new governor, Sir Hubert Young (q.v.), modified it almost out of existence.

PARASTATAL. The term refers to agencies that, under Zambia's former system of state capitalism, effectively operated as governmental subsidiaries. Most of them were economic by nature. Among the best examples were the Zambia Industrial and Mining Corporation, the Financial Development Corporation, and the Mining Development Corporation of Zambia (qq.v.). Other parastatal bodies include the Zambia Youth Service (q.v.), the National Agricultural Marketing Board, the Bank of Zambia, Zambia Railways, and Zambia Airways (qq.v.). As of the early 1970s there were already about 70 state-owned companies and statutory bodies in Zambia's parastatal sector. (*See* MWANA-KATWE, JOHN.) Following the impetus of the structural adjustment program (q.v.) in the 1990s, the vast majority of these were either sold or disbanded by the Zambia Privatisation Agency (q.v.).

PARIS MISSIONARY SOCIETY (PARIS EVANGELICAL MISSION SOCIETY; SOCIÉTÉ DES MISSIONS ÉVANGÉLIQUES). A French Protestant (Huguenot) missionary society, it began its work in southern Africa in 1835 among the Sotho (q.v.), who were ready converts. Its pioneer missionary to Zambia was François Coillard (q.v.), who first attempted to cross the Zambezi (q.v.) in July 1878. He got as far as Sesheke (q.v.), where he waited for a response from the Lozi king Lubosi (qq.v.). The favorable reply suggested that Coillard return after the capital, Lealui (q.v.), was completed. The Reverend Coillard returned to Europe for funds and supplies for a Barotseland (q.v.) mission station. He returned to the Zambezi in 1884 and contacted the Lozi leaders. The sudden outbreak of a war among the Lozi prevented Coillard's party from arriving until early 1885, when he was warmly welcomed to Lealui. A mission site was given to him 32 kilometers (20 miles) away, at Sefula. In 1887 the PMS missionaries set up a school, the first of a number of schools, mission stations, and dispensaries that they instituted throughout North-Western Rhodesia (q.v.). The Coillards were joined by Adolphe and Louis Jalla (q.v.) and their wives, among other noted PMS missionaries. Many of them played important parts in Lozi history, both through their schools and as trusted advisors to Lozi kings, especially Lewanika (q.v.).

PARLIAMENT. The Parliament of Zambia consists of the unicameral National Assembly and the president. The assembly must meet at least once a year and normally is elected every five years, unless it is dissolved earlier. It has the power of legislation and the sole power to amend the constitution. The prime minister must be a member of Parliament; he is appointed by the president and serves as his spokesman. Under the Second Republic constitution, there were 136 members: 125 were elected, 10 were chosen by the president, and a speaker was elected by the members. Under the 1964 (independence) constitution, the president was also identified as part of Parliament. Under the 1991 constitution, Parliament has 150 elected members, plus up to eight members nominated by the president. When the president joins the Parliament, the entire body becomes the National Assembly.

PARTNERSHIP. The term was used in the 1950s, before and during the existence of the Central African Federation (q.v.), to indicate that the interests of neither the Africans nor the Europeans in Central Africa (q.v.) should be subordinate to the other and that each group should recognize the rights of the other to a permanent home there. This was, at least, the definition given to it by the colonial secretary, James Griffiths (q.v.), at the second Victoria Falls Conference in 1951 (q.v.). The word was first used in the context of Central African race relations in 1935 by Sir Stewart Gore-Browne (q.v.). It was also used in 1948 by the Northern Rhodesia (q.v.) secretary for native affairs, Rowland S. Hudson (q.v.), before the African Representative Council (q.v.). Hudson encouraged "genuine partnership" between the races; "whole-hearted cooperation," he said, would be in the best interests of everyone. Nevertheless, it was the Griffiths definition that was significant, because it indicated a British move away from the doctrine of paramountcy (q.v.) put forth in 1930.

Africans realized that Europeans saw themselves as senior partners, who would have to tutor their junior partners for a long time before granting them equality. Godfrey Huggins (q.v.) noted that such a partnership was like that between a man and his horse: they work together but do not eat or sleep together. Nevertheless, the British and the government of Northern Rhodesia worked from 1951 to 1953 to find a definition of partnership that the Africans would find acceptable— presumably a justification for the impending Central African Federation, which the British saw as an experiment in racial partnership. Some "moderate" Africans accepted federation (q.v.) as being a solution to problems of racial disharmony. Kenneth Kaunda (q.v.), however, doubted the true resolve of the Europeans and saw partnership as a "partnership of the slave and the free." The fact that African education was grossly neglected, compared to that for Europeans, was proof of this. By the early 1960s, few European politicians still pretended to favor partnership, especially as federation was obviously doomed by the success of African nationalism in both Nyasaland (q.v.) and Northern Rhodesia.

PASS. More commonly known as the *chitupa* (q.v.), this was the identification certificate that Africans in Northern Rhodesia (q.v.) were required to carry as a result of a 1927 ordinance. It was designed to place limits on Africans' freedom of movement. Africans were required to show the pass to authorities upon request; a special pass was needed to move at night outside your residential area and to travel. European authorities saw it as a way to maintain order; Africans protested it as a restriction on human rights.

PASSFIELD, LORD (SIDNEY WEBB). English social reformer and economic historian, he served as secretary of state for the colonies (1929–31) and dominions (1929–30) as part of a Labour Party cabinet. As colonial secretary in 1930, he issued a white paper titled "Memorandum on Native Policy in East Africa," the so-called Passfield Memorandum. In this controversial document he extended the doctrine of paramountcy (q.v.) to Northern Rhodesia and Nyasaland (qq.v.). The policy, which stated that African interests must be considered paramount over those of immigrant peoples, was proclaimed by the Duke of Devonshire in 1923 for East Africa. Settlers in Northern Rhodesia reacted bitterly to this policy and from then on fought for amalgamation (q.v.) with Southern Rhodesia (q.v.). Previously, Europeans in Northern Rhodesia had preferred a status separate from their southern neighbor. During his time in office, Passfield also encouraged more education for Africans as a step toward Africanization in employment.

PASSIVE RESISTANCE CAMPAIGN. A special project of the United National Independence Party (q.v.) from June until November 1961, the campaign was led by Kenneth Kaunda (q.v.), who was inspired by Mahatma Gandhi. The campaign protested British changes in the Macleod Constitution (q.v.) as a result of right-wing pressures. Kaunda pledged nonviolence during the campaign, but there were a number of disturbances and attacks from July through October. (*See* CHA-CHA-CHA CAMPAIGN.)

PATEL, DIPAK K. A. Born in Lusaka (q.v.)in July 1953, he entered business after completing his O-level studies in secondary school. From 1971–90 he served as chairman and managing director of Palatine Holdings, a firm engaged in textile manufacturing, construction, tourism, and property development. In 1990 he joined the national executive committee of the new Movement for Multiparty Democracy (q.v.) and became the party's campaign manager for the 1991 elections. From November 1991 to July 1992 he served as deputy minister in the ministry of commerce and industry, and minister in several ministries: information and broadcasting services, August 1992 to April 1993; sports, youth, and child development, May 1993 to June 1994; and commerce, trade, and industry, 1994 until 1996. He resigned from the cabinet and the MMD national executive in February 1996 in a dispute over the method used to ratify the new constitution. Subsequently, he was investigated for illegal business dealings.

PEOPLE'S DEMOCRATIC CONGRESS (PEOPLE'S DEMO-CRATIC PARTY). The party was formed in August 1963 by Job Michello (q.v.) when, in anticipation of the 1964 pre-independence election, he split with Harry Nkumbula's (q.v.) African National Congress (q.v.). The party had a conservative approach to politics and received encouragement and support from conservatives like Roy Welensky and the Congo's Moise Tshombe (qq.v.). One of the main battles with the ANC during the remainder of 1963 was over the question of which faction would receive the large financial support reportedly offered by Tshombe. While some money surfaced, evidently neither group ever got the rumored £100,000. The main reason for the PDC-ANC split was that Michello and his followers were unhappy over Nkumbula's leadership. Both groups pushed the British to hold the election in May 1965 instead of January 1964, supposedly to allow adequate time for voter registration. In fact, both were struggling desperately for financial and voter support and to put together slates. Attempts at merging the groups failed until late December, just before nomination day for the candidates. Even with later adjustments, there were four constituencies where ANC and PDC candidates were both entered against the United National Independence Party (q.v.). After the merger (a last resort for the floundering factions), the ANC identity survived and the PDC folded.

PEREIRA, GONÇALO CAETANO. He was the head of a family of Goan adventurers who led an expedition from Portuguese East Africa into northeastern Zambia in 1796. The expedition was instigated in 1793, when a group of Bisa ivory (qq.v.) traders visited Pereira in Tete (q.v.) with a message from the Lunda leader, Kazembe (qq.v.). Pereira, his son, Manuel, and some Bisa traveled to Kazembe in 1796. They returned to Tete in 1798 with two ambassadors from Kazembe, announcing that the Lunda wanted to organize ivory trade with the Portuguese at Tete and had even invited them to set up a trading post near his territory. Francisco de Laçerda (q.v.) had different plans: he brought both Pereiras with him as guides during his attempt to travel through Kazembe's country. The mission ended in failure, and only the Pereiras' knowledge of the country brought many of the travelers safely back to Tete. The Pereira family continued to dominate trade in the area well into the middle of the 19th century.

PERPETUAL KINSHIP. An extension of the common Lunda-Bemba (qq.v.) practice of positional succession (q.v.), it uses the ideology of kinship to link titled positions, regardless of actual kinship ties between the two individuals occupying those titles. For example, neighboring chiefs A and B of the same matrilineal people may be actual brothers, children of the same mother and father. If, however, the original chief of A was the mother's brother of the original chief of B and had given his sister's son his chiefship, the chief of A will always be the "mother's brother" (senior) to the chief of B, who will always be A's "sister's son." Thus, the ideology of kinship structures a whole network of leadership positions, regardless of their occupants' actual blood ties.

Similarly, kinship or marriage terms are sometimes used to express the relationship between whole peoples. The people that once conquered or provided protection to another typically assume the position of "husband" to the "wifely" people, who were either conquered or requested protection.

PETAUKE. The southernmost of Eastern Province's (q.v.) six districts, it shares a border of over 160 kilometers (100 miles) with Mozambique (q.v.). The district had a population of 125,000 in 1969 and 251,000 in 1990. The town of Petauke is about 40 kilometers (25 miles) north of the Mozambique border and about 137 kilometers (85 miles) southwest of Chipata (q.v.), along the Great East Road (q.v.).

PICHEN, NASHIL. *See* KAZEMBE, NASHIL PICHEN.

PIGEONHOLES. *See* HATCH SYSTEM.

PIM, SIR ALAN. He was Britain's foremost expert on colonial finance and senior author, with S. Milligan, of the 1938 *Report of the Commission Appointed to Enquire into the Financial and Economic Position of Northern Rhodesia*. It is still recognized as the best general study of Zambia's economic history between the First and Second World Wars. In the early 1930s, Pim made similar studies of Basutoland, Swaziland, and Bechuanaland. Much of the Pim-Milligan Commission's investigation took place in 1937. Though it was appointed to see how the government might reduce spending in Northern Rhodesia (q.v.), the report, instead, recommended an increase, noting the lack of many social services. Increased investment, the report said, was needed in health services, roads, urban housing, schools, agricultural development, and secondary industries. The Second World War soon began, however, and few results were seen for quite a while. Pim also specifically noted that the mineral royalties still being accrued by the British South Africa Company (q.v.), instead of by the government, would have been sufficient for most of the needed expansion. The commission also made recommendations on modernizing the traditional government of Barotseland (q.v.). Some of the savings could assist in financing development in the region.

PINTO, FRANCISCO JOÃO. He was the chaplain for Francisco de Lacerda's (q.v.) 1798 expedition that left Tete (q.v.) in search of an overland route to the Atlantic. They reached Kazembe's (q.v.) capital on the Luapula River (q.v.), but Lacerda died before seeing him. Father Pinto took command and was finally granted an audience. No trade agreements (or even passage rights) were made, however, and after internal quarrels among the Portuguese, Father Pinto and the remnants of the group turned back in July 1799. Their return to Tete was beset with confrontations with the Africans, especially the Bisa (q.v.), and his diary records the value of their guide, Gonçalo Pereira (q.v.).

PINTO, SERPA. A Portuguese army officer who made a transcontinental trip from Angola to Mozambique (qq.v.) in the 1880s to further Portugal's territorial claims, Pinto traveled through Barotseland (q.v.), where he met the young king Lewanika (then Lubosi) (qq.v.). Pinto would have arranged the sale of arms and ammunition that Lewanika wanted, but the deal fell through when the Lozi *ngambela* and *kuta* (qq.v.) objected and forced Lewanika to expel Pinto. Later, in 1889, Pinto was a leader of Portuguese forces in Nyasaland (q.v.), when both the British and Portuguese tried to solidify their East African territorial claims.

PLATEAU TONGA. One branch of the larger grouping called Tonga (q.v.), this group of people lives in southern Zambia on the Batoka Plateau, north of Lake Kariba (qq.v.). The Tonga are linguistically (and presumably historically) related to some of their neighbors, notably the Ila, Lenje, Toka, Sala, Soli, and Leya (qq.v.). These matrilineal and patrilocal people seem to have been among the earliest of the present inhabitants of Zambia and to have arrived from the south some 500 years ago. It is a society without chiefs or much oral history. Rainmakers at the rain shrines (q.v.) do have some ritual importance and thus some political influence; and some of them were appointed government chiefs when the British tried to impose indirect rule (q.v.). The system of age mates (*basimusela*) provided some group unity, as it does in other cattle-raising societies. The Plateau Tonga adopted plow farming around the turn of the century from the Jesuit missions, growing primarily maize (q.v.) and groundnuts. They were also active in trade, making iron tools and weapons for trade with other Africans. As the 19th century progressed, the Plateau Tonga were occasionally hit by cattle raids. The Lozi and Kololo (qq.v.) were their chief attackers, but the Ndebele (q.v.) also raided them. The Plateau Tonga have also been active in modern politics. They and Southern Province (q.v.) provided consistent electoral support to Harry Nkumbula (from Ila, country) and his African National Congress (qq.v.). As early as 1937, a group of Tonga chiefs, farmers, and teachers formed the Northern Rhodesia African National Congress (q.v.) to protest local problems, but it soon folded as a result of government pressure.

PLYMOUTH BRETHREN. This British community of dissenting Christians disagreed with numerous practices of the Anglican Church, and felt that the sacraments could be performed by laymen. They also actively preached the Bible. One of their early meetings was in Plymouth, England, in 1830. They soon decided to spread the Gospel through missionary activity in foreign lands. Their first African missionary was Frederick S. Arnot (q.v.), who spent 18 months among the Lozi (q.v.) (1882–84) before moving on to Angola and Katanga (qq.v.), where he and his colleagues documented the climax and collapse of Msiri's Yeke empire (qq.v.). Following the Yeke collapse in 1891, the Plymouth Brethren relocated their work to the Luapula River and the western shores of Lake Mweru (qq.v.), from which base they proselytized again in Northern Rhodesia (q.v.) in the 1890s. One of the missionaries, Dan Crawford, interceded between the Lunda leader Kazembe (qq.v.) and the British to prevent bloodshed. At the same time, some of the brethren in Angola began to work in North-Western Rhodesia at Kaleñe Hill.

POLISH WAR REFUGEES. The impetus for the 1942–43 arrival of some 4,000 Polish war refugees in Northern Rhodesia (q.v.) seems to date to 1939, when the Legislative Council (q.v.), at London's request, discussed and rejected Governor Hubert Young's (q.v.) proposal to resettle Jewish refugees from Nazi Germany in northwestern Northern Rhodesia. Following Italy's defeat in Somalia and the liberation of Ethiopia, Lieutenant-Colonel Stewart Gore-Browne (q.v.) replaced Major Hugh McKee as director of war evacuees and refugees and was told to prepare to receive Italian internees from Eritrea in early 1942. Some 300 Polish refugees, mostly middle-class urbanites, came instead, and taxed Gore-Brown's patience with their complaints about the "primitive" conditions of the hotels and boardinghouses in Fort Jameson (q.v.) and along the southern line of rail (q.v.). By late 1943, 3,000 more Poles, including rural peasants, were brought to special camps in Abercorn, Lusaka (qq.v.), and Bwana Mkubwa. The rioters, gangsters, and attempted murderers among this lot were sent to Southern Rhodesia (q.v.) and Kenya. While some of the Polish women became nannies and domestic servants in European households, it was commonly thought that the very sight of such women doing manual labor was detrimental to European racial prestige—and that of European women in particular. Though the various Roman Catholic (q.v.) religious orders tried to serve as intermediaries, the low rank accorded these refugees was best expressed when the Lusaka Women's Institute, led by a Methodist minister's wife, accused the Polish women of soliciting the officers and enlisted men in neighboring battalions. Gore-Brown was delighted when he was relieved of these administrative duties in 1944. The last of the camps closed in 1948. Most of these refugees went to Britain; only a few stayed in Northern Rhodesia.

POLL TAX. This was an early 1930s supplement to the hut tax (q.v.). Whereas the hut tax was levied upon each hut a man claimed, thus penalizing polygynists and those caring for elderly relatives, the poll tax was levied upon all able-bodied males of 18 years or more. As part of the tax reforms suggested by Sir Stewart Gore-Brown's (q.v.) committee, the hut tax was dropped in the late 1940s, making the poll tax the main tax upon Africans.

POMBEIROS. The Portuguese name for the mestizo, Luso-African traders, who played an important role as middlemen between the Portuguese and Africans, carrying products and cultural communication in both directions. The word means "traveling agents" (Portuguese *pombo* means "road"). In Zambian history, Amaro José and P. J. Baptista (qq.v.) are often collectively called "the pombeiros."

PONDE. An important Bemba (q.v.) leader for 40 years, he ultimately held the post of Chitimukulu (q.v.) from 1916 until his death in 1923. As the sister's son (matrilineal successor) of both Chitapankwa and Mwamba II (qq.v.) (who was also Ponde's father-in-law), Ponde was given authority over the Lungu of Tafuna (qq.v.) in about 1880. This was the recently conquered country in the distant northwest corner of Bemba-controlled territory, between Isoka (q.v.) and the Luombe River. It was generally in Mwamba II's sphere of influence. Ponde became a noted military leader, especially for laying long siege to a place he was trying to conquer. In the 1890s he, like many other Bemba leaders, was busily engaged in trading ivory (q.v.) and slaves to Arab (q.v.) and east coast traders for firearms and cloth. It was undoubtedly some of Ponde's raids that were described in the early London Missionary Society (q.v.) reports of the fierce Bemba. Yet some of Ponde's villages were themselves attacked in 1893 by Sampa (q.v.) when LMS missionaries arrived in the area.

In December 1895, Ponde's forces killed Chitimbwa IV, captured his village, and carted off the spoils. It is said that Ponde was responsible for the Bemba ultimately becoming subject to the British. When Mwamba III (q.v.) died in 1898 (*see* DUPONT, JOSEPH), Ponde was determined to succeed to that title. He informed some of the representatives of the British South Africa Company (q.v.) of that fact. Two of them, Charles McKinnon and Robert Young (qq.v.), opposed Ponde's claim, partly because they feared his strong personality and militancy. He had challenged and rebuffed a number of European officials. In late 1898, a force led by McKinnon peacefully moved Ponde from Mwamba's village. But by March 1899, Ponde, determined to win, built a fortified village on a rocky hill near Kasama (q.v.). Again the British approached, and after several brief battles, they stormed and captured his village. Ponde and some followers escaped, but he surrendered a month later. He became active again about five years later, however, when he took over the southern part of Lubemba from the aged Makumba (q.v.). He became Chitimukulu in 1916 and served until his death, seven years later.

PORTUGAL. As a colonial power with territories adjacent to Zambia in both the west (Angola, q.v.) and the east (Mozambique, q.v.), Portugal's involvement with Zambian territory goes back several centuries and continued until its two territories became independent in 1975. Although two Portuguese explorers passed through the southeastern corner of Zambia as early as 1564, the real beginning of exploration came over 200 years later, when men like Lacerda, Baptista, José, Monteiro, Gamitto, Silva Pôrto, and Pinto (qq.v.) traversed Zambian land for a variety of political, economic, and adventurous reasons from 1798 to 1878. During the scramble for Africa following the Berlin Conference of 1884–85, Portugal made a determined effort to secure rights to an entire band of territory from Angola on the Atlantic Ocean to Mozambique on the Indian Ocean. This came into direct conflict with the British "Cape to Cairo" dream. Ultimately, Portugal lost in its bid for Zambian territory. As late as 1905 a decision in international arbitration by King Victor Emmanuel of Italy (q.v.) was needed to settle the boundary dispute between Portugal and Britain over the Angola-Barotseland border. Few problems arose with Portugal then until Zambian independence in 1964. Many of the Angolan and Mozambican nationalist forces had offices or even bases in Zambia. Despite the fact that ports in Portuguese Africa were crucial to Zambia's copper (q.v.) exports (not to mention a variety of imports, such as petroleum), the Zambian government canceled all trade agreements with Portugal in December 1964.

POSHO (POSO). This is the *ki*Swahili term for "rations" or, more commonly, "food allowance"; the *ci*Bemba (q.v.) term is *(li)-poso*. From the early colonial period on, Europeans were expected to provide for the feeding of their African employees in addition to paying an established fee or monthly salary. In the early 20th century, *posho* consisted of a weekly yard of calico and, sometimes, salt, which African laborers could then exchange for food in neighboring villages. With the monetization of the Northern Rhodesian economy, *posho* was converted to a cash payment. *Posho* still persists, even though it was legally abolished soon after independence.

POSITIONAL SUCCESSION. A practice common among the Lunda (q.v.) but also to some extent among the Bemba (q.v.). A successor to a traditional post receives not only the title, authority, rights, and duties of his predecessor but also takes on all of his social and political relationships to the point where he virtually "becomes" the person he succeeded. An extension of this is the concept of perpetual kinship (q.v.).

POST. An independent newspaper that went into circulation in Lusaka (q.v.) and on the Copperbelt (q.v.) as the *Weekly Post* on July 26, 1991, it was owned by a consortium of 20 business people. The independent and critical editorial line of the paper earned it the enmity of the Movement for Multiparty Democracy (q.v.) government. In mid-1992, acting editor Jowie Mwiinga was summoned to police headquarters, and MMD youth threatened to attack the *Post's* offices after it published an article criticizing President Chiluba (q.v.) for accepting a gift of an automobile from a South African businessman. In April 1994 the managing director, Fred M'membe (q.v.), and a reporter, Bright Mwape, were arrested and charged with defaming the president in an article titled "Chiluba Is a Twit," which was derived from a statement made by princess Nakatindi Wina.

By this point the *Post* was facing more than three dozen libel suits, including one by the president himself. On December 7, 1994, the government raided the offices of the *Post* (and the *Times of Zambia*, q.v.) looking for seditious materials. The papers had printed stories alledging that President Chiluba had had an extramarital affair. The president was out of the country at the time, however, and several ranking MMD members attempted to distance the party from the raid, sensing a political blunder by the police. On June 2, 1995, the government-owned printing firm, Printpak, suspended printing of the *Post* due to an outstanding debt amounting to about U.S.$1,800, though the *Post* disputed the debt.

The government's campaign against the *Post* intensified in early 1996 in two separate incidents. First, articles and columns by Fred M'membe, Bright Mwape, and Lucy Sichone (q.v.) criticized the vice president for a speech he made in Parliament (q.v.) attacking a Supreme Court decision protecting civil liberties. The three were charged with contempt of Parliament under a colonial law that prohibits nonmembers from criticizing comments made in Parliament. After hiding for 10 days, M'membe and Mwape surrendered to parliamentary authorities, but they refused to apologize for their comments. Second, the February 5 issue of the *Post* published the government's plans to hold a referendum on the controversial draft constitution in March. M'membe, Mwape, and another editor were arrested the following day and charged with possessing state secrets. The February 5 edition was also declared a banned publication and removed from circulation. Daily and archival issues of the *Post* are available over the Internet.

PRAIN, SIR RONALD. One of the most important financiers and industrialists in Zambia's history, he was born in Chile in 1907 and educated in England. In 1936 he became director of the Anglo-Metal Company; three years later he became director of Rhodesian Selection Trust, Ltd. (q.v.), and in 1943 became managing director of Roan Antelope Mine and Mufulira Mine (qq.v.). By 1950 he was, in addition to many other important directorships, chairman of all three copper (q.v.) organizations. An economic and political realist, he consistently pushed for the reform of racist economic patterns. In 1953 he announced that the Rhodesian Selection Trust would break the industrial colour bar (q.v.) before Africans broke it themselves. He thus opened up more mining jobs to Africans, despite complaints of European workers and unions. In the 1950s, Prain invested large amounts of money in development plans in Northern and Luapula Provinces (qq.v.). He has also helped finance programs to improve African education. In the early 1960s he stressed the importance of Africans and Europeans learning to work together, utilizing each other's skills in a balance profitable to all. Nevertheless, his cautious, gradualist approach did not win favor with many African nationalists.

PREFERENTIAL TRADE AREA. This trade bloc was founded at an international conference held in Lusaka (q.v.) in December 1981. Nine nations—the Comoro Islands, Djibouti, Ethiopia, Kenya, Malawi, Mauritius, Somalia, Uganda, and Zambia—signed the Preferential Trade Treaty. These nine were joined by Lesotho and Swaziland in March 1982 and by Zimbabwe and Burundi in June and December, respectively. By the time the PTA was officially inaugurated in July 1984, Rwanda had joined and the signatories had agreed to deep tariff reductions on a broad range of goods. Fulfillment of the obligations lagged, however: by the end of 1985, Zambia was the only member to have met all its obligations. Turnout at the December 1985 summit was disappointing, as only three heads of state joined President Kaunda (q.v.) there. The failure of most member states to meet their obligations meant that the PTA had a minimal impact upon trade in its first 18 months. Mauritius withdrew from the PTA in mid-1986.

PRESBYTERIAN CHURCH. The main Presbyterian missionaries to enter Zambia came as the Free Church of Scotland (q.v.). One of their early converts and evangelists was David Kaunda (q.v.), father of Zambia's first president. In 1924 the church was renamed the Church of Central Africa, Presbyterian (q.v.), a predecessor of the United Church of Zambia (q.v.).

PRESERVATION OF PUBLIC SECURITY ORDINANCE. A law promulgated in 1959 by the government, which feared that the nationalist political groups might instigate disruptions, it gave the governor extensive emergency powers. He had power, for example, to arrest and detain people without trial. The ordinance was bitterly opposed by many. It was first used on May 11, 1960, following the attack on Lillian Burton (q.v.). The governor banned the United National Independence Party (q.v.) in Western (now Copperbelt) Province (qq.v.) and declared its branches unlawful. He also restricted five UNIP leaders, including Kenneth Kaunda, Simon Kapwepwe, and M. K. Sipalo (qq.v.), from entering the province. As a result of further disturbances in August 1961, several of the ordinance's regulations were also applied to Luapula and Northern Provinces (qq.v.). Also, in both provinces branches of UNIP were declared unlawful under the Societies Ordinance (q.v.).

PRIMITIVE METHODIST MISSIONARY SOCIETY. A group at odds with the orthodox branch of Wesleyanism, it sent a few missionaries to southern Africa in the late 1880s. It was led by the Reverend Arthur Baldwin (q.v.). The missionaries were prevented from entering Bulozi by the Lozi (qq.v.) until 1891, when the Reverend François Coillard (q.v.) interceded for them. They spent two years in Bulozi before Lewanika (q.v.) allowed them to move into the territory of the Nanzela and the Ila (qq.v.), part of Lewanika's attempt to assure the Ila that he would be a peaceful overlord. The Primitive Methodists' main station was at Nkala, in the Kafue Hook (q.v.), a site often visited by the Northern Copper Company's (q.v.) European prospectors and miners.

PROTECTORATE. While Great Britain preferred to describe Northern Rhodesia (q.v.) as a protectorate, implying a request for protection and assistance from the indigenous people, in fact it was treated more like a conquered colony. Only the Lozi (q.v.) made any kind of overtures to England that could be construed as requests for protection, and the Lozi certainly did not get what they requested.

PROVINCIAL COMMISSIONER. Under the British system of indirect rule (q.v.), a provincial commissioner served as the administrative supervisor for a province. Responsible to them were the district commissioners (q.v.), who were superior to the local chiefs, for whom they were also the main source of administrative communication. The provincial commissioners were responsible to the governor of Northern Rhodesia (q.v.) and also served as appeals judges for the District Courts.

PROVINCIAL COUNCILS. Instituted by action of the Legislative Council (q.v.) and the Northern Rhodesia (q.v.) government in 1943, the Regional Councils (renamed Provincial Councils in 1945) were designed by the government to serve as forums for African opinions and grievances. They were purely advisory, without administrative or statutory functions. In effect, they were an extension of the Urban Advisory Councils (q.v.). They were to give Africans a sense of participation, no matter how illusory, in their government, and thereby stave off the growth of nationalist organizations. Some better-educated Africans did indeed try to work through the councils for awhile, until, frustrated by their ineffectiveness, they became active in the independence movement. When the Provincial (Regional) Councils were first formed, they heavily represented traditional leaders and rural interests (unless a major urban area happened to be in the region). If there was no urban area to send representatives, local African associations could choose delegates, but the majority on each of these councils were rural and traditional. Each province had at least one such council and as many as three for larger provinces. Barotseland (q.v.) had none, however, as the government of Northern Rhodesia felt that the Lozi *kuta* (qq.v.) could serve the same purpose. The provincial commissioner usually presided at the meetings of the Provincial Councils. When the territorywide African Representative Council (q.v.) was formed in 1946, its delegates were selected from each of the Provincial Councils as well as from the Urban Advisory Councils.

PUBLICATIONS BUREAU. *See* NORTHERN RHODESIA AND NYASALAND JOINT PUBLICATIONS BUREAU.

PUTA, ROBINSON. This nationalist political figure of the 1950s was also active in the trade union movement. Contrary to Lawrence Katilungu (q.v.), he felt that the unions should work closely with the African National Congress (q.v.) for mutual benefit. At one point in the mid-1950s, he was both the vice president of the African Trade Union Congress and deputy president of the ANC. He lost both positions in 1956. He later became the head of the Zambia Railways (q.v.) board. In the early 1970s, he was active in the United Progressive Party (q.v.), which, however, was quickly banned.

Q

QUELIMANE. This port city is on the Indian Ocean in Mozambique (q.v.), north of the mouth of the Zambezi River (q.v.). It was not unusual for ivory (q.v.) traders from the area of Zambia, especially the Bisa (q.v.), to bring their ivory here.

R

RAILWAY AFRICAN WORKERS TRADE UNION. Formed in the early 1950s, it was long one of the two strongest unions in Northern Rhodesia (q.v.). Its president in its formative years was Dixon Konkola (q.v.).

RAIN SHRINE. This ritual institution is common to the Plateau and Valley Tonga (qq.v.) of Southern Province (q.v.) and their neighbors. Their small villages had few normal interconnections except for a rain shrine that often served a half dozen or more villages. These shrines, sometimes at the graves of important men or at sites established by respected rainmakers (*see* LWIINDI), are still important in this region of relatively low and geographically variable rainfall. By the early 20th century, rain shrine priests acquired a number of political functions, such as settling disputes and arranging defensive military alliances. The British, looking for chiefs among these chiefless peoples, were naturally drawn to the rain shrine priests. Monze (q.v.) actually courted the British South Africa Company (q.v.) by collecting Tonga taxes on his own initiative. By doing so, however, he offended the Lozi king, Lewanika (qq.v.), and embarrassed the BSAC.

RAWLINS COMMISSION. The commission was appointed by the Northern Rhodesia (q.v.) government in 1957 to consider possible reforms in the Barotse native government. Its conservative members, however, recommended few substantive changes. The commission satisfied none of Mwanawina's (q.v.) opponents, some of whom joined the United National Independence Party (q.v.) in despair. The commission seemed designed to justify the status quo.

REFORMED TRADE UNION CONGRESS. In 1960, leaders of the Trade Union Congress (q.v.) split over the political activities of its president, Lawrence Katilungu (q.v.), who was then both acting president of the African National Congress (q.v.) and a member of the Monckton Commission (q.v.). The dissenters—including Jonathan Chivunga, Albert Kalyati (qq.v.), and Mathew Mwendapole—formed the RTUC, largely composed of the smaller unions that Katilungu had dismissed during the controversy. While it had little money and a small number of workers enrolled, it included some active members of the United National Independence Party (q.v.), some with connections in international unionism. Nevertheless, it was independent of UNIP and represented an alternative to Katilingu's politicized TUC. Katilungu lost an important union post in December 1960, and the TUC and RTUC reunited in February 1961 as the United Trade Union Congress (q.v.). Chivunga became its president.

REGIONAL COUNCILS. This is an early name for the Provincial Councils (q.v.).

RENNIE, SIR GILBERT. He was governor of Northern Rhodesia (q.v.) from 1948 to 1954, when he was appointed the Central African Federation's (q.v.) first high commissioner in London. He had been active in the colonial government for decades. In 1930, for example, he was provincial commissioner in Barotseland (q.v.). As governor, he was a strong supporter of racial partnership, assuring the Africans that the British government retained ultimate responsibility for them. Rennie stated that partnership (q.v.) could work when based on honest intention and goodwill. However, he supported such proponents of federation (q.v.) as Sir Godfrey Huggins and Sir Roy Welensky (qq.v.), and described Kenneth Kaunda (q.v.) as an agitator. As governor, he also opposed the promotion of Africans in the mines to more skilled positions. As federation approached, Rennie visited Barotseland several times to persuade the king and his *kuta* (q.v.) that the federation was not only desirable but would even enhance the status of the kingdom.

REPUBLIC OF ZAMBIA. This became the official name of Northern Rhodesia (q.v.) when it became independent on October 24, 1964. The so-called Second Republic began in 1973, when Zambia became "a one-party participatory democracy." The Third Republic began in 1991, when President Frederick Chiluba (q.v.) and the Movement for Multiparty Democracy (q.v.) party took over the government from Kenneth Kaunda (q.v.) and his United National Independence Party (q.v.).

RESERVES COMMISSIONS. Convinced that Northern Rhodesia (q.v.) should be developed as "white man's country" and that African villagers needed to be protectively isolated from European encroachment and demoralizing influences, Governor Herbert Stanley (q.v.) appointed the 1924, 1926, and 1927 Reserves Commissions to survey all lands in which the mines and white settlers had an interest. These were, respectively, the Fort Jameson (q.v.) area, the line of rail (q.v.), and the Abercorn (q.v.) area. Africans were "chased" onto the Native Reserves (q.v.), which were established between 1928 and 1930, while the newly designated Crown Lands (q.v.) they had vacated were made available for European purchase. Thus, the competing land interests of Africans and Europeans were resolved in the latter's favor. In general, the migrant labor system established by these remote and overcrowded labor reserves generated a system of rural poverty, stagnation, and underdevelopment.

RHODES, CECIL JOHN. A South African financial and political entrepreneur, his ambitions and actions opened up the land north of the Limpopo River to the British South Africa Company (q.v.). Southern, North-Eastern, and North-Western Rhodesia (qq.v.) were named for him. Born in England on July 5, 1853, he left school at the age of 16 to go to South Africa. When diamonds were discovered near Kimberley in the early 1870s, Rhodes' shrewd and timely dealings made him a fortune of some half million pounds a year. He made several trips back to England in the 1870s, earning an Oxford degree in the process. Perhaps the period from 1888 to 1891 was his busiest. In 1888 he sent his partner, Charles D. Rudd, to make a deal with Lobengula (q.v.), the powerful Ndebele (q.v.) leader. The Rudd Concession, although of questionable validity, gave Rhodes rights in much of the territory between the Limpopo and Zambezi Rivers (q.v.). He then persuaded the British to grant a charter to the BSAC in 1889, which only fueled Rhodes' fantasy of engineering a "Cape-to-Cairo" chain of British colonies. Rhodes hired agents like Sir Harry Johnston and Alfred Sharpe (qq.v.) to pursue treaty agreements with Africans in modern Malawi (q.v.) and eastern Zambia. He also had Frank Lochner (q.v.), one of his agents, negotiate and sign a treaty and concession with Lozi king Lewanika (qq.v.) in 1890. Ultimately it gave the BSAC control of land far beyond that under Lozi control. Rhodes became South Africa's prime minister in 1890, a post he held until 1897, when he resigned. He died in Cape Province, South Africa, on March 26, 1902.

RHODESIA. The name was introduced in 1895, in tribute to Cecil J. Rhodes (q.v.), for the area under British South Africa Company (q.v.) control. The British government approved its use in 1897. During the period of the Central African Federation (q.v.), the name referred to both Northern and Southern Rhodesia (qq.v.), together. After Northern Rhodesia quit the federation and became Zambia, Southern Rhodesia adopted the name for itself, dropping the "Southern" prefix. Following Rhodesia's unilateral declaration of independence (q.v.) in 1965, Rhodesia and Zambia broke many of their old commercial and communication links, even though many nationalists from Rhodesia (Zimbabwe) had offices and bases in Zambia.

RHODESIA ANGLO-AMERICAN CORPORATION, LTD. The Rhodesian branch of the Anglo-American Corporation of South Africa, Ltd. (q.v.), it was set up in 1928. By 1930 it was running major copper (q.v.) mines at Nkana and Nchanga (qq.v.) as well as the smaller and older Bwana Mkubwa Mine (q.v.). The Rhokana Mine soon followed, and copper production at its Bancroft (Chililabombwe, q.v.) Mine began in 1957. After independence in 1964, the corporation changed its name to Anglo-American Corporation of Zambia, Ltd., and then to Nchanga Consolidated Copper Mines, Ltd. (q.v.). In 1980, Nchanga and Roan Consolidated Copper Mines were joined to form Zambia Consolidated Copper Mines (q.v.).

RHODESIA COPPER COMPANY. A consolidated grouping of mining companies, it was owned by Sir Edmund Davis (q.v.).

RHODESIA REFORM PARTY. A minor party during the last couple of years of the Central African Federation (q.v.), it had a conservative orientation. It seems to have been started by John Gaunt (q.v.) in October 1960 as an offshoot of his earlier Northern Rhodesia Association. It gained greater respectability in January and February 1962, when Ian Smith (q.v.) and other right-wing dissidents from the United Federal Party (q.v.) joined with Gaunt. It claimed a middle ground between the UFP and the Dominion Party (q.v.). It opposed forced integration and the Build a Nation campaign (q.v.). By mid-March 1962, however, Winston Field (q.v.) was putting together his Rhodesian Front (q.v.), and the Rhodesia Reform Party dissipated when most of its members joined Smith and Field.

RHODESIAN FRONT. Formed in March 1962 as a merger of the Federal Dominion Party (q.v.) and several other small groups, this was the Southern Rhodesian political party led by Winston Field and Ian Smith (qq.v.) that defeated the United Federal Party (q.v.) in the December 1962 elections. Under Ian Smith, it continued to dominate the political scene in Rhodesia (Zimbabwe) into the late 1970s.

RHODESIAN MAN. *See* KABWE MAN.

RHODESIAN NATIVE LABOUR BUREAU. Apparently inspired by a suggestion by prospector Frank J. Smitheman (q.v.), the bureau was formed in Salisbury (q.v.) in August 1903 to remedy the lack of Southern Rhodesian Africans for mine and farm labor. The bureau sought its workers north of the Zambezi (q.v.), where hut tax (q.v.) collections had just begun to encourage such work. The bureau seems to have inspired the term *chibalo* (q.v.), meaning forced labor. Its agents became infamous for their ruthless recruitment tactics, including hostage taking. Its recruits suffered overcrowding, scurvy, dysentery, pneumonia, and a high mortality rate. In 1907–08, North-Western and North-Eastern Rhodesia temporarily forbade the bureau to supply recruits to certain southern mines. By 1912, news of dead recruits and a history of aggressive tax collections provoked local rebellions and the suspension of bureau recruiting in Kasempa and Zambezi Districts (qq.v.). A joint Northern and Southern Rhodesian (qq.v.) government committee met in 1913 to address the mortality issue, and Southern Rhodesia adopted regulations to limit the number of continuous hours miners could work, the number of miners working per shift, and the number of blasting shifts per day. The bureau was unable to survive increasing competition from the Katangan mines, the World War I carrier corps, and the Copperbelt (q.v.) mines, and died in the 1920s.

RHODESIAN RAILWAYS. Begun as a part of Cecil Rhodes' (q.v.) dream of "Cape to Cairo" British colonies, the railway went from South Africa through the eastern edge of Botswana (q.v.) and north through Southern Rhodesia (q.v.). In 1905 the line from Cape Town crossed the Zambezi River at Victoria Falls (qq.v.) and progressed through Lusaka to Kabwe (qq.v.). Four years later it was extended to the Congo border and reached Elisabethville (Lubumbashi) and the Katangan copper mines in 1910. Another line cut eastward from Southern Rhodesia to Mozambique (q.v.) and the ports of Beira (q.v.) and Lourenço Marques. From 1929 to 1949, it was totally owned by the British South Africa Company (q.v.) and, in Mozambique, by the Portuguese government. In 1953 its ownership was turned over to the Federation of Rhodesia and Nyasaland. When the federation broke up in 1963, the governments of Rhodesia and Zambia divided its assets and liabilities equally. Since 70 percent of the facilities were in Rhodesia, a problem arose after Rhodesia's unilateral declaration of independence (q.v.) in 1965. Seven months of bargaining ended in June 1967 with an agreement on many of the issues. The Zambia Railways Act of 1967 created Zambia Railways (q.v.) as an independent national system. The Rhodesian Railways had been crucial to the export of

Zambia's copper (q.v.), but in 1975 the TAZARA (q.v.) Railway provided an alternative route through Tanzania (q.v.).

RHODESIAN REPUBLICAN PARTY. A minor, white extremist party led by men such as Colin Cunningham (q.v.) and Dr. G. A. Smith, it contested both sets of 1962 elections and then seemingly disappeared. It ran nine candidates in the April 27 federal elections. All of them lost. It ran five candidates in late October. The two upper-roll candidates got 65 votes, just 0.2 percent of the valid votes cast.

RHODESIAN SELECTION TRUST, LTD. A major international mining company, it was set up in Northern Rhodesia (q.v.) in 1928 after the American Metal Company Limited of New York (now the American Metal Climax) acquired a major interest in the Roan Antelope Mine (q.v.). Subsidiaries were formed to handle new mines as well as the concentrators, smelters, and refineries on the Copperbelt (q.v.) that became part of the RST system. Its primary facilities were located at Mufulira, Chibuluma, Chambishi, Luanshya, and Ndola (qq.v.). On December 16, 1964, the name was changed to Roan Selection Trust, Ltd. (q.v.).

RHODESIAN TEAK. See TEAKWOOD.

RHODES-LIVINGSTONE INSTITUTE. The Rhodes-Livingstone Institute for Social Research was, at the urging of Stewart Gore-Browne (q.v.), proposed by Governor Hubert Young (q.v.) in 1934 and established in 1938, with funding from the Northern Rhodesian government and the mining companies. Initially headquartered in Livingstone and incorporating the Livingstone Museum (q.v.), the two units separated in 1946; the institute relocated to Lusaka (q.v.) in 1952. Governor Young intended this autonomous research institute to help improve race relations on the Copperbelt and line of rail (qq.v.), but its first two directors, anthropologists Godfrey Wilson (1938–41) and Max Gluckman (1942–47), broadened its mission to include a study of the effects of industrialization on African societies and, through its *Rhodes-Livingstone Journal*, the dissemination of its findings. Though it also studied the Afrikaner miners and Indian shopkeepers, most of its work focused upon Africans. Further, its officers' habit of living and speaking with Africans fostered the suspicion and hostility of white settlers, administrators, and mining companies. This was particularly true of Godfrey Wilson's work with Broken Hill's African miners in 1939 and J. Clyde Mitchell and A. L. Epstein's Copperbelt work in the early 1950s.

By the late 1950s, the institute's African research assistants were encouraged to present and publish papers, but most of its work was done by expatriate scholars. And though by 1964 the institute had fostered classic ethnographies on African peoples and more than 30 papers in anthropology, sociology, history, law, economics, and nutrition, it was a public relations failure within Northern Rhodesia (q.v.). Briefly incorporated into the University College of Rhodesias and Nyasaland (q.v.) in 1962, the institute became a research body for the University of Zambia in 1966 and was reconstituted as the University of Zambia's Institute for African Studies (qq.v.) in 1971. In 1996 it was renamed the Institute for Economic and Social Research.

RHOKANA CORPORATION, LTD. The corporation was once part of the Anglo-American Corporation of South Africa, Ltd. (q.v.), then of the Nchanga Consolidated Copper Mines, Ltd. (q.v.), and, after 1980, of Zambia Consolidated Copper Mines (q.v.). Its copper (q.v.) and cobalt came from Nkana Mine at Kitwe on the Copperbelt (qq.v.). Copper was first produced at Nkana in November 1931, and an electrolytic refinery began in 1935. In August 1933, Nkana also began producing cobalt. Over the decades, Nkana Mine was among Zambia's most productive mines.

RIDLEY REPORT. Published in June 1959, it was actually titled *Report of an Inquiry into All the Circumstances which Gave Rise to the Making of the Safeguard of Elections and Public Safety Regulations.* It was the result of the government-appointed Race Relations Committee chaired by N. C. A. Ridley. On the one hand, it seemed to recognize that racial discrimination existed and should gradually be abolished. On the other hand, however, it reported at great length on the potentially violent, antigovernment activities of the Zambia African National Congress (q.v.) and suggested that government efforts to suppress it were justified.

ROAN ANTELOPE MINE. Located at what is now the mining center and city of Luanshya (q.v.), the Roan Antelope Mine was claimed in 1902 by two Rhodesia Copper Company (q.v.) prospectors, William Collier (q.v.) and Jack O'Donohogue. Early rights were forgotten, however, and new companies began prospecting the area in 1923. The Rhodesian Selection Trust (q.v.) came into being in 1928 and controlled the mine, which began production in 1931. The disturbances of 1935 hit the mine in late May of that year, and six miners were killed. For nearly 50 years, it continued to be one of Zambia's top producing copper (q.v.) mines.

ROAN CONSOLIDATED MINES, LTD. This huge copper (q.v.) mining company is a continuation of the Rhodesian Selection Trust (q.v.), founded in 1928, which had changed its name to Roan Selection Trust (q.v.) in December 1964. RCM, Ltd., was created in January 1970, after the Zambian government took control of 51 percent of the shares of Roan Selection Trust through the Industrial Development Corporation (q.v.). In February 1975, the government also took over the company's management and sales. In 1980, Nchanga Consolidated Copper Mines (q.v.) joined RCM to form Zambia Consolidated Copper Mines (q.v.). In the mid-1990s, ZCCM was put up for sale to private investors. (*See* ZAMBIA PRIVATISATION AGENCY.)

Since the 1920s, Rhodesian Selection Trust was one of two huge mining companies dominating the economy of the country. Much of its stock was owned by Americans, especially American Metal Climax, Inc. In 1965, Roan Selection Trust was producing 45 percent of Zambia's copper, to the Anglo-American Corporation's 51 percent. Its principal producing mines were the Roan Antelope Mine, at Luanshya (qq.v), which began production in 1931, and the Mufulira Mine (1933). Its other major mines are Chibuluma (1956) and Chambishi (1965) (qq.v.).

ROAN SELECTION TRUST, LTD. This was the name of Rhodesian Selection Trust, Ltd. (q.v.), as of December 16, 1964. After the Zambian government nationalized the mining industry in 1970, the trust was reincorporated in the United States as RST International, Inc., which acquired 20 percent of the stock in Roan Consolidated Mines, Ltd. (q.v.), the corporation then controlling the trust's former holdings.

ROBERT WILLIAMS AND COMPANY. A subsidiary of Tanganyika Concessions, Ltd. (q.v.), located at Fort Rosebery (q.v.; modern Mansa), it recruited laborers for the Union Minière du Haut-Katanga (q.v.) mines in Katanga (q.v.). It was successful in both Northern and Luapula Provinces of Northern Rhodesia (qq.v.) in the early decades of the 20th century. *See* WILLIAMS, ROBERT.

ROBERTS, JOHN. One of Northern Rhodesia's (q.v.) most active European politicians during the federation (q.v.) period, he was born in England in 1919 and came to Northern Rhodesia with his parents in 1928. After serving in World War II, he learned farming in England and South Africa before acquiring his own tobacco, maize, and cattle farm in 1949 in the Broken Hill District of Northern Rhodesia. A member of the Federal Party (q.v.), he was elected to the Legislative Council (q.v.) in 1954 to take the Broken Hill seat vacated by his friend, Roy Welensky (q.v.). He was soon elected Federal Party leader in the council and became minister of health, lands, and local government. While he worked for measures to improve housing for Africans, he also demanded greater control over African trade unions and the recruitment of more locally born white policemen. He also fought for an upgrading of authority for elected European members of the council. In May 1956, he demanded, in vain, that he be named chief minister. He was re-elected to the council in March 1959 and was appointed minister of labor and mines in the Executive Council (q.v.). During the next several years of constitutional politics he attempted to get more power for the elected European members, supporting the position that Europeans should stay in charge until the eventual emergence of a mature and responsible African leadership. When a contrary constitutional decision was announced by England in February 1961, he and other United Federal Party (q.v.) ministers resigned in protest. (The Federal Party had become the United Federal Party in November 1958, and Roberts remained the leader of its Northern Rhodesian branch.)

In June 1962, recognizing the inevitability of constitutional change, Roberts represented the UFP in talks to create an electoral alliance with Harry Nkumbula (q.v) and the African National Congress (q.v.). Though their alliance against the United National Independence Party (q.v.) was successful in the October 1962 elections, the ANC left the alliance and joined UNIP in a parliamentary coalition. In April 1963, Roberts changed the name of his party to the National Progress Party (q.v.). He also started talks with Kenneth Kaunda (q.v.) about guaranteeing some European seats in a new Zambian Parliament. He pledged to help Zambia by providing a constructive opposition, advising the government with the experience and economic knowledge his party could provide. Under Roberts's leadership, the party won all 10 European seats in the 1964 elections. The NPP was dissolved in 1966.

ROCK ART. There is a considerable amount of rock painting in Zambia as well as some rock engraving. Among the better sites are Chifubwa Stream, Munwa Stream, Ayrshire Farm (qq.v.), and Nyambwezu Falls. These paintings are mainly found in northeastern Zambia, with just a few examples in the northwest and the south. Some seem to be by Late Stone Age peoples, who were perhaps similar to the San (Bushmen, q.v.), although the art does not resemble the so-called Bushman art of Southern Africa. There are however, strong similarities to East African painting. Most of these early works are naturalistic depictions of animals in red, purple, or black pigment. Human figures are far more stylized than the animals. The best paintings are at Nachitalo Hill, Mwela rocks, and Rocklands Farm (qq.v.).

A second style of painting, more abstract and schematic, is also found in Zambia. It is dated later, probably Iron Age, and in some cases was produced in the last couple of centuries. Grid patterns and a white, greasy pigment are found frequently in this newer work, along with yellow and red pigments. Among the better sites where these works are to be found are Zawi Hill (where the other style is also found), Rukuzye (qq.v.), and Nasalu.

ROCKLANDS FARM. The farm is 11 kilometers (seven miles) south of Chipata (q.v.) (Fort Jameson, q.v.) on the road to Chadiza, where there is an excellent example of African rock art (q.v.). On a granite face of a hill there is a five-foot naturalistic painting of an eland, outlined in red and shaded. It is similar to art found elsewhere in East Africa.

ROLLING STRIKES. The term described a series of 15 brief, consecutive strikes and subsequent work stoppages by the African Mineworkers Union (q.v.) at seven copper (q.v.), lead, and zinc mines between July and September 1956. Disrupting production during a period of peak world demand, these strikes reflected the mix of social, economic, and political grievances common to the federation (q.v.) era, for they were preceded that May and June by the African National Congress's line of rail (qq.v.) shop boycotts and by the miner's own protests against the industrial colour bar (q.v.). Central to these strikes was the bitter rivalry between the AMU and the older Mines African Staff Association (q.v.). Both the AMU and the African National Congress (q.v.) saw MASA as part of a "divide and rule" strategy by clever Europeans to break the AMU or to create an African middle class with no interest in the ANC's antifederation struggle. The rolling strikes ended in late August but were followed by a series of work stoppages in early September, when the AMU forbade its members to work overtime or on Saturdays and to conform to protective practices not required of European miners. The strikes and stoppages annoyed the mine companies and frightened other whites. When rumors spread about a wider, general African strike, the acting provincial governor, in the interest of law and order, declared a state of emergency on the Copperbelt (q.v.) on September 11; 32 AMU members were detained immediately; another 31 Africans, mostly ANC members, were detained shortly afterward.

ROMAN CATHOLIC. This is Zambia's largest Christian church and, after the Jehovah's Witnesses (q.v.), its second-largest denomination. The first Catholics in the country were the Jesuits, who crossed the Zambezi River (q.v.) near Victoria Falls (q.v.) in 1879. In 1902, they established missions among the Tonga (q.v.) and, in 1927, a mission at Broken Hill (q.v.). The White Fathers (q.v.), who entered from the north in 1891, were far more successful in modern Northern and Luapula Provinces (qq.v.). But though many labor migrants from these two provinces traveled to the Copperbelt (q.v.) mines from the late 1920s on, until 1931 the Roman Catholics on the Copperbelt were only served by occasional visiting priests from the White Fathers at Chilubula or the Jesuits at Broken Hill. In 1931, the government reluctantly agreed to allow the (Italian) Franciscan Fathers to open stations near Roan Antelope and Bwana Mkubwa Mines (qq.v.), and they began work near the Nkana Mine (q.v.) in 1932. Lusaka (q.v.) became an archdiocese in May 1959. Kasama (q.v.) followed a few years later. There are also six dioceses. In 1969 and 1973, Africans were named archbishops at Lusaka and Kasama.

RONDAVEL. This is an Afrikaans term for a round, brick hut with a thatched (later, corrugated iron) roof. At Roan Antelope, the first permanent housing for mineworkers were rondavels.

ROTSE (ROZI). Both are variants of "Lozi" (q.v.). The "Rotse" spelling was prevalent among missionaries, travelers, and early administrators; thus the words "Barotseland" and "Barotse."

RUBBER. Beginning in the 1880s, long before the development of Far Eastern rubber plantations, Lunda, Luvale, Kaonde, and Lamba (qq.v.) collectors (q.v.) in north-central Zambia traded latex from the *Landolphia* and *Carpodinus gracilis* shrubs to Mambari (q.v.) traders. By 1900, European traders discovered similar wild rubber resources along the Luapula River (q.v.). As eager collectors began digging up and boiling rubber roots, the administration tried to protect this potentially valuable resource from extinction by limiting trade and establishing protected reserves. Thus in 1901–02 Louis de Fries, a former trader, was based near modern Ndola (q.v.) as conservator of the Kafue Rubber Reserve. Results, though, were disappointing, and the Ndola area was abandoned for work in Northern Province (q.v.) when Johan Cornelius de Josselyn de Jong, a Dutch plant experimenter, was made first secretary of agriculture in 1905. De Jong set his sights on the Chambeshi River (q.v.), and recruited Charles Duncan Simpson, an African Lakes Company (q.v.) steamboat operator, to establish the Chambeshi rubber factory and to study rubber extraction in England. A *chitukutuku*, or traction engine (qq.v.), was shipped in to haul the machinery from the uncompleted rail line south of Ndola, but thanks to rains and frequent breakdowns, the 1913–15 trip took 19 months.

Rubber never fulfilled its promise as a cash crop for white settlers. Simpson went on leave soon after the factory went into production in 1916, and he returned to find it occupied by the army's river transport service, which ran overland from the Copperbelt (q.v.) rail line to the Luapula (q.v.) and Chambeshi Rivers and the factory's ferry site. The wily German general, Paul von Lettow-Vorbeck (q.v.), led a German assault on the factory on November 13, 1918, but there he received word of the November 11 armistice and of Germany's surrender. The factory produced a small amount of rubber in 1918, but the world market had already collapsed. The factory became a sawmill during the postwar rebuilding of Kasama (q.v.) and, then, a river transport post, before its final collapse during the 1935–36 river floods. Further Zambian rubber trials produced some 280 tons during World War II. Dunlop and Piggott Askew completed a feasibility study for a rubber plantation in Luapula Province's (q.v.) Nchelenge District in 1994, and plans for another plantation near Samfya (q.v.), south of Lake Bang-weulu (q.v.), were announced in 1995.

RUKUZYE. Site of a dam north of Chipata (q.v.), the rock surfaces of the hills provided many "canvases" for traditional rock art (q.v.). For the most part, they are red grid patterns, although a serpent's outline also appears.

RUSSELL COMMISSION. The commission of inquiry, chaired by Sir William A. Russell, was appointed to investigate the Copperbelt strike of 1935 (q.v.). The report of the commission, issued the same year, concluded that the Watch Tower Movement (q.v.) was an important cause of the disturbances and that poor treatment of African miners by their European bosses was only a secondary factor. The direct cause, however, was the inadequate manner in which a tax increase was announced to the miners, and the commission recommended the creation of a government newspaper for Africans. This, when it appeared, was called *Mutende* (q.v.).

RUSTICATION. A policy practiced by the federation government of jailing or detaining African nationalist leaders in places far from their home area for reasons of security.

S

SAA KUTA. This traditional council of the Lozi (q.v.) is a subgroup within the larger Mulongwanji (q.v.), or National Council. Its membership consisted of select *induna*s (q.v.)—the Makwambuya, Likombwa, and Linabi—who met to discuss national problems and pending policy matters. Their recommendations were then passed on to the Sikalo *kuta* (q.v.). In the 20th century, the revived *Katengo kuta* (q.v.) would often bring its suggestions to the *Saa kuta* (q.v.) for further consideration. Under British colonial rule, in the mid–20th century, the *Saa kuta* and the *Sikalo kuta* were merged for administrative purposes and became known as the *Saa Sikalo*, or the Barotse Native Government.

SAID IBN HABIB. The premier Arab explorer of 19th-century Central Africa (q.v.), Said was one of three Arab and Swahili (qq.v.) traders who, in 1845–60, traveled from Zanzibar to the Angolan coast and back again, stopping at Kazembe's Lunda

(qq.v.) and the pre-Yeke (q.v.) copper (q.v.) workings in Katanga (q.v.). There they met Portuguese agents, who escorted
them south to the Kololo (q.v.) king, Sekeletu (q.v.), in Barotseland (q.v.), and then on through Angola (q.v.), where they were
joined by Silva Pôrto (q.v.) to Benguela. David Livingstone
(q.v.) met them in Barotseland in 1853, when Said's party was
returning east with Silva Pôrto's agents, who were bound for
Tete (q.v.). Said returned to Barotseland in 1861, bringing guns
and powder to Sekeletu. In 1867–68 he went trading in Katanga
and, while en route to Ujiji, astonished Livingstone with his
cache of 5,240 pounds of ivory (q.v.), 10,500 pounds of copper,
and a great number of slaves. Said was one of the founders of
Nyangwe, the Arab trading town on the Upper Congo's Lualaba River, and was associated with the northerly shift in Arab
trading patterns in the late 19th century. While he was a friend
of Tippu Tib (q.v.), Said had no respect for King Leopold's
Congo Free State or for Tippu Tib's appointment as the Upper
Congo's provisional governor. Said died in 1889 while en route
to Zanzibar.

SAKUBITA, M. M. Born around 1930, Sakubita published a 72-
page Lozi (q.v.) story, *Liswanelo Za Luna Li Lu Siile*, in 1954. A
corrected revision *Liswanelo Za Luna Kwa Lifolofolo* (How Not to
Handle Animals) was published in 1958.

SAKWE. Located near Chadiza in Eastern Province (qq.v.), it is
the site of an unusual piece of schematic rock art (q.v.) by Late
Stone Age Zambians. Horizontal and vertical stripes produce a
checkered grid.

SALA. This small group of almost 21,000 *ci*Tonga-speaking people (1986) live immediately west of Lusaka (q.v.). Because of Ila
and Tonga (qq.v.) influences, the early Sala language has become extinct.

SALAULA. Derived from the Bemba (q.v.) verb "to select carefully," this is a current term for imported, secondhand clothes.
Itinerant African hawkers have sold such clothes for more than
60 years; for many years they were brought in from the Democratic Republic of Congo (q.v.) (Zaire). New clothing became
so expensive by the mid-1980s that some 20 Zambian trading
firms import over $4 million worth of used clothing from the
United States and Canada alone. Retail market traders buy 45-
kilogram bales of used clothing from the trading firms, then

take them to market, where they are opened in front of eager customers. Fashioning a wardrobe from secondhand clothes is no longer a source of embarrassment but of pride. And in any urban marketplace, the *salaula* section is far larger than that devoted to produce.

SALISBURY. Now called Harare, Salisbury was the name of the capital of white-ruled Rhodesia and, in 1953–63, of the Federation of the Rhodesias and Nyasaland. In earlier years, before the Copperbelt (q.v.) was fully developed, it was a magnet for Zambian migrant laborers searching for their hut tax (q.v.) monies. It was named after Lord Salisbury (q.v.).

SALISBURY, LORD. The Third Marquess of Salisbury and British statesman in the late Victorian age, he was Britain's prime minister and foreign secretary from 1886 until 1892. His granting of a charter to Cecil Rhodes for the British South Africa Company (qq.v.) in 1889 was a milestone in the colonial history of Zambia. He was also responsible for numerous other acts that opened up East, Central, and Southern Africa to direct English involvement.

SAMFYA. This archaeological site is on the western shore of Lake Bangweulu (q.v.), where "grinding grooves" are found on flat rock surfaces. The grooves are possibly from the Late Stone Age, and are each about 38 to 46 centimeters (15 to 18 inches) long, 10 centimeters (four inches) wide, and five to eight centimeters (two to three inches) deep. Similar grooves have been found in West Africa. Early Iron Age pottery has been found at Samfya that has been radiocarbon dated to about A.D. 400.

SAMPA MULENGA KAPALAKASHA. The Chitimukulu (q.v.) (i.e., Bemba, q.v., senior chief) from 1884 to 1896, he was hostile to the spread of the British South Africa Company (q.v.) influence. A younger brother of Chitimukulu III, Chitapankwa (q.v.), Sampa appears to have been egotistical and difficult. He argued with his older brothers, including Chitapankwa himself, over land they had given him. He blinded his brother-in-law in a fight over land. He had a following equipped with guns, which he supposedly got by raiding caravans.

When Mwamba II, Chileshye Kapalaula (q.v.), died in 1883, Chitapankwa wanted to appoint Sampa (q.v.) to that chiefdom, but Sampa refused, preferring to wait for Chitapankwa himself to die so he could succeed him. This angered the older brother—but he did indeed die in October 1883, and Sampa became the Chitimukulu in 1884. Many opposed him, including other Bemba chiefs, but at that time, while the Chitimukulu was the senior and paramount chief (q.v.), Mwamba III, Mubanga Chipoya (q.v.), was the strongest. Suspicion and hostility existed between the two leaders throughout their reigns, and their forces fought each other on a number of occasions. It is said that Sampa once attacked Mwamba's village but was beaten back. Sampa won over a few of Mwamba's vassals, one being Ponde (q.v.), his nephew who later also became Chitimukulu. In general, however, Sampa's control was limited to the core chiefdom of Lubemba (q.v.), and he did not dominate other Bemba chiefdoms.

Sampa's dealings with Arab (q.v.) traders contributed to his power. They advised him to avoid dealing with the Europeans, who they thought would end the lucrative slave trade (q.v.). While Sampa was more concerned about the White Fathers (q.v.) and the BSAC, his most devastating run-in was with a German administrator, Hermann von Wissman (q.v.), in mid-1893. On one of his regular raids, Sampa took his men north into Tanganyika; while attacking a Lungu (q.v.) village, his large slave-raiding force confronted Wissman's 60 soldiers, a cannon, and a Maxim gun. Despite Wissman's warning, Sampa let the battle proceed, and his men were routed. The news spread that Sampa's forces had been humiliated, and Sampa returned in shame.

Sampa had recurring arguments with three successive Bemba chiefs, Makasa III, IV, and V (qq.v.). He hoped to have one of his own sons named Makasa V, but this did not happen, as there were senior candidates available. Ironically, Mukwuka Makasa V's fear of Sampa led him to make favorable contacts with European missionaries. Sampa sent four of his warriors to assassinate Bishop Dupont (q.v.), but they did not succeed. Later (in December 1895), he invited Makasa and the White Fathers to his capital "to talk about some important affairs." They refused, fearing they were being lured into a trap. He tried again in March 1896, hoping that the priest might be able to counter the BSAC's increasing influence in his area. Again, he was turned down. Indeed, while Sampa was probably in earnest this time, neither the Europeans nor his fellow Bemba chiefs were willing to trust him. He died in mid-May 1896, presumably of an illness he contracted while leading a raid five months earlier across the Sangwe River into Nyakyusa country.

SANDYS, DUNCAN. British secretary of state for commonwealth relations and colonial affairs from 1960 to late 1964, he also replaced R. A. Butler (q.v.) as the minister responsible for Central Africa (q.v.). His 1962 visit to the Central African Federation (q.v.) stirred up excitement when the king of Barotseland (q.v.) met with him and requested that the Lozi (q.v.) be allowed to secede from Northern Rhodesia (q.v.). In May 1963, he contacted the Lozi king and invited him to a meeting with Kenneth Kaunda (q.v.) and himself in London. Sandys was responsible for the abortive Federal Review Conference (q.v.) of December 1960. He had frequent meetings with many Zambian leaders during the period when the federation was dissolving and Zambia was becoming independent.

SANGUNI. This is one of the names of the "Luanshya snake," the legendary underground creature once said to inhabit the mosquito-infested swamps of the Luanshya River near Roan Antelope Mine (q.v.). Development work at Roan began in 1927. Until Roan's 1929–32 sanitation and antimalaria campaign got under way, during which the swamps were drained and the river channeled, Roan's workers suffered such high illness and mortality rates (from malaria (q.v.) and blackwater fever as well as typhus, cholera, and pneumonia) that waggish Cape Town railway clerks advised new European recruits heading north to Roan not to bother buying roundtrip tickets. Given its endemic health problem, Roan suffered daily desertions and a continuous shortage of African laborers. The local Lamba (q.v.) declined to work at Roan, attributing the illness and rash of underground accidents to the giant *funkwe* snake, a legendary creature that lived at the river's source and wriggled through the mine shafts spewing water and poisonous gas.

When Chirupula Stephenson (q.v.) visited in 1928, Roan's general manager asked how he could be rid of the problem. Stephenson arranged transportation for headman Katanga and other elders of the chiefly Lamba clan to visit Roan to propitiate the creature and ask it to relocate. The snake evidently cooperated, though Stephenson's 1948–49 correspondence suggests that the Lamba elders had expected more compensation than the beer and the blankets they received. It is not clear how the lengendary *funkwe* snake came to be called a *sanguni* (or *nsanguni*). As the latter is a witchcraft familiar, with a human head and a snakelike or fishlike body, it might be that Roan's early African laborers attributed their epidemic health problems to witchcraft.

SARDANIS, ANDREW SOTIRIS. This Zambian businessman was one of the most important European participants in government in the early years of the Republic of Zambia. Born March 13, 1931, on Cyprus, he emigrated to Northern Rhodesia (q.v.) in 1950. He held a variety of business and management positions and stood—but lost—as a United National Independence party (q.v.) candidate in the Legislative Council (q.v.) by-elections of December 1962. In June 1965, he was appointed chairman and managing director of the Industrial Development Corporation (q.v.), a post he held until April 1970. From then until December 1970 he was managing director of the Zambia Industrial and Mining Corporation (q.v.) and its subsidiaries, the Industrial Development Corporation of Zambia and Mining Development Corporation of Zambia (qq.v.). In 1968 he was permanent secretary of the ministry of commerce, industry, and trade, and in 1969–70 he was permanent secretary of the ministry of state participation. He resigned from government at the end of 1970. In 1971 he worked briefly for a Lonrho (q.v.) subsidiary before establishing his own Lusaka consulting firm. He also acquired interests in the import business and Caterpillar franchises in the region. In the 1980s, he bought American Metal Climax (*see* RHODESIAN SELECTION TRUST, LTD.) and thus gained a seat on the Anglo-American Corporation's (q.v.) board of directors.

Sardanis also entered the banking industry by founding Meridien Bank and then acquired Banque Internationale pour l'Afrique Occidental. Meridien BIAO opened branches in over 20 countries, but its weak financial base and allegations of mismanagement and fraud led the central banks of several countries, including that of Zambia, to close down its operations. Before its 1995 closure, the Bank of Zambia (q.v.) put between K70 and K90 billion into Meridien BIAO in a futile attempt to save it. As only K4.3 billion of the K39 billion in depositors' funds was deemed recoverable, the loss of these funds during the period of the structural adjustment program's (q.v.) austerity measures became a national scandal. As of September 1995, Sardanis was under police bond at his Chisamba farm, and he and seven of his former senior managers were charged under the Banking and Financial Services Act.

SATA, MICHAEL. This former member of Parliament (q.v.) defected from the United National Independence Party (q.v.) in January 1991 and made a name for himself in Parliament by attacking alleged corruption in the regime, including accusing

Zambia Consolidated Copper Mines and the Metal Marketing Corporation (qq.v.) of charging exorbitant marketing fees for handling copper (q.v.) sales. One of President Chiluba's (q.v.) most versatile and enduring cabinet ministers, Sata was appointed the first minister of local government and housing after the 1991 elections. At the Movement for Multiparty Democracy's (q.v.) April 1992 convention, he delivered a stinging attack against tribalism and those who would limit the president's powers. The next May, President Chiluba promised a thorough investigation into the Anti-Corruption Commission's suggestion that Sata had taken kickbacks from a contract issued to one of the government's higher-bidding building contractors. That July, Sata brought suit against the *Weekly Post* (*see POST*) for reporting that he had been knocked down in a fight with the current minister of lands. By May 1993, Sata was serving as minister of labor. After the January 1994 resignations of Vernon Mwaanga, Sikota Wina (qq.v.), and Princess Nakatindi Wina during the allegations that Chiluba's cabinet members were involved in the drug trade (q.v.), Sata became minister of health. The attorney general declined to prosecute Sata on the Anti-Corruption Commission's charge that he had deposited K1.2 billion of treasury funds in a low-interest-bearing account in a bank in which he was a shareholder. Sata then played an active role in the very public, mid-1994 resignations of Vice President Levy Mwanawasa and Minister of Legal Affairs Dr. Ludwig Sondashi, whom he accused of plotting against him. One of them was later charged with alleging that very high placed Zambians not only smoked *dagga* (marijuana) but were also involved in the drug trade. In January 1995, Sata was awarded K1 million in damages from the *Weekly Post* for a series of articles attacking him; the chief justice refused, however, to issue a permanent injunction against the newspaper, on the grounds that it would inhibit free debate.

SAUCEPAN SPECIAL. The Central African Broadcasting Service (q.v.) opened an African languages radio station in Lusaka (q.v.) in 1945, but only a few towns (and few African townsfolk) had electricity. A wired radio line in Lusaka was prohibitively expensive. Africans gained wider access to radio after October 1949, when Harry Franklin (q.v.), director of the Department of Information (q.v.), persuaded the Ever Ready Company that it could sell a lot of batteries by introducing a wireless (*wayaleshi*), battery-powered, shortwave receiver. First housed in a handleless, aluminium cooking pot, the receiver was soon dubbed the "saucepan special." The receivers were distributed and sold at minimal markup, and because their glass tubes often blew, the CABS's engineering department operated an exchange system for repairs. Africans bought some 1,200 of these radio sets in the first four months alone. About 5,000 sets were in use in 1950, and over 30,000 in 1954, by which time several manufacturers were selling such sets. Zambians eagerly embraced this medium for news and entertainment. Its musical broadcasts stimulated local record sales and, with the records of Alick Nkhata and the Lusaka Radio Band (qq.v.), the birth of Zambian popular music.

SCHUCKMANNSBURG. This is a World War I site in the Caprivi Strip (q.v.). The Germans, who then controlled Caprivi, established a fort there, five kilometers (three miles) across the Zambezi River (q.v.) from Sesheke (q.v.). To secure the Zambezi border, a detachment of the British South Africa Company (q.v.) Police and a force from the Northern Rhodesia Police (q.v.) captured the fort on September 21, 1914, without a shot being fired. Control was left in the hands of the Northern Rhodesian Police.

SCOTT, ALEXANDER. Dr. Scott owned the *Central African Post* in the early 1950s and, for a brief period, was a Progressive Party leader. Considered a liberal for the time, he was nevertheless elected to the Federal Parliament and helped to found the multiracial Constitution Party (q.v.).

SCOTT, GUY. The long-time editor of *Productive Farming*, the journal of the Commercial Farmers' Bureau, Dr. Scott was a critic of the Kaunda (q.v.) regime's agricultural policies. He was elected the Mpika (q.v.) member of Parliament (q.v.) and then appointed minister of agriculture in the Movement for Multiparty Democracy (q.v.) government formed after the 1991 elections. He earned widespread praise for his management of the food relief effort following the disastrous drought of 1992. However, he and Emmanuel Kasonde (q.v.), the finance minister, were fired by President Chiluba (q.v) in April 1993 amid vague allegations of corruption. Chiluba subsequently charged that Scott had ignored proper tender procedures in awarding the transport contract for Zambian maize (q.v.) imports to a South African firm. But these sackings, along with those of three other dynamic and highly qualified cabinet ministers, were widely attributed to Chiluba's political insecurity. Scott was also criticized for his handling of an outbreak of swine fever throughout central Zambia. His ministry ordered the slaughter of all pigs in the region and compensation for farmers. As a large-scale pig farmer, Scott stood to receive a sizable compensation payment, while township dwellers, who were not supposed to be keeping pigs at all, were fined instead of compensated. This move was considered a political blunder. Scott was expelled from the MMD during the formation of the National Party (q.v.) in August 1993; he was reinstated that November. Simon Zukas (q.v.) replaced Scott as minister of agriculture.

SEBANZI HILL. An important archaeological site near Gwisho Hot Springs (q.v.), on the Kafue flats in south-central Zambia, the area has been continuously occupied since the 12th or 13th century A.D. The people there then were Early Iron Age farmers, hunters, and fishers who had large herds of cattle and goats. Their pottery closely resembles that of the 19th- and 20th-century Tonga (q.v.). Spindle whorls indicate that cotton was being spun for cloth, and the site's artifacts include cattle figurines and Zambia's first Early Iron Age smoking pipes.

SEBITUANE (SEBITWANE; SIBITWANE). The leader of the Kololo (q.v.), he was one of the more remarkable of Southern Africa's outstanding 19th-century leaders. He was born about 1800 of Sotho (q.v.) parents and became a chief of the Sotho's Fokeng Clan at about age 20 (his older brother had been killed by a lion). Living in the area of the present Orange Free State near Lesotho, the Kololo fled the region when wars started by Shaka the Zulu caused disruptions throughout South-Central Africa. Marching northward in about 1823, they were defeated by Mzilikazi's Ndebele (qq.v.). Sebituane and his followers then veered westward into the land of the Tswana peoples and further north through parts of the Kalahari Desert and the Okavango and Chobe swamps.

In the 1830s the Kololo crossed the Zambezi River at Kazungula on the eastern tip of the Caprivi Strip (qq.v.). Fearing the Ndebele (q.v.) to their south, they headed north to raid the Tonga and Ila (qq.v.) cattle herds. Sebituane tricked Tonga leaders into attending a council meeting and had them massacred. He had less luck with the Ila, though, who recaptured their cattle at night. He settled for a while at Kapoli near Kalomo (q.v.), but withdrew to Sachitema around 1840 when an Ndebele army tried to avenge an earlier Kololo cattle raid. Sebituane's men won, but fearing another Ndebele attack, they fled west, where they subdued the Lozi (q.v.), who were then involved in a civil war over royal succession (*see* SILUMELUME). In the next 10 years Sebituane conquered much of the Zambezi floodplain that was home to the Lozi (q.v.), including the southern part at Sesheke (q.v.) and further south to Linyanti (q.v.) in the Caprivi Strip. His greatest threat at the time was the Ndebele, who were repeatedly repulsed by Kololo warriors.

In addition to their battles with the Ndebele and the Lozi, Sebituane's warriors repeatedly dominated the Ila, the Nanzela (q.v.), and most of the other southern peoples. Meanwhile, Sebituane was also dealing with both Arab (q.v.) and European traders. The Arabs were eager to acquire Lozi men for their slave trade, and Sebituane could provide them. He also acquired guns from the western trade with the Mambari and Silva Pôrto (qq.v.), the Portuguese slave trader. It is interesting that Sebituane saw the need to integrate Lozi leaders into his highly centralized political and military organization, perhaps to ensure their loyalty. Thus Sipopa (q.v.), a future Lozi king, spent a number of years at Sesheke with the Kololo. In 1851, just two weeks before his death, Sebituane also welcomed Dr. David Livingstone (q.v.), hoping that Livingstone might provide him with more magic to ward off the Ndebele spears. But according to Livingstone, Sebituane died of pneumonia from an old, infected spear wound. Neighboring Ila people say, however, that Livingstone's story is not correct, that Sebituane insisted on riding the doctor's horse, which threw and killed him. His death occurred on July 7, 1851. He was ultimately succeeded by a son, Sekeletu (q.v.).

SECOND NATIONAL DEVELOPMENT PLAN. First outlined by President Kaunda (q.v.) at the Mulungushi Conference of the United National Independence Party (q.v.) in May 1971, its specifics were presented in January 1972. The plan was designed to cover the period 1972–76 and was a follow-up to the First National Development Plan. Both plans were hindered by the closing off of trade with Rhodesia (*see* UNILATERAL DECLARATION OF INDEPENDENCE) and by declining world copper (q.v.) prices. The initial projection was for a 6.8 percent annual growth rate. On the discouraging side, it projected an annual increase of only 20,000 new jobs and 67,000 new workers. Educational facilities would be improved, according to the plan, so that every child would be guaranteed a minimum of a fourth-grade education, and 80 percent would finish primary school. The greatest emphasis in the plan, however, was on agricultural development. It was hoped that rural areas could be developed and that economic and quality-of-life differences between rural and urban areas could be erased. A plan was formulated to create special intensive development zones, areas chosen for their good soil and access to transport. Ideally, such plans would help reduce food imports by utilizing sites with high production potential. Finally, the plan called for the expansion and diversification of industry and mining, and a 15 percent increase in manufacturing.

SECOND ZAMBIAN REPUBLIC. The title is that of the Zambian government after the establishment of the one-party participatory democracy on December 13, 1972. Technically, however, the new constitution was not adopted by Parliament (q.v.) and signed by President Kaunda (q.v.) until August 1973.

SECRETARY-GENERAL OF UNIP. Under the original constitution of the United National Independence Party (q.v.) there was no president. The highest position was secretary-general and was filled by Kenneth Kaunda (q.v.) in 1969. Later, under the one-party participatory democracy instituted by the 1973 Zambian Constitution Act that set up the Second Zambian Republic (q.v.), the president of UNIP was also the president of Zambia. The position of secretary-general was both a party and governmental post. He served by appointment by the president, subject to the approval of the National Committee. He had to be a member of the Central Committee of UNIP (q.v.). His duties were all party duties assigned to him by the president. He was, according to Zambia's constitution, responsible for the administration of UNIP. He was also an ex officio member of the cabinet. Perhaps of greater importance, he was to replace the president of Zambia in his absence, illness, or death, for a period up to three mouths. In 1973, the post was held by Grey Zulu (q.v.); he was replaced by Mainza Chona (q.v.) in June 1978.

SEERS REPORT. Officially titled *The Economic Survey Mission on the Economic Development of Zambia: Report of the UN/ECA/FAO Mission* and published in 1964, it set the guidelines for Zambia's First National Development Plan. Some of its recommendations were designed to ensure an economically feasible form for the goals of the politicians.

SEFULA MISSION. The first mission station in Barotseland (q.v.) of the Reverend Coillard of the Paris Mission Society (qq.v.), it was located about 32 kilometers (20 miles) south of Lealui (q.v.), a site suggested by Lewanika (q.v.). Founded in October 1886, the station, with Lewanika's permission, opened its first school in March 1887. In October 1892, Coillard moved his headquarters to a new station at Lealui, the Lozi (q.v.) capital.

SEJAMANJA. At this site of Late Stone Age rock art (q.v.) near Chadiza in Eastern Province (qq.v.), reptiles are depicted in silhouette with red pigment.

SEKELETU (SIKELETU). A son of Sebituane (q.v.) and a leader of the Kololo (q.v.). When Sebituane died on July 7, 1851, his daughter, Mamochisane (q.v.), was his chosen successor, but, preferring a family-oriented lifestyle, she abdicated in favor of her younger half brother, Sekeletu. That he was only about 18, and that his mother was a captive woman, not a Sotho (q.v.), made his succession questionable for some Kololo (q.v.). Unfortunately, he lacked the natural leadership abilities of his father. He alienated many of his own people, in addition to the conquered Lozi (q.v.) whom his father had managed to placate. He was a bitter man, obsessed with witchcraft, especially after he acquired leprosy, which forced him into seclusion. Yet he continued his father's pattern of cattle raiding against the neighbors, especially the Ila (q.v.). He also used Dr. Livingstone's (q.v.) return visit in 1853 to open up direct trade with the Atlantic coast areas of Angola (q.v.), bypassing Mambari (q.v.) middlemen. He hoped to persuade Livingstone to set up a mission among his people, thinking that it might dissuade the feared Ndebele (q.v.) from attacking. Sekeletu also had trouble among his own followers. After Mpepe (q.v.) failed in his attempt to assassinate him, Sekeletu began executing everyone he suspected of plotting against him. His brutal reign united many of his opponents, brought his kingdom to the edge of chaos, and allowed many subject peoples to assert their independence. Sekeletu died—strangled, said one Sala (q.v.) elder—in August 1863. Njekwa (q.v.), a Lozi noble, led the Lozi army and defeated the Kololo in 1864. Sipopa (q.v.) became leader of the restored Lozi kingdom.

SELBORNE, LORD. Governor of the Transvaal and high commissioner for South Africa from 1905 to 1910, he toured the Rhodesias in 1906, reporting favorably on the British South Africa

Company (q.v.) administration of the territory, even north of the Zambezi River (q.v.). He also received petitions from Lozi king Lewanika (qq.v.), who pleaded with him as representative of England to require the BSAC to fulfill its end of the concessions agreements (q.v.) and to retract its hut tax (q.v.). In October 1906, Lewanika traveled to Bulawayo (q.v.) to meet with Selborne on these matters, but the high commissioner found little merit in his arguments.

SELF-RULE. Zambia's penultimate step in the progress toward independence, self-rule was attained as the result of the Order in Council of January 3, 1964 (q.v.).

SENA. An administrative center set up by the Portuguese some time in the 16th or early 17th century, it was founded on the south bank of the lower Zambezi River (q.v.), at the Shire River confluence, about halfway between Tete (q.v.) and the Indian Ocean. Around 1700 the Portuguese became interested in the area north and west of Sena, including today's Malawi (q.v.) and Zambia. Dr. Francisco de Lacerda (q.v.) became governor at Sena in 1797, before he started on his trip to meet Kazembe (q.v.), the Lunda (q.v.) king.

SENANGA. One of the rural districts of Western Province (q.v.), it is itself divided into two separate parliamentary constituencies. The district has a border with Angola (q.v.) but also stretches east to the Zambezi River (q.v.). The town of Senanga is on the Zambezi itself and was the site of the conquest of the Subiya (q.v.) by an early Lozi leader, Mwanambinyi (qq.v.). The district had a population of 88,600 in 1969 and 135,200 in 1990.

SENGA. A *ci*Tumbuka-speaking people who live along Zambia's eastern border, they apparently came from the Katanga (q.v.) region some 200 or 300 years ago and may once have been part of the Bisa (q.v.). Another possibility is that they were originally Tumbuka (q.v.) but came under the influence of later Bisa immigrants. They do share language and similar clan names with the Tumbuka, but, like the Bisa, wove cloth from their own cotton. They bartered this cloth along with tobacco and basketwork. The Bemba (q.v.), to whom the Senga were sometimes subject, traded especially for tobacco. In the 19th century, the Senga's Luangwa (q.v.) valley homeland also became the site of such Arab slave traders (qq.v.) as Kapandansalu (q.v.)

and Koma Koma. Kapandansalu and some neighboring Arabs allied with the Bemba in 1897 to twice attack the village of Senga chief Chibale (q.v.). The Senga won both battles but only with the aid of Robert Young (q.v.) and a force of British South Africa Company (q.v.) police from Nyasaland (q.v.). This spurred the establishment of a company *boma* at Mirongo (qq.v.), near Chibale's (q.v.) village.

The Senga have a traditional senior chief, called Kambombo, but he has little political authority. He was usually the most important trader, however, and thus accumulated much material wealth. Chiefly titles are hereditary. Unlike most Zambian peoples, the Senga follow a patrilineal descent system.

SERENJE. The easternmost district of Central Province (q.v.), it had a population of nearly 53,000 in 1969 and 104,000 in 1990. The district shares its entire western border with Shaba (Katanga) Province, Democratic Republic of Congo (qq.v.) (Zaire). The town of Serenje is close to the middle of the district.

SESHEKE. Both a district and a town in modern Zambia, it is of special interest as a 19th-century community often visited by Europeans and fought over by Africans. Today, it is a district in Western (formerly Barotse) Province (q.v.). It extends north a long distance from its border with the Caprivi Strip (q.v.). Its population in 1969 was 49,000 and 64,900 in 1990. The town, on the north bank of the Zambezi River (q.v.) near where it turns eastward, is small. The area has been traditionally the home of the Subiya (q.v.), who came under Lozi (q.v.) political control early in the 18th century. With the invasion of southern Barotseland by Sebituane's Kololo (qq.v.), however, the new rulers controlled it. The Kololo used both Sesheke and Linyanti (q.v.) as major political centers, in part to keep the Ndebele (q.v.) from penetrating the upper Zambezi River valley. By the mid-1860s both Sebituane and his successor, Sekeletu (q.v.), were dead, and the Kololo were considerably weakened. The Lozi began again to assert themselves in the area around Sesheke, firmly integrating it into Barotseland in 1886, when Lewanika (q.v.) appointed Kabuka as senior *induna* (q.v.) there. Meanwhile, many Europeans passed through Sesheke. Dr. Livingstone (q.v.) entered the town in 1851, using his medical skills to win over Sebituane. The trader George Westbeech (q.v.) had a house there, and the Reverend Coillard (q.v.) waited there for permission to visit the Lozi capital at Lealui (q.v.). Ten years earlier the Lozi king, Sipopa (q.v.), had made

Sesheke the temporary capital of the Lozi, perhaps because the area was not the most secure part of the kingdom and needed his personal authority.

SEZONGO. A 19th-century leader of the Nanzela (q.v.) people, he established himself as chief at Nakalomwe in southern Zambia. His leadership of the Nanzela made him wealthy in ivory (q.v.), slaves, cattle, and *mpande* shells (q.v.). His raids against the Ila, Tonga, Nkoya, and Lozi (qq.v.) made him feared and added to his wealth and (through slaves) to the size of his following. At one point he massacred about 300 Ndebele (q.v.) who were fleeing Sebituane (q.v.). Eventually, the latter attacked Sezongo, and despite the desertion of a large force led by his younger brother, Shambala, Sezongo and his men fought a lengthy battle against the mighty Kololo (q.v.) before he was killed.

SHABA. See KATANGA.

SHAIWILA. This Lala (q.v.) chief of the 1920s settled scores with those who opposed his illegitimate succession by supporting the Watch Tower Movement of Mwana Lesa (qq.v.), who identified and killed as witches most of Shaiwila's enemies. The British eventually caught and tried Mwana Lesa and sentenced both Shaiwila and the prophet to death by hanging.

SHAMWANA, EDWARD. This prominent Lusaka (q.v.) lawyer, former High Court, (q.v.) commissioner, and manager of International Telephone and Telegraph, was, along with Valentine Musakanya (q.v.), arrested in October 1980 on charges of conspiring to overthrow the government. During his 10 years in prison, he was adopted as a prisoner of conscience by Amnesty International. In May 1981 he appeared in High Court to face treason charges. Prosecutors alleged that between April and October 1980 he had conspired with others and had recruited an armed band to overthrow the government. In January 1983 he was found guilty of treason and sentenced to hang. After a lengthy wait, his appeal was heard in August 1984, and in April 1985 the Supreme Court upheld the conviction and mandatory death sentences for Shamwana and four others; Musakanya and one other defendant were then acquitted. In late 1986 President Kaunda (q.v.) commuted the death sentences of Shamwana and his four colleagues to life imprisonment, and in July 1990 Kaunda, as part of a broad amnesty for political prisoners, freed him. Shamwana returned to his law practice. He joined the Movement for Multiparty Democracy (q.v.), which rebuked him for arguing that local government candidates should have at least a grade 7 school certificate. In November 1993 he left the MMD for the newly created National Party (q.v.) and was elected its vice president in the party's April 1995 convention elections.

SHANGOMBO. An important border town in Senanga (q.v.) District of Western Province (q.v.), it is on the eastern side of the Kwando River (q.v.), immediately across the river from Angola (q.v.). It is located on a north-south border road.

SHARPE, ALFRED. Trained as an English lawyer, Sharpe served in the colonial service in Fiji before coming to Nyasaland (q.v.) (Malawi, q.v.) as a big-game hunter. There, in 1887, he was among the European volunteers who defended the African Lakes Company (q.v.) store at Karonga, and the northern shore of modern Lake Malawi (q.v.), against Mlozi's Arabs (qq.v.). In 1890, Harry Johnston and Cecil Rhodes (qq.v.) hired Sharpe and Joseph Thomson (q.v.) to collect chiefs' and headmen's treaties for the British South Africa Company (q.v.), and to steal Katanga (q.v.) from King Leopold II before the Belgians could set foot in the region.

Sharpe's first assignment took him beyond Zumbo (q.v.) and up the Luangwa (q.v.) valley. Though he failed to get a treaty from Ngoni chief Mpezeni (qq.v.) in March 1890, and won only two treaties while among the Nsenga and Chewa (qq.v.), he declared a British Protectorate that May over the lands west of the Luangwa River (q.v.). His second expedition went through Karonga to secure the Luapula valley and Katanga. Though Lunda chief Kazembe (qq.v.) signed a treaty in September that promised him British protection, he forbade Sharpe from visiting his enemy, Yeke king Msiri (qq.v.). Sharpe and about a dozen carriers did find their way to Msiri in November, just ahead of the Belgian expeditions. But Msiri followed the advice of Frederick Arnot (q.v.), his then-absent missionary, and declined to sign away his mineral rights. On his return to Lake Mweru (q.v.), Sharpe sited the first two of 11 BSAC forts across the Tanganyika Plateau, which were designed to keep a sharp eye on the Yeke and Kazembe and on the neighboring German and Belgian territories.

Made vice-consul of the British Central African Protectorate (q.v.) in 1891, Sharpe assumed an active role in the pacification of modern Malawi. Later, as the protectorate's commissioner, he supplied Sikh and Nyasaland (qq.v.) troops during North-Eastern Rhodesia's (q.v.) subjugations of Mpezeni (q.v.) and Kazembe in 1898 and 1899, respectively.

SHILA. A *ci*Bemba (q.v.)-speaking people, they live along Lake Mweru and the Luapula River (qq.v.) valley and are primarily known as fishermen. They moved into this region sometime before the 18th century, replacing the Bwile (q.v.). They claim that their principal chieftainship, Nkuba (q.v.), is of Bemba (q.v.) origin and migrated from the east after quarreling with the Chitimukulu (q.v.). The Lunda (q.v.) defeated the Shila several times in the 18th century, with several different Nkubas (q.v.) as victims. Nkuba IV was killed by the forces of Kazembe III (q.v.) around 1760, and since then the Shila have paid tribute to the Lunda while remaining on the land.

SHIMWALULE. One of the most important leadership positions among the Bemba (q.v.), the Shimwalule is the hereditary undertaker or burial priest. He guards the main royal burial grove, Mwalule (q.v.), which is situated east of the Chambeshi River (q.v.), in the easternmost part of Bemba country. In fact, the original Shimwalule was a Bisa (q.v.) headman named Kabotwe, and his matrilineal descendants have succeeded to the position and title. In addition, he has a certain amount of secular authority as both a village headman and authority over some neighboring headmen. By custom, no Shimwalule is allowed to bury more than one Chitimukulu (q.v.). If a second one dies, the Shimwalule must be replaced before the burial occurs. This custom, though, was broken by Chimbwi Shinta in the 1890s.

SHINDE. This is a variant of Ishinde (q.v.).

SICABA (NATIONAL) PARTY. A party founded in Barotseland (q.v.) in June 1962 to contest the Legislative Council (q.v.) seats from Barotseland in the 1962 elections, its organizers were traditionalists who opposed the United National Independence Party (q.v.) and who wanted Barotseland to secede from Northern Rhodesia (q.v.). A victory, its leaders felt, would convince Great Britain that this should be allowed. The Barotse king and the *kuta* (q.v.) favored the party but did not specifically endorse it. On the other hand, during the campaign, Roy Welensky's United Federal Party (qq.v.) supplied a public relations man, three Land Rovers, and other equipment. Nevertheless, UNIP's strong campaign and the Sicaba Party's failure to get many traditionalists registered to vote produced an overwhelming UNIP victory. A 1963 alliance with the African National Congress (q.v.) failed, and the party dissolved the same year.

SICHONE, LUCY BANDA. A former United National Independence Party (q.v.) activist and Central Committee (q.v.) member, she resigned from partisan politics in the early 1990s to found and chair the Zambia Civic Education Association (q.v.), a public interest group engaged in providing civic education and legal aid to disadvantaged Zambian citizens. As UNIP secretary for legal affairs, she was among the 15 or more UNIP members detained during the bizarre "Zero Option" emergency (q.v.) of 1993. Sichone also served as the deputy secretary of the Constitutional Review Commission (q.v.), which released its report in 1995. That May she became the second (polygynous) wife of Kebby Musokotwane (q.v.), then president of UNIP. She is one of the most widely recognized and respected civic leaders in Zambia.

SIKALO KUTA. A traditional council of the Lozi (q.v.) and a subgroup within the larger Mulongwanji (q.v.), it consisted of the most important and senior members of the Mulongwanji, plus the *ngambela* and the *natamoyo* (qq.v.). This group most closely represented the interests of the king and his *ngambela* (prime minister). In addition, because of the importance of its members, its advice was given more weight by the king than that of the Saa *kuta* (q.v.), a larger group with which it interacted on governmental matters. All members of the Sikalo *kuta* were also members of the Saa *kuta*. Under British colonial rule in the mid–20th century, the Saa and Sikalo were merged for administrative purposes and became known as the Saa Sikalo, the Barotse Native Government.

SIKALUMBI, WITTINGTON K. An important nationalist politician in the 1950s, he was a member of the African National Congress (q.v.) and helped Kenneth Kaunda at the *Congress News* (qq.v.), a political newspaper. He also organized a somewhat successful campaign against the hatch system (q.v.) in 1954. By 1958 he had quit the ANC and briefly joined the Constitution Party (q.v.). In October 1958, at the inaugural meeting of the Zambian African National Congress (q.v.), he was named deputy secretary of the party. In 1959 he was arrested by the government in its sweep of ZANC leaders and rusticated (q.v.) to Namwala (q.v.). This did not prevent him from writing letters abroad for international support.

SIKHS. Soldiers and policemen from India (specifically, adherents of the Sikh religion, from East Punjab) who served with the British South Africa Company (q.v.) in the early days of BSAC rule in Central Africa (q.v.) (Malawi, q.v.). The British trusted them and recruited them for military duty because they had remained loyal to the British during the Indian Mutiny of 1857–58. Among the British victories in which they participated were those over Ponde, Mporokoso, Kazembe, and Mpezeni (qq.v.).

*SI*KOLOLO. The language of the Kololo (q.v.) people, the mid-19th-century Sotho (q.v.) invaders who conquered and married among the Lozi (q.v.). The language is basically *se*Sotho, as that was also the ethnic derivation of the Kololo. It became so widespread among the Lozi (the people affected most by the invasion) that missionaries such as the Reverend Coillard (q.v.), who set up mission schools between 1880 and 1900 among the Lozi, taught in *se*Sotho and *si*Kololo, not *si*Luyana, the language of the Lozi royal court. The language is the common language of the Lozi today, although minor changes have occurred, and it is now more commonly called either *si*Lozi (q.v.) or just Lozi.

*SI*LOZI. Also called Lozi (q.v.), it is the language of most of the Lozi people today (although *si*Luyana was the royal language in the past). Actually, the language is basically *si*Kololo (q.v.) with the added influence of other minor local languages. It is spoken by many people who are either Lozi or who are members of closely allied or neighboring peoples.

SILUMBU. He was one of the main champions of Lubosi (Lewanika) (qq.v.) in his attempt to claim the Lozi (q.v.) throne in the 1870s. Lubosi later appointed him prime minister (*ngambela*, q.v.). One knowledgeable witness, the Reverend Coillard (q.v.), called Silumbu "the most influential man of the tribe and the real ruler." In 1885, when a successful rebellion occurred among factions that lost the throne to Lubosi, Silumbu led a large army to reconquer the Bulozi (q.v.) valley and reclaim the throne for Lubosi from Tatila Akufuna (q.v.). Though Silumbu died during the civil war, Lubosi was restored to the throne, and Lewanika saw that Silumbu had an almost royal funeral.

SILUMELUME. A son of the Lozi king Mulambwa (qq.v.), who died in 1830, Silumelume's succession was challenged by his brother Mubukwanu (q.v.). The former had support among northern Lozi, whereas the latter's support was in the southern part of the kingdom. Silumelume was chosen king by the Mulongwanji (q.v.) and declared to be so by both his father's *ngambela*, Muswa, and the *natamoyo* (qq.v.). Insecure about his brother's intentions, Silumelume planned an attack upon him, with Mbunda (q.v.) warriors. A counterplot was arranged by a supporter of Mubukwanu, who persuaded the Mbunda to secretly support him. At a ceremonial Mbunda war dance before Silumelume and his council, one of the Mbunda killed Silumelume with an arrow. The kingdom remained divided and thus was vulnerable to a Kololo (q.v.) invasion.

*SI*LUYANA. The official court language today in Bulozi (q.v.) (Barotseland, q.v.). While it is spoken by the ruling dynasty, it is uncertain whether it was introduced by the region's Luyana (q.v.) conquerors or by the local people who were conquered. It is one of a number of similar languages now grouped under the term "Luyana." The common Lozi (q.v.) language, originally *si*Kololo, is now called *si*Lozi (qq.v.).

SILVA PÔRTO, ANTONIO FRANCISCO FERREIRA DA. This Portuguese ivory (q.v.), cattle, and slave trader (q.v.) was based at the Ovimbundu (*see* MAMBARI) chiefdom of Bié (modern Kuito) in Angola (q.v.) in 1845–90. He was the first European to reach Barotseland (q.v.), where he began trading in 1848. In 1854, with the help of Said ibn Habib (q.v.), his agents traveled through Lozi, Ila, Lamba, and Bisa country (qq.v.) to reach Portuguese territory at Tete on the lower Zambezi River (qq.v.). Silva Pôrto and his agents also traded with the Kuba to the north and with Msiri's Yeke (qq.v.) to the east. When civil war began brewing around Lubosi (q.v.) in 1884, Silva Pôrto left Barotseland with the malaria (q.v.)-ravaged missionary, F. S. Arnot (q.v.), bringing him through Angola (q.v.) to the coast at Benguela. In June 1890, upset with Portugal's waning influence across Central Africa (q.v.) and his mistreatment by the chief of Bié, Silva Pôrto blew himself up on a bed of Portuguese flags laid over six powder barrels.

SIMBO HILL. A site of rock art (q.v.), it is located 27 kilometers (17 miles) west of Petauke *boma* (qq.v.). It contains red-pigmented drawings of reptiles, perhaps from the Late Stone Age of Zambian prehistory. There are also more recent drawings in a greasy white paint of crude human figures and perhaps hoes or axes. Local tradition indicates that these could have been done in the 19th century.

SINDANO, HANOC CHIMPUNGWE. He was an aggressive and successful Watch Tower Movement (q.v.) leader ("prophet"), notably in Northern Province, Northern Rhodesia (qq.v.). A Tanganyika-born Mambwe (q.v.), he went to Southern Rhodesia (q.v.) as a herder in 1905. He later worked in the mines and learned about the Watch Tower (*see* JEHOVAH'S WITNESSES) from his fellow miners. Six of them, including Sindano, were deported for their religious activities in October 1917. Sindano, who had been a student of Donald Siwale (q.v.), returned to the Abercorn (q.v.) (Mbala) area to preach.

He preached disobedience to all civil authority, African as well as European, and told his followers not to work for either the Europeans or the chiefs, all of whom were "devils." He was arrested by the government in September 1918 but was acquitted. He spent several periods in jail in the next decade. Some writers indicate that, unlike other Watch Tower Movement (q.v.) leaders, he was greedy for power and material gain. He evidently pocketed collections. Nevertheless, he was an outstanding preacher, promising that the African millennium was coming and that Europeans would be pushed out of the country. Sindano's main church was at Tukamulozya in Abercorn (Mbala) District. Although still active in the movement in the mid-1930s, his influence had become minimal.

SINKALA-MEMBE, WENDY WAKAPEMBE. Born in Ndola (q.v.) in March 1959, one of 13 children in her family, she earned a full Cambridge certificate and several others in management and business. She joined Zambia Railways (q.v.) in 1977 as the country's first female shunter. She served in a variety of administrative posts before entering partisan politics and winning a parliamentary seat in the 1991 elections. She was then appointed deputy minister for Central Province (q.v.), the only female minister in the nine provinces. In 1992 she was transferred to the ministry of foreign affairs as deputy minister and, in July 1995, was made deputy minister in the ministry of local government and housing.

SIPALO, MUNUKAYUMBWA. Perhaps one of the most vigorous of the young nationalists in the African National Congress, the Zambia African National Congress, and the United National Independence Party (qq.v.) during the 1950s and 60s, he was certainly the most active in pan-African affairs and one of the best orators. Born in December 1929 in Barotseland (q.v.), he received his basic education there before studying economics at New Delhi University. While in India, he edited a magazine about Africa, was elected president of the African Student's Association in Asia, and attended the Bandung Conference. He did not finish his degree but returned to Central Africa (q.v.) via Egypt, where he worked closely with Gamal Abdel Nasser for two months in 1956. Back in Northern Rhodesia (q.v.) he joined the ANC and became private secretary to Harry Nkumbula (q.v.), its president, and a member of ANC's executive body. An aggressive and dynamic leader filled with ideas to make ANC more active, he soon became an attractive alternative to some who opposed Nkumbula's more conservative brand of leadership. In September 1957, Nkumbula had him expelled from ANC's executive, and in early 1958 he was expelled from the party. His year in the party had shaken up its members, however, and made the party much more active, for example in the beerhall boycotts (see BEERHALL SYSTEM).

He worked on the Copperbelt (q.v.) for most of 1958 before helping to form ZANC in October. As secretary, he was second only to Kenneth Kaunda (q.v.). His wide travels and stimulating oratory made him an excellent party organizer, but they were also behind the government's detaining him for several months at Feira (q.v.) in March 1959 and then charging him with sedition. He was sentenced to a year at hard labor, sharing a cell in Salisbury (q.v.) with Kaunda. When released in January 1960, he and Kaunda joined UNIP. Again, Sipalo became secretary-general to Kaunda's presidency. In April he attended a series of Afro-Asian meetings in Ghana and Guinea, addressing huge crowds. In December he joined the UNIP delegation in London at the Federal Review Conference (q.v.) and later returned for the Northern Rhodesia Constitutional Conference. Shortly thereafter he was chosen secretary of the All African People's Conference in Cairo. At UNIP's Mulungushi Conference of 1961, he was replaced as secretary because of alleged alcohol abuse. In 1962 he served as UNIP's representative in Ghana. In December 1962 he suffered serious burns from a petrol bomb attack but was back in politics within two years. In September 1964, Kaunda named him minister of health in the independence cabinet, but he was replaced the next January. He returned to the cabinet in May 1966 as minister of labor and social development and continued in the labor post until August 1967. Sipalo was one of the Barotseland UNIP leaders defeated by a Bemba-Tonga coalition when running for reelection to the Central Committee of UNIP (q.v.) in August. He resigned from the party but returned to the cabinet when Kaunda appointed him minister of agriculture. Sipalo's farewell to Zambian politics occurred in December 1968; he lost his seat in Parliament (q.v.) when the banned United Party (q.v.) helped the ANC unseat three Barotseland UNIP cabinet members in the general elections.

SIPOPA (SEPOPA; LUTANGU SIPOPA). King (Litunga, q.v.) of the Lozi (q.v.) from 1864 to 1876, he was the son of the Lozi king Mubambwa. He was known as Lutangu in his youth. Captured by the Kololo king Sebituane (qq.v.), he lived with the invaders for many years as an adopted son. When Sebituane died and was succeeded by his brutal son, Sekeletu (q.v.), in 1851, Sipopa fled the Kololo and went to a northern Lozi stronghold, Lukwakwa (q.v.), where he helped to overthrow and kill Imasiku (q.v.). He was eventually made king of the royal faction. He became close to a Lozi nobleman, Njekwa (q.v.), who was mainly responsible for the military victory over the Kololo. In 1864, Njekwa invited Sipopa to take over as Lozi king in the restored kingdom. Njekwa was then made his *ngambela* (q.v.) or prime minister.

Sipopa soon had many Lozi opponents. Some felt he had been influenced too much by the Kololo, while others pointed to his political ineptitude. He even became jealous of Njekwa and replaced him, losing the support of a large faction of traditionalists. (Only Njekwa's popularity had kept a faction from deposing Sipopa in 1869.) Sipopa turned out to be despotic and cruel, ignoring the Mulongwanji (q.v.) for a coterie of private supporters. In July 1874 he moved his capital south to Sesheke (q.v.), an area made secure in 1866 by his conquest of the local Toka and Subiya (qq.v.) peoples. He had a close relationship there with the trader George Westbeech (q.v.), who sold him guns. A revolt was brewing, however, and as he fled his capital, he was fatally shot by one of his own bodyguards.

Sipopa is favorably remembered for one major and lasting reform. The Lozi had been split on several occasions by having two semi independent leaders, one in the north and one in the south. Sipopa appointed his sister to be the southern leader (at

Nalolo, q.v.). When she died in 1871, he appointed his daughter. By having the male king at Lealui (q.v.) appoint the female ruler at Nalolo, no rival claimant to the throne was created, yet the dual capitals remained. The pattern continues today.

SITUMPA FOREST STATION. The earliest dated Iron Age site in Zambia, it is near Machili on the eastern border of Barotseland (q.v.). Radiocarbon dates suggest it may have been occupied around A.D. 100, though something closer to A.D 250 is considered more likely. Pottery fragments have been found as well as indications of iron working. The occupants of this site seems to have predated the Dambwa (q.v.) people and their Shongwe pottery traditon.

SITUPA. This is the *si*Lozi (q.v.) equivalent of the *chitupa* (q.v.), or pass (qq.v.), which the Northern Rhodesian (q.v.) government required all urban Africans to carry.

SIWALE, DONALD R. A Northern Rhodesian (q.v.) government clerk and teacher for many years, he was also an early nationalist. In 1923 he received a copy of the constitution of the North Nyasa Native Association from a former classmate at Livingstonia (q.v.). Inspired by this, Siwale, David Kaunda (q.v.), and several others organized the Mwenzo Welfare Association (q.v.) as a forum for African social and political views. In 1924 the association protested the heavy taxation of rural Africans. When Siwale was transferred, his organization folded. (Actually, Siwale and his friends had been organized informally almost 20 years previous, as they had been trained as teachers at Livingstonia in 1904 and continued to meet periodically.) In the early 1950s the elderly Siwale, now retired, was still active politically. In 1950, as a member of the Northern Provincial Council and again in 1952 as a member of the African Representative Council (q.v.), Siwale spoke out against white domination and the proposed federation (q.v.), arguing instead that Africans should be granted at least equal representation with Europeans in the Legislative and Executive Councils (qq.v.).

SIYUBO, SILUMELUME. *Ngambela* (q.v.) (prime minister) to Lozi king Mwanawina (qq.v.) for about a year in the early 1960s, he was a strong traditionalist. He accompanied Mwanawina to London in 1963 to plead for Barotseland's (q.v.) right to secede from Northern Rhodesia (q.v.). He clung to this hope even though the king eventually indicated a willingness to concede to the United National Independence Party (q.v.). Elected councillors tried to persuade the Barotse National Council (q.v.) to replace Siyubo with an elected prime minister. After a near-violent demonstration against him in Lealui (q.v.), he resigned in October 1963.

SJAMBOK. This is the Afrikaans name for the plaited leather whip with which Europeans imposed their will upon Africans during the early exploration and settlement of Northern Rhodesia (q.v.).

SKINNER, JAMES JOHN. This Lusaka (q.v.) lawyer became an active worker for the United National Independence Party (q.v.) and later became Zambia's attorney general and chief justice. Born in Dublin, Ireland, in July 1923, he was called to the Irish bar in 1946 and to the Northern Rhodesia (q.v.) bar in 1951. Considered radical by some Europeans, he supported the African nationalists in their campaigns, joining UNIP in 1960. In 1962 he was the legal advisor to UNIP as well as one of its principal campaign advisors. He wrote the *Election Workers Handbook* in 1962, a 22-page manual that was sent to UNIP officials at all levels to guide them through the election procedure. He himself was an unsuccessful UNIP candidate for the Luangwa (q.v.) national seat in 1962, but he was elected to Parliament (q.v.) in 1964.

He was appointed attorney general of Zambia in September 1964, a position he held until January 1969. He was simultaneously minister of justice (September 1964 until January 1965) and minister of legal affairs (September 1967 until January 1969). In March 1969, Skinner was appointed chief justice of Zambia. A controversy over a decision by Justice Ifor Evans (q.v.) led to Skinner's resignation in September 1969. He then became chief justice of Malawi (q.v.) in 1970.

SLAVE TRADE. Domestic slavery existed for centuries among Africans in Zambia. People became slaves either through capture in warfare, in payment for debt or for causing the death of another, or as a pledge or pawn for a senior relative who was in debt or responsible for another's death. Before the mid–19th century, those who stayed in captivity had no kin to protect or redeem them. While some slaves were allowed to accumulate property and buy their freedom, the most that domestic slaves could hope for was eventual adoption into their masters' families.

The external slave trade began primarily in the early 19th century. The Portuguese had been using slaves at the gold mines near Zumbo (q.v.) for 200 years, but near the end of the 18th century the Portuguese at Mozambique (q.v.) had begun to provide slaves for the Indian Ocean island sugar plantations of the French. Soon there was a demand for slaves in Brazil. At first, most of the slaves came from the area of the lower Zambezi River (q.v.), especially the Chewa (q.v.). The Portuguese attempted to open up slave trading with Kazembe, the Lunda (qq.v.) leader who had for years been sending slaves west to Mwata Yamvo (q.v.). At the same time, the Portuguese in Angola (q.v.) and their Mambari (q.v.) middlemen were buying slaves from Lamba, Luvale, and Lunda (qq.v.) chiefs in northwest Zambia. The early 19th century also saw Arab (q.v.) traders from Zambia coming in search of slaves and other commodities, mostly from northeastern Zambia. By the 1870s and 1880s this northeastern trade was dominated by the Bemba (q.v.), who were active in slave raiding.

In the west, the Lozi (q.v.) dominated their neighbors for the sake of the slave trade. The Portuguese themselves raided villages in southeastern Zambia in the mid and late 19th century as the demand for slaves increased, even though technically the trade was now illegal. A Portuguese-speaking Chikunda from Tete (qq.v.) named Kanyemba was a ferocious slave hunter throughout southern Zambia in the 1870s and 1880s.

The ivory (q.v.) and slave trade were interrelated, as the slaves were often used as porters. Ultimately, one of the major factors in stopping the slave trade was the coming of the British, as the missionaries, British South Africa Company (q.v.) officials, and George Grey's (q.v.) prospectors worked to eliminate the trade and served as protection against slave raiders.

SMITH, IAN. Prime minister of Southern Rhodesia (q.v.) and leader of the Rhodesian Front (q.v.) from 1964 to 1979, he was an experienced Rhodesian politician, engineering his country's unilateral declaration of independence (q.v.) in November 1965. He became the principal adversary of President Kaunda (q.v.) in matters involving Zambian-Rhodesian relations. Guerrilla forces based in Zambia and Mozambique (q.v.) harrassed and brought down Smith's government, a factor in Smith's animosity toward Zambia.

SMITHEMAN, FRANK J. Smitheman's 1896–98 prospecting party of eight Europeans was sent by Rhodesia Concessions,

Ltd., from Bulawayo (q.v.) to look for gold in the Muchinga Mountains (q.v.), west of the Luangwa River (q.v.), and thus to determine the route of the projected railway line from Bulawayo to Lake Tanganyika (q.v.). They found no minerals, but fearful of Mpezeni's hostile Ngoni (qq.v.) warriors, they built a massive stone fort (Fort Elwes) in the Irumi Hills among the Lala near the Katangan Pedicle (qq.v.). There, in late 1897, they granted refuge to Chiwala's Swahili slave traders (qq.v.), whom a Belgian punitive force had just driven from their stockade on the Luapula River (q.v.). On his return, Smitheman submitted a report to Arthur Lawley (q.v.), the British South Africa Company (q.v.) administrator of Matabeleland, on the availability and suitability of North-Eastern Rhodesia's (q.v.) peoples as laborers for the southern mines, thus anticipating the creation of the Rhodesian Native Labour Bureau (q.v.).

SMOKE THAT THUNDERS. This is the English translation of Mosi-oa-tunya, the African name for Victoria Falls (q.v.).

SOCCER. The favorite spectator sport in Zambia, its season lasts eight months. Also called "football" in Zambia (and many countries other than the United States), it is the national sport.

SOCIÉTÉ DES MISSIONS ÉVANGÉLIQUES. This is the French name of the Paris Missionary Society (q.v.), which sponsored the Reverend Coillard's (q.v.) work in Barotseland (q.v.).

SOCIETIES ORDINANCE. A law passed by the Legislative Council (q.v.) in November 1957, it was aimed at controlling nationalist political organizations. It required them to register their branches and to supply the government with detailed information about their organization, officers, and activities. Both the Zambia African National Congress and the United National Independence Party (qq.v.) were especially harassed by application of the ordinance.

SOKO, AXON JASPER (ACKSON JOSEPH). One of the early activists in the Zambia African National Congress and the United National Independence Party (qq.v.), he served in numerous government positions from 1967 to 1977, when he was dismissed from the cabinet and accused of engaging in the activities of a banned political party, the United Progressive Party (q.v.). Born in June 1930 at Chipata (q.v.), he eventually became an accountant-bookkeeper. He served as regional secretary at

Ndola (q.v.) of both ZANC and UNIP from 1959 to 1964, although he was restricted to Luwinga in 1959 because of his party activity. In 1964 he was elected to Parliament from Lundazi. In 1967 he was appointed minister of state for finance, but later that year he was switched to minister for Eastern Province. At one-year intervals he held the same position for Northern, Central, and Copperbelt Provinces. In 1971 he became minister of state for technical and vocational training. He joined the cabinet in April 1971 as minister of trade and industry. In 1973 he became minister of mines and industry, holding this position until his dismissal in April 1977.

SOKOTA, PASKALE. This Bemba (q.v.) teacher was an early member of the African National Congress (q.v.) and a member of the Legislative Council (q.v.). He was headmaster of the Kitwe African School from 1941 to 1951. In 1949 he became a member of the Western Province African Provincial Council and of the African Representative Council (q.v.). An active member of the ANC, he and Dauti Yamba (q.v.) were placed on the Legislative Council with ANC support, replacing two relatively nonpolitical occupants of its two African seats. In 1954 he was reelected for another term. He was an African representative at the Lancaster House Conference (q.v.) in London in 1952. At the Victoria Falls Conference of 1951 (q.v.), he opposed federation (q.v.). In August 1956, the younger and more militant Simon Kapwepwe (q.v.) replaced him on the ANC National Executive Committee. In 1959 he ran unsuccessfully for the Legislative Council as an Independent. In May of that year he was one of the founders of the African National Freedom Movement (q.v.).

SOLI. One of the groups of *ci*Tonga (q.v.)-speaking peoples of south-central Zambia, near Lusaka (q.v.), the Soli, during the 18th century, were among the African peoples who traded with the Portuguese at Zumbo and Feira along the Luangwa-Zambezi River (qq.v.) confluence. Nineteenth-century reports indicate that the Soli were adept iron smelters and smiths. With but one exception, the Soli chiefdoms, like those of the Lala and Ambo (q.v.), were founded by members of the Bena Nyendwa, or Vulva Clan. The system of matrilineal descent (q.v.) is followed among the Soli.

SOLWEZI. This is a district in Zambia's North-Western Province (q.v.) as well as a town about 32 kilometers (20 miles) south of the Democratic Republic of Congo (q.v.) (Zaire) border. Solwezi District had about 53,000 people in 1969 and 120,600 in 1990. The town is not particularly large, but two major roads service it. In 1969 its residents as well as its traditional leaders, by not voting yes in a national referendum, showed their displeasure with the United National Independence Party (q.v.) government for its failure to provide development for the region.

SORGHUM. Often called "kaffir corn" in Central and Southern Africa, "Guinea corn" or even "millet" (q.v.) in West Africa, sorghum is a traditional staple crop throughout much of Zambia, one still valued for its resistance to both drought and waterlogging. Sorghum's biggest drawback, though, is that its ripening seeds must be protected against birds. In those parts of Zambia where maize (q.v.) has not completely replaced sorghum, villagers go out into the fields at dawn and dusk each May and early June with bullroarers and slingshots to scare away the birds. Sorghum is commonly used for brewing beer and has been found in several Early Iron Age sites in Zambia.

SOTHO. This is a term (rhymes with "tutu") for both an ethnic and a linguistic group in Southern Africa. Most of the people in Lesotho, and some of the Africans in Southern Africa, are Sotho. Moreover, like the Swazi of Swaziland and South Africa, they are speakers of seSotho, the second largest of the four major southern Bantu language groups. The Kololo (q.v.), the mid-19th-century conquerors of Barotseland (q.v.), were a Sotho people. The Reverend Coillard of the Paris Evangelical Missionary Society (qq.v.) came to Barotseland after working among the Sotho, bringing Sotho evangelists with him. An interesting separatist church movement was set up by the Sotho evangelist, Willie Mokalapa (q.v.).

SOUTHERN AFRICAN DEVELOPMENT CO-ORDINATION CONFERENCE. This international organization of Southern African states formed in April 1980, when Zimbabwe, Malawi (q.v.), Lesotho, and Swaziland joined the old frontline states (Zambia, Tanzania, Angola, Mozambique, and Botswana, q.v.) to redirect their regional trade and development efforts in order to enlarge their markets and establish their economic independence from South Africa.

SOUTHERN PROVINCE. Located along a major part of the border with Zimbabwe, this province lies generally north and west of the area of the Zambezi River dominated by Victoria Falls and Lake Kariba (qq.v.). The province had almost a half million people in 1969 and over 946,400 in 1990. It consists of nine districts, which, in descending order by population, are Choma, Mazabuka, Monze, Kalomo, Livingstone, Namwala (q.v.), Sinazongwe, Siavonga, and Gwembe. The principal peoples of these districts are the Tonga, Toka, Ila, Leya, and Subiya (qq.v.). During the United National Independence Party's (q.v.) height of power in the late 1960s, Southern Province was considered an African National Congress (q.v.) stronghold, primarily because its leader, Harry Nkumbula (q.v.), was from this province, and had numerous contacts with its traditional leaders.

SOUTHERN RHODESIA. Known as Rhodesia from 1964 to 1979 and as Zimbabwe since 1980, it is Zambia's principal southern neighbor. It was long a source of conflict because of its long history as a white minority-ruled state.

SOUTHERN RHODESIA NATIVE LABOUR BUREAU. *See* RHODESIAN NATIVE LABOUR BUREAU.

STANLEY, SIR HERBERT JAMES. A South African appointed by the British as the first governor of Northern Rhodesia (q.v.), he served from April 1924 until he retired in 1927. One of his most popular actions took place on October 22, 1925, when he announced at Kasama (q.v.) that the poll tax (q.v.) had been reduced from 10 shillings to 7 shillings, 6 pence. However, he also stated that problem tribes would have their taxes increased as a punishment. Stanley served as high commissioner in South Africa from April 1931 to January 1935.

STEPHENSON, JOHN E. (CHIRUPULA). One of the more colorful figures in Zambian colonial history, Stephenson came to Fort Jameson, North-Eastern Rhodesia (qq.v.), in 1899 as a telegrapher for the British South Africa Company (q.v.). In 1900 he and Francis E. F. Jones were appointed collectors (q.v.) to open up the Kafue Hook (q.v.). Preaching an end to war, witchcraft, and the slave trade (q.v.), they opened the old Mkushi and Kapopo *bomas* (q.v.) among the Lala and Lima (qq.v.) peoples and, in 1901, introduced the first hut tax (q.v.). Though later repentant of his zealous tax collections, his nickname, Chirupula (the flogger), refers to the rough brand of justice he administered with his hippo-hide whip. In 1902–03, he helped open Chipawa, Mwomboshi, and Sitanda *bomas* in Soli and

Lenje (qq.v.) country, and in 1904 he opened the first Ndola (q.v.) *boma* to keep an eye on the Bwana Mkubwa Mine (q.v.) and on Chiwala's slave- and ivory-trading Swahili (qq.v.). In 1905 he quarreled with Robert Coryndon (q.v.) over the Copperbelt's (q.v.) transfer to North-Western Rhodesia (q.v.), based upon Lewanika's (q.v.) fictitious territorial claims in the Lochner Concession (q.v.), and the doubling of the hut tax.

Passed over for promotion, and resisting the perceived pressure to abandon his two African wives and children, Stephenson resigned from the BSAC in 1906. He settled among the Lala in Mkushi District and pursued a wide variety of work. Beginning as a labor recruiter for the Katangan mines, he then ran a portage service between Kabwe and Katanga (qq.v.), dabbled in rubber growing, and cut the traction engine (q.v.) road to the Chambeshi (q.v.) rubber factory. He served with the Northern Rhodesia Rifles (q.v.) before settling into citrus farming at home. In 1928 he helped curb the turnover of African laborers at Roan Antelope Mine (q.v.) by arranging the ceremonial "exorcism" of its legendary Sanguni snake (q.v.).

Stephenson became a great, if ineffective, advocate of the Lala and Lamba (q.v.) chiefs. In 1948–49 he published 52 numbers of his *Chirupula's Gazette*, a biweekly, mimeographed circular, to expound his pet peeves—the "Barotse fiction" and the danger posed by unregistered African guns—and his theory that the Lala and Lamba "priest-kings" (i.e., chiefs and village headmen) originated in Pharonic Egypt. Thereafter, Chirupula supplied a steady stream of historical recollections to William Brelsford (q.v.). His *Chirupula's Tale* (1937) is an autobiographical account of his first two years as a BSAC collector; Kathaleen S. Rukavina's *Jungle Pathfinder* (1950, 1951) is a romanticized biography. Chirupula's 1957 funeral was attended by about 60 Europeans, 700 Africans, and his surviving (third) Lala wife and nine children.

STEVENSON ROAD. This 483-kilometer-long (300-mile-long) track along the Tanzanian border between Karonga and Abercorn (q.v.) was an important communication link in the early colonization of Central Africa (q.v.). Missionaries and traders coming to the Tanganyika Plateau formerly took an onerous, 2,900-kilometer (1,800-mile) overland trek from Zanzibar to Ujiji. Envisioning a quicker water route up the Zambezi (q.v.) and Shire Rivers to Lake Nyasa (Malawi, q.v.), James Stevenson—a Glaswegian merchant, board member of the Free Church of Scotland, and director of the African Lakes Company (qq.v.)—donated some £3,000 for a permanent road linking Lakes Nyasa and Tanganyika (q.v.). Construction began in 1881, and though only 97 kilometers (60 miles) were completed, a rough portage track was in service by 1885 for the stations of the African Lakes Company, the London Missionary Society, the White Fathers, and the British South Africa Company (qq.v.). When a telegraph line was established from Karonga to Abercorn in 1889, the track became an ox wagon road with rest houses along the way. By 1900, a freight wagon service operated between Fife (q.v.) and Abercorn. During the early years of World War I, the Northern Rhodesia Rifles (q.v.) patrolled the Stevenson Road to guard against intruders from German East Africa, who constantly cut the telegraph lines.

STIRLING, DAVID. This moderate-to-liberal European politician founded the Capricorn Africa Society (q.v.) in 1949 and the multiracial Constitution Party (q.v.) in 1957.

STORRS, SIR RONALD. This popular Northern Rhodesia (q.v.) governor (1932–34) was a fine writer with a sharp intellect. The Central African climate affected his health, however, and he was transferred without having affected policy.

STRIKES OF 1935, 1940. Perhaps the most notable labor unrest in Zambia occurred during the Copperbelt (q.v.) strikes of 1935 and 1940. Although economic and social in origin, they demonstrated a rising political consciousness among Africans. They were motivated by, among other things, Africans' low wage rates and inferior food and housing conditions, compared to European miners in the same mines. Africans also resented the colour bar (q.v.), which reserved all advanced jobs for Europeans, and the insulting and even brutal behavior of Europeans toward Africans. Almost nothing was achieved by the 1935 strike, which did not last long. The 1940 strike was more vigorous and ended only when 17 strikers were killed and 65 injured during an attack by the miners on a compound office.

STRUCTURAL ADJUSTMENT PROGRAM. The term refers to the austerity measures that the International Monetary Fund (q.v.) imposes as prerequisites for further foreign aid. Zambia plunged into serious foreign debt in the mid-1970s, when copper (q.v.) prices fell below production costs and the cost of oil imports tripled. Foreign exchange earnings evaporated, spare parts became scarce, and mine production fell. President Kaunda's (q.v.) administration borrowed heavily to maintain Zambia's extensive system of price subsidies, and Zambia's debt rose from US$623 million in 1970 to US$7.2 billion in 1990, by which time Zambia was no longer able to pay the interest on its debts. In 1985, to qualify for further aid, Kaunda's regime adopted a wide range of austerity measures—currency devaluation, higher interest rates, the domestic auctioning of foreign exchange, the removal of subsidies and price controls, and a wage freeze—designed to attract foreign investment and to make Zambia's exports more competitive. But the social and political costs of the structural adjustment program—unemployment, strikes, and 1986 bread and mealiemeal (q.v.) riots in Copperbelt towns—forced Kaunda to break with the IMF in 1987. A new round of economic reforms in 1989 all but brought down President Kaunda's government (see LU-CHEMBE, MWANBA), so that by early 1991 Zambia was broke and cut off from all forms of donor aid.

President Chiluba (q.v.) took office in November 1991 and immediately implemented the IMF's structural adjustment program to gain access to aid, while simultaneously lobbying for a write-off on Zambia's US$3.1 billion debt to the World Bank and the IMF. Price subsidies were removed upon food and on health, transport, and educational services. Some parastatals—the National Agricultural Marketing Board, Zambia Airways (qq.v.), United Bus Company, and Kabwe Mine (q.v.)—were closed, while others were handed over to the Zambia Privatisation Agency (q.v.). More than 100,000 formal sector jobs (about one-quarter of all formal sector jobs) were eliminated in just four years. The consequent loss of job security during a time of ruinous inflation only encouraged the remaining employees to pilfer. The informal sector—including *salaula* (q.v.) traders and street vendors—has swelled accordingly, and the increasing numbers of extralegal charcoal burners (manufacturers) now pose serious deforestation and environmental problems to the Kafue River (q.v.) basin. The mealiemeal shortage in August 1994—attributed to collection failures in remote rural areas and to hoarding by private maize (q.v.)-buying firms in search of higher prices—suggests that the IMF's free market cure for the Zambian economy has dangerous, unanticipated consequences. Zambians have reinterpreted this program's SAP acronym to mean "Satana ali pano" (Satan is right here).

STUBBS, FRANK N. He was the African National Congress (q.v.) candidate for the Luapula (q.v.) national seat in the 1962 election. A conservative-to-moderate European, he won the seat in the December by-election after campaigning vigorously on the platform that he would quit the African National Congress (q.v.) rather than join in a governing coalition with the "radical" United National Independence Party (q.v.). When he won, however, it was discovered that Stubbs and C. E. Cousins (q.v.), also of the ANC, were the only Europeans elected by either UNIP or the ANC. As the constitution required that two of the ministers be Europeans, Stubbs came under pressure to renege on his campaign pledge to allow an all-African coalition to come to power. Harry Nkumbula (q.v.) of the ANC used the two Europeans to bargain for ministerial parity with UNIP. Stubbs announced that he would return to his constituents to discuss the situation and on December 15 returned to Lusaka (q.v.) to join the government to "serve the interests of the country." He became minister for transport and works, a post he held until UNIP decisively won the 1964 elections.

SUBIYA (SUBIA). One of the many ethnic groups in southwestern Zambia, the Subiya homeland is the area between the Chobe and Zambezi Rivers (qq.v.), south of the Zambezi. Thus most Subiya actually live in the Caprivi Strip (q.v.) of Namibia. While one group of Subiya speak *ci*Tonga, most of them are *si*Lozi speaking (qq.v.), as a result of their numerous contacts with the Lozi (q.v.). Historians believe the Subiya were pushed south out of the Zambezi floodplain when the Lozi (then the Luyi) began moving south. This was in the 17th century, when Mwanambinyi (q.v.) conquered them and set up a capital near today's Senanga (q.v.). However, it was the sixth Lozi king, Ngombala (q.v.), who brought them firmly under Lozi rule in the early 18th century. Lozi *induna*s (q.v.) were sent to the area to live and, thereby, to represent the Lozi king. Tribute was paid in grain, fish, meat, skins, ivory (q.v.), or honey. An attempted revolt by the Subiya and the Toka (q.v.) in 1865–66 was ruthlessly suppressed by Sipopa (q.v.), the Lozi king. He later attempted to win their support by restoring some of their land and giving them governmental positions.

SULIMAN, ABDULLAH IBN (BIN). A prominent Arab (q.v.) trader who lived in northern Zambia in the late 19th and early 20th century, he arrived (sent by Kumba Kumba, q.v.), leading a squad of elephant hunters. Abdullah and his men assisted Chimutwe Nsama VI of the Tabwa (qq.v.) to regain his capital from his rivals. A couple of years later, in 1884, Tippu Tib (q.v.)

again sent Abdullah to aid Chimutwe, this time against Bemba chief Mporokoso (qq.v.). A large force of Bemba, including the Mwamba (q.v.) himself, aided Mporokoso, but the Bemba eventually were repelled. Abdullah was given land for his reward, and his heirs still live in the village he built on Kaputa Stream. In 1891, Chimutwe argued with Abdullah over a woman and began interfering with his caravans. Abdullah allied himself with the Bemba, and Chimutwe was killed at his capital by the combined force. The new Nsama had Abdullah's backing. Abdullah died at his village in 1916.

SULIMAN, NASORO BIN. An Arab (q.v.) trader from Muscat and a follower of Mlozi (q.v), Suliman and his followers, upon Mlozi's defeat in 1895, set up camp near the Bemba (q.v.) leader, Mporokoso (q.v.). A British attempt to visit the Mporokoso in April 1899 was repulsed by Suliman and his followers. Eventually, the Arabs fled to Abdullah bin Suliman (q.v.), who turned over Nasoro to the British in June 1899.

SUNKA MULAMU. A *ci*Nyanja (q.v.) phrase meaning "push (me), (my) brother-in-law," by the late 1970s it came to represent motor vehicles that required jump-starts to become operational. At that time, imported automotive products like batteries became prohibitively expensive, while those produced domestically were often unreliable.

SUPREME ACTION COUNCIL. Set up by the African National Congress (q.v.) at its February 1952 conference, the council was a special nine-member leadership group. Its main duty was to fight federation (q.v.). Since work stoppages were to be a principal weapon, five of the nine seats were filled by members of the Trade Union Congress (q.v.). Kenneth Kaunda (q.v.) was a member of the council.

SUU, FRANCIS L. A Lozi (q.v.) politician active in the Sicaba Party (q.v.) of Barotseland (q.v.) in 1962, he had been an administrative secretary to Yeta III (q.v.). He was not part of the subsequent administration but had returned to the royal court in the 1950s. In April 1962, he was a member of the Barotse delegation at constitutional discussions in London. In June he helped organize the Sicaba Party and became one of its two candidates in the October 1962 Legislative Council (q.v.) elections. He was overwhelmingly defeated by Arthur Wina (q.v.), receiving only

65 votes. The next month he announced his retirement from politics and his intention to dissolve the party.

SWAHILI. Derived from the Arabic *sahil* (coast), it is both a linguistic and ethnic term. *Ki*Swahili, the Swahili language, is a Bantu language (q.v.) with many Arabic loan words. As a trade language throughout Eastern Africa, it became the common language in the Katanga (q.v.) mines and, along with English, the national language of modern Tanzania. The Swahili people proper were the urban traders of the Kenyan and Tanzanian coast who, beginning at Kilwa in the late 12th century, served the dhows of the Arab, Persian, and Indian traders from across the Indian Ocean. Unlike the Arab (q.v.) traders, mostly first-generation immigrants of demonstrable Arabic ancestry, the Swahili consider themselves a creolized people of mixed African and Arab origins. In Zambian history, however, "Swahili" came to mean any African trader (often Yao or Chewa, qq.v.) with east coast connections and who wore east coast robes, spoke *ki*Swahili, and was Muslim. In African oral histories, these nominal Swahili are often called BaNgwana, BaLungwana, or BaNyasa. A number of Swahili settled in Zambia during the course of the 19th-century slave and ivory trade (qq.v.), notably among the Tabwa and the Lamba (qq.v.) of Northern and Copperbelt Provinces (qq.v.). Given their historic association with the slave trade, neither the Swahili language nor the ethnic identity is popular in modern Zambia.

SWAKA. A small ethnic group in north-central Zambia, they probably originated as a 19th-century offshoot of their eastern neighbors, the Lala (q.v.). After the imposition of native reserves (q.v.), a serious land shortage around 1930 forced many Swaka to move west and settle among the Lamba (q.v.) people in what is now called Copperbelt Province (q.v.).

T

TABWA. A matrilineal people who straddle the Zambia-Democratic Republic of Congo (Zaire) border between Lakes Mweru and Tanganyika (qq.v.), they now speak *ci*Bemba (q.v.) and, in many ways, resemble their Bemba (q.v.) neighbors to the south. The most important Tabwa chiefship, that of Nsama (q.v.), was founded in Itabwa (q.v.) (land of the Tabwa) in the late 18th century by Nsama, local head of the chiefly Zimba (Leopard)

Clan. The Lunda king, Kazembe III (qq.v.), received tribute from them around that same time. A later offshoot of this group was the Mulilo chiefship. These early Tabwa are supposed to have worn cotton cloth, rather than the barkcloth and skins worn by their neighbors.

The strongest Tabwa leader was Nsama III, Chipili Chipioka, who soundly defeated the Arab (q.v.) traders in 1841–42 and a combined Arab-Lunda force some 20 years later. In 1867, however, a caravan led by Tippu Tib (q.v.) defeated him, and foreign traders dominated Itabwa from then on. Some Bemba groups, for example, moved into the Tabwa territory called Isenga. And though the Tabwa petitioned the colonial government to return it to them in the mid-1930s, the British were not interested. Harry Johnston (q.v.) obtained a "treaty" for the British South Africa Company (q.v.) from Tabwa chief Mulilo in 1889, and Alfred Sharpe (q.v.) obtained a similar one from Nsama a year or two later.

TAFUNA. The title was given to the paramount chief (q.v.) of the Lungu (q.v.) people of northern Zambia, near the southeastern corner of Lake Tanganyika (q.v.). Other Lungu chiefs were secondary to him. The royal capital was at Isoko (q.v.) with the exception of a brief period under Tafuna III. In 1870, Tafuna IV, Kakunga, returned the capital to Isoko, but he fled north to Kasanga around 1883 when the Bemba (q.v.) of Chitapankwa (q.v.) ravaged the area and killed Lungu chief Zombe (q.v.). No Tafuna returned to Isoko for many years, and Ponde's (q.v.) Bemba ruled the area. The Tafuna was exiled and imprisoned in 1891 after refusing to supply workers to the London Missionary Society and the African Lakes Company (qq.v.). In 1930 the Tafuna urged the Northern Rhodesian government to remove the Bemba still occupying Lungu land, but he was turned down.

TALKING DRUM. Unlike the true hourglass-shaped talking drums of West Africa, on which the sounds produced by varying the skin tension can mimic the rising and falling vowel pitches of the region's tonal languages, the talking drum (*mondo*) of Kazembe's Lunda (qq.v.) and the Bemba (q.v.) is a hollow wooden slit signal drum. Beaten with wooden sticks, it sent messages by varying the combination of beats.

TAMBO. This small ethnic group, located along the upper Luangwa River (q.v.) in extreme northeastern Zambia, is part of the

Mambwe-Lungu (q.v.) language group. In the 19th century, the Tambo grew cotton and wove their own cloth. Their traditions suggest that they broke away from the Bisa (q.v.) and moved east into unoccupied territory. While retaining the Bisa's matrilineal clan names, the Tambo and their neighbors are patrilineal, cattle-keeping people. During the 19th century, they were involved in conflicts with the Iwa (q.v.) chiefs.

TANGANYIKA CONCESSIONS, LTD. This subsidiary of the British South Africa Company (q.v.) was established in 1899 by Cecil Rhodes' associate, Robert Williams (qq.v.), who parlayed a 5,180-square-kilometer (2,000-square-mile) BSAC prospecting concession south of the Katanga (q.v.) border into a 155,400-square-kilometer (60,000-square-mile) concession from the Compagnie du Katanga and its successor, the Comité Spécial du Katanga. Under George Grey (q.v.), TANKS established the mineral wealth of the Katangan-Rhodesian Copperbelt, opened and ran the mines, hastened the end of the slave trade (q.v.) to Angola (q.v.), and determined the terminus of the future rail line from Southern Rhodesia (q.v.) and South Africa. Not surprisingly, Williams' TANKS defended Belgian king Leopold during the "red rubber" scandal in the early 1900s, when his Congo Free State was charged with mutilating Africans to enforce its mandated rubber collections. Though Union Minière du Haut-Katanga (q.v.) assumed control of the Katangan mines in 1906, TANKS owned 40 percent of its shares and arranged financing for the railroad extension from Broken Hill (q.v.) (1906) and Ndola (q.v.) (1908) to Elisabethville (modern Lubumbashi) and Katanga mines (1910). This, in turn, provided the BSAC with freight revenues from the coal and copper (q.v.) shipments to and from the Katangan mines. Until 1930, Robert Williams and Co., TANKS' labor recruiting subsidiary headquartered in Fort Rosebery (q.v.), provided a large share of the UMHK's workers, most of them from modern Luapula and Northern Provinces (qq.v.). The postwar devaluation of the Belgian franc so crippled TANK's finances that, by the early 1920s, its wealth was largely limited to its stock and purchasing rights in the UMHK.

TANGANYIKA DISTRICT. An important administrative subdivision of North-Eastern Rhodesia (q.v.) during the days of British South Africa Company (q.v.) rule, the district was home to the Bemba, Lungu, Mambwe, Tabwa (qq.v.), and their experienced warriors. The slave and ivory trade (qq.v.) were both active in the area, and interethnic fighting was also common. The district also attracted many of the early missionary groups. While Abercorn (q.v.) was the principal administrative center, there were also other *bomas* (q.v.) at Sumbu, Katwe, and Mporokoso (q.v.). At the turn of the century there were about 100 policemen stationed in the district.

TANGANYIKA ESTATE. This 11,163-square-kilometer (4,310-square-mile) territory in the Abercorn and Isoka (qq.v.) areas of northeastern Zambia was acquired by the British South Africa Company (q.v.) from the African Lakes Company (q.v.). The Reserves Commission (q.v.) of 1927 persuaded the BSAC to give up parts of it to allow more Europeans to acquire the land for coffee plantations. Despite African protests, the Crown Lands and Native Reserves (qq.v.) (Tanganyika District) Order in Council of 1929 created such lands. The attempt to attract more Europeans was notoriously unsuccessful.

TANZAM RAILWAY. *See* TAZARA.

TAZAMA. *See* TANZANIA-ZAMBIA OIL PIPELINE.

TANZANIA. This country, Zambia's northeastern neighbor, was created in 1964 by the union of two independent states, Tanganyika and Zanzibar. The TAZARA (q.v.) railway could never have been built without the cooperation of Tanzania and its former president, Julius Nyerere (q.v.), who was a close friend and advisor to Zambia's Kenneth Kaunda (q.v.).

TANZANIA-ZAMBIA OIL PIPELINE. This 1,705-kilometer (1059-mile) pipeline from the port at Dar es Salaam, Tanzania (q.v.), to the Ndola (q.v.) oil refinery was completed in 1968, as part of the larger effort to reduce Zambia's dependence upon the uncertain rail route through what were then white minority-ruled Rhodesia and South Africa. TAZAMA celebrated its 25th anniversary in 1993, when its annual pumping rate of 1.1 million tonnes per year was expected to improve once its rehabilitation work was complete.

TANZANIA-ZAMBIA RAILWAY AUTHORITY. *See* TAZARA.

TAZARA. The acronym for the Tanzania-Zambia Railway Authority, Zambia's main import and export transport artery from 1975–80, the Tanzam Railway is now commonly called the TA-

ZARA. As early as 1961, Kenneth Kaunda (q.v.) was discussing the need for a new rail line to the Indian Ocean, one not controlled by hostile, white regimes. Though Rhodesia's 1965 unilateral declaration of independence (q.v.) only exacerbated Zambia's need, neither Britain, America, the World Bank, nor the United Nations were willing to fund it. Then, in 1967, the Peoples' Republic of China offered to build such a railway, offering a US$400 million interest-free loan and the necessary equipment and technicians. Construction, which began in 1970 and ended in 1975, involved 25,000 polite and smiling Chinese technicians and 100,000 African laborers. Paralleling the Great North Road (q.v.), this 1,860-kilometer (1160-mile) railway runs from the Tanzanian port of Dar es Salaam, over 300 bridges, through ten kilometers (six miles) of tunnels to within a kilometer or two of the Zambia Railways (q.v.) line at Kapiri Mposhi (q.v.).

Problems soon arose, as neither the railway nor the port at Dar were able to bear the weight or volume of Zambia's total imports and exports. Narrow embankments were washed away by rains, and the Chinese locomotives (eventually replaced by German ones) proved unequal to some of the line's long, steep grades. When spare parts and railway wagons became scarce, stocks accumulated on the docks at Dar, where ships waiting to load and unload clogged the port. Tanzanian and Zambian authorities were soon accusing one another of incompetence and corruption. In fact, the Chinese had provided technical and managerial training to 1,200 TAZARA trainees, but these were soon lured away by the higher salaries available in the private sector. By October 1978, the TAZARA became so hopelessly clogged that Zambia was forced to revert to the southern railway line through white-ruled Rhodesia. The Chinese did send out 250 advisors to refurbish the TAZARA in the early 1980s, and while the TAZARA made its first profit around 1985, Zambia was pleased to regain access to the southern rail line to South Africa's ports once Zimbabwe became a black majority-ruled state.

TEAKWOOD. An export product of Zambia, the product is important enough that the industry was nationalized by the Mulungushi Declaration (q.v.) of 1968. The slow-growing teak forests are most often found in the Sesheke and Senanga districts of Western Province (qq.v.), where they are commercially exploited. The product is variously known as Rhodesian teak, Zambezi redwood, or *mukushi*. Its scientific name is *Baikiaea plurijuga*. At first used only for mining timber and railway sleepers, its beauty has made it popular for furniture and parquet floors.

TEMBE. These stockaded villages, belonging to Arab slave traders (qq.v.), were found primarily in the Luangwa (q.v.) valley of northeastern Zambia in the late 19th century.

TEMBO, CHRISTON. Appointed deputy to General Masheke, the army commander, in October 1980, Tembo became chief of the army in April 1985, after Grey Zulu (q.v.) was made the United National Independence Party's (q.v.) secretary-general, and General Masheke became minister of defense. Tembo was replaced as army head, in January 1987, by Lieutenant General Gary Kalenge. He was later made ambassador to West Germany. He was arrested and accused of participating in a coup plot in October 1988, along with five other military officers and three civilians. In August 1989 it was announced that Tembo, along with three other senior officers, had been charged with treason for plotting to overthrow the government. In July 1990 Zambia's High Court (q.v.) rejected Tembo's confession to treason as inadmissible, saying that it had been extracted under duress. On July 25, President Kaunda (q.v.) announced that Tembo, along with other persons held on conspiracy charges, had been granted amnesty. He was released on July 31 and immediately expressed an interest in joining the newly formed Movement for Multiparty Democracy (q.v.). The granting of his amnesty came in the midst of serious rioting in Lusaka (q.v.), which began over the increase in the price of mealiemeal (q.v.) but which soon took on antigovernment overtones. President Chiluba (q.v.) appointed Tembo minister of tourism when the MMD took power after the 1991 elections.

TEMBO, FRANKLIN. One of the founders and the first chairman in 1932 of the Abercorn Native Welfare Association (q.v.), within a few years he had switched to the Kasama Native Welfare Association (q.v.), becoming its secretary in 1937. His activities in these associations in the 1930s made him an early advocate of African autonomy. (Sources are unclear as to whether this is the same man as the Edward Franklin Tembo who was a cofounder of the Livingstone Native Welfare Association, q.v., in 1930.)

TEMPLE, MERFYN M. A Methodist minister in Lusaka (q.v.) and author of several books on the church in Zambia, notably *Afri-*

can Angelus and *Rain on the Earth,* the Reverend Temple was active in various liberal, multiracial groups, including the Constitution Party (q.v.) of which he was chairman. As the United National Independence Party (q.v.) began to rise in the early 1960s, Temple became an active campaigner for European support of UNIP. In 1964 he was appointed the first director of the Zambia Youth Services (q.v.).

TETE. Located on the lower Zambezi River (q.v.) between its confluences with the Luangwa and the Shire Rivers, the town was an important trading center for many centuries. Arab (q.v.) traders presumably passed through Tete in the 12th or 13th centuries on their way to Ingombe Ilede (q.v.). A Jesuit mission and Portuguese traders and officials were based there in the 17th century. Early in the next century, gold was discovered in the vicinity, attracting more people. Meanwhile, the Bisa (q.v.) came south to Tete with their ivory (q.v.), as did the Lunda of Kazembe (qq.v.). Later, slaves were brought from the north for trade. At the same time, Portuguese explorers like Lacerda, Monteiro, and Gamitto (qq.v.) began their trips to Zambia from Tete, and Silva Pôrto (q.v.) ended his Zambian trip there. Today, it is part of Mozambique (q.v.).

THIRD NON-ALIGNED SUMMIT CONFERENCE. This prestigious meeting of representatives of states was held in Lusaka (q.v.), Zambia, in late 1970. The speeches and debates in Mulungushi Hall concentrated on Southern African issues. The largest Third World summit conference up to that time, it condemned the white-ruled countries of southern Africa and urged that drastic action be taken against them.

THIRD ZAMBIAN REPUBLIC. The constitution of the Third Republic was promulgated in August 1991, prior to the 1991 elections. It was based on the report of the Mvunga Commission (q.v.), which had been appointed by President Kaunda (q.v.). This constitution represented a compromise between the United National Independence Party (q.v.) government and its ad hoc opposition, the Movement for Multiparty Democracy (q.v.). The latter succeeded in having language added enhancing Parliament's (q.v.) legislative powers in the Third Republic. The new constitution, however, still granted considerable discretionary powers to the president. Once the MMD came to power later in the year, it reopened the Mvunga Commission and, in 1993, opened a new Constitutional Review Commission (q.v.), which, under the chairmanship of John Mwanakatwe (q.v.), released its report in 1995.

THOMAS, J. H. This British secretary of state for dominion affairs from June 1930 until November 1935 refused a request in 1931 by the Southern Rhodesian (q.v.) government (with support by some elected members of the Northern Rhodesian Legislative Council) that a conference be held to consider amalgamation (q.v.) of the two territories. He believed that Northern Rhodesia needed time to develop as a separate entity.

THOMSON, JAMES MOFFAT. See MOFFAT THOMSON, JAMES.

THOMSON, JOSEPH. A noted East African hunter and explorer, Thomson, like Alfred Sharpe (q.v.), was hired by Cecil Rhodes (q.v.) in 1890 to collect concessionary treaties for the British South Africa Company (q.v.), and to steal Katanga from Belgium's King Leopold II by obtaining a treaty from Yeke king Msiri (qq.v.). Thomson's caravan left Kotakota, on the western shore of Lake Nyasa (Malawi) in August 1890 and traveled among the Bisa, Aushi, Lala, and Lamba (qq.v.) peoples and through the Katanga Pedicle (q.v.) to the area of modern Sakania. He reached Lamba chief Mushili (qq.v.), the namesake of Yeke king Msiri, in November, and made a brief visit to Lenje (q.v.) chief Chipepo before heading back to Mushili's. The sick porters he left there started a local smallpox epidemic. Thomson abandoned his attempt to reach Msiri and turned back for Nyasaland (q.v.). Ngoni chief Mpezeni (qq.v.) again declined to deal with him, and Thomson blamed this on the interference of Karl Wiese (q.v.), the German trader with interests in Portuguese East Africa (Mozambique, q.v.). Though the BSAC based its initial claims to the Copperbelt's (q.v.) mineral wealth on Thomson's treaty with Mushili, the Colonial Office put little stock in his 14 vaguely worded treaties. Thus in 1906 the BSAC transferred the Copperbelt from North-Eastern to North-Western Rhodesia (qq.v.), basing its claims on the terms of the Lochner Concession from Lozi king Lewanika (qq.v.).

THUMB PIANO. See KALIMBA.

TIMES OF ZAMBIA. Taken over by the United National Independence Party (q.v.) in 1975, presumably because of criticism of the government, this is Zambia's largest newspaper. Even when it was owned by the multinational corporation Lonrho (q.v.), it got much of its information from government agencies, notably the Zambia Information Services (q.v.). It is now published in Lusaka (q.v.). It was founded in 1944 as the *Northern News* (q.v.) and was aimed toward a European readership until 1963. As a twice weekly, it was under the ownership of Roy Welensky (q.v.) and, later, the Argus newspaper chain of South Africa. Under the ownership of Lonrho, it became the *Times of Zambia* on July 1, 1965. Six weeks earlier, Richard Hall (author of several books on Zambia) had become editor; and the paper became a moderate, slightly progovernment paper, with some coverage of international news supplementing a national and local emphasis. It was then published in Ndola (q.v.). Under Dunston Kamana, editor in the early 1970s, however, the *Times* became critical of some UNIP politicians and government inefficiency. Early in 1972 Kamana was replaced when the government appointed its own editor, Vernon Mwaanga (q.v.). UNIP took over the paper in 1975. In the early 1990s it was privatized by the Zambia Privatisation Agency (q.v.).

TIPPU TIB (TIPPOO TIB). One of Africa's best-known Arab (q.v.) traders, this native of Zanzibar was actually named Hamed ibn Muhammed el Murjebi. The Africans knew him as both Tippu Tib and Pembamoto. His first trip to Central Africa (q.v.) was evidently in 1863–64, when he traveled in search of ivory (q.v.). In 1866 he returned and visited Bemba chief Mwamba (qq.v.) and the old and powerful Tabwa chief Nsama (qq.v.). Tippu Tib coveted Nsama's huge storehouses of ivory and copper (q.v.), and in 1967 his Arab fighters defeated Nsama using guns against the Tabwa's spears and bows. A thousand slaves, 30 tons of ivory, and 10 tons of copper were taken, according to the biography that appeared in 1906 based on his records. His use of guns revolutionized regional warfare, as Tippu's Lungu (q.v.) allies and other Africans saw how easily the mighty Nsama was beaten. After this victory Tippu Tib returned to the coast through Bemba territory, where he had left his half brother, Kumba Kumba (q.v.). Tippu Tib returned to trade in 1869–70, visiting Tabwa country as well as several of the Bemba chiefs, including Mwamba and Chitimukulu (q.v.). He then set up a permanent trade depot at Nsama's village, headed by Kumba Kumba, and made his way west into Katanga (q.v.). Kakunga, a member of the Lungu chiefly family, used Tippu's help to defeat his opponents and become Tafuna IV at Isoko (qq.v.). Tippu's force also helped Lukwesa, a Lunda leader, regain his position as Kazembe (q.v.). Later in his life, King Leopold II of Belgium made Tippu provisional governor of the Upper Congo. He later accompanied Henry Stanley on the Emin Pasha relief expedition. In his old age he retired to Zanzibar, where he died of malaria (q.v.) in 1905.

TOBACCO. Tobacco was first imported into Africa in the early 19th century, but the Gwembe Tonga and the Senga (qq.v.) were exporting it within just a few decades. Around 1914, Europeans were growing tobacco on large farms near Fort Jameson (q.v.) for export. It became Northern Rhodesia's (q.v.) main export in 1926–27, but its market slowly collapsed until after World War II. It was an increasingly popular crop in Zambia, especially since World War II; by the mid-1970s, Zambia was averaging over 6,000 metric tons per year, with Virginia tobacco being the most popular. While Virginia flue-cured tobacco is produced mainly in central and southern Zambia, burley is produced in Eastern Province (q.v.), and small plots of Turkish tobacco grow in scattered parts of northeastern Zambia.

TOBACCO ASSOCIATION OF ZAMBIA. Originally begun as the northern (i.e., Northern Rhodesian, q.v.) branch of the Rhodesian Tobacco Association, the association changed its name after independence. Its purpose is to develop and promote the national tobacco industry, but it also provides its members with agricultural extension, marketing, and crop insurance services, which are funded by a 1 percent levy on tobacco sales.

TODD, REGINALD STEPHEN GARFIELD. Todd was president of the United Rhodesia Party and, from 1953 to 1958, prime minister of Southern Rhodesia (q.v.). Born in New Zealand in 1908, he was a missionary in Southern Rhodesia from 1934 until he became prime minister in 1953. He was first elected to Parliament (q.v.) in 1946. In 1959 he helped form the Central Africa Party (q.v.), which was briefly active in Northern as well as Southern Rhodesia during the middle part of the decade of federation (q.v.). Todd's moderately liberal view of race relations and political rights for Africans found sympathy among some Northern Rhodesian (q.v.) liberals such as Sir John Moffat (q.v.). These same views, though, caused his removal from the prime minister's seat after his party deemed him too radical.

TOKA. This small ethnic group lives in southern Zambia, to the north and east of Victoria Falls (q.v.). The people are sometimes called the southern Tonga (q.v.), and are part of the *ci*Tonga (q.v.)-speaking language group. Like the 19th-century Tonga, they were politically decentralized, cattle-keeping farmers and traders and, as such, were targeted by raiders from the stronger and more cohesive Kololo, Ndebele, and Lozi (qq.v.). On the other hand, Toka groups helped overthrow Lubosi (Lewanika) (qq.v.) for a brief period, almost tricked Sebituane (q.v.) into an ambush, and raided the Gwembe (Valley) (q.v.) Tonga in the 1850s. They were severely weakened by the smallpox epidemic of 1892–93 and by the rinderpest epidemic of 1895. In the 1890s the Toka entered the migrant labor system, working in the Southern African mines. The Lozi considered them their vassals. The 1900 Lewanika Concession (q.v.) allowed the British South Africa Company (q.v.) to provide land grants in Toka territory to outsiders.

TOMBOSHALO. A Lungu (q.v.) leader around the beginning of the 20th century, Tomboshalo refused to accept the authority of Bemba chief Kaliminwa (qq.v.). Tomboshalo had been a slave of the Ngoni (q.v.) for a time in his youth and, when freed, lived at the London Missionary Society mission at Nyamukolo (qq.v.). His father's land was then under Chief Kaliminwa. Encouraged by LMS missionary James Hemans (q.v.), he led a band armed with spears and bows and publicly defied the conquering chief's authority. Headmen of several neighboring villages joined in the defiance. The native commissioner (q.v.) intervened and finally got Tomboshalo to recognize Kaliminwa's authority. But the next year, in May 1904, Tomboshalo again protested the Bemba rule and was jailed for his persistence.

TONGA. Both a linguistic and an ethnic term, the Tonga language family includes the Lenje, Soli, and Ila (qq.v.). These three peoples are not counted, however, among the *ci*Tonga (q.v.) speakers of Zambia, which constitute nearly 12 percent of Zambia's population (795,600 in 1986) and is limited to the Tonga, Toka, Totela (q.v.), Leya (q.v.), and Subiya (q.v.). There are, in addition, nearly another 70,000 *ci*Tonga speakers in Zimbabwe and Botswana (q.v.).

Ethnically, there are about 800,000 Plateau and Gwembe Tonga (qq.v.) in Zambia alone. They live in Southern Province (q.v.), south of the Kafue River (q.v.) and along the western half of the Zambezi River (q.v.) border with Zimbabwe. Ceramics from the archaeological site of Sebanzi Hill (q.v.) strongly suggest that the ancestors of today's Tonga peoples were living in southern Zambia by the 12th or 13th century. Living in small, decentralized villages and with no complex political organization, the Tonga people developed little ethnic consciousness. When the British came, they appointed chiefs, sometimes choosing the local rainmaker. (*See* PLATEAU TONGA for information applicable to most Tonga.)

TOTELA. The Totela are one of the smaller groups in southwestern Zambia. They were under Lozi (q.v.) domination from the time of the mid–18th century reign of Ngombala (q.v.), the sixth Lozi king. They occasionally intermarried with the Lozi, who loaned them cattle because of their good pasture area south of the Lumbe River (q.v.). A noted traveler, Emil Holub (q.v.), described the Totela as excellent ironworkers, second in southern Africa only to the Zulu. Their ironwork was an important trade item for them.

TOWN BEMBA (*CI*COPPERBELTI; *CI*TAUNI). Town Bemba is based upon the *ci*Bemba (q.v.) spoken by the majority of the Copperbelt's (q.v.) labor migrants and other immigrants and incorporates a host of English loan words. It is the rapidly and continuously changing vernacular language of the urban Copperbelt and is best described in A. L. Epstein's classic 1959 paper, "Linguistic Innovation and Culture on the Copperbelt," which was reprinted in his *Scenes from African Urban Life* (1992).

TRACTION ENGINE (CHITUKUTUKU). From 1906 to 1916, wood-burning, steam-powered traction engines were used to haul trailers of heavy freight through modern Zambia's tsetse (q.v.)-infested bush. First introduced by George Grey's Tanganyika Concessions, Ltd. (qq.v.), to bring a smelting furnace and mining gear from the Broken Hill (q.v.) railhead to Kansanshi (q.v.) Mine, such engines were also used to transport copper (q.v.) and supplies to and from the Katangan rail line and to bring supplies to the Anglo-Belgian Boundary Commission of 1911–13. Chirupula Stephenson (q.v.) blazed much of the Great North Road (q.v.) when, in 1913–15, he cut the road for the traction engine hauling machinery from Kashitu Siding (near Kapiri Mposhi, q.v.) to the short-lived Chambishi rubber factory north of Mpika (q.v.) (*see* RUBBER). During World War I, Arthur Davison (q.v.) worked on the crew whose two traction engines helped transport two 40-foot armed motor launches from the Congo's Kambove railhead to counter German steamers on Lake Tanganyika (q.v.). While such engines could plow through brush and smaller trees, they required advance teams to cut rough tracks, to supply their constant firewood and water requirements, and to lay corduroy bridges across marsh or water hazards.

TRADE UNION CONGRESS. Founded by Lawrence Katilungu (q.v.) in 1950, the TUC was a federation of many of the newly formed African trade unions. The African Mineworkers Union (q.v.), of which Katilungu was also president, was the most prominent of the member unions. Dixon Konkola (q.v.) replaced him as the TUC's president in 1955. In 1960, Katilungu's participation on the Monckton Commission (q.v.) and his position as acting president of the African National Congress (q.v.) caused bitter controversy within the TUC, and many unions formed the Reformed Trade Union Congress (q.v.). When he was replaced as leader of the AMU in December 1960, the TUC and the RTUC reunited as the United Trade Union Congress (q.v.).

TRADE UNIONS AND TRADE DISPUTES ORDINANCE. This ordinance, designed to create stable industrial relations, was passed in December 1964 and went into effect early the next year. It stopped trade unions from receiving outside assistance, especially financial aid, and established the Zambia Congress of Trade Unions (q.v.) with which all unions were encouraged to affiliate. The law gave considerable power to the registrar of trade unions, to the minister of labor, and to the ZCTU. The law required secret ballots in union elections and, to prevent the proliferation of minor unions, required that each registered trade union have a minimum of 100 members.

TRANSITIONAL DEVELOPMENT PLAN. Inaugurated in January 1965, this plan, following the pattern of the Emergency Development Plan of 1964, emphasized educational expansion. It carried on the primary and secondary education projects of the earlier plan and established a goal of universal primary education. Its budget of £35 million also added projects for developing a university and teacher-training colleges, along with adult education. The plan ended in July 1966, when the First National Development Plan was begun.

TRYPANOSOMIASIS. Commonly known as sleeping sickness, this disease affects both animals and humans across Africa in a wide area on both sides of the equator. Much of Zambia experiences it. Spread by the tsetse (q.v.) fly, it can be deadly, thus many infested areas are sparsely inhabited and undercultivated. In Zambia, attempts by the government to inoculate the cattle met serious resistance, spurred on in the 1950s by the African National Congress (q.v.), which warned that inoculations would harm the cattle. One notable resistance incident occurred in 1958 at Choma (q.v.).

TSETSE FLY. This horsefly-like insect is the principal transmitter of trypanosomiasis (q.v.). It is associated with wild game herds and belts of shady bush.

TSHOMBE, MOISE. Tshombe was the leader of the Conakat Party based in Katanga (q.v.) Province of the Congo in the early 1960s. He led a secessionist movement, attempting to withdraw Katanga from the Congo. Although this uprising was finally quelled with the aid of United Nations troops, Tshombe later became prime minister of the Congo (Democratic Republic of Congo, q.v., or Zaire) in the 1960s. As a conservative politician supported in part by the financial backing of mining interests, he also became involved in Zambian politics. Roy Welensky (q.v.) evidently attempted to set up alliances and aid agreements between Tshombe and leaders of Zambia's African National Congress (q.v.) such as Lawrence Katilungu and Harry Nkumbula (qq.v.). Dixon Konkola's Central African People's Union (qq.v.) was another possible connection for Tshombe. Although some money from Katanga sources evidently reached these party leaders, Kenneth Kaunda (q.v.) himself made two trips to visit Tshombe, once as president of Pan-African Freedom Movement (q.v.), to whose goals of pan-Africanism he reportedly urged Tshombe to commit himself. He also urged Tshombe to discontinue his support of the more conservative African nationalists.

TUMBUKA. Tumbuka refers to both a linguistic group and an ethnic group. The nearly 330,000 (1986) *ci*Tumbuka-speaking people in Zambia include the Tumbuka, the Senga, and the Yombe (qq.v.). Another 400,000 or more *ci*Tumbuka speakers live in Malawi (q.v.).

As an ethnic group, the Tumbuka live near the eastern border of Zambia, near the Senga and the Ngoni (qq.v.). They are apparently related to the Senga, but their lands were invaded by the Zwagendaba's Ngoni (q.v.) around 1855, and Mbelwa was elected the Ngoni chief there. The Tumbuka were some of the earliest inhabitants of Zambia and are linked with the Yombe in the myth of Vinkakanimba (qq.v.). They lived in villages or small scattered hamlets, without centralized chiefdoms. Corporate matrilineal descent (q.v.) groups were the main units of social organization. After 1855 came years of Ngoni domination, and many traditions and customs were lost. With the coming of colonialism, however, a Tumbuka consciousness reemerged. And in early 1909 the Tumbuka were very receptive to the preaching of Elliot Kamwana (q.v.), a noted Watch Tower Movement (q.v.) leader.

TWA. Twa is the name of swamp-dwelling fishing peoples of the Kafue Flats, the Lukanga Swamp, and the eastern marshes of Lake Mweru and Lake Bangweulu (qq.v.), long assumed to be relics of Zambia's original Stone Age inhabitants. Though Zambians in these areas identify neighboring peoples as Twa, few claim the name for themselves. It seems to indicate social inferiority.

TWIN RIVERS KOPJE. This site, about 30 kilometers (18 miles) southwest of Lusaka (q.v.), has produced artifacts from the Zambian Middle Stone Age. Radiocarbon dates associated with the crude stone flakes and other objects suggest a date around 21,000 B.C.

U

UNDI. The principal chiefship of the Chewa (q.v.) people of south-eastern Zambia, the Undi is perhaps the oldest continuous chiefly dynasty in Zambia. The first Undi split from a line of Luba (q.v.) emigrants in the 16th century and moved west, where the Portuguese reported an Undi capital at Mano in 1614. Undi's dominion, which extended to include his fellow Phiri clansmen who remained in Malawi (q.v.), was called "Maravi" (the basis for the modern Malawi's name). Portuguese travels into modern Zambia generally passed through this chiefdom. At first, Undi sold the Portuguese ivory (q.v.), but gold was discovered near his capital around 1760 and in two outlying regions in 1800. In return for payment of tribute, the Chewa allowed the Portuguese and their slaves to mine the gold. Settlers and armed hunters soon followed, and the Undi saw the gradual loss of his regional authority and power.

In 1958 the reigning Undi went to London with Harry Nkumbula (q.v.) for talks at the Colonial Office. The same Undi attended the Federal Review Conference (q.v.) in 1960 and joined Kenneth Kaunda and Joshua Nkomo (qq.v.) in their famous walkout.

UNGA. A small ethnic group, the Unga are believed to have split off from the Bemba (q.v.) in the mid–18th century, when Bemba immigrants were traveling around the northern end of Lake Bangweulu (q.v.). The *ci*Bemba (q.v.)-speaking Unga are fishing peoples of the Bangweulu swamps; they traded their fish and otter skins for iron and other products. Although their swamp life made them less vulnerable to attack than other peoples, they were subjected to a series of raids by the Yeke (q.v.) in the late 19th century. They were somewhat more successful at evading early European administrators, and they became notorious tax defaulters who all but dared the collectors (q.v.) to enter the swamps.

UNILATERAL DECLARATION OF INDEPENDENCE. In April 1964, just months before Malawi (q.v.) and Zambia became independent, black majority-ruled states, the white electorate in Southern Rhodesia (q.v.) voted in the Rhodesian Front Party and Prime Minister Ian Smith (qq.v.). To preserve Rhodesia's white minority rule against any further pressure for racial partnership, Smith declared Rhodesia's independence from Great Britain on November 11, 1965. Britain went through the motions of mounting an international campaign of economic sanctions against the Rhodesian rebels. Zambia joined in, but soon became the main victim of the sanctions, which cut off its oil supply and, in the days before the TAZARA (q.v.) railway, its international transport route through Rhodesia. Ultimately, Zambia's people bore the costs of finding or creating new power sources and transport routes, of returning to colonial-era emergency regulations, of hosting Joshua Nkomo's (q.v.) ZIPRA freedom fighters, and of their government's May 1977 declaration of war against what Zambia National Broadcasting Services (q.v.) used to call "the regime of fascist rebel leader Ian Smith."

UNION CHURCH OF THE COPPERBELT. In 1925, while extending their work to the African townsfolk of Ndola and Bwana Mkubwa (qq.v.), the South African Baptists at Kafulafuta Mission (q.v.) were delighted to discover an embryonic, but auto-mous and nondenominational, African congregation in Ndola, one largely composed of second-generation Christians from Nyasaland (q.v.), like Ndola *boma* (q.v.) clerk Ernest A. Mwamba (q.v.). That year it elected its own board of elders, baptized 64 members, and financed its own evangelist to the larger region. This congregation, the Union Church of the Copperbelt, built its own church in 1927, and similar ones were built in Roan Antelope and Nchanga (qq.v.) in the next few years.

While the Reverend Arthur J. Cross became their visiting advisor, neither he nor the South African Baptists at Kafulafuta Mission did anything to compromise the Union Church's political or financial autonomy. And it retained its autonomy after 1936, when the UCCB became the core—and a financially contributing member—of the newly created, collaborative effort known as the United Missions in the Copperbelt (q.v.). The UCCB, though, suffered from the general shortage of African ministers and catechists and from frequent turnover in members and personnel. Thus, in or around 1945, it was incorporated into the Church of Central Africa (q.v.) in Rhodesia, a predecessor of the United Church of Zambia (q.v.), which then had four African ministers on the Copperbelt.

UNION MINIÈRE DU HAUT-KATANGA. This Belgian mining company was formed on October 28, 1906, to take over the operation of Katanga Mines from George Grey and Tanganyika Concessions, Ltd. (qq.v.). It remained the principal owner of Katanga Mines for over half a century. As such, as it was the employer of many African labor migrants from Northern and Luapula Provinces (qq.v.), most of them recruited by Robert Williams and Company (q.v.).

UNITED AFRICAN CONGRESS. In about May 1959, the president of the Rhodesian African Railway Workers Union, Dixon Konkola (q.v.), and a small group of followers organized the United African Congress, promising a nonviolent campaign for self-government. In June the UAC joined with the like-minded new group, the African National Freedom Movement (q.v.), to create the United National Freedom Party (q.v.).

UNITED CENTRAL AFRICA ASSOCIATION. The predecessor of the Federal Party and the United Federal Party (qq.v), the association was created in the 1940s to campaign for a federation (q.v.) of Northern Rhodesia, Southern Rhodesia, and Nyasaland (qq.v.). When the British accepted the idea, and the first federal elections were called in 1953, the association entered them as the Federal Party.

UNITED CHURCH OF ZAMBIA. After the Jehovah's Witnesses (q.v.) and Roman Catholics (q.v.), the United Church is the third largest denomination in Zambia. Although organized in 1958, it actually grew out of church unity movements over the previous three decades. The Union Church of the Copperbelt (q.v.), which formed in 1925, was perhaps the first such collaboration. The Presbyterian groups united as the Church of Central Africa (q.v.) in Rhodesia, and the Paris Evangelical Mission (*see* PARIS MISSIONARY SOCIETY) became the Church of Barotseland. In 1958 all of these came together along with the Methodists, the London Missionary Society (q.v.), and the Free Church of Scotland (q.v.) to create the United Church of Central Africa in Rhodesia. In 1965, its name was changed to the United Church of Zambia. Its synod headquarters are in Lusaka (q.v.).

UNITED DEMOCRATIC PARTY. The short-lived political party founded in June 1992 by Enoch Kavindele (q.v.), a millionaire businessman and United National Independence Party (q.v.) presidential aspirant. The UDP never won a parliamentary seat, but it did hold 42 local council seats by the time that it was dissolved in November 1993. Kavindele subsequently joined the Movement for Multiparty Democracy (q.v.), and was appointed chairman of its finance and economic committee.

UNITED FEDERAL PARTY. In 1958, this federal-level party controlled the territorial legislatures of all three parts of the Central African Federation (q.v.) (Nyasaland, Northern Rhodesia, Southern Rhodesia, qq.v.). In addition, it controlled the federal Parliament (q.v.). It was created by a merger of the Federal Party (q.v.) and the United Rhodesia Party (basically a Southern Rhodesian party). While negotiations for the merger began early in 1957, the union did not occur until March 1958. While Roy Welensky (q.v.) was spokesman for the party at the federal level, his protégé, John Roberts (q.v.), was the man in charge in Northern Rhodesia (q.v.).

In June 1962, when it became apparent that the federation was doomed, Roberts and the UFP arranged an alliance with the African National Congress (q.v.) for the October 1962 elections in Northern Rhodesia and promoted such African front groups as the National Republican Party and the Central African People's Union (qq.v.). In preparation for the election, the UFP began recruiting African members. In November 1961, Welensky also started the unsuccessful Build-a-Nation Campaign (q.v.). The 1962 campaign did not change many minds. To most Africans, the UFP was the party of white supremacy and the unpopular federation; to Europeans, it represented responsible, "civilized" government and personal security. The election resulted in a stalemate. The UFP won all but one of the 14 upper-roll seats but none of the lower-roll seats. It did, however, win two African seats in the national constituencies. Thus it ended up with 15 of the 34 seats in the Legislative Council (q.v.). If combined with the ANC's five seats, a "conservative" coalition could control the council. After a period of indecision, however, Harry Nkumbula (q.v.) of the ANC formed a coalition with Kenneth Kaunda's (q.v.) 14 United National Independence Party's (q.v.) legislators, instead. Six months later, in April 1963, John Roberts changed the name of the Northern Rhodesian branch of the UFP to the National Progress Party (q.v.).

UNITED MINEWORKERS UNION. This name was adopted by the old Mines African Staff Association (q.v.) in 1963, when it claimed that it represented all mine employees. The African Mineworkers Union (q.v.) bitterly contested that claim. Before the year was finished, the UMU was dissolved and reorganized as the Mines Local Staff Association (q.v.). It was closely associated with the United National Independence Party, which opposed the AMU's connections with the African National Congress (q.v.).

UNITED MISSIONS IN THE COPPERBELT. Following the General Missionary Conference's (q.v.) call for greater cooperation among Protestant churches in serving the Copperbelt's (q.v.) African townsfolk, the Reverend Reginald J. B. (Mike) Moore of the London Missionary Society (q.v.) came to the Copperbelt in 1933 and won the support of the (African) Union Church of the Copperbelt (q.v.) and the mine authorities. In 1936, this resulted in the creation of the UMCB, a nominally collaborative effort by the London Missionary Society, the South African Baptist Missionary Society, the Free Church of Scotland Mission (q.v.), the Methodist Mission Society, the Universities' Mission to Central Africa (q.v.), the United Society for Christian Literature, and the South African Presbyterian Church.

The Reverend Arthur J. Cross, former advisor to the UCCB, left his position with the South African Baptists at Kafulafuta Mission (q.v.) to lead the UMCB "team" from its headquarters at Mindolo, just three kilometers (two miles) northwest of Kitwe (q.v.).

In 1937, the UMCB opened schools at Mindolo, Luanshya (q.v.), Mufulira (q.v.), and Nchanga (q.v.); it started adult schools and the Women's Centre at Mindolo in 1939; and, in 1940, for a few brief years it was charged with the management of all the Copperbelt schools. But the UMCB never received the funds or personnel its leaders had anticipated and had to shelve its plans for a teacher training school at Mindolo. Its resources were severely strained during World War II. The Reverend Moore became an active promoter of the African trade union movement and had to resign. He died of cancer in 1943, and the Reverend Cross died of a heart attack in 1945. By then, the UMCB had effectively collapsed. Some missions wanted out of the Copperbelt; others, who had put more into the Copperbelt effort, went their separate ways; and others were unhappy with the UMCB's emphasis upon social work. The UMCB was eventually replaced by the Copperbelt Christian Service Council in 1955 and the Mindolo Ecumenical Centre (q.v.) in 1958.

UNITED NATIONAL FREEDOM PARTY. This small, short-lived party was an important predecessor of the United National Independence Party (q.v.). It was created in June 1959 from the merger of the African National Freedom Movement and the United African Congress (qq.v.). Dixon Konkola (q.v.) became its president-general, while Solomon Kalulu and Harry Banda (qq.v.) became vice president and secretary-general. They publicly stated that their true leader was the imprisoned Kenneth Kaunda (q.v.); most of the party's members came from the recently banned Zambia African National Congress (q.v.). These leaders opposed both Harry Nkumbula (of the African National Congress) and the federation (qq.v.), and called for immediate self-government. The party then merged with the African National Independence Party (q.v.) to form UNIP later in 1959.

UNITED NATIONAL INDEPENDENCE PARTY. The ruling party of Zambia from 1963 until 1991, it was, from 1972–90, the only legal party during the course of the Second Republic's "one-party participatory democracy." When the Zambia African National Congress (q.v.) was banned in March 1959, and most of its major leaders rusticated (q.v.) by the government, the African National Congress (q.v.) was left as the only significant African party in Northern Rhodesia (q.v.). In September, though, the ANC split again, and that October one of the dissidents, Mainza Chona (q.v.), joined UNIP, which had just recently formed from the September amalgamation (q.v.) of the African National Independence Party and the United National Freedom Party (qq.v.), each of which had been formed to keep ZANC's spirit alive.

The goal of UNIP at this point was to dismantle federation (q.v.) by legal, nonviolent means and to boycott the Monckton Commission (q.v.), which was to make recommendations to the Federal Review Conference (q.v.). UNIP found its strength limited to areas of Bemba (q.v.) influence, mostly the northeastern part of the country and the Copperbelt (q.v.) mining towns. As ZANC leaders emerged from their government restrictions in late 1959, they joined UNIP and broadened the party's geographical base. Kenneth Kaunda (q.v.) was released from prison on January 9, 1960, and on January 31 was elected president of UNIP at a party conference, with Chona becoming deputy president. The party's immediate concern was to organize and expand its membership. It was successful at both. Although it was banned on the Copperbelt in May (the ban was lifted in November) and was widely opposed by chiefs and the government, UNIP claimed over 300,000 members by the end of 1960. In December 1960 it had representatives in London at the Federal Review Conference. Its actions there and at the subsequent talks on the Northern Rhodesian constitution led almost directly to Great Britain's decision to disband the Central African Federation (q.v.). Although the next stages in ending federation and bringing independence saw numerous conflicts between UNIP and British leaders over the composition of interim legislatures and the framing of elections, UNIP had won its crucial battle by early 1961. Most of 1961 and 1962 were spent in improving UNIP's organization and preparing for the October 1962 Legislative Council (q.v.) elections. UNIP sought support from members of the labor union movement and financial aid and acceptance from other successful African countries. Leaders from Ghana, Liberia, and Tanganyika provided both approval and economic assistance.

At first, UNIP's organizational structure was similar to that of the ANC. It had a president and other national officers at the top. Kaunda took special pains to maintain a regional, ethnic, and linguistic balance among the members of the Central Committee of UNIP (q.v.), the party's permanent executive. There were also eight provincial divisions, each of which had considerable freedom because of inadequate communication and controls from the center. Kaunda reformed this late in 1961, changing the eight provincial sections into 24 regional organizations, each with a full-time organizing secretary appointed by and responsible to the Central Committee. In addition, the Youth and Women's Brigades were integrated more closely into the party. Finally, the party's National Council (the chief policymaking organ, which was called into session by the Central Committee) was expanded and made more national in membership: it now also included the 24 regional secretaries. All this organization was crucial, as the 1962 elections were vigorously fought.

To win control of the Legislative Council, UNIP needed European support. The complicated election formula required a mixture of support to win the national constituencies so as to provide some party with a majority in the Legislative Council. UNIP had several hundred white members in 1962, with Sir Stewart Gore-Browne, James Skinner, and Merfyn Temple (qq.v.) being the most notable. Skinner provided excellent help by publishing a brochure to guide UNIP members through the maze of election rules and procedures. UNIP was also the only party to stage a major drive to register new voters, even forming registration schools to help voters through the government's literacy tests.

In the crucial 1962 elections, UNIP won 12 lower-roll seats (with 78.2 percent of the vote) but only one upper-roll seat (19.8 percent of the vote), plus the national seat reserved for Asians. Thus it had 14 of the Legislative Council's 34 seats. After considerable deliberation, the ANC brought its five seats into a coalition with UNIP, and the two groups prepared a ruling cabinet. The six ministerial positions in the cabinet were divided equally, with Kenneth Kaunda, Simon Kapwepwe, and Reuben Kamanga (qq.v.) holding UNIP's three. Four parliamentary secretaries and the chief whip were also UNIP men. It was this core that led Northern Rhodesia and UNIP through the final steps leading to independence. Prior to that, however, elections were again held, in January 1964. This time, the parliamentary elections were based upon universal adult suffrage. UNIP's two main competitors in 1962 were now much weaker. The UFP had dissolved, and its successor, the National Progress Party (q.v.) competed for—and won—only the 10 seats reserved for Europeans. The ANC was torn by internal dissension. As a result, UNIP won 55 of the regular seats to ANC's 10, 24 of which were not contested. In the 41 contested races, UNIP won 69.6 percent of the votes. Thus at independence UNIP had a 55–20 majority in Parliament.

The next important year for UNIP was 1967. A new party constitution had been passed by the party's National Council at a meeting in June 1966 (and formally adopted at the general conference in August 1967). A major change in the party structure was that Central Committee posts would be contested on an individual basis, rather than on a carefully balanced "team" ticket. As a result, there was a bitter party election at the 1967 General Conference, in which the ethnic and regional divisions within UNIP surfaced, as coalitions of different ethnic groups campaigned along tribal lines (*see* UNITY IN THE EAST MOVEMENT). This caused considerable grief within the party, and such divisions continue to fuel the current (1996) opposition to President Frederick Chiluba's (q.v.) ruling party, the Movement for Multiparty Democracy (q.v.). While the *ci*Bemba (q.v.)-speakers and their allies tended to dominate the party elections, President Kaunda used his cabinet appointments to placate the losing groups.

General elections were again scheduled for December 1968. As the ruling party, UNIP could run on its record against its only active opponent, the ANC. Another potential opponent, the United Party (q.v.), had been banned in August 1966. UNIP's hopes to expand its convincing parliamentary majority were not to be, as the ANC, in spite of its weak finances, won handily in both Southern and Barotse Provinces (qq.v.). In the newly expanded Parliament, UNIP was left with 81 seats, the ANC with 23, and there was one independent. After the election, the intraparty rivalry in UNIP surfaced again. In August 1969, a meeting of the party's National Council was abruptly closed by the president because of a motion to oust Simon Kapwepwe as vice president. He later resigned but was persuaded by Kaunda to stay until the party's next elections. At the same time, Kaunda dissolved the Central Committee and took over party power as its secretary-general. He then appointed three ministers of state to aid him in party administration, finance, and publicity.

Kaunda appointed the Chuula Commission (q.v.) to draft a new party constitution. The results were highly controversial, however, and its key proposals concerning the Central Committee were rejected. Finally a General Conference at Mulungushi in May 1971 approved a new party constitution and endorsed the list of new Central Committee members submitted by the National Council. Soon, however, Simon Kapwepwe and Justin Chimba (q.v.) bolted from UNIP to form the United Progressive Party (q.v.) in August 1971. The existence of the UPP was a further sign that ethnic sectionalism was still a major problem for UNIP.

With the coming of the Second Zambian Republic and its creation of a one-party state, the role of UNIP became even more important to Zambia, and its constitution effectively became a direct instrument of the government. The party president was, by definition, Zambia's president. Once selected as UNIP president by the party's General Conference, he was automatically the only candidate for election as Zambia's president. The people could only vote yes or no for this one and only candidate, and only a national majority of no votes would compel UNIP to reconsider its choice of party president. Voter turnouts fell accordingly, and large numbers of no votes came from the former ANC strongholds in Southern and Barotse Provinces.

To contest Kaunda's hold on the party and national presidency, Harry Nkumbula (q.v.) and Simon Kapwepwe joined UNIP in time for the 1978 General Conference and ran for party president. Overnight, the eligibility rules for party office candidates were rewritten so that their brief tenure as UNIP members disqualified them from running. Though the constitutionality of this maneuver was challenged in the courts, the Supreme Court eventually determined that UNIP was just another private club (!) and as such it could alter its constitution whenever and however it pleased.

Neither Kaunda nor UNIP fared well after the collapse of copper (q.v.) prices in the late 1970s. The UNIP General Conference of August 1988 approved a variety of structural changes, including enlargement of the Central Committee to 68 members. Of these, 41 would be elected from a list approved by the National Council, seven would be appointed by the president, and the remaining 20 would be cabinet ministers. In addition, a Committee of Chairmen was created, composed of UNIP's general-secretary, the prime minister, the secretary of state for defense and security, the (eight) provincial Central Committee members, and the heads of the Central Committee's nine subcommittees. These changes were seen as tightening the control of the UNIP elite over its governance.

By the late 1980s, the Mineworkers Union of Zambia (q.v.)

and Zambia's Trade Union Congress (q.v.) had weathered popular confrontations with Kaunda and his party, and the leaders of these unions then put together the Movement for Multiparty Democracy and forced Kaunda to hold the 1991 multiparty elections that drove Kaunda and UNIP from power.

In March 1992, President Chiluba declared a state of emergency following the discovery of an alleged plot to destabilize the government. This so-called "Zero Option" (q.v.) affair led to the detention of several top UNIP officials, including three of Kenneth Kaunda's sons.

Kaunda stepped down as party head, and Kebby Musokotwane (q.v.) assumed that post at the UNIP National Congress in September 1992. In late October 1994, however, Kaunda announced that he was reentering the political fray and intended to run for president in the 1996 national elections. Musokotwane refused to step down, arguing that Kaunda's nomination would depend upon UNIP's future party elections. This dispute divided the party into two factions, and it only worsened in December 1994, when a group of Central Committee members attempted to impeach and suspend both Musokotwane and the party's vice president, Malimba Masheke, a Kaunda supporter. They appointed Patrick Mvunga (q.v.) as interim party president. The government, however, would recognize only leaders elected at the 1992 party congress. In the extraordinary party congress held in Lusaka in June 1995, Musokotwane won only 17 percent of the votes, and Kaunda was reelected party leader. Kaunda moved to purge the party of Musokotwane's supporters, trying to remove Dingiswayo Banda (q.v.) from his post as leader of UNIP's parliamentary opposition. The government, however, warned Kaunda not to meddle in parliamentary affairs.

UNITED PARTY. Reportedly founded in March 1966, the United Party held its inaugural general conference in Lusaka (q.v.) in May 1966. Its leaders were both members of Parliament (q.v.): Mufaya Mumbuna (q.v.), former vice president of the African National Congress (q.v.), was elected president, and Dickson Chikulo of the United National Independence Party (q.v.) was made treasurer. After registration as a party, it was officially recognized by the speaker in the National Assembly on July 20, 1966. To counteract that move, UNIP and ANC joined in amending the constitution to require any member to resign from Parliament if he changed his party after his election. Thus the seats were contested in a by-election, and UNIP won them both. Meanwhile, allegations of corruption forced two Lozi (q.v.)-speaking UNIP cabinet ministers—Nalumino Mundia (q.v.) and Mubiana Nalilungwe—to leave the cabinet in January 1966.

Mundia was dismissed from the party and the the Parliament in March 1967 and was soon involved with the United Party and elected its president. The UP gained strength, especially in Barotseland (q.v.), where people were very upset with the government's decision to curtail the Witwatersrand Native Labour Association's (q.v.) labor recruitment to South Africa. The UP organized heavily on the Copperbelt (q.v.), drawing from previous UNIP supporters. UNIP, however, did not idly accept this, and the UP accused it of confiscating party literature, refusing permission for meetings in Barotseland, and refusing to recognize the election of a chief who supposedly was a UP supporter. UP officials were arrested (then acquitted) on weak grounds, its supporters were beaten by gangs of UNIP youths, and the party was generally harassed by lower-level UNIP officials. After an incident in which two UNIP officials died at the hands of some UP members, the UP was banned on August 14, 1966, and Mundia was detained. Many UP supporters then joined the ANC, which was preparing for the December 1968 general elections. A loose alliance formed, with Mundia and other former UP members running for most of the Barotseland seats in Parliament. The ANC won 6 of the 11 Barotseland seats, defeating three of the four Lozi cabinet ministers in the process. Most of the victory was due to UP organization. Mundia won his seat and became an ANC leader in Parliament.

UNITED PEOPLE'S PARTY. The party was formed October 1, 1972, by a number of former members of the United Progressive Party (q.v.), some of them recently freed from detention. Its goal was to fight the plan for a one-party state. The leaders announced that Simon Kapwepwe (q.v.) would head it when he was freed from detention. It was banned on October 19, 1972, and its leaders were arrested.

UNITED PROGRESSIVE PARTY. This party was legal for only about six months, and was one of the principal reasons for the creation of a one-party state in Zambia. At the beginning of August 1971, there were reports in Zambia that dissident United National Independence Party (q.v.) members had formed a new political party. Four Bemba (q.v.) members of

Parliament (q.v.) were disciplined by President Kaunda (q.v.) for their connections with the United Progressive Party. Simon Kapwepwe (q.v.), a former vice president, resigned from his cabinet position on August 21, 1971, and announced that he was the actual leader of the UPP. He said that the party's goal was to "stamp out all forms of capitalism, tribalism, and sectionalism." UNIP supporters reacted negatively, demanding a one-party state, and harassing and intimidating UPP supporters. Over 100 UPP supporters were detained. Of its leaders, only Kapwepwe remained free. In the by-elections on December 21, 1971, Kapwepwe won back his seat in Parliament. Growing unemployment due to an economic recession accounted for part of his success and his party's following. On February 4, 1972, the UPP was banned, and Kapwepwe and many more followers were detained without trial. In March 1972, some members of the UPP formed the Democratic People's Party (q.v.). That April, two government ministers and UPP members, Axon Soko (q.v.) and Zongani Banda, were dismissed from the government "for engaging in activities of a banned opposition party."

UNITED TRADE UNION CONGRESS. The congress was formed in early 1961 by a merger of the rival Trade Union Congress and Reformed Trade Union Congress (qq.v.). Its leadership consisted mostly of the old RTUC leaders, with Jonathan Chivunga (q.v.) as president. The leaders were largely United National Independence Party (q.v.) supporters. The party was weakened considerably in July 1962 when the African Mineworkers Union (q.v.) withdrew. Its leadership became split by factionalism, and UNIP finally stepped in and called for new elections. The Zambian government paid £5,614 in 1965 to wipe out its debt so that a newly formed Zambia Congress of Trade Unions (q.v.) could begin fresh.

UNITY IN THE EAST MOVEMENT. The movement was a splinter group of *si*Lozi and *ci*Nyanja (q.v.) speakers who broke from the United National Independence Party (q.v.). They formed the movement after the 1967 Central Committee of UNIP (q.v.) elections, in which a *ci*Bemba (q.v.)-speaking faction led by Simon Kapwepwe (q.v.) swept all but one of the contested seats. Moreover, Reuben Kamanga (q.v.) from Eastern Province (q.v.) lost his position as UNIP deputy president to Simon Kapwepwe from Northern Province (q.v.). The formation of the Unity in the East Movement was further evidence of the sectional and ethnic tensions within UNIP. These tensions ultimately led to the declaration of the Second Zambian Republic's (q.v.) one-party state.

UNIVERSITIES' MISSION TO CENTRAL AFRICA. Supported by the social elite in Britain's Church of England, the UMCA was created in response to David Livingstone's (q.v.) 1857 appeal to Oxford and Cambridge Universities. Its first mission was in Malawi's (q.v.) Shire highlands in 1861, where disease, hunger, and slave raids soon prompted its withdrawal to Zanzibar, from 1864–81. Thus in the early years of British South Africa Company (q.v.) rule, white settlers at Fort Jameson (q.v.) were served by a priest under the bishop of Likoma, in Nyasaland (q.v.), while those in Livingstone (q.v.) and along the line of rail (q.v.) were served by a priest under the archbishop of Cape Town. The UMCA's Diocese of Northern Rhodesia was created in 1909 but only on condition that it not neglect its European members. Its first African priest, the Reverend Leonard M. Kamungu of Nyasaland, was ordained that same year, and its newly consecrated bishop, John Hine, arrived in Livingstone in 1910. Hine was immediately involved in a dispute with his white congregation for suggesting that its African members might use the whites' new church.

Unlike other Northern Rhodesian mission societies, the UMCA's efforts were split between European and African members. Its work at Livingstone, Broken Hill, Fort Jameson, and Ndola (qq.v.) was largely directed at whites, while widely scattered stations were established among the Nsenga, Tonga, Aushi, and Lala (qq.v.), thus upsetting the ethnically exclusive territories claimed by other Protestant missions. In spite of its racially divided mission, the UMCA adopted a progressive, pro-African stance on a variety of social issues. It fought, but lost, the battle with the 1924 Reserves Commission (q.v.) to remove 2,500 Africans from the North Charterland Exploration Company's (q.v.) concession in Eastern Province (q.v.). It was among the missions that lobbied for the creation of the Native Education Department in 1925 and was especially critical of the funding cutbacks for mission-run primary schools in the 1930s. Its bishop gave testimony to Governor Hubert Young's (q.v.) 1938 commission on reforming African taxation. And in 1945 its bishop was appoined an "unofficial" (q.v.) African representative to the Legislative Council (q.v.). The UMCA is perhaps best known for educating and ordaining Africans for pastoral duties.

UNIVERSITY COLLEGE OF RHODESIAS AND NYASALAND. This multiracial college of the Central African Federation (q.v.), established in 1955 and opened in 1957, was the last of the five postwar college affiliates of the University of London and its School of Oriental and African Studies in Tropical Africa. Located in Salisbury (q.v.) (now Harare), it offered Africans from Northern Rhodesia (q.v.) an alternative to Fort Hare College in South Africa and Makerere in Uganda—at least until Southern Rhodesia's (q.v.) unilateral declaration of independence (q.v.) and the opening of the University of Zambia (q.v.) in 1965–66. In 1961, 61 Africans from Northern Rhodesia were enrolled at Salisbury. The other four postwar university colleges— Achimota (Ghana), Ibadan (Nigeria), Khartoum (Sudan), and Makerere—were established between 1946 and 1949.

UNIVERSITY OF ZAMBIA. Founded in 1965, the university opened its doors to its first students in March 1966. In 1969 it had about 1,000 full-time students. It is located in Lusaka (q.v.) and graduated its first class in 1969. Its first engineers graduated in 1971, and its medical school produced its first graduates in 1972. In 1973 the university opened its schools of agriculture and of mines. It has now some 2,700 staff members and 4,600 students. UNZA students have a long history of public protests against government policies, and the university is frequently closed to curb these demonstrations. In January 1993 the university announced that government scholarships would be withheld from students who boycotted classes, joined demonstrations, or failed to complete their courses on time. Though students were again reminded of the costs of university closures in October 1994 and asked to steer clear of politics, student leaders claim the small size of the parliamentary opposition makes their involvement obligatory. UNZA suffers shameful plumbing, sewage, and furnishings problems. Its faculty and other staff salaries have long been hopelessly inadequate. Some 350 faculty members struck for higher salaries and amenities throughout much of 1994. In 1991–94 the university lost about 150 lecturers to neighboring countries offering higher salaries. Zambian postgraduate education appears to be at a critical juncture.

UNOFFICIALS. This term is used to describe those members of the colonial Legislative Council (q.v.) who did not hold their seats because of membership in the official colonial administration. It was a particularly important step for the territory when, in 1945, the number of unofficials in the territory's Executive Council outnumbered the officials. In Northern Rhodesia (q.v.) during the 1930s, most of the unofficials were Europeans who urged amalgamation (q.v.) with Southern Rhodesia (q.v.). For many years, the leader of the unofficials was Sir Stewart Gore-Browne (q.v.), but he was replaced in 1946 by Sir Roy Welensky (q.v.).

UPPER ROLL. This is one part of a system of qualified franchise by which eligible voters were divided into two voting categories, an upper roll and a lower roll. The 1962 constitution for Northern Rhodesia (q.v.) provided for this arrangement. Placement on the upper roll was determined by meeting qualifications based on education, income, property, or community status. The upper roll consisted mostly of Europeans, while the lower roll consisted almost exclusively of Africans. Once membership on the two rolls was determined, the election machinery required candidates to receive proportions of votes from each roll in order to win certain "national" seats. Each roll also voted independently for other seats.

URBAN ADVISORY COUNCILS. The first urban advisory councils were established on the Copperbelt (q.v.) by the Northern Rhodesian (q.v.) government in 1938. The councils could meet only four times a year but were designed to alert the government to opinion trends among the Africans as well as to advise it on matters of welfare and other difficulties that Africans faced outside the mine compounds. The African members of the councils were appointed by the district commissioner (q.v.). Generally speaking, these councils had little influence and accomplished less. Members failed to represent their fellow workers adequately. In both Lusaka and Broken Hill (qq.v.), the same appointees remained for five years. Yet the government saw these councils as a step toward political evolution and a way of airing grievances. National political consciousness in the late 1940s was not channeled through these councils. Nevertheless, in 1942–43, the government arranged to expand the councils to towns outside the Copperbelt and to add Provincial Councils (q.v.) to the structure. After World War II some council members were to be elected, which brought them closer to reflecting African opinion. They were still only advisory, however, and their only real link with the European-controlled local government was the district commissioner (q.v.).

USHI. Ushi is a common variant of the ethnic name Aushi (q.v.). The assumption behind this usage is that the initial "a" of Aushi, as in old Nyasaland (Malawi), is the Bantu plural personal prefix and that the proper root word is "Ushi" (*see* BANTU LANGUAGES). Yet since an Aushi person is a *mu*-Aushi, the Aushi area is called *ubw*Aushi, and their language is *ci*Aushi, the true ethnonym seems to be "Aushi" rather than "Ushi."

V

VAKAKAYE RIOTS. These antiadministration protests took place in 1956 in North-Western Province (q.v.) of Northern Rhodesia (q.v.). Several hundred people participated, urged on by Nyampenji, a chieftainess who objected when the colonial administration withdrew its recognition of her in 1946. She resented her lack of control over the new Luvale Native Authority (qq.v.). Her followers denounced controls by modern authorities, and opposed increased taxes.

VALLEY TONGA. This is another term for the Gwembe Tonga (q.v.).

VAN EEDEN, GUILLAUME FRANÇOIS MARAIS. Van Eeden was a leader in several European parties in Central Africa (q.v.). He was born in Fort Jameson, Northern Rhodesia (q.v.), and was elected to its Legislative Council (q.v.) in 1948. He resigned to pursue his successful run for the Kafue seat in the Federal Parliament. In 1955 he left the United Federal Party (q.v.) and helped Winston Field form and lead the Northern Rhodesia Commonwealth Party (qq.v.). But in 1958 he helped form the Federal Dominion Party (q.v.). In March 1961, however, he resigned from the Dominion Party and announced that he would support the efforts of the UFP. By 1963 he was working with John Roberts in the National Progress Party (qq.v.), the heir of the UFP.

VAN OOST, FATHER ACHILLE. Born in France in 1859 and ordained in 1883, Father van Oost entered North-Eastern Rhodesia (q.v.) from German East Africa with the White Fathers (q.v.) in 1891. He helped establish Old Mambwe (q.v.) mission, preceding Father Dupont (q.v.). Dealing mainly with the Bemba (q.v.) chiefs, his first meeting was with Chilangwa in August

1892. In January 1894 a visit to a Bemba headman named Chit-
ika led him (and his companion, Father Depaillat) to a series of
meetings with an important chief, Makasa V, a son of Chitimukulu (qq.v.). The meetings occurred over a 15-month period
and were cordial on both sides, despite the priest's opposition
to Makasa's part in the slave trade (q.v.). Attempts by Makasa
to set up a visit to Sampa (q.v.) miscarried. However, Sampa
did invite the priests to choose a site for a new mission near
him. On that trip, Father van Oost died of blackwater fever on
April 20, 1895.

VICTOR EMMANUEL. *See* KING VICTOR EMMANUEL OF
ITALY.

VICTORIA FALLS. The falls were named for England's Queen
Victoria by David Livingstone (q.v.) in November 1855. They
are called by the Lozi (q.v.) "Mosi-oa-Tunya," or The Smoke
that Thunders. A majestic tourist attraction near the town of
Livingstone (q.v.), in Zambia, the falls are on the Zambezi
River (q.v.) and are thus shared by Zambia and Zimbabwe. A
footbridge built over the Knife Edge (*see* KNIFE-EDGE
BRIDGE) in 1969 improved the view from the Zambian side.
The falls are fairly new in the course of history, as geological
evidence points out that 30,000 years ago the falls were about
eight kilometers (five miles) downstream until the present
gorges were formed. At 103 meters (338 feet) high and 1,700
meters (5,602 feet) wide, they are twice as high and half again
as wide as Niagara Falls. Water flow runs about 20,000 cubic
meters per minute in November and December, and 550,000
cubic meters per minute in March and April. The first railway
and road bridge across the gorge just below the falls was built
in 1905 and is 200 meters (219 yards) long.

VICTORIA FALLS CONFERENCE, 1949. The conference, sometimes called "the first Victoria Falls conference," was an informal meeting of leading white politicians from Northern and
Southern Rhodesia and Nyasaland (qq.v.). It was led by Roy
Welensky and Godfrey Huggins (qq.v.), with the goal of invest-
igating the possibility of federation (q.v.) in Central Africa
(q.v.). The idea of amalgamation (q.v.) was abandoned but a
proposal for federation in which control of native affairs would
be retained by the territorial governments was entertained, the
delegates clearly believing that African participation in the political life of the federal state was decades away. The British

government refused to extend official recognition to the conference.

VICTORIA FALLS CONFERENCE, 1951. The so-called second Victoria Falls Conference was convened by the British government and the three Central African territorial governments. An agreement was reached to form a Central African Federation (q.v.), and the conference's basic ideas were used in drafting a later plan for federation (q.v.). Although the African Councils (q.v.) were represented at this meeting, the African representatives from Northern Rhodesia and Nyasaland (qq.v.) refused to accept the agreement. The term "partnership" (q.v.) was introduced to the conference by the British colonial secretary, James Griffiths (q.v.).

VICTORIA FALLS CONFERENCE, 1963. This conference included leaders of all three Central African governments, both African and European. Its purpose was to decide the date for the end of the Central African Federation (q.v.). They agreed on December 31, 1963.

VINKAKANIMBA. According to Yombe (q.v.) tradition, Vinkakanimba was an elephant hunter from Uganda who followed the herds south and entered the territory of Uyombe. He became the first Yombe chief, with his capital at Zuzu. With him in his travels were five men who became the founders of most of the Tumbuka (q.v.) chiefdom's royal clans. He died after being defeated in a battle with the chief of Kambombo. His son, Mughanga, succeeded him.

VOICE OF UNIP. The *Voice* was the official publication of the United National Independence Party (q.v.). It was started in 1960 by UNIP's chief publicist, Sikota Wina (q.v.), whose writing was often more inflammatory than the words of his party leaders. But the paper was a much-read source of nationalist information, especially prior to independence.

VORSTER, JOHANNES BALTHAZAR. Vorster was prime minister of South Africa from September 1966 until September 1978. In 1967 he bluntly warned Zambia not to use violence with South Africa or "we will hit you so hard that you will never forget it." Kaunda's (q.v.) reply, that Zambia could defend itself and that Vorster was seeking a fight when Zambia had threatened no one, led Vorster to reply that South Africa desired peaceful relations with Zambia. In mid-1968 a series of letters and other contacts between Vorster and President Kaunda frankly discussed relations between their countries. Both were concerned that the Rhodesia question be settled without fighting. Further evidence of mutual concern over the Rhodesia-Zimbabwe question was demonstrated by the two leaders' mid-1970s attempts to persuade the opposing forces to begin reasonable negotiations. Notable in this regard was the December 1974 Lusaka Agreement on the subject of Rhodesian constitutional talks. According to the agreement, neither side would lay down preconditions for the talks.

W

WADDINGTON, SIR E. J. Waddington was governor of Northern Rhodesia (q.v.) from 1941 to 1948. His first major problem occurred in 1942 when the (European) Mineworkers Union led by Frank Maybank, a socialist, threatened to disrupt production on the Copperbelt (q.v.) unless the government responded to a wide range of grievances. Waddington ultimately called in the Southern Rhodesia Armored Car Regiment, which arrested Maybank and his top assistants. In 1942, Waddington set up a War Committee within the Executive Council that included "unofficials" of the Legislative Council (qq.v.). This led him to agree in 1944 to the establishment of an unofficial-member majority in the Legislative Council, which took effect the next year. During the war years, Waddington was active in the Inter-Territorial Conference (q.v.) with the governors of Nyasaland and Southern Rhodesia (qq.v.). When the subject of amalgamation (q.v.) of the territories was raised, he opposed it. He favored instead a council form of inter-territorial cooperation on common interests. His position won, and at the end of 1944 he announced the creation of the Central African Council (q.v.).

WALLACE, SIR LAWRENCE AUBREY. Wallace was the British South Africa Company's (q.v.) administrator of North-Eastern Rhodesia (q.v.) from April 1907 to January 1909. He then became administrator of North-Western Rhodesia (q.v.), a position he held until the two areas were combined and he was made administrator for the amalgamated Northern Rhodesia (q.v.). He served in that capacity from August 1911 to March 1921. Born in Natal, South Africa, he worked as a civil engineer and surveyor. He also built railways in Argentina before coming to Central Africa (q.v.). Regarding job reservations (*see* COLOUR BAR), he was willing to sacrifice African interests in favor of the settlers. He did, however, oppose excessive criminal punishment. In 1913 he suggested to the directors of the BSAC that an Advisory Council would be useful. It was instituted, after considerable debate, in 1918.

WALUBITA, MUHELI. Walubita served as *ngambela* (q.v.) (prime minister) of Barotseland from 1948 to 1956, succeeding Sikota Wina (q.v.). King Mwanawina (q.v.) wanted Akabeswa Imasiku (q.v.), a relative by marriage, to hold the position, but resident commissioner A. F. B. Glennie (q.v.) prevailed. Walubita was born in 1897 at Kazungula (q.v.). His father was chief councilor (*liashimba*) at Sesheke (q.v.). He was educated both there and in Barotseland at the Paris Mission Society (q.v.) schools. He received administrative experience as clerk in the Mwandi *kuta* (q.v.) and as secretary to the chief at Sesheke. When his father died, Walubita succeeded him as *liashimba* at Sesheke in 1938. In 1945 King Imwiko (q.v.) appointed him educational *induna* (q.v.) of Barotseland, and in 1947 he switched to *induna* for agricultural development. In 1948 he became *ngambela*. In the mid-1950s a dispute arose over whether the Barotseland national government was open to the modernizing element among the Lozi (q.v.). Walubita opposed the conservative Imwiko on this question. When Imwiko again indicated that he wanted Imasiku as *ngambela*, Walubita resigned in early 1956.

WARE, HARRY. Ware was a hunter and trader who arrived in Africa around 1880, making a number of journeys north to the Zambezi River (q.v.). By advertising in European papers, he worked as a guide for British sportsmen wishing to hunt in South-Central Africa, promising also to show them Victoria Falls (q.v.). In June 1889 he arrived in the Lozi capital, Lealui (qq.v.), seeking a mining concession from Lewanika (q.v.) to prospect and dig for gold and other minerals in certain distant parts of the Lozi empire. Working on behalf of a South African mining syndicate, he received a mineral concession to the Batoka territory, an area larger than Ireland, for a period of 20 years. Ware, on his part, promised to pay Lewanika £200 a year plus a 4 percent royalty on the mineral output. In October 1889, Ware sold his concession to two speculators, who several weeks later sold it to Cecil Rhodes' British South Africa Company (qq.v.). Ware won over the Lozi leaders, in part, through gifts of Martini-Henry rifles, ammunition, blankets, and clothes. The Reverend Coillard (q.v.) told Lewanika that a concession to Ware might lead to the British protection he was seeking. At the same time, Coillard secretly hoped that it would bring "civilization" to the area. Instead, it brought the BSAC, with its royal charter to promulgate laws, maintain a police force, and acquire new concessions (*see* LOCHNER CONCESSION).

WARE CONCESSION, 1889. *See* WARE, HARRY.

WATCH TOWER BIBLE AND TRACT SOCIETY. *See* JEHOVAH'S WITNESSES.

WATCH TOWER MOVEMENT. The movement was a loose network of populist, millenarian social movements led by such prophets as Elliot Kamwana, Hanoc Sindano, Tomo Nyirenda, and Jeremiah Gondwe (qq.v.) from 1910–35, when some of these separatist communities were reabsorbed into the Watch Tower Bible and Tract Society. In general, these prophets preached an imminent Second Coming—one sometimes led by black Americans—that would liberate Africans from poverty, sickness, death, and European colonial rule. Though often characterized as a protopolitical movement among migrant laborers, the Watch Tower Movement was primarily based in the uncertainties of rural life. It was particularly popular in the Luapula River valley and the upper Kafue River basin (qq.v.), regions of small and subordinated peoples with ineffective leaders. Among the Lala and Lamba (qq.v.), for example, the Watch Tower prophets railed as much against the traditional chiefs as against the colonial regime and offered baptism as a means of controlling witchcraft. Building upon the work of earlier millenarian prophets like Mupumani Cheso (q.v.), the Watch Tower Movement was an alternative African form of Christianity in which divine intervention would deliver the material wealth of the Europeans to all Africans who adopted "true" beliefs and practices.

WAYALESHI. *See* SAUCEPAN SPECIAL.

WE. "We" is used occasionally to designate the Gwembe Tonga (q.v.).

WEATHERLEY, POULETT. Weatherley was a European explorer and sportsman who lived for several years (especially 1895–98) near the Bemba chiefs Mporokoso and Ponde (qq.v.) in the area between Lakes Mweru and Tanganyika (qq.v.). He was the first European to circumnavigate Lake Bangweulu (q.v.). His informative communications, notably with Sir Harry Johnston (q.v.) of the British South Africa Company (q.v.), were insightful and helped shape policy. He also had the respect of Mporokoso, who agreed to sign a peace settlement in December 1896 if Weatherley was the European contact. The BSAC refused. Some of his reports were published in the *British Central Africa Gazette.*

WEBB, SIDNEY. Later Lord Passfield (q.v.).

WEEKLY POST. See POST.

WELENSKY, SIR ROY (ROLAND). Welensky was a major European politician from the mid-1930s until the mid-1960s. Born January 20, 1907, in Salisbury, Southern Rhodesia (qq.v.), to Lithuanian immigrant parents, Welensky received a minimal education and worked in stores and on the railway as a teenager. He was the heavyweight boxing champion of Rhodesia from 1926 to 1928. He was a railway engine driver and became active in trade unions in Broken Hill (q.v.) in the 1930s. He was elected to the Legislative Council (q.v.) of Northern Rhodesia (q.v.) in 1938 and formed the Northern Rhodesia Labour Party (q.v.) in 1941. He consistently opposed African competition for "European jobs." In 1946 he was chosen chairman of the "unofficials" (q.v.) in the Legislative Council. He campaigned vigorously for amalgamation (q.v.) of the two Rhodesias, working closely with Godfrey Huggins (q.v.) of Southern Rhodesia. From the time of the Victoria Falls Conference of 1949 (q.v.), however, Welensky worked for federation (q.v.) instead. When federation was achieved in 1953, he became minister of communications and posts. He became deputy prime minister in 1955 and prime minister in 1956.

It was clear from the beginning of federation that Welensky, a white supremacist, was being groomed to succeed Huggins. Meanwhile, in 1953, Welensky had helped form the Federal Party (q.v.) to contest the first federation elections. Welensky and Huggins pledged themselves to the concept of "partnership" among "civilized peoples," a category used by whites to exclude Africans. Their victory and Huggins' 1956 retirement made Welensky both prime minister of the federation and leader of the Federal Party. In March 1958, the formal merging of the Federal Party with the United Rhodesia Party resulted in a new group, the United Federal Party (q.v.). As federal prime minister, Welensky fought immediately for complete independence from British control through dominion status. He also opposed any liberalization of the Northern Rhodesian constitution that might promote greater African representation. He counted on the Federal Review Conference (q.v.) of 1960 to bring greater independence for the federation and constantly lobbied for it in London. The abortive conference, however, brought greater independence for Nyasaland and Northern Rhodesia. At the end of 1963, despite all of his efforts, Welensky's federation folded. His book, *Welensky's 4000 Days* (1964), tells his story.

Sir Roy tried a parliamentary comeback in 1964, but was decisively defeated by the Rhodesian Front (q.v.) candidate. He then settled down in Salisbury (q.v.). Compared with his white compatriots there, Welensky sounded surprisingly moderate. As late as 1977, for example, he spoke out in favor of turning the Rhodesian government over to its African majority.

WELFARE ASSOCIATIONS. The associations were a 1930s and 1940s social phenomenon throughout Northern Rhodesia (q.v.), promoting brotherhood and mutual support between African townsfolk. They also provided an outlet for grievances against Europeans and conservative African chiefs. As such, they were early examples of African nationalist political consciousness.

The first one in Northern Rhodesia was the Mwenzo Welfare Association (q.v.). Inspired by an association in Nyasaland (q.v.), this group was started by Donald Siwale and David Kaunda (qq.v.), among others. It did not last long, but in 1930 an association began in Livingstone (q.v.). In the next decade or so, important welfare associations began in Ndola, Broken Hill, Lusaka, Mazabuka, Choma, Luanshya, Abercorn, Kasama, and Fort Jameson (qq.v.). On May 18, 1946, the associations united in a Federation of African Societies of Northern Rhodesia (q.v.). In 1948 the federation became the Northern Rhodesia African Congress (q.v.), the first truly nationalist body among Africans in Northern Rhodesia.

WEMBA. Wemba is a typographical variant of Bemba (q.v.). A "w" beneath a circumflex (^) was an early variant for the International Phonetic Alphabet's /ß/ sound. In most Zambian languages, the voiced bilabial fricative found at the beginning of a word is a soft "b," which sounds like a cross between a "b" and a "v". Most typewriters lack this circumflex character, and a plain "w" was used instead. Modern Zambian language orthographies simply use a "b".

WENELA. *See* WITWATERSRAND NATIVE LABOUR ASSOCIATION.

WESTBEECH, GEORGE. Westbeech was an English hunter and trader who spent 26 years in southern Africa, much of it as a semiofficial commercial agent for the Lozi (q.v.). Arriving in Natal in 1862, he soon traveled in Matabeleland, where he established a business relationship with George A. Phillips that lasted over 20 years. Westbeech would dominate trade in Barotseland (q.v.), while Phillips controlled trade in Matabeleland. They gained the confidence of the old Ndebele chief Mzilikazi and his successor, Lobengula (qq.v.). They accompanied the latter on a long trip in 1868 and in 1870 attended his installation. This friendship allowed them to prevent Lobengula from raiding the Lozi, which increased Westbeech's influence among the Lozi. Meanwhile, Westbeech gained the personal respect of Lozi kings Sipopa and Lewanika (qq.v.), allowing him extensive trade and hunting privileges. In turn he helped many European hunters and missionaries to travel to Barotseland. The Reverends Arnot and Coillard (qq.v.), for example, owed him a great deal for smoothing their way with Lewanika.

Westbeech opened up and improved wagon routes and established a trading community at Pandamatenga, south of Victoria Falls (q.v.), in the tsetse-free no-man's-land between the Lozi, the Ndebele, and the Tswana. The upper Zambezi River (q.v.) became his personal highway, as he exported large quantities of ivory (q.v.) and brought in items for trade. His close friendships with Lozi leaders and other Africans, their respect for his integrity, and his fluency in African languages led to his success in Africa. He was considered to be a headman by Lozi leaders and became a member of the Barotse council of state. In 1875 he married the daughter of a Transvaal farmer. He died of liver disease July 17, 1888, in the Transvaal. His diary contains many interesting insights for historians of this period.

WESTERN PROVINCE. Formerly called Barotseland and Barotse Province (qq.v.), this is the southwesternmost of Zambia's nine provinces. It had 410,100 people in 1969 and 607,500 in 1990.

It has six administrative districts: Seseke, Senanga, Mongu, Lukulu, Kalabo, and Kaoma (formerly Mankoya) (qq.v.). It is bordered on the west by Angola (q.v.) and on the south by the Caprivi Strip (q.v.). In 1969, President Kaunda (q.v.) decreed that the area formerly called Barotseland or Barotse Province would be a fully integrated part of Zambia and would be called "Western Province." Before then, "Western Province" was the name of modern Copperbelt Province (q.v.). Even earlier in Zambian history, the term "Western Province" included the areas today encompassed by both Copperbelt and North-Western Provinces (q.v.).

WHITE FATHERS. This Roman Catholic (q.v.) order was founded in 1848 by Cardinal Lavigerie to do mission work in Algeria. Its missionaries came southward from their mission fields in Uganda and Tanganyika to establish a mission at Mambwe Mwela on the Stevenson Road (qq.v.) in July 1891. They also established a mission station at Kayambi (q.v.) in July 1895. By 1918 the order was active in most of Northern Province (q.v.), Zambia. Their primary work was among the Bemba (q.v.). Much of the important early work is in the stories of Father van Oost and Father Joseph Dupont (qq.v.).

WIESE, KARL. Wiese was a German hunter, trader, and amateur ethnographer who lived among Mpezeni's Ngoni (qq.v.) in 1885. He married an African slave trader (q.v.) from Tete (q.v.) and assembled his own corps of armed African retainers. Though Mpezeni had refused the British South Africa Company's (q.v.) treaty requests from Alfred Sharpe and Joseph Thomson (qq.v.) in 1890, Wiese, then working for the Portuguese, claimed to have won exclusive mining and commercial rights from Mpezeni in 1891. Neither Harry Johnston (q.v.) nor the Foreign Office recognized his claim, so Wiese fabricated the story that Mpezeni's land was rich in gold and in 1893, he sold his claim to a group of London investors. Backed by the BSAC in 1895, they acquired a 25,900-square-kilometer (10,000-square-mile) concession, which became the North Charterland Exploration Company (q.v.). Though Mpezeni had no knowledge of this, the concession included his entire territory.

Wiese and North Charterland's prospectors returned to Ngoniland in 1896, but Mpezeni's son and war captain, Nsingu, and the Ngoni warriors resented their presence and land claims and killed two Europeans in 1897. Finding themselves surrounded, Wiese and his companions sent out an urgent call for help, which brought in the Central African Rifles (with its artillery and Maxim guns) from Blantyre to rescue Wiese's party. Nsingu was captured, tried, and shot; Mpezeni surrendered; and 12,000 cattle were confiscated. This ended the so-called Ngoni rebellion, although, in point of fact, the Ngoni had no part in North Charterland's concession and had never recognized the sovereignty of either the BSAC or Queen Victoria.

WILLIAMS, ROBERT. Williams was a friend of Cecil Rhodes (q.v.), the founder (1891) of the Zambezi Exploring Company (q.v.), and founder (1899) of Tanganyika Concessions, Ltd. (q.v.). Tanganyika Concessions soon acquired large prospecting concessions in Northern Rhodesia (q.v.) and neighboring Katanga (q.v.). In 1899 and 1901–02, George Grey (q.v.) led two expeditions that confirmed the enormous mineral wealth of the Central African Copperbelt. Grey and Tanganyika Concessions actually ran the Katanga mines until 1906, and Williams' Robert Williams and Company (q.v.), based in Fort Rosebery (Mansa), supplied the Katanga mines with labor migrants from Northern and Luapula Provinces (qq.v.). In 1912, Williams obtained a Portuguese concession to build Angola's Benguela Railway (qq.v.); it was completed in 1931.

WINA, ARTHUR NUTULUTI LUBINDA. This elder brother of Sikota Wina (q.v.) and son of a noted Lozi *ngambela*, Shemakono Wina (qq.v.), studied at Makerere University in Uganda and at UCLA in California. While there, he was named the United National Independence Party's (q.v.) representative in the United States. Once home, he became UNIP's treasurer and won a decisive victory against the Lozi's secessionist Sicaba Party (q.v.) in the 1962 elections. He served as Zambia's first minister of finance (1964 to 1967), when his Lozi constituents abandoned UNIP in favor of the African National Congress and United Party (qq.v.) coalition candidate. Wina retired into private business but was appointed chairman of the Zambia State Insurance Company in 1971.

He returned to politics in 1991 as a founder, Parliament (q.v.) member, and first chairman of the Movement for Multiparty Democracy (q.v.) in the days before it became a political party. Were it not for his frail health, it is likely that he, rather than Frederick Chiluba (q.v.), would have become its president and presidential candidate. After the October 1991 elections, President Chiluba appointed Wina minister of education. In April

1993, under vague allegations of corruption, Wina was fired, an act widely interpreted as a sign of Chiluba's political insecurity. Wina became one of 10 members of Parliament who resigned from the MMD in August 1993 to form the opposition National Party (q.v.), claiming that the MDD was overrun with "corrupt opportunists and drug barons." Arthur Wina was chairman of the NP. He died in Johannesburg of heart disease in August 1995. In the by-election that followed, Wina's Kalabo seat was retaken by UNIP.

WINA, SHEMAKONO KALONGA. Wina was *ngambela* (prime minister) of Barotseland (qq.v.) from 1941–48 and the father of two important Zambian cabinet officials, Arthur and Sikota Wina (qq.v.). Born in 1878, he was the son of an *induna* (q.v.) based in Lealui (q.v.). After his education in Paris Mission Society (q.v.) schools, he married one of Lewanika's (q.v.) daughters in 1905. He was an *induna* at Sesheke (q.v.) until 1922, when his father died and he succeeded him as *induna* Wina Lioma at Lealui. In 1936 he joined Daniel Akafuna as his chief councilor at the Balovale *kuta* (q.v). The British government disbanded that *kuta* in 1941, detaching the Balovale (Zambezi, q.v.) District from Barotseland (q.v.). Wina's cooperation with the British, notably his support of the war effort and his longtime personal friendship with the king, Yeta (q.v.), combined with his natural leadership ability, made him an obvious choice as *ngambela*. He was also made acting paramount chief (q.v.). He remained as *ngambela* under King Imwiko but was dismissed by King Mwanawina (qq.v.) in 1948. The two had clashed when Wina supported Mwene Mutondo in an earlier dispute with Mwanawina. Mwanawina spread a number of accusations against Wina and then announced to the resident commissioner that Wina should not remain as *ngambela*. He thus retired.

WINA, SIKOTA. As a member of the United National Independence Party (q.v.), Wina was a nationalist activist and member of the Zambian government until his temporary retirement from politics in 1976. The younger brother of Arthur Wina (q.v.) and son of Shemakono Wina (q.v.), he was born in 1931 at Mongu (q.v.). He enrolled at Fort Hare College in South Africa in 1953 but was expelled in 1955 for planning a protest strike as secretary of the student representative council. He returned to Lusaka (q.v.) and became an editor for the Department of Information (q.v.). He resigned in January 1957, when he was hired as editor of Nchanga's (q.v.) African paper, *Drum*, but within a year he switched to *African Life*, an independent magazine for Africans. The latter post gave him a chance to hone his talents as a political journalist, but it also got him—as a secret member of Zambia African National Congress (q.v.) central committee—arrested as a possible subversive during the 1959 Copperbelt Emergency (*see* ROLLING STRIKES), and he was rusticated (q.v.) to Luwingu in Northern Province (q.v.) from March to November 1959. Upon his release he immediately joined UNIP and became director-general of its international and publicity bureau. In 1960 and 1961 he was a member of UNIP's delegation at constitutional conferences in London and a member of the UNIP Executive Committee.

In 1962, he declared Roy Welensky (q.v.) a "prohibited immigrant." Kenneth Kaunda (q.v.) chastised him for racial remarks and forced him to resign as UNIP's director of elections. Two months later, however, he organized UNIP's Committee of Thirty (q.v.), a body designed to map out the party's policies and campaign strategy. He successfully ran for the Legislative Council (q.v.) in 1962, and was named chief whip in the first African government. Three weeks later, however, he was also made parliamentary secretary for local government and social welfare (serving under Kaunda). He remained the government's chief whip until 1971. Reelected to Parliament in 1964, he became, in succession, minister of health, minister of local government, and minister of information, broadcasting, and tourism. He was a member of the central committee of UNIP (q.v.) and chairman of its election, publicity, and strategy committee. In 1976 he returned to his position as chairman of the Zambian Publishing Company.

The December 1979 report of the parliamentary committee on parastatal (q.v.) corporations charged Wina with using the Zambian Publishing Company to make large loans to senior executives on very favorable terms. Wina denied the charges but was dismissed by President Kaunda in August 1980. In 1983, he was detained five months in an Indian jail on charges of Mandrax smuggling. After returning to Zambia on a Sudanese passport—issued to a "Mr. Hussein"—he presented himself as a victim of political persecution (*see* DRUG TRADE). He had become a prominent critic of President Kaunda and, at UNIP's fifth national convention in March 1990, he circulated an open letter accusing the leadership of betraying the people and its own democratic principles. Wina and his wife, Nakatindi Wina, returned to Parliament as members of the Movement for Multiparty Democracy (q.v.), and Wina became deputy speaker of the assembly. When similar allegations of drug trafficking against President Chiluba's (q.v.) cabinet arose 1993, Wina and his wife resigned their government posts.

WISSMANN, HERMANN VON. Wissmann was the imperial commissioner for German East Africa near the end of the 19th century. In 1893, in an attempt to deter the slave trade (q.v.) in the area between Lakes Malawi and Tanganyika (qq.v.), he intercepted a large slave-raiding force led by the Bemba Chitimukulu, Sampa (qq.v.). The Bemba force was just inside German territory and heading south when it approached the stockaded village of a Lungu headman, Nondo. Inside were Wissmann, 60 trained soldiers, a cannon, and a Maxim gun. The Bemba approached late on July 6, fired a few shots, and gradually moved a large force (the Germans estimated 5,000) within striking range of the stockade. The next morning Wissmann talked with Sampa's emissary, who suggested that the Germans would be spared if they left quickly. Wissmann warned them of the futility of waging a battle against European arms. A few shots were fired from the stockade, Wissmann threw out a grenade, and then the Germans riddled the Bemba front lines with their Maxim gun. Sampa's forces were routed, and the story quickly spread to other Bemba leaders. While the Bemba remained hostile to the European invaders, they acquired a healthy respect for European military capabilities.

WITCHCRAFT ORDINANCE, 1914. The ordinance (also called the Witchcraft Suppression Proclamation) attempted to outlaw African witchcraft (*ubuloshi; ubufwiti*) by punishing witchcraft accusations, the use of divination or the poison ordeal (*mwafi*) to identify a witch (*muloshi; mfwiti*), and the execution of a witch. Colonial rule seems to have exacerbated witchcraft fears, first, by generating new interpersonal tensions, often expressed in witchcraft accusations, and second, by fostering political rivalries between chiefs.

One cannot, in fact, outlaw the belief in witchcraft. Thus, as elsewhere on the continent, most Africans perceived this ordinance as a "witchcraft protection act." While it did nothing to prevent people from using medicines to bring illness and death to fellow village residents, it effectively forbade their victims from protecting themselves and the deceased victims' relatives from exacting revenge. As seen in the later *banyama* (q.v.) scares, this ordinance seemed to ally the Europeans with the witches. The Watch Tower and Muchape Movements (qq.v.), on the other hand, responded to Africans' fear of witchcraft.

WITWATERSRAND NATIVE LABOUR ASSOCIATION. Although labor had flowed from Zambia to Johannesburg for decades, the flow intensified in 1940 when agents of the Johannesburg-based WENELA began recruiting in Barotseland (q.v.) for the South African mines. As many as 6,000 men traveled annually from Barotseland to South Africa, where they earned about £5 a month. WENELA paid the Litunga (q.v.) of Barotseland an annual fee for each worker recruited. In 1964 this fee was doubled to 24 shillings per head, an increase of about £5000 a year. In 1966, the Zambian minister of labor, also a Lozi (q.v.), prohibited all further WENELA recruitment in Barotseland, depriving the area of its greatest single source of cash income. President Kaunda (q.v.) defended this measure, saying that all ties helpful to the continuation of racism in South Africa must be severed. The Lozi thus became further alienated from Kaunda's United National Independence Party (q.v.) government and, for the time being, were attracted to the new United Party (q.v.).

WORTHINGTON, FRANK VIGERS. Worthington was acting administrator of North-Western Rhodesia (q.v.) from April to July 1904. A British South Africa Company (q.v.) official, he and Colonel Colin Harding (q.v.) were signatories of the concession by King Lewanika (q.v.) in October 1900. He later served as the secretary for native affairs.

Y

YAMBA, DAUTI. Yamba was a teacher and a nationalist politician in the 1940s and 1950s. He visited South Africa and came back with the idea of forming an African Congress. Meanwhile, he became headmaster of the Luanshya African School (1941–46) and was then appointed education councilor to the Lunda Native Authority (q.v.). In May 1946, he was a major organizer of the Federation of African Societies (q.v.), which became the Northern Rhodesia African Congress (q.v.) two years later. Yamba had been secretary of the Luanshya Native Welfare Association (q.v.) and was elected president of the new federation. In 1951 he was chosen by the African Representative Council (q.v.) to fill one of the two African seats on the Legislative Council of Northern Rhodesia (qq.v.). When the council voted in 1953 on the formation of the Central African Federation (q.v.), Yamba was one of only four to vote against it. In 1953, Yamba was chosen (through indirect election) as one of the two African representatives from Northern Rhodesia to the federal Parliament (q.v.). He was ridiculed by Prime Minister Godfrey Huggins (q.v.) when Yamba spoke out during a debate, arguing that Huggins' brand of "partnership" would not be meaningful unless federal legislation established true racial equality. His efforts as a member of Parliment proved futile, but he served until March 1962. In the Northern Rhodesia general election of 1962, he ran as a member of the African National Congress (q.v.) for a Northern Province seat in the Legislative Council but received only 87 votes out of almost 4,000. Prior to that, in 1959, he had been active as a founding organizer of the African National Freedom Movement (q.v.).

YAO. The Yao, who live to the east of Lake Malawi in Malawi (qq.v.), had important historical contacts with Zambian peoples. As the leading traders of East Central Africa, the Yao were middlemen in the trade between the Indian Ocean ports and the Bisa (q.v.) (and thus also Kazembe's Lunda, qq.v.) of Zambia. Ivory (q.v.) was an important commodity in this trade. Ngoni (q.v.) men also regularly married Yao women.

YEKE. Yeke (meaning "hunters") refers to the Sumbwa Nyamwezi ivory (q.v.) hunters and traders from western Tanzania (q.v.) who came to Katanga (q.v.) about 1845. Using their superior firearms to protect themselves from Luba (q.v.) raiders and to exploit chiefly rivalries, Msiri (q.v.) led the Yeke in establishing (1856–60) their Katangan ivory, slave, and copper (q.v.) trading empire, which, in turn, received cloth, guns, and powder from Portuguese and Mambari (q.v.) traders from the west coast and from Arab (q.v.) and African traders from the east coast.

The Yeke conquered most of Katanga. They collected tribute from the Kaonde, Lamba, and Lala (qq.v.), and raided the Aushi, Bisa, and Unga (q.v.). They also expanded the old Katanga copper mines and manufactured superb bracelet wire. The Yeke and their trading partners ended Mwata Yamvo's (q.v.) 18th-century Central African trading empire and, by moving the eastern trade routes farther north, isolated Kazembe's Lunda (qq.v.), annexed their western territories, and warred with them in the 1870s. Frederick Arnot and the Plymouth Brethren (qq.v.) had a mission near Msiri's capital (1886–92), and documented the apex and demise of his empire.

King Leopold II of Belgium, hearing of Cecil Rhodes' (q.v.) plan to steal Katanga (*see* ALFRED SHARPE; JOSEPH THOMSON), sent three expeditions in 1891 to establish Leopold's sovereignty over Katanga. But while Msiri stalled, the local Sanga began a general revolt that cut off the Yeke's food and powder supplies. The third Belgian expedition, resolved to force Msiri's consent, shot him to death in a brief but heated confrontation. The Belgians installed Msiri's son as his successor, and the Yeke warriors soon joined their efforts to establish a new, Belgian empire in Katanga.

YETA I. He was one of the earliest of Lozi (q.v.) kings. According to some lists, he succeeded the founder of the Lozi state, Mboo (q.v.). He has been referred to as the consolidator of the kingdom, during whose reign (perhaps late 17th or early 18th century) the kingship in Kalabo (q.v.) was recognized by both the Lozi and their neighbors. He is still remembered in Lozi praise songs. Among his other accomplishments was the creation of a Lozi bureaucracy through the institution of *induna*s (q.v.).

YETA III. He was the son of the Lozi king, Lewanika (qq.v.). He was known as Litia until he became Litunga (q.v.) on March 13, 1916, as Yeta III. Forty-two years old at the time, Yeta had received excellent training. He was among the first Lozi to attend the Paris Missionary Society's (q.v.) school and served as chief of Sesheke (q.v.) from 1891 to 1916. Upon becoming Litunga, he brought a number of educated, young Lozi of royal blood into the highest councils. They were well informed about the position of their kingdom vis-à-vis the British South Africa Company (q.v.). Since the BSAC had not provided health care, education, and transport services, they argued, the BSAC's mineral concessions were void. Yeta also argued that the BSAC had reneged on its pledge to contribute a share of the hut tax (q.v.) to the Lozi treasury. When British Crown rule replaced BSAC rule in 1924, Yeta and his advisors, though not totally satisfied, accepted a financial package worked out by Governor Herbert Stanley (q.v.). A highlight of Yeta's reign was his 1938 visit to London for the coronation of George VI. A low point was the controversy over the Zambezi District (q.v.) that same year. He was struck by paralysis and left speechless in early 1939 and remained that way before reluctantly resigning in 1945. He died the next year.

YOMBE. The Yombe are one of Zambia's smaller ethnic groups. They are a *ci*Tumbuka-speaking people and live in Zambia's easternmost territory. Their ruling clan is the Wowo. The Yombe cultivate maize (q.v.), beans, and millet. Their territory, called Uyombe, was inhabited by the Bisa (q.v.) until the coming of Vinkakanimba (q.v.).

YOUNG, SIR HUBERT. Young was colonial governor of Northern Rhodesia (q.v.) from 1934 to 1938. He did not want Northern Rhodesia to adopt South Africa's racial policies, and he did not think that Southern Rhodesia (q.v.) should be absorbed into South Africa. But he also felt that the interests of the European minority should not be subordinated to those of the African majority. He tried but failed to convince the British colonial secretary, William Ormsby-Gore (q.v.), that the mineral claims of the British South Africa Company (q.v.) to the Copperbelt (q.v.) were extremely weak and that the territory could use its income to improve social services and public works.

YOUNG, ROBERT. Young was an official with the British South Africa Company (q.v.) for about two decades, until his retirement at Chinsali (q.v.) in 1916. At first only an assistant collector (q.v.), he made an important contribution to Zambia's history by writing a history of the Bemba (q.v.). Included was a chronological list of Bemba leaders. In 1897 he was assigned to build a *boma* at Mirongo (q.v.), where he set up his residency. In August 1904, Young set up a new post at Chinsali, where be became a commissioner for the BSAC. There he gained the respect of David Kaunda (q.v.), father of Zambia's president. In his two decades of work, he dealt with most of the Bemba chiefs of the day.

YUBYA. Yubya was the seventh king of the Lozi (q.v.). He was noted for his extravagant standard of living. His flaunting of wealth and his monopoly over tribute stirred resentment among his *induna*s (q.v.). As a result, he introduced a system whereby the *induna*s could take a portion of his tribute for themselves. He probably ruled in the early to mid–18th century.

Z

Z-VOTE. The term refers to the Zambian Voter's Observation Team (q.v.) in the 1991 elections.

ZAIRE PEDICLE. *See* KATANGA PEDICLE.

ZAIRE REPUBLIC. *See* DEMOCRATIC REPUBLIC OF CONGO.

ZAMANGLO. *See* ANGLO-AMERICAN CORPORATION OF SOUTH AFRICA, LTD.

ZAMBESIA. Zambesia used to refer to the territory of modern Zambia and Zimbabwe. The Zambezi River (q.v.) intersected the area, thus leading many to refer to northern Zambesia and southern Zambesia.

ZAMBEZI DISTRICT. This district (formerly called Balovale District) is located in North-Western Province (q.v.), along the upper sections of the Zambezi River (q.v.). It had over 61,000 people in 1969 and 70,000 in 1990, mostly Lunda and Luvale (qq.v.) peoples. The district became part of a controversy in the late 1930s when it was still administered as part of Barotseland (q.v.), despite its non-Lozi population. Residents complained, and in 1938 the government appointed a commission led by Sir Philip MacDonell (q.v.) to investigate the question. It made its report in 1939, but the government did not act on it until July 1941, when it removed almost all of the district from the control of the Barotse king and transferred it to Kaonde-Lunda (later Western) Province (q.v.).

ZAMBEZI EXPLORING COMPANY. The company was a predecessor of Tanganyika Concessions, Ltd. (q.v.). It was a subsidiary of the British South Africa Company (q.v.) and was founded in 1891 by Robert Williams (q.v.), a friend of Cecil Rhodes (q.v.). Convinced of the location of a large supply of minerals, Williams obtained a concession for 5,180 square kilometers (2,000 square miles) near the source of the Kafue River (q.v.), and sent George Grey (q.v.) to explore it.

ZAMBEZI PLAIN. The plain covers an area along both sides of the upper Zambezi River (q.v.). It is sometimes called Bulozi by the Lozi (qq.v.), who consider it the heart of their country. It is about 160 kilometers (100 miles) long and between 16 and 48 kilometers (10 and 30 miles) wide.

ZAMBEZI REDWOOD. *See* TEAKWOOD.

ZAMBEZI (ZAMBESI) RIVER. The river is 3,542 kilometers (2,200 miles) long and is one of Africa's greatest rivers. It starts near

Kaleñe Hill in the northern tip of North-Western Province (q.v.) and moves south through Western Province (q.v.) (*see* ZAMBEZI PLAIN). Early on it picks up a major tributary, the Kabompo River (q.v.). It then heads east, forming the Rhodesia-Zambia border. It tumbles over Victoria Falls (q.v.) and then enters Lake Kariba (q.v.). The Kariba Dam (q.v.) slows it down and sends a controlled flow in a northeasterly direction. Past the Kariba Dam, the Kafue River and the Luangwa River (qq.v.) join the Zambezi. Passing Feira (q.v.) it leaves the country and continues east and then southeast through Mozambique (q.v.), past the towns of Tete and Sena (qq.v.) on its way to the Indian Ocean south of Quelimane (q.v.). Europeans did not fully appreciate the significance of this river until the reports of Dr. David Livingstone (q.v.) reached the world.

ZAMBIA. The word Zambia became prominent on October 24, 1958, when Kenneth Kaunda (q.v.) and his followers named their new party the Zambia African National Congress (q.v.), but the exact origin of the word is in doubt. It was obviously derived from the Zambezi River (q.v.), which flows through much of the country, and from the word Zambesia (q.v.). In 1953 Arthur Wina (q.v.), in a poem he wrote while attending Makerere College in Uganda, used the word to refer to his country. Stories differ as to who suggested the name at the first ZANC meeting. Regardless, the group preferred it to the other suggestions, Muchinga (after the Muchinga Mountains, q.v., in eastern Zambia) or Zambesia.

ZAMBIA AFRICAN NATIONAL CONGRESS. ZANC was founded on October 24, 1958, by some of the younger, more militant members of the African National Congress (q.v.). A split had been brewing in the ANC for some time over a variety of issues but especially over leader Harry Nkumbula's (q.v.) conciliatory nationalist stance and his apparent willingness to participate in the 1959 Legislative Council (q.v.) elections. The leaders of ZANC, the quickly adopted acronym, pledged to boycott the elections and the so-called Benson Constitution (q.v.) because of its poor provisions for African electoral participation. The founding of this party brought the name Zambia to public use for the first time. The presidency of ZANC was given to Kenneth Kaunda (q.v.); Munukayumbwa Sipalo (q.v.) was general secretary, and Simon Kapwepwe (q.v.) was treasurer. Their deputies were Paul Kalichini, W. K. Sikalumbi, and Reuben Kamanga (qq.v.), respectively. Sikota Wina, Grey Zulu, and Lewis Changufu (qq.v.) were added to the executive com-mittee. All these officers were officially elected at a general con-ference in Broken Hill (q.v.) on November 8, 1958.

The immediate goals of ZANC were to establish an effective African boycott of the 1959 election and to replace the ANC as the territory's major nationalist party. It made quick strides toward the latter goal, as ZANC leaders, many of them from Luapula and Northern Provinces (qq.v.), brought thousands of former ANC members from those provinces into the new party. On the other hand, its success in the south and west was never what the leaders desired. The ANC managed to hold support in all parts of the country, even in some ZANC strong-holds. Nevertheless, ZANC's campaign to boycott the elections (primarily by not registering) began to succeed enough by Jan-uary 1959 that the government was concerned. Likewise, the registration of ZANC branches under the Societies Ordinance (q.v.) was confused because a number of ANC branches had neglected to inform the government after their conversion to the ZANC. By February, the government was increasingly anx-ious about the ZANC threat. Public meetings were held despite police bans, and the rhetoric of some ZANC leaders sounded extreme to some Europeans, despite Kaunda's constant pledge of nonviolence.

Nyasaland's (q.v.) March 2 declaration of a state of emer-gency was probably the final motivation for the government to act. On March 11, 1959, ZANC was banned and most of its leaders were arrested and rusticated (q.v.) to distant provinces. Governor Benson (q.v.) even compared ZANC's leaders with Murder Incorporated, Chicago's "organization of killers" in the 1930s. Although the results of the March 20 election showed that 85 percent of the registered Africans voted, only one-quarter of the anticipated African voters had registered. By the time most ZANC leaders were freed in early 1960, a new organization, the United National Independence Party (q.v.), had been created as a successor to ZANC and only awaited the release of its true leaders.

ZAMBIA AFRICAN NATIONAL DEMOCRATIC UNION. The union was a minor party that never attained much following or prominence. Its formation was announced in May 1969. Its leaders had previously been involved with both the African National Congress and the United Party (qq.v.), of which it was considered to be a small splinter.

ZAMBIA AGRICULTURAL DEVELOPMENT BANK. The bank is a government agency; it was formed in 1982 to take over the operations of the Agricultural Finance Corporation and the Cattle Finance Company. Its start-up was delayed by the government's failure to pay its initial capital contribution of K15 million. Over the course of the 1980s it followed in the tradition of its predecessors, failing to rationalize the smallholder lending market by maintaining subsidized lending rates at the behest of Zambia's governing elite.

ZAMBIA AIRWAYS. The airways was a parastatal (q.v.) body formed in 1967 by the Zambian government with the assistance of Alitalia Airlines. It became the national airline, replacing the federation's Central African Airways (q.v.), the assets of which were distributed among Zambia, Malawi (q.v.), and Rhodesia at the end of 1967. It had service to Europe as well as to a number of African countries. Zambia Airways was liquidated in December 1994 and was replaced by such licensed private firms as Aero Zambia and Zambia Express Airways, which is linked to South African Airways.

ZAMBIA ALLIANCE OF WOMEN. The alliance began in 1982; it is affiliated with the International Alliance of Women. Its objectives are to promote the social and economic status of women and children and to raise awareness of issues of concern to women. It has been involved in the renovation of facilities for women at the University Teaching Hospital in Lusaka (q.v.), agroforestry projects, preschool classes, water and sanitation projects, and educational seminars on the Law of Succession of 1989, which is designed to protect a woman's property rights after the divorce or death of her husband.

ZAMBIA ASSOCIATION FOR RESEARCH AND DEVELOPMENT. The association was formed in October 1984 to encourage research on the position of women in Zambia and grew out of the socioeconomic research group, which functioned in the mid- to late-1970s. ZARD collects and disseminates information and documents on women and runs workshops and a resource center. Its emphasis is on action-oriented and participatory research. ZARD has also been involved in disseminating information about the 1989 Law of Succession, which is designed to protect a woman's property rights after divorce or the death of her husband.

ZAMBIA ASSOCIATION OF UNIVERSITY WOMEN. The association was organized in 1980 to combat antifemale biases in educational materials and to improve the position of women through education, community programs, and the defense of their legal rights. The ZAUW also conducts programs to help combat diarrhea in the poorer areas of Lusaka (q.v.).

ZAMBIA CIVIC EDUCATION ASSOCIATION. The association is a nonpartisan civic education group which was founded by Lucy Sichone (q.v.). The ZCEA educates citizens about their rights, urges residents of poor areas to take action to obtain their due city council services, takes up the causes of persons mistreated by the authorities, and works with the police to improve their relations with local communities. It carries out these goals by providing civic education in the schools, paralegal training, and legal aid in public interest cases; arranging public debates; issuing simplified pamphlets on laws and government; and running projects dealing with police-community relations and citizen responsibilities.

ZAMBIA CONFEDERATION OF INDUSTRIES AND CHAMBERS OF COMMERCE. The confederation is the successor to the first chambers of commerce, which date back to the 1930s, though under a variety of different names. ZACCI goals are to speak for the business community with a single voice and to link the business community with the government. Its activities include organizing business forums, coordinating trade missions, and disseminating business news. It also publishes *Profit*, a monthly business magazine.

ZAMBIA CONGRESS OF TRADE UNIONS. The congress was established early in 1965 by Parliament's (q.v.) Trade Unions and Trade Disputes Ordinance (q.v.) of December 1964. Its purpose was to be an umbrella organization to which all trade unions would affiliate. It nearly reached that goal. In 1975, under President Newstead Zimba (q.v.), it had 16 affiliated unions, with a membership of about 142,000 members, of whom 40,000 belonged to the Mineworkers Union of Zambia (q.v.). It replaced the old United Trade Union Congress (q.v.), which had fragmented and was deeply in debt. The 1964 ordinance not only passed important rules for unions but also defined the powers of the ZCTU. All affiliated unions, for example, were required to pay the ZCTU a part of their collected dues, and its approval was required for certain decisions such as a strike ballot, strikes, amalgamation (q.v.), or dissolution. In effect, the ZCTU was a branch of the United National Independence Party (q.v.), for not only did the minister of labor appoint its first officers, but the ordinance gave him the authority to dissolve it without challenge.

By 1975, however, declining living standards and government-imposed wage ceilings and subsidies cuts brought about a rift between the unions, on the one hand, and UNIP and the government on the other; the ZCTU assumed the role of an extraparliamentary opposition party. In 1980, for example, ZCTU called for UNIP to reduce government's role in the economy and to encourage private investment instead. The ZCTU maintained that competiton between the public and private sectors was good, and it criticized the performance of public enterprises. But conditions in the 1980s were hard on the ZCTU; recession and retrenchment in the early 1980s cut ZCTU membership from 500,000 to 380,000.

In January 1981, following the MUZ's threat of an election boycott, UNIP expelled 17 executive committee members of the MUZ and the ZCTU. The MUZ then staged a popular, eight-day strike to assert the independence of their union posts from UNIP membership, and the leaders were readmitted to UNIP in April. That July, after the Railway Workers Union of Zambia struck to protest government-imposed management changes and MUZ members burned the minister of mines' official car, MUZ vice chairman, Timothy Walamba, together with Frederick Chiluba, Newstead Zimba (qq.v.), and Chitalu Sampa (then chairman, general secretary, and Assistant Secretary, respectively, of the ZCTU), were detained for advocating industrial unrest and the overthrow of the government. They were released in November 1981 after the High Court (q.v.) dismissed all charges.

Though Frederick Chiluba and ZCTU leaders played prominent roles in the 1990 formation and 1991 electoral victory of the ad hoc Movement for Multiparty Democracy (q.v.), job retrenchments in the mines and other industries led Francis Kaunda (q.v.) and his MUZ—along with 11 other unions, including the Zambia Union of Financial and Allied Workers and the Zambia National Union of Teachers—to break from President Fackson Shamenda's ZCTU in 1994, threatening a considerable loss of members and their annual dues contributions.

ZAMBIA CONSOLIDATED COPPER MINES. In view of the copper (q.v.) industry's problems, and to avoid duplication of plants, personnel, and equipment, President Kaunda (q.v.) ordered the merger of the Nchanga Consolidated Copper and Roan Consolidated Mines (qq.v.) in 1980. The ZCCM, the product of this merger, was established by 1982. In their subsequent review of the Zambian copper (q.v.) industry, ZCCM's managers showed Kaunda that copper sales, then worth only 51 percent of their early 1970s indexed value, could no longer generate the foreign exchange needed to subsidize the country's manufacturing and agricultural sectors. The ZCCM then reemphasized cobalt over copper production and began closing down some of its less profitable mines and plants, including Bwana Mkubwa Mine (q.v.) (closed in 1984), Konkola III shaft, Chambishi Mine (q.v.) (closed in 1987), and the Luanshya (q.v.) smelter and Ndola Copper Refinery tank house. In 1995, the ZCCM registered with the new Lusaka Stock Exchange (q.v.) and was seeking the advice of international merchant bankers on how best to become private. The Anglo-American Corporation (q.v.) preferred that the ZCCM be sold as a single unit to a consortium in which it would be the majority shareholder.

ZAMBIA COOPERATIVE FEDERATION. The ZCF was established by the government to serve as the central organization for Zambia's producer cooperatives. Local cooperative societies join together to form district unions, which join together to form provincial unions, and these, in turn, constitute the ZCF. At its general meeting of December 1991, the ZCF decided to become a private body on its own, without the intervention of the Zambia Privatisation Agency (q.v.). It became the marketing agency for agricultural inputs and maize (q.v.) sales after NAMBoard's (q.v.) dissolution in 1989, and the effort put too much of a strain on the organization. While it still undertakes marketing efforts, it only does so on a contractual basis and not at the direction of the government. It is attempting to rebuild itself and to revitalize its constituent, local societies. As of March 1995, the ZCF was owed K25 billion in unpaid farmers' loans, much of which was presumably due to interest charges. Not surprisingly, its farm-to-farm recovery program had little luck in locating delinquent borrowers.

ZAMBIA COUNCIL FOR SOCIAL DEVELOPMENT. Formed in Kabwe (q.v.) in 1974, the ZCSD began as a collective comprised of parastatal (q.v.) and nongovernmental organizations. It went into decline in the latter half of the 1980s, when external donors withdrew their support, citing the ZCSD's poor management and loss of grassroots contact. A thorough evaluation of its practices, procedures, and structure was conducted in early 1991. With 72 affiliated members as of 1993, the ZCSD coordinates social development activities, provides referral services, and promotes programs to alleviate ignorance, hunger, and disease.

ZAMBIA DAILY MAIL. The *Daily Mail* is a government-owned daily newspaper, published in Lusaka (q.v.). It originated in 1960 as a weekly, the *African Mail* (which was assisted financially by the London *Observer*). In 1962 it became the *Central African Mail* (q.v.) and fought for independence and against federation (q.v.). The Zambian government bought the paper in early 1965 and changed its name to the *Zambian Mail* when the *Observer* stopped its financial support. The government instructed its editors to explain and support government policies while also reflecting public opinion. It was published only twice weekly for several years. Primarily appealing to the educated, urban reader, it tends to focus upon Zambian coverage at the expense of international news. Its daily circulation in 1975 was 32,000. The Zambia Privatisation Agency (q.v.) privatized both the *Zambia Daily Mail* and the *Times of Zambia* (q.v.).

ZAMBIA DEMOCRATIC CONGRESS. The Congress was formed in September 1995 by two young turks—former deputy ministers—who had been expelled from the Movement for Multiparty Democracy (q.v.) party for "indiscipline," apparently a reference to the public remarks they made concerning the necessity of taking decisive action against drug traffickers (*see* DRUG TRADE) regardless of their level of leadership.

ZAMBIA EXPATRIATE MINERS ASSOCIATION. ZEMA was formed after independence by a merger of the Mines Workers Society and the Mines Officials and Salaried Staff Association. Attempts to get it to merge with the Zambia Mineworkers Union (q.v.) proved futile because of doubts and fears on both sides. Early in 1969 the minister of labor announced that he no longer recognized ZEMA. Since expatriates came only on fixed-period contracts, the issue eventually resolved itself.

ZAMBIA INDEPENDENT MONITORING TEAM. ZIMT was formed to monitor the 1991 elections. It suffered from organizational problems from the start; it was headed by David Phiri, a golfing partner of President Kenneth Kaunda (q.v.), so ZIMT's political independence was always in doubt. Furthermore, the Zambian Elections Monitoring Coordinating Committee (*see* FOUNDATION FOR DEMOCRATIC PROCESS) was established as a separate monitoring group. ZIMT languished after the 1991 elections. In July 1993 Dr. Mashekwa Nalumango, a ZIMT leader, called a meeting in an attempt to revive the group, but the turnout was poor, and some of its original members publicly distanced themselves from Dr. Nalumango's effort, saying that ZIMT had been dissolved after the elections. In late 1994, however, ZIMT reaffirmed its legal existence and sponsored a workshop on the electoral process. It also monitored some polling stations in the November 1993 by-elections.

ZAMBIA INDUSTRIAL AND MINING CORPORATION. ZIMCO was founded as a parastatal (q.v.) holding company in 1969. Its duty was to oversee the government's interests in mining, industrial, and commercial enterprises. It held 51 percent interest in the Industrial Development Corporation, the Mining Development Corporation, the Financial Development Corporation (qq.v.), the National Import and Export Corporation, and a half dozen other parastatal constituent members of the ZIMCO umbrella organization. Its chairman of the board was President Kaunda (q.v.). In 1975 it had 87,000 employees and owned assets of about K1.5 billion. In essence, it established state control over about 80 percent of Zambia's formal economic sector. As such, it became the central target of the Zambia Privatisation Agency (q.v.). It was scheduled to be dissolved at the end of December 1994 and all its affairs wrapped up by March 1995. In the course of its rapid demise, few safeguards were established to prevent the demoralized and soon-to-be redundant employees from plundering the assets of its many subsidiaries.

ZAMBIA INFORMATION SERVICES. The ZIS is an office of the ministry of information and broadcasting; its press section is the official distributor of governmental news both inside and outside the country. The ZIS also makes films and recordings about current events, publishes several semimonthly magazines, some in English and others in local languages, and serves some diplomatic goals. Its predecessors were the Northern

Rhodesian and the federal departments of information (see DE-PARTMENT OF INFORMATION).

ZAMBIA MINEWORKERS UNION. The ZMU became the name of the African Mineworkers Union (q.v.) as of January 1965. In April 1966, the AMU merged with the Mines Police Association and the Mines Local Staff Association to form the Mineworkers Union of Zambia (q.v.). During the brief existence of the ZMU, it had one notable impact on the country: it was behind the huge 1966 strike that crippled the industry for a time.

ZAMBIA NATIONAL BROADCASTING SERVICES. The government-controlled ZNBS was founded January 1, 1966. It manages both television services and shortwave radio broadcasting. The services operate in English on both radio and television and in seven Zambian languages on the radio. The general service radio network is only in English and includes BBC programs in addition to locally produced educational and entertainment programs. The home service network broadcasts in eight languages, and its biggest difficulty is allowing each language to get equal air time. Rural reception, even when batteries are available, is often spotty; in October 1993 the People's Republic of China loaned Zambia US$10 million to buy more radio transmitters. Though the ZNBS offers little or nothing in the way of educational programming, it has a 30 percent share in Multichoice, a South African purveyor of a pay-TV dish system.

ZAMBIA NATIONAL FARMERS UNION. The ZNFU was formed in 1910 and has operated under a variety of names over the years. In 1992, the Commercial Farmers' Bureau adopted the name to reflect its inclusion of both small- and large-scale farmers. The ZNFU's affiliated organizations include the Tobacco Association of Zambia (q.v.), the Zambia Farm Employers' Association, the Zambia Seed Producers' Association, the Zambia Export Growers' Association, the Zambia Coffee Growers' Association, the Wildlife Producers' Association of Zambia, the Agricultural Conservation Association of Zambia, and the Young Farmers' Union of Zambia. The ZNFU had about 1,600 members as of mid-1994. In August of that year it opened the Agricultural Commodity Exchange in Lusaka (q.v.) in order to reestablish an orderly agricultural marketing organization once the government withdrew its former services. The ZNFU publishes a monthly magazine, *Productive Farming*, produces a weekly radio program, provides extension services to its members, and represents farmers' interests in government and policymaking bodies.

ZAMBIA NATIONAL PROVIDENT FUND. The ZNPF was established in 1966 to provide pensions and permanent disability stipends to all employed Zambian citizens. Like the U.S. Social Security system, it requires monthly contributions from both employer and employee. Domestic servants, though, are rarely registered with the ZNPF, even though a 1973 amendment to the ZNPF bill of 1965 required employers of urban domestic servants to make regular contributions to their pensions. Aside from cases of permanent disability, one must be 45 years old and fully retired to begin to collect one's benefits. The age qualification tends to work against rural Zambians, who in many cases do not know, and lack any documentary evidence of, when they were born.

ZAMBIA POLICE FORCE. Transformed from the old Northern Rhodesia Police (q.v.), the ZPF was established by the independence constitution as one of the national public (civil) services. The commissioner of police is appointed by the president. Zambia's police force is notoriously underpaid, and its officers are widely (if often unfairly) suspected of corrupt practices associated with the drug trade (q.v.).

ZAMBIA PRIVATISATION AGENCY. This independent, limited-term agency was created in response to the World Bank and International Monetary Fund's structural adjustment program (qq.v.) for the Zambian economy. Its purpose is to divest the government of most of its many parastatal (q.v.) companies and to end Zambia's former system of state capitalism, in which one parastatal holding company—Zambia Industrial and Mining Corporation (q.v.)—controlled 80 percent of the country's formal economic sector. In 1993–94, 16 parastatals worth over US$60 million—including Zambia Airways (q.v.), the United Bus Company, the National Agricultural Marketing Board (q.v.), cement plants, and a brewery—were either closed or sold to private buyers. Another 33 parastatals, including Chambeshi Mine (q.v.), were to be privatized in 1995. The resulting unemployment, loss of job security, and demoralization posed serious threats to President Frederick Chiluba's (q.v.) administration and his party's prospects in the 1996 elections.

By mid-1997, the ZPA reported completing the privatization of 211 of a total of 326 companies to be privatized.

ZAMBIA RAILWAYS. Founded as a parastatal (q.v.) body in 1967, the ZR developed out of the dissolution of Rhodesian Railways at the end of federation (qq.v.). Following Rhodesia's unilateral declaration of independence (q.v.) in 1965, negotiations resulted in a division of the rolling stock. The ZR operates the north-south, Kitwe to Livingstone (qq.v.), line of rail; the TAZARA (q.v.) railway is under its own authority. This 85-year-old transport system has seen better days, and in June 1993 the ZR took out half-page ads in the *Times* and the *Daily Mail* to counter the rumor that its carriage service was a death trap. The long-term deterioration of its permanent way, though, has meant 15-kilometer-per-hour speed restrictions. Thus the railway has lost much of its transport business to South African tractor-trailer trucks, and passenger service dropped 40 percent between 1970 and 1994. The World Bank gave the ZR US$18 million for repairs in 1993, and in 1995 the ZR sold off surplus houses and five new locomotives as part of a K10 billion retrenchment bill.

ZAMBIA REVENUE AUTHORITY. The ZRA was formally launched in March 1994. It has the power to bring tax evaders to court through the public prosecutor's office. In the first few months, ZRA was successful in collecting revenues, though it faced the challenges of an expanding tax base and forged tax exemption certificate schemes. In 1995, the ZRA introduced the value-added tax system to Zambia.

ZAMBIA YOUTH SERVICE. The ZYS was a parastatal (q.v.) body formed in 1964 with the goal of tackling the problem of unemployed urban youth. The Reverend Merfyn Temple (q.v.) was appointed its first director. Anyone aged 16 to 25 who did not complete or go beyond secondary school could join the ZYS. Its camps were designed to provide training to fill the nation's future needs. Boys were trained in the trades and in modern agricultural practices. Girls received training in home economics and in running village cooperatives. For a number of years it was considered successful and even received international financial support, despite the fact that during the 1969 judiciary crisis, ZYS members stormed and ransacked the High Court (q.v.) building. In 1971 the ZYS was replaced by the Zambia National Service. Most of the members of the ZYS were recruited from the Youth Brigade of the United National Independence Party (q.v.).

ZAMBIAN ELECTIONS MONITORING COORDINATION COMMITTEE. *See* FOUNDATION FOR DEMOCRATIC PROCESS.

ZAMBIAN HUMANISM. The Zambian counterpart to President Julius Nyerere's (q.v.) Ujamaa or African socialism, the national ideology of Tanzania, Zambian humanism was the ideology propounded by President Kenneth Kaunda (q.v.). It stressed the inherent worth of individual human beings within the larger context of societal cooperation and was said to hold the middle ground between the twin evils of capitalism and communism. Class consciousness and the pursuit of personal gain and material possessions were denounced as violations of Zambian humanism, even as the gap between Zambia's many poor and its privileged few was widening and becoming increasingly permanent. This disparity between the ideals and realities of Zambian society fed a general sense of cynicism and mistrust toward the government.

ZAMBIAN POUND. The pound was the principal unit of currency in Zambia until January 1968, when it was replaced by the kwacha (q.v.).

ZAMBIAN VOTER'S OBSERVATION TEAM (Z-VOTE). The Z-vote was a joint elections monitoring enterprise of the Carter Center in Atlanta, Georgia, and the National Democratic Institute for International Affairs in Washington, D.C., to observe Zambia's multiparty elections of October 31 and November 1, 1991, both of which were subsequently certified as largely free and fair.

ZAMBIANIZATION. A primary goal set down by President Kaunda just after independence, Zambianization was the policy by which European, Asian, and African expatriates were replaced by Zambian citizens in employment of all kinds—industry, business, civil service, defense, the judiciary, and the professions. Zambian citizens of European and Asian origin were not excluded, but the policy clearly emphasized the placement of African citizens in middle- and upper-level positions. At the time of independence, qualified African citizens were often in short supply, and a number of stop-gap measures and training programs were instituted toward the goal of full Zambianization (*see* MULUNGUSHI DECLARATION). In November 1971, a Zambianisation Commission was set up to speed up the hiring and promotion process and to check on the need for expatriates. In November 1994 the secretary of the Federation of Employers suggested that the commission had outlived its usefulness and should be dissolved.

ZAMENGLISH. The Zambian variety of the delightful demotic English spoken throughout Southern Central Africa, Zamenglish incorporates elements of Town Bemba (q.v.) and Town Nyanja. It adds or omits prepositions in unexpected places, alters verbs, and ends interrogative sentences with the phrase "isn't it?" The word "too" invariably means "very" (rather than "also"), so the sentence "That one is too movious" refers to someone who is always on the move.

ZAMROCK. Zamrock was the preeminent pop music style of the 1970s. The Ghanaian Afrorock group Osibisa came to Zambia in 1972 and inspired a younger generation of Zambian musicians to marry the hard rock sounds of Cream, Led Zeppelin, and Jimi Hendrix with traditional Zambian music. Though assisted by President Kaunda's (q.v.) 1976 decree that domestic radio broadcasts should highlight Zambian music, Zambian pop musicians were (and are) hampered by the shortage of foreign exchange, by the consequent shortage and expense of imported instruments and equipment, by archaic recording facilities, and by the increasing expense of recorded music and players. Zamrock musicians include Smokey Haangala, Ricky Ilonga, Keith Mlevhu, Paul Ngozi (deceased), and such groups as the Black Power Band, Blackfoot, and Witch. Zamrock has always been an eclectic musical style; while some Zamrock groups, like the 5 Revolutions Band, drifted into Kalindula (q.v.) music in the eighties, others adapted to the continuous popularity of Congolese- (Zairean-) style rumba or the new sounds of reggae.

ZAWI HILL. This Late Stone Age site is about 27 kilometers (17 miles) north of Chipata (q.v.). Two groups of early Zambian rock art (q.v.) are found there. The more faded and probably older group is naturalistic and depicts an eland and a large bird, perhaps an ostrich, both in red pigment. The other painting, a short distance away on the large vertical rock face near the top of the hill, is schematic art.

ZERO OPTION EMERGENCY. In February 1993 the *Times of Zambia* (q.v.) announced it had acquired a copy of a document called "Zero Option" being circulated by a faction of the Central Committee of UNIP (q.v.). It reportedly included plans to destabilize Zambia (and President Chiluba's, q.v., government) through riots, strikes, and armed insurrection, all of it backed by secret funding from Iran, Iraq, Syria, and the Palestine Liberation Organization (an improbable terrorist alliance). That March, the minister of home affairs announced the discovery of an AK-47 arms cache at farms in Mansa (q.v.) District. Kebby Musokotwane (q.v.), then United National Independence Party (q.v.) president, said the plan had never been considered by the Central Committee and was not party policy; he implied he knew its author's identity and that it was part of a plot to remove him from UNIP's leadership. At least 15 UNIP members were detained—including senior army officers, former cabinet ministers, and the former heads of intelligence and broadcasting—and Parliament (q.v.) approved a state declaration of emergency. The six detainees who were released in April claimed that the "Zero Option" document had been circulated at a Central Committee meeting the previous February. A senior government official was then allegedly kidnapped and put under a death sentence to obtain the release of the other detainees. All detainees were released on May 20, the kidnapped official was released on May 22, and a retired army colonel and two others were arrested in connection with the alleged kidnapping on May 24. The state of emergency, widely criticized as an alarming drift away from Zambia's democratic liberalization, was lifted by President Chiluba on May 25. Not long afterward, a significant number of Movement for Multiparty Democracy (q.v.) members, many of them from Eastern and Southern Provinces (qq.v.), left the MMD to form the new National Party (q.v.).

ZIMBA, NEWSTEAD LEWIS. Lewis was an officer in the Zambia Congress of Trade Unions (q.v.) from 1972 until about 1990. A teacher by profession, he was made a headmaster in Ndola (q.v.) in 1967. In 1971 he became full-time president of the National Union of Teachers, an affiliate of the ZCTU. He was an outspoken political activist and among the 17 trade union officers who were expelled from the United National Independence Congress (q.v.) in January 1981 and, as the ZCTU's general-secretary, was one of the four union leaders detained from June until November 1981 for fomenting political unrest leading to the overthrow of the government. He eventually joined the ad hoc Movement for Multiparty Democracy (q.v), won a parliamentary seat in the 1991 elections, and joined President Frederick Chiluba's (q.v.) cabinet. During the "Zero Option" (q.v.) emergency of 1993, Zimba was minister of home affairs.

ZOMBE. A strong Lungu (q.v.) leader of the late 19th century, Zombe was a grandson of Tafuna I but not himself holder of the Tafuna (q.v.) chieftainship. His stockaded village was along the Lucheche River, southeast of the southern end of Lake Tanganyika, and northeast of Isoko (qq.v.). Both David Livingstone and Joseph Thomson (qq.v.) visited his village. Zombe was involved in several clashes with the Bemba (q.v.) and was at first incredibly successful. In 1872 he withstood a three-month siege by Chitapankwa (q.v.) and, with other Lungu reinforcements, routed the Bemba leader and his Swahili (q.v.) allies. Many of the Bemba guns were left behind as they fled. By 1880 Zombe was so powerful that he evicted Tafuna IV Kakunga from Isoko. Kakunga went to the Bemba, especially Chitapankwa, for aid. The latter recruited forces from Bemba chiefs Makasa and Nkula and possibly from the Mambwe chief Kela (qq.v.). Early in the 1880s this huge force moved on Zombe's large village and crushed Zombe, killing him and destroying his village. In 1893 the administrative center of Abercorn (q.v.) was founded near the site.

ZUKAS, SIMON BER. Zukas was a Lithuanian immigrant who later became a civil engineer. He was a political activist and close friend of early African trade unionists and nationalists. The government deported him in 1952. He and his parents came from Lithuania to the Copperbelt (q.v.) in the 1930s, and Zukas became a sergeant in the King's African Rifles. He began to question colonialism when he had to put down an African riot in Buganda and later questioned the morality of the colour bar (q.v.) while a student at the University of Cape Town. In the late 1940s his "radical" and even "communist" ideas made him active in groups such as the Anti-Federation Action Committee in Ndola (q.v.), where he published the *Freedom Newsletter* with coeditors Reuben Kamanga, Justin Chimba, and Mungoni Liso (qq.v.). In 1951 they all joined the African National Congress (q.v.). In 1952, he was deported to England for his "communist" activities. Nevertheless, he continued to keep in touch with the nationalists both through correspondence and personally, as when Harry Nkumbula (q.v.) traveled to London. After self-government under Kenneth Kaunda (q.v.) was granted in 1964, Zukas was given a hero's welcome back to Zambia by his earlier political companions. Following the Movement for Multiparty Democracy's (q.v.) victories in the 1991 elections, Zukas assumed a series of cabinet posts in President Frederick Chiluba's (q.v.) administration. He began in the office of the president, then replaced Dr. Guy Scott (q.v.) as minister of agriculture in April 1993, and became minister of works in June 1995.

ZULU, ALEXANDER GREY. Zulu was a prominent Zambian nationalist in the 1950s and 1960s and held a great many governmental and political posts. Born in 1924 in Chipata (q.v.), he was educated at the noted Munali Secondary School (q.v.) in Northern Rhodesia (q.v.). In the early 1950s he became interested in the cooperative movement and in 1953 became an accountant of the Kabwe Cooperative Marketing Union. By 1962 he had become its first African manager. Meanwhile, he had become active in the Zambia African National Congress (q.v.) with Kaunda and Kapwepwe (qq.v.), joining its first executive committee in November 1958. In March 1959 they were all jailed. By 1962 he was involved full-time in politics and was active in the United National Independence Party (q.v.). In the Legislative Council (q.v.) election that year he won his Copperbelt (q.v.) seat by an overwhelming 12,000 votes. At that time Grey Zulu was one of UNIP's five national trustees. Joining the new government first as parliamentary secretary for local government and social welfare, a few weeks later (in January 1963) he moved to the ministry of native affairs. With the coming of self-government in 1964, however, he was named minister of commerce and industry, of transport and works (September 1964), of mines and cooperatives (January 1965), of lands and mines (January 1967), of home affairs (September 1967), and of defense (January 1970), a crucial post considering the guerrilla action in neighboring Rhodesia. In 1973 he left that post to become secretary-general of UNIP. He was replaced in that position in June 1978, when he was made chairman of UNIP's defense and security committee. Zulu was Kenneth Kaunda's faithful right-hand man, and it was generally assumed that Zulu would be the one to succeed him in any emergency.

In August 1980, Zulu became embroiled in a National Assembly debate about a constitutional amendment to create the post of secretary of state for defense and security specifically for him. The amendment encountered opposition, but it passed by a significant majority. Zulu became UNIP's secretary-general in April 1985. However, he did not stand for reelection to the Central Committee (q.v.) at the party's August 1991 Congress, immediately preceding the multiparty elections of October 1991.

ZUMBO. A Portuguese outpost on the northeastern confluence of the Zambezi and Luangwa Rivers (qq.v.), Zumbo is located across the Luangwa from Feira (q.v.). Portuguese traders operated from there as early at 1700. By 1752 they bought ivory and copper (qq.v.) from Zambian peoples. By the beginning of the 19th century, Lamba, Ambo, and even Toka (qq.v.) traders were traveling in the area. Items received in return included beads and Goan and Indian cloth. In 1804, Zumbo was destroyed by a neighboring chief, and the Portuguese abandoned it in 1836. In 1862 they reopened it for trade, mainly in ivory, but slaves also passed through en route to Brazil. Since the Portuguese government did not have much control at Zumbo, traders were free to form their own armies (see CHIKUNDA). The Bemba, Bisa, and Nsenga (qq.v.) all exchanged ivory for muzzle-loading guns. In 1888 the Nsenga chief Mburuma laid siege to Zumbo, but the Portuguese strengthened their armed forces there and appointed a governor in 1890. During these two centuries, the Zambezi played a major role in the Portuguese gold trade, primarily from the people south of the Zambezi River.

ZWANGENDABA. Zwangendaba was an Nguni Clan military leader who fled the power of his overlord, Shaka Zulu, after a battle on the Mhlatuze River in Natal in 1818. Fleeing north with his people through Swaziland and Mozambique (q.v.), he collected a large following during his 30-year exodus. These Ngoni (q.v.), as they came to be called, crossed the Zambezi River (q.v.) in 1835. They spent six years among the Senga (q.v.), adding recruits, and then bypassed Bemba (q.v.) country, ending up near the Fipa people in the Tanzanian section of southern Lake Tanganyika (q.v.). The Ngoni were nomadic herdsmen. They were also excellent warriors and terrorized farmers en route. Zwangendaba died at Ufipa in 1848, and the Ngoni moved south again into Zambia and Malawi (q.v.) under such leaders as Mpezeni, Mperembe (qq.v.), and Mbelwa.

Bibliography

1. General
   a. General and Information Guides
   b. Demographic Statistics
   c. Travel and Description
   d. Bibliographies

2. Cultural
   a. Fine Arts
   b. Linguistics
   c. Literature

3. Economic
   a. Agriculture
   b. Commerce and Business
   c. Development
   d. Industry
      i. Mining
      ii. Other
   e. Transportation and Communications

4. Historic
   a. Archaeology
   b. Precolonial
   c. Company and Colonial Rule
   d. Postindependence

5. Political
   a. Constitution, Law, and Government
      i. Law and Justice
      ii. Administration
      iii. Other
   b. Humanism
   c. Politics and Political Parties
   d. Race Relations
   e. Foreign Affairs

6. Scientific
   a. Geography
   b. Geology
   c. Medicine
   d. Natural Science and Zoology

7. Social
  a. Anthropology and Sociology
     i. General
     ii. Rural
     iii. Urban
  b. Education
  c. Religion and Missions

1. General

1.a. General. General and Information Guides

Brelsford, W. V., ed. *Handbook to the Federation of Rhodesia and Nyasaland*. London: Cassell, 1960.

Brown, A. Samler, and G. Gordon Brown. *The South and East African Year Book and Guide*. London: Sampson Low, Marston, 1925.

Burdette, Marcia M. *Zambia: Between Two Worlds*. Boulder: Westview, 1988.

Clements, Frank. *Getting to Know Southern Rhodesia, Zambia, and Malawi*. New York: Coward-McCann, 1964.

Davies, B. H., ed. *Zambia in Maps*. London: University of London Press, 1971.

Dickie, John, and Alan Rake. *Who's Who in Africa: The Political Military and Social Leaders of Africa*. London: African Development, 1973.

Dresang, Eliza T. *The Land and People of Zambia*. Philadelphia: Lippincott, 1975.

Faber, Mike. *Zambia—The Moulding of a Nation*. London: African Bureau, 1968.

Fagan, B. M., ed. *The Victoria Falls: A Handbook to the Victoria Falls, the Batoka Gorge, and Part of the Upper Zambezi River*. 2nd ed. Lusaka: Northern Rhodesia Commission for the Preservation of Natural and Historical Monuments and Relics, 1964.

Gordon-Brown, A., ed. *The Year Book and Guide to Southern Africa, 1950*. London: Sampson Low, Marston, 1950.

Gregor, Gordon. "Tourism in Zambia." *Horizon* 9 (1967).

Hailey, Lord W. *An African Survey: A Study of Problems Arising in Africa South of the Sahara*. Rev. ed. London: Oxford University Press, 1956.

Hall, H. *Zambia*. London: Pall Mall, 1965.

Handbook to the Federation of Rhodesia and Nyasaland. Salisbury: Government Printer, 1960.

Hanna, A. J. *The Story of the Rhodesias and Nyasaland*. London: Faber and Faber, 1960.

Illustrated Handbook of North-Eastern Rhodesia. Fort Jameson: Administration Press, 1906.

James, Selwyn. *South of the Congo.* New York: Random House, 1943.

Mlenga, Kelvin G. *Who Is Who in Zambia.* Lusaka: Zambia Information Service, 1968.

————. *Who's Who in Zambia, 1979.* Ndola: Roan Consolidated Mines, 1979.

Norton, John, ed. *Guide to Southern Africa.* London: Robert Hale, 1969.

The Occasional Papers of the Rhodes-Livingstone Museum. Nos. 1–16. Atlantic Highlands, N.J.: Humanities, 1975.

Ogrizek, Dore, ed. *South and Central Africa.* New York: McGraw-Hill, 1954.

Pirie, George. "North-Eastern Rhodesia: Its People and Products." *Journal of the African Society* 5, 6 (1905, 1906).

Pitch, Anthony. *Inside Zambia—and Out.* Cape Town: Timmins, 1967.

Rake, Alan. *Who's Who in Africa: Leaders for the 1990s.* Metuchen, N.J.: Scarecrow Press, 1992.

Segal, Aaron. "Zambia." In *The Traveler's Africa.* Ed. Philip M. Allen and Aaron Segal. New York: Hopkinson and Blake, 1973.

Sumaili, Fanuel K. M. *Zambia in the 1990s.* Lusaka: PWPA of Zambia, 1991.

Tanser, G. H. *British Central African Territories: Southern Rhodesia, Northern Rhodesia, and Nyasaland.* Cape Town: Juta, 1952.

Universities' Mission to Central Africa. *Beyond the Waters that Thunder: A Book about Northern Rhodesia.* Westminster: UMCA Publications Board, 1932.

Where to Stay in Zambia. Lusaka: Zambia National Tourist Bureau, 1967.

Wilson, Tim, ed. *A Brief Guide to Northern Rhodesia.* Lusaka: Government Printer, 1960.

Wood, Anthony St. John. *Northern Rhodesia: The Human Background.* London: Pall Mall, 1961.

Woods, Jonah. *A Guide Book to the Victoria Falls.* Bulawayo: Manning, 1960.

Zambia Information Services. *Zambia Today: A Handbook to the Republic of Zambia.* Lusaka: Government Printer, 1964.

1.b. General. Demographic Statistics

Bettison, D. G. *Numerical Data on African Dwellers in Lusaka Northern Rhodesia.* Livingstone: Rhodes-Livingstone Institute, 1960.

Chilivumbo, A. *Migration and Uneven Rural Development in Africa: The Case of Zambia.* Lanham, Md.: University Press of America, 1985.

Hedlund, Hans, and Mats Lundahl. *Migration and Change in Rural Zambia.* Uppsala: Scandinavian Institute of African Studies, 1983.

Heisler, Helmuth. *Urbanization and the Government of Migration: The Inter-Relation of Urban and Rural Life in Zambia.* New York: St. Martin's, 1984.

Jackman, Mary Elizabeth. *Recent Population Movements in Zambia*. Lusaka: University of Zambia, Institute for African Studies, 1973.

Kay, George. *Maps of the Distribution and Density of Africa: Population in Zambia*. Lusaka: University of Zambia, Institute for Social Research, 1967.

————. *A Social Geography of Zambia: A Survey of Population Patterns in a Developing Country*. London: University of London Press, 1967.

Kuczynski, R. B. *Demographic Survey of the British Colonial Empire. Part 2*. London: Oxford University Press, 1949.

Msimuko, A. K., and Elizabeth Khasiani. "Population Policy and Development in Zambia." *African Social Research* 31 (1981).

Ohadike, Patrick O. *Demographic Perspectives in Zambia: Rural-Urban Growth and Social Change*. Zambian Paper no. 15. Lusaka: University of Zambia, Institute for African Studies, 1981.

Ohadike, Patrick O., and Habtemariam Tesfaghiorghis. *The Population of Zambia*. New York: CIRCRED, UN, 1975.

Zambia. *1980 Population and Housing Census of Zambia*. 5 vols. Lusaka: Central Statistical Office, 1985–88. (1, *Administrative Report*; 2, *Demographic and Socio-Economic Characteristics*; 3, *Major Findings and Conclusions*; 4, *Fertility and Mortality Levels and Trends*; 5, *Demographic Projections*.)

Zambia. *Women and Men in Zambia: Facts and Figures*. Lusaka: Central Statistical Office, 1991.

1.c. General. Travel and Description

Bent, Newell, Jr. *Jungle Giants*. Norwood, Mass.: Plimpton, 1936.

Berghegge, F. "Account of a Journey in Central Africa." *Rhodesiana* 3 (1958).

Bigland, Eileen. *The Lake of the Royal Crocodiles*. New York: Macmillan, 1939.

————. *Pattern in Black and White*. London: Drummond, 1940.

Butt, G. E. *My Travels in North-West Rhodesia*. London: Dalton, 1909.

Cambell, J. S. "I Knew Lewanika." *Northern Rhodesia Journal* 1 (1950).

Chapman, James. *Travels in the Interior of South Africa, 1849–1863*. 2 vols. London: Bell & Daldy, 1868.

Colville, Olivia. *One Thousand Miles in a Manchilla: Travel and Sport in Nyasaland, Angoniland, and Rhodesia*. London: Scott, 1911.

Cullen, Lucy Pope. *Beyond the Smoke that Thunders*. New York: Oxford University Press, 1940.

Curzon, Marquess. *Tales of Travel*. London: Hodder and Stoughton, 1923.

Dann, H. C. *Romance of the Posts of Rhodesia and Nyasaland*. London: Godden, 1940.

Davidson, H. Frances. *South and South Central Africa*. Elgin: Brethren, 1915.

Debenham, Frank. *The Way to Ilala*. London: Longmans, Green, 1955.

Decle, Lionel. *Three Years in Savage Africa*. New York: M. F. Mansfield, 1898.

Duffy, Kevin. *Black Elephant Hunter*. London: Davies, 1960.

Gibbons, Alfred St. Hill. *Africa from South to North through Marotseland*. London: Lane, 1904.

———. *Exploration and Hunting in Central Africa, 1895–1896*. London: Methuen, 1898.

———. "Journey in Marotse and Mashikolumbwe Countries." *Geographical Journal* 9 (1897).

Giraud, Victor. *Les Lacs de l'Afrique Equatoriale*. Paris, 1890.

Glave, E. J. "Glave in the Heart of Africa." *Century Magazine*, no. 30 (1896).

Gouldsbury, C. *An African Year*. London: Arnold, 1912.

Gouldsbury, C., and H. Sheane. *The Great Plateau of Northern Rhodesia: Being Some Impressions of the Tanganyika Plateau*. London: Arnold, 1911.

Goy, Madame M. K. *Alone in Africa, or, Seven Years on the Zambezi*. London: Nisbet, 1901.

Harding, Colonel C. *In Remotest Barotseland*. London: Hurst and Blackett, 1905.

Hazard, C. J. "Recollections of North-Western Rhodesia in the Early 1900's." *Northern Rhodesia Journal* 3 (1959).

Hobson, Dick. *Tales of Zambia*. London: Zambia Society Trust, 1996.

Holub, Emil. "Journey through Central East Africa." *Proceedings of the Royal Geographical Society* 2 (1880).

———. *Seven Years in South Africa*. 2 vols. Boston: Houghton, Mifflin, 1881.

———. *Von der Capstadt ins Land der Maschukulmbe. Reisen im Sudlichen Afrika in der Jahren, 1883–1887*. 2 vols. Vienna, 1890.

Hubbard, Mary G. *African Gamble*. New York: Putnam, 1937.

Hubbard, Wynant Davis. *Ibama*. Greenwich, Conn.: New York Graphic Society, 1962.

King, Ralph W., and John P. DeSmidt. *The Rhodesias and Nyasaland: A Pictorial Tour of Central Africa*. Capetown: Timmins, n.d.

Letcher, Owen. *Big Game Hunting in North-Eastern Rhodesia*. London: John Long, 1911.

Long, Basil. *Sir Drummond Chaplin*. London: Oxford University Press, 1941.

Mackintosh, C. W. *The New Zambezi Trail: A Record of Two Journeys to Northern Western Rhodesia, 1903–1920*. London: Marshall, 1922.

Mansfield, Charlotte. *Via Rhodesia: A Journey through Southern Africa*. London: S. Paul, 1913.

Marcosson, Isaac F. *An African Adventure*, New York: Lane, 1921.

Oswell, W. Edward. *Wm. Cotton Oswell: Hunter and Explorer.* 2 vols. London: Heinemann, 1900.

Payne, Faith Naegeli. "Zambia's Kasaba Bay." *Africa Report* 2 (1966).

Pretorius, P. J. *Jungle Man: The Autobiography of Major P. J. Pretorius.* New York: Dutton, 1948.

Read, Grantly Dick. *No Time for Fear.* New York: Harper, 1955.

Schulz, A., and A. Hammar. *The New Africa, Journey up the Chobe, etc.* London, 1897.

Scott, E. D. *Some Letters from South Africa, 1894–1932.* London: Sherratt and Hughes, 1903.

Selous, F. C. *A Hunter's Wanderings in Africa.* London, 1881.

––––––. *Travel and Adventure in South-East Africa.* London, 1893.

Sharpe, Alfred. "Travels in the Northern Province and Katanga." *Northern Rhodesia Journal* 3 (1957).

Statham, J. C. B. *With My Wife across Africa by Canoe and Caravan.* London: Simpkin, Marshall, Hamilton, Kent, 1924.

Tabler, W. C. *The Far Interior.* Cape Town: Balkema, 1956.

Thwaits, B. C. "Trekking from Kalomo to Mongu in 1906." *Northern Rhodesia Journal* 3 (1957).

"Undiscovered Zambia." *Africa Report* 17 (1972).

Wadia, Ardaser Sorabjee N. *The Romance of Rhodesia: Being Impressions of a Sight-Seeing Tour to Southern and Northern Rhodesia.* London: Dent, 1947.

Waugh, Evelyn. *Tourist in Africa.* Boston: Little, Brown, 1960.

1.d. General. Bibliographies

Bardouille, Raj. *Research on Zambian Women in Retrospect and Prospect: An Annotated Bibliography.* Lusaka: Swedish International Development Agency, 1992.

Bliss, Anne M., and J. A. Rigg. *Zambia.* World Bibliographical Series vol. 51. Oxford: Clio, 1984.

Chitambo, A. M. *Women in Zambia: A Bibliographical Guide and Directory.* Lusaka: Women and Law in Southern Africa Research Project, 1991.

Derricourt, B. M. *Supplementary Bibliography of the Archaeology of Zambia, 1967–1973.* Lusaka: Government Printer, 1975.

Jones, Ruth. *Bibliography for South-East Central Africa and Madagascar.* London: International African Institute, 1961.

Leigh, Carol. "Zambia: Politics and Economics since Independence." *Southern African Update* (Johannesburg)(1991).

Musiker, Naomi. *Kaunda's Zambia, 1964–1991: A Select and Annotated Bibliography.* Bibliographical Series no. 26. Johannesburg: South African Institute of International Affairs, 1993.

Mwanza, Ilsa. *Bibliography of Zambian Theses: List of M.A. and Ph.D. Theses on Zambia*. Lusaka: University of Zambia, Institute for African Studies, 1987.

Phillipson, D. W. *An Annotated Bibliography of the Archaeology of Zambia*. Lusaka: Government Printer. 1968.

Rau, William. *A Bibliography of Pre-Independence Zambia: The Social Sciences*. Boston: Hall, 1978.

Rhodesia and Nyasaland. *A Select Bibliography of Recent Publications Concerning the Federation of Rhodesia and Nyasaland*. Salisbury: Federal Information Department, 1960.

Rooke, A. P., and W. C. Msiska. *Bibliography of Oral Literature Projects in Zambia*. Library Occasional Publication no. 1. Lusaka: University of Zambia, 1981.

Rotberg, Robert I. "Then and Now in Central Africa." *Africa Report* 13 (1968).

Williams, Geoffrey J. *Independent Zambia: A Bibliography of the Social Sciences*. Boston: Hall, 1984.

2. Cultural

2.a. Cultural. Fine Arts

Bantje, H. "Kaonde Song and Ritual." *Annales, Sciences Humaines* 95 (Musée Royale de l'Afrique Centrale, Tervuren) (1978).

Bender, Wolfgang. *Sweet Mother: Modern African Music*. Trans. Wolfgang Freis. Chicago: University of Chicago Press, 1991.

Brelsford, W. V. "Some Reflections on Bemba Geometric Decorative Art." *Bantu Studies* 12 (1937).

———. "Notes on Some Northern Rhodesian Bowstands." *Man*, no. 40 (1940).

———. *African Dances*. Lusaka: Government Printer, 1948.

———. *African Dances of Northern Rhodesia*. Livingstone: Rhodes-Livingstone Museum, 1948.

Brown, Ernest D. "Drums of Life: Royal Music and Social Life in Western Zambia." Ph.D. diss., University of Washington, 1984.

Chaplin, J. H. "Some Aspects of Folk Art in Northern Rhodesia." *Man*, 63 (1963).

Clark, J. D., and B. M. Fagan. "Charcoals, Sands, and Channel-decorated Pottery from Northern Rhodesia." *American Anthropologist* 67 (1966).

Cooper, C. "Village Crafts in Barotseland." *Rhodes-Livingstone Journal* 11 (1951).

Epskamp, Kees P. "Historical Outline of the Development of Zambian National Theatre." *Canadian Journal of African Studies* 21 (1987).

Goodall, Elizabeth, et al. *Prehistoric Rock Art of the Federation of Rhodesia and Nyasaland.* Salisbury: National Publications Trust, Rhodesia and Nyasaland, 1959.

Graham, Ronnie. *The World of African Music: Stern's Guide to Contemporary African Music.* Vol. 2. Chicago: Pluto, 1992.

Ijzermans, Jan J. "Music and Theory of the Possession Cult Leaders in Chibale, Serenje District, Zambia." *Ethnomusicology* 39 (1995).

Jones, A. M. *African Music in Northern Rhodesia and Some Other Places.* Lusaka: Government Printer, 1949.

Jones, A. M., and L. Kombe. *The Icila Dance, Old Style.* Roodepoort: Longmans, Green, 1952.

Malamusi, Moya Aliya. "The Zambian Popular Music Scene." *Jazzforschung* 16 (Graz, Austria)(1984).

Mensah, Atta Annan. *Music and Dance in Zambia.* Lusaka: Zambia Information Services, 1971.

Mwesa, Mapoma I. "The Determinants of Style in the Music of Ing'omba." Ph.D. diss., University of California-Los Angeles, 1980.

Summers, H., ed. *Prehistoric Rock Art of the Federation of Rhodesia and Nyasaland.* London: Chatto and Windus, 1959.

Turner, Edith. "Zambia's Kankanga Dances: The Changing Life of Ritual." *Performing Arts Journal* 10 (1987).

Veerbeek, Leon. "L'Historie dans les chants et les danses populaires: la zone culturelle Bemba du Haut-Shaba (Zaire)." *Enquêtes et Documents d'Histoire Africaine* 10 (1992).

———. "Initiation et mariage dans la chanson populaire des Bemba du Zaire." *Annales, Sciences Humaines* 139 (Musée Royale de l'Afrique Centrale Tervuren) (1993).

2.b. Cultural. Linguistics

Barnes, B. H., and C. M. Doke. "The Pronunciation of the Bemba Language." *Bantu Studies* 3 (1927).

Epstein, A. L. "Linguistic Innovation and Culture on the Copperbelt, Northern Rhodesia." *Southwestern Journal of Anthropology* 15 (1959).

Fortune, G. "A Note on the Languages of Barotseland." Paper prepared for the Conference on the History of the Central African Peoples. Lusaka, 1963.

Jacottet, E. *Etudes sur les langues du Haut-Zambeze: textes originaux.* Paris, 1896.

Kashoki, Mubanga E. *A Phonemic Analysis of Bemba.* Manchester: Manchester University Press for University of Zambia, Institute for Social Research, 1968.

———. *The Factor of Language in Zambia.* Lusaka: Kenneth Kaunda Foundation, 1990.

Musonda, M., and Mubanga E. Kashoki. "Lexical Adaptability in Bemba and Lunda: Some Implications for Present Day Communication." *African Social Research* 34 (1982).

Mytton, Graham. "Multilingualism in Zambia." Paper no. 7. Zambia Broadcasting Services Research Project, 1973, Lusaka.

Ohannessian, Sirarpi, and Mubanga E. Kashoki. *Language in Zambia.* London: International African Institute, 1977.

Sambeck, J. van. *A Bemba Grammar.* London: Longmans, Green, 1955.

Serpell, Robert. "Linguistic Flexibility in Urban Zambian School Children." *Studies in Child Language and Multilingualism: Annals of the New York Academy of Sciences* 345 (1980).

Sims, G. W. *An Elementary Grammar of Cibemba.* Basutoland: Morija Printing Works, 1959.

2.c. Cultural. Literature

Bantu, Joseph. *A Straw in the Eye.* Lusaka: Kenneth Kaunda Foundation, 1989.

Cancel, Robert. "Inshimi Structure and Themes: The Tabwa Oral Narrative Tradition." Ph.D. diss., University of Wisconsin-Madison, 1981.

———. "Broadcasting Oral Traditions: The 'Logic' of Narrative Variants, the Problem of 'Message.' " *African Studies Review* 29 (1986).

———. *Allegorical Speculation in an Oral Society: The Tabwa Narrative Tradition.* Berkeley: University of California Press, 1988.

Chalinga, G. B. M. *Maloko miwa Makande (Old Luyana Proverbs).* Lusaka: Northern Rhodesia Publications Bureau, 1960.

Chileshe, John. "Literacy, Literature, and Ideological Formation: The Zambian Case." Ph.D. diss., University of Sussex, 1983.

———. "Literature in English from Zambia:A Bibliography of Published Works to 1986." *Research in African Literatures* 19 (1988).

Chongo, Julius. *Fumbi Khoboo!* Lusaka: NECZAM, 1972.

Dauphin-Tinturier, A.-M. "Communication et tradition dans l'univers Bemba, Zambie." *Genve-Afrique* 27 (1989).

Herdeck, Donald E. *African Authors: A Companion to Black African Writing.* Vol. 1, 1300–1973. Washington, D.C.: Black Orpheus, 1973.

Higgs, Peter Lawrence. "Culture and Value Changes in Zambian School Literature." Ph.D. diss., University of California-Los Angeles, 1979.

Jahn, Janheiz, Ulla Schild, and Almut Nordmann. *Who's Who in African Literature.* Tubingen: Horst Erdmann, 1972.

Kerr, David, and Garikayi Soniwa. *Matteo Sakala.* Ndola: Multimedia, 1978.

Liwaniso, Mufalo, ed. *Voices of Zambia.* Lusaka: NECZAM, 1971.

Lutato, Kalunga Stanley. "The Influence of Oral Narrative Traditions on the Novels of Stephen A. Mpashi." Ph.D. diss., University of Wisconsin-Madison, 1980.

M'Bay, Kazadi Ntole. *Chants, marriage et société au Bushi: textes litteraires et contexte*. Lubumbashi: Celta, 1978.

Masiye, Andreya. *Before Dawn*. Lusaka: National Education Company of Zambia, 1971.

Maxwell, Kevin B. *Bemba Myth and Ritual: The Impact of Literacy on an Oral Culture*. New York: P. Lang, ca. 1983.

Moyo, P. C., T. W. C. Sumaili, and J. A. Moody, eds. *Oral Traditions in Southern Africa*. 4 vols. Lusaka: University of Zambia, Institute for African Studies, 1986.

Mulaisho, Dominic. *Tongue of the Dumb*. London: Heinemann, 1971.

Mulaisho, Killian. *Tragedy of Pride*. Ndola: Multimedia, 1988.

Phiri, Gideon. *Victims of Fate*. Lusaka: NECZAM, 1972.

Reed, John. "Zambian Fiction." In *The Writing of East and Central Africa*, ed. G. D. Killian. London: Heinemann, 1984.

Shaw, Mabel. *A Treasure of Darkness: An Idyll of African Child Life*. London: Longmans, Green, 1936.

Sibale, Grieve. *Between Two Worlds*. Lusaka: NECZAM, 1979.

Torrend, J. *Specimens of Bantu Folklore from Northern Rhodesia*. London: Kegan Paul, Trench, Trubner, 1921.

Wendland, Ernst Richard. "Stylistic Form and Communicative Function in the Nyanja Radio Narratives of Julius Chongo." Ph.D. diss., University of Wisconsin-Madison, 1979.

3. Economic

3.a. Economic. Agriculture

Allan, William. *The African Husbandman*. Edinburgh: Oliver and Boyd, 1965.

Carr, Marilyn, ed. *Women and Food Security: The Experience of the SADCC Countries*. London: IT, 1991.

Dixon-Fyle, Mac. "Agricultural Improvement and Political Protest on the Tonga Plateau, Northern Rhodesia." *Journal of African History* 18 (1977).

Dodge, Doris J. *Agricultural Policy and Performance in Zambia*. Berkeley: University of California, Institute of International Studies, 1977.

Donkin, J. "Marketing Organizations of Zambia." *Monthly Agricultural Bulletin* (Lusaka)(August 1967).

Eraser, Robert H. "Land Settlement in the Eastern Province of Northern Rhodesia." *Rhodes-Livingstone Journal* 3 (1945).

Fenichel, Allen, and Bruce Smith. "A Successful Failure: Integrated Rural Development in Zambia." *World Development* 20 (1992).

Francis, P. "Ox Draught Power and Agricultural Transformation in Northern Zambia." *Agricultural Systems* 27 (1988).

Geisler, Gisela. "Who Is Losing Out? Structural Adjustment, Gender, and the Agricultural Sector in Zambia." *Journal of Modern African Studies* 30 (1992).

Good, Kenneth. "Systemic Agricultural Mismanagement: The 1985 'Bumper' Harvest in Zambia." *Journal of Modern African Studies* 24 (1986).

Hellen, J. A. *Rural Economic Development in Zambia, 1890–1964*. Munich: Weltforum-Verlag, 1968.

Hobson, R. H. "Rubber: A Footnote to Northern Rhodesian History." Occasional Paper no. 13. Rhodes-Livingstone Museum, 1960, Livingstone.

Honeybone, David, and Alan Marter, eds. *Poverty and Wealth in Rural Zambia*. Lusaka: University of Zambia, Rural Development Studies Bureau, 1979.

Kakeya, M. "Agricultural Change and Its Mechanism in the Bemba Villages of Northeastern Zambia." *African Studies Monograph* (supp.) no. 6 (Kyoto University, Research Committee for African Area Studies) (1987).

Kakeya, M., and Y. Sugiyama. "Chitemene, Finger Millet, and Bemba Culture: A Socio-Ecological Study of Slash-and-Burn Cultivation in Northeastern Zambia." *African Studies Monograph* (supp.) no. 4 (Kyoto University, Research Committee for African Area Studies) (1984).

Kay, George. "Changing Patterns of Settlement and Land Use in the Eastern Province of Northern Rhodesia." Occasional Papers in Geography no. 2, University of Hull, 1964, Hull.

————. "Agricultural Progress in Zambia's Eastern Province." *Journal of Administration Overseas* 5 (1966).

————. "A Regional Framework for Rural Development in Zambia." *African Affairs* 67 (1968).

Keller, Bonnie, and Dorcas Mbewe. "Impact of Present Agriculture Policies on the Role of Women, Extension, and Household Food Security." In *Strategies for Implementing National Policies in Extension and Food Security for Rural Women*. Rome: UN/FAO, 1988.

————. "Policy and Planning for the Empowerment of Zambia's Women Farmers." *Canadian Journal of Development* 12 (1991).

Kydd, Jonathon. "Coffee after Copper? Structural Adjustment, Liberalisation, and Agriculture in Zambia." *Journal of Modern African Studies* 26 (1988).

Levin, Nora. "Cooperation Brings a Grassroots Revolution." *Africa Report* 17 (1972).

Lombard, C. Stephen. "Agriculture in Zambia since Independence." *East Africa* 8 (Nairobi) (1971).

————. *The Growth of Co-operatives in Zambia, 1914–1971*. Lusaka: University of Zambia, Institute for African Studies, 1971.

———. "Farming Co-operatives in the Development of Zambian Agriculture." *Journal of Modern African Studies* 10 (1972).

Makings, S. M. *Agricultural Change in Northern Rhodesia and Zambia, 1946–1985.* Stanford: Stanford University Press, 1968.

Marter, Alan, and David Honeybone. *The Economic Resources of Rural Households and the Distribution of Agricultural Development.* Lusaka: University of Zambia, Rural Development Studies Bureau, 1976.

Meyer, Robert. "A Cross-Cultural Examination of Organizational Structure and Control: The Zambian Agricultural Sector." *Journal of Asian and African Studies* 27 (1992).

Moore, Henrietta, and Megan Vaughn. *Cutting Down Trees: Gender, Nutrition, and Agricultural Change in Northern Province of Zambia, 1890–1990.* London: Currey, 1994.

Nadeau, Emile George. "Peasant-Based Agricultural Development: Problems and Prospects in Zambia." Ph.D. diss., University of Wisconsin-Madison, 1977.

Ndiaye, Serigne, and Andrew J. Sofranko. "Importance of Labor in Adoption of a Modern Farm Input." *Rural Sociology* 53 (1988).

Peter, David U. *Land Usage in Barotseland.* Communication no. 19. Lusaka: Rhodes-Livingstone Institute, 1960.

Pletcher, James R. "The Political Uses of Agricultural Markets in Zambia." *Journal of Modern African Studies* 24 (1986).

Quick, Stephen A. "Bureaucracy and Rural Socialism in Zambia." *Journal of Modern African Studies* 15 (1977).

———. *Humanism or Technocracy? Zambia's Farming Co-operatives, 1965–1972.* Zambian Paper no. 12. Manchester: Manchester University Press, 1978.

Rakodi, Carole. "Urban Agriculture: Research Questions and Zambian Evidence." *Journal of Modern African Studies* 26 (1988).

Ranger, T. O. *The Agricultural History of Zambia.* Lusaka: NECZAM, 1971.

Safilios-Rothschild, C. *The Implications of the Roles of Women in Agriculture.* New York: Population Council, 1985.

Sano, Hans-Otto. "Agricultural Policy Changes in Zambia during the 1980s." Working Paper no. 88.4. Centre for Development Research, 1988, Copenhagen.

———. "The IMF and Zambia: The Contradictions of Exchange Rate Auctioning and Desubsidization of Agriculture." *African Affairs* 87 (1988).

———. "From Labour Reserve to Maize Reserve: The Maize Boom in the Northern Province in Zambia." Working Paper no. 89.3. Centre for Development Research, 1989, Copenhagen.

———. *Big State, Small Farmers: The Search for an Agricultural Strategy for Crisis-Ridden Zambia.* Copenhagen: Centre for Development Research, 1990.

Schültz, Jurgen. *Land Use in Zambia*. Afrika-Studien no. 95. Munich: Ifo-Institute für Wirtschaftsforschung, 1976.

Scudder, Thayer. *Gathering among African Woodland Savannah Cultivators: The Gwembe Tonga*. Lusaka: University of Zambia, Institute for African Studies, 1971.

Stolen, K. A. "Peasants and Agricultural Change in Northern Zambia." Occasional Paper no. 4. International Development Programme, Agricultural University of Norway, 1983.

Stromgaard, Peter. "Field Studies of Land Use under Chitimene Shifting Cultivation, Zambia." *Geografisk Tidsskrift* 84 (1984).

———. "Prospects of Improved Farming Systems in a Shifting Cultivation Area in Zambia." *Quarterly Journal of International Agriculture* 23 (1984).

———. "A Subsistence Society under Pressure: The Bemba of Northern Zambia." *Africa* 55 (1985).

———. "The Grassland Mound System of the Asia Mambwe of Zambia." *Tools and Tillage* 6 (1988).

———. "Adaptive Strategies in the Breakdown of Shifting Cultivation: The Case of the Mambwe, Lamba, and Lala of Northern Zambia." *Human Ecology* 17 (1989).

———. "Peasant Household Economy in Rural Zambia: The Dilemma of Small-Scale Farmers in Transition." *Fennia* 168 (1990).

Trapnell, C. G. *The Soils, Vegetation, and Agriculture of North-Eastern Rhodesia*. Lusaka: Government Printer, 1943.

———. "Ecological Results of Woodland Burning Experiments in Northern Rhodesia." *Journal of Ecology* 47 (1959).

Trapnell, C. G., and N. Clothier. *The Soils, Vegetation, and Agricultural Systems of North-Western Rhodesia*. 2nd ed. Lusaka: Government Printer, 1967.

Van Horn, Laurel. "The Agricultural History of Barotseland, 1840–1964." In *The Roots of Rural Poverty in Central and Southern Africa*, ed. Robin Palmer and Neil Parsons. Berkeley: University of California Press, 1977.

Wiggins, Steve. "Against the Odds: Managing Agricultural Projects in Africa: Evidence from Sierra, Leone, and Zambia." *International Review of Administrative Sciences* 58 (1992).

Wood, Adrian Paul, and Richard W. A. Vokes, eds. *The Dynamics of Agricultural Policy and Reform in Zambia*. Ames: Iowa State University Press, 1990.

Wood, Adrian Paul. "Food Production and the Changing Structure of Zambian Agriculture." In *Food Systems in Central and Southern Africa*. London: University of London, School of African and Oriental Studies, 1985.

3.b. Economic. Commerce and Business

Banda, Gabriel. *Adjusting to Adjustment in Zambia: Women's and Young People's Responses to a Changing Economy.* Oxfam Research Paper no. 4. Oxford, UK: Oxfam UK and Ireland, 1990.

Barclays Bank D.C.O. *Zambia: An Economic Survey.* Lusaka: Government Printer, 1968.

Bardouille, Raj. "The Sexual Division of Labour in the Urban Informal Sector: Case Studies of Some Townships in Lusaka," *African Social Research* 32 (1981).

Beveridge, Andrew. "Converts to Capitalism: The Emergence of African Entrepreneurs in Lusaka, Zambia." Ph.D. diss., Yale University, 1973.

Beveridge, Andrew A., and Anthony R. Oberschall. *African Businessmen and Development in Zambia.* Princeton: Princeton University Press, 1979.

Chiposa, Sylvester. "Kaunda Penalizes Black Marketeers," *New African* (May 1988) (London).

Chitala, D. "SEP Joins Sido in Uphill Battle." *African Business* 67 (London) (1984).

Goodman, S. H. "Investment Policy in Zambia." In *After Mulungushi: The Economics of Zambian Humanism,* ed. B. de G. Fortman. Nairobi: East African, 1969.

Hansen, Karen Tranberg. "The Black Market and Women Traders in Lusaka, Zambia." In *Women and the State in Africa,* ed. Jane Parpart and Kathleen Staudt. Boulder: Lynne Rienner, 1989.

Harvey, Charles. "The Control of Credit in Zambia." *Journal of Modern African Studies* 11 (1973).

Hentz, James J. "Multinational Corporations at the Interstices of Domestic and International Politics: The Case of the H. J. Heinz Company in Zambia and Zimbabwe." *Journal of Commonwealth and Comparative Politics* 32 (1994).

Hobson, Dick. *Showtime: A History of the Agricultural and Commercial Society of Zambia, 1914–1976.* Lusaka: Agricultural and Commercial Society of Zambia, 1979.

Husbands, Winston, and Shelia Thompson. "The Host Society and the Consequences of Tourism in Livingstone, Zambia." *International Journal of Urban and Regional Research* 14 (1990).

Milimo, John T., and Yacob Fisseha. "Rural Small-Scale Enterprises in Zambia: Results of a 1985 Country-Wide Survey." Michigan State University Working Paper no. 28. Rural Development Studies Bureau and Michigan State University, 1986, Lusaka.

Musambachime, M. Chambikalenshi. "The Role of Kasenga (Eastern Shaba) in the Development of Mweru-Luapula Fishery." *African Studies Review* 38 (1995).

"Recycling Sacks to Save Zambia Foreign Exchange." *Market South East* 3 (London) (1989).

Resources and Opportunities in the Rhodesias and Nyasaland: A Guide to Commerce and Industry in the Territories. Nairobi: Guides and Handbooks of Africa Publishing Co., 1963.

Siyolwe, Yolisha W. "Makwebo Women: A Study of the Socio-Economic Activities of a Select Group of Women Traders in Lusaka, Zambia, 1980–1990." Masters thesis, University of Oxford, 1994.

Turner, K. "New Zambian Economic Program Involves Takeover of Some Firms, Limit on Repatriation of Profits." *International Commerce,* April 29, 1968.

————. *Small-Scale Enterprises in Zambia and Schemes for Their Development: Some Specific Strategies.* Lusaka: University of Zambia, Institute for African Studies, 1985.

Woodruff, H. W. *The Federation of Rhodesia and Nyasaland (Southern Rhodesia, Northern Rhodesia, and Nyasaland): Economic and Commercial Conditions.* London: HMSO, 1955.

"Zambian Industrial and Commercial Association." *Southern African Connection* 2 (Sandton, Transvaal) (1987).

3.c. Economic. Development

Adam, Christopher. "Fiscal Adjustment, Financial Liberalization, and the Dynamics of Inflation: Some Evidence from Zambia." *World Development* 23 (1995).

Applegate, Michael J. "A Nonlinear Multisectoral Simulation of Devaluation and Import Substitution in Zambia." *Journal of Developing Areas* 24 (1990).

Baldwin, R. E. *Economic Development and Export Growth: A Study of Northern Rhodesia, 1920–1960.* Berkeley: University of California Press, 1966.

Bamberger, Michael, Biswapriya Sanyal, and Nelson Valverde. *Evaluation of Site and Service Projects: The Experience from Lusaka, Zambia.* World Bank Staff Working Paper no. 548. Washington, D.C.: World Bank, 1982.

Barber, William J. "Federation and the Distribution of Economic Benefits." In *A New Deal in Central Africa,* ed. C. Leys and C. Pratt. London: Heinemann, 1960.

————. *The Economy of British Central Africa: A Case Study of Economic Development in a Dualistic Society.* Stanford: Stanford University Press, 1961.

Bates, Robert H. *Rural Responses to Industrialization: A Study of Village Zambia.* New Haven: Yale University Press, 1976.

Burawoy, Michael. "The Hidden Abode of Underdevelopment: Labour Process and the State in Zambia." *Politics and Society* 11 (1982).

Cheru, Fantu. "Zambia: The IMF's Newest 'Bantustan.' " In *The Silent*

Revolution in Africa: Debt, Development, and Democracy. London: Zed, 1989.

Chidumayo, E. N. "Environment and Development in Zambia: An Overview." In *Proceedings of the National Seminar on Environment and Development.* Occasional Study no. 10. Lusaka: Zambia Geographical Association, 1979.

Chilivumbo, Alifeyo. *Migration and Uneven Rural Development in Africa: The Case of Zambia.* Lanham, Md.: University Press of America, ca. 1985.

Clements, Frank. *Kariba: The Struggle with the River God.* New York: Putnam's, 1960.

Curry, Robert L. "Problems in Acquiring Mineral Revenues for Financing Economic Development: A Case Study of Zambia during 1970–1978." *American Journal of Economics and Sociology* 43 (1984).

Daniel, Philip. "Zambia: Structural Adjustment or Downward Spiral?" *IDS Bulletin* 16 (Sussex) (1985).

Due, Jean M. "Liberalization and Privatization in Tanzania and Zambia." *World Development* 21 (1993).

Elliott, C., ed. *Constraints on the Economic Development of Zambia.* Nairobi: Oxford University Press, 1971.

Fortman, B. de G., ed. *After Mulungushi: The Economics of Zambian Humanism.* Nairobi: East African, 1969.

Gappert, Gary. *Capital Expenditure and Transitional Planning in Zambia.* Syracuse: Syracuse University, Program of East African Studies, 1966.

Geisler, Gisela. "Silences Speak Louder than Claims: Gender, Household, and Agricultural Development in Southern Africa." *World Development* 21 (1993).

Good, Kenneth. "Debt and the One-Party State in Zambia." *Journal of Modern African Studies* 27 (1989).

Gran, Guy. "From the Official Future to a Participatory Future: Rethinking Development Policy and Practice in Rural Zambia." *Africa Today* 30 (1983).

Gregory, Sir Theodore. *Ernest Oppenheimer and the Economic Development of Southern Africa.* New York: Oxford University Press, 1962.

Gulhati, Ravi, and Uday Sekhar. "Industrial Strategy for Late Starters: The Experience of Kenya, Tanzania, and Zambia." *World Development* 10 (1982).

Hancock, W. K. *Survey of British Commonwealth Affairs.* Vol. 1. *Problems of Economic Policy, 1918–39.* London: Oxford University Press, 1942.

Hansen, Art. "The Illusion of Local Sustainability and Self-Sufficiency: Famine in a Border Area of Northwestern Zambia." *Human Organization* 53 (1994).

Hansen, Karen Tranberg. "Planning Productive Work for Married

Women in a Low-income Settlement in Lusaka: The Case for a Small-Scale Handicrafts Industry." *African Social Research* 33 (1982).

———. " 'The Work History': Disaggregating the Changing Terms of Poor Women's Entry into Lusaska's Labor Force." Working Papers on Women in International Development, no. 134. East Lansing: Michigan State University, 1987.

Hansen, Karen Tranberg, and Leslie Ashbaugh. "Women on the Front Line: Development Issues in Southern Africa." *Women and International Development Journal* 2 (1991).

Harvey, Charles. "The Structure of Zambian Development." In *Development Paths in Africa and China*, ed. Ukandi Damachi, Guy Routh, and Abdel-Rahman E. Ali Taha. London: Macmillan, 1978.

Hawkins, Jeffrey J., Jr. "Understanding the Failure of IMF Reform: The Zambian Case." *World Development* 19 (1991).

Howatch, David. *Shadow of the Dam*. New York: Macmillan, 1961.

International Labour Organisation. *Youth Employment and Youth Employment Programmes in Africa. A Comparative Sub-Regional Study: The Case of Zambia*. Addis Ababa: International Labour Organisation, 1986.

Jolly, Richard. "The Seers Report in Retrospect." *African Social Research* 11 (1971).

Jules-Rosette, Bennetta. "Alternative Urban Adaptations: Zambian Cottage Industries as Sources of Social and Economic Innovation." *Human Organization* 38,3 (1979).

Kaunda, K. D. *Economic Revolution in Zambia*. Lusaka: Government Printer, 1968.

———. *Zambia: Towards Economic Independence. Address to the National Council of UNIP at Mulungushi, April 19, 1968*. Lusaka: Government Printer, 1968.

———. "Zambia's Economic Reforms." *African Affairs* 67 (1968).

Kayizzi-Mugwera, Steve. "External Shocks and Adjustment in a Mineral-Dependent Economy: A Short-Run Model for Zambia." *World Development* 19 (1991).

Knauder, Stephanie. *Shacks and Mansions: An Analysis of the Integrated Housing Policy of Zambia*. Lusaka: Multimedia, 1982.

Libby, Ronald T. "Transnational Class Alliances in Zambia." *Comparative Politics* 15 (1983).

Maembe, Edward, and Jim Tomecko. *Economic Promotion in an Interated Upgrading Project: The Case of Kalingalinga Township, Lusaka*. Institute for African Studies Commissioned Studies Report, no. 1. Lusaka: Institute for African Studies, University of Zambia, 1987.

Makgetla, Neva Seidman. "Theoretical and Practical Implications of IMF Conditionality in Zambia." *Journal of Modern African Studies* 24 (1986).

Meijer, Fons. "Structural Adjustment and Diversification in Zambia." *Development and Change* 21 (1990).

Munachonga, Monica. "Income Allocation and Marriage Options in Urban Zambia." In *A Home Divided: Women and Income in the Third World*, ed. Daisy Dwyer and Judith Bruce. Stanford: Stanford University Press, 1988.

Muntemba, Maud. "'Thwarted Development: A Case Study of Economic Change in the Kabwe Rural District of Zambia, 1902–1970." In *The Roots of Rural Poverty in Central and Southern Africa*, ed. Robin Palmer and Neil Parsons. Berkeley: University of California Press, 1977.

Myers, Robert J. "Rural Manpower in Planning in Zambia." *International Labour Review* 102 (1970).

Oden, Berti'l, and Haroub Othman, eds. *Regional Cooperation in Southern Africa*. Seminar Proceedings no. 22. Uppsala: Scandinavian Institute of African Studies, 1989.

O'Keefe, Phil, and Barry Munslow, eds. *Energy and Development in Southern Africa*. Uppsala: Scandinavian Insitute of African Studies, 1985.

Rakodi, Carole. "Upgrading in Chawama, Lusaka: Displacement or Differentiation?" *Urban Studies* 25 (1988).

———. "After the Project Has Ended: The Role of a Non-Governmental Organization in Improving the Conditions of the Urban Poor in Lusaka." *Community Development Journal* 25,1 (1990).

Report of the Commission Appointed to Enquire into the Financial and Economic Position of Northern Rhodesia (Pim-Milligan Report). Colonial no. 145. London: HMSO, 1938.

Rothchild, D. "Rural-Urban Inequities and Resource Allocation in Zambia." *Journal of Commonwealth Political Studies* 10 (1972).

Sanyal, Biswapriya. "Who Gets What, Where, Why and How: A Critical Look at the Housing Subsidies in Zambia." *Development and Change* 12 (1981).

———. "Organizing the Self-Employed: The Politics of the Urban Informal Sector." *International Labour Review* 130,1 (1991).

Scarritt, James R. "European Adjustment to Economic Reforms and Political Consolidation in Zambia." *Issue* 3 (1973).

Schlyter, Ann. *Twenty Years of Development in George, Zambia*. Stockholm: Swedish Council for Building Research, 1991.

———. "Time Series Analysis: A Longitudinal Study of Housing Quality in Lusaka." In *Housing the Poor in the Developing World: Methods of Analysis, Case Studies, and Policy*, ed. A. Graham Tipple and Kenneth G. Willis. London: Routledge, 1991.

Schuster, Ilsa M. Glazer. "Marginal Lives: Conflict and Contradiction in the Position of Female Traders in Lusaka, Zambia." In *Women and World in Africa*, ed. Edna Bay. Boulder, Colo.: Westview Press, 1982.

Scudder, Thayer. "The Kariba Case: Man-Made Lakes and Resource Development in Africa." *Bulletin of the Atomic Scientists* (December 1965).

Seers, Dudley. "The Use of a Modified Input-Output System for an Economic Program in Zambia." *Institute of Development Studies Communications* 50 (University of Sussex) (1970).

Seymour, Anthony. "Squatters, Migrants, and the Urban Poor: A Study of Attitudes Towards Inequality with Special Reference to Squatter Settlements in Lusaka, Zambia." Ph.D. diss., University of Sussex, 1976.

Shaw, Timothy M. *Dependence and Underdevelopment: The Development and Foreign Policies of Zambia*. Athens: Ohio University, Center for International Studies, 1976.

Siddle, D. J. "Rural Development in Zambia: A Spatial Analysis." *Journal of Modern African Studies* 8 (1970).

Simonis, Heide, and Udo Ernest Simonis, eds. *Socio-Economic Development in Dual Economies: The Example of Zambia*. Munich: Weltforum Verlag, 1971.

St. Jorre, John de. "Zambia's Economy: Progress and Perils." *Africa Report* 12 (1967).

Steel, William F. "Recent Policy Reform and Industrial Adjustment in Zambia and Ghana." *Journal of Modern African Studies* 26 (1988).

Thøgersen, Karsten, and Jørgen E. Andersen. *Urban Planning in Zambia: The Case of Lusaka*. Copenhagen: Royal Danish Academy of Fine Arts, School of Architecture, 1983.

Thomas, P. A. "Zambian Economic Reforms." *Canadian Journal of African Studies* 2 (1968).

Thompson, C. B., and H. W. Woodruff. *Economic Development in Rhodesia and Nyasaland*. London: Dennis Dobson, 1954.

Todd, Dave M., and Christopher P. Shaw. "The Informal Sector and Zambia's Employment Crisis." *Journal of Modern African Studies* 18 (1980).

Turok, Ben, ed. *Development in Zambia: A Reader*. London: Zed, 1979.

United Nations, Economic Commission for Africa. *Report of the Economic Survey Mission on the Development of Zambia*. Ndola: Falcon, 1964.

Van der Hoven, Ralph. "Zambia's Economic Dependence and the Satisfaction of Basic Needs." *International Labour Review* 121 (1982).

Woldring, Klass, and Chibwe Chibaye, eds. *Beyond Political Independence: Zambia's Development Predicament in the 1980s*. Berlin: Mouton, 1984.

Wulf, Jurgen. "Zambia under the IMF regime." *African Affairs* 87 (1988).

———. "Floating Exchange Rates in Developing Countries: The Case of Zambia." *Journal of Modern African States* 27 (1989).

Young, R., and John Loxley. *Zambia: An Assessment of Zambia's Structural Adjustment Experience*. Ottawa: North-South Institute, 1990.

Zambia, Republic of. *Second National Development Plan*. Lusaka: Ministry of Development Planning and National Guidance, 1971.

3.d.i. Economic. Industry. Mining

Bancroft, J. A. *Mining in Northern Rhodesia.* London: British South Africa Company, 1961.

Bates, Robert. H. "Input Structures, Output Functions, and Systems Capacity: A Study of the Mineworkers' Union of Zambia." *Journal of Politics* 32 (1970).

——. *Unions, Parties, and Political Development: A Study of Mine-Workers in Zambia.* New Haven: Yale University Press, 1971.

Berger, Elena L. *Labor, Race, and Colonial Rule: The Copperbelt from 1924 to Independence.* Oxford: Clarendon, 1974.

Bostock, M., and C. Harvey, eds. *Economic Independence and Zambia Copper: A Case Study of Foreign Investment.* New York: Praeger, 1972.

Bradley, Kenneth. *Copper Venture: The Discovery and Development of Roan Antelope and Mufulira.* London: Mufilira Copper Mines, 1962.

Brauer, Dieter. "The Painful Process of Structural Adjustment." *Development and Cooperation* 3 (Baden-Baden) (1985).

Burdette, Marcia. "The Dynamics of Nationalization between Multinational Companies and Peripheral States: Negotiations between AMAX, Inc., the Anglo American Corporation of South Africa, Ltd., and the Government of the Republic of Zambia." Ph.D. diss., Columbia University, 1979.

——. "Were the Copper Nationalizations Worthwhile?" In *Beyond Political Independence: Zambia's Development Predicament in the 1980s,* ed. Klaas Woldring. Berlin: Mouton, 1984.

Chiposa, Sylvester. "Zambia Still Haunted by Copper Dependence." *African Business* 82 (London) (1985).

Cobbe, James H. "Case Study No. 2: Copper in Zambia." In *Governments and Mining Companies in Developing Countries,* ed. James H. Cobbe. Boulder: Westview, 1979.

Copperbelt of Zambia, Mining Industry Year Book, 1966. Kitwe: Copper Industry Service Bureau, 1967.

Cunningham, Simon. *The Copper Industry in Zambia: Foreign Mining Companies in a Developing Country.* New York: Praeger, 1981.

Daniel, Phillip. *Africanisation, Nationalisation, and Inequity: Mining Labour and the Copperbelt in Zambian Development.* Paper in Industrial Relations and Labour no. 4. Cambridge: Cambridge University Press, 1979.

Faber, M. L. O., and J. G. Potter. *Towards Economic Independence: Papers on the Nationalization of the Copper Industry in Zambia.* London: Cambridge University Press, 1966.

Gann, L. H. "The Northern Rhodesian Copper Industry and the World of Copper, 1923–62." *Rhodes-Livingstone Journal* 18 (1955).

Hearing, Roger. "When Copper Was King." *Africa Report* 33 (1988).

A History of the Mineral Rights of Northern Rhodesia. London: Maxwell Stamp, 1961.

Innes, Duncan. *Anglo American and the Rise of Modern South Africa.* New York: Monthly Review Press, 1984.

Mezger, Dorothea. *Copper in the World Economy.* Trans. Pete Burgess. New York: Monthly Review Press, 1980.

Mhango, Mkwapatira. "Zambian Mining: Grim Outlook." *New African* (London) (1984).

Mhone, Guy C. Z. *The Political Economy of a Dual Labor Market in Africa: The Copper Industry and Dependency in Zambia, 1929–1969.* Rutherford, N.J.: Fairleigh Dickinson University Press, ca. 1982.

Moore, R. J. B. *These African Copper Miners: A Study of the Industrial Revolution in Northern Rhodesia, with Principal Reference to the Copper Mining Industry.* London: Livingstone, 1948.

O'Faircheallaigh, Ciaran. "Mineral Taxation, Mineral Revenues, and Mine Investment in Zambia, 1964–83. *American Journal of Economics and Sociology* 45 (1986).

Ohadike, Patrick O. *Development of and Factors in this Employment of African Migrants in the Copper Mines of Zambia, 1940–1966.* Manchester: Manchester University Press [for] University of Zambia, Institute for Social Research, 1969.

Pagni, Lucien. "Zambia: Copper, a Fickle Friend." *Courier* 121 (Brussels) (1990).

Perrings, Charles. "Consciousness Conflict and Proletarianization: An Assessment of the 1935 Mineworkers' Strike on the Northern Rhodesian Copperbelt." *Journal of Southern African Studies* 4 (1978).

Prain, R. L. "The Stabilization of Labor in the Rhodesian Copperbelt." *African Affairs* 121 (1956).

———. *Copper: The Anatomy of an Industry.* London: Mining Journal Books, 1975.

Rhodesian Selection Trust Group of Companies. *The African Mine Worker on the Copperbelt of Northern Rhodesia.* Salisbury: RST, 1960.

Roan Consolidated Mines, Ltd. *Zambia's Mining Industry: The First 50 Years.* Ndola: Public Relations Department, Roan Consolidated Mines, Ltd., 1978.

Saasa, Oliver C. *Zambia's Policies towards Foreign Investment: The Case of the Mining and Non-Mining Sectors.* Research Report no. 79. Uppsala: Scandinavian Institute of African Studies, 1987.

Shafer, Michael. "Capturing the Mineral Multinationals: Advantage or Disadvantage?" *International Organization* 37 (1983).

Sklar, Richard L. *Corporate Power in an African State: The Political Impact of Multinational Mining Companies in Zambia.* Berkeley: University of California Press, 1975.

Spearpoint, F. "The African Native and the Rhodesian Copper Mines." *Journal of the Royal African Society* 36 (1937).

"Zambia: Copper Annual Report, 1988." *Africa Research Bulletin: Economic, Financial, and Technical Series* 25 (1988).

"Zambia's Copper-Toyota Barter Controversy." *Market South East* 4 (London), 4,1 (1990): 4–5.

"Zambia: Expats—Indispensible or Good Riddance?" *New African Development* (London) (October 1980).

"Zambia Focus." *African Business* (London) (November 1982).

"Zambia: Fund Boost for Minerals Exploration." *EASA* 2 (London) (1989).

"Zambia: World Bank Copper Loan Agreed at Last." *Africa Economic Digest* 5 (London) (1984).

"ZCCM Looks Ahead." *Southern African Economist* 3 (Harare) (1990).

"Africa Monitor: Zambia." *Africa Insight* 19 (Pretoria) (1989).

3.d.ii. Economic. Industry. Other

Angi, C., and T. Coombe. "Training Programs and Employment Opportunities for Primary School Leavers in Zambia. " *Manpower and Unemployment Research in Africa* (Lusaka) (November 1969).

Berg, E. J., and J. Butler. "Trade Unions." In *Political Parties and National Integration in Tropical Africa*, ed. J. S. Coleman and C. G. Rosberg. Berkeley: University of California Press, 1964.

Bettison, David G. "Factors in the Determination of Wage Rates in Central Africa." *Rhodes-Livingstone Journal* 28 (1960).

Brelsford, W. V. *Fishermen of the Bangweolu Swamps*. Paper no. 12. Livingstone: Rhodes-Livingstone Institute, Papers, 1946.

Clausen, Lars. "On Attitudes Towards Industrial Conflict in Zambian Industry." *African Social Research* 2 (1966).

Davis, J. M., ed. *Modern Industry and the African*. London: Macmillan, 1933.

Fincham, Robin. "Economic Dependence and the Development of Industry in Zambia." *Journal of Modern African Studies* 18 (1980).

Fosh, Patricia, and Zahid Kazi. "The Industrial Relations Systems of Two ex-British Colonies: Zambia and Singapore." *Round Table* 319 (1991).

Gertzel, Cherry. "Industrial Relations in Zambia to 1975." In *Industrial Relations in Africa*, ed. Ukandi Damachi et al. New York: Macmillan, 1979.

Heisler, Helmut. "The African Workforce of Zambia." *Civilizations* 21 (1971).

Holly, R. "The Skilled Manpower Constraint." In *Constraints on the Economic Development of Zambia*, ed. C. Elliott. Nairobi: Oxford University Press, 1971.

Johns, Sheridan. "The Parastatal Sector." In *Administration in Zambia*, ed. William Tordoff. Manchester: Manchester University Press, 1980.

Kamva, A. "Small-Scale Industries in Zambia: A Case Study of Selected Enterprises on the Copperbelt." *African Social Research* 33 (1982).

Mufune, Pempelani. "Industrial Participatory Democracy: Zambia's System of Work Place Democracy." *African Quarterly* 26 (1987).

Philpott, R. "The Mulobezi-Mongu Labor Route." *Rhodes-Livingstone Journal* 3 (1945).

Read, Margaret. "Migrant Labor and Its Effect on Tribal Life." *International Labour Review* 46 (1942).

Sanderson, F. E. "The Development of Labor Migration from Nyasaland, 1819–1914." *Journal of African History* 2 (1961).

Scudder, Thayer. "Fishermen of the Zambezi." *Rhodes-Livingstone Journal* 27 (1960).

Seidman, Ann. *The Need for an Industrial Strategy in Zambia*. Lusaka: University of Zambia, 1973.

———. "The Distorted Growth of Import-Substitution Industry: The Zambian Case." *Journal of Modern African Studies* 12 (1974).

Turok, Ben. "Zambia's System of State Capitalism." *Development and Change* 11 (1980).

———. "Control in the Parastatal Sector of Zambia." *Journal of Modern African Studies* 19 (1981).

Van Velsen, Jaap. "Labor Migration as a Positive Factor in the Continuity of Tonga Tribal Society." *Economic Development and Cultural Change* 8 (1960).

Vingerhoets, Jan W., and Ad M. Sannen. *Fabrication of Copper Semi-Manufactures in Zambia: A Preliminary Assessment*. Eindhoven and Tilburg (The Netherlands): Technical University, Eindhoven and Tilburg University, 1985.

Young, Alistair. "Patterns of Development in Zambian Manufacturing Industry since Independence." *Eastern African Economic Review* 1 (1969).

———. *Industrial Diversification in Zambia*. New York: Praeger, 1973.

3.e. Economic. Transportation and Communications

Arnold, Guy, and Ruth Weiss. *Strategic Highways of Africa*. London: Freeman, 1977.

Bailey, Martin. *Freedom Railway: China and the Tanzania-Zambia Link*. London: Collings, 1978.

Briggs, John. "The Tanzania-Zambia Railway: Review and Prospects." *Geography* 77 (1992).

Bushell, Chris. "Uncorking Zambia's Rail Bottleneck." *Africa Economic Digest* (London) (February 1980).

Chiposa, Sylvester. "Zambia-Zimbabwe: Trading, Travelling Like Never Before." *African Business* (London) (August 1980).

Chipungu, Samuel N. "The Evolution of Peasant Forms of Transport in Zambia: The Experience of the Southern Province, 1900–1975." History Seminar Paper. University of Zambia, 1988, Lusaka.

Craig, J. "Zambia-Botswana Road Link: Some Border Problems." In *Zambia and the World*. Lusaka: University of Zambia, 1970.

Due, John F. "The Problems of Rail Transport in Tropical Africa." *Journal of Developing Areas* 13 (1979).

———. "Trends in Rail Transport in Zambia and Tanzania." *Utafiti* 8 (Nairobi) (1986).

Fraenkel, Peter. *Wayaleshi*. London: Weidenfeld and Nicolson, 1959.

Gleave, M. B. "The Dar es Salaam Transport Corridor: An Appraisal." *African Affairs* 91 (1992).

Griffiths, Ieuan L. "Transport and Communications in the Relationship of a Land-Locked State: Zambia." In *Transport in Africa: Proceedings of a Seminar*. Edinburgh: University of Edinburgh Press, 1973.

Haefele, E. T., and E. G. Steinberg. *Government Controls on Transport: An African Case*. Washington, D. C.: Brookings, 1986.

Hall, Richard, and Hugh Peyman. *The Great Uhuru Railway: China's Showpiece in Africa*. London: Gollancz, 1977.

Howard, Carol. "Zambia-Tanzania: Keeping Tazara on the Rails." *Africa Economic Digest* (London), September 5, 1980.

Juma, S. "End of the Line for Tazara Railway?" *Concord Weekly* 46 (London) (1985).

Kamlomo, R. "Malawi and Zambia Agree on Road Transport Cooperation." *This Is Malawi* 18 (Blantyre) (1988).

Kasoma, Francis. "The Role of News Coverage in Adult Education." *Journal of Adult Education* 1 (Lusaka) (1982).

———. *The Press in Zambia*. Lusaka: Multimedia, 1986.

Lungu, Gatian F. "The Church, Labour, and the Press in Zambia: The Role of Critical Observers in a One-Party State." *African Affairs* 85 (1986).

Moeller, Philip W. *Field Report: An Assessment of Transport Infrastructures Relative to Zambian Coastal Linkage*. Washington, D.C.: USAID, 1980.

Musole, G. "The Zambia Dossier and Something More." *SADCC Energy* 8 (Lusaka) (1990).

Mutukwa, Kasuka S. "Tanzania-Zambia Railway: Imperial Dream Becomes Pan-African Reality." *Africa Report* 17 (1972).

———. *Politics of the Tanzania-Zambia Railway Project*. Washington, D.C.: University Press of America, 1977.

Mwase, Ngila. "The Tanzania-Zambia Railway: The Chinese Loan and the Pre-Investment Analysis Revisited." *Journal of Modern African Studies* 21 (1983).

———. "The Development Impact of the Tanzania-Zambia Railway." *Zimbabwe Journal of Economics* 1 (1984).

Mytton, Graham. *Listening, Looking, and Learning: Report on a National Mass Media Audience Survey in Zambia, 1970–73.* Lusaka: University of Zambia, Institute for African Studies, 1974.

Nwaffisi, Samwilu. "Zambia Broadcasting Corporation News: A Content Analysis." *Africa Media Review* 3 (Nairobi) (1989).

Nyirenda, Juma Esau. "Radio Broadcasting for Rural Development in Zambia." *Journal of Adult Education* 1 (Lusaka) (1982).

"Press Gagged." *Africa Events* 6 (Dar es Salaam) (1990).

Rusinga, Andrew. "Beira Corridor Freight 'Costs Less.' " *African Business* (London) (November 1986).

Segal, Aaron. "The Tanganyika-Zambia Railway Project." *Africa Report* 9 (1964).

"Tazara Revisted." *Africa Events* 7 (Dar es Salaam) (1991).

"Tazara's Financial Problems." *Africa Research Bulletin: Economic, Financial, and Technical Series* 21 (1984).

"This Is Your Captain Speaking [Zambia Airways]." *Southern African Economist* 2 (Harare) (1989).

Yu, George T. "Working on the Railroad: China and the Tanzania-Zambia Railway." *Asian Survey* 11 (1971).

"Zambia: Lifelines to the Sea." *Courier* (Brussels) (July-August 1979).

"Zambia: Opposition Groups Warned." *Africa Research Bulletin: Political, Social, and Cultural Series* (Crediton, Devon), May 1, 1980.

"Zambia Railways Need a Clear Strategy." *EASA* 2 (London) (1988).

Zambia, Republic of. Ministry of Power, Transport, and Communications. *Annual Report, 1987.* Lusaka: Government Printer, 1987.

"Zambia's Transport Capacity Hit by Forex Shortage." *Market South East* 3 (London) (1989).

4. Historic

4.a. Historic. Archaeology

Bisson, Michael S. "Prehistoric Copper Mining in Northwestern Zambia." *Archaeology* 27 (1974).

———. "Copper Currency in Central Africa: The Archaeological Evidence." *World Archaeology* 6 (1975).

———. "The Prehistoric Copper Mines of Zambia." Ph.D. diss., University of California-Santa Barbara, 1976.

———. "Trade and Tribute: Archaeological Evidence for the Origin of States in South Central Africa." *Cahiers d'Etudes Africaines* 22 (1982).

———. "A Survey of Late Stone Age and Iron Age Sites at Luano, Zambia." *World Archaeology* 24 (1992).

Clark, Desmond J. *The Stone Age Cultures of Northern Rhodesia.* Cape Town: South African Archaeological Society, 1950.

——. "Pre-European Copper Working in South Central Africa." *Roan Antelope* (May 1957).

——. "Digging up History." *Northern Rhodesia Journal* 3 (1958).

——. *Kalambo Falls Prehistoric Site*. Vol. 1. Cambridge: Cambridge University Press, 1969.

——. *Kalambo Falls Prehistoric Site*. Vol. 2. Cambridge: Cambridge University Press, 1974.

——. "J. Desmond Clark (A Personal Memoir)," In *The Pastmasters: Eleven Modern Pioneers of Archaeology*, ed. Glyn Daniel and Christopher Chippendale. New York: Thames and Hudson, 1989.

——. "A Personal Memoir." In *A History of African Archaeology*, ed. Peter Robertshaw. London: Currey, 1990.

Derricourt, Robin M. "People of the Lakes: Archaeological Studies in Northern Zambia." Zambian Paper no. 13. University of Zambia, Institute for African Studies, 1980, Lusaka.

——. *Man on the Kafue: The Archaeology and History of the Itezhitezhi Area of Zambia*. New York: Barber, 1985.

Fagan, Brian M. "Iron Age in Zambia." *Current Anthropology* (1956).

——. "The Iron Age Sequence in the Southern Province of Northern Rhodesia." *Journal of African History* 4 (1963).

——. *Iron Age Cultures in Zambia*. Vols. 1, 2. London: Chatto and Windus, 1966, 1967.

——. "Gundu and Ndonde, Basanga, and Mwanamaimpa." *Azania* 13 (1978).

Fagan, Brian M., and Francis L. van Noten. *The Hunter-Gatherers of Gwisho*. Tervuren: Musée Royale de l'Afrique Centrale, 1971.

Fagan, Brian M., and B. W. Phillipson. "Sebanzi: The Iron Age Sequence at Lochinvar and the Tonga." *Journal of the Royal Anthropological Institute* 96 (1965).

Gabel, Creighton. *Stone Age Hunters of the Kafue: The Gwisho A Site*. Brookline: Boston University Press, 1966.

Lancaster, Chet S., and A. Pohorilenko. "Ingombe Ilede and the Zimbabwe Culture." *International Journal of African Historical Studies* 9 (1976).

Miller, Sheryl F. "Contacts between the Later Stone Age and the Early Iron Age in Southern Central Africa." *Azania* 4 (1969).

——. "The Nachikufan Industries of the Zambian Later Stone Age." Ph.D. diss., University of California-Berkeley, 1969.

——. "The Age of the Nachikufan Industries in Zambia." *South African Archaeological Bulletin* 26 (1971).

——. "The Archaeological Sequence of the Zambian Later Stone Age." *Proceedings of the Panafrican Congress on Prehistory* 6 (1973).

Mills, E. A. C., and N. T. Filmer. "Chondwe Iron Age Site, Ndola, Zambia." *Azania* 7 (1972).

Phillipson, David W. "The Early Iron Age Site at Kapwirimbwe, Lusaka." *Azania* 3 (1968).

———. "The Early Iron Age in Zambia—Regional Variants and Some Tentative Conclusions." *Journal of African History* 9 (1968).

———. "The Prehistoric Sequence at Nakapapula Rock Shelter, Zambia." *Proceedings of the Prehistoric Society* 35 (1969).

———. "Excavations at Twickenham Road, Lusaka." *Azania* 6 (1970).

———. "Notes on the Later Prehistoric Radiocarbon Chronology of Eastern and Southern Africa." *Journal of African History* 11 (1970).

———. "An Early Iron Age Site on the Lubusi River, Kaoma District, Zambia." *Zambia Museum Journal* 2 (1971).

———. "Early Iron Age Sites on the Zambian Copperbelt." *Azania* 7 (1972).

———. "Zambian Rock Paintings." *World Archaeology* 3 (1972).

———. "Iron Age History and Archaeology in Zambia." *Journal of African History* 16 (1974).

———. "The Iron Age in Zambia." Historical Association of Zambia, Pamphlet no. 5. Lusaka: NECZAM, 1975.

———. *The Prehistory of Eastern Zambia.* Nairobi: British Institute in Eastern Africa, 1976.

———. *The Later Prehistory of Eastern and Southern Africa.* New York: Africana, 1977.

———. "Early Food-Production in Central and Southern Africa." In *From Hunters to Farmers: The Causes and Consequences of Food Production in Africa,* ed. J. Desmond Clark and Steven A. Brandt. Berkeley: University of California Press, 1984.

———. *African Archaeology.* Cambridge: Cambridge University Press, 1985.

Phillipson, Laurel. "A Survey of Upper Pleistocene and Holocene Industries in the Upper Zambezi Valley." Ph.D. diss., University of California-Berkeley, 1975.

———. "Survey of the Stone Age Archaeology of the Upper Zambezi Valley, II: Excavations at Kandanda." *Azania* 11 (1976).

Sampson, C. Garth. *The Stone Age Archaeology of Southern Africa.* New York: Academic, 1974.

Savage, D. K. "Identifying Industries in South Central Africa: The Zambian Wilton Example." Ph.D. diss., University of California-Berkeley, 1983.

Stringer, Christopher B. "An Archaic Character in the Broken Hill Innominate E. 719." *American Journal of Physical Anthropology* 71 (1986).

Vogel, Joseph O. *Kamangoza: An Introduction to the Iron Age Cultures of the Victoria Falls Region.* Nairobi: Oxford University Press, 1971.

———. *Kumadzulo: An Early Iron Age Village Site in Southern Zambia.* Lusaka: Oxford University Press, 1971.

————. *Simbusenga: The Archaeology of the Intermediate Period of the Southern Zambian Iron Age*. Lusaka: Oxford University Press, 1975.

Vogel, Joseph O., and N. M. Katanekwa. "Early Iron Age Pottery from Western Zambia." *Azania* 11 (1976).

4.b. Historic. Precolonial

Adams, Henry Gardiner. *The Life and Adventures of Dr. Livingstone in the Interior of South Africa*. London: Blackwood, 1870. Previously published as *Dr. Livingston: His Life and Adventures in the Interior of South Africa*. London, 1857.

Alimen, H. *The Prehistory of Africa*. London: Hutchinson, 1957.

Alpers, E. A. "North of the Zambezi." In *The Middle Age of African History*, ed. Oliver Roland. London: Oxford University Press, 1967.

Anderson, W. H. *On the Trail of Livingstone*. Mountain View, Calif.: Pacific Press, 1919.

Baxter, T. William. "Slave Raiders in North-Eastern Rhodesia." *Northern Rhodesia Journal* 1 (1950).

————. "The Barotse Concessions." *Northern Rhodesia Journal* 3, 4 (1951).

————. "The Concessions of Northern Rhodesia." *Occasional Papers of the National Archives of Rhodesia and Nyasaland* 1 (1963).

Bertrand, Alice E. *Alfred Bertrand, Explorer and Captain of Cavalry*. London: RTS, 1926.

Birmingham, David. "Central Africa and the Atlantic Slave Trade." In *The Middle Age of African History*, ed. Roland Oliver. London: Oxford University Press, 1967.

Blaikie, William Garden. *The Personal Life of David Livingstone*. New York: Harper, 1881.

Bontinck, François. "La double traversée de l'Afrique par trois 'Arabes' de Zanzibar, 1845–1860." *Etudes d'Histoire Africaine* 6 (1974).

Bradley, K. "Statesmen: Coryndon and Lewanika in North Western Rhodesia." *African Observer* 5 (1936).

Brelsford, W. V. *The Succession of Bemba Chiefs: A Guide for District Officers*. Lusaka: Government Printer, 1944.

————. *Generation of Men: The European Pioneers of Northern Rhodesia*. Lusaka: Manning, 1965.

Brode, Heinrich. *Tippoo Tib: The Story of His Career in Central Africa*. London: Arnold, 1907.

Burton, Richard F., trans. *The Lands of Cazembe: Lacerda's Journey to Cazembe in 1798*. London, 1873.

Cairns, H. A. C. *Prelude to Imperialism: British Reactions to Central African Society, 1840–1890*. London: Routledge and Kegan Paul, 1965.

Campbell, Dugald. *In the Heart of Bantuland: A Record of Twenty-Nine Years' Pioneering in Central Africa among the Bantu Peoples*. London: Seeley Service, 1922.

Campbell, R. J. *Livingstone.* New York: Dodd, Mead, 1930.

Caplan, Gerald L. "Barotseland's Scramble for Protection." *Journal of African History* 10 (1969).

Chamberlain, D. *Some Letters from Livingstone.* London: Oxford University Press, 1940.

Chambliss, J. E. *The Life and Labors of David Livingstone.* Philadelphia: Hubbard, 1875.

Chibanza, S. J. "Kaonde History." *Central Bantu Historical Texts.* Vol. 1. Lusaka: Rhodes-Livingstone Institute, 1961.

Clarence-Smith, W. Gervase. "Slaves, Commoners, and Landlords in Bulozi c. 1875 to 1906." *Journal of African History* 20 (1979).

Clark, J. Desmond. *The Stone Age Cultures of Northern Rhodesia.* Cape Town: South African Archaeological Society, 1950.

―――. "A Note on the Pre-Bantu Inhabitants of Northern Rhodesia and Nyasaland." *Northern Rhodesia Journal* 1 (1950–52).

―――. *The Prehistory of Southern Africa.* Harmondsworth: Pelican, 1959.

Clay, Gervas. "Barotseland in the 19th Century between 1801 and 1864." *Proceedings of the Conference on the History of the Central African Peoples.* Lusaka: Rhodes-Livingstone Institute, 1963.

―――. *Your Friend Lewanika, Litunga of Barotseland, 1842–1916.* London: Chatto and Windus, 1968.

Coupland, Sir Reginald. *The Exploitation of East Africa, 1856–1890: The Slave Trade and the Scramble.* London: Faber and Faber, 1939.

―――. *Livingstone's Last Journey.* London: Collins, 1945.

Cunnison, I. G. "History on the Luapula." *Rhodes-Livingstone Institute Papers* 21 (1951).

―――. "Kazembe and the Portuguese." *Journal of African History* 2 (1961).

―――. "Kazembe and the Arabs." In *The Zambesian Past,* ed. Eric Stokes and Richard Brown. Manchester: Manchester University Press, 1966.

Derricourt, Robin M. *Man on the Kafue: The Archaeology and History of the Itezhitezhi Area of Zambia.* New York: Barber, 1985.

Derricourt, Robin N., and Robert J. Papstein. "Lukolwe and the Mbwela of North-Western Zambia." *Azania* 11 (1977).

Fagan, Brian M. "Pre-European Ironworking in Central Africa, with Special Reference to Northern Rhodesia." *Journal of African History* 2 (1961).

―――. *Southern Africa.* London: Thames and Hudson, 1965.

―――, ed. *A Short History of Zambia, from the Earliest Times until A.D. 1900.* Nairobi: Oxford University Press, 1966.

―――. "Early Farmers and Traders North of the Zambezi." In *The Middle Age of African History,* ed. Roland Oliver. London: Oxford University Press, 1967.

Farrant, Leda. *Tippu Tib and the East African Slave Trade*. New York: St. Martin's, 1976.

Finger, Charles, J. *David Livingstone: Explorer and Prophet*. Garden City, N.Y.: Doubleday, Page, 1927.

Fisher, W. Singleton, and Julyan Boyle. *Africa Looks Ahead: The Life Stories of Walter and Anna Fisher of Central Africa*. London: Pickering and Inglis, 1948.

Gamitto, Antonio Candido Pedroso. *King Kazambe and the Marave, Cheva, Bisa, Bemba, Lunda, and Other Peoples of Southern Africa, Being the Diary of the Portuguese Expedition to that Potentate in the Years 1831 and 1832*. Trans. Ian Cunnison. 2 vols. Lisbon: Junta de Investigaçoes do Ultramar, 1960.

Gann, Lewis. "The End of the Slave Trade in British Central Africa, 1889–1912." *Rhodes-Livingstone Journal* 16 (1954).

Gelfand, R. *Livingstone the Doctor: His Life and Travels*. Oxford: Blackwell, 1957.

Gross, Felix. *Rhodes of Africa*. London: Cassell, 1956.

Hall, R. N. *Prehistoric Rhodesia*. London: Unwin, 1909.

Hall, Richard. "Portuguese Expeditions in Zambia." In *A Short History of Zambia from the Earliest Times until A.D. 1900*, ed. Brian M. Fagan. Nairobi: Oxford University Press, 1966.

Hanna, A. J. *The Beginnings of Nyasaland and North-Eastern Rhodesia, 1859–1895*. Oxford: Clarendon, 1956.

Harding, Colonel Colin. *Far Bugles*. London: Simpkin Marshall, 1933.

Harrington, H. T. "The Taming of North-Eastern Rhodesia." *Northern Rhodesia Journal* 2 (1954).

Hawthorne, John. *Dan Crawford: The Gatherer of the People*. London: Pickering and Inglis, n.d.

Hole, H. M. *The Making of Rhodesia*. London: Macmillan, 1926.

———. *The Passing of the Black Kings*. London: Allen, 1932.

Holmberg, A. *African Tribes and European Agencies: Colonialism and Humanitarianism in British South and East Africa, 1870–1895*. Goteberg: Akedemiforlaget, 1966.

Holub, Emil. *Emil Holub's Travels North of the Zambezi*. Trans. Christa Johns, ed. Ladislav Holy. Manchester: Manchester University Press, 1975.

Hudson, R. "Memories of Abandoned Bomas: No. 4 Nalolo." *Northern Rhodesia Journal* 2 (1953).

Hughes, Thomas. *David Livingstone*. London: Macmillan, 1897.

Hunt, B. L. "Lewanika Visits Livingstone." *Northern Rhodesia Journal* 5 (1964).

Isaacman, Allen. "Ex-Slaves, Transfrontiersmen, and the Slave Trade: The Chikunda of the Zambezi Valley, 1850–1900." In *Africans in Bond-

age: Studies in Slavery and the Slave Trade, ed. Paul E. Lovejoy. Madison: University of Wisconsin, African Studies Program, 1986.

Jalla, Adolphe, and Emma. *Pioneers par les Ma-Rotse*. Florence: Imprimerie Claudienne, 1903.

Johnston, Sir Harry. *British Central Africa*. London, 1896.

Johnston, James. *Reality versus Romance in South-Central Africa*. New York: Revell, 1893.

Lack, R. A. *Visit to Lewanika, King of the Barotse*. London: Simpkin Marshall, 1902.

Langham, R. W. M. "Thornton and Rumsey of Mbesuma Ranch." *Northern Rhodesia Journal* 4 (1960).

Langworthy, H. W. *Zambia before 1890: Aspects of Pre-Colonial History*. London: Longmans, 1972.

Lawley, Arthur. "From Bulawayo to the Victoria Falls: A Mission to King Lewanika." *Blackwood's Magazine* (December 1898).

Livingstone, David. *Missionary Travels and Researches in South Africa*. London, 1857.

———. *The Last Journals of David Livingstone in Central Africa*. Ed. H. Waller. Vol. 1. London, 1874.

———. *The Zambezi Expedition of David Livingstone, 1858–1863*. Ed. J. P. R. Wallis. Vol. 1. *The Journals*. Vol. 2. *The Journals, Continued, with Letters and Despatches Therefrom*. Oppenheimer Series. London: Chatto and Windus, 1956.

Livingstone, David, and Charles Livingstone. *Narrative of an Expedition to the Zambezi and Its Tributaries; and of the Discovers of the Lakes Shirwa and Nyassa, 1858–1864*. New York, 1866.

Macnair, J. *Livingstone the Liberator*. London: Collins, 1940.

———, ed. *Livingstone's Travels*. London: Dent, 1954.

MacQueen, James. "Journeys of Silva Porto with the Arabs from Benguela to Ibo and Mozambique through Africa, 1852–1854." *Journals of the Royal Geographic Society* 30 (1860).

Mainga, Mutumba. "New Light on the Origin of the Lozi." *Proceedings of the Conference on the History of the Central African Peoples*. Lusaka: Rhodes-Livingstone Institute, 1963.

———. "The Lozi Kingdom." In *A Short History of Zambia from the Earliest Times until A.D. 1900*, ed. Brian M. Fagan. Nairobi: Oxford University Press, 1966.

———. *Bulozi under the Luyana Kings*. London: Longmans, 1973.

———. "The Origin of the Lozi: Some Oral Traditions." In *The Zambesian Past*, ed. Eric Stokes and Richard Brown. Manchester: Manchester University Press, 1966.

Marwick, M. G. "History and Tradition in East Central Africa through the Eyes of the North Rhodesian Cewa." *Journal of African History* 4 (1963).

Mathers, E. P. *Zambesia: England's El Dorado in Africa*. London: King, Sell, & Railton, 1892.

McDonald, J. G. *Rhodes: A Life*. London: Allan, 1927.

Miller, Basil. *David Livingstone: Explorer-Missionary*. Grand Rapids, Mich.: Zondervan, 1941.

Miller, Joseph C. "Lineages, Ideology, and the History of Slavery in Western Central Africa." In *The Ideology of Slavery in Africa*, ed. Paul E. Lovejoy. Beverly Hills: Sage, 1981.

———. *Way of Death: Merchant Capitalism and the Angolan Slave Trade, 1730–1830*. Madison: University of Wisconsin Press, 1988.

Millin, Sarah Gertrude. *Rhodes*. Rev. ed. London: Chatto and Windus, 1952.

Miracle, Marvin P. "Plateau Tonga Entrepreneurs in Historical Interregional Trade." *Rhodes-Livingstone Journal* 26 (1959).

———. "Aboriginal Trade among the Senga and Nsenga of Northern Rhodesia." *Ethnology* 1 (1962).

———. "Ivory Trade and the Migration of the Northern Rhodesian Senga." *Cahiers d'Etudes Africaines* 3 (1963).

Mitchell, Lewis. *Life of Rhodes*. London: Arnold, 1910.

———. *The Life and Times of the Right Honorable Cecil John Rhodes, 1853–1902*. 2 vols. New York: Kennerly, 1910.

Munday, J. T. "Kankomba." *Central Bantu Historical Texts*. Vol. 1. Lusaka: Rhodes-Livingstone Institute, 1961.

Mupatu, Y. W. *Mulambwa Santulu U Amuhela Bo Mweve* (King Mulambwa Welcomes the Mbunda Chiefs). London: Macmillan, 1958.

———. *Bulozi Sapili* (Barotseland in the Past). Cape Town: Oxford University Press, 1959.

Mushindo, Paul. *The Life of a Zambian Evangelist: The Reminiscences of Rev. Paul B. Mushindo*. Lusaka: University of Zambia, Institute for African Studies, 1973.

Muuka, L. S. "The Colonization of Barotseland in the 17th Century." *Proceedings of the Conference on the History of the Central African Peoples*. Lusaka: Rhodes-Livingstone Institute, 1963.

———. "The Colonization of Barotseland in the 17th Century." In *The Zambesian Past*, ed. Eric Stokes and Richard Brown. Manchester: Manchester University Press, 1966.

Nalilungwe, Mubuana. *Makolo Ki Ba* (The Coming of the Kololo). Rev. ed. Cape Town, Lusaka: NECZAM, 1972.

O'Brien, Dan. "Chiefs of Rain-Chiefs of Ruling: A Reinterpretation of Pre-Colonial Tonga (Zambia) Social and Political Structure." *Africa* 53 (Manchester) (1983).

Oliver, Roland A. *Sir Harry Johnston and the Scramble for Africa*. London: Chatto and Windus, 1957.

————, ed. *The Middle Age of African History*. London: Oxford University Press, 1967.

Omer-Cooper, J. D. *The Zulu Aftermath*. London: Longmans, 1966.

Pachai, B., ed. *Livingstone: Man of Africa*. New York: Longmans, 1973.

Papstein, Robert J. "The Upper Zambezi: A History of the Luvale People, 1000–1900." Ph.D. diss., University of California-Los Angeles, 1978.

Piomer, William. *Cecil Rhodes*. New York: Appleton, 1933.

Polack, W. G. *David Livingstone*. St. Louis: Concordia, 1929.

Poole, Edward Humphrey Lane. "An Early Portuguese Settlement in Northern Rhodesia." *Journal of the African Society* 30 (1931).

————. *The Native Tribes of the East Luangwa Province of Northern Rhodesia.* Livingstone: Government Printer, 1934.

————. *The Native Tribes of the Eastern Province of Northern Rhodesia: Notes, on Their Migration and History*. Lusaka: Government Printer, 1938.

Radziwell, Princess Catherine. *Cecil Rhodes: Man and Empire-Maker*. New York: Funk and Wagnalls, 1918.

Ranger, T. O. *Aspects of Central African History*. London: Heinemann, 1968.

Read, Margaret. "The Moral Code of the Ngoni and Their Former Military State." *Africa* 11 (1938).

Reefe, Thomas Q. *The Rainbow and the Kings: A History of the Luba Empire to 1891*. Berkeley: University of California Press, 1981.

————. "The Societies of the Eastern Savanna," In *History of Central Africa*, ed. David Birmingham and Phyllis M. Martin. Vol. 1. London: Longmans, 1983.

Roberts, Andrew Dunlap, ed. "The History of Ahdullah ibn Suliman." *African Social Research* 4 (1967).

Roberts, John S. *The Life and Explorations of David Livingstone*. Boston, 1875.

Roberts, Andrew Dunlop. "Migrations from the Congo (A.D. 1500 to 1850)." In *A Short History of Zambi from the Earliest Times until A.D. 1900*, ed. Brian M. Fagan. Nairobi: Oxford University Press, 1966.

————."The History of the Bemba." In *The Middle Age of African History*, ed. Roland Oliver. London: Oxford University Press, 1967.

————. "The Nineteenth Century in Zambia." In *Aspects of Central African History*, ed. T. O. Ranger. London: Heinemann, 1968.

————. "Chronology of the Bemba (North-Eastern Zambia)." *Journal of African History* 2 (1970).

————. *A History of the Bemba*. Madison: University of Wisconsin Press, 1973.

Rukavina, Kathaleen Stevens. *Jungle Pathfinder: The Biography of Chirupula Stephenson*. London: Hutchinson, 1952.

Sakubita, M. M. *Za Luna Li Lu Siile* (Our Vanishing Past). Lusaka: NEC-ZAM, 1972.

Schapera, I., ed. *David Livingstone, Family Letters, 1841–1856.* 2 vols. London: Chatto and Windus, 1959.

———. *Livingstone's Private Journals, 1851–1853.* London: Chatto and Windus, 1960.

———. *Livingstone's Missionary Correspondence, 1841–1856.* London: Chatto and Windus, 1961.

———. *Livingstone's Africa Journals.* 2 vols. London: Chatto and Windus, 1963.

Schecter, Robert E. "History and Historiography on a Frontier of Lunda Expansion: The Origins and Early Development of the Kanongesha." Ph.D. diss., University of Wisconsin-Madison, 1980.

Seaver, G. *David Livingstone: His Life and Letters.* New York: Harper, 1957.

Serpa Pinto, A. de. *How I Crossed Africa from the Atlantic to the Indian Ocean.* 2 vols. Philadelphia: Lippincott, 1881.

Siegel, Brian. "Chipimpi, Vulgar Clans, and Lala-Lamba Ethnohistory," In *Culture and Contradiction: Dialectics of Wealth, Power and Symbol,* ed. Hermine G. De Soto. San Francisco: Mellen Research University Press, 1992.

Smith, Alison. "The Southern Sector of the Interior, 1840–1884." In *History of East Africa,* ed. Roland Oliver and Mathew Gervase. Vol. 1. Oxford: Clarendon, 1963.

Smith, E. W. "Sebitwane and the Makololo." *African Studies* 16 (1956).

Stirke, D. E. C. *Barotseland: Eight Years among the Barotse.* London: John Ball Sons and Danielson, 1922.

Stokes, K., and Richard Brown, eds. *The Zambesian Past: Studies in Central African History.* Manchester: Manchester University Press, 1966.

Swann, A. J. *Fighting the Slave Hunters in Central Africa.* London: Seeley, 1910.

Tabler, Edward C., ed. *Trade and Travel in Early Barotseland: The Diaries of George Westbeech, 1885–1888, and Captain Norman MacLeod, 1875–1876.* London: Chatto and Windus, 1963.

———. *The Zambezi Papers of Richard Thornton.* Vol. 1, 1858–1860. Vol. 2, 1860–1863. Robins Series no. 4. London: Chatto and Windus, 1963.

Thomas, F. M. *Historical Notes on the Bisa Tribe, Northern Rhodesia.* Communication no. 3. Lusaka: Rhodes-Livingstone Institute, 1962.

Tippu Tib. "Maisha ya Hamed bin Muhammed." *Journal of the East African Swahili Committee* (supp.) 28, 29 (1958, 1959).

Van Binsbergen, Wim M. J. "Likota lya Bankoya: Memory, Myth, and History." *Cahiers d'Etudes Africaines* 27 (1987).

———. *Tears of Rain: Ethnicity and History in Central Western Zambia.* London: Kegan Paul, 1992.

Vansina, Jan. "South of the Congo." In *The Dawn of African History,* ed. Roland Oliver. London: Oxford University Press, 1961.

———. "Long Distance Trade Routes in Central Africa." *Journal of African History* 3 (1962).

———. *Paths in the Rainforests: Toward a History of Political Tradition in Equatorial Africa.* Madison: University of Wisconsin Press, 1990.

Vellut, Jean-Luc. "Notes sur le Lunda et la frontière Luso-africaine (1700–1900)." *Etudes d'Histoire Africaine* 3 (1972).

Venning, J. H. "Early Days in Balovale." *Northern Rhodesia Journal* 2 (1955).

Verbeek, Leon. *Filiation et usurpation: histoire socio-politique de la region entre Luapula et Copperbelt.* Tervuren: Musée Royale de l'Afrique Centrale, 1987.

Vogel, Joseph O. "Subsistence Settlement Systems in the Prehistory of Southwestern Zambia." *Human Ecology* 14 (1986).

Waller, H., ed. *Last Journals of David Livingstone.* London, 1874.

Wallis, J. P. R., ed. *The Barotseland Journal of James Stevenson-Hamilton: 1898–1899.* London: Chatto and Windus, 1953.

———. *The Zambezi Expedition of David Livingstone.* 2 vols. London: Chatto and Windus, 1956.

White, C. M. N. "The Balovale Peoples and Their Historical Background." *Rhodes-Livingstone Journal* 8 (1948).

———."The History of the Lunda-Lubale Peoples." *Rhodes-Livingstone Journal* 8 (1949).

Williams, Basil. *Cecil Rhodes.* New York: Henry Holt, 1921.

Woodhouse, C. M., and John G. Lockhart. *Cecil Rhodes.* London: Hodder and Stoughton, 1963.

Wright, Marcia. *Women in Peril: Life Stories of Four Captives.* Lusaka: NECZAM, 1984.

4.c. Historic. Company and Colonial Rule

Akafuna, Ishee Kwandu Sikota. "Lewanika in England, 1902. *Northern Rhodesia Journal* 2 (1953).

Allighan, Garry. *The Welensky Story.* London: Macdonald, 1962.

Alport, Lord. *The Sudden Assignment: Being a Record of Service in Central Africa during the Last Controversial Years of the Federation of Rhodesia and Nyasaland, 1961–1963.* London: Hodder and Stoughton, 1965.

Ambler, Charles. "Alcohol, Racial Segregation, and Popular Politics in Northern Rhodesia." *Journal of African History* 30 (1990).

———. "Alcohol and the Control of Labor on the Copperbelt." In *Liquor and Labor in Southern Africa*, ed. Jonathan Crush and Charles Ambler. Athens: Ohio University Press, 1992.

An Account of the Disturbances in Northern Rhodesia. Lusaka: Government Printer, 1961.

Assimeng, J. M. "Sectarian Allegiance and Political Authority: The Watch Tower Society in Zambia." *Journal of Modern African Studies* 8 (1970).

Banda, H. K., and Harry Nkumbula. *Federation in Central Africa.* London: 1951.

Barber, W. J. "Federation and the Distribution of Economic Benefits." In *A New Deal in Central Africa,* ed. C. Leys and C. Pratt. London: Heinemann, 1960.

Barnes, J. A. "African Separatist Churches." *Rhodes-Livingstone Journal* 9 (1950).

Barton, Frank. "Portrait of a Failure: Sir Roy Welensky" *Africa South* 3, 4 (1959).

Bate, H. Maclear. *Report on the Rhodesias.* London: Melrose, 1953.

Baxter, G. H., and P. W. Jodgens. "The Constitutional Status of the Federation of Rhodesia and Nyasaland." *International Affairs* (October 1957).

Berger, Elena L. *Labour, Race, and Colonial Rule: The Copperbelt from 1924 to Independence.* Oxford: Clarendon, 1974.

Billing, M. G. "Tribal Rule and Modern Politics in Northern Rhodesia." *African Affairs* 58 (1969).

Black, Colin. *Rhodesia and Nyasaland.* New York: Macmillan, 1961.

Bradley, Kenneth G. *The Story of Northern Rhodesia.* Rev. ed. London: Longmans, Green, 1946.

Brelsford, W. V. *The Story of the Northern Rhodesia Regiment.* Lusaka: Government Printer, 1954.

Broomfield, Gerald W. *1960—Last Chance in the Federation.* London: Universities' Mission to Central Africa, 1960.

Cambridge History of the British Empire. Vol. 3. *The Empire Commonwealth, 1870–1919: South Africa, Rhodesia, and the Protectorates.* Cambridge: Cambridge University Press, 1936.

Castle, Barbara. "Labour and Central Africa." *Africa South* 3, 4 (1959).

Chandos, Viscount (Oliver Lyttelton). *The Memoirs of.* London: Bodley Head, 1962.

Chanock, Martin. "Making Customary Law: Men, Women, and Courts in Colonial Northern Rhodesia." In *African Women and the Law: Historical Perspectives,* ed. Jean Hay and Marcia Wright. Boston: Boston University, African Studies Center, 1982.

———. *Law, Custom, and Social Order: The Colonial Experience in Malawi and Zambia.* Cambridge: Cambridge University Press, 1985.

Charlton, Leslie. *Spark in the Stubble: Colin Morris of Zambia.* London: Epworth, 1969.

Chauncey, George. "The Locus of Reproduction: Women's Labour in the Zambian Copperbelt, 1927–1953." *Journal of Southern African Studies* 7 (1981).

Chikulo, B. C. "End of an Era: An Analysis of the 1991 Zambian Presidential and Parliamentary Elections." *Politikon* 20 (1993).

Chipungua, Samuel N. "The State Technology and Peasant Differentiation in Zambia: A Case Study of the Southern Province, 1930–1986." Lusaka: Historical Association of Zambia, 1988.

———. "Accumulation from Within: The Boma Class and the Native Treasury in Colonial Zambia." In *Guardians in Their Time: Experiences of Zambians under Colonial Rule, 1890–1964*, ed. Samuel N. Chipungu. London: Macmillan, 1992.

———. "African Leadership under Indirect Rule in Colonial Zambia." In *Guardians in Their Time: Experiences of Zambians under Colonial Rule, 1890–1964*, ed. Samuel N. Chipungu. London: Macmillan, 1992.

———, ed. *Guardians in Their Time: Experiences of Zambians under Colonial Rule, 1890–1964*. London: Macmillan, 1992.

Chona, Mainza. "Northern Rhodesia's Time for Changes." *Africa South in Exile* 5 (1961).

Clay, G. C. R. *History of the Mankoya District*. Communication no. 4. Lusaka: Rhodes-Livingstone Institute, 1966.

Clegg, E. *Race and Politics: Partnership in the Federation of Rhodesia and Nyasaland*. London: Oxford University Press, 1960.

Cliffe, Lionel. "Labour Migration and Peasant Differentiation: Zambian Experiences." *Journal of Peasant Studies* 5 (1978).

Crawford, D. *Thinking Black: Twenty-Two Years without a Break in the Long Grass of Central Africa*. London: Morgan and Scott, 1912.

Creighton, T. R. M. *The Anatomy of Partnership: Southern Rhodesia and the Central African Federation*. London: Faber and Faber, 1960.

———. "The Future of the Federation." *Africa South Is Exile* 5 (1961).

Dann, H. C. *Romance of the Posts of Rhodesia and Nyasaland*. London: Godden, 1940.

Datta, Kusum. "The Policy of Indirect Rule in Northern Rhodesia (Zambia), 1924–1953." Ph.D. diss., University of London, 1976.

———. "Farm Labour, Agrarian Capital, and the State in Colonial Zambia: The African Labour Corps, 1942–1952." *Journal of Southern African Studies* 14 (1988).

———. "The Political Economy of Rural Development in Colonial Zambia: The Case of the Ushi-Kabende, 1947–1953." *International Journal of African Historical Studies* 21 (1988).

Davidson, A. B. "African Resistance and Rebellion against the Imposition of Colonial Rule." In *Emerging Themes of African History: Proceedings of the International Congress of African Historians*, ed. T. O. Ranger. Nairobi: East African, 1968.

Davis, J. A., and J. K. Baker, eds. *Southern Africa in Transition*. London: Pall Mall, 1966.

Dixon-Fyle, Mac. "Politics and Agrarian Change among the Plateau Tonga of Northern Rhodesia, c. 1924–1963." Ph.D. diss., University of London, 1976.

————. "Agricultural Improvement and Political Protest on the Tonga Plateau, Northern Rhodesia." *Journal of African History* 18 (1977).

Dunn, Cyril. *Central African Witness.* London: Gollancz, 1959.

Epstein, A. L. *Politics in an Urban African Community.* Lusaka: Manchester University Press for Rhodes-Livingstone Institute, 1958.

Evans, I. L. *The British in Tropical Africa.* Cambridge: Cambridge University Press, 1958.

Farwell, Byron. *The Great War in Africa, 1914–1918.* New York: Norton, 1986.

Fernandez, J. W. "The Lumpa Uprising: Why?" *Africa Report* 9 (1964).

Fetter, Bruce. *The Creation of Elisabethville, 1910–1940.* Stanford: Hoover Institution Press, 1976.

————. *Colonial Rule and Regional Imbalance in Central Africa.* Boulder, Colo.: Westview, 1983.

————. "Relocating Central Africa's Biological Reproduction, 1923–1963." *International Journal of African Historical Studies* 19 (1986).

Fields, Karen E. *Revival and Rebellion in Colonial Central Africa.* Princeton: Princeton University Press, 1985.

Foster, George M. "Colonial Administration in Northern Rhodesia in 1962." *Human Organization* 46 (1987).

Franck, T. M. *Race and Nationalism: The Struggle for Power in Rhodesia-Nyasaland.* London: Allen and Unwin, 1960.

Franklin, H. *Unholy Wedlock: The Failure of the Central Africa Federation.* London: Allen and Unwin, 1963.

Gadsen, Fay. "Education and Society in Colonial Zambia." In *Guardians in Their Time: Experiences of Zambians under Colonial Rule, 1890–1964,* ed. Samuel N. Chipungu. London: Macmillan, 1992.

Gale, W. D. *Deserve to Be Great: The Story of Rhodesia and Nyasaland.* Bulawayo: Manning, 1960.

Gann, L. H. *The Birth of a Plural Society: The Development of Northern Rhodesia under the British South Africa Company.* Lusaka: Manchester University Press for Rhodes-Livingstone Institute, 1958.

————. *A History of Northern Rhodesia: Early Days to 1953.* London: Chatto and Windus, 1964.

Gelfand, Michael. *Northern Rhodesia in the Days of the Charter: A Medical and Social Study, 1878–1924.* Oxford: Blackwell, 1961.

Gibbs, Henry. *Africa on a Tightrope.* London: Jarrolds, ca. 1954.

Gibbs, Peter. *Avalanche in Central Africa.* London: Barker, 1961.

Glennie, A. F. B. "The Administration Officer Today: Barotseland." *Corona* 2 (1959).

Gregory, Joel W., and Elias Mandala. "Dimensions of Conflict: Emigrant Labor from Colonial Malawi and Zambia, 1900–1945." In *African Population and Capitalism: Historical Perspectives,* ed. Dennis D. Cordell and Joel W. Gregory. 2d ed. Madison: University of Wisconsin Press, 1994.

Gribble, Howard. *The Price of Copper.* London: Universities' Mission to Central Africa, n.d. (ca. 1962).

Griffiths, James. *Livingstone's Africa, Yesterday and Today.* London: Epworth, 1958.

Gussman, Boris. *Out in the Mid-Day Sun.* London: Allen and Unwin, 1962.

Hailey, Lord. *Native Administration in British African Territories.* Part 11. *Central Africa.* London: HMSO, 1950.

Hall, Richard. *Kaunda—Founder of Zambia.* London: Longmans, 1964.

———. *Zambia, 1890–1964: The Colonial Period.* London: Longmans, 1976.

Hansen, Karen Tranberg. "Labor Migration and Urban Child Labor During the Colonial Period in Zambia." In *Demography from Scanty Evidence: Central Africa in the Colonial Era,* ed. Bruce Fetter. Boulder, Colo.: Lynne Rienner, 1990.

Harding, C. *Frontier Patrols: A History of the British South Africa Police and Other Rhodesian Forces.* London: Bell, 1937.

Hatch, John. *Two African Statesmen: Kaunda of Zambia, Nyerere of Tanzania.* Chicago: Regnery, 1976.

Henderson, Ian. "The Origins of Nationalism in East and Central Africa: The Zambian Case." *Journal of African History* 11 (1970).

Heward, Christine. "The Rise of Alice Lenshina." *New Society,* August 13, 1964.

Hodgkin, T. *African Political Parties.* Harmondsworth: Penguin, 1961.

Holleman, J. F., and S. Biesheuvel. *White Mine Workers in Northern Rhodesia, 1959–1960.* Leiden: Afrika-Studiencentrum, 1973.

Hooker, J. R. "Welfare Associations and Other Instruments of Accommodation in the Rhodesias between the World Wars." *Comparative Studies in Society and History* 9 (1966).

Hoppers, Wim. "Industrial Training and Labor Market Segmentation in Zambia: A Historical Analysis." *African Studies Review* 29 (1986).

Hutchinson, Robert, and George Martelli. *Robert's People: The Life of Sir Robert Williams, Bart., 1860–1938.* London: Chatto and Windus, 1971.

Indakwa, John. *Expansion of British Rule in the Interior of Central Africa.* Washington, D.C.: University Press of America, 1977.

Jones, N. S. Carey. "Native Treasuries in Northern Rhodesia. " *Rhodes-Livingstone Journal* 2 (1944).

Jones, Arthur Creech. "Central Africa (II), the Challenge of Federation." *Africa South* 2 (1957).

Jones, Marilyn Y. "The Politics of White Agrarian Settlement in Northern Rhodesia, 1898–1928." M.A. thesis, University of Sussex, 1974.

Kamayoyo, N. "Anatomy of Underdevelopment in Bulozi: The Case of Lyaluyi, 1890–1924." M.A. thesis, University of Zambia, 1988.

Kanduza, Ackson M. "The Impact of Railway Rates and Customs Agreements on Farming in Northern Rhodesia/Zambia, 1910–1939: The

Case of Maize and Cattle Farming." M.A. thesis, University of Zambia, 1979.

———. "The Tobacco Industry in Northern Rhodesia, 1912–1938." *International Journal of African Historical Studies* 16 (1983).

———. *The Political Economy of Underdevelopment in Northern Rhodesia, 1919–1960: A Case Study of Customs Tariff and Railway Freight Policies.* Lanham, Md.: University Press of America, 1986.

———. "Towards a History of Ideas in Zambia." In *Guardians in Their Time: Experiences of Zambians under Colonial Rule, 1890–1964,* ed. Samuel N. Chipungu. London: Macmillan, 1992.

Kaunda, Kenneth. *Dominion Status for Central Africa.* London: UCD and MUF, 1957.

———. "Rider and Horse in Northern Rhodesia." *Africa South* 3 (1959).

———. *Zambia Shall Be Free: An Autobiography.* London: Heinemann, 1962.

———. *Africa's Freedom.* London: Allen and Unwin, 1964.

Kaunda, Kenneth, and C. Morris. *Black Government.* Lusaka: United Society for Christian Literature, 1960.

Keatley, Patrick. "Monckton and Cleopatra." *Africa South in Exile* 5 (1961).

———. "The Guilty Partner." *Africa South in Exile* 6 (1961).

———. *The Politics of Partnership: The Federation of Rhodesia and Nyasaland.* London: Penguin, 1963.

Keet, Dot. "The African Representative Council, 1946–1958: A Focus on African Political Leadership and the Politics of Northern Rhodesia." M.A. thesis, University of Zambia, 1975.

Kirkman, W. *Unscrambling an Empire—A Critique of British Colonial Policy, 1956–1966.* London: Chatto and Windus, 1966.

Kirkwood, Kenneth. "British Central Africa: Politics under Federation." *Annals of American Academy of Political Science* (March 1955).

Leys, Colin, and Cranford Pratt. *A New Deal in Central Africa.* New York: Praeger, 1961.

Luchembe, Chipasha. "Ethnic Stereotypes, Violence, and Labour in Early Colonial Zambia, 1889–1924." In *Guardians in Their Time: Experiences of Zambians under Colonial Rule, 1890–1964,* ed. Samuel N. Chipungu. London: Macmillan, 1992.

Macmillan, Hugh. "The Historiography of Transition on the Zambian Copperbelt—Another View." *Journal of Southern African Studies* 19,4 (1993).

Macpherson, Fergus. *Kenneth Kaunda of Zambia.* London: Oxford University Press, 1974.

———. *Anatomy of a Conquest: The British Occupation of Zambia, 1884–1924.* Burnt Mill, Harlow, Essex, U.K.: Longmans, 1981.

Mason, P. *The Birth of a Dilemma: The Conquest and Settlement of Rhodesia.* London: Oxford University Press, 1958.

——. *Year of Decision: Rhodesia and Nyasaland in 1960.* London: Oxford University Press, 1960.

Matongo, Albert B. K. "Popular Culture in a Colonial Society: Another Look at Mbeni and Kalela Dances on the Copperbelt, 1930–64." In *Guardians in Their Time: Experiences of Zambians under Colonial Rule, 1890–1964,* ed. Samuel N. Chipungu. London: Macmillan, 1992.

Mbikusita, Godwin. *Yeta III's Visit to England, 1937.* Lusaka: Government Printer, 1940.

McWilliams, M. D. "The Central African Liberals" *Africa South* 3 (1958).

Meebelo, Henry. *Reaction to Colonialism: A Prelude to the Politics of Independence in Northern Zambia, 1893–1939.* Manchester: Manchester University Press, 1971.

——. *African Proletarians and Colonial Capitalism.* Lusaka: Kenneth Kaunda Foundation, 1986.

Melady, T. *Kenneth Kaunda of Zambia: Selections from His Writings.* New York: Praeger, 1964.

Memorandum on Native Policy in Northern Rhodesia (Gardiner-Brown Report). Lusaka: Government Printer, 1950.

Mhone, Guy C. Z. *The Political Economy of a Dual Labor Market in Africa: The Copper Industry and Dependency in Zambia, 1929–1969.* Rutherford, N.J.: Fairleigh Dickinson University Press, ca. 1982.

Mittelbeeler, Emmet V. "After Federation: Some Predictions." *Africa Report* 8 (1963).

Momba, Jotham C. "Peasant Differentiation and Rural Party in Colonial Zambia." *Journal of Southern African Studies* 11 (1985).

Morris, Colin. *The Hour after Midnight: A Missionary's Experiences of the Racial and Political Struggle in Northern Rhodesia.* London: Longmans, 1961.

——. *A Humanist in Africa: Letters to Colin M. Morris from Kenneth D. Kaunda, President of Zambia.* Nashville, Tenn.: Abingdon, 1966.

Mpashi, S. *Betty Kaunda.* London: Longmans, 1969.

Mtepuka, Elias M. "Central African Federation (I), the Attack." *Africa South* 1 (1957).

Mulford, David. *The Northern Rhodesia General Election, 1962.* London: Oxford University Press, 1964.

——. *Zambia: The Politics of Independence, 1957–1964.* London: Oxford University Press, 1967.

Munger, Edwin. *President Kenneth Kaunda of Zambia: An Extraordinary Human Being Facing Extraordinary Problems.* Field Staff Report, Central and Southern Africa, 14. 2. Hanover, N.H.: American Universities Field Staff, 1970.

Muntemba, Maud Shimwaayi, ed. *Zambian Land and Labour Studies*. Vol. 4. Lusaka: National Archives of Zambia, 1973.

———. "Rural Underdevelopment in Zambia: Kabwe Rural District, 1850–1970." Ph.D. diss., University of California-Los Angeles, 1977.

———. "Thwarted Development: A Case Study of Economic Change in the Kabwe Rural District of Zambia, 1902–70." In *The Roots of Rural Poverty in Central anad Southern Africa*, ed. R. Palmer and N. Parsons. London: Heinemann, 1977.

———. "Women and Agricultural Change in the Railway Region of Zambia: Dispossession and Counterstrategies." In *Women and Work in Africa*, ed. Edna Bay. Boulder, Colo.: Westview, 1982.

———. "Women as Food Producers and Suppliers in the Twentieth Century: The Case of Zambia." *Development Dialogue* 1 (1982).

Musambachime, Mwelwa C. "The Impact of Rumour: The Case of the Banyama (Vampire Men) Scare in Northern Rhodesia, 1930–1964." Seminar Paper. University of Zambia, School of Humanities and Social Sciences, n.d.

———. "Development and Growth of the Fishing Industry in Mweru-Luapula, 1920–1964." Ph.D. diss., University of Wisconsin-Madison, 1981.

———. "The Social and Economic Effects of Sleeping Sickness in Mweru-Luapula, 1906–1922." *African Economic History* 10 (1981).

———. "Northern Rhodesian Tax Stamps as an Aid to Chronology." *History in Africa* 14 (1987).

———. "Rural Political Protest: The 1953 Disturbances in Mweru-Luapula." *International Journal of African Historical Studies* 20 (1987).

———. "Impact of Cattle Diseases on the Cattle Industry in Colonial Zambia." Seminar Paper. University of Zambia, History Department, 1988.

———. "Protest Migrations in Mweru-Luapula, 1900–1940." *African Studies* 47 (1988).

———. "Military Violence against Civilians: The Case of the Congolese and Zairean Military in the Pedicle, 1890–1988." *International Journal of African Historical Studies* 23 (1990).

———. "Dauti Yamba's Contribution to the Rise and Growth of Nationalism in Zambia, 1941–1964." *African Affairs* 90 (1991)

———. "Colonialism and the Environment in Zambia, 1860–1964." In *Guardians in Their Time: Experiences of Zambians under Colonial Rule, 1890–1964*, ed. Samuel N. Chipungu. London: Macmillan, 1992.

———. "The Ubutwa Society in Eastern Shaba and Northeast Zambia to 1920." *International Journal of African Historical Studies* 27 (1994).

———. "The Role of Kasenga (Eastern Shaba) in the Development of Mweru-Luapula Fishery." *African Studies Review* 38 (1995).

Mvunga, M. P. *The Colonial Foundation of Zambia's Land Tenure System*. Lusaka: NECZAM, 1980.

Mvusi, Thandile R. M. "Creation of Unemployment in Northern Rhodesia, 1899–1936." Ph.D. diss., Northwestern University, 1984.

Mwalukanga, G. M. "Constraints on the Development of Cotton Production in Northern Rhodesia, 1900–1945: The Case of Eastern Luangwa." M.A. diss., University of Zambia, 1984.

Nationalism in Colonial Africa. London: Muller, 1956.

Needham, D. E. *Iron Age to Independence: A History of Central Africa*. New York: Longmans, 1975.

"Northern Rhodesia—Some Observations on the 1964 Elections." *Africa Report* 9 (1964).

Palmer, Robin, ed. *Zambian Land and Labour Studies*. 3 vols. Occasional Paper. Lusaka: National Archives of Zambia, 1973–76.

————. "The Zambian Peasantry under Colonialism, 1900–1930." In *The Evolving Structure of Zambian Society*, ed. Robin Fincham and John Markakis. Edinburgh: University of Edinburgh, Centre of African Studies, 1980.

————. "Land Alienations and Agricultural Conflict in Colonial Zambia." In *Imperialism, Colonialism, and Hunger: East and Central Africa*, ed. Robert I. Rotberg. Lexington, Mass.: Heath, 1983.

Palmer, Robin, and Neil Parsons, eds. *The Roots of Rural Poverty in Central and Southern Africa*. London: Heinemann, 1977.

Papstein, Robert J. "The Transformation of Oral History under the Colonial State." In *Papers Presented to the International Oral History Conference, 24–26 October 1980*. Vol. 2. Amsterdam: University of Amsterdam, 1980.

————. "The Political Economy of Ethnicity: The Example of Northwestern Zambia." *Tijdschrift voor Geschiedenis* 98 (1985).

————. "From Ethnic Identity to Tribalism: The Upper Zambezi Region of Zambia, 1830–1981." In *The Creation of Tribalism in Southern Africa*, ed. Leroy Vail. London: Currey, 1989.

Parpart, Jane L. *Labor and Capital on the African Copperbelt*. Philadelphia: Temple University Press, 1983.

————. "Class and Gender on the Copperbelt: Women in Northern Rhodesian Copper Mining Communities, 1926–1964." In *Women and Class in Africa*, ed. Claire Robertson and Iris Berger. New York: Africana, 1986.

————. "The Household and the Mine Shaft: Gender and Class Struggles on the Zambian Copperbelt, 1924–1964." *Journal of Southern African Studies* 13 (1986).

————. "Sexuality and Power on the Zambian Copperbelt, 1926–1964." In *Patriarchy and Class: African Women in the Home and the Workforce*, ed. Sharon B. Stichter and Jane L. Parpart. Boulder, Colo.: Westview, 1988.

———. "Where Is Your Mother?" Gender, Urban Marriage, and Colonial Discourse on the Zambian Copperbelt, 1924–1945." *International Journal of African Historical Studies* 27 (1994).

Perham, Margery, ed. *Ten Africans*. London: Faber and Faber, 1936.

Perrings, Charles. "Consciousness, Conflict, and Proletarianisation: An Assessment of the 1935 Mineworkers' Strike on the Northern Rhodesian Copperbelt." *Journal of Southern African Studies* 4 (1977).

———. *Black Mineworkers in Central Africa: Industrial Strategies and the Evolution of an African Proletariat in the Copperbelt, 1911–1941*. New York: Africana, 1979.

Phillips, C. E. Lucas. *The Vision Splendid: The Future of a Central African Federation*. London: Heinemann, 1960.

Phiri, Bizeck Jube. "The Capricorn Africa Society Revisited: The Impact of Liberalism in Zambia's Colonial History, 1949–1963." *International Journal of African Historical Studies* 24 (1991).

Pim, Alan. "Anthropological Problems of Indirect Rule in Northern Rhodesia." *Man* 38 (1938).

Pollock, Norman H., Jr. *Nyasaland and Northern Rhodesia: Corridor to the North*. Pittsburgh: Duquesne University Press, 1971.

Prins, Gwyn. *The Hidden Hippopotamus: Reappraisal in an African History: The Early Colonial Experience in Western Zambia*. Cambridge: Cambridge University Press, 1980.

———, ed. "Self-Help Education at Makapulwa School: An Autobiography by Yuyi W. Mupatu, with Contributions from R. B. Muteto and A. L. Mufungulwa." Communication no. 16. Lusaka: University of Zambia, Institute for African Studies, 1980.

———. "The Battle for Control of the Camera in Late Nineteenth-Century Western Zambia." *African Affairs* 89 (1990).

Ranger, T. O. "The 'Ethiopian' Episode in Barotseland, 1900–1905." *The Rhodes-Livingstone Journal* 37 (1965).

———. "Connections between 'Primary Resistance' Movements and Modern Mass Nationalism in East and Central Africa." Part 1. *Journal of African History* 9 (1968).

———. "Nationality and Nationalism: The Case of Barotseland." *Journal of the Historical Society of Nigeria* 4 (1968).

———. "Making Northern Rhodesia Imperial: Variations on a Royal Theme, 1924–38." *African Affairs* 79 (1980).

Reed, John. "The Salisbury Talks." *Africa South in Exile* 5 (1961).

Report of the Committee Appointed to Inquire into the Constitution of the Barotse Native Government Together with the Comments Thereon of the National Council (Rawlins Committee). Lusaka: Government Printer, 1957.

Report on Native Taxation. Lusaka: Government Printer, 1938

Report of the Advisory Commission on the Review of the Constitution of Rhode-

sia and Nyasaland (Monckton Commission). Cmmd. 1148. London: HMSO, 1960.

Roberts, Andrew Dunlop. "The Political History of 20th-Century Zambia." In *Aspects of Central African History*, ed. T. O. Ranger. London: Heinemann, 1968.

———."The Lumpa Church of Alice Lenshina." In *Protest and Power in Black Africa*, ed. P. I. Rotberg and A. A. Mazrui. New York: Oxford University Press, 1970.

———. *The Lumpa Church of Alice Lenshina*. New York: Oxford University Press, 1972.

———. *A History of Zambia*. New York: Africana, 1976.

Rogerson, C., and B. Tucker. "Commercialization and Corporate Capital in the Sorghum Beer Industry of Central Africa." *Geoforum* 16 (1985).

Rotberg, Robert I. "Inconclusive Election in Northern Rhodesia." *Africa Report* 7 (1962).

———. "The Lenshina Movement of Northern Rhodesia," *Rhodes-Livingstone Journal* 29 (1963).

———. "The Missionary Factor in the Occupation of Trans-Zambezia." *Northern Rhodesia Journal* 5 (1964).

———. "The Federation Movement in British East and Central Africa, 1889–1953." *Journal of Commonwealth Political Studies* 2 (1964).

———. *A Political History of Tropical Africa*. New York: Harcourt, Brace, World, 1965.

———. *The Rise of Nationalism in Central Africa: The Making of Malawi and Zambia, 1873–1964*. Cambridge: Harvard University Press, 1965.

———. "White Rule and the Federation of British Central Africa." In *Southern Africa in Transition*. New York: Praeger, 1966.

———. *Black Heart: Gore-Brown and the Politics of Multiracial Zambia*. Berkeley: University of California Press, 1977.

Rotberg, Robert I., and A. A. Mazrui, eds. *Protest and Power in Black Africa*. New York: Oxford University Press, 1970.

Rothman, Norman. "African Urban Development in the Colonial Period: A Study of Lusaka, 1905–1964." Ph.D. diss., Northwestern University, 1972.

Sanger, Clyde. *Central African Emergency*. London: Heinemann, 1960.

———. "A Long Time Dying: Central African Federation." *Africa South in Exile* 6 (1961).

Seleti, Yona Ngalaba. "Entrepreneurship in Colonial Zambia." In *Guardians in Their Time: Experiences of Zambians under Colonial Rule, 1890–1964*, ed. Samuel N. Chipungu. London: Macmillan, 1992.

Shepperson, G. "The Politics of African Church Separatist Movements in British Central Africa, 1892–1916." *Africa* 24 (1954).

Siegel, Brian. "Bomas, Missions, and Mines: The Making of Centers on the Zambian Copperbelt." *African Studies Review* 31 (1988).

Sikalumbi, W. K. *Before UNIP.* Lusaka: National Educational Company of Zambia, n.d.

Slinn, Peter. "Commercial Concessions and Politics during the Colonial Period: The Role of the British South Africa Company in Northern Rhodesia, 1890–1964." *African Affairs* 70 (1971).

Smyth, Rosalyn. "Propaganda and Politics: The History of Mutende during the Second World War." *Zambia Journal of History* 1 (1981).

————. "War Propaganda during the Second World War in Northern Rhodesia." *African Affairs* 83 (1984).

Sokoni, J., and M. Temple. *Kaunda of Zambia.* London: Nelson, 1964.

Spiro, H. J. "The Rhodesias and Nyasaland." In *Five African States: Responses to Diversity,* ed. Gwendolen M. Carter. London: Pall Mall, 1964.

Stephenson, John E. "The John E. Stephenson Papers." 1945–56 correspondence. Yale University Library, Manuscripts and Archives, African Collection, vol. 8—Zambia, n.d.

Stokes, George. "Memories of Abandoned Bomas, No. 12: Old Fife (Period 1900–1919)." *Northern Rhodesia Journal* 3 (1957).

Stonehouse, John. "A Central African Report." *Africa South* 4 (1959).

Summers, Roger, and L. H. Gann. "Robert Edward Codrington, 1869–1908." *Northern Rhodesia Journal* 3 (1956).

Taylor, Don. *Rainbow on the Zambesi.* London: Museum, 1953.

————. *The Rhodesian: The Life of Sir Roy Welensky.* London: Museum, 1955.

Theal, G. M. *Records of South-Eastern Africa.* Vols. 1–9. Cape Town, 1898.

Vail, Leroy. "Ecology and History: The Example of Eastern Zambia." *Journal of Southern African Studies* 2 (1977).

————. "The Political Economy of East-Central Africa." In *History of Central Africa,* ed. David Birmingham and Phyllis M. Martin. Vol. 2. London: Longmans, 1983.

Van Horn, Laurel. "The Agricultural History of Barotseland, 1840–1964." In *The Roots of Rural Poverty in Central and Southern Africa,* ed. Robin Palmer and Neil Parsons. London, 1977.

Van Onselen, Charles. *Chibaro: African Mine Labour in Southern Rhodesia, 1900–1933.* London: Pluto, 1976.

Vickery, Kenneth P. "The Making of a Peasantry: Imperialism and the Tonga Plateau Economy, 1890–1936." Ph.D. diss., Yale University, 1978.

————. "Saving Settlers: Maize Control in Northern Rhodesia." *Journal of Southern African Studies* 11 (1985).

————. *Black and White in Southern Zambia: The Tonga Economy and British Imperialism, 1890–1939.* New York: Greenwood, 1986.

————. "The Second World War Revival of Forced Labor in the Rhodesias." *International Journal of African Historical Studies* 22 (1989).

Walker, E. A. *A History of Southern Africa.* London: Longmans, 1957.

Wallace, L. A. "Beginning of Native Administration in Northern Rhodesia." *Journal of the African Society* 21 (1922).

Welensky, Sir Roy. *Welensky's 4000 Days: The Life and Death of the Federation of Rhodesia and Nyasaland.* London: Collins, 1964.

Werbner, R. P. "Federal Administration, Rank, and Civil Strife among the Bemba Royals and Nobles." *Africa* 37 (1967).

White, Luise. "Vampire Priests of Central Africa: African Debates about Labor and Religion in Colonial Northern Zambia." *Comparative Studies in Society and History* 35 (1993).

———. "Tsetse Visions: Narratives of Blood and Bugs in Colonial Northern Rhodesia, 1931–9." *Journal of African History* 36 (1995).

Williams, R. *How I Became a Governor.* London: Murray, 1913.

Williams, S. *Central Africa: The Economies of Inequality.* London: Fabian Commonwealth Bureau, 1960.

Wills, A. J. *An Introduction to the History of Central Africa.* 3d ed. London: Oxford University Press, 1973.

Wright, Marcia. "Justice, Women, and the Legal Order in Abercorn, North-Eastern Rhodesia." In *African Women and the Law: Historical Perspectives*, ed. Jean Hay and Marcia Wright. Boston: Boston University, African Studies Center, 1982.

———. "Technology, Marriage, and Women's Work in the History of Maize-Growers in Mazabuka, Zambia: A Reconnaissance." *Journal of Southern African Studies* 10 (1983).

———. " 'Tambalika': Perspectives on a Colonial Magistrate." *African Affairs* 85 (1986).

———. *Strategies of Slaves and Women: Life Stories from East/Central Africa.* New York: Barber, 1993.

Yorke, Edmund. "The Spectre of a Second Chilembwe: Government, Missions, and Social Control in Wartime Northern Rhodesia, 1914–18." *Journal of African History* 31 (1990).

4.d. Historic. Postindependence

Brown, R. "Zambia and Rhodesia: A Study in Contrast." *Current History* 48 (1965).

Cross, Sholto. "Politics and Criticism in Zambia." *Journal of Southern African Studies* 1 (1974).

Garrison, Lloyd. "Africa's Good Guy under Pressure." *New York Times Magazine,* August 7, 1966.

Gregor, Gordon. "President Kaunda—Champion of the Common Man." *Horizon,* January 12, 1968.

Hall, Richard. "Zambia and Rhodesia: Links and Fetters." *Africa Report* 11 (1966).

———. "Zambia's Search for Political Stability." *World Today* 25 (1969).

Heron, Alastair. "Zambia: Key Point in Africa." *World Today* 21 (1965).

Hunter, Guy. "Unification of Zambia's Two Economies." *Optima* 16 (1966).

Jennings, Peggy, and Paul Changuion Jr. "On Voluntary Service In Zambia." *Horizon* 9 (1967).

Kaunda, Kenneth. *Zambia: Independence and Beyond: The Speeches of Kenneth Kaunda*, ed. Colin Legum. London: Nelson, 1966.

———. *Economic Revolution in Zambia*. Lusaka: Government Printer, 1968.

———. *Zambia: Towards Economic Independence*. Address to the National Council of UNIP at Mulungushi, April 19, 1968. Lusaka: Government Printer, 1968.

———. *Zambia's Guidelines for the Next Decade*. Lusaka: Government Printer, 1968.

———. *Africa in the Sixties: The Decade of Decision and Definition*. Lusaka: Zambia News Agency, 1969.

———. *I Wish to Inform the Nation*. Lusaka: Government Printer, 1969.

———. *Towards Complete Independence*. Lusaka: Government Printer, 1969.

———. *Take up the Challenge*. Lusaka: Government Printer, 1970.

———. *A Path for the Future*. Lusaka: Zambia Information Services, 1971.

———. *Address to Parliament on the Opening of the Third Session of the Second National Assembly, January 8, 1971*. Lusaka: Government Printer, 1971.

Keith, Grace. *The Fading Colour Bar*. London: Robert Hale, 1966.

Leech, John. "Zambia Seeks a Route to Fuller Independence." *Issue* 2 (1972).

Legum, Colin D., ed. *Zambia, Independence and Beyond: The Speeches of Kenneth Kaunda*. London: Nelson, 1966.

Macpherson, Fergus. *Kenneth Kaunda of Zambia*. London: Oxford University Press, 1974.

Martin, A. *Minding Their Own Business: Zambia's Struggle against Western Control*. London: Hutchinson, 1972.

Musambachime, Mwelwa C. "The Impact of Rapid Population Growth and Economic Decline on the Quality of Education: The Case of Zambia." *Review of African Political Economy* 48 (1990).

Mwangila, Goodwin. *The Kapwepwe Diaries*. Lusaka: Multimedia, 1986.

O'Brien, Dan. 1982. "Party, Polity, and Bureaucracy: The Zambian Education Debate, 1974–1977." *African Affairs* 81 (1982).

Ostrander, F. T. "Zambia in the Aftermath of Rhodesian UDI: Logistical and Economic Problems." *African Forum* 2 (1967).

Prins, Gwyn. "Self Defence Against Invented Tradition: An Example from Zambia." In *Fonti Orali/Oral Sources/Sources orales*, ed. B. Bernardi, C. Poni, and A. Triulzi. Milan: Franco Angeli, 1978.

Rotberg, Robert I. "What Future for Barotseland?" *Africa Report* 8 (1963).
————. "Tribalism and Politics in Zambia." *Africa Report* 12 (1967).
Sklar, Richard L. "Zambia's Response to the Rhodesian UDI." In *Politics in Zambia*, ed W. Tordoff. Berkeley: University of California Press, 1974.
Sutcliffe, R. B. "Crisis on the Copperbelt." *World Today* 22 (1966).
————. Zambia and the Strains of UDI." *World Today* 23 (1967).
Welch, Claude E., Jr. "Zambia and Lesotho—the Transfer of Power." *Africa Report* 9 (1964).
Wele, P. M. *Kaunda and the Mushala Rebellion: The Untold Story*. Lusaka: Multimedia, 1987.
Zambia, 1964–1974: A Decade of Achievement. Lusaka: Zambia Information Services, 1974.
Zambia: Six Years After. Lusaka: Zambia Information Services, 1970.

5. Political

5.a.i. Political. Constitiution, Law, and Government. Law and Justice

Bradley, Kenneth. *Native Courts and Authorities in Northern Rhodesia*. London: Longmans, Green, 1948.
Canter, Richard S. "Dispute Settlement and Dispute Processing in Zambia: Individual Choice versus Societal Constraints." In *The Disputing Process: Law in Ten Societies*, ed. Laura Nader and H. F. Todd. New York: Columbia University Press, 1978.
Coldham, Simon. "The Law of Succession in Zambia: Recent Proposals for Reform." *Journal of African Law* 27,2 (1983).
————. "The Wills and Administration of Estates Act 1989 and the Intestate Succession Act 1989 of Zambia." *Journal of African Law* 33,1 (1989).
Colson, Elizabeth. "From Chief's Court to Local Court: The Evolution of Local Courts in Zambia." In *Freedom and Constraint: A Memorial Tribute to Max Gluckman*, ed. H. A. Aronoff. Assen (The Netherlands): Van Gorcum, 1976.
Epstein, A. L. "Some Aspects of the Conflict of Law and Urban Courts in Northern Rhodesia." *Rhodes-Livingstone Journal* 12 (1951).
————. "The Role of the African Courts in Urban Communities of the Copperbelt in Northern Rhodesia." *Rhodes-Livingstone Journal* 13 (1953).
————. *The Administration of Justice and the Urban African*. Study 7. London: Colonial Research Studies, 1953.
————. *Juridical Techniques and the Judicial Process*. Manchester: Manchester University Press for Rhodes-Livingstone Institute, 1954.
Hamalengwa, Munyonzwe. "The Political Economy of Human Rights in Africa." *Philosophy and Social Action* 9 (1983).

————. *Thoughts Are Free: Prison Experience and Reflections on Law and Politics in General*. Don Mills, Ont.: Africa in Canada, 1991.

————. "The Legal System of Zambia." In *Monistic or Pluralistic Legal Culture? Anthropological and Ethnological Foundations of Traditional and Modern Legal Systems*, ed. Peter Sack, Carl Wellman, and Mitsukuni Vasaki. Berlin: Duncker and Humblot, 1991.

Hatchard, John. "Crime and Penal Policy in Zambia." *Journal of Modern African Studies* 23 (1985).

Himonga, Chuma N. "Family Property Disputes: The Predicament of Women and Children in a Zambian Urban Community." Ph.D. diss., London School of Economics and Political Science, 1985.

————. "Property Disputes in Law and Practice: Dissolution of Marriage in Zambia." In *Women and Law in Southern Africa*, ed. Alice Armstrong. Harare: Zimbabwe Publishing House, 1987.

Laws of Zambia, 1964. Lusaka: Government Printer, 1965.

"The Legal Organization of a New State—Zambia." *Review of Contemporary Law* 12 (1965).

Longwe, S. H., and R. Shakakata, eds. *Women's Rights in Zambia. Proceedings of the Second National Women's Conference Held at Mindolo Ecumenical Foundation, Kitwe*. Lusaka: Zambia Association for Research and Development, 1985.

Mindolo Ecumenical Foundation. *A Seminar on Widowhood, Law of Succession, and the Church in Zambia*. Kitwe: Mindolo Ecumenical Foundation, 1991.

Mumba, Norah M. *A Song in the Night: A Personal Account of Widowhood in Zambia*. Lusaka: Multimedia Publications, 1992.

Mvunga, Mphanza P. "A Call for Reform in the Law of Succession in Zambia." *Zango: Zambian Journal of Contemporary Issues* 4 (1978).

————. "Law and Social Change: A Case Study in the Customary Law of Inheritance in Zambia." *African Social Research* 28 (1979).

————. *The Colonial Foundation of Zambia's Land Tenure System*. Lusaka: NECZAM, 1980.

Mwaanga, Vernon J. *The Other Society: A Detainee's Diary*. Lusaka: Fleetwood, 1986.

Ndulo, Muna, and Kaye Turner, eds. *Civil Liberties Cases in Zambia*. Oxford: Oxford University Press, 1984.

Ng'ong'ola, Clement. "The Post Colonial Era in Relation to Land Exploration Laws in Botswana, Malawi, Zambia, and Zimbabwe." *International and Comparative Law Quarterly* 41 (1992).

Nkwilimba, Mapanza, and Roy Clarke, eds. *Gabon Aftermath: The Mistreatment of the Football Widows*. Lusaka: Zambia Association for Research and Development, 1994.

Roberts, Andrew Dunlop. "Zambia: White Judges under Attack." *Round Table* 236 (1969).

White, C. M. N. "The Changing Scope of Urban Native Courts in Northern Rhodesia." *Journal of African Law* 8 (1964).

5.a.ii. Political. Constitution, Law, and Government.
Administration

Bates, Robert, and Paul Collier. "The Politics and Economics of Policy Reform in Zambia." In *Political and Economic Interactions in Economic Policy Reform: Evidence from Other Countries*, ed. Robert Bates and Anne O. Krueger. London: Blackwell, 1993.

Bell, Michael W. "Government Revenue Stabilisation in Primary Producing Countries." *Journal of Modern African Studies* 21 (1983).

Byrne, W. J. "The Elasticity of the Tax system of Zambia." *World Development* 11 (1983).

Chilufya, Gregory, and F. Harry Cummings. "Standards in Monitoring and Evaluation: The Case of the Planning Division of Zambia's Ministry of Agriculture." *Canadian Journal of Development Studies* 15 (1994).

DeJong, Lammert, and Jan Kees Van Donge. "Communication and Ward Development Committees in Chipata: A Zambian Case-Study of Administrative Inertia." *Journal of Modern African Studies* 21 (1983).

Dresang, D. L. "Ethnic Politics, Representative Bureaucracy, and Development Administration: The Zambian Case." *American Political Science Review* 77 (1974).

Glennie, A. F. B. "The Administration Officer Today: Barotseland." *Corona* 2 (1959).

Greenfield, C. C. "Manpower Planning in Zambia." *Journal of Administration Overseas* 7 (1968).

Harvey, C. R. M. "The Fiscal System." In *Constraints on the Economic Development of Zambia*, ed. C. Elliott. Nairobi: Oxford University Press, 1971.

Heisler, Helmuth. "Continuity and Change in Zambian Administration." *Journal of Local Administration Overseas* 4 (1965).

Hudson, W. J. S. "Local Government Reorganization in Isoka District." *Journal of Local Administration Overseas* 4 (1965).

Kasongo, Anthony B., and A. Graham Tipple. "An Analysis of Policy Towards Squatters in Kitwe, Zambia." *Third World Planning Review* 12,2 (1990).

Martin, Robert. "The Ombudsman in Zambia." *Journal of Modern African Studies* 15 (1977).

Mukwena, Royson M. "Zambia's Local Administration Act, 1980: A critical Appraisal of the Integration Objective." *Public Administration and Development* 12 (1992).

Mulwanda, Mpanjilwa, and Emmanuel Mutale. "Never Mind the People, the Shanties Must Go: The Politics of Urban Land in Zambia." *Cities* 11,5 (1994).

Nkomo, Mokubung O. "A Comparative Study of Zambia and Mozambique: Africanization, Professionalization, and Bureaucracy in the African, Postcolonial State." *Journal of Black Studies* 16 (1986).

Ohadike, Patrick O. "Counting Heads in Africa: The Experience of Zambia, 1963 and 1969." *Journal of Administration Overseas* 9 (1970).

Rakodi, Carole. "The Local State and Urban Local Government in Zambia." *Public Administration and Development* 8 (1988).

Schaffer, Bernard, ed. *Administrative Training and Development: A Comparative Study of East Africa, Zambia, Pakistan, and India.* New York: Praeger, 1974.

Taylor, P. L. "Local Government Training in Zambia." *Journal of Local Administration Overseas* 5 (1966).

Tordoff, William. "Provincial and District Government in Zambia." *Journal of Administration Overseas* 8 (1968).

———. "The Administration of Development in Zambia." In *Collected Seminar Papers on Bureaucratic Change in New States.* London: University of London, Institute of Commonwealth Studies, 1971.

———. "Provincial and Local Government in Zambia." *Journal of Administration Overseas* 9 (1970).

———, ed. *Administration in Zambia.* Manchester: Manchester University Press, 1980.

Tordoff, William, and Ralph A. Young. "Decentralization and Public Sector Reform in Zambia." *Journal of Southern African Studies* 20 (1994).

Wood, G. "Administrative Training in Zambia." In *Administrative Training and Development: A Comparative Study of East Africa, Zambia, Pakistan, and India,* ed. Bernard Schaffer. New York: Praeger, 1974.

5.a.iii. Political. Constitution, Law, and Government. Other

Apthorpe, Raymond, ed. *From Tribal Rule to Modern Government.* Lusaka: Rhodes-Livingstone Institute, 1959.

Baxter, G. H., and P. W. Jodgens. "The Constitutional Status of the Federation of Rhodesia and Nyasaland." *International Affairs* (October 1957).

Baylies, Carolyn. "The State and Class Formation in Zambia." Ph.D. diss., University of Wisconsin-Madison, 1978.

———. "The State and the Growth of Indigenous Capital: Zambia's Economic Reforms and Their Aftermath." In *The Evolving Structure of Zambian Society,* ed. Robin Fincham and John. Edinburgh: University of Edinburgh, Centre of African Studies, 1980.

Baylies, Carolyn, and Morris Szeftel. "The Rise of a Zambian Capitalist Class in the 1970s." *Journal of Southern African Studies* 8 (1982).

Caplan, G. L. "Barotseland: The Secessionist Challenge to Zambia." *Journal of Modern African Studies* 6 (1968).

————. *The Elites of Barotseland, 1878–1969: A Political History of Zambia's Western Province.* Berkeley: University of California Press, 1970.

Chitoshi, C. M. "The Role of the Local Government Association of Zambia." *Planning and Administration* 14 (1987).

Clay, Gervas. "African Urban Advisory Councils in the Northern Rhodesia Copperbelt." *Journal of African Administration* 1 (1949).

Cliffe, Lionel. "Labour Migration and Peasant Differentiation: Zambian Experiences." In *Development in Zambia: A Reader*, ed. Ben Turok. London: Zed, 1979.

Cross, Sholto. "Politics and Criticism in Zambia." *Journal of Southern African Studies* 1 (1974).

Davidson, J. W. *The Northern Rhodesian Legislative Council.* London: Faber and Faber, 1948.

Gregor, Gordon. "Sea Cadets of Land-Locked Zambia." *Horizon* 9 (1967).

Gupta, Anirudha. "The Zambian National Assembly: Study of the African Legislature." *Parliamentary Affairs* 19 (1965–66).

Heatha, F. M. N. "The Growth of African Councils on the Copperbelt of Northern Rhodesia." *Journal of African Administration* 5 (1953).

Molteno, Robert. *The Zambian Community and Its Government.* Lusaka: NECZAM, 1974.

Moore, Robert C. *The Political Reality of Freedom of the Press in Zambia.* Lanham, Md.: University Press of America, ca. 1992.

Mudenda, G. "Class Formation and Class Struggle in Contemporary Zambia." In *Proletarianization and Class Struggle in Africa*, ed. Bernard Magubane and Nzongola-Ntalaja. San Francisco: Synthesis, 1983.

Parpart, Jane, and Timothy Shaw. "Contradictions and Coalition: Class Fractions in Zambia, 1964 to 1984." *Africa Today* 30 (1983).

Peaslee, Amos J. "Constitution of Zambia." *Constitution of Nations, I: Africa.* The Hague: Martinus Nijhoff, 1965.

Rakudi, Carole. "The Local State and Urban Local Government in Zambia." *Public Administration and Development* 8 (1988).

Scarritt, James. "The Analysis of Social Class, Political Participation, and Public Policy in Zambia." *Africa Today* 30 (1983).

Shaw, Timothy. "The Political Economy of Zambia." *Current History* (March 1980).

Silverman, Philip. "Local Elites and the Image of a Nation: The Incorporation of Barotseland within Zambia." Ph. D. diss., Cornell University, 1968.

Southall, Tony. "Zambia: Class Formation and Government Policy in the 1970s." *Journal of Southern African Studies* 7 (1980).

Szeftel, Morris. "Conflict, Spoils, and Class Formation in Zambia." Ph.D. diss., Manchester University, 1978.

Tordoff, William, and Robert Molteno. "Parliament." In *Politics in Zambia*, ed. William Tordoff. Berkeley: University of California Press, 1974.

5.b. Political. Humanism

Kandeke, Timothy. *Fundamentals of Zambian Humanism*. Lusaka: NEC-ZAM, 1981.

Kaunda, Kenneth. *A Humanist in Africa: Letters to Colin Morris from Kenneth Kaunda, President of Zambia*. London: Longmans, 1966.

———. *A Guide to the Implementation of Humanism*. Lusaka: Government Printer, 1967.

———. *Humanism in Zambia*. Lusaka: Government Printer, 1967.

———. *Humanism in Zambia and a Guide to Its Implementation*. Lusaka: Government Printer, 1968.

———. "Ideology and Humanism." *Pan-Africa Journal* 1 (1968).

———. *Ten Thoughts on Humanism*. Kitwe: Veritas, 1970.

Lacy, Creighton. "Christian Humanism in Zambia." *Christian Century*, February 16, 1972.

Meebelo, Henry S. "The Concept of Man-Centeredness in Zambian Humanism." *African Review* 3 (1973).

———. *Main Currents of Zambian Humanist Thought*. New York: Oxford University Press, 1973.

Molteno, Robert. "Zambian Humanism: The Way Ahead." *African Review* 3 (1973).

Soremekun, F. "The Challenge of Nation-Building: Neo-Humanism and Politics in Zambia, 1967–1969." *Geneve-Afrique* 9 (1970).

———. "Kenneth Kaunda's Cosmic Humanism." *Geneve-Afrique* 9 (1970).

———. "Zambia's Cultural Revolution." *East Africa Journal* 7 (Nairobi) (1970).

Zambia, Republic of. "Humanism and Our Foreign Policy." In *Humanism Radio Commentaries*, nos. 1–42. Lusaka: Ministry of Development Planning and National Guidance, 1972.

Zulu, J. B. *Zambian Humanism*. Lusaka: NECZAM, 1970.

5.c. Political. Politics and Political Parties

Billing, M. G. "Tribal Rule and Modern Politics in Northern Rhodesia." *African Affairs* 58 (1969).

Bjornlund, Eric, Michael Bratton, and Clark Gibson. "Observing Multiparty Elections in Africa: Lessons from Zambia." *African Affairs* 91 (1992).

Bratton, Michael. *The Local Politics of Rural Development: Peasant and Party-State in Zambia*. Hanover: University Press of New England, 1980.

———. "Zambia Starts Over." *Journal of Democracy* 3 (1992).

Bratton, Michael, and Beatrice Liatto-Katunda. "A Focus Group Assessment of Political Attitudes in Zambia." *African Affairs* 93 (1994).

Burnell, Peter. "Zambia at the Crossroads." *World Affairs* 157 (1994).

Chan, Stephan. "Zambia's Foreign Policy—Elitism and Power." *Round Table* 302 (1987).

Chaput, Michael, ed. *Patterns of Elite Formation and Distribution in Kenya, Senegal, Tanzania, and Zambia.* Syracuse: Syracuse University, Program of East African Studies, 1968.

Chikulo, Bornwell C. "The Impact of Elections in Zambia's One-Party Second Republic." *Africa Today* 35 (1988).

Donge, Jan Kees van. "An Episode from the Independence Struggle in Zambia: A Case Study from Mwase Lundazi." *African Affairs* 84 (1985).

Geisler, Gisela. "Sisters under the Skin: Women and the Women's League in Zambia." *Journal of Modern Africa* 25 (1987).

———. "Troubled Sisterhood: Women and Politics in Southern Africa: Case Studies from Zambia, Zimbabwe, and Botswana." *African Affairs* 94 (1995).

Gertzel, Cherry, et al. "Zambia's Final Experience of Inter-Party Elections: The By-Elections of December 1971." *Kronick van Afrika* 12 (1972).

Gertzel, Cherry, ed. *The Dynamics of the One-Party State in Zambia.* Manchester: Manchester University Press, 1984.

Good, Kenneth. "Zambia and the Liberation of South Africa." *Journal of Modern African Studies* 25 (1987).

Hall, Richard. "Zambia's Search for Political Stability." *World Today* 25 (1969).

Hamalengwa, Munyonzwe. *Class Struggles in Zambia, 1889–1989, and the Fall of Kenneth Kaunda, 1990–1991.* Lanham, Md.: University Press of America, 1992.

Harries-Jones, Peter. *Freedom and Labour: Mobilization and Political Control on the Zambian Copperbelt.* New York: Schocken, 1975.

Mijere, Nsolo. "The State and Development: A Study of the Dominance of the Political Class in Zambia." *Africa Today* 35 (1988).

Molteno, R. V. "Zambia and the One-Party State." *East Africa Journal* 9 (1972).

Momba, Jotham C. "The State, Rural Class Formation, and Peasant Participation in Zambia: The Case of Southern Province." *African Affairs* 88 (1989).

Mtshali, B. Vulindlela. "South Africa and Zambia's 1968 Election." *Kronick van Afrika* 2 (1970).

Mufune, Pempelani. "The Formation of Dominant Classes in Zambia: Critical Notes." *Africa Today* 35 (1988).

Ollawa, Patrick. *Participatory Democracy in Zambia: Political Economy of*

National Development. Elms Court, Ilfracombe, Devon, UK: Stockwell, 1979.

Panter-Brick, Keith. "Prospects for Democracy in Zambia." *Government and Opposition* 29 (1994).

"Party Merger in Zambia." *Afriscope* 3 (Lagos) (1973).

Pettman, Jan. "Zambia's Second Republic—the Establishment of a One-Party State." *Journal of Modern African Studies* 12 (1974).

Phiri, Bizeck Jube. "Zambia: The Myth and Realities of One-Party Participatory Democracy." *Geneve-Afrique* 29 (1991).

Rasmussen, Thomas. "Political Competition and One-Party Dominance in Zambia." *Journal of Modern African Studies* 7 (1969).

Scarritt, J. R. "Adoption of Political Styles by African Politicians in the Rhodesias." *Midwest Journal of Political Science* 10 (1966).

———. "Political Values and the Political Process in Zambia." *Bulletin of the Institute for Social Research, University of Zambia* 1 (1966).

———. "The Zambian Election—Triumph or Tragedy?" *Africa Today* 16 (1969).

———. Elite Values, Ideology, and Power in Post-Independence Zambia." *African Studies Review* 14 (1971).

———. "President Kenneth Kaunda's Annual Address to the Zambian National Assembly: A Contextual Content Analysis of Changing Rhetoric, 1965–83." *Journal of Modern African Studies* 25 (1987).

Scott, Ian. "Political Money and Party Organisation in Zambia." *Journal of Modern African Studies* 20 (1982).

Scott, Ian, and R. V. Molteno. "The Zambian General Elections." *Africa Report* 14 (1969).

Segal, Ronald. *Political Africa: A Who's Who of Personalities and Parties.* New York: Praeger, 1961.

Shafer, D. Michael. "Sectors, States, and Social Forces: Korea and Zambia Confront Economic Restructuring." *Comparative Politics* 22 (1990).

Sichone, Owen B. "One-Party Participatory Democracy and Socialist Orientation: The Depoliticization of the Masses in Post-Colonial Zambia." In *Democracy and the One-Party State in Africa,* ed. Peter Meyns and Dani Wadada Nabudere. Hamburg: Institut fur Afrika-Kunde, 1989.

Silverman, Philip. "National Commitment among Local Elites in Western Zambia." *Journal of Modern African Studies* 22 (1984).

Szeftel, Morris. "Political Graft and the Spoils System in Zambia: The State as a Resource in Itself." *Review of African Political Economy* 24 (1982).

Tordoff, William. "Political Crisis in Zambia." *Africa Quarterly* 10 (1970).

Tordoff, William, and Ian Scott. "Political Parties: Structures and Policies." In *Politics in Zambia,* ed. William Tordoff. Berkeley: University of California Press, 1974.

Woldring, Klaas. "Corruption and Inefficiency in Zambia: Recent Inquiries and Their Results." *Africa Today* 30 (1983).

Young, H. A. "The 1968 General Elections." In *Zambia in Maps*, ed D. H. Davies. London: University of London Press, 1971.

Zambia, Republic of. *Report of the National Commission on the Establishment of a One-Party Participatory Democracy in Zambia.* Lusaka: Government Printer, 1972.

———. *The Constitution of the United National Independence Party.* Lusaka: Government Printer, 1973.

———. *UNIP National Policies for the Next Decade, 1974–1984.* Lusaka: Zambia Information Service, 1974.

5.d. Political. Race Relations

Berger, Elena L. *Labor, Race, and Colonial Rule: The Copperbelt from 1924 to Independence.* Oxford: Clarendon, 1974.

Burawoy, Michael. *The Colour of Class on the Copper Mines.* Lusaka: University of Zambia, Institute for African Studies, 1972.

Clegg, E. *Race and Politics: Partnership in the Federation of Rhodesia and Nyasaland.* London: Oxford University Press, 1960.

Dotson, F., and L. O. *The Indian Minority of Zambia, Rhodesia, and Malawi.* New Haven: Yale University Press, 1968.

Franck, T. M. *Race and Nationalism: The Struggle for Power in Rhodesia-Nyasaland.* London: Allen and Unwin, 1960.

Gray, J. R. *The Two Nations: Aspects of the Development of Race Relations in the Rhodesias and Nyasaland.* London: Oxford University Press, 1960.

Matejko, Alexander. "Blacks and Whites in Zambia." *Ethnicity* 3, 4 (1976).

Mhango, Mkwapatira. "Zambia: Asian Shops Returned." *New African* (London) (October 1988).

Rotberg, Robert I. "Race, Relations, and Politics in Colonial Zambia: The Elwell Incident." *Race* 7 (1965).

5.e. Political. Foreign Affairs

Anglin, D. G. "Confrontation in Southern Africa: Zambia and Portugal." *International Journal* 25 (1970).

———. "Zambia and the Recognition of Biafra." *African Review* 1 (1971).

———. "The Politics of Transit Routes in Land-Locked Southern Africa." In *Land-Locked Countries of Africa*, ed. Z. Cervenka. Uppsala: Scandinavian Institute of African Studies, 1973.

———. "Reorientation of Zambia's External Relations-Disengagement from Southern Africa and Integration with East Africa: A Transaction Analysis." In *Cooperation and Conflict in Southern Africa: Papers on a*

Regional Subsystem, ed. T. M. Shaw and K. A. Heard. Washington, D.C.: University Press of America, 1977.

————. "Zambia and Southern African 'Detente.' " *International Journal* 30 (1975).

————. "Zambia and the Southern African Liberation Movements." In *Politics of Africa: Dependence and Development*, ed. T. M. Shaw and K. A. Heard. New York: Africana Publishing for Dalhousie University Press, 1979.

————. "Zambian versus Malawian Approaches to Political Change in Southern Africa." In *Profiles of Self-Determination*, ed. David S. Chanaiwa. Northridge: California State University Foundation, 1976.

Anglin, D. G., and Timothy Shaw. *Zambia's Foreign Policy: Studies in Diplomacy and Dependence*. Boulder, Colo.: Westview, 1979.

Ballance, F. *Zambia and the East African Community*. Syracuse: Syracuse University Program of Eastern African Studies. 1971.

Bone, Marion. "The Foreign Policy of Zambia." In *The Other Powers: Studies in the Foreign Policies of Small States*, ed. Ronald P. Barston. New York: Barnes and Noble, 1973.

Burdette, Marcia. "The Mines, Class Power, and Foreign Policy in Zambia." *Journal of Southern African Studies* 10 (1984).

Caplan, G. L. "Zambia, Barotseland, and the Liberation of Southern Africa." *Africa Today* 15 (1969).

Chan, Stephen. *Kaunda and Southern Africa: Image and Reality in Foreign Policy*. New York: St. Martin's, 1992.

Cliffe, Lionel. "Zambia in the Context of Southern Africa." In *The Evolving Structure of Zambian Society*, ed. Robin Fincham and John Markakis. Edinburgh: University of Edinburgh, Centre of African Studies, 1980.

Delius, Anthony. "Africa's Guerrillas Extend Their Fight." *Reporter*, October 5, 1967.

Eriksen, Karen. "Zambia: Class Formation and Detente." *Review of African Political Economy* 9 (1978).

Grundy, Kenneth. "Host Countries and the Southern African Liberation Struggle." *Africa Quarterly* 10 (1970).

————. *Confrontation and Accommodation in Southern Africa: The Limits of Independence*. Berkeley: University of California Press, 1973.

Hall, R. *The High Price of Principles: Kaunda and the White South*. London: Hodder and Stoughton, 1969.

Hanlon, Joseph. *Beggar Your Neighbours: Apartheid Power in Southern Africa*. London: Currey, 1986.

Hill, C. R. "The Botswana-Zambia Boundary Question: A Note of Warning." *Round Table* 252 (1973).

Levin, Nora. "Cooperation Brings a Grassroots Revolution." *Africa Report* 17 (1972).

Martin, Anthony. *Minding Their Own Business: Zambia's Struggle against Western Control.* London: Hutchinson, 1972.

Martin, David, and Phyllis Johnson. *The Chitepo Assassinations.* Harare: Zimbabwe Publishing, 1985.

McKay, V. P. "The Propaganda Battle for Zambia." *Africa Today* 18 (1971).

Molteno, R. V. *Africa and South Africa—The Implications of South Africa's "Outward-Looking" Policy.* London: Africa Bureau, 1971.

———. "South Africa's Forward Policy in Africa." *Round Table* 243 (1971).

Mtshalia, B. Vulindlela. "Zambia's Foreign Policy." *Current History* 58 (1970).

———. "Zambia's Foreign Policy Problems" *African Social Research* 11 (1971)

———. "Zambia and the White South," In *Land-Locked Countries of South Africa*, ed. Cervenka Zdenek. Uppsala: Scandinavian Institute of African Studies, 1973.

Mujaya, M. S. "Zambia's Foreign Policy: A Study." Political Science Paper no. 7. Dar es Salaam: University of Dar es Salaam, 1970.

Mwaanga, Vernon. "Zambia's Policy toward Southern Africa."In *Southern Africa in Perspective Essays in Regional Politics*, ed. C. P. Potholm and R. Dale. New York: Free Press, 1972.

———. "U. S.-African Relations: The View from Zambia." *Africa Report* 19 (1974).

———. "Zambia's Foreign Policy: To Play a Full Part in the Affairs of the Human Family." *Enterprise* 3 (1974).

Nolutshungu, Sam C. *South Africa in Africa: A Study of Ideology and Foreign Policy.* New York: Africana, 1975.

Oudes, Bruce. "Kaunda's Diplomatic Offensive." *Africa Report* 20 (1975).

Pettmann, Jan. *Zambia: Security and Conflict.* New York: St. Martin's, 1974.

Shamuyarira, Nathan M. "The Lusaka Manifesto." *East Africa Journal* (November 1969).

Shaw, Timothy. "Southern Africa: Cooperation and Conflict in an International Sub-System." *Journal of Modern African Studies* 12 (1974).

———. "Regional Cooperation and Conflict in Africa." *International Journal* 30 (1975).

———. *Dependence and Underdevelopment: The Development and Foreign Policies of Zambia.* Athens: Ohio University, Center for International Studies, 1976.

———. "The Foreign Policy of Zambia." *Journal of Modern African Studies* 14 (1976).

———. "The Foreign Policy System of Zambia." *African Studies Review* 19 (1976).

Stockwell, John. *In Search of Enemies.* New York: Norton, 1978.

Thompson, Carol B. *Challenge to Imperialism: The Frontline States in the Liberation of Zimbabwe.* Boulder, Colo.: Westview, 1986.

Tostensen, Arne. *Dependence and Collective Self-Reliance in Southern Africa: The Case of SADCC.* Research Report no. 62. Uppsala: Scandinavian Institute of African Studies, 1982.

Zambia and the World: Essays on Problems Relating to Zambia's Foreign Policy. Lusaka: University of Zambia, Faculty of Humanities and Social Studies, 1970.

Zimba, B. H. "Zambian Policy towards Zaire, 1974–78." M.A. thesis, Carleton University, 1979.

6. Scientific

6.a. Scientific. Geography

Bond, G. "The Origin of the Victoria Falls." In *The Victoria Falls: A Handbook to the Victoria Falls, the Batoka Gorges and Part of the Upper Zambezi Valley,* ed Brian M. Fagan. Livingstone: Livingstone Commission for the Preservation of Natural and Historical Monuments and Relics, 1964.

Bradshaw, Benjamin F. "Notes on the Chobe River, South Central Africa." *Proceedings of the Royal Geographical Society* 3 (1881).

Lawton, R. M. "A Study of the Dynamic Ecology of Zambian Vegetation." *Journal of Ecology* 66 (1978).

MacDonald, John F. *Zambesi River.* London: Macmillan, 1955.

Malaisse, F. "L'homme dans la forêt claire zambezienne: contribution à l'étude de l'ecosysteme forêt claire (Miombo)." *African Economic History* 7 (1979).

William, Geoffrey J., ed. *Lusaka and Its Environs: A Geographical Study of a Planned Capital City in Tropical Africa.* Lusaka: Zambia Geographical Asociation, Handbook Series, no. 9, 1986.

6.b. Scientific. Geology

Cahen, L., and J. Lepersonne. "Equivalence entre le systeme du Kalahari du Congo Belge et les Kalahari beds d'Afrique australe." *Mem. Soc. Belge Geol.* 8 (1952).

Dixey, F. "The Geology of the Upper Zambezi Valley." In *The Stone Age Cultures of Northern Rhodesia,* ed. Clark J. Desmond. Cape Town: South African Archaeological Society, 1950.

Gair, H. S. *The Karroo System and Coal Resources of the Gwembe District, North-East Section.* Lusaka: Government Printer, 1959.

Garlick, W. G. "Geomorphology." In *The Geology of the Northern Rhodesian Copperbelt,* ed. F. Mendelsohn. London: Macdonald, 1961.

———. "The Sygnetic Theory." In *The Geology of the Northern Rhodesian Copperbelt*, ed. F. Mendelsohn. London: Macdonald, 1961.

Hutchon, Brian. *The Geology of the Kariba Area*. Report no. 3. Lusaka: Geological Survey Department, 1958.

Mendelsohn, F., ed. *The Geology of the Northern Rhodesian Copperbelt*. London: Macdonald, 1961.

Pelletier, R. A. *Mineral Resources of South-Central Africa*. Cape Town: Oxford University Press, 1964.

Phillips, K. A. *The Geology and Metalliferous Deposits of the Luiri Hill Area (Mumbwa District): Explanation of Degree Sheet 1527, N.W. Quarter*. Report no. 4. Lusaka: Northern Rhodesia, Department of Geological Survey, 1958.

Reeve, W. H. *The Geology and Mineral Resources of Northern Rhodesia*. Vol. 1. Lusaka: Government Printer, 1963.

Taverner-Smith, R. *The Karroo System and Coal Resources of the Gwembe District, South-West Section*. Lusaka: Government Printer, 1960.

6.c. Scientific. Medicine

Agbabiaka, T. "Campaign of Hope?" *African Concord* 169 (London) (1987).

Brooks, Elizabeth. "The Population Dilemma: 'A People's World or a World of People.'" *Zango: Zambian Journal of Contemporary Issues* 6 (1979).

Dillon-Malone, Clive. "Mutumwa Nchimi Healers and Wizardry Beliefs in Zambia." *Social Science and Medicine* 26 (1988).

Doell, E. W. *Hospital in the Bush*. London: Johnson, 1957.

Freund, Paul J. "Health Care in a Declining Economy: The Case of Zambia." *Social Science and Medicine* 23 (1986).

———. "Information for Health Development." *World Health Forum* 7 (Geneva) (1986).

Friend, Paul J., and Katele Kalumba. *UNICEF/GRZ Monitoring and Evaluation Study of Child Health and Nutrition in Western and Northern Provinces, Zambia*. Lusaka: University of Zambia, Institute for African Studies, 1984.

Gelfand, M. *Northern Rhodesia in the Days of the Charter: A Medical and Social Study, 1878–1924*. Oxford: Blackwell, 1961.

Geloo, Zarina. "HIV Positive, Abortion Negative: New Group Campaigns for Mothers' Right to Choose." *Africa South* (Harare) (May 1991).

Griffith, P. G. "Leprosy in Northern Rhodesia." *Science and Medicine in Central Africa*. London: Pergamon, 1965.

Haworth, A., M. Mwanalushi, and D. M. Todd. *Community Response to Alcohol-Related Problems in Zambia*. Vol. 1. *Historical and Background In-*

formation. Lusaka: University of Zambia, Institute for African Studies, 1981.

———. "Acting in Good Time against the Drug Menace." *World Health Forum* 9 (1988).

Hira, Subhash K. "Sexually Transmitted Disease: A Menace to Mothers and Children." *World Health Forum* 7 (1986).

Howe, J. "AIDS: A Poor Prognosis." *Africa Health* 9 (December–January 1987).

Inambao, A. W., E. L. Makubalo, and F. K. Wurapa. "Revitalizing Primary Health Care." *World Health Forum* 8 (1987).

Kapilikisha, Mutale. "AIDS: 'Zambians Seem to be Getting the Message.'" *New African* (London) (January 1990).

Kauppinen, M. *National Nutrition Surveillance Programme: Annual Report*. Lusaka: Ministry of Health, 1985.

Leeson, Joyce. "Traditional Medicines: Still Plenty to Offer." *Africa Report* 15 (October 1970).

Massam, B. H., et al. "Applying Operations Research to Health Planning: Locating Health Centres in Zambia." *Health Policy and Planning* 1 (Oxford) (1986).

Morna, Colleen Lowe. "Zambia: AIDS Programme with a Human Face." *New African* (March 1989).

Mouli, V. Chandra. *All against AIDS: The Copperbelt Health Education Project, Zambia*. London: Action Aid, 1992.

Musambachime, Mwelwa C. "The Social and Economic Effects of Sleeping Sickness in Mweru-Luapula, 1906–1922." *African Economic History* 10 (1981).

———. "Impact of Cattle Diseases on the Cattle Industry in Colonial Zambia." Seminar Paper. University of Zambia, History Department, 1988.

Mwansa, Lengwe Katembula. "Rural-Urban Health Care Service Imbalances in Zambia: Forces and Outcomes." *Journal of Social Development in Africa* 4 (1989).

Pagni, Lucien. "Education and Health." *Courier* 121 (1990).

Phillips, C. M. "Problems of Blindness in Northern Rhodesia." In *Science and Medicine in Central Africa*. London: Pergamon, 1965.

Pollock, Norman H., Jr. *The Struggle against Sleeping Sickness in Nyasaland and Northern Rhodesia, 1900–1922*. Athens: Ohio University, Center for International Studies, 1969.

Sabatier, Renee. *AIDS and the Third World*. Alexandria, Va.: Panos Institute, 1986.

Serpell, Robert. *Mobilizing Local Resources in Africa for Persons with Learning Difficulties or Mental Handicaps*. Oslo: Norwegian Association for the Mentally Retarded, 1983.

———. "Social and Psychological Constructs in Health Records: The

Need for Adaptation to Different Sociocultural Environments." In *Psychosocial Factors Affecting Health*, ed. M. Lipkin and K. Kupka. New York: Praeger, 1983.

————. "Childhood Disability in Sociocultural Context: Assessment and Information Needs for Effective Services." In *Health and Cross-Cultural Psychology: Towards Applications*, ed. P. R. Dasen, J. W. Berry, and N. Sartorius. Newbury Park, Calif.: Sage, 1988.

Serpell, Robert, D. Nabuzoka, S. Ng'andu, and I. M. Sinyangwe. "The Development of a Community-Based Strategy for the Habilitation of Disabled Children in Zambia: A Case of Action-Oriented Health Systems Research." *Disabilities and Impairments* 2 (1988).

Siandwazi, Catherine. *Household Food Security and Nutrition in Zambia*. Lusaka: University of Zambia, Institute for African Studies, 1992.

Smith, V. X. "Excessive Drinking and Alcoholism in the Republic of Zambia." M.A. thesis, Howard University, 1973.

Swab, Janice Coffey. "Food and Health: The Zambian Experience." *Africa Today* 40 (1993).

Turner, V. W. *Lunda Medicine and the Treatment of Diseases*. Occasional Paper no. 15. Livingstone: Rhodes-Livingstone Museum, 1964.

————. "A Ndembu Doctor in Practice." In *Magic, Faith, and Healing*, ed. Ari Kiev. Glencoe, Ill.: Free Press, 1964.

Twumasi, Patrick A., and Paul J. Freund. "Local Politicization of Primary Health Care as an Instrument for Development: A Case Study of Community Health Workers in Zambia. *Social Science and Medicine* 20 (1985).

Webster, M. H. "Medical Aspects of the Kariba Hydro-Electric Scheme." In *Man-Made Lakes and Human Health*, ed. N. F. Stanley and M. P. Alpers. New York: Academic, 1975.

Williams, Glen. *From Fear to Hope: AIDS Care and Prevention at Chikankata Hospital*. London: Action Aid, 1990.

"Zambia: AIDS Alert." *Africa Research Bulletin: Political, Social and Cultural Studies* 23 (Crediton, Devon) (1986).

Zambia, Republic of, and UNICEF. *Situation Analysis of Children and Women in Zambia*. Lusaka: UNICEF, 1986.

6.d. Scientific. Natural Science and Zoology

Ansell, W. F. H. *The Mammals of Northern Rhodesia*. Lusaka: Government Printer, 1960.

Banage, W. S. "Wild Life Conservation and Its Problems in Zambia." In *Proceedings of the National Seminar on Environment and Development*. Occasional Study no. 10. Lusaka: Zambia Geographical Association, 1979.

Cohn, Roger. "Zambia: The People's War on Poaching." *Audubon* 96 (1994).

Fairweather, W. G. *Northern Rhodesia: Meterological Report and Statistical Survey.* London: Waterlow, 1925.

Fanshawe, D. B. *Fifty Common Trees of Northern Rhodesia.* Lusaka: Government Printer, 1962.

Ford, John. *The Role of Trypanosomiasis in African Ecology.* Oxford: Clarendon, 1971.

Gibson, Clark C. "Transforming Rural Hunters into Conservationists: An Assessment of Community-Based Wildlife Management Programs in Africa." *World Development* 23 (1995).

Horscroft, F. D. M. "Vegetation." In *The Geology of the Northern Rhodesian Copperbelt,* ed. F. Mendelsohn. London: Macdonald, 1961.

Jackson, P. B. N. *Fishes of Northern Rhodesia.* Lusaka: Government Printer, 1961.

Lagus, Charles. *Operation Noah.* London: Kimber, 1960.

Marks, Stuart A. *The Imperial Lion: Human Dimensions of Wildlife Management in Central Africa.* Boulder, Colo.: Westview, 1984.

Mathessen, Peter, and Bob Doutwaite. "The Impact of Tsetse Fly Control Campaigns on African Wildlife." *Oryx* 4 (1985).

Owens, Mark. "Two against the Odds: Our Fight to Save Zambia's Elephants." *International Wildlife* 22 (1992).

Trapnell, C. G., J. D. Martin, and W. Allan. *Vegetation-Soil Map of Northern Rhodesia.* Lusaka: Government Printer, 1947.

Trapnell, C. G., and I. Langdale-Brown. "The Natural Vegetation of East Africa." In *The Natural Resources of East Africa,* ed. E. W. Russell. Nairobi: East African I Bureau, 1962.

7. Social

7.a.i. Social. Anthropology and Sociology. General

Ashbaugh, Leslie, "The Great East Road: Gender, Generation, and Rural-to-Urban Migration in the Eastern Province of Zambia." Ph.D. diss., Northwestern University, 1996.

Barnes, J. A. "The Material Culture of the Fort Jameson Ngoni." Occasional Papers no. 1. Livingstone: Rhodes-Livingstone Museum, 1948.

———. "Some Aspects of Political Development among the Fort Jameson Ngoni." *African Studies* 7 (1948).

———. "Measures of Divorce Frequency in Simple Societies." *Journal of the Royal Anthropological Institute* 79 (1949).

———. *Marriage in a Changing Society.* Paper no. 20. Livingstone: Rhodes-Livingstone Institute, 1951.

———. "The Perception of History in a Plural Society: A Study of an Ngoni Group in Northern Rhodesia." *Human Relations* 4 (1951).

Bates, Robert H. *A Study of Village Zambia*. New Haven: Yale University Press, 1976.

Brooks, Elizabeth. "Social Work Intervention: A Search for Relevance in the Zambian Context." Ph.D. diss., University of Zambia, 1980.

Brown, Richard. "Anthropology and Colonial Rule: Godfrey Wilson and the Rhodes-Livingstone Institute." In *Anthropology and the Colonial Encounter*, ed. Talal Asad. London: Ithaca, 1973.

———. "Passages in the Life of a White Anthropologist: M. H. Gluckman in Northern Rhodesia." *Journal of African History* 20 (1979).

Colson, Elizabeth. *Social Consequences of Resettlement*. Atlantic Highlands, N.J.: Humanities, 1971.

———. "Max Gluckman and the Study of Divorce." In *Cross-examination: Essays in Memory of Max Gluckman*, ed. Peter H. Gulliver. Leiden: Brill, 1978.

Dahlschen, Edith. *Children in Zambia*. Lusaka: National Educational Company of Zambia, 1972.

Epstein, A. L. "Divorce, Law, and Stability of Marriage among the Lunda of Kazembe." *Rhodes-Livingstone Journal* 14 (1954).

Ferguson, James. "Mobile Workers, Modernist Narratives: A Critique of the Historiography of Transition on the Zambian Copperbelt." *Journal of Southern African Studies* 16 (1990).

———. "The Country and the City on the Copperbelt." *Cultural Anthropology* 7 (1992).

Geisler, Gisela. "Sisters under the Skin: Women and the Women's League in Zambia." *Journal of Modern African Studies* 25 (1987).

Geisler, Gisela, and Karen Tranberg Hansen. "Structural Adjustment, the Rural-Urban Interface, and Gender Relations in Zambia." In *Women in the Age of Economic Transformation: Gender Impacts of Reform in Post-Socialist and Developing Countries*, ed. Steven Pressman, Nahid Aslanbeigui, and Gale Summerfield. London: Routledge, 1994.

Gluckman, Max. "Kinship and Marriage among the Lozi of Northern Rhodesia and the Zulu in Natal." In *African Systems of Kinship and Marriage*, ed. A. R. Radcliffe-Brown and C. D. Forde. London: Oxford University Press, 1950.

Hall, Barbara, ed. *Tell Me, Josephine*. New York: Simon and Schuster, 1964.

Hicks, R. E. "Similarities and Differences in Occupational Prestige Ratings: A Comparative Study of Two Cultural Groups in Zambia." *African Social Research* 3.

Kapferer, Bruce. *Co-operation Leadership and Village Structure*. Manchester: University of Zambia, Institute for Social Research, 1967.

Kay, G. *Social Aspects of Village Regrouping in Zambia*. Hull: University of Hull, 1967.

Lancaster, Chet. "Battle of the Sexes in Zambia: A Reply to Karla Poewe." *American Anthropologist* 81 (1979).

Long, N. *Social Change and the Individual: A Study of the Social and Religious Responses to Innovation in a Zambian Rural Community.* Manchester: Manchester University Press, 1968.

Mahdi, A. A. *Rape and Attempted Rape in Zambia: A Study of Statistical Trends in the Copperbelt Province of Zambia, 1970–1989.* Lusaka: Institute of Human Relations, 1992.

Mitchell, J. Clyde. *The Kalela Dance.* Manchester: Manchester University Press, 1956.

———. "Aspects of African Marriage on the Copperbelt of Northern Rhodesia." *Rhodes-Livingstone Journal* 22 (1957).

Mlenga, Kelvin. "The Role of Youth in Zambia's Changing Society." *Horizon* 10 (1968).

Musambachime, Mwelwa C. "The University of Zambia's Institute for African Studies and Social Science Research in Central Africa, 1938–1988." *History in Africa* 20 (1993).

Ohadike, Patrick O. "Aspects of Domesticity and Family Relationship: A Survey Study of the Family Household in Zambia." *Journal of Asian and African Studies* 6 (1971).

Phillips, Arthur, ed. "Marriage Laws in Africa." *Survey of African Marriage and Social Change.* London: Oxford University Press, 1953.

Phiri, Elizabeth C. *Violence Against Women in Zambia.* Lusaka: Young Women's Christian Association Council of Zambia, 1993.

Poewe, Karla. "Women, Horticulture, and Society in Sub-Saharan Africa: Some Comments." *American Anthropologist* 81 (1979).

Powdermaker, Hortense. "Communication and Social Change Based on a Field Study in Northern Rhodesia." *Transactions of the New York Academy of Sciences,* ser. 2, 17 (1955).

———. "Social Change through Imagery and Values of Teen-Age Africans in Northern Rhodesia." *American Anthropologist* 58 (1956).

Rennie, J. Keith, and C. E. Robbins, eds. *Social Problems in Zambia.* Lusaka: University of Zambia, School of Humanities and Social Sciences, Committee on Student Publications, 1976.

Richards, Audrey I. *Bemba Marriage and Present Economic Conditions.* Paper no. 4. Livingstone: Rhodes-Livingstone Institute, 1940.

———. "Variations in Family Structure among the Central Bantu." In *African Systems of Kinship and Marriage,* ed. A. R. Radcliffe-Brown and C. D. Forde. London: Oxford University Press, 1950.

Ritchie, J. F. *The African as Suckling and as Adult.* Paper no. 9. Livingstone: Rhodes-Livingstone Institute, 1943.

E. L. Deregowska, comp. *Some Aspects of Social Change in Africa South of the Sahara, 1959–1966.* Lusaka: University of Zambia, Institute for Social Research, 1966.

Van Binsbergen, Wim M. J. "Occam, Francis Bacon, and the Transformation of Zambian Society." *Cultures et developpement* 9 (1977).

Van Donge, Jan Kees. "Understanding Rural Zambia Today: The Relevance of the Rhodes-Livingstone Institute." *Africa* 55 (1985).

Werbner, Richard P. "The Manchester School in South-Central Africa." *Annual Review of Anthropology* 13 (1984).

Wilson, Godfrey, and Monica Wilson. *Analysis of Social Change, Based on Observations in Central Africa.* Cambridge: Cambridge University Press, 1954.

7.a.ii. Social. Anthropology and Sociology. Rural

Apthorpe, Raymond. "Northern Rhodesia: Clanship, Chieftainship, and Nsenga Political Adaptation." In *From Tribal Rule to Modern Government.* Lusaka: Rhodes-Livingstone Institute, 1959.

———. "Problems of African Political History: The Nsenga of Northern Rhodesia." *Rhodes-Livingstone Journal* 28 (1960).

Auslander, Mark. " 'Open the Wombs!' The Symbolic Politics of Modern Ngoni Witchfinding." In *Modernity and Its Malcontents: Ritual and Power in Postcolonial Africa,* ed. Jean Comaroff and John Comaroff. Chicago: University of Chicago Press, 1993.

Barnes, J. A. "The Fort Jameson Ngoni." In *Seven Tribes of British Central Africa,* ed. Elizabeth Colson and Max Gluckman. London: Oxford University Press, 1951.

———. "History in a Changing Society." *Rhodes-Livingstone Journal* 11 (1951).

———. *Politics in a Changing Society.* London: Oxford University Press, 1954.

Bates, Robert H. *Rural Responses to Industrialization: A Study of Village Zambia.* New Haven: Yale University Press, 1976.

Bertrand, Alfred. *The Kingdom of the Barotsi: Upper Zambesia.* London, 1898.

Bond, G. C. "Kinship and Conflict in a Yombe Village." *Africa* 52 (1972).

———. *The Politics of Change in a Zambian Community.* Chicago: University of Chicago Press, 1976.

Brelsford, W. V. "The Bemba Trident." *NADA* 13 (Salisbury) (1935).

———. "Notes on Some Northern Rhodesian Bowstands." *Man* 40 (1940).

———. *Aspects of Bemba Chieftainship.* Communication no. 2. Livingstone: Rhodes-Livingstone Institute, 1944.

———. *The Tribes of Northern Rhodesia.* Lusaka: Government Printer, 1956.

———. *The Tribes of Zambia.* 2nd ed. Lusaka: Government Printer, 1965.

Burles, R. S. "The Katengo Council Elections." *Journal of African Administration* 4 (1952).

Canter, Richard S. *National and International Events and the Incidence of*

Ethnic Conflict: Lenje-Rhodesian Relations in Zambia. Working Paper no. 3. Boston: Boston University, African Studies Center, 1976.

Caplan, G. L. *The Elites of Barotseland, 1878–1969: A Political History of Zambia's Western Province.* Berkeley: University of California Press, 1970.

Chiwale, J. C. *Royal Praises and Praise-names of the Lunda-Kazembe of Northern Rhodesia: Their Meaning and Historical Background.* Central Bantu Historical Text no. 3. Communication no. 25. Lusaka: Rhodes-Livingstone Institute, 1962.

Clark, J. Desmond. "The Bushmen Hunters of the Barotse Forests." *Northern Rhodesia Journal* 1 (1950).

Colson, Elizabeth. "The Plateau Tonga of Northern Rhodesia." In *Seven Tribes of British Central Africa,* ed Elizabeth Colson and Max Gluckman. London: Oxford University Press, 1951.

———. "Every Day Life among the Cattle-Keeping Plateau Tonga." *Rhodes-Livingstone Museum Papers,* new ser. 9 (1953).

———. "Ancestral Spirits and Social Structure among the Plateau Tonga." *International Archives of Ethnography* 47 (1954).

———. *Marriage and the Family among the Plateau Tonga of Northern Rhodesia.* Manchester: Manchester University Press, 1958.

———. "Marriage and the Family among the Plateau Tonga of Northern Rhodesia." *Rhodes-Livingstone Journal* 1 (1958).

———. "The Resilience of Matriliny: Gwembe and Plateau Tonga Adaptations." In *The Versatility of Kinship,* ed. Linda S. Cordell and Stephen Beckerman. New York: Academic, 1980.

———. "Land Law and Land Holding among Valley Tonga of Zambia." *Journal of Anthropological Research* 42 (1986).

———. *For Prayer and Profit: The Ritual, Economic, and Social Importance of Beer in Gwembe District, Zambia, 1950–1982.* Stanford: Stanford University Press, 1988.

Colson, Elizabeth, and Max Gluckman, eds. *Seven Tribes of British Central Africa.* London: Oxford University Press, 1951.

Colson, Elizabeth, and Thayder Scudder. "Gwembe Tonga Matrilineality and Virlocality." *American Anthropologist* 82 (1980).

Coxhead, J. C. *The Native Tribes of Northern Rhodesia.* Occasional Paper no. 5. London: Royal Anthropological Institute, 1914.

Crehan, Kate. "Munkunashi: An Exploration of Some Effects of the Penetration of Capital in North-Western Zambia." *Journal of Southern African Studies* 8 (1981).

———. "Women and Development in North Western Zambia: From Food Producer to Housewife." *Review of African Political Economy* 27–28 (1983).

———. "Bishimi and Social Studies: The Production of Knowledge in a Zambian Village." *African Affairs* 84 (1985).

——. *Co-operatives in Chizela: Ideology and Practical Realities*. Lusaka: University of Zambia, Institute for African Studies, 1989.

——. "Structures of Meaning and Structures of Interest: Peasants and Planners in North-Western Zambia." In *Cultural Struggle and Development in Southern Africa*, ed. Preben Kaarsholm. Harare: Baobab, 1991.

——. *The Fractured Community: Landscapes of Power and Gender in Rural Zambia*. Berkeley: University of California Press, 1997.

Cunnison, I. *Kinship and Local Organization on the Luapula: A Preliminary Account of Some Aspects of Luapula Organization*. Livingstone: Rhodes-Livingstone Institute, 1950.

——. "Headmanship and the Ritual of Luapula Villages." *Africa* 26 (1956).

——. "Perpetual Kinship: A Political Institution of the Luapula People." *Rhodes-Livingstone Journal* 20 (1956).

——. *The Luapula Peoples of Northern Rhodesia*, Manchester: Manchester University Press, 1959.

——, ed. and trans. *Historical Traditions of the Eastern Lunda, by Mwata Kazembe XIV*. Communication no. 23. Lusaka: Rhodes-Livingstone Institute, 1962.

Dixon-Fyle, Mac. "Reflections on Economic and Social Change among the Plateau Tonga of Northern Rhodesia." *International Journal of African Historical Studies* 16 (1983).

Doke, Clement M. *The Lambas of Northern Rhodesia: A Study of Their Customs and Beliefs*. London: Harrap, 1931.

Fielder, Robin J. "Economic Spheres in Pre- and Post-Colonial Ila Society." *African Social Research* 28 (1979).

Fortes, M. , and E. E. Evans-Pritchard, eds. *African Political Systems*. London: Oxford University Press, 1940.

Frankenberg, Ronald. "Economic Anthropology or Political Economy: The Barotse Social Formation." In *The New Economic Anthropology*, ed. J. Clammer. London: Macmillan, 1978.

Gatter, P. "Indigenous and Institutional Thought in the Practice of Rural Development: A Study of an Ushi Chiefdom in Luapula, Zambia." Ph.D. diss., University of London, 1990.

Geisler, Gisela. "Moving with Tradition: The Politics of Marriage Amongst the Toka of Zambia." *Canadian Journal of African Studies* 26 (1992).

——. "Who Is Losing Out? Structural Adjustment, Gender, and the Agricultural Sector in Zambia." *Journal of Modern African Studies* 30,1 (1992).

Gibbons, A. St. "Marotseland and the Tribes of the Upper Zambesi." *Proceedings of the Royal Colonial Institute* no. 29 (1897–98).

Glennie, A. F. B. "The Barotse System of Government." *Journal of African Administration* 4 (1952).

Gluckman, Max. *Economy of the Central Barotse Plain.* Paper no. 7. Livingstone: Rhodes-Livingstone Institute, 1941.

―――. *Administrative Organization of the Barotse Native Authorities, with a Plan for Reforming Theme.* Communication no. 1. Livingstone: Rhodes-Livingstone Institute, 1943.

―――. *Essays on Lozi Land and Royal Property.* Paper no. 10. Livingstone: Rhodes-Livingstone Institute, 1943.

―――. "African Land Tenure." *Rhodes-Livingstone Journal* 3 (1945).

―――. "Zambesi River Kingdom." *Libertas* 5 (1945).

―――. "The Lozi of Barotseland in North-Western Rhodesia." In *Seven Tribes of British Central Africa,* ed. Elizabeth Colson and Max Gluckman. Manchester: Manchester University Press, 1951.

―――. "Succession and Civil War among the Bemba: An Exercise in Anthropological Theory." *Rhodes-Livingstone Journal* 16 (1954).

―――. *The Judicial Process among the Barotse of Northern Rhodesia.* Glencoe, Ill.: Free Press, 1955.

―――. *Custom and Conflict in Africa.* Oxford: Blackwell, 1955.

―――. "Technical Vocabulary of Barotse Jurisprudence." *American Anthropologist* (October 1959).

―――. "Anthropological Problems Arising out of the African Industrial Revolution." In *Social Change in Modern Africa,* ed. A. W. Southall. London: Oxford University Press, 1961.

―――. *Order and Rebellion in Tribal Africa.* London: Cohen and West, 1963.

―――. *Politics, Law, and Ritual in Tribal Society: Some Problems in Social Anthropology.* Oxford: Oxford University Press, 1965.

―――. *The Ideas of Barotse Jurisprudence.* Atlantic Highlands, N.J.: Humanities, 1965.

Hedlund, Hans, and Mats Lundahl. "The Economic Role of Beer in Rural Zambia." *Human Organization* 43 (1984).

Holy, Ladislav. *Strategies and Norms in a Changing Matilineal Society: Descent, Succession, and Inheritance among the Toka of Zambia.* Cambridge: Cambridge University Press, 1986.

Hudson, R. S. , and H. K. Prescot. "The Election of a 'Ngambela' in Barotseland." *Man* 24 (1924).

Ikacana, N. S. *Litaba za Makwangwa* (Traditions of the Kwangwa). Lusaka: Northern Rhodesia Publications Bureau, 1964.

―――. *Litaba za Sicaba sa Malozi.* Rev. ed. Cape Town: Oxford University Press, 1959.

―――. *The Story of the Barotse Nation.* Lusaka: Lusaka Publications Bureau, 1961.

Jalla, Louis. *Sur les Rives du Zambeze: notes ethnographiques.* Paris: Societe des missions evangeliques, 1928.

Jaspan, M. A. "The Ila-Tonga Peoples of North-Western Rhodesia." *Eth-*

nographic Survey of Africa, West Central Africa. Part 4. London: International African Institute, 1953.

Jones, Stanley. "Mankoya in 1925 to 1927." *Northern Rhodesia Journal* 4 (1959).

Jordan, E. Knowles. "Mongu in 1908." *Northern Rhodesia Journal* 4 (1959).

————. "Chinsali in 1920–1922." *Northern Rhodesia Journal* 5 (1964).

Kay, George. *Chief Kalaba's Village.* Manchester: Manchester University Press, 1964.

Kazembe XIV. "Historical Traditions of the Eastern Lunda." Trans. I. Cunnison. *Central Bantu Historical Texts—II.* Lusaka: 1962.

Krige, Eileen. J., and J. D. Krige. *The Realm of a Rain-Queen: A Study of the Pattern of Lovedu Society.* London: Oxford University Press, 1943.

Kumar, Shubh K. "Effect of Seasonal Food Shortage on Agricultural Production in Zambia." *World Development* 16 (1988).

Labrecque, E. "Le tribu des Babemba: I. Les origines des Babemba." *Anthropos* 28 (1933).

Lancaster, Chet S. *The Goba of the Zambezi: Sex Roles, Economics, and Change.* Norman: University of Oklahoma Press, 1981.

Mackintosh, C. W. *Yeta III, Paramount Chief of the Barotse (Northern Rhodesia): A Sketch of His Life.* London: Pickering and Inglis, 1937.

————. *Lewanika, Paramount Chief of the Barotse.* London: Lutterworth, 1942.

Marks, Stuart A. *Large Mammals and a Brave People: Subsistence Hunters in Zambia.* Seattle: University of Washington Press, 1976.

Marwick, M. G. "History and Tradition in East Central Africa through the Eyes of the Northern Rhodesian Cewa." *Journal of African History* 4 (1963).

————. *Sorcery in Its Social Setting: A Study of the Northern Rhodesian Cewa.* Manchester: Manchester University Press, 1965.

McCulloch, M. *The Lunda, Luena, and Related Tribes of North Western Rhodesia and Adjoining Territories.* London: International African Institute, 1951.

Mitchell, J. Clyde (with M. Gluckman and J. A. Barnes). "The Village Headman in British Central Africa." *Africa* 19 (1949).

Moore, Henrietta, and Megan Vaughan. "Cutting down Trees: Women, Nutrition and Agricultural Change in the Northern Province of Zambia, 1920–1986." *African Affairs* 86 (1987).

————. *Cutting down Trees: Gender, Nutrition, and Agricultural Change in Northern Province of Zambia, 1890–1990.* London: Currey, 1994.

Mpashi, S. A. *Abapatili Bafika Ku Babemba.* Lusaka: Oxford University Press, 1966.

Palmer, R. H. *Lewanika's Country.* Canada: Privately printed, 1955.

Poewe, Karla O. "Matriliny and Capitalism: the Development of Incipient Classes in Luapula, Zambia." *Dialectical Anthropology* 3 (1978).

———. "Matriliny in the Throes of Change: Kinship, Descent, and Marriage in Luapula, Zambia." *Africa* 48 (1978).

———. "Religion, Matriliny and Change: Jehovah's Witnesses and Seventh Day Adventists in Luapula, Zambia." *American Ethnologist* 5 (1978).

———. "Regional and Village Economic Activities: Prosperity and Stagnation in Luapula, Zambia." *African Studies Review* 22 (1979).

———. "Matrilineal Ideology: The Economic Activities of Women in Luapula, Zambia." In *The Versatility of Kinship*, ed. Linda S. Cordell and Stephen Beckerman. New York: Academic, 1980.

———. *Matrilineal Ideology: Male-Female Dynamics in Luapula, Zambia.* New York: Academic, 1981.

Poewe, Karla O., and Peter R. Lovell. "Marriage, Descent, and Kinship: On the Differential Primacy of Institutions in Longana and Luapula." *Africa* 50 (1980).

Pottier, Johann. "The Transformation of a Defunct Labour Reserve: The Case of the Mambwe People of Zambia." Ph.D. diss., University of Sussex, 1980.

———. "Defunct Labour Reserve? Mambwe Villages in the Post-Migration Economy." *Africa* 53 (1983).

———. *Migrants No More: Settlement and Survival in Mambwe Villages, Zambia.* Bloomington: Indiana University Press, 1988.

Pritchett, James A. "Continuity and Change in an African Society: The Kanongesha Lunda of Mwinilunga, Zambia." Ph.D. diss., Harvard University, 1990.

Reynolds, P. *Dance Civet Cat: Child Labour in the Zambezi Valley.* Athens: Ohio University Press, 1991.

Richards, Audrey I. "Motherright among the Central Bantu." *Essays Presented to C. G. Seligman*, ed. E. E. Evans-Pritchard, R. Fitch, B. Malinowski, and I. Schaperal. London: Keegan Paul, 1933.

———. "Bow-Stand or Trident?" *Man* 35 (1935).

———. "Tribal Government in Transition: The Bemba of North-Eastern Rhodesia." *Supplement to the Journal of the Royal African Society* 34 (1935).

———. "A Modern Movement of Witchfinders." *Africa* 8 (1935).

———. "The Life of Bwembya, a Native of Northern Rhodesia." In *Ten Africans*, ed. M. Perham. London: Faber and Faber, 1936.

———. *Land, Labour, and Diet in Northern Rhodesia: An Economic Study of the Bemba Tribe.* London: Oxford University Press, 1939.

———. "The Political System of the Bemba Tribe—North Eastern Rhodesia." In *African Political Systems*, ed. M. Fortes and E. E. Evans-Pritchard. London: Oxford University Press, 1940.

———. *Hunger and Work in a Savage Tribe*. Glencoe, Ill.: Free Press, 1948.

———. "The Bemba of North-Eastern Rhodesia." In *Seven Tribes of British Central Africa*, ed. Elizabeth Colson and Max Gluckman. London: Oxford University Press, 1951.

———. *Chisungu, a Girl's Initiation Ceremony among the Bemba of Northern Rhodesia*. New York: Grove, 1956.

———. "The Village Census in the Study of Culture Contacts." In *Methods of Study of Culture Contacts in Africa*. New York: Oxford University Press, 1958.

Richardson, E. M. *Aushi Village Structure in the Fort Rosebery District of Northern Rhodesia*. Communication no. 13. Lusaka: Rhodes-Livingstone Institute, 1959.

Scudder, Thayer, and Elizabeth Colson. "Long-Term Field Research in Gwembe Valley, Zambia." In *Long-Term Field Research in Social Anthropology*, ed. George M. Foster et al. New York: Academic, 1978.

Shaw, Mabel. *Dawn in Africa: Stories of Girl Life*. London: Edinburgh House, 1932.

Sichone, O. B. "Labour Migration, Peasant Farming, and Rural Development in Winamwanga." Ph.D. diss., Cambridge University, 1991.

Siegel, Brian. "Centers on the Periphery: Rural Development in Ndola Rural Central." In *Small Urban Centers in Rural Development in Africa*, ed. Aidan Southall. Madison: University of Wisconsin, African Studies Program, 1979.

———. "Farms or Gardens: Ethnicity and Enterprise on the Rural Zambian Copperbelt." Ph.D. diss., University of Wisconsin, 1984.

———. "The 'Wild' and 'Lazy' Lamba: Ethnic Stereotypes on the Central African Copperbelt." In *The Creation of Tribalism in Southern Africa*, ed. Leroy Vail. London: Currey, 1989.

Sikota. "Notes—Lewanika in England, 1902." *Northern Rhodesian Journal* 2 (1953).

Skjonsberg, Else. *Change in an African Village: Kefa Speaks*. West Hartford, Conn.: Kumarian, 1989.

Slaski, J. "Peoples of the Lower Luapula Valley." *Ethnographic Survey of Africa, East Central Africa*. Part 2. London: International African Institute, 1951.

Smith, E. W., and A. M. Dale. *The Ila-Speaking People of Northern Rhodesia*. 2 vols. New York: Macmillan, 1920.

Stefaniszyn, Bronislaw. *Social and Ritual Life of the Ambo of Northern Rhodesia*. London: Oxford University Press, 1964.

Stokes, Eric. "Barotseland: The Survival of an African State." In *The Zambesian Past*, ed. Eric Stokes and Richard Brown. Manchester: Manchester University Press, 1966.

Thomson, J. Moffat. *Memorandum on the Native Tribes and Tribal Areas of Northern Rhodesia*. Lusaka: Government Printer, 1934.

Tuden, Arthur. "Ila Slavery." *Rhodes-Livingstone Journal* 24 (1958).

Tumbo-Masabo, Zubeida and Rita Liljestrom, eds. *Chelewa, Chelewa: The Dilemma of Teenage Girls.* Uppsala: Scandinavian Institute of African Studies, 1994.

Turner, Edith L. B. *The Spirit and the Drum: A Memoir of Africa.* Tucson: University of Arizona Press, 1987.

Turner, Thomas, and Pat O'Connor. "Women in the Zambian Civil Service: A Case of Equal Opportunities?" *Public Administration and Development* 14 (1994).

Turner, Victor W. *The Lozi Peoples of North-Western Rhodesia.* London: International African Institute, 1952.

———. *Lunda Rites and Ceremonies.* Livingstone: Rhodes-Livingstone Museum, 1953.

———. "A Lunda Love-Story and Its Consequences." *Rhodes-Livingstone Journal* 19 (1955).

———. *Schism and Continuity in an African (Ndembu) Society.* Manchester: Manchester University Press, 1957.

———. "Symbols in Ndembu Ritual." *Closed Systems and Open Minds.* Chicago: Aldine, 1964.

———. "A Ndembu Doctor in Practice." In *Magic, Faith and Healing,* ed. Ari Kiev. Glencoe, Ill.: Free Press, 1964.

———. *The Forest of Symbols: Aspects of Ndembu Ritual.* Ithaca: Cornell University Press, 1967.

———. *The Drums of Affliction.* London: Oxford University Press, 1968.

———. *Revelation and Divination in Ndembu Ritual.* Ithaca: Cornell University Press, 1975.

Van Binsbergen, Wim M. J. "The Infancy of Edward Shelonga: An Extended Case from the Zambian Nkoya." In *In Search of Health: Essays in Medical Anthropology,* ed. S. van der Geest and K. W. van der Veen. Amsterdam: University of Amsterdam, 1979.

———. "The Unit of Study and the Interpretation of Ethnicity: Studying the Nkoya of Western Zambia." *Journal of Southern African Studies* 8 (1981).

———. "Rural Communities in the Central African Context: The Nkoya of Central Western Zambia." In *Les communautes rurales, première partie: sociétés sans écruiture.* Paris: Dessain and Tolra, 1983.

———. "From Tribe to Ethnicity in Western Zambia: The Unit of Study as an Ideological Problem." In *Old Modes of Production and Capitalist Encroachment,* ed. Wim M. J. Van Binsbergen and Peter L. Geschiere. London: Kegan Paul, 1985.

———. "The Post-Colonial State, 'State Penetration' and the Nkoya Experience in Central Western Zambia." In *State and Local Community in Africa,* ed. Wim M. J. van Binsbergen, F. Reijntjens, and G. Hesseling. Brussels: Centre d'Etudes et de Documentation de l'Afrique, 1986.

———. "Chiefs and the State in Independent Zambia." *Journal of Legal Pluralism and Unofficial Law* 25–26 (1987).

Van Donge, Jan Kees. "Farmers, Politicians, and Bureaucrats: A Zambian Case Study." *Journal of Development Studies* 19 (1982).

———. "Rural-Urban Migration and the Rural Alternative in Mwasi Lundazi, Eastern Province, Zambia." *African Studies Review* 27 (1984).

Van Velsen, Jaap. "Labour Migration as a Positive Factor in the Continuity of Tonga Tribal Society." *Economic Development and Cultural Change* 8 (1960).

Vansina, Jan. *Kingdoms of the Savanna.* Madison: University of Wisconsin Press, 1966.

Watson, W. *Tribal Cohesion in a Money Economy: A Study of the Mambwe People of Northern Rhodesia.* Lusaka: Manchester University Press, 1958.

Watt, Nigel. "Lewanika's Visit to Edinburgh." *Northern Rhodesian Journal* 2 (1953).

White, C. M. N. *Witchcraft, Divination, and Magic.* Lusaka: Northern Rhodesia Government, 1947.

———. *The Material Culture of the Lunda-Luvale Peoples.* Occasional Paper no. 3. Livingstone: Rhodes-Livingstone Museum, 1948.

———. "Luvale Political Organization and the Luvale Lineage." In *Tribal Rule to Modern Government.* Lusaka: Rhodes-Livingstone Institute, 1959.

———. *An Outline of Luvale Social and Political Organization.* Manchester: Manchester University Press, 1960.

———. *Elements in Luvale Beliefs and Rituals.* Paper no. 32. Lusaka: Rhodes-Livingstone Institute 1961.

———. "The Ethnohistory of the Upper Zambesi." *African Studies* 21 (1962).

Whiteley, Wilfred. "Bemba and Related People of Northern Rhodesia." In *Ethnographic Survey of Africa, East Central African.* Part 2. London: International African Institute, 1951.

Winterbottom, J. M. "Outline Histories of Two Northern Rhodesian Tribes." *Rhodes-Livingstone Journal* 9 (1950).

7.a.iii. Social. Anthropology and Sociology. Urban

Epstein, A. L. "The Network and Urban Social Organization." *Rhodes-Livingstone Journal* 29 (1961).

———. *Ethos and Identity: Three Studies in Ethnicity.* London: Tavistock, 1978.

———. *Urbanization and Kinship: The Domestic Domain on the Copperbelt of Zambia, 1950–1956.* New York: Academic, 1981.

———. *Scenes from African Urban Life: Collected Copperbelt Essays.* Edinburgh: Edinburgh University Press, 1992.

Gluckman, Max. "From Tribe to Town." *Nation* (Sydney) September 24, 1960.

Hansen, Karen Tranberg. "Married Women and Work: Exploration from an Urban Case Study." *African Social Research* 20 (1975).

———. "The Urban Informal Sector as a Development Issue: Poor Women and Work in Lusaka, Zambia." *Urban Anthropology* 9 (1980).

———. "When Sex Becomes a Critical Variable: Married Women and Domestic Work in Lusaka, Zambia." *African Social Research* 30 (1980).

———. "Lusaka's Squatters: Past and Present." *African Studies Review* 25 (1982).

———. "Negotiating Sex and Gender in Urban Zambia." *Journal of Southern African Studies* 10 (1984).

———. "Budgeting against Uncertainty: Cross-Class and Transtethnic Redistribution Mechanisms in Urban Zambia." *African Urban Studies* 21 (1985).

———. "Domestic Service in Zambia." *Journal of Southern African Studies* 13 (1986).

———. "Household Work as a Man's Job: Sex and Gender in Domestic Service in Zambia." *Anthropology Today* 13 (1986).

———. *Distant Companions: Servants and Employers in Zambia, 1900–1985.* Ithaca: Cornell University Press, 1989.

———. "Body Politics: Sexuality, Gender, and Domestic Service in Zambia." *Journal of Women's History* 2 (1990).

———. "Domestic Trials: Power and Autonomy in Domestic Service in Zambia." *American Ethnologist* 17 (1990).

———. "After Copper Town: The Past in the Present in Urban Zambia." *Journal of Anthropological Research* 47 (1991).

———. "Cookstoves and Charcoal Braziers: Culinary Practices, Gender, and Class in Zambia." In *African Encounters with Domesticity*, ed. Karen Tranberg Hansen. New Brunswick: Rutgers University Press, 1992.

———. "Gender and Housing: The Case of Domestic Service in Lusaka, Zambia." *Africa* 62,2 (1992).

———. "White Women in a Changing World: Employment, Voluntary Work, and Sex in Post-World War II Northern Rhodesia." In *Western Women and Imperialism*, ed. Nupur Chaudri and Margaret Stroebel. Bloomington: Indiana University Press, 1992.

———. "Dealing with Used Clothing: *Salaula* and the Construction of Identity in Zambia's Third Republic." *Public Culture* 6 (1994).

———. *Keeping House in Lusaka.* New York: Columbia University Press, 1997.

Harries-Jones, Peter. *Freedom and Labour: Mobilization and Political Control on the Zambian Copperbelt.* New York: St. Martin's, 1975.

———. " 'A House Should Have a Ceiling': Unintended Consequences of Development Planning in Zambia." In *Perceptions of Development*, ed. Sandra Wailman. Cambridge: Cambridge University Press, 1977.

Heisler, Helmut. "Creation of a Stabilized Urban Society: A Turning Point in the Development of Northern Rhodesia/Zambia." *African Affairs* 70 (1971).

———. *Urbanization and the Government of Migration*. New York: St. Martin's, 1974.

Jules-Rosette, Bennetta. *Symbols of Change: Urban Transition in a Zambian Community*. Norwood, N.J. : Ablex, ca. 1981.

Keller, Bonnie B. "Marriage and Medicine: Women's Search for Love and Luck." *African Social Research* 26 (1978).

———. "Marriage by Elopement." *African Social Research* 27 (1979).

Mitchell, J. Clyde. *African Urbanization in Ndola and Luanshya*. Communication no. 6. Lusaka: Rhodes-Livingstone Institute, 1954.

———. "Power and Prestige among Africans in Northern Rhodesia: An Experiment." *Proceedings and Transactions of the Rhodesian Scientific Association* 45 (1957).

———, ed. *Social Networks in Urban Situations: Analyses of Personal Relationships in Central African Towns*. Manchester: University of Zambia, Social Research Institute, 1969.

———. *Cities, Society, and Social Perception: A Central African Perspective*. Oxford: Clarendon, 1987.

Mitchell, J. Clyde, and A. L. Epstein. "Occupational Prestige and Social Status among Urban Africans in Northern Rhodesia." *Africa* 29 (1959).

Mlenga, Kelvin. "Rural-Urban Migration—A Perennial Problem." *Horizon* 9 (1967).

Ohadike, Patrick O. "The Nature and Extent of Urbanization in Zambia." *Journal of African and Asian Studies* 4 (1969).

Parkin, David, ed. *Town and Country in Central and Eastern Africa*. Lusaka: International African Institute, 1976.

Powdermaker, H. *Copper Town*. New York: Harper and Row, 1962.

Read, Margaret. "Migrant Labour and Its Effect on Tribal Life." *International Labour Review* 45 (1942).

Roeber, Carter A. "Shylocks and Mabisinesi: Trust, Informal Credit, and Commercial Culture in Kabwe, Zambia." Ph.D. diss., Northwestern University, 1995.

Schuster, Ilsa M. Glazer. *New Women of Lusaka*. Palo Alto: Mayfield, 1979.

Simmance, Alan J. F. *Urbanization in Zambia*. New York: Ford Foundation, 1972.

Van den Berghe, Leo, ed. *Hard Times in the City*. Vol. 3 of *Studies in Zambian Society*. Lusaka: University of Zambia, 1978.

Wilson, Godfrey. *An Essay on the Economics of Detribalization in Northern Rhodesia*. Part 1. Papers no. 5 and 6. Lusaka: Rhodes-Livingstone Institute, 1942.

7.b. Social. Education

Achola, Paul P. W. *Implementing Educational Policies in Zambia*. Washington, D.C.: World Bank, 1990.

Ahmed, Mushtag. "Functional Literacy Experimental Pilot Project in Zambia: Reasons for Drop-Out." *Indian Journal of Adult Education* 33 (1972).

Banda, C. J. "The Primary School-Leavers Problem in Zambia: Official Policies and Attempted Solutions." M.Ed. thesis, University of Zambia, 1981.

Bullington, Robert Adrian. "African Education in Northern Rhodesia." *Science Education* 47 (1964).

Careccio, J. "Mathematical Heritage of Zambia." *Arithmetic Teachers* 17 (1970).

Carmody, Brendan P. "Denominational Secondary Schooling in Post-Independence Zambia: A Case Study." *African Affairs* 89 (1990).

Chilongo, Gramatiel I. N. "Adult Education in Aid of Agricultural Development." *Journal of Adult Education* 1 (1982).

Chiposaa, Sylvester. "Universities Get the Squeeze." *New African* 21–22 (1986).

———. "Zambia Universities' Brain Drain." *New African* 43 (1987).

Chirwa, M. K. T. "Maize Growing as a Core Subject in Teaching Functional Literacy in Northwestern Province." *Journal of Adult Education* 2 (1983).

Clarke, Roy H. "Schooling as an Obstacle to Development in Zambia." In *Education and Development*, ed. R. Garrett. London: Croom Helm, 1985.

Coombe, Trevor. "The Origins of Secondary Education in Zambia, Part II: Anatomy of a Decision, 1934–1936." *African Social Research* 4 (1967).

———. "The Origins of Secondary Education in Zambia, Part III: Anatomy of a Decision, 1937–1939." *African Social Research* 5 (1968).

Csapo, M. "Special Educational Developments in Zambia." *International Journal of Educational Development* 7 (1987).

Draisma, Tom. *The Struggle against Underdevelopment in Zambia since Independence: What Role for Education?* Amsterdam: Free University Press, 1987.

Etheredge, D. A. "The Role of Education in Economic Development: The Example of Zambia." *Journal of Administration Overseas* 6 (1967).

Ezeilo, Bernice. "Validating Danger: Munthu Test and Porteus Maze Test in Zambia." *International Journal of Psychology* 13 (1978).

Fox, Frederic. *14 Africans vs. One American*. New York: Macmillan, 1962.

Higgs, Peter L. "Culture and Africanization in Zambian School Literature." Ph.D. diss., University of California-Los Angeles, 1978.

———. "The Introduction of English as the Medium of Instruction in Zambian Schools." *Zambia Educational Review* 2 (1980).

Hoppers, Wim. "The Aftermath of Failure: Experiences of primary School-Leavers in Rural Zambia." *African Social Research* 29 (1980).

———. *Education in a Rural Society: Primary Pupils and School Leavers in Mwinilunga, Zambia.* The Hague: CESO, 1981.

Jones, Thomas Jesse. *Education in East Africa.* New York: Phelps-Stokes Fund, ca. 1924.

Kabamba, Juliano M. *Use Studies of Public Libraries: The Benefits of Community-Based Information Services in Zambia.* Lusaka: University of Zambia, Institute for African Studies, 1988.

Kashoki, Mubanga E. "Educational Reform without Social Reform: The Case of Zambia." *Third World Quarterly* 2 (1980).

Kelly, M. J. *Education in a Declining Economy: The Case of Zambia.* Analytical Case Study no. 8. Washington, D.C.: EDI, 1991.

Kingsley, Phillip R. "Rural Zambian Values and Attitudes Concerning Cognitive Competence." In *From a Different Perspective: Studies of Behavior Across Cultures,* ed. I. R. Lagunes and Y. H. Poortinga. Berwyn, Penn.: Swets North America, 1985.

Kuntz, Marthe. "Education indigène sur le Haut-Zambesi." *Le Monde Non Chretien* 3 (1932).

Lungwangwa, Geoffrey. *The Impact of Structural Adjustment on the Quality of Basic Education in Zambia.* Lusaka: University of Zambia, Institute for African Studies, 1992.

Lungwangwa, Geoffrey, and Oliver Saasa, eds. *Educational Policy and Human Resource Development in Zambia.* Lusaka: University of Zambia, Institute for African Studies, 1991.

Macdonald, Roderick. "Reflections on Education in Central Africa." *Africa Report* 8 (1963).

Maimbolwa-Sinyangwe, Irene M. "Sex Differences in Progression in Zambian Secondary Schools." Seminar paper, University of Zambia, Educational Research Bureau, 1987.

Mhango, Mkwapatira. "Zambian Educational Hopes Dashed." *New African* (March 1984).

———. "Why Lusaka University Was Closed." *New African* (April 1984).

Molteno, R. V. "Our University and Our Community." *Jewel of Africa* 2 (1970).

Mortimer, M. "History of the Barotse National School: 1907 to 1957." *The Northern Rhodesia Journal* 3 (1957).

M'tonga, Mapooa. "Children's Games and Play in Zambia." Ph.D. diss., Queen's University, Belfast, 1985.

Musambachime, Mwelwa C. "The Impact of Rapid Population Growth and Economic Decline on the Quality of Education: The Case of Zambia." *Review of African Political Economy* 48 (1990).

Mwanakatwe, J. M. "The Progress of Education in Zambia since Independence." *Optima* 17 (1967).

————. *The Growth of Education in Zambia since Independence*. Lusaka: Oxford University Press, 1968.

————. "Reflections on the Use of English as a Medium of Instruction in Schools." *Bulletin of the Zambia Language Group* 2 (1976).

Ng'andu, Sophie M. Kasonde. "Aspects of the Upbringing and Education of Children with Special Needs in a Rural Zambian Bemba Culture." M.Phil. thesis, University of London, 1986.

Nyeko, J. "The Development of Female Education in Northern Rhodesia, 1925–1963: The Case of Central Province." M.A. thesis, University of Zambia, 1983.

Pagni, Lucien. "ACP-Zambia: Education and Training." *Courier* 85 (1984).

Peters, H. *Education and Achievement: Contribution of Education and Development of Elites among the Plateau Tonga*. Zambian Paper no. 16. Lusaka: University of Zambia, 1976.

Robertson, James S. "Education in Zambia." In *Education in Southern Africa*, ed. B. Rose. London: Collier-Macmillan, 1970.

Saxby, John. "The Politics of Education in Zambia." Ph.D. diss., University of Toronto, 1980.

Schana, S. C. B. "Which Language? A Brief History of the Medium of Instruction Issue in Northern Rhodesia." *Zambia Educational Review* 2 (1980).

Schuster, Ilsa. "Kinship, Life Cycle, and Education in Lusaka." *Journal of Comparative Family Studies* 18 (1987).

Scudder, Thayer, and Elizabeth Colson. *Secondary Education and the Formation of an Elite: The Impact of Education on Gwembe District*. New York: Academic, 1980.

Seleketi, Clayton. "The Medium of Instruction in Zambia's Primary Schools." M.A. thesis, University of Zambia, 1985.

Serpell Robert. *Culture's Influence on Behavior*. London: Methuen, 1976.

————. "Learning to Say It Better: A Challenge for Zambian Education." In *Language and Education in Zambia*, ed. L. N. Omondi and Y. T. Simukoko. Communication no. 14. Lusaka: University of Zambia, Institute for African Studies, 1978.

————. "The Cultural Context of Language Learning: Problems Confronting English Teachers in Zambia." *English Teachers Journal* 5 (1981).

————. "Measures of Perception, Skills, and Intelligence: The Growth of a New Perspective on Children in a Third World Country." In *Review of Child Development Research*, ed. W. W. Hartup. Vol. 6. Chicago: University of Chicago Press, 1982.

————. "Dimensions endogènes de l 'intelligence chez les A-Chewa et autres peuples africains." In *La recherche ontercultureelle*, ed. J. Retschitski, M. Bossel-Lagos, and P. Dasen. Vol. 2. Paris: Harmattan, 1989.

————. *The Significance of Schooling: Life-Journeys in an African Society.* Cambridge: Cambridge University Press, 1993.

Shaw, Mabel. *God's Candlelights: An Educational Venture in Northern Rhodesia.* London: Livingstone, 1941.

Shifferaw, M. "Educational Policy and Practice Affecting Females in Zambian Secondary Schools." Ph.D. diss., University of Wisconsin-Milwaukee, 1982.

Tembo, L. P. *The African University, Issues and Perspectives: Speeches by L. H. K. Goma.* Zambian Paper no. 14. Lusaka: University of Zambia, Institute for African Studies, 1981.

Wilkin, D. "To the Bottom of the Heap: Educational Deprivation and Its Social Implications in the Northwestern Province of Zambia, 1906–1945." Ph.D. diss., Syracuse University, 1983.

Wincott, N. E. "Education and the Development of Urban Society in Zambia." In *Malawi Past and Present*, B. Pachai. Manchester: University of Manchester Press, 1967.

7.c. Social. Religion and Missions

Addison, James Thayer. *Francois Coillard.* Hartford, Conn.: Church Missions Publishing, 1924.

Arnot, F. S. *From Natal to the Upper Zambezi: First Year among the Barotse.* Glasgow, 1883.

————. *Garenganze; or, Seven Years Pioneer Mission Work on Central Africa.* London, 1889.

————. *Garanganze West and East.* Glasgow: Pickering and Inglis, 1902.

————. *Missionary Travels in Central Africa.* Bath: Office of "Echoes of Service," 1914.

Baeta, C. G., ed. *Christianity in Tropical Africa: Studies Presented and Discussed at the Seventh International African Seminar, University of Ghana, April 1965.* London: Oxford University Press, 1968.

Baker, Ernest. *The Life and Explorations of F. S. Arnot.* London: Seeley, Service, 1921.

Baldwin, A. *A Missionary Outpost in Central Africa (The Story of the Baila Mission).* London: Hammond, 1914.

————. *Rev. Henry Buckenham, Pioneer Missionary.* London: Johnson, 1920.

Banda, R. S. L. "The Educational Policy and Activities of the Dutch Reformed Church Mission in Zambia to 1976." M.Ed. thesis, University of Zambia, 1981.

Batungwa, Ives Chituba. "The Role of the Church in the Democratization Process in Africa: The Zambian Experience." *Courier* 134 (1992).

Bloom, A. G. *The History of the Universities' Mission to Central Africa.* Vol. 3, 1933–1957. London: Universities' Mission to Central Africa, 1962.

Bolink, Peter. *Towards Church Union in Zambia: A Study of Missionary Co-operation and Church-Union Efforts in Central Africa*. Franeker (The Netherlands): Wever, 1967.

Bond, George C. "Ancestors and Protestants: Religious Coexistence in the Social Field of a Zambian Community." *American Ethnologist* 14 (1987).

Carmody, Brendan Patrick. "The Nature and Consequences of Conversion in Jesuit Education at Chikuni, 1905–78." Ph.D. diss., University of California-Berkeley, 1986.

———. *Conversion and Jesuit Schooling in Zambia*. Leiden: Brill, 1992.

Chapman, William. *A Pathfinder in South Central Africa: A Story of Pioneer Missionary Work and Adventure*. London: Hammond, 1909.

Chisenga, B. "Chitambo Mission: A History of Mission Education and Its Impact on Lala Society of Serenje District, 1906–64." M.A. thesis, University of Zambia, 1987.

Coillard, François. *La Mission au Zambeze*. Paris, 1880.

———. *A Lealuyi: lettres recentes de Coillard*. Paris, 1892.

———. *Zambesia: Work among the Barotse*. Glasgow, 1894.

———. *On the Threshold of Central Africa*. London, 1897.

———. *Sur le Haut-Zambeze voyages et travaux de mission*. Paris, 1898.

———. *The Valley of the Upper Zambezi* (two letters). London, 1898.

Colson, Elizabeth. "Converts and Tradition: The Impact of Christianity on Valley Tonga Religion." *Southwestern Journal of Anthropology* 26 (1970).

———. "A Continuing Dialogue: Prophets and Local Shrines among the Tonga of Zambia." In *Regional Cults*, ed. Richard Werbner. New York: Academic, 1976.

Corbeil, J. J. *Mbusa: Sacred Emblems of the Bemba*. London: Ethnographica Publishers, 1982.

Cross, Sholto. "A Prophet Not without Honor." In *African Perspectives*, ed. Christopher Allen and R. W. Johnson. Cambridge: Cambridge University Press, 1970.

———. "The Watch Tower Movement in South Central Africa, 1908–1945." Ph.D. diss., Oxford University, 1972.

———. "Social History and Millenial Movements: The Watch Tower in South Central Africa." *Social Compass* 24 (1977).

Dillon-Malone, Clive M. *The Korsten Basketmakers*. Lusaka: University of Zambia, Institute for African Studies, 1978.

Dieterlen, H. *François Coillard*. Paris: Société des Missions Evangéliques, 1921.

Doke, Clement M. *Trekking in South Central Africa, 1913–1919*. Roodeport: South African Baptist Historical Society, 1975.

Ellis, James J. *Fred Stanley Arnot: Missionary, Explorer, Benefactor*. London: Pickering and Inglis, 192?.

Epstein, A. L. "The Millennium and the Self: Jehovah's Witnesses on the Copperbelt in the '50s." *Anthropos* 81 (1986).

Favre, Edward. *François Coillard, 1834–1904.* 3 vols. Paris: Société des Missions Evangéliques, 1908.

Garvey, Brian. "The Development of the White Fathers Mission among the Bemba-Speaking Peoples, 1891–1964." Ph.D diss., University of London, 1974.

———. "Bemba Chiefs and Catholic Missions, 1898–1935." *Journal of African History* 18 (1977).

Groves, C. P. *The Planting of Christianity in Africa.* 4 vols. London: Lutterworth, 1948–58.

Grubb, Norman R. *C. T. Studd, Athlete and Pioneer.* Grand Rapids, Mich.: Zondervan, 1937.

Guthrie, Charles. "The Emergence and Decline of a Mission-Educated Elite in North-Eastern Zambia, 1895–1964." Ph.D. diss., Indiana University, 1978.

Hinfelaar, Hugo F. "Religious Change among Bemba-Speaking Women." Ph.D. diss., University of London, 1989.

Hooker, J. R. "Witnesses and Watchtower in the Rhodesias and Nyasaland." *Journal of African History* 6 (1965).

Howell, A. E. *Bishop Dupont: King of the Brigands.* Franklin, Pa.: News-Herald, 1949.

Ipenburg, A. *Lubwa: The Presbyterian Mission and the Eastern Bemba.* Lusaka: Historical Association of Zambia, 1984.

Jacottet, E. *Contes et traditions du Haut-Zambeze.* Paris, 1895.

Johnson, Walton. *Worship and Freedom: A Black American Church in Zambia.* London: International African Institute, 1977.

Jules-Rosette, Bennetta. *African Apostles.* Ithaca: Cornell University Press, 1975.

———. "Prophecy and Leadership in the Maranke Church: A Case Study in Continuity and Change." In *African Christianity,* ed. George Bond, Walton Johnson, and Sheila S. Walker. New York: Academic, 1979.

———, ed. *The New Religions of Africa: Priests and Priestesses in Contemporary Cults and Churches.* Norwood, N.J.: Ablex, 1979.

———. "Changing Aspects of Women's Initiation in Southern Africa." *Canadian Journal of African Studies* 13 (1980).

———. *Symbols of Change: Urban Transition in a Zambian Community.* Norwood, N.J.: Ablex, 1981.

Kerswell, Kate L. *Romance and Reality of Missionary Life in Northern Rhodesia.* London: Hammond, 1913.

Lungu, Gatian F. "The Church, Labour, and the Press in Zambia: The Role of Critical Observers in a One-Party State." *African Affairs* 85 (1986).

MacConnachie, J. *An Artisan Missionary on the Zambesi: Being the Life Story of William Thomson Waddell.* Edinburgh: Oliphant, Anderson, Ferrier, 1910.

Mackintosh, C. W. *Coillard of the Zambezi.* London: Fisher and Unwin, 1907.

———. *Some Pioneer Missions of Northern Rhodesia and Nyasaland.* Livingstone: Rhodes-Livingstone Museum, 1950.

Macqueen, James. *News from Barotseland, 1898–1916.* Magazine of the Paris Evangelical Missionary Society.

Maxwell, Kevin B. *Bemba Myth and Ritual: The Impact of Literacy on an Oral Culture.* New York: Lang, 1983.

Merle, Davis J., et al. *Modern Industry and the African: An Enquiry into the Effect of the Copper Mines of Central Africa upon Native Society and the Work of Christian Missions.* London: Macmillan, 1933.

Mhoswa, A. "A Study of the Educational Contribution of the Jesuit Mission at Chikuni and the Adventist Mission at Rusangu, 1905–1964." M.Ed. thesis, University of Zambia, 1980.

Milingo, Emmanuel. *The World in Between: Christian Healing and the Struggle for Spiritual Survival.* Maryknoll, N.Y.: Orbis, 1984.

Mills, Dora S. *Is It Worth While?* London: Universities' Mission to Central Africa, 1912.

Morrill, Leslie, and Madge Haines. *Livingstone: Trail Blazer for God.* Mountain View, Calif.: Pacific, 1959.

Morris, Colin. *The Hour after Midnight: A Missionary's Experiences of the Racial and Political Struggle in Northern Rhodesia.* London: Longmans, 1961.

Morrow, Sean. "Some Social Consequences of Mission Education: The Case of Mbereshi, 1915–1940." *History in Zambia* 11 (1981).

———. "Motives and Methods of the London Missionary Society in Northern Rhodesia, 1887–1941." Ph.D. diss., University of Sussex, 1984.

———. "'No Girl Leaves the School Unmarried': Mabel Shaw and the Education of Girls at Mbereshi, Northern Rhodesia, 1915–1940." *International Journal of African Historical Studies* 19 (1986).

Mushindo, Paul. *The Life of a Zambian Evangelist: The Reminiscences of Rev. Paul B. Mushindo.* Lusaka: University of Zambia, Institute for African Studies, 1973.

Peters, H. "The Contribution of Education to the Development of Elites amongst the Plateau Tonga of Zambia: A Comparative Study of School Leavers from Two Mission Schools, 1930–1965." Ph.D. diss., University of Illinois, 1976.

Ragsdale, J. "Educational Development of Zambia as Influenced by Protestant Missions, 1880–1945." D.Ed. diss., Lehigh University, 1973.

Ranger, T. O. "The Mwana Lesa Movement of 1925." In *Themes in the*

Christian History of Central Africa, ed. T. O. Ranger and J. Weller. London: Heinemann, 1975.

———. "Religious Movements and Politics in Sub-Saharan Africa." *African Studies Review* 20 (1986).

Ranger, T. O., and J. Weller. eds. *Themes in the Christian History of Central Africa*. London: Heinemann, 1975.

Rotberg, R. I. "The Missionary Factor in the Occupation of Trans-Zambezia." *Northern Rhodesia Journal* 5 (1984).

———. *Christian Missions and the Creation of Northern Rhodesia, 1880–1924*. Princeton: Princeton University Press, 1985.

Sakala, Richard. "Scientific Socialism Causes Schisms in Zambia." *All Africa Press Service Bulletin* (supp.) 12 (1982).

Shepperson, G. "The Politics of African Church Separatist Movements in British Central Africa, 1892–1916." *Africa* 24 (1954).

———. "Church and Sect in Central Africa." *Rhodes-Livingstone Journal* 33 (1963).

Shillito, Edward. *François Coillard, a Wayfaring Man*. London: SCM, 1923.

Smith, Julia A. *Sunshine and Shade in Central Africa*. London: Dalton, 1908.

Smith, Edwin William. *The Way of the White Fields in Rhodesia*. London: World Dominion, 1928.

———. *The Blessed Missionaries*. Cape Town: Oxford University Press, 1950.

———. *Great Lion of Bechuanaland: The Life and Times of Roger Price, Missionary*. London: Independent, 1957.

Stevenson, Wy. C. *Year of Doom, 1975: The Story of Jehovah's Witnesses*. London: Hutchinson, 1967.

Stone, W. Vernon. "The Livingstone Mission to the Bemba." *The Bulletin of the Society for African Church History* 2 (1968).

Tanguy, Francois. "Kayambi: The First White Fathers' Mission in Northern Rhodesia." Trans. Clifford Green. *Northern Rhodesia Journal* 2 (1954).

———. *Imilandu Ya Babemba*. Lusaka: Oxford University Press, 1966.

Taylor, H. J. *Cape Town to Kafue*. London: Hammond, 1915.

Taylor, H. J., and Dorothea Lehmann. *Christians of the Copperbelt. The Growth of the Church in Northern Rhodesia*. London: SCM, 1961.

Temple, Merfyn M. *African Angelus*. London: Cargate, 1950.

———. *Rain on the Earth: Scenes of the Church in Northern Rhodesia*. London: Cargate, 1956.

Ter Haar, Gerrie, and Stephen Ellis. "Spirit Possession and Healing in Modern Zambia: An Analysis of Letters to Archbishop Milongo." *African Affairs* 87 (1988).

"Turbulent Priests." *Africa Confidential*, February 8, 1991.

Van Binsbergen, Wim M. J. *Religious Change in Zambia: Exploratory Essays*. London: Kegan Paul, 1981.

Verbeek, Leon. *Mythe et culte de Kipimpi (Rep. du Zaire)*. Bandundu: CEEBA, 1982.

———. *Le monde des espirits au sud-est du Shaba et au nord de la Zambie*. Rome: Libreria Ateneo Salesiano, 1990.

Verstraelen-Gilhuis, G. *From Dutch Mission to Reformed Church in Zambia*. Wever: Fraenker, 1982.

Weissling, Lee E. "The Effects of a Religious Mission on Rural Development: A Case Study of Lwawu, Northwestern Province, Zambia." *Canadian Journal of African Studies* 24 (1990).

White, Luise. "Vampire Priests of Central Africa: African Debates about Labor and Religion in Colonial Northern Zambia." *Comparative Studies in Society and History* 35 (1993).

Wilson, George Herbert. *The History of the Universities' Mission to Central Africa*. Westminster: UMCA, 1936.

"Zambia: Clergy Attacks Marxist Courses." *New African Development* (November 1979).

"Zambia: Double 'S' Sword." *Africa Confidential*, May 12, 1982.

About the Authors

John J. Grotpeter, author of the first edition of the *Historical Dictionary of Zambia* (1979), was professor of political science at the St. Louis College of Pharmacy, where he also held an endowed chair as the William S. and Edith C. Bucke Professor of Liberal Arts. He was the founder and, for twenty-five years, director of the college's liberal arts division. He completed his doctoral dissertation in 1965 on the early political history of Swaziland, Basutoland, and Bechuanaland. He was the author of several books as well as many articles, book reviews, and conference papers, including the *Historical Dictionary of Swaziland* (1975) and the *Historical Dictionary of Namibia* (1994).

Brian V. Siegel teaches anthropology and the sociology of religion in the Sociology Department at Furman University. His particular interest in the Lamba and other peoples of the Central African Copperbelt derives from his earlier study of ethnic stereotypes and antagonisms in the rural Zambian Copperbelt. He received his Ph.D. in anthropology from the University of Wisconsin-Madison in 1983.

James R. Pletcher received his Ph.D. from the University of Wisconsin-Madison in political science in 1981. Since 1983 he has taught at Denison University in Granville, Ohio. His dissertation and subsequent publications have explored the political manipulation of the maize market in Zambia. He has also worked on agricultural development and marketing issues in Malaysia. He is currently working on the process of maize market liberalization in Zambia and the process of agricultural policymaking.